Adobe® CREATIVE SUITE® 6
INTRODUCTORY

Contents

Adobe **Flash CS6**

CHAPTER ONE
Creating a Simple Animated Web Banner

CHAPTER TWO
Drawing with Flash

Adobe **Creative Suite 6**

CHAPTER INTEGRATION 1
Importing Files between Photoshop and Flash

Adobe **Dreamweaver CS6**

CHAPTER ONE
Creating a New Web Site
with Dreamweaver

CHAPTER TWO
Designing a Web Site
Using a Template and CSS

CHAPTER THREE
Adding Graphics
and Links

Adobe **Creative Suite 6**

CHAPTER INTEGRATION 2
Inserting Flash and Photoshop Files in Dreamweaver

Appendices

APPENDIX A
Project Planning Guidelines

APPENDIX B
Graphic Design Overview

Preface

The Shelly Cashman Series® offers the finest textbooks in computer education. We are proud of the fact that our Adobe books have been so well received. To build upon the innovation, quality and realibility you have come to expect from the Shelly Cashman Series, we now introduce a new text to fit a semester course covering the Adobe® Creative Suite®! Coverage of the newest features and concepts pertaining to Photoshop®, Flash®, and Dreamweaver® including the new content-aware controls; a new, easier, user experience in Flash with animations, advanced correction tools, the use of HTML5 and CSS3 standards, how to create mobile Web sites, and coverage of social networking to ensure relevancy and application of contemporary skills.

For this Creative Suite 6 text, the Shelly Cashman Series development team carefully reviewed our pedagogy and analyzed its effectiveness in teaching today's student. Students today read less, but need to retain more. They not only need to be able to perform skills, but to retain those skills and know how to apply them to different settings. Today's students need to be continually engaged and challenged to retain what they're learning.

With this Creative Suite 6 text, we continue our commitment to focusing on the user and how they learn best.

Objectives of This Textbook

Adobe Creative Suite 6: Introductory is intended for a course that offers an introduction to Photoshop, Flash, and Dreamweaver. No previous experience with Adobe software is assumed, and no mathematics beyond the high school freshman level is required.

The objectives of this book are:

- To teach graphic and Web design skills using student-focused exercises
- To expose students to image editing and graphic design fundamentals
- To develop an exercise-oriented approach that promotes learning by doing
- To encourage independent study and to help those who are working alone

The Shelly Cashman Approach

A Proven Pedagogy with an Emphasis on Project Planning

Each chapter presents a practical problem to be solved, within a project planning framework. The project orientation is strengthened by the use of Plan Ahead boxes, that encourage critical thinking about how to proceed at various points in the project. Step-by-step instructions with supporting screens guide students through the steps. Instructional steps are supported by the Q&A, Experimental Step, and BTW features.

A Visually Engaging Book that Maintains Student Interest

The step-by-step tasks, with supporting figures, provide a rich visual experience for the student. Call-outs on the screens that present both explanatory and navigational information provide students with information they need, when they need to know it. Each chapter presents a real-world scenario with current topics and new CS6 features.

Supporting Reference Materials (online Quick Reference, Appendices)

The appendices provide additional information about the application at hand, such as the Help Feature, Using Adobe Bridge, and Publishing to a Web Server, as well as a new appendix, For Mac Users. With the online Quick Reference, students can quickly look up information about a single task, such as keyboard shortcuts, and find page references of where in the book the task is illustrated.

Integration of the World Wide Web

The World Wide Web is integrated into the Adobe Creative Suite 6 learning experience by (1) BTW annotations; (2) an online Quick Reference Summary Web page; and (3) using online Help for each application.

End-of-Chapter Student Activities

Extensive end of chapter activities provide a variety of reinforcement opportunities for students where they can apply and expand their skills through individual and group work. To complete some of these assignments, you will be required to use the Data Files for Students. Visit http://www.cengage.com/ct/studentdownload for detailed access instructions or contact your instructor for information about accessing the required files.

Textbook Emphasis

Currency

All of the new CS6 features, including the new Content-Aware Patch and Move tools, the new Crop Tool, the new Blur gallery and others are covered

For Mac Users

Mac user information is covered in a new appendix, making this textbook work for either a PC or MAC platform

Publishing to a Web Server

New appendix discusses considerations for publishing to a web server including how to choose Web services and the process of going live

New Images

Updated photos in chapter project with topics of interest geared toward students

HTM5 and CSS3

Engaging coverage of the latest HTML5 and CSS3 standards including style sheets which provide students with a solid understanding of professional Web design

Professional Web Design

Explore creative designed centered solutions for creating a business and personal site that captures the attention of your targeted audience

Mobile Web Site

Design a mobile Web site using a Web standards approach for delivering content beyond the desktop

Web Accessibility

Integration of guidelines and standards for Web accessibility and disability access to the Web

Instructor Resources

The Instructor Resources include both teaching and testing aids that can be accessed via the Instructor Resouce CD or at www.cengage.com/login.

Instructor's Manual Includes lecture notes summarizing the chapter sections, figures and boxed elements found in every chapter, teacher tips, classroom activities, lab activities, and quick quizzes in Microsoft Word files.

Syllabus Easily customizable sample syllabi that cover policies, assignments, exams, and other course information.

Figure Files Illustrations for every figure in the textbook in electronic form.

PowerPoint Presentations A multimedia lecture presentation system that provides slides for each chapter. Presentations are based on chapter objectives. Ideal for using with distance learning classes and fully customizable.

Solutions to Exercises Includes solutions for all end-of-chapter and chapter reinforcement exercises.

Test Bank & Test Engine Test Bank includes 112 questions for every chapter, featuring objective-based and critical thinking question types, including page number references and figure references, when appropriate. Also included is the test engine, ExamView, the ultimate tool for your objective-based testing needs.

Data Files for Students To complete some of the end of chapter assignments, students will be required to use the Data Files for Students. Students can visit www.cengage.com/ct/studentdownload for detailed instructions about accessing the required files.

Learn Online

CengageBrain.com is the premier destination for purchasing or renting Cengage Learning textbooks, ebooks, eChapters and study tools, at a significant discount (eBooks up to 50% off Print). In addition, CengageBrain.com provides direct access to all digital products including eBooks, eChapters and digital solutions (i.e. CourseMate, SAM) regardless of where purchased. The following are some examples of what is available for this product on www.cengagebrain.com.

Student Companion Site Many Learn It Online activities, including quizzing and games, are available for no additional cost at www.cenagebrain.com to help reinforce chapter terms and concepts.

Adobe Creative Suite 6 CourseMate CourseMate with eBook for Adobe Creative Suite 6 keeps today's students engaged and involved in the learning experience. Adobe Creative Suite 6 CourseMate includes an integrated and multi-media rich eBook, and a variety of interactive learning tools, including quizzes, activities, videos, and other resources that specifically reinforce and build on the concepts presented in the chapter. These interactive activities are tracked within CourseMate's Engagement Tracker, making it easy to assess students' retention of concepts. All of these resources enable students to get more comfortable using technology and help prepare students to use the Internet as a tool to enrich their lives. Available Spring 2013.

About Our Covers

The Shelly Cashman Series is continually updating our approach and content to reflect the way today's students learn and experience new technology. This focus on student success is reflected on our covers, which feature real students from Bryant University using the Shelly Cashman Series in their courses, and reflect the varied ages and backgrounds of the students learning with our books. When you use the Shelly Cashman Series, you can be assured that you are learning computer skills using the most effective courseware available.

Textbook Walk-Through

BTW

Screen Resolution
If your system has a high-resolution monitor with a screen resolution of 1280 × 800 or higher, lowering that resolution to 1024 × 768 might cause some images to be distorted because of a difference in the aspect ratio. If you want to keep your high-resolution setting, be aware that the location of on-screen tools might vary slightly from the book.

Overview

As you read this chapter, you will learn how to edit the photo shown in Figure 1–1a on the previous page by performing these general tasks:

- Customize the workspace.
- Display and navigate a photo at various magnifications.
- Crop a photo effectively.
- Create and modify a border.
- Stroke a selection.
- Resize and print a photo.
- Save, close, and then reopen a photo.
- Add stroked text to the photo.
- Save a photo for the Web.
- Use Photoshop Help.

Plan Ahead

General Project Guidelines

When editing a photo, the actions you perform and decisions you make will affect the appearance and characteristics of the finished product. As you edit a photo, such as the one shown in Figure 1–1a, you should follow these general guidelines:

1. **Find an appropriate image or photo.** Keep in mind the purpose and the graphic needs of the project when choosing an image or photo. Decide ahead of time on the file type and decide if the image will be used on the Web. An eye-catching graphic image should convey a theme that is understood universally. The photo should grab the attention of viewers and draw them into the picture, whether in print or on the Web.

2. **Determine how to edit the photo to highlight the theme.** As you edit, use standard design principles, and keep in mind your subject, your audience, the required size and shape of the graphic, color decisions, the rule of thirds, the golden rectangle, and other design principles. Decide which parts of the photo portray your message and which parts are visual clutter. Crop the photo as needed.

3. **Identify finishing touches that will further enhance the photo.** The overall appearance of a photo significantly affects its ability to communicate clearly. You might want to add text or a border.

4. **Prepare for publication.** Resize the photo as needed to fit the allotted space. Save the photo on a storage medium, such as a hard drive, USB flash drive, or CD. Print the photo or publish it to the Web.

Using Sel...

BTW | **By The Way Boxes**

To Use the Rectangular Marquee Tool

The following step selects the tall basket in the lower-left corner of the Baskets Edited image using the Rectangular Marquee Tool. You will use the Elliptical Marquee Tool later in this chapter.

1

- With the Rectangular Marquee Tool selected on the Tools panel, drag to draw a rectangle around the tall basket in the lower-left corner to create a marquee selection. Drag close to the basket itself, as shown in Figure 2–6.

Experiment

- Practice drawing rectangular and elliptical marquees. Press SHIFT+M to switch between the two. SHIFT+DRAG to look at the effects. Press and hold the SPACEBAR key while you drag to reposition the current marquee. When you are finished, redraw a rectangle around the basket.

Q&A

What was the black box that appeared as I created the marquee?

That was the Transformation Values indicator to help show you exactly where you are in the image.

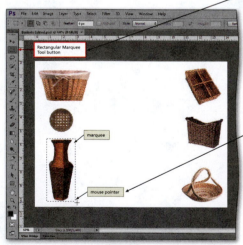

Figure 2–6

Photoshop Chapter

Other Ways
1. Press M key or SHIFT+M until Rectangular Marquee Tool is active, drag selection

The Move Tool

The Move Tool on the Photoshop Tools panel is used to move or make other changes to selections. Activating the Move Tool by clicking the Move Tool button, or by pressing the V key on the keyboard, enables you to move the selection border and its contents by dragging in the document window. When you first use the Move Tool, the mouse pointer displays a black arrowhead with scissors. To move the selection in a straight line, press and hold the SHIFT key while dragging. If you press and hold the ALT key while dragging, you duplicate or move only a copy of the selected area, effectively copying and pasting the selection. While duplicating, the mouse pointer changes to a black arrowhead with a white arrowhead behind it.

When you move selections, you need to be careful about overlapping images. As you will learn in Chapter 3, Photoshop might layer or overlap portions of images when you move them. While that sometimes is preferred when creating collages or composite images, it is undesirable if an important object is obscured. Close tracing while creating selections and careful placement of moved selections will prevent unwanted layering.

2

- Click Tahoma or a similar font in the list.

- Click the 'Set the font style' box arrow to display the list of font styles (Figure 1–68).

Q&A Why does the list not include other styles, such as italics?

Available font styles depend on the chosen font and the capability of the printer to reproduce that font. This font has only regular and bold styles.

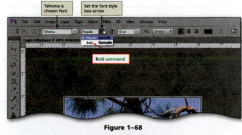

Figure 1–68

3

- Click Bold to choose a bold font style.

- Select the value in the 'Set the font size' box, and then type 36 to replace the size (Figure 1–69).

Figure 1–69

4

- Click the 'Set the text color' box to open the Color Picker (Text Color) dialog box.

- Click a white color in the upper-left corner of the color field (Figure 1–70).

Q&A What do the numerical boxes indicate?

Each color mode uses a numerical method called a color model, or color space, to describe the color. Some companies use specific numbers to create exact colors for branding purposes.

5

- Click the OK button in the Color Picker (Text Color) dialog box to apply white as the text color on the options bar.

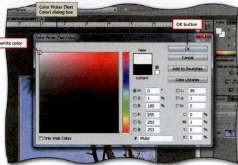

Figure 1–70

To Insert Text

With the type tool selected, you drag a bounding box in the document window to insert text. A **bounding box** is similar to a text box in other applications, with a dotted outline and sizing handles. As you drag, the mouse pointer changes to a small, open book outline. After typing the text in the bounding box, you use the 'Commit

Textbook Walk-Through

To Use the Zoom Tool

The following steps zoom in on the eagle for careful editing later in the chapter.

1
- Click the Zoom Tool button on the Tools panel to select the Zoom Tool.
- Move the mouse pointer into the document window to display the magnifying glass mouse pointer (Figure 1–30).

Q&A Why does my mouse pointer display a minus sign?

Someone may have previously zoomed out and the setting has carried over. Click the Zoom In button on the options bar.

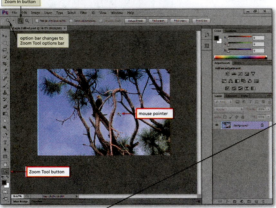

Figure 1–30

2
- Click the eagle three times to zoom in (Figure 1–31).

Experiment
- On the options bar, click the Zoom In button and then click the photo. Click the Zoom Out button and then click the photo. ALT+click the photo to zoom in the opposite direction from the options bar setting. Zoom to 50% magnification.

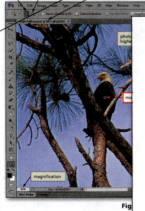

Fig...

Other Ways
1. Press Z, click document window
2. Press CTRL+PLUS SIGN (+) or CTRL+MINUS SIGN (−)
3. On View menu, click Zoom In or Zoom Out

Experiment Steps within our step-by-step instructions, encourage students to explore, experiment, and take advantage of the features of Adobe Photoshop CS5. These steps are not necessary to complete the projects, but are designed to increase the confidence with the software and build problem-solving skills.

Other Ways boxes that follow many of the step sequences explain the other ways to complete the task presented.

1
- If necessary, click the Timeline tab to display the Timeline, and then click in Frame 24 on the Timeline to select that frame.
- Click Insert on the Application bar to display the Insert menu.
- Point to Timeline on the Insert menu to display the Timeline submenu (Figure 1–51).

Figure 1–51

2
- Click Keyframe on the Timeline submenu to insert a new keyframe at Frame 24 (Figure 1–52).

Q&A What does the white box at Frame 23 indicate?

It indicates the final frame in which the contents of the previous keyframe are displayed. Whatever is on the stage at Frame 1 (the previous keyframe) appears for a total length of time of 23 frames when the animation runs.

Figure 1–52

Other Ways
1. Right-click frame in Timeline, click Insert Keyframe

Chapter Summary

In this chapter, you gained a broad knowledge of Flash. First, you started Flash and explored the Flash workspace. You created a new Flash document, changed the stage settings, imported a bitmap, and then converted it to a vector. You then exported a vector graphic. Using the Timeline, you created a shape tween animation and then published the animation. You learned how to use Adobe Community Help. Finally, you learned how to quit Flash.

The items listed below include all the new Flash skills you have learned in this chapter:

1. Start Flash (FL 4)
2. Select the Essentials Workspace (FL 6)
3. Create a New ActionScript 3.0 Document (FL 8)
4. Show and Hide Panels (FL 16)
5. Save a Flash Document (FL 17)
6. Disable Auto-Recovery (FL 20)
7. Import a Bitmap (FL 22)
8. Resize the Stage (FL 25)
9. Trace a Bitmap (FL 29)
10. Select and Move a Shape (FL 32)
11. Revert a Document (FL 33)
12. Create a Keyframe (FL 35)
13. Delete Shapes (FL 37)
14. Create a Shape Tween (FL 39)
15. Test the Animation (FL 41)
16. Export a File (FL 43)
17. Configure Publish Settings and Publish Files (FL 45)
18. View Published Files (FL 48)
19. Write ActionScript Code to Stop an Animation (FL 51)
20. Publish an Animation (FL 53)
21. Access Flash Help (FL 54)
22. Use the Help Search Box (FL 55)
23. Quit Flash (FL 57)

Apply Your Knowledge

Reinforce the skills and apply the concepts you learned in this chapter.

Creating and Publishing a Flash Animation

Instructions: Start Flash and perform the customization steps found on pages FL 6 through FL 7. You will create an animation as part of an advertisement for a preschool. In the animation, a caterpillar morphs into a butterfly, as shown in Figure 1–84. First, you will create a new ActionScript 3.0 document. Then you will import and trace two bitmaps at different keyframes. Next, you will create a shape tween to create a morphing animation. Finally, you will publish and view the HTML and SWF files.

Chapter Summary includes a concluding paragraph, followed by a listing of the tasks completed within a chapter together with the pages on which the step-by-step, screen-by-screen explanations appear.

Apply Your Knowledge usually requires students to open and manipulate a file from the Data Files that parallels the activities learned in the chapter.

Textbook Walk-Through

STUDENT ASSIGNMENTS

Apply Your Knowledge

Reinforce the skills and apply the concepts you learned in this chapter.

Planning a Web Site

Instructions: Plan a simple Web site and complete a one-page report in preparation for developing it.

Perform the following tasks:

1. Identify which type of Web site you will design — personal, organizational/topical, or commercial. Write a brief paragraph describing the site's overall purpose and its targeted audience. Create a name for your site.

2. List at least three general goals for your Web site. You will fine-tune these goals into a mission statement in a subsequent chapter.

3. List elements in addition to text — photos, music, animation, and so forth — that you could include on your Web site to support your general goals.

4. List the design tools you expect to use to develop your Web site.

5. List an available domain name and URL for your site.

6. Submit your report to your instructor and be prepared to discuss your report with the class.

Extend Your Knowledge

Extend the skills you learned in this chapter and experiment with new skills. You may need to use Help to complete the assignment.

Learning about HTML

Instructions: Perform the following tasks:

1. Open a Web browser and type the URL, www.cengagebrain.com into the Address or Location bar.

2. If necessary, press the ALT key to access your browser's menu system. Browse through your menu system for the View Source or Page Source command. Click the command to open a window that displays the HTML, similar to Figure 23.

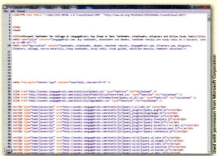

Figure 23

Used with permission from Microsoft Corporation

Continued >

Extend Your Knowledge

projects at the end of each chapter allow students to extend and expand on the skills learned within the chapter. Students use critical thinking to experiment with new skills to complete each project.

Extend Your Knowledge *continued*

3. Make a list of ten HTML tags, noted within angle brackets: < and >. Note that an HTML tag that begins with a slash (/) is an ending to a previous tag; hence, you do not have to list the ending tags.

4. Use a search engine, such as Google, to look up the definition of each of the HTML tags.

5. Submit a report, as directed by your instructor, listing each tag and its definition.

Make It Right

Analyze a project and correct all errors and/or improve the design.

Color-Blind Accessibility Issues

Problem: Protanomaly or protanopia is a specific kind of color blindness where the red shades and hues are seen more weakly. Figure 24a shows a Web site as seen by a person with normal color vision. Figure 24b shows a Web site as seen by a person who is color blind, specifically with prot-anomaly. Notice that it would be impossible for a color-blind person to discern which fields were required. Several free Web tools exist to test Web sites for color issues. You are to evaluate your school's Web site for issues related to color blindness.

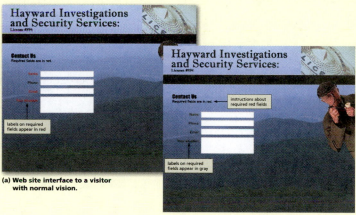

(a) Web site interface to a visitor with normal vision.

(b) Web site interface to a color-blind visitor.

Figure 24

Instructions: Perform the following steps:

1. Open a Web browser and navigate to your school's Web site. Observe the colors and graphics.

2. Click the link in the Address bar to select it.

3. Press CTRL + C to copy the selected link to the system Clipboard.

4. Open a second Web browser window and then type `colorfilter.wickline.org` in the Address bar. Press the ENTER key to go to the Color Filter Web site.

Continued >

Make It Right projects call on students to analyze a file, discover errors in it, and fix them using the skills they learned in the chapter.

Textbook Walk-Through

A local diner is advertising a breakfast special with a Flash banner on its Web site. With the Flash file open, press the ENTER key to play the animation. Note the animation does not work (it simply switches from the egg to the fried egg with no morphing) and there is a broken line in the green area of the Timeline, indicating the shape tween is broken.

Remembering that bitmaps must be traced (and converted to shapes) before a shape tween can be applied, check Frames 1 and 24 and ensure both contain traced bitmaps. (*Hint*: A converted shape appears with a gray dotted overlay.)

Change the document properties, as specified by your instructor. Save the file as Make It Right 1-1 Eggs Fixed and publish the HTML and SWF files with the name, Make it Right 1-1 Eggs Fixed. Submit the revised document in the format specified by your instructor.

In the Lab

Design and/or create a project using the guidelines, concepts, and skills presented in this chapter. Labs are listed in order of increasing difficulty.

Lab 1: Creating a Slide Show

Problem: A florist has asked you to create a slide show for his Web site. Using Flash, you create a slide show where each image appears for three seconds and loops endlessly. One frame from the slide show is displayed in Figure 1–86.

Note: To complete this assignment, you will be required to use the Data Files for Students. Visit www.cengage.com/ct/studentdownload for detailed instructions or contact your instructor for information about accessing the required files.

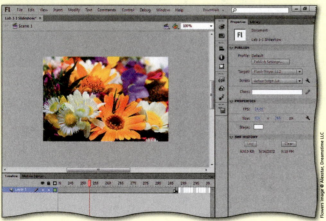

Figure 1–86

Flowers Image © Aleoztar, Dreamstime LLC

Continued >

In the Lab assignments require students to utilize the chapter concepts and techniques to solve problems on a computer.

In the Lab *continued*

    c. Which search found the more relevant links?

    d. Did you find any duplicates in the metasearch? What about in the standard search?

    e. Did either search engine use a filter? What other settings did the search engine provide: Such settings might include bolding your search terms, excluding explicit content, or limiting the number of hits per page.

7. Submit your findings as specified by your instructor.

Cases and Places

Apply your creative thinking and problem-solving skills to design and implement a solution.

1: Create a Usability Survey

Academic

Your school recently updated its Web site. The school administration has selected a team to develop a usability survey or questionnaire that you can give to a group of users (including students, parents, and instructors) to evaluate the new Web site. Identify the types of information you hope to gain by distributing this survey or questionnaire. Create a usability survey using your word processing program. Be sure to carefully word the questions to collect the specific feedback you want. For example, asking "Do you like the Web site?" is not as helpful as asking "What do you like about the Web site?" Give the survey or questionnaire to at least five people, including at least one from each group identified above. Allow participants to complete the survey or questionnaire and then look at the results. Did the survey results provide the type of information you were seeking? If not, reword your questions to be more specific, and redistribute the survey to another group of participants. Apply your creative thinking and problem-solving skills to design and implement a solution.

2: Use Trial Software

Personal

You would like to try some of the other applications in the Adobe Creative Suite 6. Go to the Web site http://www.adobe.com/downloads/ and point to any application, such as InDesign or After Effects. When the links appear below the application, click Try. When the Trial Web site appears, click the Download button. (If you are on a lab machine, please check with your instructor before downloading and installing new software.) Install the software per the instructions. Once installed, open the software and try creating a simple file. Explore the menus. Look at the panels and toolbars. Write a summary of your experience and submit it as directed by your instructor.

3: Research Web Design Software

Professional

Your friend owns a small nail salon and wants a Web site to advertise her business. She knows of your interest in Web design and wants you to recommend software to her. Using Web search tools, investigate the differences between the Adobe Creative Suite and other kinds of Web creation software such as Microsoft Expression Web or Office application software to determine which might be the best choice to create her Web site. Consider things such as price, user-friendliness, the learning curve, the output, and accessibility when doing your research. Write a summary and submit it as directed by your instructor.

Found within the Cases and Places exercises, the **Personal** activities call on students to create an open-ended project that relates to their personal lives.

Introduction to Adobe Creative Suite 6 and Web Design

Objectives

You will have mastered the material in this project when you can:

- Define the purpose of the Adobe Creative Suite 6

- Explain the differences between the package versions of Adobe CS6

- Characterize Web design

- Describe the Internet and its associated key terms

- Describe the World Wide Web and its associated key terms

- List the types and purposes of Web sites

- Define Web servers, publishing, and hosting

- Categorize Web browsers and identify their purpose

- Explain HTML and CSS in relation to Web design

- Identify the types of tools used to create Web pages

- Describe how to plan a Web site

- Describe how to select a host for a Web site

- Identify the steps in creating, managing, and updating a Web site

Introduction to Adobe Creative Suite 6 and Web Design

Introduction

Before you begin to use the applications in Adobe Creative Suite 6, you should understand the role of the suite and how the suite applications interact. You will learn how Adobe packages the applications as well as how they relate to Web development, the Internet, and the World Wide Web. The **Adobe Creative Suite 6**, also known as **Adobe CS6**, is a collection of applications to perform graphic design, animation, video editing, publishing, and Web development. Adobe CS6 includes more than 15 applications distributed in five different packages based on purpose and level of complexity. As the industry-standard software for graphic design, professional designers as well as amateurs use the Adobe Creative Suite 6 to edit photos, create animations and illustrations, edit video, and publish both print and Web publications.

Because much of the Adobe-created content that designers develop ends up on the Web, it is important to understand the hardware and software protocols used by the Internet and the World Wide Web. The Internet is a worldwide network of connected computers and computer networks, made up of millions of users using a vast range of technologies. Trillions of Web pages, providing information on any subject you can imagine, currently are available on the World Wide Web. People use the Internet to search for information, to communicate with others around the world, and to seek entertainment. Students register for classes, pay tuition, and find out final grades using this computer network. Stores and individuals sell their products using computer connectivity, and most industries rely on the Internet and the World Wide Web for business transactions.

In this chapter, you will learn about the purpose of the individual applications in Adobe CS6 and some basics about Web design, the Internet, hardware, and software. You will be introduced to Web browsers, types and purposes of Web sites, development tools, and the process of planning and developing a Web site.

Adobe Creative Suite 6

Adobe CS6 is a suite, or collection, of many applications, including those you might have heard of, such as Photoshop, Flash, and Dreamweaver, as well as some applications you might not be familiar with, such as Contribute, Encore, and Audition. You can purchase the applications within the suite individually, but Adobe also packages its suite products into groups, geared for specific tasks and users. For example, the **Design Standard** package includes industry-standard software for editing digital images, creating vector graphics, and laying out high-quality print documents with elegant typography. In addition, it includes software to create e-books and interactive digital documents. The **Design Premium** package helps you create content, such as digital magazines, online content, Web sites based on current Internet standards, and digital content for mobile devices such as smartphones and tablets. The **Web Premium** package provides everything you need to create and deliver standards-based Web sites, including content for cross-platform digital devices and apps. The **Production Premium** package is used for video production with powerful audio and video-editing tools, work flow improvements, and advanced compositing effects. The **Master Collection** package includes all of the Adobe CS6 products.

Table 1 displays individual products in Adobe Creative Suite 6 and the packages in which they are included.

Table 1 Adobe Creative Suite 6 Applications and Packages

Software	Design Standard	Design Premium	Web Premium	Production Premium	Master Collection
Acrobat X Pro	X	X	X		X
After Effects				X	X
Audition				X	X
Bridge	X	X	X	X	X
Contribute			X		X
Device Central	X	X	X	X	X
Dreamweaver		X	X		
Encore				X	X
Fireworks		X	X		X
Flash		X	X	X	X
Flash Catalyst		X	X	X	X
Illustrator	X	X	X	X	X
InDesign	X	X			X
Photoshop	X	X	X	X	X
Premiere				X	X

The Adobe CS6 Applications

This book introduces you to three of the most popular, industry-leading applications in the Adobe Creative Suite 6: Photoshop, Flash, and Dreamweaver. Appendix E also introduces Adobe Bridge, the suite's file management system. It is important, however, to be familiar with the general purpose of each of the applications in the suite. Table 2 on the next page describes the purpose of some of the individual products in Adobe Creative Suite 6.

As you work through this book, you will learn the basics of Photoshop, Flash, and Dreamweaver — the three most popular of the Adobe CS6 applications. You will learn about basic photo editing, manipulation selections in photos, and effectively using layers in Photoshop. In Flash, you will learn how to draw vector art, use keyframes, and create symbols and instances while creating animations for the Web. As you study Dreamweaver, you will learn how to create a Web page in a local site; add other pages, links, and images; and create tables in advanced page layouts. In the appendices, you will be introduced to graphic design, the Adobe CS6 Help system, Adobe Bridge, and uploading files to Web servers.

Table 2 Adobe Creative Suite 6 Software Applications and Purpose	
Software	**Purpose/User Application**
Acrobat	Create and edit PDF (Portable Document Format) files with text and media content
After Effects	Create and edit sophisticated motion graphics and cinematic visual effects
Audition	Perform audio production tasks with tools, including recording, mixing, and sound restoration
Bridge	Manage files and media with centralized access and organizational tools
Contribute	Publish and manage Web sites, integrating authoring, reviewing, and publishing in an easy-to-use editor
Device Central	Test content for mobile phones, tablets, and consumer electronic devices
Dreamweaver	Author and edit Web pages with visual and code-level tools
Encore	Create and manage DVDs, Blu-ray discs, and Web files with content from other applications
Fireworks	Create optimized graphics for the Web and other devices
Flash	Create and edit interactive content and experiences for desktop users, the Web, and other electronic devices
Illustrator	Create and edit vector artwork for any project with drawing tools, brushes, and advanced typography
InDesign	Design desktop publishing page layouts for print or digital distribution
Photoshop	Edit photos and create digital images with advanced filtering, correction, and painting tools
Premiere	Edit video and audio in native formats with cross-platform capabilities

Windows vs. Mac OS

The figures in this book use the Windows operating system; however, Adobe CS6 applications look very similar whether you are using either the Windows or the Mac Operating System. Both versions present the same tools and similar menus. One of the main differences is in the approach to shortcut keys. Windows uses the CTRL key to access many of the shortcuts in the Adobe Creative Suite 6; Mac OS uses the CMD key represented by the symbol ⌘ and sometimes the OPT key represented by the symbol ⌥.

The Windows and Mac versions also differ in the look and feel of the operating system standard dialog boxes, such as New, Open, Save, and Print. As dialog boxes are introduced throughout the book, the corresponding figures are displayed in Windows; Mac users should refer to Appendix G for specifics about the dialog boxes.

Whether you use Windows or Mac OS, you will find the steps in this book work with either system.

The Internet and the World Wide Web

Many people use the terms, Internet, and, World Wide Web, interchangeably, but that is not entirely accurate. The difference has to do with the physical networks required to create connections versus the collections of documents and files referred to as Web pages and Web sites.

Internet

Most people today have had exposure to the Internet at school, in their homes, at their jobs, or at their local library. The **Internet** is a worldwide collection of computers and computer networks that links billions of computers used by businesses, government, educational institutions, organizations, and individuals using modems, phone lines, television cables, satellite links, fiber-optic connections, other communications devices, and multimedia (Figure 1). The Internet is the infrastructure or the physical networks of computers.

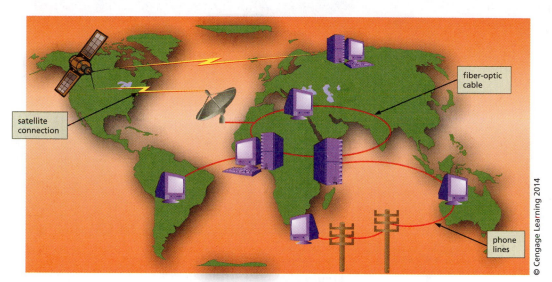

Figure 1

A **network** is a collection of two or more computers that are connected for the purpose of sharing resources and information. High-, medium-, and low-speed data lines connect networks. These data lines permit data (including text, graphical images, and audio and video data) to move from one computer to another. An **Internet service provider (ISP)** is a company that has a permanent connection to the Internet. ISPs use high- or medium-speed data lines to allow individuals and companies to connect to the Internet. An Internet connection at home generally is a DSL or cable data line that connects to an ISP. Businesses typically use high-speed connectivity methods, including T-1 leased lines, OC3 leased lines, and other high-capacity methods.

World Wide Web

The **World Wide Web**, also called the **Web**, consists of a collection of linked documents composed in Hypertext Markup Language (HTML). To support multimedia, the Web relies on the **Hypertext Transfer Protocol (HTTP)**, which is a set of rules for exchanging text, graphic, sound, video, and other multimedia files. Web users must have Web browser software, such as Microsoft Internet Explorer or Google Chrome, installed on their computers in order to view and navigate Web pages.

Users with computers connected to the Internet can access a variety of services, including e-mail, social networking, and the World Wide Web where they can find information at many different types of Web sites (Figure 2 on the next page).

Figure 2

The Cloud

Cloud computing, or the **cloud**, as it is called, is the delivery of computing services using the Internet. Many software and hardware companies that used to sell or provide physical products are now providing those products using Web services. A **Web service** is a software technology delivered to consumers over the Internet, rather than as an installed application on their computers. For example, instead of a company purchasing and installing health benefits management software, the company instead could access the software from the cloud, without having to buy or install anything. These cloud services share resources, software, and information as they distribute their product to computers and other devices as a utility. The advantages are many. The cloud frees information technology departments (IT) from the responsibilities associated with installation, maintenance, and increased user demand. Cloud providers are responsible for all infrastructure and repair of cloud-based products, in addition to meeting surges in demand and ensuring that the service is reliable.

What Is Web Design?

Web design or **Web development** is the process of planning, creating, testing, and implementing a Web page or Web site. A Web designer or developer must think about the information architecture, hardware, software, user interface, site structure, navigation, layout, colors, fonts, text, graphics, sound, video, and, most important, meeting the needs and goals of the Web site purpose or owner. The Adobe Creative

Suite 6 can help you design standards-based Web pages and Web sites — sites that adhere to standard protocols and design recommendations of the World Wide Web Consortium (W3C).

A **Web page** is a document or resource suitable for use on the World Wide Web. Because the Web supports text, files, graphics, sound, and video, a Web page can include any of these multimedia elements. Users access Web pages through a Web browser and display pages on a screen, which might be a computer monitor or a mobile device. The Web is ever changing and consists of trillions of Web pages. Because of the ease of creating Web pages, both new Web sites and pages with updated content are being added all the time.

A **Web site** is a related collection of Web pages, created and maintained by an individual, company, educational institution, or other organization. Each Web site contains a **home page**, which is the first document users see when they access the Web site. The home page often serves as an index or table of contents to other documents and files displayed on the site, as shown in Figure 3.

Figure 3

Many people think of Web design in relation to the Web page that they can see using a Web browser. This kind of access into the Web sometimes is called the **presentation layer** or **tier**. Much of the design and navigational functionality is developed in the presentation tier, as it displays application data in a user-friendly format and provides user controls. The coding to create the presentation tier is called **client-side coding** — the user is the client and the Web browser performs the commands. Client-side computing enables the Web site to have different, changing content depending on user input, environmental conditions (such as the time of day), or other variables. If the Web site accepts data entry, the client-side processing in the presentation tier ensures that valid data is entered into the Web form.

Behind the scenes, programming implements the navigation and calculations that must occur in order to fulfill the requirements of the Web site. Also called **server-side coding**, this code is not accessible to or visible by the casual Web site visitor. It is executed and stored on the computer that hosts the Web site, storing the Web pages and collecting data permanently (Figure 4).

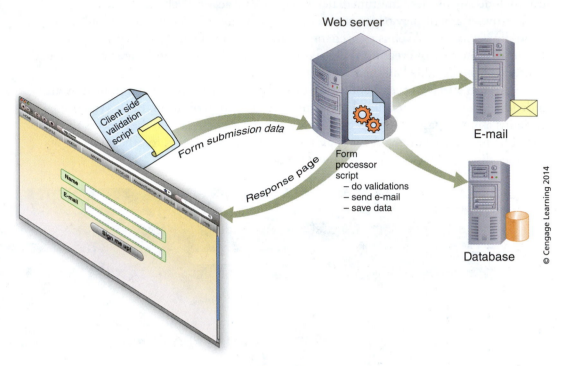

Figure 4

Whereas beginning Web designers typically include all of the processing in a single file, more advanced programmers use a tier structure. Like other application programs, tiers or layers delineate and necessarily separate the parts of the Web site for organization, development, maintenance, and security.

Types of Web Sites

The types of sites found on the Web can be personal, organizational/topical, or commercial. A Web site's type differs from its purpose. The type is defined as the category of site, and is determined by the company or individual responsible for the site's creation. For example, the purpose of a site by a company might be to sell its products. An overview of personal, organizational/topical, and commercial Web sites follows, along with the individual design challenges they present.

Personal Web Sites

Individuals create their own personal Web sites for a range of communication purposes. You might use a personal Web site to promote your employment credentials, share news and photos with friends and family, or share a common interest or hobby with fellow enthusiasts. Depending on your site's purpose, you might include your résumé, blog, photo gallery, biography, e-mail address, or a description. Families can share photographs, video and audio clips, stories, schedules, or other information through Web sites. Many individual Web sites allow password protection, which protects the content from unauthorized persons.

Creating a personal Web site is typically less complex than creating other types of sites. Working independently means you must assume all the roles necessary to build the Web site. Web roles are discussed later in this chapter. Despite these challenges, you can publish a successful Web site to promote yourself and your services, or simply tell the world what you are all about. You also can use a **content management system (CMS)** to allow you to focus on the content of your site and not its structure. The Web offers a range of tools for creating personal sites using CMS tools such as Windows Live or Joomla.

Blogging or social networking tools are free alternatives to creating a personal Web site. Although lacking the full range of Web page elements, Facebook, for example, can give you a presence on the Web by allowing you to communicate and share information with your friends; LinkedIn can present your résumé, references, and business connections to potential employers (Figure 5).

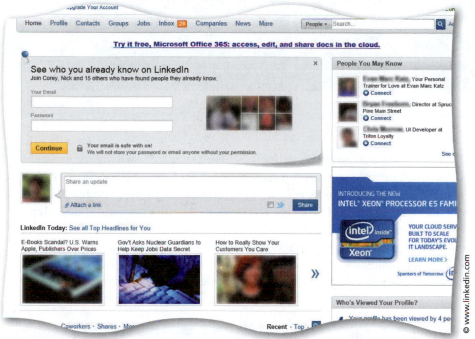

Figure 5

Organizational and Topical Web Sites

An organizational Web site is one that is owned by any type of group, association, or organization, whether it is a professional or amateur group. For example, if you belong to the Photoshop Enthusiasts of North America, you might volunteer to create an organizational Web site to promote member accomplishments or to encourage support and participation. Conversely, as a photographer, you might choose to design a topical Web site devoted to black-and-white photography to share your knowledge with others, including tips for amateurs, photo galleries, and online resources. A site that is focused on a specific subject is called a topical Web site. The purpose of both types of sites is to provide resources to the Web site visitors.

Professional, nonprofit, international, social, volunteer, and various other types of organizations abound on the Web, as do Web sites devoted to every topic imaginable. As you browse the Web, however, you will find that some organizational and topical Web sites lack accurate, timely, objective, and authoritative content. You must evaluate a Web site's content for these four elements carefully. Figure 6 on the next page shows an example of an organizational Web site developed by Calvary United Methodist Church of Brownsburg, Indiana.

Figure 6

Colleges, universities, and other schools use Web sites to distribute information about areas of study, provide course information, or register students for classes online. Instructors use their Web sites to issue announcements, post questions on reading material, list contact information, and provide easy access to lecture notes and slides. Many instructors today use course management software, such as Blackboard or Oncourse, adopted by their respective schools, to upload course content. In addition to keeping in contact with current students, university Web sites, like the Indiana University Purdue University Indianapolis site shown in Figure 7, provide a range of information to a variety of visitors, including prospective students, parents, faculty, and staff.

Figure 7

Commercial Web Sites

The goal of a commercial Web site is to promote and sell products or services of a business, from the smallest home-based business to the largest international enterprise. **Electronic commerce (e-commerce)** is the buying and selling of goods and services on the Internet. In addition to advertising and selling, companies may provide technical and product support for their customers as well as the ability to browse product catalogs and comparison shop. Figure 8 shows Cengage.com, which is a company that sells and distributes book-related materials online.

Figure 8

Search Tools

Search tools are commercial Web sites that locate specific information on the Web based on a user's search requirements. A **search engine** is a Web-based search tool that locates a Web page using a word or phrase found in the page. To find Web pages on particular topics using a popular search engine, such as Google, Bing, or Ask.com, you enter a term or phrase, called a **keyword,** in the search engine's text box and click a button usually labeled Search or Go. The search engine compares your search keywords or phrases within the contents of its database of pages and then displays a list of relevant pages. A match between a keyword search and the resulting occurrence is called a hit.

Search engine optimization (SEO) is the process of designing a Web page to increase the likelihood that the page will appear high in a search engine's search results list. Search engine optimization tools include metatags, descriptive page titles, relevant inbound links from other sites, and clearly written text.

Hardware and Software

The hardware and software needed for the creation and maintenance of Web pages and Web sites includes Web servers, Web browsers, and HTML.

Web Servers

Web pages are stored on a **Web server**, or **host**, which is a computer that stores and sends (serves) requested Web pages and other files. Any computer that has Web server software installed and is connected to the Internet can act as a Web server. Every Web site is stored on, and runs from, one or more Web servers. A large Web site might be spread over several servers in different geographic locations.

To make the Web pages that you have developed available to your audience, you have to publish those pages. **Publishing** is the process of copying the Web pages and associated files, such as graphics and audio, to a Web server. Once a Web page is published, anyone who has access to the Internet can view it, regardless of where the Web server is located. For example, although the U.S. Department of Labor Web site is stored on a Web server somewhere in the United States, it can be viewed by anyone, anywhere in the world. Once a Web page is published, it can be read by almost any computer — whether you use the Mac, Windows, or Linux operating system — and on any type of computer hardware. For more information on publishing to a Web server, see Appendix C, Publishing a Web Site.

Web Browsers

To display a Web page on any type of Web site, a computer needs to have a Web browser installed. A **Web browser**, also called a **browser**, is a program that interprets and displays Web pages and enables you to view and interact with a Web page. Microsoft Internet Explorer, Mozilla Firefox, Google Chrome, and Apple Safari are popular browsers. Browsers provide a variety of features, including the capability to locate Web pages, to move forward and backward among Web pages, to add a favorite, to bookmark a Web page, and to set security settings.

To locate a Web page using a browser, you type the Web page's Uniform Resource Locator (URL) in the browser's Address or Location bar. A **Uniform Resource Locator (URL)** is the address of a document or other file accessible on the Internet. Web page URLs can be found in a wide range of places, including school catalogs, business cards, product packaging, and advertisements. Figure 9 shows an example of a URL on the Web and explains its parts.

Hyperlinks are an essential part of the World Wide Web. A **hyperlink**, also called a **link**, is an element used to connect one Web page to another Web page on the same server or to Web pages on different Web servers located anywhere in the world. Clicking a hyperlink allows you to move quickly from one Web page to another, without concern for where the Web pages reside or where they are stored. You can also click hyperlinks to move to a different section of the same Web page.

Many different Web page elements, including text, graphics, and animations, can serve as hyperlinks. Figure 10 shows examples of several different Web page elements used as hyperlinks.

protocol   domain name   path   Web page name

http://www.usps.com/household/stampcollecting/welcome.htm

Figure 9

logo hyperlink   button hyperlink   text hyperlink

navigation hyperlinks

graphic hyperlink

Figure 10

© Cengage Learning 2014

What Is Hypertext Markup Language?

When you access a Web page with your browser, the Web server reads through a coded page line by line and executes the code to display the finished page. **Hypertext Markup Language (HTML)** is the language used to develop basic Web pages. To view the HTML source code for a Web page using Internet Explorer, right-click the Web page, and then click View source. Web site programming allows you to turn a simple, static HTML page into a dynamic Web page by using various programming languages within the HTML code. Web programming languages, such as PHP and ASP, provide user interaction to fill in an online application, post your Facebook status, submit a dinner review at Yelp, purchase your textbooks online, or request an online Groupon coupon, for example.

HTML is **platform independent**, meaning you can create, or code, an HTML file on one type of computer, and then use a browser on another type of computer to view that file as a Web page. The page looks the same regardless of what platform you are using. One of the greatest benefits of Web technology is that the same Web page can be viewed on many different types of digital hardware, including mobile devices like smartphones. The newest HTML standard is **HTML5**, representing the fifth major revision of the core Web language. Web developers use HTML5 to display their sites on a variety of smartphones, tablets, and computers without tailoring the code for specific hardware. HTML5 supports in-browser multimedia by adding simple tags to play audio and video elements. HTML5 enables developers to write less JavaScript code (a scripting Web language), which makes the site easier to code and update.

What Is CSS?

Cascading Style Sheets (CSS) are collections of formatting definitions that affect the appearance of Web page elements. You can use CSS **styles** to format text, images, headings, tables, and so forth. Using CSS, you can make a formatting change in one place and update all the Web pages that contain that same formatting. CSS layouts are used to create a similar look and feel across Web sites. They also are used to reduce the amount of work and HTML code generated by consolidating display properties into a single file.

Creating Web Pages

You can create Web pages and Web sites using a variety of tools, including text editors, application software, Web design software, animation software, and graphic manipulation/creation software.

Text Editors

As you learned earlier in this chapter, you can write HTML code to create Web sites. HTML code typically is written using a text editor. A **text editor**, such as Notepad, is a program that allows a user to enter, change, save, and print text, such as HTML. Text editors do not have many advanced features, but they do allow you to develop HTML documents easily. A **value-added text editor (VATE)** such as TextPad is a more robust text editor that uses color schemes for HTML code, along with the ability to record macros, run programs, and preview Web pages. An **HTML text editor** such as EditPlus is a program that provides basic text-editing functions, as well as more advanced features such as color coding for various HTML tags, menus to insert HTML tags, and spell checkers. An **HTML object editor** such as EiffelStudio provides the additional functionality of an outline editor that allows you to expand and collapse HTML objects and properties, edit parameters, and view graphics attached to the expanded objects. Figure 11 displays some features of HTML text editors.

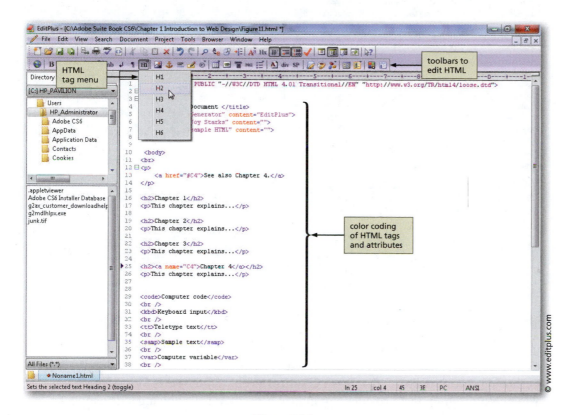

Figure 11

Application Software

Many popular software applications also provide features that enable you to develop Web pages easily. Microsoft Word, Excel, and PowerPoint, for example, have a Save as Web Page option that converts a document into an HTML file by automatically adding HTML tags to the document. Adobe Acrobat also has an export feature that creates HTML files. Each of these applications allows you to add hyperlinks, drop-down boxes, option buttons, or scrolling text to the Web page. These applications make it simple to save any document, spreadsheet, database, or presentation to display as a Web page. Corporate policies, procedure manuals, and PowerPoint presentations, for example, easily can be saved as Web pages and published to the company's intranet. Figure 12 on the next page displays an Excel spreadsheet saved as a Web page.

Although using application software to create Web pages is easy, it often produces extraneous, nonstandard code. The Web pages typically will lack much of the functionality of Web design software. Additionally, application software–created Web pages work better with specific associated browsers. For example, a Web page created using Microsoft Word will appear perfectly in the Microsoft browser, Internet Explorer, but might not appear correctly using Mozilla Firefox.

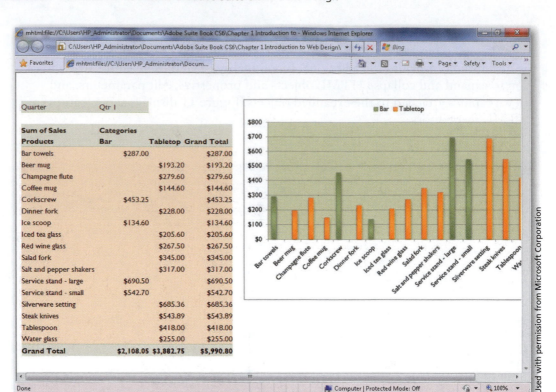

Used with permission from Microsoft Corporation

Figure 12

Web Design Software

Many people create Web pages using Web design software such as Adobe Dreamweaver, Amaya, or CoffeeCup. Most Web design software, also called Web authoring software, uses a **WYSIWYG editor (What You See Is What You Get)**, which is a program that provides a graphical user interface, allowing a developer to preview the Web page during its development.

Advantages of using a Web authoring program like Dreamweaver include the ability to create Web sites quickly and easily with helpful tools to enhance the design. Authoring programs also help you to manage the folders and files in which you create, build, and manage Web sites and Internet applications.

Dreamweaver contains coding tools and features that include references for HTML, CSS, and other scripting languages, as well as editors that allow you to edit the code directly (Figure 13). It also provides the tools that help you author accessible content. **Web accessibility** means that people with disabilities can access and use the Web pages you create. More specifically, Web accessibility means that people with disabilities can perceive, navigate, and interact with the Web. Web accessibility also benefits others, including older people with changing abilities. Dreamweaver uses accessible pages that comply with government guidelines and Section 508 of the Federal Rehabilitation Act.

Animation Software

Many Web pages benefit from animation to explain things such as process flow or production concepts; many sites use animation as an attention getter. Computer animation encompasses a variety of techniques, the unifying factor being that the animation is created digitally on a computer, including two-dimensional (2D) animation and three-dimensional (3D) animation.

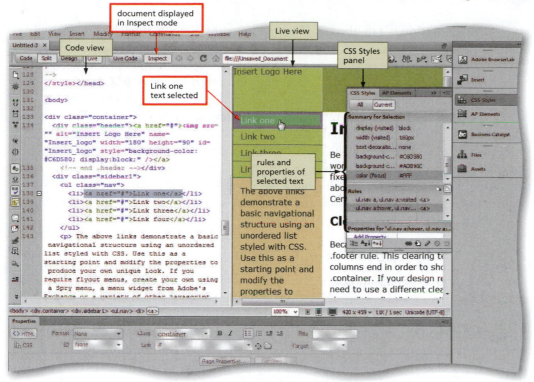

Figure 13

2D animation is created or edited using bitmap or vector graphics with computerized versions of traditional animation techniques such as rotation and morphing. For example, cel animation is a type of 2D animation based on a series of frames or cels in which the object is redrawn in each consecutive cel to depict motion. The motion of animation is perceived by the viewer as a series of frames. Onion Skinning animation, a term taken from the type of transparent paper that graphic artists use to follow their animation, allows the animation artist to see a faint outline of the previous cel in order to draw the changes for the next cel. Path-based animation moves an object along a predetermined path on the screen.

Adobe Flash is a popular animation-generating software (Figure 14). Toon Boom and TV Paint are used widely as well. Some users create animations from packaged animations and clip art, such as those found in Microsoft PowerPoint.

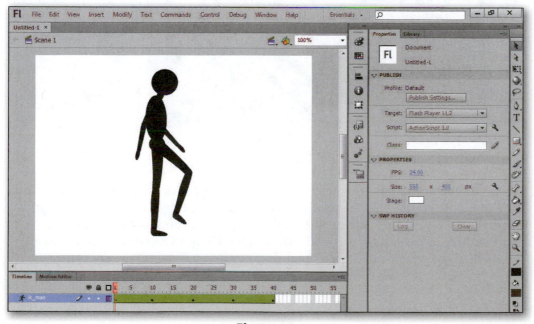

Figure 14

3D animation is a method in which an animator digitally models and manipulates graphics to create animation. Computer animators create a three-dimensional "model" to start with and use the computer to modify small sections of an object, using software such as 3ds Max, Maya, or Poser. **Computer-generated imagery (CGI)** is the application of 3D computer graphics to create dynamic and static special effects in Web design, art, video games, films, television, simulations, and printed media. For example, in a process called rigging, animators manipulate a mesh using a digital skeletal structure to control the mesh. Various other techniques can be applied, such as mathematical functions, physical functions such as gravity, special effects such as fire and water, and the use of motion capture, to name but a few. Well-made 3D animations can be difficult to distinguish from live action and commonly are used as visual effects for movies.

Graphic Manipulation/Creation Software

Sometimes photos appear on the Web in their original, unedited state; but more commonly, photos and graphics benefit from being edited before being used on the Web. Manipulating photos and graphics is an important tool in graphic design. As you learned earlier in the chapter, programs like Photoshop provide many ways to edit, create, store, and optimize graphics (Figure 15). Some users edit graphics with a less-expensive, scaled-down version of Photoshop called Photoshop Elements. Still others use shareware programs such as GIMP (GNU Image Manipulation Program).

Figure 15

Computer graphics can be classified into two distinct categories: raster graphics and vector graphics. Raster graphics represent images by using rectangular grids of pixels; vector graphics use geometrical shapes such as arcs, points, lines, and shapes to represent images. Appendix B, Graphic Design Overview, presents more information on graphic design.

Planning a Web Site

The first step in building your first Web site is to design a detailed plan to ensure success. Defining your site's purpose, its target audience, the intended Web platform, and the proposed design is a crucial aspect of Web development. You need to make sure that visitors are immediately drawn into your site through captivating content, a compelling call to action, ease of use, and a sense of community.

Planning Basics

Those who rush into publishing their Web site without proper planning usually design sites that are unorganized and difficult to navigate. Visitors to this type of Web site often lose interest quickly and do not return. As you begin planning your Web site, consider the following guidelines to ensure that you set and attain realistic goals.

Purpose and Goal   Determine the purpose and goal of your Web site. Create a focus by developing a mission statement, which conveys the intention of the Web site. Consider the 10 basic types of Web sites mentioned previously. Will your Web site consist of one basic type or a combination of two or more types? For example, a business Web site's purpose may be to market new products and services or provide customer support. By focusing on the goals that you hope to achieve, you can effectively plan a site that fits your organization's business model.

Target Audience   Knowing your target audience is essential to good design because the needs of your intended visitors help shape the content of a site as well as its look and feel. Figure 16 shows the Web site for a popular outdoor company named REI that is customized to its target audience. The intended audience at the REI site is anyone who enjoys nature and outdoor adventures. Notice the image on the REI home page during the month of January is customized to the time of the year. Visitors in the

Figure 16

winter most likely are focused on snow activities including sledding and skiing, and interested in clothing that provides warmth during the winter season. Easy navigation using a wide variety of links is provided for the major categories of products sold at REI. A search tool at the top of the site enables quick and easy navigation to the desired products. Knowing the information that your target audience is searching for simplifies their purchasing experience at this site. Creating a welcoming, easy-to-navigate experience is vital to any site, so consider the characteristics of your target audience such as interest, gender, education, age range, income, profession/job field, and computer proficiency.

Multiplatform Display   Where will your target audience view your Web site? Will it be displayed on a Mac laptop using Safari, a Windows tablet using Internet Explorer, an Android phone on a built-in browser, or a desktop PC using Mozilla Firefox? Planning for Web presentation involves verifying that your site will function in a variety of browsers based on the intended layout and in different screen resolutions. **Screen resolution** refers to the number of pixels in a display, such as 1280 × 800. The layout of a Web site can change depending on the user's screen resolution. Creating a multi-platform Web page, also called a **cross-platform site,** that provides a similar display experience across various screen sizes, resolutions, browsers, and devices is supported by a new code environment called HTML5 and CSS3, which are explained later in the chapter. Web developers must plan their sites to deploy on any device without worrying that the device itself will not support a particular graphic or effect used in the page.

Design

A Web site consists of more than information and links. A well-designed Web site creates a positive interaction with the user by focusing on a visual, aesthetically pleasing way to present information. Web users prefer a simple, clean, and functional design. Avoid a cluttered design that uses multiple fonts, inconsistent icons, flashing ads, and ubiquitous links. Consider the following Web design principles when creating a memorable site.

Focal Point   A mixture of elements including text, colors, and images all compete for your attention when you open a Web page. A design element called a **focal point** provides a dominating element that captures your attention. In Figure 17, the United States Department of Agriculture nutrition site uses a dominant image as a focal point to immediately draw your attention to and illustrate the purpose of this site — choosing a plate full of healthy foods. A focal point in your site may be an element such as a prominent header, company logo, or central product image. Notice the amount of white space in the site in Figure 17. **White space** is the empty space around the focal point and other design elements that enables important aspects of the page to stand out. White space does not have to be white; it can be the background color of the page. Appropriate use of white space can lead the user's eye to important content. When a Web page lacks a clear focal point and white space, competing images, flashing text, and abundant text can confuse the user.

Color as a Design Tool   Color effectively can convey information that adds interest and vitality to your site. Color should be aesthetically pleasing to your target audience and suit the content of the page. For example, in Figure 16 on the previous page, the gray and white colors fit the page's winter theme. When designing Web pages for

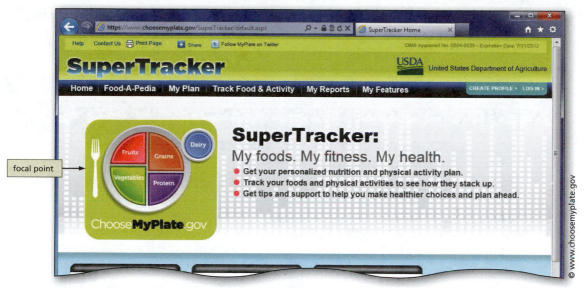

focal point

Figure 17

a business environment, consider the company's branding colors. In Figure 18, the site for the Cengage Learning publishing company incorporates the colors in the logo shown in the upper-left corner of the page. The blue color scheme of this page reinforces the site's overall message and identity.

company logo

Figure 18

The most common misuse of color is a background color that detracts from the readability of the text. How much time would you spend on a site featuring a bright yellow background and white text? A bright yellow background strains the eyes, making it impossible to read the text. Keep in mind that people use color to categorize objects in their everyday lives. Colors in the cool color group such as green and blue tend to have a calming effect. Similarly, many companies use color in their Web design to help users identify and categorize their brand with just one glance. For example, red is associated with power and energy, making it a good color for a sports car. Table 3 describes the common colors and their related meanings.

Table 3 Common Color Meanings	
Color	**Description**
Blue	Trust, security, conservative, technology (The most common color used on the Web)
Green	Nature, money, earth, health, good luck
White	Purity, cleanliness, innocence, precision
Red	Power, danger, passion, love, energy
Black	Sophistication, power, death, fear
Gray	Intellect, elegance, modesty
Orange	Energy, balance, warmth, brightness
Yellow	Cheer, optimism, joy, honesty
Brown	Reliability, earth, comfort
Purple	Mystery, spirituality, arrogance, royalty

Text Design   Like other Web elements, good **typography**, or the appearance and arrangement of the characters that make up your text, is vital to the success of your Web page. Adding text is not just about placing letters on a site, but rather using text as a page design element to improve readability. The introductory text of a Web page should instantly convey the purpose of the site. A Web site visitor will more likely read a short and well-structured introduction while skipping longer paragraphs of text. In the Web site for the Fish restaurant shown in Figure 19, the shading on the left provides a focal point for the text. The introductory text is short, useful, and interesting. A call to action initiated by the text requests that you view the menus. The site clearly defines what its targeted audience wants to view first — the menus.

text design

call to action

© www.fishrestaurantcharleston.com

Figure 19

On an opening page, shorter text can captivate your audience. But when longer paragraphs are necessary to provide more detailed information, the text should be easy to read. A font face or font family is the typeface that will be applied to the text by a

Web browser. Select fonts with good readability — especially when developing pages for smaller, mobile devices.

Image Design Images provide an instant focal point to any site and give viewers an immediate cue about page content. In the Fish restaurant example in Figure 19, the image of Asian food on the home page conveys the flavor of the cuisine and the ambiance of this restaurant. Even a cursory glance at this opening communicates a positive impression for that type of cuisine and atmosphere.

An image can stimulate visual interest, market a product, display a company logo, illustrate a process, or provide graphical information. Visitors' eyes are naturally drawn to photos of people. Creating a balance between the number of images and text elements is vital to achieving an uncluttered appearance. An image leaves a stronger impression because our brains are drawn to familiar, real-life objects rather than words alone.

Accessibility Guidelines

In your planning phase, you must ensure your site is accessible to all users. Imagine if your school's Web site was not accessible to all students regardless of physical limitations. For schools and government entities it is not only unwise, but also likely in violation of federal law. Section 508, which was added as an amendment in 1998 to the Rehabilitation Act, requires that electronic and information technology that is developed by or purchased by federal agencies be accessible to people with disabilities (www.section508.gov). Businesses seek the largest possible audience and recognize the positive return on investment (ROI) for the extra costs of building a site accessible to all customers. Table 4 categorizes the major types of disabilities. Each requires certain kinds of adaptations in the design of the Web content, but ultimately everyone benefits from helpful illustrations and clear navigation.

Table 4 Disability Types and Design Strategies		
Disability	**Description**	**Design Strategies**
Cognitive	Autism, learning disabilities, distractibility, inability to focus on large amounts of information	Keep text short. Break up text with headings. Use meaningful graphics.
Hearing	Deafness	Provide a transcription or summary of audio elements.
Motor	Inability to move mouse or use touch screen, slower response time	Minimize scrolling.
Visual	Blindness, poor vision, color blindness	Describe images in text (which may be read aloud by a screen reader). Use a large, easy-to-read font.

As a Web designer, removing barriers so people with disabilities have equal access to the Web is a moral and often a legal obligation under the Americans with Disabilities Act (ADA). For example, a visually impaired person often uses a screen reader, which is a software application that can vocalize screen content. A Web site image should contain information called **alternative text** describing the picture for the screen. The **World Wide Web Consortium (W3C)**, an international standards organization for the World Wide Web, provides Web standards, language specifications, and accessibility recommendations at www.w3.org to promote the growth of the Web. Forward-thinking Web developers plan their sites with accessibility in mind because it is the right thing to do. Accessibility needs to be an integral part of Web design planning rather than an afterthought. Throughout this text, accessibility is illustrated as each aspect of Web page development is covered.

Role of Social Networking

Planning a site extends beyond selecting content and following accessibility rules. Modern Web sites enable users to interact with one another and share information. These sites create a sense of community with two-way conversations between site visitors and business responses, including product reviews, targeted e-mail, a Facebook and Twitter marketing presence, YouTube links to new product video demonstrations, and blog feedback. These online interactions allow businesses to give their customers a voice and help them improve their products, services, and customer satisfaction. A Web site can provide customer reviews and ratings to help other customers. In addition, many sites incorporate Facebook pages and Twitter follower links by providing logos and inviting visitors to connect with them.

As shown in Figure 20, the publishing company Cengage Learning provides a Facebook and Twitter logo on its opening page to allow a user to "like" or "follow" its product line. When a visitor "likes" a business, he or she becomes a fan on Facebook, promoting that business to all of the visitor's personal contacts. Cengage Learning leverages Facebook and Twitter to provide instructors and students with the latest technology innovations, educational research, and e-book ventures. This social networking resource offers the customer a location to share learning success stories, ask questions, and post new ways to integrate classroom solutions. This presence creates an interwoven community of friends and colleagues who quickly can learn about the business from others who have liked or followed it.

(a) Cengage Learning page

(b) Linked Facebook presence

(c) Linked Twitter presence

Figure 20

Web Site Hosting

Creating a good Web site begins with planning the content and structure. But selecting a Web server host, which makes a Web site visible to the world through a unique URL, is another important consideration. Each Web site requires a Web server running continuously to deliver your Web pages to visitors quickly.

Obtain a Domain Name   To allow visitors to access your Web site, you must obtain a domain name. Visitors access Web sites via an IP address or a domain name. An **IP address (Internet Protocol address)** is a number that uniquely identifies each computer or device connected to the Internet. A **domain name** is the text version of an IP address. The **Domain Name System (DNS)** is an Internet service that translates domain names into their corresponding IP addresses. The **Accredited Registrar Directory** provides a listing of domain name registrars accredited by the **Internet Corporation for Assigned Names and Numbers (ICANN)**. Your most difficult task likely will be to find a name that is not registered. Expect to pay approximately $8 to $50 per year for a domain name.

For example, a small hair salon named Shear Styles contacts a domain registrar, Network Solutions — which is shown in Figure 21 — to create a site for its Web presence. The salon would like the URL www.shearstyles.com, but must first verify if that URL is available. As a Web domain registrar, Network Solutions determines if the site is available and the yearly cost of that domain name. The domain name ends with an extension such as .com (commercial entity), .net (network), .gov (government agency), .org (organization), or .edu (education) to represent the type of site. Domain names should be easy to recall or should reflect the organization's name so that people easily can find the site.

enter URL to determine if domain name is available

possible domain extensions

© www.networksolutions.com

Figure 21

Obtain Server Space   Locate an ISP that will host your Web site. Recall that an ISP is a business that has a permanent Internet connection. ISPs offer connections to individuals and companies for free or for a fee. Typically, an ISP for your home Internet connection provides a small amount of server space for free to host a personal site.

If you select an ISP that provides free server space, your visitors will typically be subjected to advertisements and pop-up windows. Other options to explore for free or inexpensive server space include online communities, such as Bravenet (http://bravenet .com), Biz.ly (www.biz.ly), and webs.com (www.webs.com); and your educational institution's Web server. If the purpose of your Web site is to sell a product or service or to promote a professional organization, you should consider a fee-based ISP. Shop around to determine the best fit for your site. When selecting an ISP, consider the following questions and how they apply to your particular situation and Web site:

1. What is the monthly fee? Are setup fees charged?

2. How much server space is provided for the monthly fee? Is there unlimited storage? Can you purchase additional space? If so, how much does it cost?

3. How much bandwidth is available to download multimedia files?

4. Is your site hosted on a single dedicated server or cloud-hosted servers? (Cloud hosting forms a network of connected servers that are located in different locations across the world, providing multiple backup opportunities.)

5. What is the average server uptime on a monthly basis? What is the average server downtime?

6. What are the server specifications? Can the server handle heavy usage? Does it have battery backup power?

7. Are **server logs**, which keep track of the number of accesses, available?

8. What technical support does the ISP provide, and when is it available?

9. Does the server on which the Web site will reside have CGI and PHP scripting capabilities, and provide support for Active Server Pages (ASP), SQL Database, and File Transfer Protocol (FTP)?

10. Does the server on which the Web site will reside support e-commerce with **Secure Sockets Layer (SSL)** for encrypting confidential data such as credit card numbers? Are additional fees required for these capabilities?

Publish the Web Site   You must publish, or upload, a finished Web site from your computer to a host server where your site then will be accessible to anyone on the Internet. Publishing, or uploading, is the process of transmitting all the files that constitute your Web site from your computer to the top directory, also called the root folder on the selected server or host computer. The files that make up your Web site can include Web pages, PDF documents, images, audio, video, animation, and others. You can use a variety of tools and methods to manage the upload task. Some of the more popular of these are **FTP (File Transfer Protocol)** and Web authoring programs such as Dreamweaver. These tools allow you to link to a remote server, enter a password, and then upload your files. Dreamweaver contains a built-in function similar to independent FTP programs.

Project Management

After completing the planning phase, the next step is to create, manage, and update the site. In most businesses, a **Webmaster** or Web project manager is in charge of delivering the site. Large commercial organizations employ a Web development team, shown in Figure 22, which includes project managers, designers, programmers, a marketing group, a legal team to deal with copyright materials and permissions, editors, and strategic managers. The Webmaster works within the budget for site development, creates a schedule from start to end, and defines the quality of the work completed. The members of a Web team continue their roles throughout the development, testing, and maintenance of the site to keep the information current.

Testing the Site

A Web site's usability or ease of use is an integral part of the site's success. Due to the complexity of most Web sites with multimedia, interaction, and navigation, each page in a site must be tested on various browsers, operating systems, and platforms. Testing can take place at almost any stage of site development, but earlier is better. Among other things, the testing process verifies that the site is free of spelling and grammatical errors, all the links work correctly, and graphics appear as designed.

BTW

Test Web Pages
To test a Web page, you can use the Adobe BrowserLab at https://browserlab.adobe.com to see how your pages are displayed in a variety of browsers and versions of browsers. The best way to test a site is to use actual users. Each user independently reviews each page and records his or her feedback. In addition to the basic testing, safety testing with e-commerce sites is especially imperative where credit card numbers and personal information are part of the purchasing process. These security tests should report any possible vulnerabilities and recommendations to address them.

Figure 22

Maintaining the Site

An outdated Web site gives the impression that the site has been abandoned, making the visitor lose trust in the information on the site. In the long run, performing ongoing maintenance is usually less expensive than overhauling a site that is significantly out of date. Content on any site should be routinely reviewed for accuracy, currency, and alignment with the site's purpose. A Web site is a living entity, requiring the addition of updated images, topics, and videos at regular intervals. The site should be reviewed periodically for obsolete information and broken links. Use internal statistics from your ISP reports to track each visitor's behavior to determine popular pages within your site, how visitors found your site, their countries of origin, the browsers they are using, and the number of people visiting your site. Learning to use and apply the information derived from the server log will help you make your Web site successful.

BTW

Load Testing
A Web site testing process called load testing simulates the operation of hundreds or thousands of simultaneous visitors to determine how well a site performs under a heavy load.

Chapter Summary

This chapter introduced you to the Adobe Creative Suite 6 software and its various applications. You learned how Adobe packages its suite components and the basic functions of the software. You then learned about the Internet and the World Wide Web, along with the types and purposes of Web sites and browsers. As an introduction to Web design, you learned about the role of HTML, animation, and graphics. You learned about hardware used in creating and maintaining Web sites. You were introduced to various kinds of software applications that can help you create standards-based, compliant, and accessible Web sites. Finally, you learned about the steps involved in planning, designing, creating, publishing, and maintaining a Web site.

The items listed below include all the new concepts you have learned in this chapter:

1. Adobe Creative Suite 6 (CS 2)
2. The Internet and the World Wide Web (CS 4)
3. What Is Web Design? (CS 6)
4. Types of Web Sites (CS 8)
5. Hardware and Software (CS 12)
6. Creating Web Pages (CS 14)
7. Planning a Web Site (CS 19)
8. Web Site Hosting (CS 24)
9. Project Management (CS 26)

Apply Your Knowledge

Reinforce the skills and apply the concepts you learned in this chapter.

Planning a Web Site

Instructions: Plan a simple Web site and complete a one-page report in preparation for developing it.

Perform the following tasks:

1. Identify which type of Web site you will design — personal, organizational/topical, or commercial. Write a brief paragraph describing the site's overall purpose and its targeted audience. Create a name for your site.

2. List at least three general goals for your Web site. You will fine-tune these goals into a mission statement in a subsequent chapter.

3. List elements in addition to text — photos, music, animation, and so forth — that you could include on your Web site to support your general goals.

4. List the design tools you expect to use to develop your Web site.

5. List an available domain name and URL for your site.

6. Submit your report to your instructor and be prepared to discuss your report with the class.

Extend Your Knowledge

Extend the skills you learned in this chapter and experiment with new skills. You may need to use Help to complete the assignment.

Learning about HTML

Instructions: Perform the following tasks:

1. Open a Web browser and type the URL, `www.cengagebrain.com` into the Address or Location bar.

2. If necessary, press the ALT key to access your browser's menu system. Browse through your menu system for the View Source or Page Source command. Click the command to open a window that displays the HTML, similar to Figure 23.

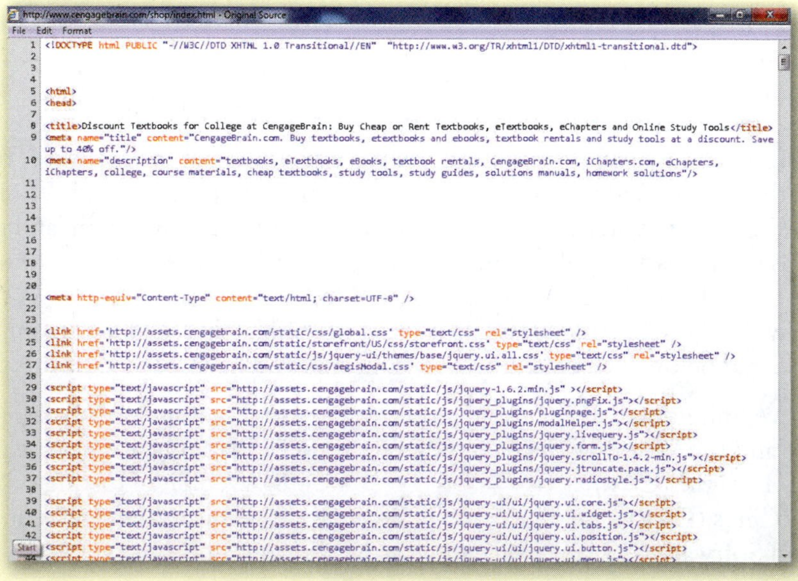

Figure 23

Used with permission from Microsoft Corporation

Continued >

Extend Your Knowledge *continued*

3. Make a list of ten HTML tags, noted within angle brackets: < and >. Note that an HTML tag that begins with a slash (/) is an ending to a previous tag; hence, you do not have to list the ending tags.

4. Use a search engine, such as Google, to look up the definition of each of the HTML tags.

5. Submit a report, as directed by your instructor, listing each tag and its definition.

Make It Right

Analyze a project and correct all errors and/or improve the design.

Color-Blind Accessibility Issues

Problem: Protanomaly or protanopia is a specific kind of color blindness where the red shades and hues are seen more weakly. Figure 24a shows a Web site as seen by a person with normal color vision. Figure 24b shows a Web site as seen by a person who is color blind, specifically with protanomaly. Notice that it would be impossible for a color-blind person to discern which fields were required. Several free Web tools exist to test Web sites for color issues. You are to evaluate your school's Web site for issues related to color blindness.

(a) Web site interface to a visitor with normal vision.

(b) Web site interface to a color-blind visitor.

Figure 24

Instructions: Perform the following steps:

1. Open a Web browser and navigate to your school's Web site. Observe the colors and graphics.

2. Click the link in the Address bar to select it.

3. Press CTRL + c to copy the selected link to the system Clipboard.

4. Open a second Web browser window and then type `colorfilter.wickline.org` in the Address bar. Press the ENTER key to go to the Color Filter Web site.

Continued >

Make It Right *continued*

5. When the Web site appears, click the Type a URL box, delete its contents, and then press CTRL + V to paste your school's URL into the box.

6. If necessary, click the pick a color filter box arrow and then choose protanopia in the list.

7. Click the Fetch and Filter button.

8. When the Web site appears, observe again the colors and graphics.

9. Write a summary of the differences and submit it as directed by your instructor.

In the Lab

Lab 1: Using the Internet

Problem: According to a study by the Pew Internet & American Life Project, many students rely on the Internet to help them in their academic work. Survey five students to find out how they use the Internet for their studies. When they answer, listen to see if they mention items a through f, as outlined in Step 2.

Instructions: Perform the following steps:

1. Tabulate how many of the five students use the Internet for each of the following purposes:

   a. To look up information; to act as a reference library; or to get sources for reports, presentations, and projects

   b. To access podcasts, lecture notes, or other instructor-provided resources

   c. To collaborate with classmates on projects, or to study or share class notes with classmates

   d. To keep track of class schedules, assignments, and syllabi

   e. To communicate with their instructors and to submit assignments and receive feedback

   f. To participate in a virtual class, with all interactions between student and instructor — including lectures — occurring only online

2. Ask the students whether they have access to the Internet during class time under teacher direction, or only outside of class or during lab time. As a follow-up question, ask how effective they think that approach is.

3. Find out how students primarily access the Internet to do their schoolwork: school computer lab, personal computer at home or dorm, library computers, iPad or other tablet computer, or smartphone.

4. Summarize the importance of the Internet to students, according to the results of your survey.

In the Lab

Lab 2: Investigating the Adobe Creative Suite 6

Problem: You are thinking about buying the Production Premium package of Adobe Creative Suite 6. Before purchasing the software, you decide to investigate some of the lesser-known applications in the suite to make sure the Production Premium package will be your best choice. Use the Web and a search engine to research Adobe Encore CS6 and Adobe Audition CS6. Find three different Web sites that discuss each application, including a personal Web site, an organizational or topical Web site, and a commercial Web site. Look for content that is accurate, timely, objective, and authoritative. Seek out descriptions of the software, how the software is used, the learning curve, and the products that are produced with the software. Write a few paragraphs about each of the two applications based on your research. Include the citation information from the Web site.

In the Lab

Lab 3: Using Metasearch Engines

Problem: A metasearch engine is a search tool that sends requests to several other search engines or databases and aggregates the results into a single list, enabling users to search across several search engines at the same time.

Instructions:

1. Open a Web browser, type the URL `www.dogpile.com` into the Address or Location bar (Figure 25), and then press the ENTER key.

Figure 25

2. Type `Adobe CS6` in the Search for box and then press the Go Fetch! button.

3. When the results appear, look at the metasearch information related to where the search term was found, such as Found on Yahoo! Search or Sponsored: Ads by Google.

4. Choose results from four different sites, including one sponsored result and one site found from multiple search engines. Click the results and look at the Web page.

5. Perform the same search with a standard search engine such as Bing or Google. Note the similarities and the differences between the standard search engine and the metasearch engine.

6. Write a few paragraphs to answer the following questions:

   a. In the metasearch, why do you think the site was found at multiple search engines? Or, why do you think the site was only found in one search engine?

   b. Why are some results listed as Sponsored Ads? Were sponsored advertisements found in both searches? How were the sponsored advertisements differentiated from the regular or organic hits?

Continued >

In the Lab *continued*

 c. Which search found the more relevant links?

 d. Did you find any duplicates in the metasearch? What about in the standard search?

 e. Did either search engine use a filter? What other settings did the search engine provide: Such settings might include bolding your search terms, excluding explicit content, or limiting the number of hits per page.

7. Submit your findings as specified by your instructor.

Cases and Places

Apply your creative thinking and problem-solving skills to design and implement a solution.

1: Create a Usability Survey

Academic

Your school recently updated its Web site. The school administration has selected a team to develop a usability survey or questionnaire that you can give to a group of users (including students, parents, and instructors) to evaluate the new Web site. Identify the types of information you hope to gain by distributing this survey or questionnaire. Create a usability survey using your word processing program. Be sure to carefully word the questions to collect the specific feedback you want. For example, asking "Do you like the Web site?" is not as helpful as asking "What do you like about the Web site?" Give the survey or questionnaire to at least five people, including at least one from each group identified above. Allow participants to complete the survey or questionnaire and then look at the results. Did the survey results provide the type of information you were seeking? If not, reword your questions to be more specific, and redistribute the survey to another group of participants. Apply your creative thinking and problem-solving skills to design and implement a solution.

2: Use Trial Software

Personal

You would like to try some of the other applications in the Adobe Creative Suite 6. Go to the Web site http://www.adobe.com/downloads/ and point to any application, such as InDesign or After Effects. When the links appear below the application, click Try. When the Trial Web site appears, click the Download button. (If you are on a lab machine, please check with your instructor before downloading and installing new software.) Install the software per the instructions. Once installed, open the software and try creating a simple file. Explore the menus. Look at the panels and tool-bars. Write a summary of your experience and submit it as directed by your instructor.

3: Research Web Design Software

Professional

Your friend owns a small nail salon and wants a Web site to advertise her business. She knows of your interest in Web design and wants you to recommend software to her. Using Web search tools, investigate the differences between the Adobe Creative Suite and other kinds of Web creation software such as Microsoft Expression Web or Office application software to determine which might be the best choice to create her Web site. Consider things such as price, user-friendliness, the learning curve, the output, and accessibility when doing your research. Write a summary and submit it as directed by your instructor.

1 | Editing a Photo

Objectives

You will have mastered the material in this chapter when you can:

- Start Photoshop and customize the Photoshop workspace
- Open a photo
- Identify parts of the Photoshop workspace
- Explain file types
- View a photo using the Zoom Tool, Navigator panel, and the Hand Tool
- Display rulers
- Crop a photo using the rule of thirds overlay

- Save a photo for both print and the Web
- Create a border
- Open a recent file
- Resize a photo
- Insert text and stroke
- Print a photo
- Access Photoshop Help
- Close a file and quit Photoshop

1 | Editing a Photo

What Is Photoshop CS6?

Photoshop CS6 is a popular image-editing software program produced by Adobe Systems Incorporated. **Image-editing software** refers to computer programs that allow you to create and modify **digital images**, or pictures in electronic form. One type of digital image is a digital **photograph**, or **photo**, which is a picture taken with a camera and stored as a digitized file. The photo then is converted into a print or a slide, or used in another file. Other types of digital images include scanned images, or electronic forms of original artwork created from scratch. Digital images are used in graphic applications, advertising, print publishing, and on the Web. Personal uses include private photos, online photo sharing, scrapbooking, blogging, and social networking, among others. Image-editing software, such as Photoshop, can be used for basic adjustments such as rotating, cropping, or resizing, as well as for more advanced manipulations, such as airbrushing, retouching, photo repair, changing the contrast of images and balancing or combining elements of different images. Because Photoshop allows you to save multilayered, composite images and then return later to extract parts of those images, it works well for repurposing a wide variety of graphic-related files.

Photoshop CS6 is part of the **Adobe Creative Suite 6** and comes packaged with most of the suite versions. It also is sold and used independently as a stand-alone application. Photoshop CS6 is available for both the PC and Macintosh computer platforms. Photoshop CS6 Extended includes all of the features of Photoshop CS6 and some new features for working with 3D imagery, motion-based content, and advanced image analysis. The chapters in this book use Photoshop CS6 on the PC platform, running the Windows 7 operating system; however, Photoshop looks very similar on the Windows and the Mac operating systems. Both versions present the same tools and similar menus. One of the main differences is in the approach to shortcut keys. Windows uses the CTRL key to access many of the shortcuts in the Adobe Creative Suite; MacOS uses the CMD key represented by the symbol ⌘ and sometimes the OPT key represented by the symbol ⌥. As system dialog boxes are presented in the chapters, the corresponding steps for Mac users are presented in Appendix G, the For Mac Users appendix.

To illustrate the features of Photoshop CS6, this book presents a series of chapters that use Photoshop to edit photos similar to those you will encounter in academic and business environments, as well as photos for personal use.

Project Planning Guidelines

The process of editing a photo requires careful analysis and planning. As a starting point, choose a photo that correctly expresses your desired subject or theme. Once the theme is determined, analyze the intended audience. Define a plan for editing that enhances the photo, eliminates visual clutter, improves color and contrast, and corrects defects. Always work on a duplicate of an original image. Finally, determine the file format and print style that will be most successful at delivering the message. Details of these guidelines are provided in Appendix A, Project Planning Guidelines. In addition, each chapter in this book provides practical applications of these planning considerations.

Project — Postcard Graphic

A **postcard** is a rectangular piece of mail intended for writing and sending without an envelope. People use postcards for greetings, announcements, reminders, and business contacts. Many times, a postcard is an effective marketing tool used to generate prospective leads at a relatively low cost. One of the most popular uses for postcards involves pictures. Businesses and organizations produce a postcard with a photo or graphic on one side and a short description with room to write a brief correspondence on the other. People purchase picture postcards to mail to friends or to serve as reminders of their vacation. Sometimes a picture postcard is mailed to attract attention and direct people to Web sites or business locations. A postcard graphic must portray clearly its message or theme in an eye-catching manner, keeping in mind the relevant audience.

Most postcards are rectangular, at least 3½ inches high and 5 inches long — some are larger. A common size is 4 inches by 6 inches. A picture postcard might contain text printed over the picture or a border to add interest. A graphic designed for a postcard should be of high quality, use strong color, and deliver a message in the clearest, most attractive, and most effective way possible.

The project in this chapter uses Photoshop to enhance a photograph of an eagle and add text to create a postcard for use by a wildlife park. The original photo is displayed in Figure 1–1a. The edited photo is displayed in Figure 1–1b. The enhancements will emphasize the eagle by positioning the scene to make the layout appear more visually appealing and to crop some of the background. A gray border will frame the scene. Text will be added to identify the location. Finally, the photo will be resized to fit on a postcard and then optimized for the park's Web site.

What's New in CS6?
Photoshop CS6 has many new features, including an advanced cropping tool, Content Aware Move and Patch tools, Paragraph and Character Style panels, a new Blur gallery, as well as many others. To see more, press the F1 key and then click the What's new link.

(a) Original photo

(b) Edited photo

source: NASA

Figure 1–1

BTW

Screen Resolution
If your system has a high-resolution monitor with a screen resolution of 1280 × 800 or higher, lowering that resolution to 1024 × 768 might cause some images to be distorted because of a difference in the aspect ratio. If you want to keep your high-resolution setting, be aware that the location of on-screen tools might vary slightly from the book.

Overview

As you read this chapter, you will learn how to edit the photo shown in Figure 1–1a on the previous page by performing these general tasks:

- Customize the workspace.
- Display and navigate a photo at various magnifications.
- Crop a photo effectively.
- Create and modify a border.
- Stroke a selection.
- Resize and print a photo.
- Save, close, and then reopen a photo.
- Add stroked text to the photo.
- Save a photo for the Web.
- Use Photoshop Help.

Plan Ahead

General Project Guidelines

When editing a photo, the actions you perform and decisions you make will affect the appearance and characteristics of the finished product. As you edit a photo, such as the one shown in Figure 1–1a, you should follow these general guidelines:

1. **Find an appropriate image or photo.** Keep in mind the purpose and the graphic needs of the project when choosing an image or photo. Decide ahead of time on the file type and decide if the image will be used on the Web. An eye-catching graphic image should convey a theme that is understood universally. The photo should grab the attention of viewers and draw them into the picture, whether in print or on the Web.

2. **Determine how to edit the photo to highlight the theme.** As you edit, use standard design principles, and keep in mind your subject, your audience, the required size and shape of the graphic, color decisions, the rule of thirds, the golden rectangle, and other design principles. Decide which parts of the photo portray your message and which parts are visual clutter. Crop the photo as needed.

3. **Identify finishing touches that will further enhance the photo.** The overall appearance of a photo significantly affects its ability to communicate clearly. You might want to add text or a border.

4. **Prepare for publication.** Resize the photo as needed to fit the allotted space. Save the photo on a storage medium, such as a hard drive, USB flash drive, or CD. Print the photo or publish it to the Web.

When necessary, more specific details concerning the above guidelines are presented at appropriate points in the chapter. The chapter also will identify the actions performed and decisions made regarding these guidelines during the creation of the edited photo shown in Figure 1–1b on the previous page.

BTW

By The Way Boxes
For a complete list of the BTWs found in the margins of this book, visit the BTW chapter resource on the student companion site located at www .cengagebrain.com.

Starting Photoshop

If you are using a computer to step through the project in this chapter, and you want your screen to match the figures in this book, you should change your screen's resolution to 1024 × 768. For information about how to change a screen's resolution, read Appendix F, the Changing Screen Resolution appendix.

To Start Photoshop

The following steps, which assume Windows 7 is running, start Photoshop, based on a typical installation. You may need to ask your instructor how to start Photoshop for your computer.

1

- Click the Start button on the Windows 7 taskbar to display the Start menu.

- Type Photoshop CS6 as the search text in the 'Search programs and files' text box, and watch the search results appear on the Start menu (Figure 1–2).

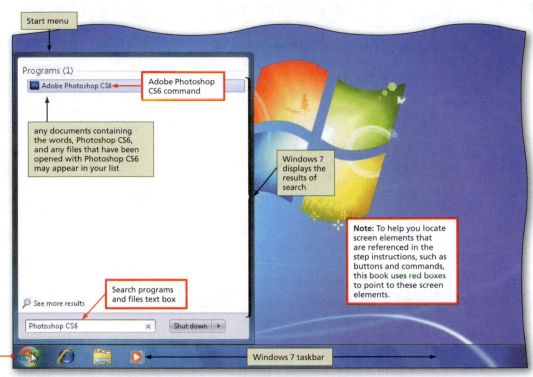

Figure 1–2

2

- Click Adobe Photoshop CS6 in the search results on the Start menu to start Photoshop.

- After a few moments, when the Photoshop window is displayed, if the window is not maximized, click the Maximize button next to the Close button on the Application bar to maximize the window (Figure 1–3).

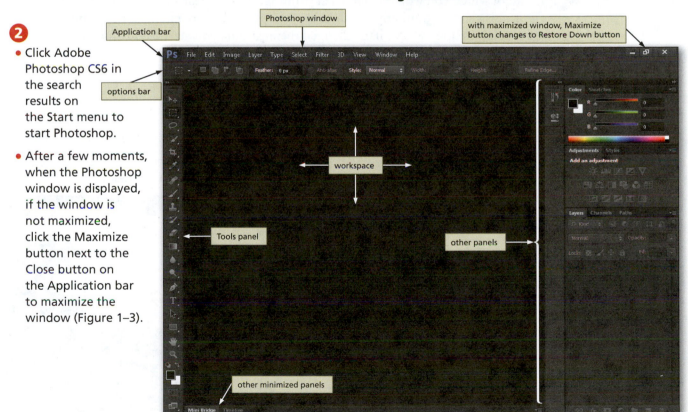

Figure 1–3

Other Ways	
1. Double-click Photoshop icon on desktop, if the icon is present	2. Click Adobe Photoshop CS6 on Start menu

MAC For a detailed example of this procedure using the Mac operating system, refer to the steps on page APP 76 of the For Mac Users appendix at the end of this book.

BTW

Q&A
For a complete list of the Q&As found in many of the step-by-step sequences in this book, visit the Q&A chapter resource on the student companion site located at www.cengagebrain.com.

Customizing the Photoshop Workspace

The screen in Figure 1–3 on the previous page shows how the Photoshop workspace looks the first time you start Photoshop after installation on most computers. Photoshop does not open a blank or default photo automatically; rather, the Application bar and the options bar appear across the top of the screen with a work area below the options bar. The Tools panel is displayed on the left; other panels are displayed on the right and across the bottom. The work area and panels are referred to collectively as the **workspace**.

As you work in Photoshop, the panels, the selected tool, and the options bar settings might change. Therefore, if you want your screen to match the figures in this book, you should restore the default workspace, select the default tool, and reset the options bar. In addition, users might change the default color for the workspace. For more information about how to change other advanced Photoshop settings, see the Changing Screen Resolution appendix.

Because of a default preference setting, each time you start Photoshop, the Photoshop workspace is displayed the same way it was the last time you used Photoshop. If you (or another user) move the panels while working in Photoshop, they will appear in their new locations the next time you start Photoshop. You can create and save your own workspaces, or use Photoshop's saved workspaces that show groups of panels used for certain tasks. For example, the Painting workspace displays the Brush panel, the Brush presets panel, and the Swatches panel, among others — all of which you would need when painting. You will learn more about panels later in this chapter. Similarly, if values on the options bar are changed or a different tool is selected, they will remain changed the next time you start Photoshop. If you want to return the workspace to its default settings, follow these steps each time you start Photoshop.

To Select the Essentials Workspace

The default workspace, called Essentials, displays commonly used panels. The following steps select the Essentials workspace and reset its default values.

1
- Click Window on the Application bar to display the Window menu.
- Point to Workspace on the Window menu to display the Workspace submenu (Figure 1–4).

🔍 **Experiment**
- Click each of the workspaces that are displayed in the list to view the different panel configurations. Notice that Photoshop displays a check mark on the menu, next to the chosen workspace. When you are finished, click Window on the Application bar and then point to Workspace again to display the submenu.

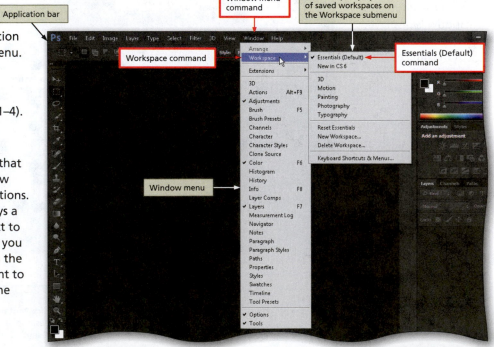

Figure 1–4

2

• Click Essentials (Default) on the Workspace submenu to select the default workspace panels.

• Click Window on the Application bar and then point to Workspace again to display the submenu (Figure 1–5).

Q&A What does the New Workspace command do?

The New Workspace command displays a dialog box where you can create a new workspace based on the currently displayed panels. You also can delete a workspace from the Workspace submenu.

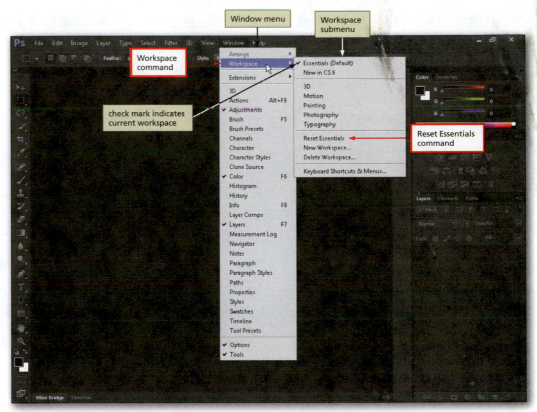

Figure 1–5

3

• Click Reset Essentials to restore the workspace to its default settings and reposition any panels that might have been moved (Figure 1–6).

Q&A My screen did not change. Did I do something wrong?

If Photoshop is a new installation on your system, you might notice few changes on your screen.

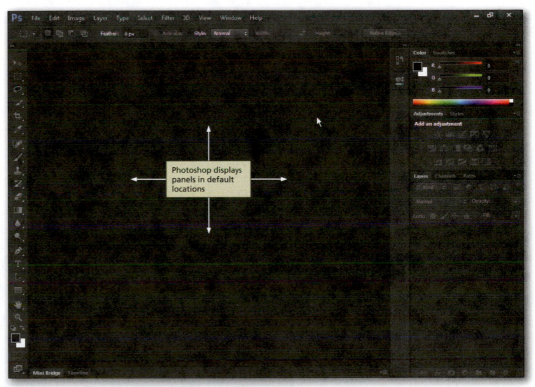

Figure 1–6

To Select the Default Tool

The following step selects the Rectangular Marquee Tool, which is the default tool for a new installation of Photoshop. When you select a tool on the Tools panel, the options bar reflects the settings of that tool.

1

- If the tools on the Tools panel appear in two columns, click the double arrow at the top of the Tools panel.

- If necessary, click the second button from the top on the Tools panel to select it (Figure 1–7).

- If the button does not display a square icon, right-click the button and then click Rectangular Marquee Tool on the context menu.

Q&A
What appears when I point to the button?

When you point to many objects in the Photoshop workspace, such as a tool or button, Photoshop displays a tool tip. A **tool tip** is a short, on-screen note associated with the object to which you are pointing, which helps you identify the object. This button's name is the Rectangular Marquee Tool.

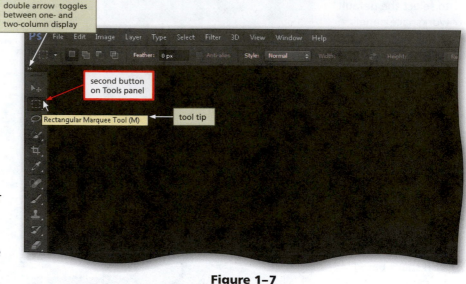

Figure 1–7

Other Ways
1. Press M

To Reset the Options Bar

As you work through the chapters, editing and creating images, you will find that the options bar is **context sensitive**, which means it changes as you select different tools. In addition, the options and settings are retained for the next time you use Photoshop. To match the figures in this book, you should reset the options bar, using a context menu, each time you start Photoshop. A **context menu**, or **shortcut menu**, appears when you right-click some objects in the Photoshop workspace. The menu displays commands representing the active tool, selection, or panel.

The following steps reset all tool settings in the options bar using a context menu.

1

- Right-click the Rectangular Marquee Tool icon on the options bar to display its context menu (Figure 1–8).

Q&A
Why is my icon elliptical?

It is possible that a previous user has used the Elliptical Marquee Tool. Press SHIFT+M to return to the Rectangular Marquee Tool.

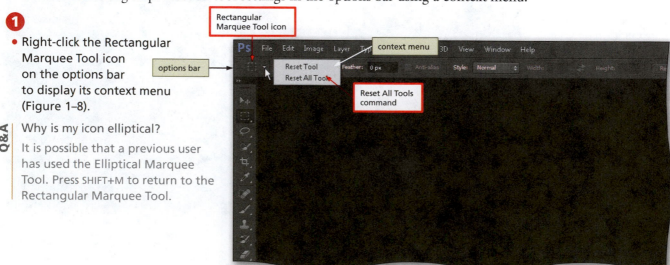

Figure 1–8

2

- Click Reset All Tools to display a confirmation dialog box (Figure 1–9).

3

- Click the OK button to restore the tools to their default settings.

Figure 1–9

To Reset the Interface Color

Photoshop CS6 allows the user to choose from among four different color schemes for the interface: Black, Dark Gray, Medium Gray, and Light Gray. The color scheme you choose depends upon your personal preferences for contrast, focus, and readability.

The following steps reset the interface color to Medium Gray, which displays the work area in dark gray and the panels in medium gray.

1

- Click Edit on the Application bar, and then point to Preferences to display the Preferences submenu (Figure 1–10).

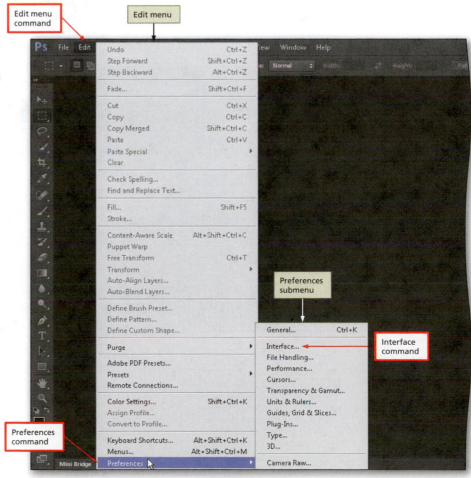

Figure 1–10

2

- Click Interface on the Preferences submenu to display the Preferences dialog box.

- In the Appearance area, click the third button, Medium Gray, to change the interface color (Figure 1–11).

 Q&A

What other preferences can I change?

You can change things such as the color of certain display features, the number of states in the History panel, and the unit of measure, among others.

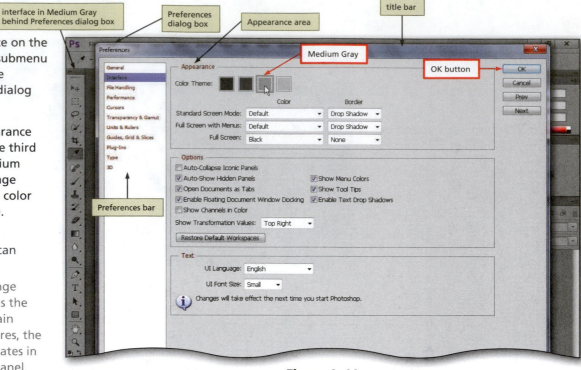

Figure 1–11

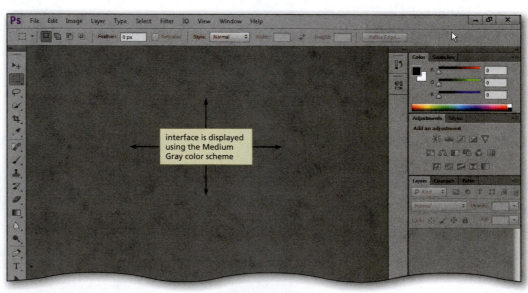

Experiment

- One at a time, click each of the four color schemes and notice how the interface changes. You can drag the title bar of the Preferences dialog box to move it out of the way, if necessary.

3

- Click the OK button in the Preferences dialog box to close the dialog box and return to the Photoshop workspace (Figure 1–12).

Figure 1–12

Other Ways

1. Press CTRL+K, click Interface on Preferences bar, click desired color scheme, click OK button

2. Right-click any button on vertical dock of panels, click Interface Options, click desired color scheme, click OK button

Opening a Photo

To open a photo in Photoshop, it must be stored as a digital file on your computer system or on an external storage device. To **open** a photo, you bring a copy of the file from the storage location to the screen where you can **edit**, or make changes to, the photo. The changes do not become permanent, however, until you **save** or store the changed file on a storage device. The photos used in this book are included in the Data Files for Students. Visit www.cengage.com/ct/studentdownload for detailed instructions or contact your instructor for information about accessing the required files. Your instructor may designate a different location for the photos.

Plan Ahead

Find an appropriate image or photo.

Sometimes a person or business gives you a specific photo to use in a project. Other times, you are assigned a theme and asked to find or take the photo. An eye-catching graphic image should convey a visual message that is not expressed easily with words. Keep the audience in mind as you choose a photo. Photos generally fall into one of four categories:

- In advertising, a photo might show a product, service, result, model, or benefit.

- In a public service setting, a photo might represent a topic of interest, nature, signage, buildings, or a photo of historical importance.

- In industry, a photo might display a process, product, work organization, employee, facility, layout, equipment, safety, result, or culture.

- For personal or journalistic use, a photo might be a portrait, scenery, action shot, or event.

To Open a File

The following steps open the Eagle file from the Data Files for Students. Visit www.cengage.com/ct/studentdownload for detailed instructions or contact your instructor for information about accessing the required files.

1
- Click File on the Application bar to display the File menu (Figure 1–13).

Q&A Do I need the Data Files for Students?

You will need the Data Files for Students to complete the activities and exercises in this book. See your instructor for information on how to acquire the necessary files.

Q&A Can I use a shortcut key to open a file?

Yes, the shortcut keys are displayed on the menu. In this textbook, the shortcut keys also are displayed at the end of each series of steps in the Other Ways box.

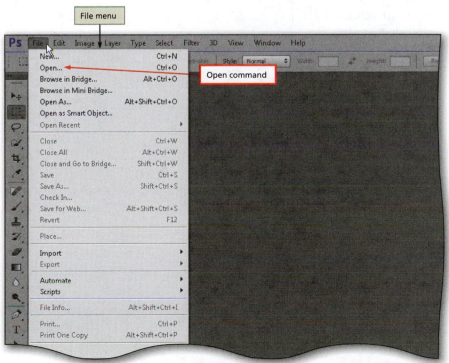

Figure 1–13

2

- Click Open on the File menu to display the Open dialog box.

- Click the Look in box arrow to display a list of the available storage locations on your system (Figure 1–14).

Q&A

What do the other buttons in the Open dialog box do?

To the right of the Look in box arrow are buttons to help you navigate folders, create folders, and change the view. Links to common storage locations are found in the Navigation pane on the left.

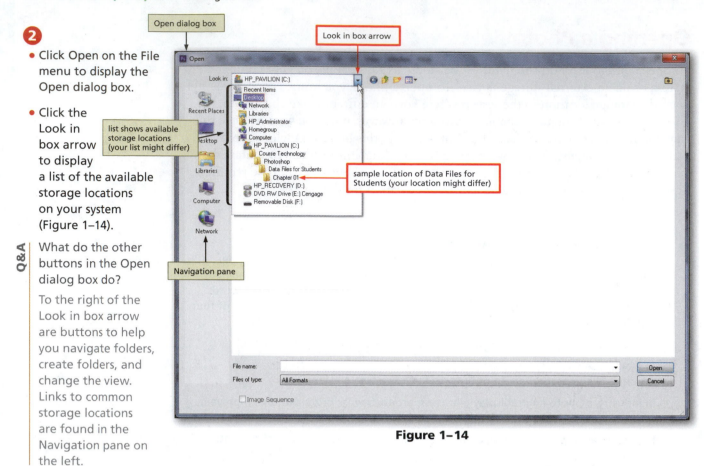

Figure 1–14

3

- Click the storage location of the Data Files for Students, as specified by your instructor, to display its contents (Figure 1–15).

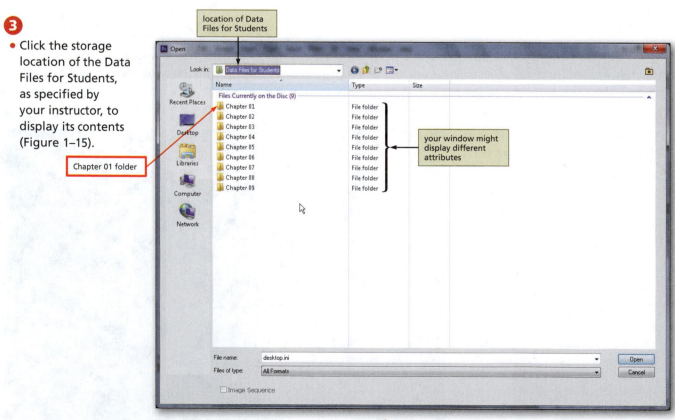

Figure 1–15

4

• Double-click the Photoshop folder and then double-click the Chapter 01 folder.

• Click the file, Eagle, to select the file to be opened (Figure 1–16).

Q&A Why is my file list different?

Your list might vary. In addition, the files in Figure 1–16 are displayed in List view. Click the View Menu button to verify your view.

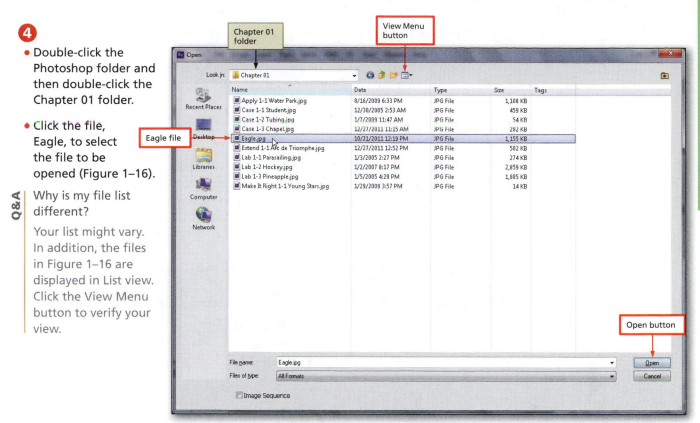

Chapter 01 folder

View Menu button

Eagle file

Open button

Figure 1–16

5

• Click the Open button to open the selected file and display the photo in the Photoshop workspace (Figure 1–17).

Q&A Can I edit a printed photo?

Most of the images you will use in this book already are stored in digital format; however, when you have a print copy of a picture, rather than a digital file stored on your system, it sometimes is

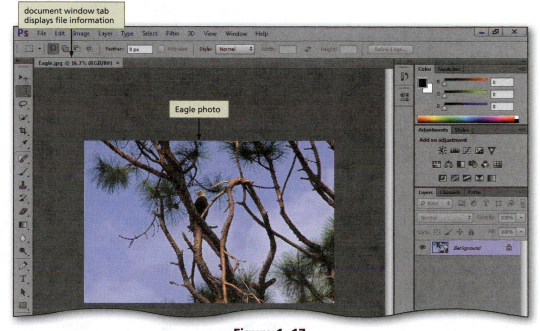

document window tab displays file information

Eagle photo

Figure 1–17

necessary to scan the picture using a scanner. A **scanner** is a device used to convert a hard copy into a digital form for storage, retrieval, or other electronic purposes. Photoshop allows you to bring a copy from the scanner directly into the workspace.

MAC For a detailed example of this procedure using the Mac operating system, refer to the steps on pages APP 77 through APP 79 of the For Mac Users appendix.

Other Ways

1. Press CTRL+O, select file, click Open button

2. In Windows, right-click file, click Open with, click Adobe Photoshop CS6

The Photoshop Workspace

The Photoshop workspace consists of a variety of components to make your work more efficient and to make your photo documents look more professional. The following sections discuss these components.

The Application Bar

The Application bar appears at the top of the workspace (Figure 1–18). The Application bar contains the application button and the menu. On the far right side of the Application bar are the common window clip controls.

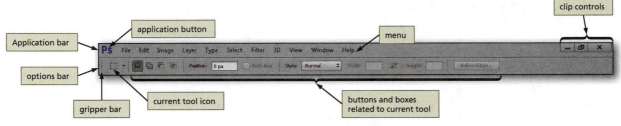

Figure 1–18

Hidden Menu Commands
When Photoshop first is installed, all of the menu commands within a menu appear when you click the menu name. To hide seldom-used menu commands, you can click the Menus command on the Edit menu and follow the on-screen instructions. A **hidden command** does not appear immediately on a menu.

Show All Menu Items
If menu commands have been hidden, a Show All Menu Items command will appear at the bottom of the menu list. Click the Show All Menu Items command, or press and hold the CTRL key when you click the menu name to display all menu commands, including hidden ones.

The menu displays the Photoshop menu names. Each **menu** contains a list of commands you can use to perform tasks such as opening, saving, printing, and editing photos. To display a menu, such as the View menu, click the View menu name on the Application bar. If you point to a command on a menu that has an arrow on its right edge, a **submenu**, or secondary menu, displays another list of commands. (See Figure 1–10 on page PS 9).

The Options Bar

The options bar (Figure 1–18) appears below the Application bar. Sometimes called the control panel, the options bar contains buttons and boxes that allow you to perform tasks more quickly than when using the Application bar and related menus. Most buttons on the options bar display words or images to help you remember their functions. When you point to a button or box on the options bar, a tool tip is displayed below the mouse pointer. The options bar changes to reflect the tool currently selected on the Tools panel. For example, a tool related to text might display a font box on the options bar, whereas a tool related to painting will display a brush button. The selected tool always appears as an icon on the left side of the options bar. As each tool is discussed, the associated options bar will be explained in more detail.

You can **float**, or move, the options bar in the workspace by dragging the gray gripper bar on the left side of the options bar. You can **dock** or reattach the options bar below the Application bar by resetting the workspace. To hide or show the options bar, click Options on the Window menu.

The Tools Panel

On the left side of the workspace is the Tools panel. The Tools panel is a group of **tools**, or buttons, organized into a toolbar. As with the options bar, you can float, dock, hide, or show the Tools panel. Each tool on the Tools panel displays a **tool icon**. When you point to the tool icon, a tool tip displays the name of the tool, including its shortcut key. You can expand some tools to show hidden tools beneath them. Expandable tools display a small triangle in the lower-right corner of the tool icon. Click and hold the tool button or right-click to see or select one of its hidden tools from the context menu. The default tool names and their corresponding shortcut keys are listed in Figure 1–19.

When you click a tool on the Tools panel, Photoshop selects the button and changes the options bar as necessary. When using a tool from the Tools panel, the mouse pointer changes to reflect the selected tool.

The Tools panel is organized by purpose. At the very top of the panel is a button to display the panel in two columns, followed underneath by the gripper bar. Below that, the selection tools appear, then the crop and slice tools, followed by retouching, painting, drawing and type, annotation, measuring, and navigation tools. At the bottom of the Tools panel are buttons to set colors, create a quick mask, and change screen modes.

As each tool is introduced throughout this book, its function and options bar characteristics will be explained further.

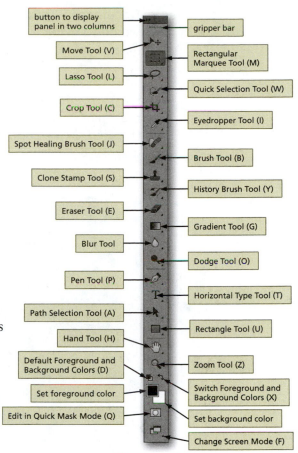

Figure 1–19

The Document Window

The **document window** is the windowed area within the workspace that displays the active file or image. The document window contains the document window tab, the display area, scroll bars, and a status bar (Figure 1–20).

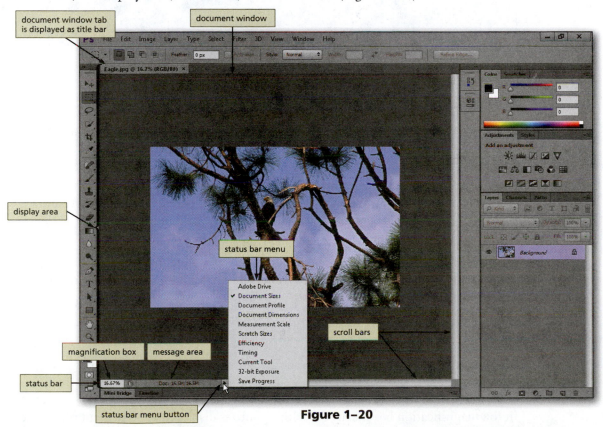

Figure 1–20

Document Window Tab When a file is open, Photoshop displays a **document window tab** at the top of the document window that shows the name of the file, the magnification, the color mode, and a Close button. If you have multiple files open, each has its own document window tab.

To **float** the document window in the display area, drag the document window tab. When the document window is floating, the document Window tab expands across the top of the document window and displays Minimize, Maximize, and Close buttons (Figure 1–21). To **dock** the document window again, or lock it in its previous location, drag the document window tab close to the options bar.

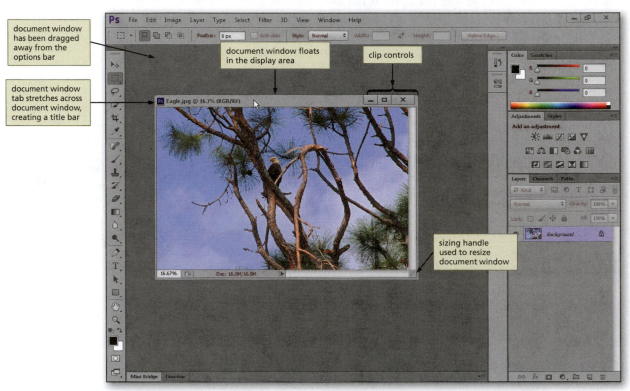

document window has been dragged away from the options bar

document window floats in the display area

clip controls

document window tab stretches across document window, creating a title bar

Eagle.jpg @ 16.7% (RGB/#)

sizing handle used to resize document window

Figure 1–21

Adobe Suite Workspaces
The workspaces of the various applications in Adobe Creative Suite 6 share the same appearance to make it easy to move between applications. The toolbars, panels, and workspace are located in the same positions. Many shortcut keys are the same. Common menu terminology reduces the learning curve.

To **minimize** a document window, drag the document window tab away from the options bar so that the window floats, and then click the Minimize button. A minimized document window does not appear in the workspace; rather, it appears as a second Photoshop button on the Windows taskbar.

In Photoshop, a maximized document window fills the entire screen; you cannot see the menus or panels. To **maximize** a document window, drag the document window tab away from the options bar so that it floats, and then click the Maximize button. To return the document window to a floating state, click the Restore Down button on the document window title bar.

Display Area The **display area** is the portion of the document window that displays the photo or image. You perform most tool tasks and edit the photo in the display area.

Scroll Bars **Scroll bars** appear on the right and bottom of the document window. When the photo is bigger than the document window, the scroll bars become active and display scroll arrows and scroll boxes to move the image up, down, left, and right.

Status Bar Across the bottom of the document window, Photoshop displays the **status bar**. The status bar contains a magnification box. **Magnification** refers to the percentage of enlargement or reduction on the screen. For example, a 50% indication in the magnification box means the entire photo is displayed at 50 percent of its actual size. Changing the magnification does not change the size of the photo physically; it merely displays it on the screen at a different size. You can type a new percentage in the magnification box to display a different view of the photo.

Next to the magnification box is the **message area**. Messages can display information about the file size, the current tool, or the document dimensions. When you first start Photoshop, the message area displays information about the document size in storage.

On the right side of the status bar is the status bar menu button, which, when clicked, displays a status bar menu (Figure 1–20 on page PS 15). You use the status bar menu to change the message area or to change to other versions of the document.

Your installation of Photoshop might display rulers at the top and left of the document window. You will learn about rulers later in this chapter.

Panels

A **panel** is a collection of graphically displayed choices and commands related to a specific tool or feature, such as those involving colors, brushes, actions, or layers (Figure 1–22). Panels help you monitor and modify your work. Each panel displays a panel tab with the name of the panel and a panel menu button. When you click the panel menu button, also called the panel menu icon, Photoshop displays a context-sensitive panel menu that allows you to make changes to the panel. Some panels have a status bar across the bottom. A panel can display buttons, boxes, sliders, scroll bars, or drop-down lists.

BTW

Panels vs. Palettes
In previous versions of the Adobe Creative Suite, the panels were called palettes. In all of the CS6 applications, panels can be grouped, stacked, or docked in the workspace, just as palettes were.

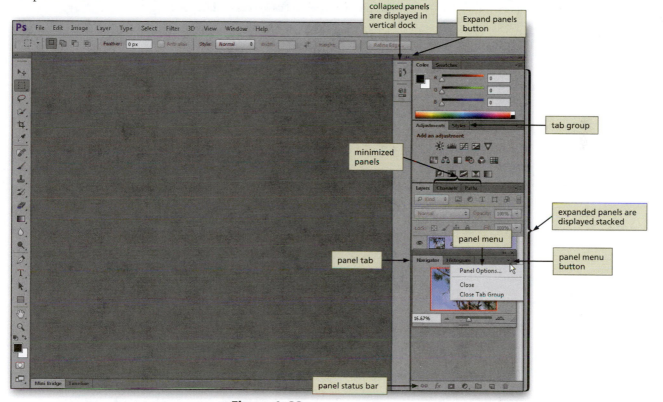

Figure 1–22

Several panels appear in the Essentials workspace. Some panels are expanded to display their contents, and are grouped by general purpose. A **panel group** or **tab group** displays several panels horizontally. The panel group is docked vertically on the right side of the workspace. Other open panels are displayed along the bottom or as icons or buttons in a vertical dock between the document window and the expanded panels. Panels are **collapsed** when they appear as an icon or button, or **expanded**

More Panel Options
If you want to display panels as buttons rather than as minimized or expanded pallets, right-click the panel tab, and then click Collapse to Icons on the context menu. A panel icon displays the name of the panel and its associated icon as a button.

Adobe Bridge
When organizing your photos into folders, or if you want to rate your photos, it might be more convenient to use Adobe Bridge CS6. See Appendix E, the Using Adobe Bridge CS6 appendix, for more information.

when they display their contents. Panels are **minimized** when they display only their tab. To collapse or expand a panel group, click the double arrow at the top of the panel or double-click its tab. To close a panel, click Close on the panel menu. To redisplay the panel, click the panel name on the Window menu or use a panel shortcut key.

You can arrange and reposition panels either individually or in groups. To move them individually, drag their tabs; to move a group, drag the area to the right of the tabs. To float a panel in the workspace, drag its tab outside of the vertical dock. You can create a **stack** of floating panels by dragging a panel tab to a location below another floating panel and docking it.

Sometimes you might want to hide all the panels to display more of the document window. To hide all panels, press the TAB key. Press the TAB key again to display the panels.

Photoshop comes with 29 panels, described in Table 1–1. As each panel is introduced throughout this book, its function and characteristics will be explained further.

Table 1–1 Photoshop Panels

Panel Name	Purpose
3D	To show the 3D layer components, settings, and options of the associated 3D file — available in Photoshop Extended only
Actions	To record, play, edit, and delete individual actions
Adjustments	To create nondestructive adjustment layers with color and tonal adjustments
Brush	To select preset brushes and design custom brushes
Brush Presets	To create, load, save, and manage preset brush tips
Channels	To create and manage channels
Character	To provide options for formatting characters
Character Styles	To create, load, save, and manage character styles
Clone Source	To set up and manipulate sample sources for the Clone Stamp Tools or Healing Brush Tools
Color	To display the color values for the current foreground and background colors
Histogram	To view tonal and color information about an image
History	To jump to any recent state of the image created during the current working session
Info	To display color values and document status information
Layer Comps	To display multiple compositions of a page layout
Layers	To show and hide layers, create new layers, and work with groups of layers
Mini Bridge	To assist in navigating folders and files, and to access other modules in the suite
Measurement Log	To record measurement data about a measured object — available in Photoshop Extended only
Navigator	To change the view or magnification of the photo using a thumbnail display
Notes	To insert, edit, and delete notes attached to files
Options	To display options and settings for the currently selected tool
Paragraph	To change the formatting of columns and paragraphs
Paragraph Styles	To create, load, save, and manage paragraph styles
Paths	To manipulate each saved path, the current work path, and the current vector mask
Properties	To display characteristics about the file and to assist in creating precise, editable pixel- and vector-based masks
Styles	To view and select preset styles
Swatches	To select and store colors that you need to use often
Timeline	To create a sequence of images or frames, displayed as motion over time
Tools	To select tools
Tool Presets	To save and reuse tool settings

File Types

A **file type** refers to the internal characteristics of digital files; it designates the operational or structural characteristics of a file. Each digital file, graphic or otherwise, is stored with specific kinds of formatting related to how the file appears on the screen, how it prints, and the software it uses to do so. Computer systems use the file type to help users open the file with the appropriate software. A **file extension**, in most computer systems, is a three- or four-letter suffix after the file name that distinguishes the file type. For example, Eagle.jpg refers to a file named Eagle with the extension and file type JPG. A period separates the file name and its extension. When you are exploring files on your system, you might see the file extensions as part of the file name, or you might see a column of information about file types.

Graphic files are created and stored using many different file types and extensions. The type of file sometimes is determined by the hardware or software used to create the file. Other times, the user has a choice in applying a file type and makes the decision based on the file size, the intended purpose of the graphic file — such as whether the file is to be used on the Web — or the desired color mode.

Several common graphic file types are listed in Table 1–2.

BTW

File Extensions
The default setting for file extensions in Photoshop is to use a lowercase three-letter extension. If you want to change the extension, do the following: Press SHIFT+CTRL+S to access the Save As dialog box. In the File name text box, type the file name, period, and new extension within quotation marks. Click the Save button.

BTW

File Name Characters
A file name can have a maximum of 260 characters, including spaces. The only invalid characters are the backslash (\), forward slash (/), colon (:), asterisk (*), question mark (?), quotation mark ("), less than symbol (<), greater than symbol (>), and vertical bar (|).

Table 1–2 Graphic File Types		
File Extension	**File Type**	**Description**
BMP	Bitmap	BMP is a standard Windows image format used on DOS and Windows-compatible computers. BMP format supports many different color modes.
EPS	Encapsulated PostScript	EPS files can contain both bitmap and vector graphics. Almost all graphics, illustration, and page-layout programs support the EPS format, which can be used to transfer PostScript artwork between applications.
GIF	Graphics Interchange Format	GIF commonly is used to display graphics and images on Web pages. It is a compressed format designed to minimize file size and electronic transfer time.
JPG or JPEG	Joint Photographic Experts Group	JPG files commonly are used to display photographs on Web pages. JPG format supports many different color modes. JPG retains all color information in an RGB image, unlike GIF format. Most digital cameras produce JPG files.
PDF	Portable Document Format	PDF is a flexible file format based on the PostScript imaging model that is cross-platform and cross-application. PDF files accurately display and preserve fonts, page layouts, and graphics. PDF files can contain electronic document search and navigation features such as hyperlinks.
PSD	Photoshop Document	PSD format is the default file format in Photoshop and the only format that supports all Photoshop features. Other Adobe applications can import PSD files directly and preserve many Photoshop features because of the tight integration among Adobe products.
RAW	Photoshop Raw	RAW format is a flexible file format used for transferring images between applications and computer platforms. There are no pixel or file size restrictions in this format. Documents saved in the Photoshop Raw format cannot contain layers.
TIF or TIFF	Tagged Image File Format	TIF is a flexible bitmap image format supported by almost all paint, image-editing, and page-layout applications. This format often is used for files that are to be exchanged between applications or computer platforms. Most desktop scanners can produce TIF images.

Saving Files
While Photoshop is saving your file, it briefly displays a Working in Background shape. In addition, your USB drive might have a light that flashes during the save process. The new file name appears on the document window tab.

Saving a Photo

As you make changes to a file in Photoshop, the computer stores it in memory. If you turn off the computer or if you lose electrical power, the file in memory is lost. If you plan to use the photo later, you must save it on a storage device such as a USB flash drive, hard disk, or in cloud storage.

While you are editing, to preserve the most features such as layers, effects, masks, and styles, Photoshop recommends that you save photos in the **PSD format**. PSD, which stands for Photoshop Document Format, is the default file format for files created from scratch in Photoshop, and supports files up to 2 gigabytes (GB) in size. The PSD format also maximizes portability among other Adobe versions and applications.

To Save a File in the PSD Format

The following steps save the photo on a USB flash drive using the file name, Eagle Edited. In addition to saving in the PSD format, you will save the photo with a new file name and in a new location, so that the original photo is preserved in case you need to start again. Even though you have yet to edit the photo, it is a good practice to save a copy of the file on your personal storage device early in the process. A **folder** is a specific location on a storage medium, represented visually by a file folder icon. Folders are good ways to organize files. In this book, you will create a folder for each chapter.

1

● With a USB flash drive connected to one of the computer's USB ports, click File on the Application bar to display the File menu (Figure 1–23).

Q&A

Do I have to save to a USB flash drive?

No. You can save to any device or folder.

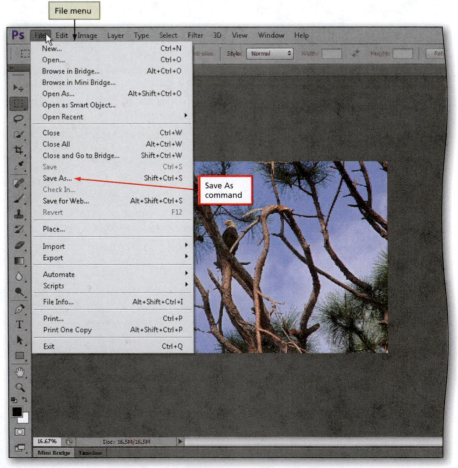

Figure 1–23

2

- Click Save As to display the Save As dialog box.

- Type **Eagle Edited** in the File name text box to change the file name. Do not press the ENTER key after typing the file name.

- Click the Save in box arrow to display the list of available drives (Figure 1–24).

Q&A

What if my USB flash drive has a different name or letter?

It is very likely that your USB flash drive will have a different name and drive letter and be connected to a different port. Verify that the device in your list is correct.

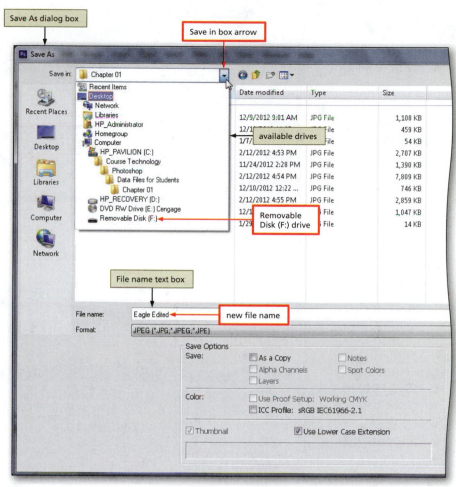

Figure 1–24

3

- Click Removable Disk (F:), or the name of your USB flash drive, in the list of available storage devices to select that drive as the new save location.

- Click the Create New Folder button on the Save As dialog box toolbar to create a new folder on the selected storage device.

- When the new folder appears, type **Chapter 01** to change the name of the folder, and then press the ENTER key (Figure 1–25).

Q&A

Why is my list of drives arranged and named differently?

The size of the Save As dialog box and your computer's configuration determine how the list is displayed and how the drives are named.

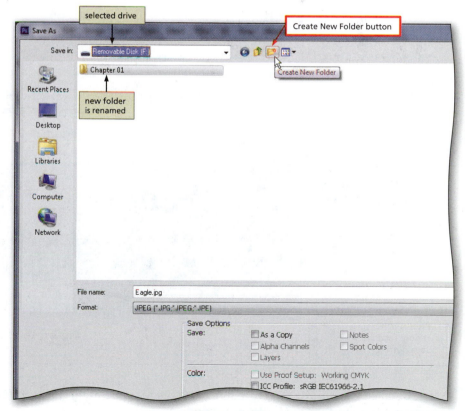

Figure 1–25

4

- Double-click the new folder to open it.

- Click the Format button to display the list of available file formats (Figure 1–26).

Do I have to use the same file name?

It is good practice to identify the relationship of this photo to the original by using at least part of the original file name with some notation about its status.

new folder

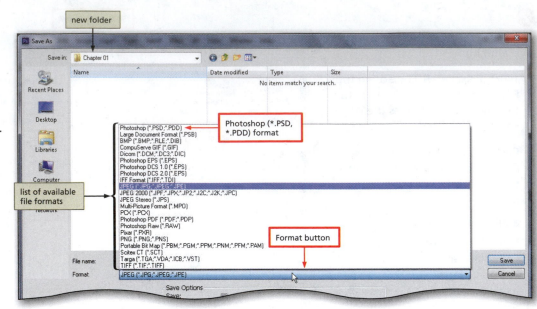

Photoshop (*.PSD, *.PDD) format

list of available file formats

Format button

Figure 1–26

5

- Click Photoshop (*.PSD, *.PDD) to select the file type (Figure 1–27).

What is PDD?

The **PDD format** is used with images created by Photo Deluxe and other software packages. Some older digital cameras produce files with a PDD extension as well.

chosen folder

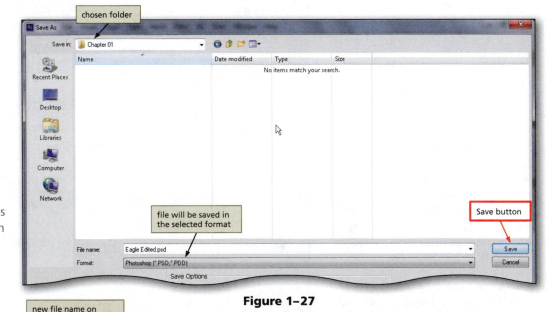

file will be saved in the selected format

Save button

Figure 1–27

6

- Click the Save button to save the document on the selected drive with the new file name (Figure 1–28).

new file name on document window tab

Figure 1–28

Other Ways

1. Press SHIFT+CTRL+S, choose settings, click Save button

For a detailed example of this procedure using the Mac operating system, refer to the steps on pages APP 79 through APP 80 of the For Mac Users appendix.

Viewing Photos

Photoshop allows you to view photos in many different ways, by adjusting the document window and by using different tools and panels. Using good navigation techniques to view images can help you edit the details of a photo or check for problems. For example, you might want to zoom in on a specific portion of the photo or move to a different location in a large photo. You might want to use a ruler to measure certain portions of the photo. Or you might want to view the image without the distraction of the panels and menu. Zooming, navigating, scrolling, and changing the screen mode are some ways to view the document window and its photo.

Zooming

To make careful edits in a photo, you sometimes need to change the magnification, or **zoom**. Zooming allows you to focus on certain parts of the photo, such as a specific person in a crowd scene or details in a complicated picture. A magnification of 100% means the photo is displayed at its actual size. Zooming in enlarges the percentage of magnification of the photo; zooming out reduces the magnification. Note that zooming does not change the size of the photo; it merely changes the appearance of the photo in the document window.

The Zoom Tool button displays a magnifying glass icon on the Tools panel. You also can press the z key to select the Zoom Tool. Choosing one over the other is a matter of personal choice. Most people use the shortcut key. Others sometimes choose the button because of its proximity to the mouse pointer at the time.

When you use the Zoom tool, each click magnifies the image to the next preset percentage. When positioned in the photo, the Zoom Tool mouse pointer displays a magnifying glass, with either a plus sign, indicating an increase in magnification, or a minus sign, indicating a decrease in magnification. Right-clicking with the Zoom Tool in the photo displays a context menu with options to zoom in or zoom out, among others.

Figure 1–29 displays the Zoom Tool options bar, with buttons to zoom in and out. Other options include check boxes used when working with multiple photos, displaying the actual pixels, fitting the entire photo on the screen, filling the screen, and displaying the photo at its print size.

BTW

Ways to Zoom
There are many ways to zoom, including the Zoom tool, the Zoom buttons, the magnification box, and the Navigator panel. How you zoom depends on your personal preference and whether you want to change the current tool.

BTW

Scrubby Zoom
If you click the Scrubby Zoom check box, you can drag to the left in the image to zoom out, or to the right to zoom in.

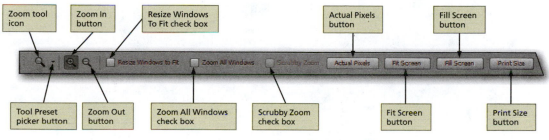

Figure 1–29

To Use the Zoom Tool

The following steps zoom in on the eagle for careful editing later in the chapter.

1

- Click the Zoom Tool button on the Tools panel to select the Zoom Tool.

- Move the mouse pointer into the document window to display the magnifying glass mouse pointer (Figure 1–30).

Q&A

Why does my mouse pointer display a minus sign?

Someone may have previously zoomed out and the setting has carried over. Click the Zoom In button on the options bar.

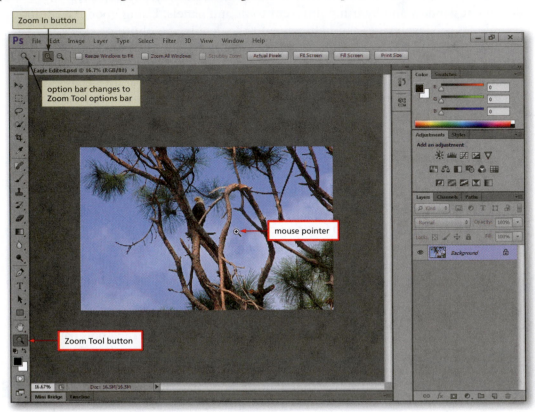

Figure 1–30

2

- Click the eagle three times to zoom in (Figure 1–31).

 Experiment

- On the options bar, click the Zoom In button and then click the photo. Click the Zoom Out button and then click the photo. ALT+click the photo to zoom in the opposite direction from the options bar setting. Zoom to 50% magnification.

Other Ways

1. Press Z, click document window

2. Press CTRL+PLUS SIGN (+) or CTRL+MINUS SIGN (-)

3. On View menu, click Zoom In or Zoom Out

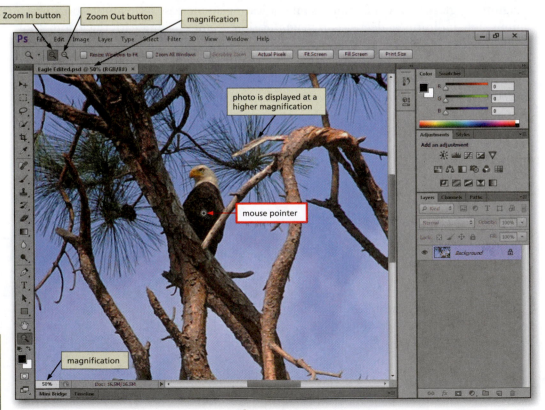

Figure 1–31

The Navigator Panel

Another convenient way to zoom and move around the photo is to use the Navigator panel. The Navigator panel (Figure 1–32) is used to change the view of your document window using a thumbnail display. To display the Navigator panel, select Navigator from the Window menu.

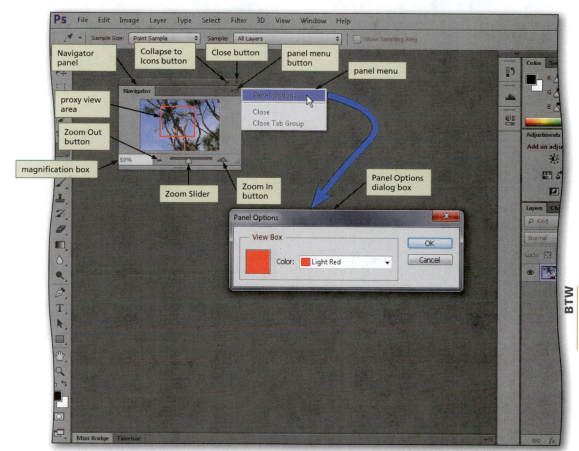

Figure 1–32

The rectangle with the red border in the Navigator panel is called the **proxy view area** or **view box**, which outlines the currently viewable area in the window. Dragging the proxy view area changes the portion of the photo that is displayed in the document window. In the lower portion of the Navigator panel, you can type in the desired magnification, or you can use the slider or buttons to increase or decrease the magnification.

In Figure 1–32, the Navigator panel menu appears when you click the panel menu button. The Panel Options command displays the Panel Options dialog box.

BTW

Moving Panels
If you want to move a panel to the workspace, as is shown in Figure 1-32, simply drag the panel tab.

BTW

Quick Reference
For a table that lists how to complete the tasks covered in this book using the mouse, menus, context menus and keyboard, see the Quick Reference Summary at the back of the book or visit the student companion site located at www.cengagebrain.com.

To Use the Navigator Panel

The following steps display and use the Navigator panel to reposition the view of the photo using the proxy view area.

1
- Click Window on the Application bar to display the Window menu (Figure 1–33).

Q&A

What two panels are already on the vertical dock of panels?

In the Essentials workspace, the History panel and Properties panel appear on the dock.

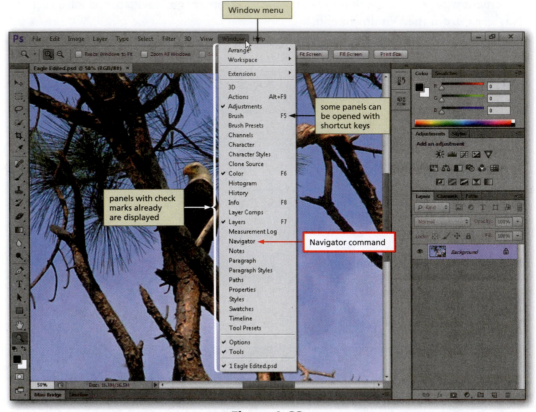

Figure 1–33

2
- Click Navigator on the Window menu to display the Navigator panel (Figure 1–34).

Q&A

Why would I choose the Navigator panel over other methods of moving around the screen?

When you are using a different tool on the Tools panel, such as a text tool or brush tool, it is easier to use the Navigator panel to zoom in or out and move around in the photo. That way, you do not have to change to the Zoom Tool, perform the zoom, and then change back to your editing tool.

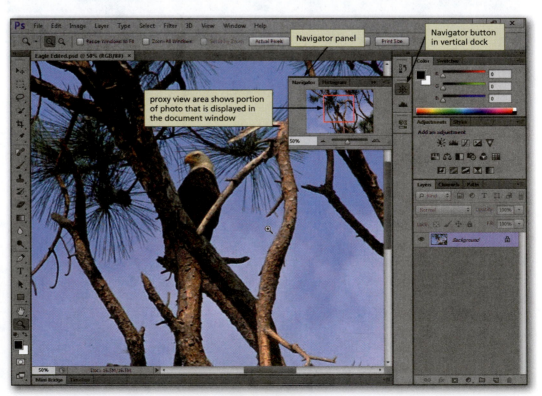

Figure 1–34

3

- Drag the proxy view area on the Navigator Panel to display the upper-right portion of the photo (Figure 1–35).

Experiment

- Drag the proxy view area to display different portions of the photo. Drag the Zoom Slider and try clicking the Zoom In and Zoom Out buttons on the Navigator panel. When you are finished, return to 50% magnification, and drag the proxy view area to display the upper-right portion of the photo.

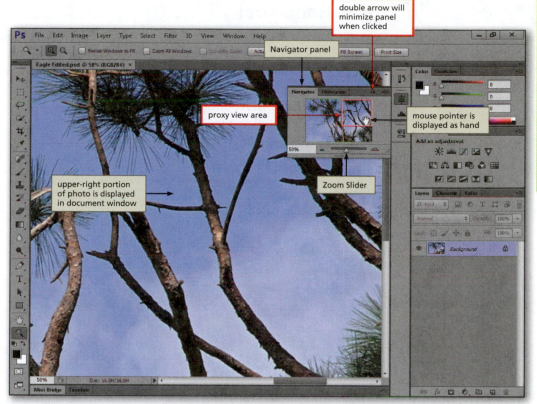

Figure 1–35

To Minimize the Navigator Panel

The following step minimizes the Navigator panel so that it is displayed as a button in the vertical dock of buttons. In the right portion of the panel's title bar, the double arrow, sometimes called the Collapse to Icons button, minimizes a panel.

1

- Click the double arrow at the top of the Navigator panel (Figure 1–36).

Q&A

How would I move or close the panel?

To move the panel, drag the panel tab. To close the panel, click Close on the panel menu, or if the panel is floating, click the panel's Close button.

Figure 1–36

Other Ways

1. On vertical dock, click Navigator button

The Hand Tool

You also can use the Hand Tool to move around in the photo if the photo has been magnified to be larger than the document window. To use the Hand Tool, click the Hand Tool button on the Tools panel, and then drag in the display area of the document window.

The Hand Tool options bar (Figure 1–37) displays boxes and buttons to assist you in scrolling and manipulating the document window.

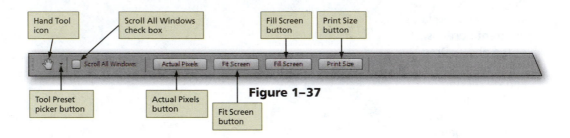

Figure 1–37

To Use the Hand Tool

The following step uses the Hand Tool to view a different part of the photo.

1
- Click the Hand Tool button on the Tools panel to select the Hand Tool.

- Drag in the document window to display the center portion of the photo (Figure 1–38).

Q&A What is the other tool grouped with the Hand Tool?

Grouped with the Hand Tool is the Rotate View Tool. It is used to rotate the entire image, nondestructively, for fine editing.

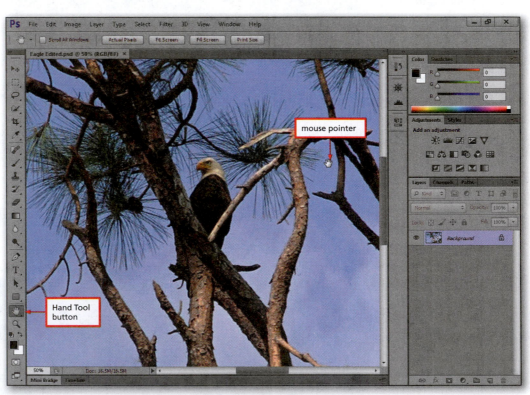

Figure 1–38

Other Ways
1. Press H, drag photo

To Change the Magnification

The following steps use the Magnification box on the status bar to change the magnification.

1
- Double-click the Magnification box on the status bar to select the current magnification (Figure 1–39).

magnification selected in Magnification box

status bar

Figure 1–39

2
- Type 20 and then press the ENTER key to change the magnification (Figure 1–40).

photo is displayed at new magnification

magnification is changed

Figure 1–40

Other Ways

1. On Navigator panel, type percentage in Magnification box

To Display Rulers

To make careful edits in a photo, sometimes it is necessary to use precise measurements in addition to zooming and navigating. In these cases, you should change the Photoshop document window to view the rulers. **Rulers** appear on the top and left sides of the document window. Rulers help you position images or elements precisely. As you move your mouse pointer over a photo, markers on the ruler display the mouse pointer's position.

The following steps display the rulers in the document window.

1

- Click View on the Application bar to display the View menu (Figure 1–41).

Q&A

What unit of measurement do the rulers use?

Rulers display inches by default, but you can right-click a ruler to change the increment to pixels, centimeters, or other units of measurement.

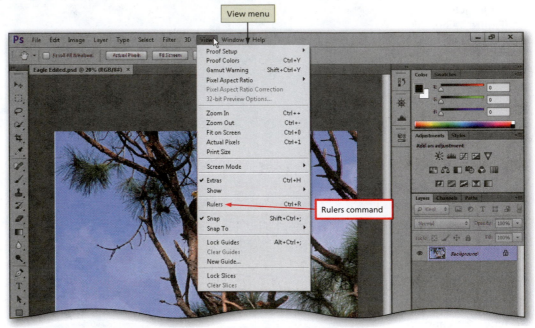

Figure 1–41

2

- Click Rulers to display the rulers in the document window (Figure 1–42).

Q&A

Is the photo really 42 × 26 inches?

The resolution from photos taken with digital cameras is measured in **megapixels** or millions of pixels. The more megapixels you have, the better the photo resolution; however, it translates to very large print sizes. You will resize the photo later in the chapter.

Figure 1–42

Other Ways
1. Press CTRL+R

Screen Modes

To change the way the panels, bars, and document window appear, Photoshop includes three **screen modes**, or ways to view the document window. The Change Screen Mode button is located at the bottom of the Tools panel (Figure 1–42) and toggles among the screen modes. Standard screen mode displays the Application bar, document window, scroll bars, and visible panels. Full screen mode displays only the image and rulers, if they are visible, on a black background. Full screen mode with menu enlarges the document window to fill the workspace with no title bar, status bar, or scroll bars. A fourth way to view the screen is to hide the panels using the TAB key. Pressing the TAB key again redisplays the panels.

Choosing a mode depends on what you are trying to accomplish. While editing a single photo, standard screen mode may be the best, especially for beginners. If you are working on multiple files, screen space is at a premium and you might want to use one of the full screen modes.

Editing the Photo

Editing, or making corrections and changes to a photo, involves a wide variety of tasks such as changing or emphasizing the focus of interest, recoloring portions of the photo, correcting defects, adding new artwork, or changing the file type for specific purposes. Editing also is called **post-processing**, because it includes actions you take after the picture has been processed by the camera or scanner.

Table 1–3 suggests typical categories and types of edits you might perform on photos; there are many others. These edits commonly overlap, and, when performed in combination, they can even create new editing varieties. You will learn more about edits as you work through the chapters in this book.

Table 1–3 Photo Edits	
Category	**Types of Edits**
Transformations	Cropping, slicing, changing the aspect, rotating, leveling, mirroring, warping, skewing, distorting, flipping, and changing the perspective
Enhancements and Layering	Filters, layers, clones, borders, artwork, text, animation, painting, morphing, ordering, styles, masks, cutaways, selections, depth perception, anti-aliasing, moves, shapes, rasterizing
Color	Correction, contrast, blending, modes and systems, separations, screening, levels, ruling, trapping, matching, black and white
Correction	Sharpening, red-eye, tears, correcting distortion, retouching, reducing noise, blur, dodge, burn
File Type	Camera raw, print, Web, animated images
Resolution	Resampling, resizing, collinear editing, interpolation, editing pixel dimensions and document sizes

Editing the Eagle Edited photo will involve three steps. First, you will crop the photo to remove excessive background. Next, you will add a border and stroke it with color. Finally, you will resize the photo to fit the intended use and size requirements, inserting text for the postcard.

BTW

Screen Modes
You also can use the View menu to change Screen Modes as well as pressing the F key on the keyboard.

BTW

Cropping
To evaluate an image for cropping, make a printout. Using two L shapes cut from paper, form a size and shape rectangle to isolate a portion of the image. Draw lines on the printout to use as a guide when cropping in Photoshop.

BTW

When Not to Crop
At times, cropping the photo is not desirable. For example, when you are working with older photos that convey a specific setting or location, the background might contain details that help evoke the setting, such as furniture, clothing worn by people in the background, or toys or vehicles from a particular time period. Retaining these details can help viewers recall the time and place of the original photo.

Plan Ahead

BTW

Rotate and Crop
You can rotate the image around the cropping area by moving the mouse pointer just outside of one of the cropping handles. When the mouse pointer changes to a curved arrow, drag to rotate. If you are using the Perspective Crop Tool, the rotation mouse pointer rotates the crop area rather than the image.

BTW

Straighten and Crop
If you click the Straighten button on the options bar, you can drag a line in the crop area. The image will rotate to match the angle of the line. This is useful when the image is out of alignment. You should try to drag across a natural line within the image.

BTW

Trimming vs. Cropping
The Trim command also crops an image by removing unwanted portions of the photo, but in a different way from the Crop Tool. The Trim command, on the Image menu, trims surrounding transparent pixels or background pixels of the color you specify.

> **Determine how to edit the photo to highlight the theme.**
> You always should perform editing with design principles in mind. Look at your photo carefully. Are there parts that detract from the central figure? Would the theme be illustrated better by only displaying a portion of the photo? If you want to emphasize a single object on a fairly solid background, you might need to crop, or trim, extraneous space around the object. Decide which parts of the photo portray your message and which parts are visual clutter.
>
> - Use the rule of thirds to position visual lines.
> - Crop the photo to remove excess background.
> - Rotate the photo if necessary.

Cropping

The first step in editing the eagle photo is to **crop**, or cut away, some of the extra sky and branches so the photo focuses on the eagle. Photographers try to compose and capture images full-frame, which means the object of interest fills the dimensions of the photo. When that is not possible, photographers and graphic artists crop the photo either to create an illusion of full-frame, to fit unusual shapes in layouts, or to make the image more dramatic. From a design point of view, sometimes it is necessary to crop a photo to straighten an image, remove distracting elements, or simplify the subject. The goal of most cropping is to make the most important feature in the original photo stand out. Cropping sometimes is used to convert a digital photo's proportions to those typical for traditional photos.

Most photographers and graphic artists use the **rule of thirds**, also called the principle of thirds, when placing the focus of interest. Imagine that the scene is divided into thirds both vertically and horizontally. The intersections of these imaginary lines suggest four positions for placing the focus of interest. The position you select depends on the subject and its presentation in the photo. For instance, there might be a shadow, path, or visual line you wish to include. In the case of moving objects, you generally should leave space in front of them, into which they theoretically can move. When eyes are involved, it is better to leave space on the side toward which the person or animal is looking, so they do not appear to look directly out of the setting.

Because the eagle photo will be used on a postcard, the photo's orientation should be **landscape**, or horizontal. In most cases, you should try to crop to a rectangular shape with an approximate short-side to long-side ratio of 5:8. Sometimes called the **golden rectangle**, a 5:8 ratio emulates natural geometric forms such as flowers, leaves, shells, and butterflies. Most digital cameras take pictures with a similar ratio.

The Crop Tool allows you to select the portion of the photo you wish to retain. Photoshop automatically displays handles and a rule of thirds overlay for further adjustments, if necessary. Then, when you press the ENTER key, the rest of the photo is cropped, or removed. You can choose to permanently delete the cropped pixels on the options bar. The cropping handles continue to appear until you choose another tool.

The Crop Tool is grouped with the Perspective Crop Tool. In a **perspective crop**, when you drag one of the cropping handles, the other handles stay in place, which creates a distortion.

The Crop Tool options bar displays boxes and buttons to assist cropping activities (Figure 1–43). You can specify the aspect ratio, or the exact height and width of the crop. The options bar also contains buttons to rotate or straighten the photo, as well as a View button menu to change the overlay grid.

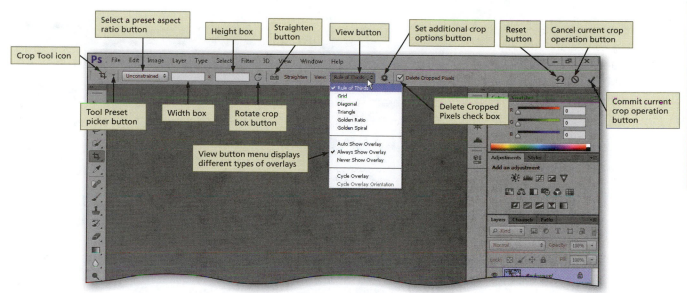

Figure 1–43

To Crop a Photo

To make the eagle the focus of the photo, the extra background will be cropped to provide a line of sight to the left, keeping as much of the tree as possible. The following steps crop the photo of the eagle.

1

- Click the Crop Tool button on the Tools panel to select the Crop Tool.

- Click the photo to display the rule of thirds grid.

- If necessary, click the Delete Cropped Pixels check box on the options bar, so that it displays a check mark (Figure 1–44).

 Experiment

- On the options bar, click the View button, and then, one at a time, choose different overlays. Click the photo to display the overlay each time. When you are finished, click the View button again and then click Rule of Thirds.

Figure 1–44

● SHIFT+CTRL+drag the lower-right cropping handle until the right vertical gridline aligns with the eagle (Figure 1–45).

Q&A

Why should I hold down the SHIFT and CTRL keys while dragging?

SHIFT+CTRL+dragging maintains the aspect ratio of both the grid overlay and the image.

Figure 1–45

● Within the cropping area, drag the photo straight up, until the upper-right intersection of the grid is centered over the eagle (Figure 1–46).

Q&A

What if I change my mind or make a mistake when cropping?

If you make a mistake while dragging the cropping area and want to start over, you can click the Cancel current crop operation button or press the ESC key, which cancels the selection. If you already have performed the crop and then change your mind, you have several choices. You can click the Undo command on the Edit menu, or you can press CTRL+Z to undo the last edit.

Figure 1–46

● Press the ENTER key to complete the crop (Figure 1–47).

🔍 **Experiment**

● If you want to practice cropping, drag a cropping handle again. After each crop, press CTRL+Z to undo the crop.

Other Ways

1. Press C, drag in photo, on options bar click 'Commit current crop operation' button
2. Select portion of image, on Image menu click Crop, press ENTER key

Figure 1–47

To Select the Default Tool Again

If you do not want to use the Crop Tool any longer, or you do not want to see the cropping handles, select any other tool on the Tools panel. The following step selects the default tool again, as you did at the beginning of the chapter.

 On the Tools panel, click the Rectangular Marquee Tool button to select the tool.

Creating a Border

A **border** is a decorative edge on a photo or a portion of a photo. Photoshop provides many ways to create a border, ranging from simple color transformations around the edge of the photo to predefined decorated layers to stylized photo frames.

A border helps define the edge of the photo, especially when the photo might be set on colored paper or on a Web page with a background texture. A border visually separates the photo from the rest of the page, while focusing the viewer's attention. Rounded borders soften the images in a photo. Square borders are more formal. Decorative borders on a static photo can add interest and amusement but easily can detract from the focus on a busier photo. **Blended borders** are not a solid fill; rather, they blend a fill color from the outer edge toward the middle, sometimes providing a three-dimensional effect. A border that complements the photo in style, color, and juxtaposition is best. In the eagle photo, you will create a border using selections of 75 black pixels with 25 pixels of overlapping white. A **pixel** is an individual dot of light that is the basic unit used to create digital images.

BTW

Selections
When you select all, Photoshop displays the photo with a marquee around all four edges. The selection tools on the Tools panel also can help you make selections in the photo. The Rectangular Marquee, Lasso, Quick Selection, and Magic Wand tools will be discussed in Chapter 2.

Identify finishing touches that will further enhance the photo.
Adding a border or decorative frame around a photo sometimes can be an effective way to highlight or make the photo stand out on the page. A border should frame the subject, rather than become the subject. If a border is required by the customer or needed for layout placement, choose a color and width that neither overwhelms nor overlaps any detail in the photo. Using a border color that complements one of the colors already in the photo creates a strong, visually connected image. For more information about graphic design concepts, read Appendix B, Graphic Design Overview.

Plan Ahead

To Create a Selection

Specifying or isolating an area of your photo for editing is called making a **selection**. Selecting specific areas allows you to edit and apply special effects to portions of your image, while leaving the unselected areas untouched.

Selections can be simple shapes such as rectangles or ovals, or unusually shaped areas of a photo, outlining specific objects. Selections can be the entire photo or as small a portion as one pixel. A selection displays a marquee in Photoshop. A **marquee** is a flashing or pulsating border, sometimes called marching ants.

In the case of the Eagle Edited photo, you will make a selection around the edge of the photo to create a border. The steps on the next page select the photo.

1

- On the Application bar, click Select to display the Select menu (Figure 1–48).

Figure 1–48

2

- On the Select menu, click the All command to display the selection marquee around the entire photo (Figure 1–49).

Q&A

Am I selecting all of the photo?

You are identifying the pixels along the edge of the image. Some commands apply to all of the pixels within the selection border, such as copying, deleting, or filling; other commands, such as stroking, apply only to the pixels along the edge of the selection.

Figure 1–49

Other Ways

1. To select all, press CTRL+A

To Stroke a Selection

A **stroke** is a colored outline or edge. When stroking a selection, you must specify the number of pixels to include in the stroke and the desired color. You also must decide whether to apply the stroke outside the selection border, inside the selection border, or centered on the selection border. Other stroke settings include blending modes and opacity, which you will learn about in a later chapter. The following steps stroke a selection.

1

• With the photograph still selected, click Edit on the Application bar to display the Edit menu (Figure 1–50).

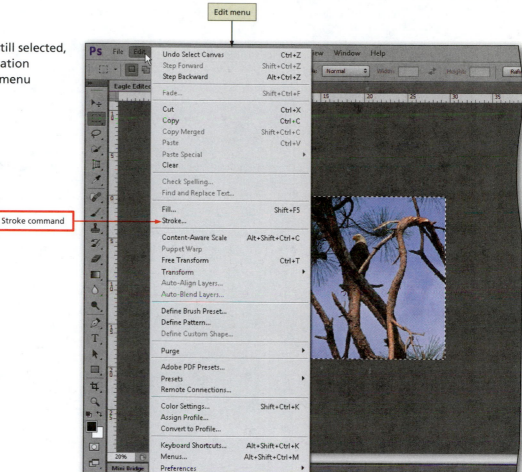

Figure 1–50

2

• Click Stroke to display the Stroke dialog box.

• Type 75 in the Width box (Figure 1–51).

Q&A

Do I need to select a color?

No, the default value is the foreground color, black. If your foreground color is not black, click the Cancel button, press the D key to choose the default colors and start again with Step 1.

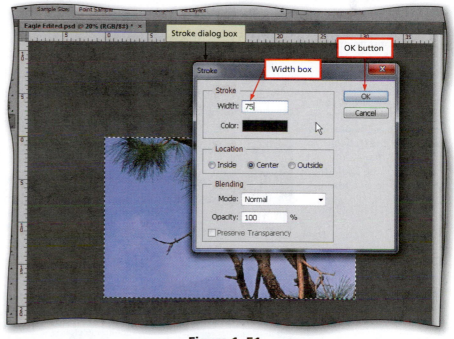

Figure 1–51

3

● Click the OK button in the Stroke dialog box to apply the stroke (Figure 1–52).

Q&A

What does the asterisk mean in the document window tab?

The asterisk means you have made changes to the photo since your last save. Once you save the file, the asterisk no longer is displayed.

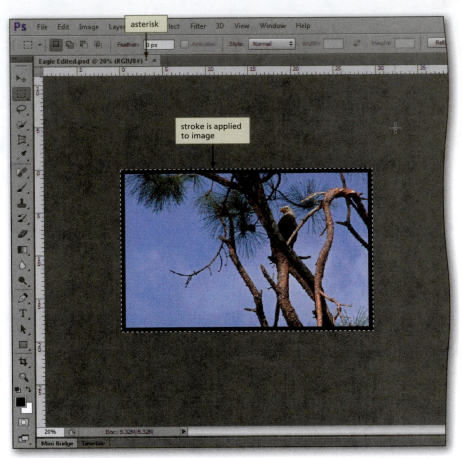

Figure 1–52

Modifying Selections

You can modify the selection in several different ways. In the eagle photo, you will modify the selection border by increasing the number of pixels along the border so you can add a second color at that location. Table 1–4 displays the Modify commands on the Select menu.

Table 1–4 Modify Commands	
Type of Modification	**Result**
Border	This command allows you to select a width of pixels, from 1 to 200, to be split evenly on either side of the existing selection marquee.
Smooth	This command allows you to select a number of pixels in a radius around the selection. Photoshop adds or removes pixels in that radius to smooth sharp corners and jagged lines, reducing patchiness.
Expand	The border is increased by a number of pixels from 1 to 100.
Contract	The border is decreased by a number of pixels from 1 to 100.
Feather	This command creates a feather edge with a width from 0 to 250 pixels.

To Modify a Selection

The following steps modify the selection by changing the border selection area.

1

- On the Application bar, click Select, and then point to Modify to display the Modify submenu (Figure 1–53).

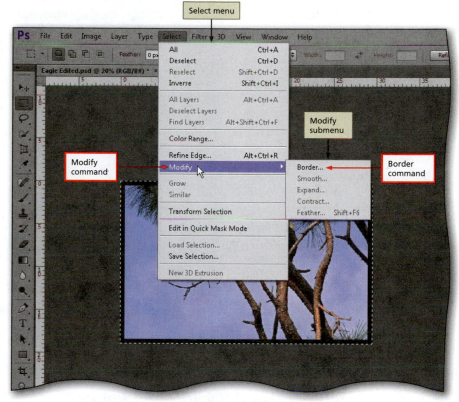

Figure 1–53

2

- Click Border on the Modify submenu to display the Border Selection dialog box.

Q&A

Could I use the Contract command to contract the selection?

No, you must specify the border first. The Contract command is **grayed out**, or **unavailable**, so you cannot select it, before choosing the Border command.

- Type 50 in the Width box to create a border selection on each side of the marquee (Figure 1–54).

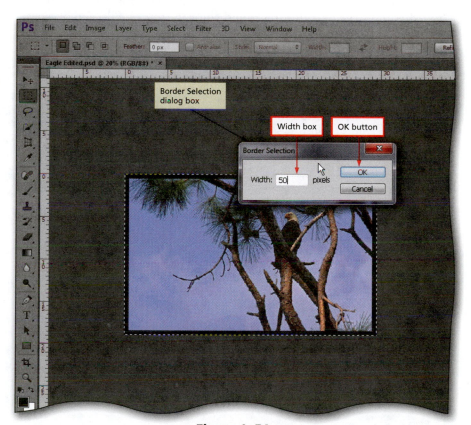

Figure 1–54

• Click the OK button in the Border Selection dialog box to define the selection (Figure 1–55).

Q&A

My display shows two marquees around the photo. Did I do something wrong?

No. Your version of Photoshop might be using a different screen mode or resolution.

 Experiment

• To practice smoothing the border, click the Select menu, point to Modify, and then click Smooth. Enter a value in the Sample Radius box and then click the OK button. Notice the change in the marquee. Press CTRL+Z to undo the Smooth command.

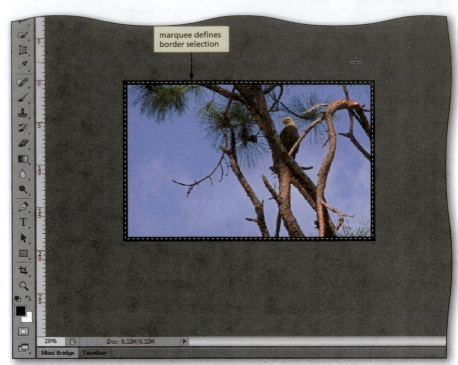

Figure 1–55

To Switch Foreground and Background Colors

On the Tools panel, the default foreground color is black and the default background color is white. Photoshop uses the default foreground color in strokes, fills, and brushes — in the previous steps when you stroked, the pixels became black. To create a rounded gray border, you will use a white, overlapping stroke. The following step switches the foreground and background colors so white is over black.

1

• Click the Switch Foreground and Background Colors button to reverse the colors (Figure 1–56).

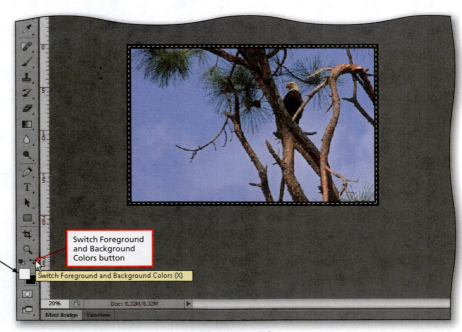

Figure 1–56

Other Ways
1. Press X

To Stroke Again

To create the gray border, you will stroke the selection again, this time with white, and using a narrower width.

1 Click Edit on the Application bar to display the Edit menu.

2 Click Stroke to display the Stroke dialog box.

3 Type 25 in the Width box to set the width of the stroke.

4 Click the OK button to apply the stroke (Figure 1–57).

white is stroked over the black to create a gray border

Figure 1–57

To Deselect

Because the border is complete, you should remove the selection indicator, or **deselect** it, so the marquee no longer appears. The following step removes the selection.

• Click Select on the Application bar, and then click Deselect to remove the selection (Figure 1–58).

selection no longer is displayed

Figure 1–58

Other Ways
1. Press CTRL+D

To Switch Foreground and Background Colors Again

The following step switches the foreground and background colors back to black over white.

1 On the Tools panel, click the Switch Foreground and Background Colors button again to reverse the colors.

Saving Photos
When you save a photo on a storage device, it also remains in main memory and is displayed on the screen.

Saving a Photo with the Same File Name

Because you have made many edits to the photo, it is a good idea to save the photo again. When you saved the document the first time, you assigned the file name, Eagle Edited. When you use the following procedure, Photoshop automatically assigns the same file name to the photo, and it is stored in the same location.

To Save a File with the Same File Name

The following step saves the Eagle Edited file with the changes you made.

1

• On the Application bar, click File to display the File menu, and then click Save to save the photo with the same file name.

Other Ways
1. Press CTRL+S

To Close a File

The following step closes the Eagle Edited document window without quitting Photoshop.

1

• Click the Close button on the document window tab (Figure 1–59) to close the document window and the image file.

• If Photoshop displays a dialog box asking you to save again, click the No button.

Figure 1–59

 MAC For a detailed example of this procedure using the Mac operating system, refer to the steps on page APP 81 of the For Mac Users appendix.

Other Ways	
1. Press CTRL+W	2. On File menu, click Close

Break Point: If you wish to take a break, this is a good place to do so. You can quit Photoshop now. To resume at a later time, start Photoshop, and continue following the steps from this location forward.

Opening a Recent File in Photoshop

Once you have created and saved a document, you may need to retrieve it from your storage medium. For example, you might want to edit the photo further or print it. Photoshop maintains a list of recently used files to give you quick access to them for further editing. The list is maintained from session to session.

To Open a Recent File

Earlier in this chapter, you saved your edited photo on a USB flash drive, using the file name, Eagle Edited. The following steps open the Eagle Edited file using the Open Recent list.

1

• Click File on the Application bar and then point to Open Recent to display the Open Recent submenu (Figure 1–60).

Q&A What does the Clear Recent File List command do?

If you click the Clear Recent File List command, your Recent list will be emptied. To open a file, you then would have to click Open on the File menu and navigate to the location of the file.

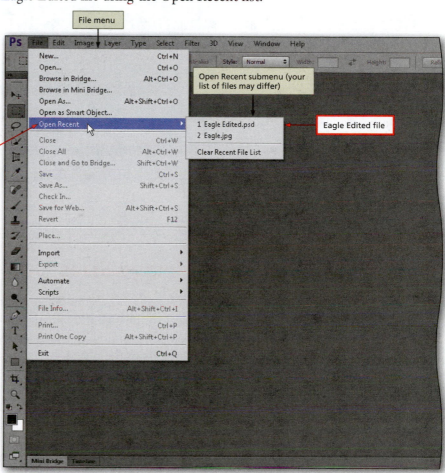

Figure 1–60

2
- Click the Eagle Edited file to open it.

- If necessary, change the magnification to 25% (Figure 1–61).

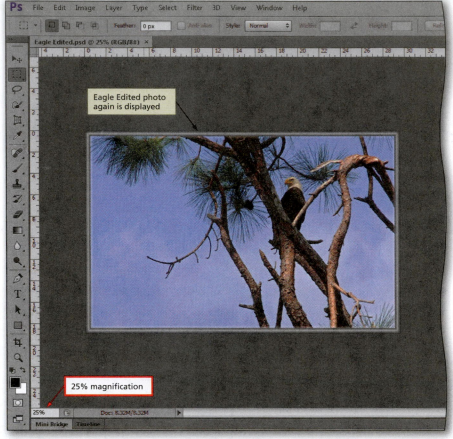

Eagle Edited photo again is displayed

25% magnification

Figure 1–61

BTW

Document Size
Cropping reduces the storage size of the document, which is the size of the saved, flattened file in Adobe Photoshop format. The document window status bar displays the new document size after cropping.

Changing Image Sizes

Sometimes it is necessary to resize an image to fit within certain space limitations. **Resize** means to scale or change the dimensions of the photo. Zooming in or dragging a corner of the document window to change the size is not the same as actually changing the dimensions of the photo. Resizing in a page layout program, such as Publisher, QuarkXPress, or InDesign, merely stretches the pixels. In Photoshop, resizing means adding to or subtracting from the number of pixels.

Photoshop uses a mathematical process called **interpolation**, or **resampling**, when it changes the number of pixels. The program interpolates or calculates how to add new pixels to the photo to match those already there. Photoshop samples the pixels and reproduces them to determine where and how to enlarge or reduce the photo.

When you resize a photo, you must consider many things, such as the type of file, the width, the height, and the resolution. **Resolution** refers to the number of pixels per inch, printed on a page or displayed on a monitor. Not all photos lend themselves to resizing. Some file types lose quality and sharpness when resized. Fine details cannot be interpolated from low-resolution photos. Resizing works best for small changes where exact dimensions are critical. If possible, it usually is better to take a photo at the highest feasible resolution or rescan the image at a higher resolution rather than resize it later.

In those cases where it is impossible to create the photo at the proper size, Photoshop helps you resize or **scale** your photos for print or online media.

**Plan
Ahead**

Prepare for publication.
Keep in mind the golden rectangle of well-designed photos and the limitations of your space. Resize the photo. Print a copy and evaluate its visual appeal. If you are going to publish the photo to the Web, determine the following:

- Typical download speed of your audience
- Browser considerations
- Number of colors
- File type

Finally, save the photo with a descriptive name indicating its completion.

To Resize the Image

Because the eagle photo will be printed on a postcard at a specific size, you will change the height to 4 inches. The following steps resize the image to create a custom-sized photo for printing.

1

- Click Image on the Application bar to display the Image menu (Figure 1–62).

Q&A What is the difference between Image Size and Canvas size?

Increasing the canvas size adds space around an existing image. Decreasing the canvas size is the same as cropping.

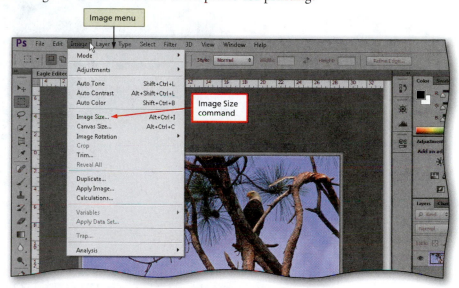

Figure 1–62

2

- Click Image Size to display the Image Size dialog box.

- In the Document Size area, double-click the value in the Height box and then type 4 to replace the previous value (Figure 1–63).

Q&A Why did the width change?

When you change the width or height, Photoshop automatically adjusts the other dimension to maintain the proportions of the photo. Your exact width might differ slightly depending on how closely you cropped the original photo.

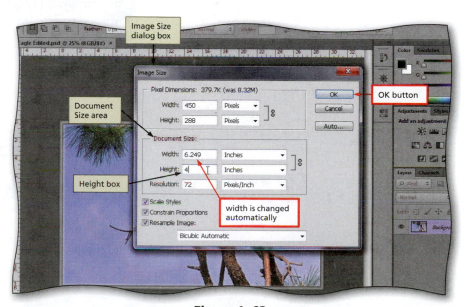

Figure 1–63

3
- Click the OK button to finish resizing the image.

- Change the magnification to 100% (Figure 1–64).

  Experiment

- Click the status bar menu button and then click Document Dimensions to verify that the image size has been changed. Then, click the status bar menu button again and then click Document Sizes to redisplay the document size.

Figure 1–64

Other Ways

1. Press ALT+CTRL+I, change settings, click OK button

Inserting Text

The next steps use a type tool to create text for the postcard. On the Tools panel, the default type tool is the Horizontal Type Tool. The options bar for the Horizontal Type Tool (Figure 1–65) includes boxes and buttons typical of those found in a word processing toolbar, including font family, font style, font size, and justification. A Create warped text button allows you to create text in specialized formations, similar to the WordArt tool in Microsoft Word. On the right side of the options bar are buttons to cancel and commit editing changes. In a future chapter, you will learn about the Character and Paragraph panels that provide additional tools for manipulating text.

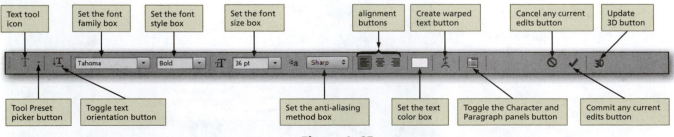

Figure 1–65

To Select the Horizontal Type Tool

The following step selects the Horizontal Type Tool on the Tools panel.

- Click the Horizontal Type Tool on the Tools panel to select it (Figure 1–66).

- If the solid T icon does not appear on the button, right-click the button to display its context menu, then click Horizontal Type Tool in the list.

Horizontal Type Tool button

Horizontal Type Tool (T)

Figure 1–66

Other Ways

1. Press T

To Set Font Options

The following steps select font settings on the options bar. In addition to the font and alignment options, when you click the 'Set the text color' box, Photoshop uses color picker tools, such as a color field and color model boxes, to help you select the text color.

- On the options bar, click the 'Set the font family' box arrow to display the list of font families.

- Scroll in the list to display the Tahoma font family (Figure 1–67).

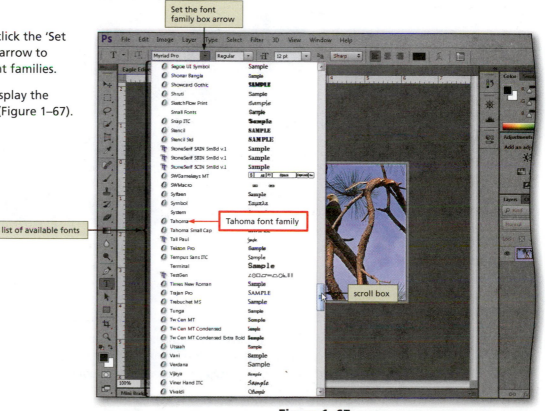

Set the font family box arrow

list of available fonts

Tahoma font family

scroll box

Figure 1–67

- Click Tahoma or a similar font in the list.

- Click the 'Set the font style' box arrow to display the list of font styles (Figure 1–68).

Why does the list not include other styles, such as italics?

Available font styles depend on the chosen font and the capability of the printer to reproduce that font. This font has only regular and bold styles.

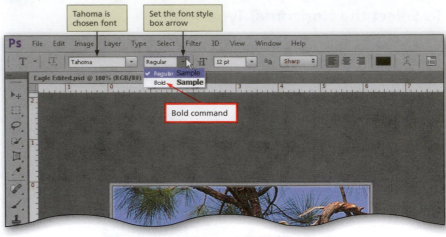

Figure 1–68

- Click Bold to choose a bold font style.

- Select the value in the 'Set the font size' box, and then type 3 6 to replace the size (Figure 1–69).

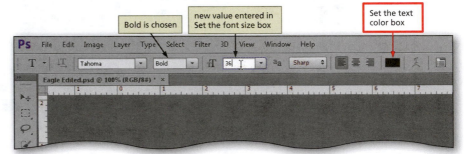

Figure 1–69

- Click the 'Set the text color' box to open the Color Picker (Text Color) dialog box.

- Click a white color in the upper-left corner of the color field (Figure 1–70).

What do the numerical boxes indicate?

Each color mode uses a numerical method called a color model, or color space, to describe the color. Some companies use specific numbers to create exact colors for branding purposes.

- Click the OK button in the Color Picker (Text Color) dialog box to apply white as the text color on the options bar.

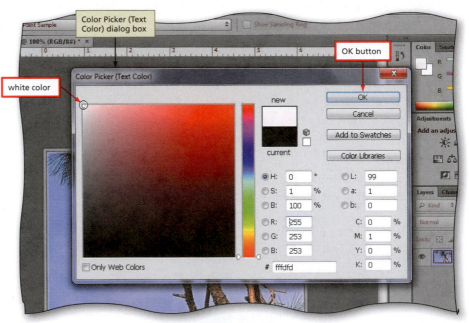

Figure 1–70

To Insert Text

With the type tool selected, you drag a bounding box in the document window to insert text. A **bounding box** is similar to a text box in other applications, with a dotted outline and sizing handles. As you drag, the mouse pointer changes to a small, open book outline. After typing the text in the bounding box, you use the 'Commit any current edits' button to complete the entry. Then, if the size of the bounding box needs to be adjusted, you can drag the sizing handles. The mouse pointer becomes an insertion point when positioned over the text. You will learn about other type tools and features in a later chapter.

The following steps enter text on the postcard.

1

- With the Horizontal Type Tool still selected, drag a bounding box in the lower-right portion of the photo, approximately 2.5 inches wide and 2 inches tall, as shown in Figure 1–71.

Q&A

What is the new notation on the Layers panel?

When you create a bounding box, Photoshop separates the text from the rest of the picture in its own layer. You will learn more about layers in a future chapter.

Figure 1–71

2

- Type National and then press the ENTER key.

- Type Wildlife and then press the ENTER key.

- Type Park to complete the text (Figure 1–72).

Q&A

Can I make changes and corrections to the text?

Yes, you can click anywhere in the text box, use the ARROW keys, the BACKSPACE key, and the DELETE key just as you do in word processing. If your bounding box is too small, you can drag the sizing handles.

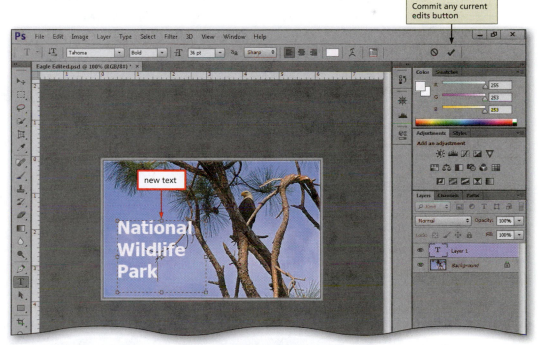

Figure 1–72

3

- On the options bar, click the 'Commit any current edits' button to finish the new layer.

To Stroke Text

Earlier in this chapter, you added a stroke of color to a selection as you created a border for the postcard. The following steps stroke the text with black to make the letters stand out. You will use the Layer Style dialog box to create the stroke.

1

• With the new layer still selected on the Layer's panel, click the 'Add a layer style' button on the Layers panel status bar (Figure 1–73).

Q&A

Could I use the Stroke command on the Edit menu to stroke text?

No. The Stroke command on the Edit menu is for selections only. Because this is an entire layer, you need to use a layer style.

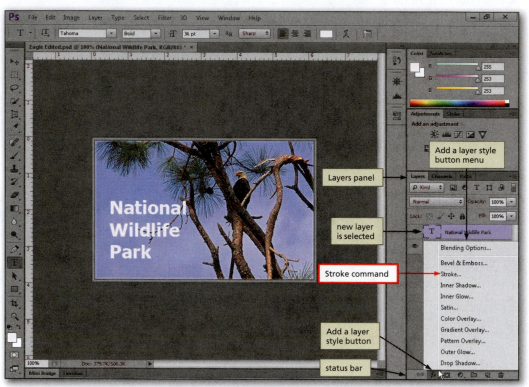

Figure 1–73

2

• Click Stroke in the list of layer styles to display the Layer Style dialog box.

• Type 1 in the Size box to create 1 pixel of black stroke (Figure 1–74).

Q&A

What should I do if my color does not appear as black?

Black is the default color; however, a previous user on your computer may have changed the color. Click the Color box to display a Color Picker dialog box. Click black and then click the OK button.

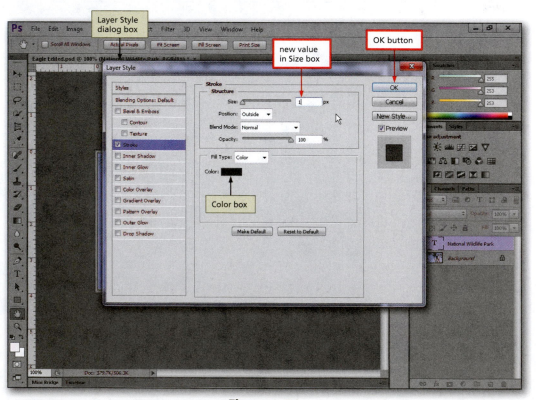

Figure 1–74

- Click the OK button in the Layer Style dialog box to accept the settings and add the stroke (Figure 1–75).

- Press the D key to reset the default colors on the Tools panel.

Figure 1–75

To Save a File with a Different Name

Many graphic designers will save multiple copies of the same photo with various edits. Because this photo has been resized to print properly, you need to save it with a different name, as performed in the following step.

- Click File on the Application bar and then click Save As to display the Save As dialog box.

- In the Save As dialog box, type `Eagle Resized with Text` in the File name text box.

- If necessary, click the Save in box arrow and then click Removable Disk (F:), or the location of your USB flash drive and appropriate folder in the list.

- If necessary, click the Format button and then click Photoshop (*.PSD, *.PDD) to select the format type (Figure 1–76).

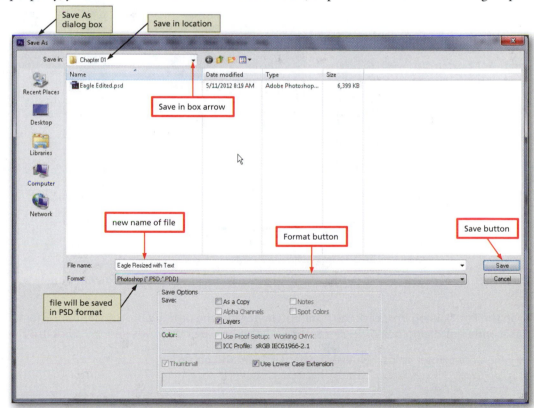

Figure 1–76

- Click the Save button to save the image with the new name.

- If Photoshop displays a Photoshop Format Options dialog box, click the OK button to accept the settings and close the dialog box.

Printing a Photo

The photo now can be printed, saved, taken to a professional print shop, or sent online to a printing service. A printed version of the photo is called a **hard copy** or **printout**. You can print one copy using the Print One Copy command on the File menu, or to display the Print dialog box, you can click Print on the File menu, which offers you more printing options.

The Print One Copy command sends the printout to the default printer. If you are not sure which printer is your default printer, choose the Print command. In the Print dialog box, click the Printer box arrow and choose your current printer. You will learn more about the Print dialog box in Chapter 2.

To Print a Photo

The following steps print the photo created in this chapter.

- Ready the printer according to the printer instructions.

- Click File on the Application bar, and then click Print to display the Print dialog box.

- If necessary, click the Printer box arrow and then select your printer from the list. Do not change any other settings (Figure 1–77).

Q&A

Does Photoshop have a Print button?

No. Photoshop's Print commands are available on the File menu or by using shortcut keys.

Figure 1–77

- In the Print dialog box, click the Print button to start the printing process. If your system displays a second Print dialog box or a Print Settings dialog box, unique to your printer, click its Print button.

- When the printer stops, retrieve the hard copy of the photo.

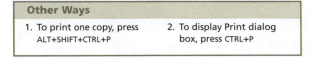

Other Ways
1. To print one copy, press ALT+SHIFT+CTRL+P   2. To display Print dialog box, press CTRL+P

Saving a Photo for Use on the Web

When preparing photos for the Web, you often need to compromise between the quality of the display and the file size. Web users do not want to wait while large photos load from Web servers to their individual computer systems. To solve this problem, Photoshop provides several commands to compress the file size of an image while optimizing its online display quality. Additionally, Photoshop allows you to save the photo in a variety of formats such as **GIF**, which is a compressed graphic format designed to minimize file size and electronic transfer time, or as an **HTML** (Hypertext Markup Language) file, which contains all the necessary information to display your photo in a Web browser.

Therefore, you have two choices in Photoshop for creating Web images: the Zoomify command and the Save for Web command. When you **zoomify**, you create a high-resolution image for the Web, complete with a background and tools for navigation, panning, and zooming. To zoomify, click Export on the File menu and then click Zoomify. In the Zoomify Export dialog box, you set various Web and export options. Photoshop creates the HTML code and accompanying files for you to upload to a Web server.

If you do not want the extra HTML files for the background, navigation, and zooming, you can create a single graphic file by using the Save for Web command. The resulting graphic can be used on the Web or on a variety of mobile devices.

Optimization is the process of changing the photo to make it most effective for its purpose. The Save for Web command allows you to preview optimized images in different file formats, and with different file attributes, for precise optimization. You can view multiple versions of a photo simultaneously and modify settings as you preview the image.

BTW

Reviewing the HTML Code
If you want to review the HTML code later, you can either open the file in Photoshop, access the Save for Web dialog box, and then click the Preview button; or, you can double-click the HTML file to open it in a browser, click View on the Browser's menu bar, and then click Source.

To Preview using the Save for Web Dialog Box

To optimize the eagle photo for use on the Web, you need to make decisions about the file size, and how long it might take to load on a Web page, as you preview the image. These kinds of decisions must take into consideration the audience and the nature of the Web page. For example, Web pages geared for college campuses probably could assume a faster download time than those that target a wide range of home users. An e-commerce site that needs high-quality photography to sell its product will make certain choices in color and resolution.

The hardware and software of Web users also is taken into consideration. For instance, if a Web photo contains more colors than the user's monitor can display, a browser might **dither**, or approximate, the colors that it cannot display, by blending colors that it can. Dithering might not be appropriate for some Web pages, because it increases the file size and, therefore, causes the page to load more slowly.

Many other appearance settings play a role in the quality of Web graphics, some of which are subjective in nature. As you become more experienced in Photoshop, you will learn how to make choices about dithering, colors, texture, image size, and other settings.

The step on the next page uses the Save for Web command to display previews for four possible Web formats.

- With the Eagle Resized with Text photo open, click File on the Application bar to display the File menu and then click Save for Web to display the Save for Web dialog box.

- Click the 4-Up tab to display four versions of the photo (Figure 1–78).

Q&A

Why are there four frames?

Photoshop displays four previews — the original photo and three others that are converted to different resolutions to optimize download times.

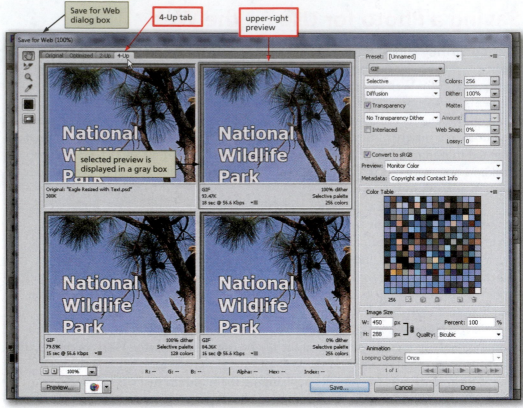

Figure 1–78

Other Ways

1. Press ALT+SHIFT+CTRL+S

To Choose a Download Speed

For faster downloads when the photo is displayed as a Web graphic, you can choose a download speed that will be similar to that of your target audience. The **annotation area** below each preview in the Save for Web dialog box provides optimization information such as the size of the optimized file and the estimated download time using the selected modem speed. You will learn more about other settings in the Save for Web dialog box in a later chapter.

The following steps change the download speed to 512 kilobytes per second (Kbps).

- Click the upper-right preview, if necessary, to choose a high quality version of the photo.

- In the annotation area below the upper-right preview, click the 'Select download speed' button to display the list of connection speeds (Figure 1–79).

Figure 1–79

2

- In the list, click Size/Download Time (512 Kbps Cable/DSL) or another appropriate speed (Figure 1–80).

Q&A

How fast will the picture download?

In Figure 1–78, the speed was 18 seconds at 56.6 Kbps. At 512 Kbps, the photo will download in 3 seconds, as shown in Figure 1–80. Your download times might differ slightly.

Experiment

- Click the Select download speed button to display the list of connection speeds and then click various connection speeds to see how the download times are affected. When finished, click Size/Download Time (512 Kbps Cable/DSL) in the list.

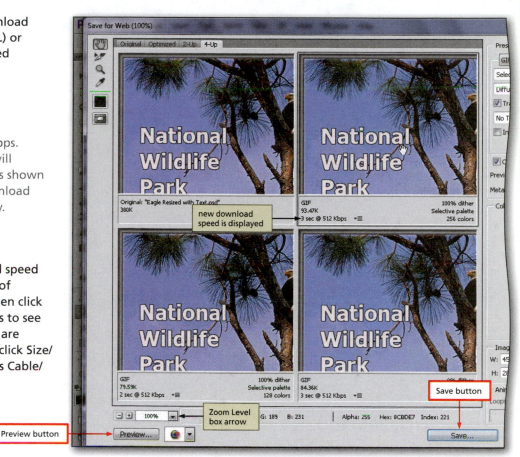

Figure 1–80

Other Ways

1. Right-click annotation area, select download speed

BTW

Save for Web Preview
If you want the entire photo to display in the Save for Web dialog box, click the Zoom Level box arrow and then click Fit in View.

To Preview the Photo on the Web

Before uploading a photo to the Web, it is always a good idea to preview it to check for errors. When Photoshop displays a Web preview of any photo, it also displays the characteristics of the file and the HTML code used to create the preview. The steps on the next page preview the image in a browser.

Figure 1–81

1

- Click the Preview button (shown in Figure 1–80 on the previous page) to display the photo in a Web browser.

- If necessary, double-click the browser's application bar to maximize the browser window (Figure 1–81).

When I clicked the Preview button, the HTML code displayed in Notepad. Should it open in a browser?

If Photoshop cannot detect a default browser on your system, you may have to click the box arrow next to the Preview button (Figure 1–80), and then click Edit List to add your browser.

How would I use the HTML code?

As a Web designer, you might copy and paste the code into a text editor or Web creation software, replacing BrowserPreview with the name of the file. After saving, the code, the HTML file, and the photo would need to be uploaded to a server.

2

- Click the Close button on the browser's application bar to close the browser window. If necessary, click the Adobe Photoshop CS6 button on the Windows taskbar to return to the Save for Web dialog box.

BTW

Saving for Web

In the Save Optimized As dialog box, you can click the Format button to choose one of three ways to save for the Web. The Images only option saves the photo itself in a Web-friendly format as a GIF file. The HTML only option saves the coding that creates the Web page, but not the photo. The HTML and Images option saves the Web page and creates an accompanying folder named Images to go with the Web page file. Inside the Images folder is a GIF version of the photo.

BTW

CS6 Device Central

Device Central, available in Photoshop CS6, the extended version, enables you to preview how Photoshop files will look on a variety of mobile devices. An emulator or mock-up displays the device and preview. Photoshop supports most cell phone displays, portable electronic devices, and MP3 players with video. In the Device Central window, you can adjust settings for lighting, scaling, and alignment.

To Save the Photo for the Web

When you click the Save button in the Save for Web dialog box, Photoshop displays the Save Optimized As dialog box, where you will name the Web file. The following steps save the Photo for the Web.

- In the Save for Web dialog box (Figure 1–80 on page PS 55), click the Save button to display the Save Optimized As dialog box.

- Type `Eagle-for-Web` in the File name text box.

- If necessary, click the Save in box arrow and then click Removable Disk (F:), or the location of your USB flash drive. Double-click the appropriate folder in the list (Figure 1–82).

Q&A

Why are the words in the file name hyphenated?

For ease of use, it is standard for Web graphics to have no spaces in their file names.

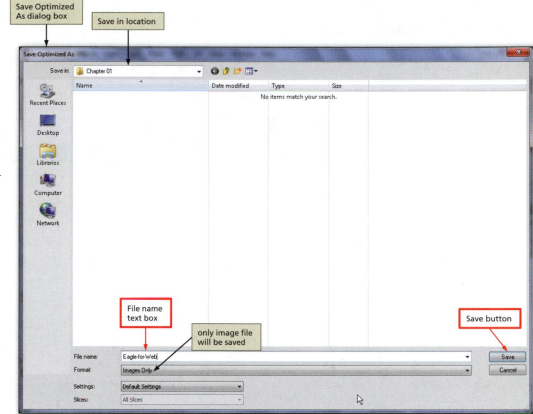

Figure 1–82

- Click the Save button in the Save Optimized As dialog box to save the file.

Photoshop Help

At anytime while you are using Photoshop, you can get answers to questions by using **Photoshop Help**. You activate Photoshop Help either by clicking Help on the Application bar or by pressing the F1 key. The Help menu includes commands to display more information about your copy of Photoshop, as well as a list of how-to guides for common tasks. The Photoshop Online Help command connects you, through the Adobe Photoshop Support Center on the Web, to a wealth of assistance, including tutorials with detailed instructions accompanied by illustrations and videos. Used properly, this form of online assistance can increase your productivity and reduce your frustration by minimizing the time you spend learning how to use Photoshop. Additional information about using Photoshop Help is available in Appendix D, the Using Photoshop Help appendix.

BTW

Community Help
Community Help is an integrated Web environment that includes Photoshop Help and gives you access to community-generated content moderated by Adobe and industry experts. Comments from users help guide you to an answer.

To Access Photoshop Help

The next step displays Photoshop Help online. You must be connected to the Web if you plan to perform these steps on a computer.

1

- With Photoshop open on your system, press the F1 key to access the Photoshop Help / Help and tutorials page.

- If necessary, double-click the application bar to maximize the window (Figure 1–83).

Q&A

My page looks different. Did I do something wrong?

No. Adobe updates the Help pages frequently. Your page will differ.

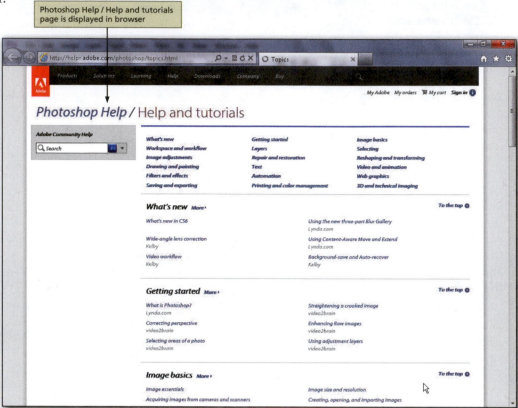

Photoshop Help / Help and tutorials page is displayed in browser

Figure 1–83

Other Ways

1. On Help menu, click Photoshop Online Help

To Use the Help Search Box

The Search box allows you to type words or phrases about which you want additional information and help, such as cropping or printing images. When you press the ENTER key, Photoshop Help responds by displaying a list of topics related to the word or phrase you typed.

The following steps use the Search box to obtain information about the Tools panel.

1
- Click the Search box and then type `Tools panel` to enter the search topic (Figure 1–84).

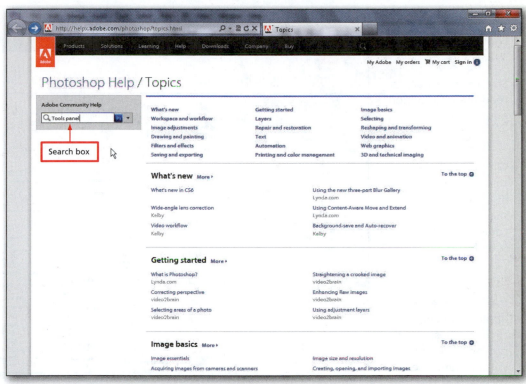

Figure 1–84

2
- Press the ENTER key to display the relevant links (Figure 1–85).

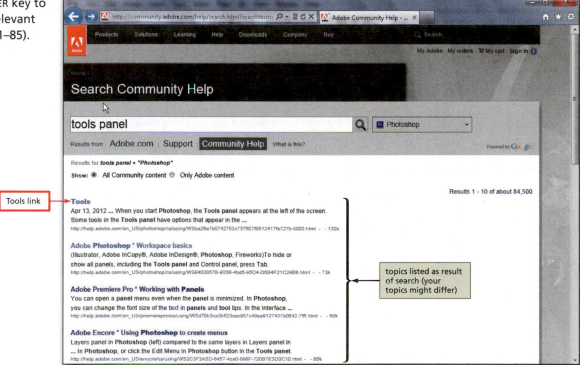

Figure 1–85

3

- Click the link, Tools, to display the contents (Figure 1–86).

- Scroll as necessary to read the information about tools.

 Experiment

- Click other links to view more information, or search for other topics using the Search box.

4

- In the browser application bar, click the Close button to close the window, and then, if necessary, click the Adobe Photoshop CS6 button on the taskbar to return to Photoshop.

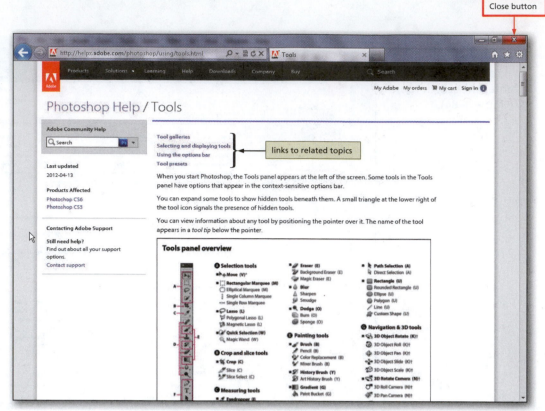

Figure 1–86

Other Ways

1. On Help menu, click Photoshop Online Help, enter search topic

To Quit Photoshop

The following step quits Photoshop and returns control to Windows.

1

- Click the Close button on the right side of the Application bar to close the window.

- If Photoshop displays a dialog box asking you to save changes, click the No button.

MAC For a detailed example of this procedure using the Mac operating system, refer to the steps on page APP 82 of the For Mac Users appendix.

Other Ways

1. On File menu, click Exit
2. Press CTRL+Q

Chapter Summary

In this chapter, you gained a broad knowledge of Photoshop. First, you learned how to start Photoshop. You were introduced to the Photoshop workspace. You learned how to open a photo, change the magnification, zoom, and display rulers. You learned about design issues related to the placement of visual points of interest. You then learned how to crop a photo to eliminate extraneous background. After you added a blended border, you resized the image and added text. Once you saved the photo, you learned how to print it. You used the Save for Web command to optimize and save a Web version. You learned how to use Adobe Help to research specific help topics. Finally, you learned how to quit Photoshop.

The items listed below include all the new Photoshop skills you have learned in this chapter:

1. Start Photoshop (PS 4)
2. Select the Essentials Workspace (PS 6)
3. Select the Default Tool (PS 8)
4. Reset the Options Bar (PS 8)
5. Reset the Interface Color (PS 9)
6. Open a File (PS 11)
7. Save a File in the PSD Format (PS 20)
8. Use the Zoom Tool (PS 24)
9. Use the Navigator Panel (PS 26)
10. Minimize the Navigator Panel (PS 27)
11. Use the Hand Tool (PS 28)
12. Change the Magnification (PS 29)
13. Display Rulers (PS 30)
14. Crop a Photo (PS 33)
15. Create a Selection (PS 35)
16. Stroke a Selection (PS 36)
17. Modify a Selection (PS 39)
18. Switch Foreground and Background Colors (PS 40)
19. Deselect (PS 41)
20. Save a File with the Same File Name (PS 42)
21. Close a File (PS 42)
22. Open a Recent File (PS 43)
23. Resize the Image (PS 45)
24. Select the Horizontal Type Tool (PS 47)
25. Set Font Options (PS 47)
26. Insert Text (PS 48)
27. Stroke Text (PS 50)
28. Save a File with a Different Name (PS 51)
29. Print a Photo (PS 52)
30. Preview using the Save for Web Dialog Box (PS 53)
31. Choose a Download Speed (PS 54)
32. Preview the Photo on the Web (PS 55)
33. Save the Photo for the Web (PS 56)
34. Access Photoshop Help (PS 58)
35. Use the Help Search Box (PS 58)
36. Quit Photoshop (PS 60)

Apply Your Knowledge

Reinforce the skills and apply the concepts you learned in this chapter.

Editing a Photo in the Photoshop Workspace

Instructions: Start Photoshop and perform the customization steps found on pages PS 6 through PS 10. Open the Apply 1-1 Water Park file in the Chapter 01 folder from the Data Files for Students. Visit www.cengage.com/ct/studentdownload for detailed instructions or contact your instructor for information about accessing the required files.

First, you will save the photo in the PSD format, then you will crop the photo, add a white border, and save the edited photo, as shown in Figure 1–87 on the next page. Next, you will resize the photo for printing and print one copy. Finally, you will reopen your edited photo, and then you will optimize it for the Web, save it, and close it.

Continued >

Apply Your Knowledge *continued*

Source: Mali Jones

Figure 1–87

Perform the following tasks:

1. On the File menu, click Save As. When Photoshop displays the Save As dialog box, navigate to your storage device and then double-click the appropriate folder, if necessary. In the File name box, type `Apply 1-1 Water Park Edited`. Click the Format button and choose the PSD file format. Click the Save button to save the file.

2. Use the Zoom Tool to zoom the photo to 50% magnification, if necessary.

3. Use the Hand Tool to reposition the photo in the workspace to view different areas of the zoomed photo.

4. Use the Navigator panel to zoom out to 16.67%.

5. Use the Crop Tool to crop the photo, retaining the top patio of the water slide and the child on the right slide as shown in Figure 1–87. When using the Crop Tool, you might want to use the 'Rotate the crop box between portrait and landscape orientation' button. Include more water than sky. Use the rule of thirds guide to position the child in the lower-right intersection. (*Hint:* If your cropping selection does not look correct, you can press the ESC key to clear the selection before you press the ENTER key. Immediately after cropping the photo, you can click Undo on the Edit menu to undo the crop action.)

6. Select a different tool so the cropping handles no longer are displayed.

7. To create the border:

    a. If necessary, press the D key to select the default colors. Press the x key to reverse the foreground and background colors, so that white displays over black on the Tools panel.

    b. Press CTRL+A to select all of the photo.

    c. Use the Select menu to modify the border to 100 pixels.

    d. Use the Stroke command on the Edit menu to stroke the selection with white.

    e. Press CTRL+D to clear your selection when you are finished creating the border.

8. Press CTRL+S to save the Apply 1-1 Water Park Edited photo with the same file name in the same location.

9. Use the Image menu to resize the photo width to 5 inches wide to create a custom-sized photo for printing.

10. Save the resized file as Apply 1-1 Water Park for Print.

11. Print the photo and then close the file. If Photoshop displays a dialog box about saving again, click the No button.

12. Open the Apply 1-1 Water Park for Print file using the Open Recent list.

13. Save the photo for the Web, displaying it in the 4-Up tab. Select the preview that looks the best for your download speed.

14. Preview the optimized photo in your browser. Close the browser.

15. Save the optimized file with the name, Apply-1-1-Water-Park-for-Web.

16. Close the Apply 1-1 Water Park for Print file without saving it and quit Photoshop.

Extend Your Knowledge

Extend the skills you learned in this chapter and experiment with new skills. You may need to use Help to complete the assignment.

Exploring Crop Tool Options

Instructions: Start Photoshop and perform the customization steps found on pages PS 6 through PS 10. Open the Extend 1-1 Arc de Triomphe file in the Chapter 01 folder from the Data Files for Students and save it on your storage device as Extend 1-1 Arc de Triomphe Edited in the PSD file format. Visit www.cengage.com/ct/studentdownload for detailed instructions or contact your instructor for information about accessing the required files.

    The photo (Figure 1–88) is to be added to a book about Paris; therefore, the structure should be centered, straightened, and display in a 5 × 7 format.

Figure 1–88

Continued >

Perform the following tasks:

1. Use Help to read about the Crop Tool's Straighten button and the Aspect Ratio button.
2. Select the Crop Tool. On the options bar, click the Straighten button, and then drag in the photo, across a line that should be straight in the upper portion of the monument.
3. Use the 'Select a preset aspect ratio' button to choose a 5 × 7 forced ratio. Drag a corner cropping handle inward, keeping the arc within the grid. Drag the picture to center it within the cropping area.
4. Click the 'Delete cropped pixels' check box, if necessary, and then crop the photo.
5. Review Table 1–4 on page PS 38. Use the commands on the Modify submenu to set the border options of your choice. Stroke the selection with a color of your choice.
6. After viewing the resulting border, use the History panel to go back to the photo's cropped state.
7. Repeat Steps 5 and 6 several times to experiment with different border widths and colors, then apply the border that best complements the photo and save the changes to the photo.
8. Close the photo and quit Photoshop.

Make It Right

Analyze a project and correct all errors and/or improve the design.

Changing a Photo's Focus and Optimizing It for the Web

Instructions: Start Photoshop and perform the customization steps found on pages PS 6 through PS 10. Open the Make It Right 1-1 Young Stars file in the Chapter 01 folder from the Data Files for Students and save it on your storage device as Make It Right 1-1 Young Stars Edited in the PSD file format. Visit www.cengage.com/ct/studentdownload for detailed instructions or contact your instructor for information about accessing the required files.

Members of your Astronomy Club have selected the Young Stars photo (Figure 1–89) for the club's Web site. You are tasked with editing the photo to focus more clearly on the cluster of stars and its trailing dust blanket, and then optimizing the photo for the Web.

Source: NASA/JPL-Caltech/Harvard-Smithsonian CFA

Figure 1–89

View the photo in different screen modes and at different magnifications. Keeping the rule of thirds and the golden rectangle concepts in mind, crop the photo to change its focal point and resave it. Then save the photo for the Web as Make-It-Right-1-1-Young-Stars-for-Web.

In the Lab

Design and/or create a project using the guidelines, concepts, and skills presented in this chapter. Labs are listed in order of increasing difficulty.

Lab 1: Cropping a Photo and Adding a Smooth Border

Problem: An extreme sports magazine has accepted the submission of your parasailing photo, but they would like you to crop the photo more, add a smooth border, and resize it. The edited photo is displayed in Figure 1–90.

Note: To complete this assignment, you will be required to use the Data Files for Students. Visit www.cengage.com/ct/studentdownload for detailed instructions or contact your instructor for information about accessing the required files.

Figure 1–90

Instructions: Perform the following tasks:

1. Start Photoshop.
2. Click Window on the application bar, point to Workspace, and then click Essentials (Default). Repeat the process and click Reset Essentials to reset the Essentials workspace.
3. Select the second button on the Tools panel to reset the Tools panel.
4. Right-click the Rectangular Marquee Tool icon on the options bar, and then click Reset all Tools to reset the options bar.
5. Press the D key to select the default colors. If black is not over white at the bottom of the Tools panel, click the Switch foreground and background colors button.
6. Open the file, Lab 1-1 Parasailing, from the Chapter 01 folder of the Data Files for Students or from a location specified by your instructor.
7. Click Save As on the File menu, and then type the new file name, Lab 1-1 Parasailing Edited. Navigate to your storage location, if necessary. Click the Format button and choose the PSD format. Click the Save button.
8. Use the Magnification box to zoom the photo to 25% magnification, if necessary.
9. If the rulers do not appear, press CTRL+R to view the rulers.
10. Select the Crop Tool. Click the photo to display the rule of thirds grid. SHIFT+drag the lower-right cropping handle until the sail is positioned at the upper-right intersection of the rule of thirds grid.
11. Press the ENTER key. If your crop does not seem correct, click the Undo command on the Edit menu and repeat Step 10.
12. Select another tool so the cropping handles no longer are displayed.
13. Save the photo again.
14. Press CTRL+A to select all of the photo. Click Select on the Application bar, point to Modify to display the Modify submenu, and then click Border to display the Border Selection dialog box. Type 100 in the Width box, and then click the OK button.

Continued >

In the Lab continued

15. Display the Modify submenu again, and click Smooth. Type 50 in the Smooth Radius box, and then click the OK button to create a second marquee with smoothed corners.

16. If white is not the foreground color, press the x key to switch the foreground and background colors. Click Edit on the Application bar and then click Stroke. Type 50 in the Width box. Click the Inside option button in the Location area. Click the OK button to stroke the selection. Press CTRL+D to deselect.

17. Click the Image Size command on the Image menu. When the Image Size dialog box is displayed, in the Document Size area, type 4 in the Width box. Click the OK button.

18. Press CTRL+S to save the file again.

19. Use the Print One Copy command on the File menu to print a copy of the photo.

20. Close your file and quit Photoshop.

21. Send the photo as an e-mail attachment to your instructor, or submit it in the format specified by your instructor.

In the Lab

Lab 2: Creating a Smoothed Border

Problem: The local hockey team is preparing a flyer to advertise its next game. The marketing department would like you to take one of the pictures from the last game and crop it to show just the face-off players and the official. Because the flyer will be printed on white paper, you should create a white border, so the photo blends into the background and adds to the ice rink effect. The edited photo is displayed in Figure 1–91.

Figure 1–91

Note: To complete this assignment, you will be required to use the Data Files for Students. Visit www.cengage.com/ct/studentdownload for detailed instructions or contact your instructor for information about accessing the required files.

Instructions: Perform the following tasks:

1. Start Photoshop. Perform the customization steps found on pages PS 6 through PS 10.

2. Open the file, Lab 1-2 Hockey, from the Chapter 01 folder of the Data Files for Students or from a location specified by your instructor.

3. Use the Save As command on the File menu to save the file on your storage device with the name, Lab 1-2 Hockey Edited, in the PSD format.

4. Click the Zoom Tool button on the Tools panel. Click the official in the photo to center the photo in the display. Zoom as necessary so you can make precise edits.

5. Crop the picture to display only the official and the two hockey players ready for the face-off. The vertical line of the hockey stick and the visual line of the official should be positioned using the rule of thirds.

6. Select a different tool so the cropping handles no longer are displayed.

7. Save the photo again with the same name.

8. Close the file and open it again using the Recent submenu.

9. Press CTRL+A to select all of the photo.

10. To create the border, do the following:

   a. On the Select menu, point to Modify, and then click Border.

   b. When the Border Selection dialog box is displayed, type 100 in the Width Box. Click the OK button.

   c. On the Select menu, open the Modify submenu, and then click Smooth.

   d. When the Smooth Selection dialog box is displayed, type 50 in the Sample Radius box to smooth the corners. Click the OK button.

   e. Press SHIFT+F5 to access the Fill command.

   f. When the Fill dialog box is displayed, click the Use box arrow and then click White in the list.

   g. Click the Mode box arrow and then click Normal in the list, if necessary.

   h. If necessary, type 100 in the Opacity box. Click the OK button.

   i. Press CTRL+D to deselect the border.

11. Save the photo again.

12. Use the Print One Copy command on the File menu to print a copy of the photo.

13. Close the document window.

14. Quit Photoshop.

15. Submit the assignment in the format specified by your instructor.

In the Lab

Lab 3: Preparing a Photo for the Web

Problem: As an independent consultant in Web site design, you have been hired by the Pineapple Growers Association to prepare a photo of an exotic pineapple growing in a field for use on the association's Web site. The edited photo is displayed in Figure 1–92.

Note: To complete this assignment, you will be required to use the Data Files for Students. Visit www.cengage.com/ct/student-download for detailed instructions or contact your instructor for information about accessing the required files.

Instructions: Perform the following tasks:
Start Photoshop. Perform the customization steps found on pages PS 6 through PS 10. Open the file, Lab 1-3 Pineapple, from the Chapter 01 folder of the Data Files for Students. Save the file in the PSD format with the name Lab 1-3 Pineapple Edited. Resize the photo to 500 pixels wide. Zoom to 50% magnification. Search Photoshop Help for help related to optimization. Read about optimizing for the Web. Print a copy of the help topic and then close the Adobe Help window.

     Use the Save for Web dialog box to view the 4-Up tab. Choose the best-looking preview. Select the connection speed of

Figure 1–92

Continued >

In the Lab *continued*

your Internet connection. Save the Web version of the photo using the name, Lab-1-3-Pineapple-for-Web. For extra credit, upload the Web version to a Web server. See Appendix C for information on publishing to a Web server. See your instructor for ways to submit this assignment.

Cases and Places

Apply your creative thinking and problem-solving skills to design and implement a solution.

Note: To complete these assignments, you may be required to use the Data Files for Students. Visit www.cengage.com/ct/studentdownload for detailed instructions or contact your instructor for information about accessing the required files.

1: Crop a Photo for a Class Directory

Academic

As a member of your high school reunion committee, it is your task to assemble the class photo directory. You are to edit a high school student photo and prepare it for print in the reunion directory. The photo needs to fit in a space 1.75 inches high and 1.33 inches wide. Each photo needs to have approximately .25 inches above the head. After starting Photoshop and resetting the workspace, select the photo, Case 1-1 Student, from the Chapter 01 folder of the Data Files for Students. Save the photo on your USB flash drive storage device as Case 1-1 Student Edited, using the PSD format. Resize the photo to match the requirements. Use the rulers to help you crop the photo for .25 inches above the top of the student's head. Save the photo again and print a copy for your instructor.

2: Create a Photo for a Social Networking Site

Personal

You would like to place a photo of your recent tubing adventure on your social networking page. The photo you have is of two people. You need to crop out the other person who is tubing. After starting Photoshop and resetting the workspace, select the photo, Case 1-2 Tubing, from the Chapter 01 folder of the Data Files for Students. Save the photo on your USB flash drive storage device as Case 1-2 Tubing Edited, using the PSD format. Crop the photo to remove one of the tubes, keeping in mind the rule of thirds, the golden rectangle, and the direction of the action. Save the photo for the Web and upload it to Facebook or another Web server as directed by your instructor.

3: Creating a Photo for a Brochure

Professional

You are an intern with an event planning business. The company is planning to send out a trifold brochure about local churches and chapels used for weddings. The photo named Case 1-3 Chapel is located in the Chapter 01 folder of the Data Files for Students. Save the photo on your USB flash drive storage device as Case 1-3 Chapel Edited, using the PSD format. Resize the photo to be 3.5 inches wide. Create a black border of 10 pixels. Save the file again and print a copy for your instructor.

2 | Using Selection Tools and Shortcut Keys

Adobe product screenshot(s) reprinted with permission from Adobe Systems Incorporated

Objectives

You will have mastered the material in this chapter when you can:

- Explain the terms layout, perspective, and storyboard

- Describe selection tools

- Select objects using the marquee tools

- Move and duplicate selections

- Use the History panel

- Use the Grow command and Refine Edges to adjust selections

- Employ the lasso tools

- Subtract areas from selections

- Use grids, guides, and snapping

- Select objects using the Quick Selection and Magic Wand Tools

- Print to a PDF file

- Use, create, and test new keyboard shortcuts

2 | Using Selection Tools and Shortcut Keys

Introduction

In Chapter 1, you learned about the Photoshop interface, as well as navigation and zooming techniques. You cropped and resized a photo, added a border and text, and saved the photo for both Web and print media. You learned about Online Help, along with opening, saving, and printing photos. This chapter continues to emphasize those topics and presents some new ones.

Recall that when you make a selection, you are specifying or isolating an area of your photo for editing. By selecting specific areas, you can edit and apply special effects to portions of your image, while leaving the unselected areas untouched. The new topics covered in this chapter include the marquee tools used to select rectangular or elliptical areas, the lasso tools used to select free-form segments or shapes, and the Quick Selection and Magic Wand Tools used to select consistently colored areas. You will learn how to use the Move Tool to duplicate and scale. Finally, you will print to a PDF file and create a new keyboard shortcut.

Project — Advertisement Graphic

An advertisement, or ad, is a form of communication that promotes a product or service to a potential customer. An advertisement tries to persuade consumers to purchase a product or service. An advertisement typically has a single message directed toward a target audience.

A graphic designed for advertising, sometimes called an **advertising piece**, needs to catch the customer's eye and entice him or her to purchase the product. A clear graphic with strong contrast, item repetition, and visual lines tells the story and enhances text that might be added later. Chapter 2 illustrates the creation of a retail store advertising piece. You will begin with the image in Figure 2–1a that shows individual wicker baskets. You then will manipulate the image by selecting, editing, and moving the objects to produce a more attractive layout, creating Figure 2–1b for use in the advertisement.

Overview

As you read this chapter, you will learn how to create the advertisement graphic shown in Figure 2–1b by performing these general tasks:

- Select portions of the photo.
- Copy, move, and scale selections.
- Eliminate white space in and among objects in selected areas.
- Retrace editing steps using the History panel.
- Refine edges of selections.
- Print to a PDF file.
- Create a new shortcut key.

(a) Original image

(b) Edited image

Figure 2–1

**Plan
Ahead**

General Project Guidelines

When editing a photo, the actions you perform and decisions you make will affect the appearance and characteristics of the finished product. As you edit a photo, such as the one shown in Figure 2–1a, you should follow these general guidelines:

1. **Choose the correct tool.** When you need to copy and paste portions of your photo, consider carefully which Photoshop selection tool to use. You want the procedure to be efficient and produce a clear image. Keep in mind the shape and background of the photo you want to copy, as well as your expertise with various tools.

2. **Plan your duplications.** Use a storyboard or make a list of the items you plan to duplicate, and then decide whether it will be an exact duplication or a manipulated one, called a **transformed copy**. The decision depends on the visual effect you want to achieve and the customer requirements.

3. **Use grids and guides.** When you are working with exact measurements, close cropping and moving, or just want to align things easily, use grids and guides to display nonprinting lines across the document window. Use the Photoshop snapping function to align selections. Visual estimations of size and location are easier to perceive when using these guides.

4. **Create files in portable formats.** You might have to distribute your artwork in a variety of formats, depending on its use. Portability is an important consideration. It usually is safe to begin work in the Photoshop PSD format and then use the Save as command or Print command to convert your work to the PDF format. PDF files are platform and software independent.

When necessary, more specific details concerning the above guidelines are presented at appropriate points in the chapter. The chapter also will identify the actions performed and decisions made regarding these guidelines during the creation of the edited photo shown in Figure 2–1b.

Creating an Advertising Piece

Figure 2–2 illustrates the design decisions made to create the advertising piece. Using an attractive layout containing multiple objects is a good marketing strategy; such a piece visually and subconsciously can encourage the viewer to purchase more than one item. **Layout** refers to placing visual elements into a pleasing and understandable arrangement; in the basket advertisement, the layout is suggestive of how the product or products might look in a buyer's home. Advertising artists and product designers try to determine how the target consumer will use the product and group objects accordingly in the layout.

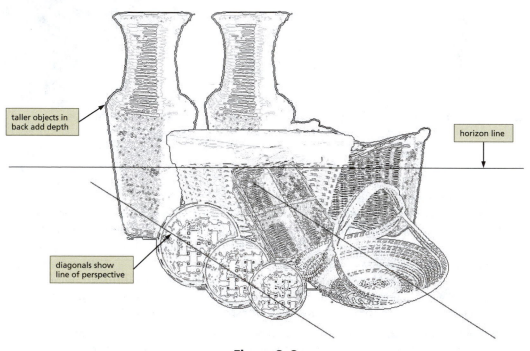

taller objects in
back add depth

horizon line

diagonals show
line of perspective

Figure 2–2

From a design point of view, creating visual diagonal lines creates perspective. **Perspective** is the technique photographers, designers, and artists use to create the illusion of three dimensions on a flat or two-dimensional surface. Perspective is a means of fooling the eye by making it appear as if there is depth or receding space in an image. Adjusting the sizes and juxtaposing the objects creates asymmetrical balance and visual tension between the featured products. For example, in Figure 2–2, the height of the tall baskets leads the viewer's eye to the background, as does the diagonal alignment of smaller pieces in front of the larger ones.

The **horizon line** in perspective drawing is a virtual horizontal line across the picture. The placement of the horizon line determines from where the viewer seems to be looking, such as down from a high place or up from close to the ground. In the basket advertisement, the horizon line runs across the middle of the drawing.

Using white space, or nonimage area, is effective in directing the viewer to notice what is important. The products grouped this way are, in a sense, framed by the white space.

This product layout also helps other members of the design team when it is time to make decisions about type placement. The group of products can be shifted up or down, as one image, to accommodate the layout and text, including the font sizes, placement, title, description, and price information. Recall that the rule of thirds offers a useful means to make effective layouts for images and text.

Designing a preliminary layout sketch, similar to Figure 2–2, to help you make choices about placement, size, perspective, and spacing, is referred to as creating a **storyboard** or **rough**.

To Start Photoshop

If you are stepping through this project on a computer and you want your screen to match the figures in this book, then you should change your computer's resolution to 1024×768 and reset the panels, tools, and colors. For more information about how to change the resolution on your computer and other advanced Photoshop settings, read Appendix F, the Changing Screen Resolution appendix.

The following steps, which assume Windows 7 is running, start Photoshop based on a typical installation. You may need to ask your instructor how to start Photoshop for your system.

1 Click the Start button on the Windows 7 taskbar to display the Start menu and then type `Photoshop CS6` in the 'Search programs and files' box.

2 Click Adobe Photoshop CS6 in the list to start Photoshop.

3 If the Photoshop window is not maximized, click the Maximize button next to the Close button on the Application bar to maximize the window.

To Reset the Workspace

As discussed in Chapter 1, it is helpful to reset the workspace so that the tools and panels appear in their default positions. The following steps select the Essentials workspace.

1 Click Window on the Application bar to display the Window menu, and then point to Workspace to display the Workspace submenu.

2 Click Essentials (Default) on the Workspace submenu to select the default workspace panels.

3 Click Window on the Application bar, and then point to Workspace again to display the list.

4 Click Reset Essentials to restore the workspace to its default settings and reposition any panels that may have been moved.

To Reset the Tools and the Options Bar

Recall that the Tools panel and the options bar retain their settings from previous Photoshop sessions. The following steps select the Rectangular Marquee Tool and reset all tool settings in the options bar.

1 If the tools in the Tools panel appear in two columns, click the double arrow at the top of the Tools panel.

2 If necessary, click the Rectangular Marquee Tool button on the Tools panel to select it.

3 Right-click the Rectangular Marquee Tool icon on the options bar to display the context menu, and then click Reset All Tools. When Photoshop displays a confirmation dialog box, click the OK button to restore the tools to their default settings.

To Set the Interface and Default Colors

Recall that Photoshop retains the interface color scheme, as well as the foreground and background colors, from session to session. The following steps set the interface to Medium Gray and the foreground and background colors to black over white.

1 Click Edit on the Application bar to display the Edit menu. Point to Preferences and then click Interface on the Preferences submenu to display the Preferences dialog box.

2 If necessary, click the third button, Medium Gray, to change the interface color scheme.

3 Click the OK button to close the Preferences dialog box.

4 Press the D key to reset the default foreground and background colors. If black is not over white on the Tools panel, press the X key.

To Open a File

To open a file in Photoshop, it must be stored as a digital file on your computer system or on an external storage device. To complete this assignment, you will be required to use the Data Files for Students. Visit www.cengage.com/ct/studentdownload for detailed instructions or contact your instructor for information about accessing the required files. The following steps open the Baskets file from the Data Files for Students.

1 With the Photoshop window open, click File on the Application bar, and then click Open to display the Open dialog box.

2 In the Open dialog box, click the Look in box arrow to display the list of available locations, and then click the location of the Photoshop Data Files for Students.

3 Double-click the Chapter 02 folder to display its contents. Double-click the file, Baskets, to open it.

4 When Photoshop displays the image in the document window, if the magnification shown on the status bar is not 60%, double-click the magnification box on the document window status bar, type 6 0, and then press the ENTER key to change the magnification (Figure 2–3).

BTW
Document Window Status Bar
The status bar of the document window in Figure 2–3 shows the current document size. To display the document dimensions, click the status bar menu button, and then click Document Dimensions.

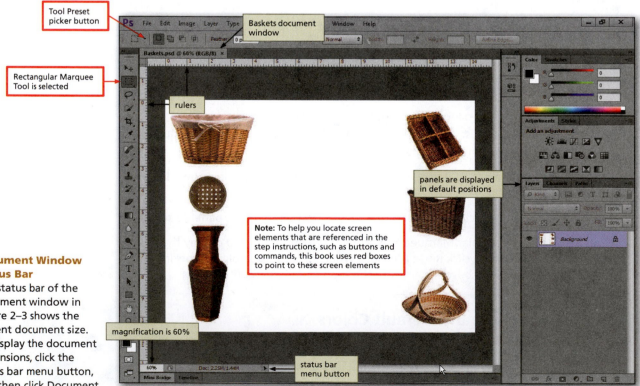

Figure 2–3

To View Rulers

The following steps display the rulers in the document window to facilitate making precise measurements.

1 If the rulers are not shown on the top and left sides of the document window, press CTRL+R to display the rulers in the workspace.

2 If necessary, right-click the horizontal ruler and then click Inches on the context menu to display the rulers in inches.

To Save a Photo

Even though you have yet to edit the photo, it is a good practice to save the file on your personal storage device early in the process. The following steps save the photo with the name Baskets Edited in a new folder named Chapter 02.

1 With your USB flash drive connected to one of the computer's USB ports, click File on the Application bar to display the File menu and then click Save As to display the Save As dialog box.

2 In the File name text box, type `Baskets Edited` to rename the file. Do not press the ENTER key after typing the file name.

3 Click the Save in box arrow, and then click Removable Disk (F:), or the location associated with your USB flash drive, in the list, if necessary.

4 On the Save As dialog box toolbar, click the Create New Folder button to create a new folder on the selected storage device.

5 When the new folder appears, type `Chapter 02` to change the name of the folder, and then press the ENTER key. Double-click the new folder to open it.

6 Click the Save button in the Save As dialog box to save the file in the new folder.

The Marquee Tools

The **marquee tools** allow you to draw a marquee that selects a portion of the document window. Marquee tools are useful when the part of an image or photo that you wish to select fits into a rectangular or an elliptical shape. Photoshop has four marquee tools that appear in a context menu when you click the tool and hold down the mouse button, or when you right-click the tool. You can select any of the marquee tools from this context menu. Recall that Photoshop offers the added flexibility of selecting a tool with a single letter shortcut key. Pressing the M key activates the current marquee tool.

The Rectangular Marquee Tool is the default marquee tool that selects a rectangular or square portion of the image or photo. The Elliptical Marquee Tool allows you to select an ellipsis, oval, or circular area.

Dragging with the Rectangular or Elliptical Marquee Tools creates a marquee drawn from a corner. If you press the SHIFT key while dragging a marquee, Photoshop constrains the proportions of the shape, creating a perfect square or circle. If you press the ALT key while drawing a selection, Photoshop creates the marquee from the center. Pressing SHIFT+ALT starts from the center and constrains the proportions.

BTW

Marquee Tool Selection
If you are using a different tool and want to activate the marquee tools, you can click the Rectangular Marquee Tool button on the Tools panel or press the M key on the keyboard to select the tool. Once the tool is selected, pressing SHIFT+M toggles between the Rectangular and Elliptical Marquee tools. You must choose the Single Row and Single Column Marquee tools from the context menu – there are no keyboard shortcuts.

The Single Row Marquee Tool allows you to select a single row of pixels. The Single Column Marquee Tool allows you to select a single column of pixels. A single click in the document window then creates the selection. Because a single row or column of pixels is so small, it is easier to use these two marquee tools at higher magnifications.

<table>
<tr><td>**Plan Ahead**</td><td>

Choose the correct tool.
When you need to copy, paste, and move portions of your photo, consider carefully which selection tool to use. You want the procedure to be efficient and produce a clear image. Keep in mind the following as you choose a selection tool:

- The shape of the selection
- The background around the selection
- The contrast between the selection and its surroundings
- The proximity of the selection to other objects
- Your expertise in using the tool
- The availability of other pointing devices, such as a graphics tablet
- The destination of the paste

</td></tr>
</table>

Table 2–1 describes the four marquee tools.

BTW

Single Row and Single Column Marquee Tools
To create interesting backgrounds, wallpapers, and color ribbons using the Single Row or Single Column Marquee tools, choose a colorful photo and create a single row or single column marquee. Press CTRL+T to display the bounding box. Then drag the sizing handles until the selection fills the document window.

Table 2–1 The Marquee Tools

Tool	Purpose	Shortcut	Button
Rectangular Marquee	Selects a rectangular or square portion of the document window	M SHIFT+M toggles to Elliptical Marquee	
Elliptical Marquee	Selects an elliptical, oval, or circular portion of the document window	M SHIFT+M toggles to Rectangular Marquee	
Single Row Marquee	Selects a single row of pixels in the document window	(none)	
Single Column Marquee	Selects a single column of pixels in the document window	(none)	

The options bar associated with each of the marquee tools contains many buttons and settings to draw effective marquees (Figure 2–4). The options bar displays an icon for the chosen marquee on the left, followed by the Tool Preset picker. The Tool Preset picker allows you to save and reuse toolbar settings.

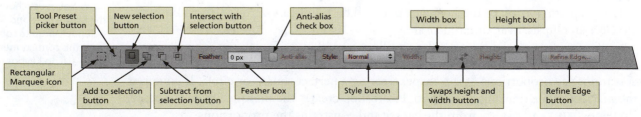

Figure 2–4

The next four buttons to the right adjust the selection. When selected, the New selection button allows you to start a new marquee.

The 'Add to selection' button draws a rectangle or ellipsis and adds it to any current selection. The 'Add to selection' button is useful for selecting the extra corners of an L-shaped object or for shapes that do not fit within a single rectangle or ellipsis. To activate the 'Add to selection' button, you can click it on the options bar, or press and hold the SHIFT key while dragging a second selection. When adding to a selection, the mouse pointer changes to a crosshair with a plus sign.

The 'Subtract from selection' button allows you to deselect or remove a portion of an existing selection. The new rectangle or ellipsis is removed from the original selection. It is useful for removing block portions of the background around oddly shaped images, or for deselecting ornamentation in an object. To activate the 'Subtract from selection' button, you can click it on the options bar, or press and hold the ALT key while dragging. When subtracting from a selection, the mouse pointer changes to a crosshair with a minus sign.

The 'Intersect with selection' button allows you to draw a second rectangle or ellipsis across a portion of the previously selected area, resulting in a selection border only around the area in which the two selections overlap. To activate the 'Intersect with selection' button, you click it on the options bar, or hold down the SHIFT and ALT keys while dragging. When creating an intersection, the mouse pointer changes to a crosshair with an X.

To the right of the selection buttons, the options bar displays a Feather box. **Feathering** softens the edges of the selection. In traditional photography, feathering is called **vignetting,** which creates a soft-edged border around an image that blends into the background. Feathering sometimes is used in wedding photos or when a haloed effect is desired. The width of the feather is measured in pixels. When using the Elliptical Marquee Tool, you can further specify blending by selecting the Anti-alias check box. **Anti-aliasing** softens the block-like, staircase look of rounded corners. Figure 2–5 shows a rectangle with no feathering, one with 10 pixels of feathering, an ellipsis with no anti-aliasing, and one created with a check mark in the Anti-alias check box.

BTW

The Tool Preset Picker
Most tools display a Tool Preset picker on the options bar. When you click the button, Photoshop displays a list of settings used during the current Photoshop session or previously saved options bar settings. The list makes it easier to save and reuse tool settings. You can load, edit, and create libraries of tool presets in conjunction with the Tool Presets panel. To choose a tool preset, click the Tool Preset picker in the options bar, and then select a preset from the list.

BTW

Anti-Aliasing
Anti-aliasing is available for the Elliptical Marquee Tool, the Lasso Tool, the Polygonal Lasso Tool, the Magnetic Lasso Tool, and the Magic Wand Tool. You must specify this option before applying these tools. Once a selection is created, you cannot add anti-aliasing.

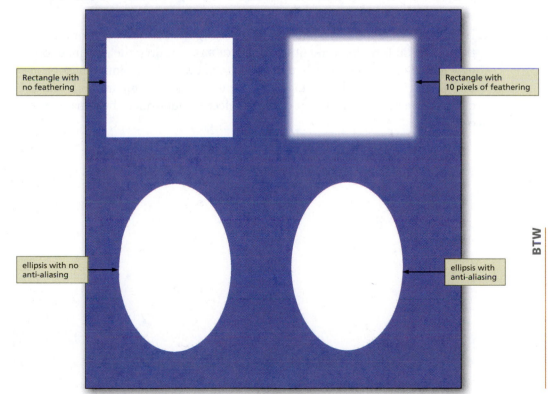

Rectangle with no feathering

Rectangle with 10 pixels of feathering

ellipsis with no anti-aliasing

ellipsis with anti-aliasing

Figure 2–5

Scrubby Sliders
You can drag some options bar labels in Photoshop. When you point to the label, a **scrubby slider** that looks like a pointing finger appears. Dragging the scrubby slider changes the value in the accompanying text box on the options bar. For example, the Feather box label on the Rectangular Marquee Tool options bar is a scrubby slider.

Layers
A layer is a portion of the image superimposed, or separated, from other parts of the document. Think of layers as sheets of clear film stacked one on top of the other. In Chapter 3, you will learn how to change the composition of an image by changing the order and attributes of layers.

Deleting Selections
You can delete a selection by pressing the DELETE key on the keyboard. Photoshop will display a Fill dialog box. Click the OK button. If you delete by accident, press CTRL+Z to bring the selection back.

When using the Rectangular Marquee Tool or the Elliptical Marquee Tool, you can click the Style button (Figure 2–4 on page PS 76) to choose how the size of the marquee selection is determined. A Normal style sets the selection marquee proportions by dragging. A Fixed Ratio style sets a height-to-width ratio using decimal values. For example, to draw a marquee twice as wide as it is high, enter 2 for the width and 1 for the height, and then drag in the photo. A Fixed Size style allows you to specify exact pixel values for the marquee's height and width. Photoshop enables the Width box and Height box when you choose a style other than Normal. A button between the two boxes swaps the values, if desired.

Sometimes you need to make subtle changes to a selection marquee. For example, if the border or edge of a selection seems to be jagged or hazy, or if the colors at the edge of a selection bleed slightly across the marquee, you can use the Refine Edge button. When clicked, it opens a dialog box in which you can increase or decrease the radius of the marquee, change the contrast, and smooth the selection border.

Once you have drawn a marquee, you can choose from other options for further manipulation of the selected area. Right-clicking a selection displays a context menu that provides access to many other useful commands such as deselecting, reselecting, or selecting the **inverse**, which means selecting everything in the image outside of the current selection. The context menu also enables you to create layers, apply color fills and strokes, and make other changes that you will learn about in future chapters.

If you make a mistake or change your mind when drawing a marquee, you can do one of three things:

1. If you want to start over, and the New selection button is selected on the options bar, you can click somewhere else in the document window to deselect the marquee; then simply draw a new marquee. Deselecting also is available as a command on the Select menu and on the context menu. The shortcut for deselecting is CTRL+D.

2. If you have already drawn the marquee but want to move or reposition it, and the New selection button is selected on the options bar, you can drag the selection to the new location.

3. If you want to reposition while you are creating the marquee, do not release the mouse button. Press and hold the SPACEBAR key, drag the marquee to the new location, and then release the SPACEBAR key. At that point, you can continue dragging to finish drawing the marquee. Repositioning in this manner can be done while using any of the four selection adjustment buttons on the options bar.

To Use the Rectangular Marquee Tool

The following step selects the tall basket in the lower-left corner of the Baskets Edited image using the Rectangular Marquee Tool. You will use the Elliptical Marquee Tool later in this chapter.

 1

- With the Rectangular Marquee Tool selected on the Tools panel, drag to draw a rectangle around the tall basket in the lower-left corner to create a marquee selection. Drag close to the basket itself, as shown in Figure 2–6.

Experiment

- Practice drawing rectangular and elliptical marquees. Press SHIFT+M to switch between the two. SHIFT+DRAG to look at the effects. Press and hold the SPACEBAR key while you drag to reposition the current marquee. When you are finished, redraw a rectangle around the basket.

Q&A | What was the black box that appeared as I created the marquee?

That was the Transformation Values indicator to help show you exactly where you are in the image.

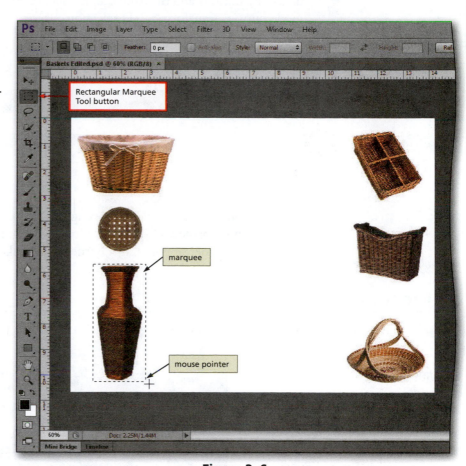

Figure 2–6

Other Ways

1. Press M key or SHIFT+M until Rectangular Marquee Tool is active, drag selection

The Move Tool

The Move Tool on the Photoshop Tools panel is used to move or make other changes to selections. Activating the Move Tool by clicking the Move Tool button, or by pressing the v key on the keyboard, enables you to move the selection border and its contents by dragging in the document window. When you first use the Move Tool, the mouse pointer displays a black arrowhead with scissors. To move the selection in a straight line, press and hold the SHIFT key while dragging. If you press and hold the ALT key while dragging, you duplicate or move only a copy of the selected area, effectively copying and pasting the selection. While duplicating, the mouse pointer changes to a black arrowhead with a white arrowhead behind it.

When you move selections, you need to be careful about overlapping images. As you will learn in Chapter 3, Photoshop might layer or overlap portions of images when you move them. While that sometimes is preferred when creating collages or composite images, it is undesirable if an important object is obscured. Close tracing while creating selections and careful placement of moved selections will prevent unwanted layering.

The Move Tool options bar displays tools to help define the scope of the move (Figure 2–7). Later, as you learn about layers, you will use the Auto-Select check box to select layer groupings or single layers. The Show Transform Controls check box causes Photoshop to display transformation controls on the selection. The align and distribute buttons and the Auto-Align Layers button also are used with layers. The 3D mode buttons transform a 3-D selection.

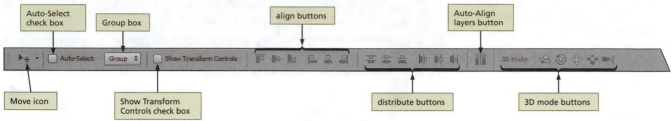

Figure 2–7

As you use the Move Tool throughout this chapter, be careful to position your mouse pointer inside the selection before moving. Do not try to move a selection by dragging its border. If you drag a border by mistake, press the ESC key.

To Use the Move Tool

The following steps use the Move Tool to move the basket up and to the right.

1

• With the basket still selected, click the Move Tool button on the Tools panel to activate the Move Tool.

• If necessary, on the options bar, click the Auto-Select check box so it does not display a check mark. If necessary, click the Show Transform Controls check box so it does not display a check mark (Figure 2–8).

Q&A

Are there any other tools nested with the Move Tool?

No, the Move Tool does not have a context menu. Tools with a context menu display a small black rectangle in the lower-right corner.

Figure 2–8

2

- Position your mouse pointer over the basket, within the marquee. Drag the selection to a position in the upper-center portion of the photo (Figure 2–9). Do not press any other keys.

Q&A

My document window shows a black square. What did I do wrong?

It is possible that the default colors on your system were changed by another user. Press CTRL+Z to undo the move. Press the D key to select the default foreground and background colors. If black is not on top at the bottom of the Tools panel, press the X key to exchange the black and white colors.

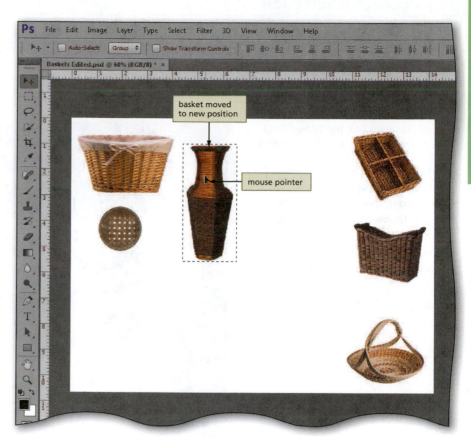

Figure 2–9

Other Ways

1. Press V, drag selection

Plan your duplications.

Creating a storyboard, either by hand or by using software, allows you to plan your image and make decisions about copies and placement. Some graphic artists annotate each copy in the storyboard with information about size, shape, location, and the tool they plan to use (Figure 2–2 on page PS 72). For example, when you paste or drag a new copy of an image into a photo, you have two choices. You can keep the copy as an exact duplicate, or you can transform the copy. The choice depends on the visual effect you want to achieve and the customer requirements. Notating those requirements on your storyboard ahead of time will facilitate creating your image.

Use an exact copy of a logo or border to create a tiled background. Commercial applications may create duplications to represent growth; or several duplications beside each other can emphasize a brand. Sometimes artists will duplicate an item several times when creating a quick sketch or a rough draft. Across photos, exact duplicates maintain consistency and product identification.

Transforming a copy or section provides additional flexibility and diversity. You might want to create the illusion of multiple, different items to promote sales. Scaling, skewing, warping, and distorting provide interest and differentiation, and sometimes can correct lens errors. Flipping, rotating, or changing the perspective of the copy adds visual excitement to reproductions and creates the illusion of three dimensions.

Plan Ahead

To Duplicate a Selection

Recall that pressing and holding the ALT key while dragging with the Move Tool creates a copy, or duplicates, the selection. SHIFT+dragging moves the selection in a straight line. Using both the SHIFT and ALT keys while dragging duplicates and moves the copy in a straight line. The following step accesses the Move Tool and creates a copy of the selected basket.

1

• If necessary, click the Move Tool button to select the Move Tool.

• Press and hold the SHIFT and ALT keys while dragging to duplicate and move the selection to the right. Move the selection just far enough that the white portion of the selection does not overlap the original tall basket (Figure 2–10).

Figure 2–10

Other Ways

1. Press CTRL+C, press CTRL+V, press V, drag selection

2. Press V, ALT+drag selection

To Deselect

The following step deselects the baskets.

1 On the Select menu, click Deselect.

The Quick Selection Tool

The Quick Selection Tool draws a selection quickly using the mouse. As you drag, Photoshop creates a selection automatically, expanding outward to find and follow the defined edges in the image. The Quick Selection Tool is nested with the Magic Wand Tool on the Tools panel. You can access either tool from the context menu or by pressing the w key; if the Magic Wand Tool has been used previously, press SHIFT+W to access the Quick Selection Tool.

Dragging a quick selection is almost like painting a stroke with a brush. The Quick Selection Tool does not create a rectangular or oval selection; rather, it looks for a contrast in color and aligns the selection border to that contrast. It is most useful for isolated objects or parts of an image that contain a contrasting background. When using the Quick Selection Tool, the mouse pointer changes to a brush tip that displays a circle with a centered cross inside. You can decrease or increase the size of the brush tip by using the LEFT BRACKET ([) or RIGHT BRACKET (]) keys respectively, or by using the options bar.

The Quick Selection Tool options bar (Figure 2–11) displays the size of the brush and contains some of the same buttons as other selection tools. It also contains an Auto-Enhance check box that reduces roughness in the selection boundary when the box is checked.

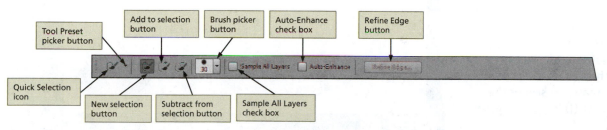

Figure 2–11

To Use the Quick Selection Tool

The following steps use the Quick Selection Tool to select the basket in the middle on the right.

1

- Click the Quick Selection Tool button on the Tools panel to select it. If the tool icon does not display a brush, right-click the button and then click Quick Selection Tool on the context menu.

- On the options bar, click the New selection button, if necessary.

- Click the Auto-Enhance check box so it displays a check mark (Figure 2–12).

Q&A What does the Auto-Enhance feature do?

Auto-Enhance reduces the block-like edges in the selection border and adjusts the selection further toward the edges of the image.

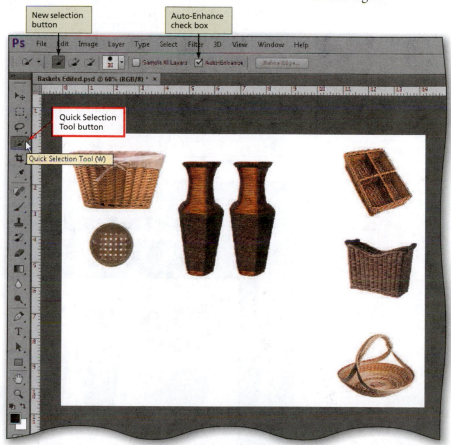

Figure 2–12

2

- Move the mouse pointer to the lower-right corner of the middle basket on the right, and then slowly drag up and left to select only the basket (Figure 2–13).

Q&A

What should I do if I make a mistake with the Quick Selection Tool?

If you make a mistake and want to start over, you can deselect by pressing CTRL+D, and then begin again.

Experiment

- Practice resizing the mouse pointer by using the LEFT BRACKET ([) key to decrease the size or the RIGHT BRACKET (]) key to increase the size.

Figure 2–13

Other Ways

1. Press W or SHIFT+W until Quick Selection Tool is active, drag selection

To Move a Selection

The following steps move the basket using the Move Tool. If you make a mistake while moving, press CTRL+Z and then move the basket again.

1 On the Tools panel, click the Move Tool button to select the tool.

2 Drag the selection left and slightly up, as shown in Figure 2–14. Do not press any other keys.

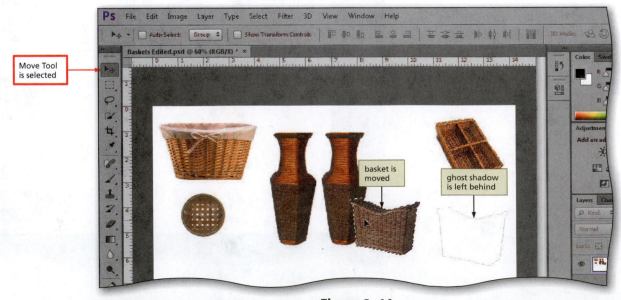

Figure 2–14

The History Panel

The History panel appears when you click the History button on the vertical dock of minimized panels. The History panel records each step, called a **state**, as you edit a photo (Figure 2–15). Photoshop displays the initial state of the document at the top of the panel. Each time you apply a change to an image, the new state of that image is added to the bottom of the panel. Each state lists the name of the tool or command used to change the image.

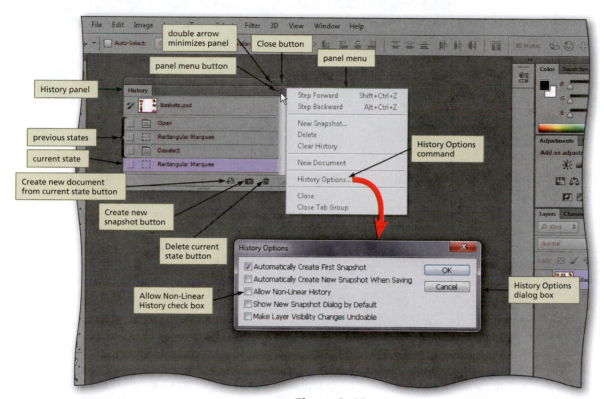

Figure 2–15

Like the Navigator panel that you learned about in Chapter 1, the History panel also has a panel menu where you can clear all states, change the history settings, or dock the panel. Buttons on the History panel status bar allow you to create a new document from a state, save the selected state, or delete it. The panel can be minimized by clicking the History button on the vertical dock or by clicking the double arrow at the top of the panel. To redisplay a minimized History panel, click the History button on the vertical dock, or choose it from the Window menu.

BTW

Using the History Panel Menu
The History panel menu has commands you can use to step forward and step backward through the listed states on the History panel.

To Display the History Panel

The following step displays the History panel.

1
• Click the History button on the vertical dock of minimized panels (Figure 2–16).

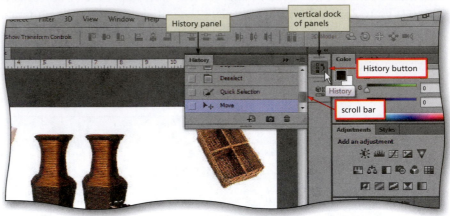

Figure 2–16

BTW

The History Panel
The History panel will list a Duplicate state when you use the ALT key to copy a selection. The word Paste will appear next to the state when you use the Copy and Paste commands from the keyboard or from the menu. The Copy command alone does not affect how the image looks; it merely sends a copy to the system Clipboard. Therefore, it does not appear as a state.

Using the History Panel

You can use the History panel in several different ways. When you select one of the states, Photoshop displays the image the way it looked at that point, when that change first was applied. Some users access the History panel to undo mistakes. Others use it to try out or experiment with different edits. By clicking a state, you can view the state temporarily or start working again from that point. You can step forward and backward through the states in the History panel by clicking them, or by pressing CTRL+SHIFT+Z or CTRL+ALT+Z, respectively.

Selecting a state and then changing the image in any way eliminates all the states in the History panel that came after it; however, if you select a state and change the image by accident, you can use the Undo command or CTRL+Z to restore the eliminated states. If you select the Allow Non-Linear History check box in the History Options dialog box (Figure 2–15 on the previous page) deleting a state deletes only that state.

You can use the History panel to jump to any recent state of the image created during the current working session by clicking the state. Alternatively, you also can give a state a new name, called a **snapshot**. Naming a snapshot identifies a state and distinguishes it from other states. Snapshots are stored at the top of the History panel and make it easy to compare effects. For example, you can take a snapshot before and after a series of transformations. Then, by clicking between the two snapshots in the History panel, you can see the total effect, or choose the before snapshot and start over. To create a snapshot, right-click the state and then click New Snapshot on the context menu, or click the Create new snapshot button on the History panel status bar. Snapshots do not save with the image; closing an image deletes its snapshots.

Not all steps appear in the History panel. For instance, changes to panels, color settings, actions, and preferences are not displayed in the History panel, because they are not changes to a particular image.

By default, the History panel lists the previous 20 states. You can change the number of remembered states by changing a preference setting (see the Changing Screen Resolution appendix). Photoshop deletes older states automatically to free more memory. Once you close and reopen the document, all states and snapshots from the last working session are cleared from the panel.

To Undo Changes Using the History Panel

Notice in Figure 2–14 on page PS 84 that a shadow appears in the previous location of the basket. This shadow, called a ghost shadow, sometimes occurs when using any of the selection tools, especially when fringe pixels are faded — they were not included in the selection marquee. Therefore, you need to return to the previous state and try again. The following step uses the History Panel to undo the Move command.

1

- If necessary, scroll down in the History panel to display the last few states.

- Click the Quick Selection state in the History panel to go back one step and undo the move (Figure 2–17). Do not press any other keys.

Q&A Could I have pressed CTRL+Z to undo the move?

Yes, if you only need to undo one step, pressing CTRL+Z will work. If you need to go back more than one step, you can press CTRL+ALT+Z or use the History panel.

Q&A What is the box to the left of each state?

When selected, that box sets the source for painting a clone-like image using the Art History Brush Tool.

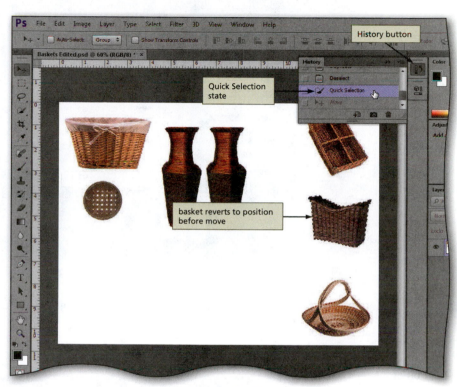

Figure 2–17

Other Ways

1. Press CTRL+ALT+Z

To Minimize the History Panel

Recall in Chapter 1 that you minimized the Navigator panel by clicking the double arrow at the top of the panel. You also can minimize a panel by clicking the panel button on the vertical dock, as demonstrated in the following step.

1 Click the History button to minimize the panel.

Refining Edges

Each of the selection tools has a Refine Edge button located on its options bar, as shown in Figure 2–11 on page PS 83. Clicking the Refine Edge button displays a dialog box where you can make choices about improving selections with jagged edges, soft transitions, hazy borders, or fine details, and improve the quality of a selection's edges. Additionally, it allows you to view the selection on different backgrounds to facilitate editing (Figure 2–18 on the next page).

BTW

Moving Among History Panel States
Photoshop uses many function keys to move easily among the states in the History panel. To step forward, press SHIFT+CTRL+Z. To step backward, press CTRL+ALT+Z. You also can use the History panel menu to step forward and backward.

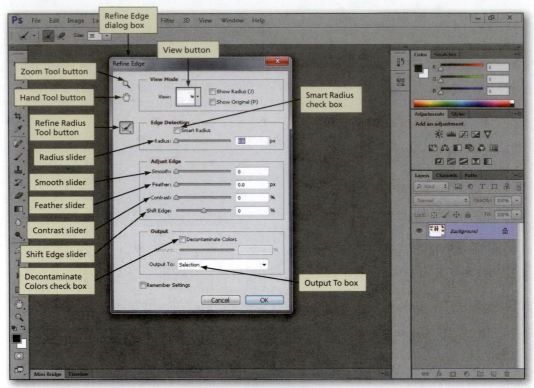

Figure 2–18

Table 2–2 displays some of the controls in the Refine Edge dialog box and their functions.

Table 2–2 Controls and Buttons in the Refine Edge Dialog Box	
Control or Button	**Function**
View Mode	Allows you to choose the background of the selection and show the radius, original, or both views
Smart Radius check box	Adjusts the radius edges automatically
Radius slider	Adjusts the size of the selection boundary by pixels
Smooth slider	Reduces irregular areas in the selection boundary to create a smoother outline with values from 0 to 100 pixels
Feather slider	Softens the edges of the selection for blending into backgrounds using values from 0 to 250 pixels
Contrast slider	Sharpens the selection edges to remove any hazy or extraneous pixels, sometimes called fuzzy artifacts or noise; increasing the contrast percentage can remove excessive noise near selection edges caused by a high radius setting
Shift Edge	Moves soft-edged borders helping remove or include background colors from selection edges
Decontaminate Colors check box	Replaces fringe color
Output To	Sets the output to a mask, layer, or new document
Remember Settings check box	Saves all settings in the dialog box for use on another selection
Zoom Tool button	Zooms selection in or out
Hand Tool button	Moves portion of the document window that is displayed
Refine Radius Tool button	Precisely adjusts the border area in which edge refinement occurs; pressing SHIFT+E toggles to the Erase Refinements Tool button
Erase Refinements Tool button	Precisely adjusts the border area in which edge refinement occurs; pressing SHIFT+E toggles to the Refine Radius Tool button

The various settings in the Refine Edge dialog box take practice to use intuitively. The more experience you have adjusting the settings, the more comfortable you will feel with the controls. To improve selections for images on a contrasting background, you should first increase the radius and then increase the contrast to sharpen the edges. For grayscale images or selections where the colors of the object and the background are similar, try smoothing first, then feathering. For all selections, you might need to adjust the Contract/Expand slider.

To Refine Edges

The following steps refine the edge of the selection.

- On the Tools panel, click the Quick Selection Tool button to select it (Figure 2–19).

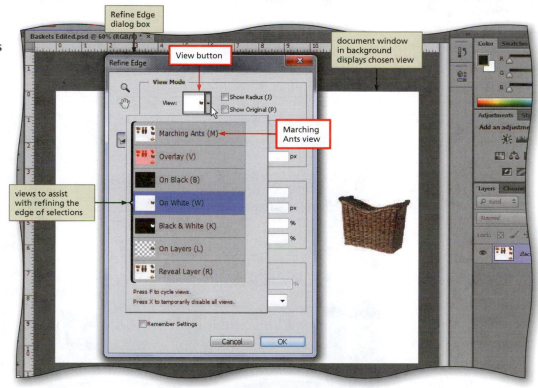

Figure 2–19

- On the Quick Selection Tool options bar, click the Refine Edge button to display the Refine Edge dialog box.

- Click the View button to display the refine edge views (Figure 2–20).

Experiment

- One at a time, click each of the views and notice how the background of the document window changes. Drag the title bar of the dialog box, if necessary to move the dialog box out of the way.

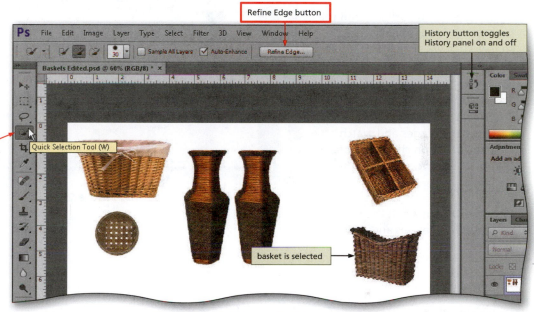

Figure 2–20

3

- Double-click Marching Ants to view the selection as a marquee.

- Drag the Radius slider until the Radius box displays approximately 20 pixels to increase the radius of the selection.

- Drag the Contrast slider until the Contrast box displays 40% to increase the contrast between the selection and its surrounding.

- Drag the Shift Edge slider until the percentage is approximately 75% to include a wider range of border colors (Figure 2–21).

 Experiment

- Drag the Shift Edge slider to various percentages and watch how the selection changes. Return the slider to 75%.

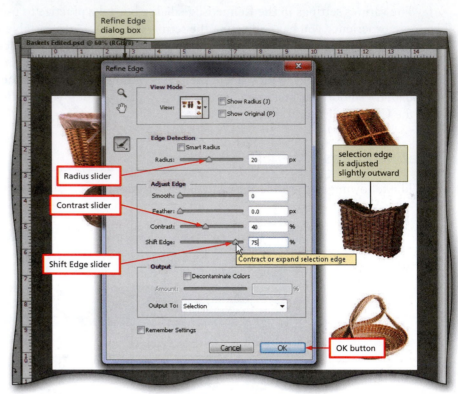

Figure 2–21

4

- Click the OK button in the Refine Edge dialog box to apply the changes and close the dialog box.

Other Ways

1. Press ALT+CTRL+R, choose settings, click OK button

2. Right-click selection, click Refine Edge, choose settings, click OK button

3. On Select menu, click Refine Edge, choose settings, click OK button

To Move Again

The following steps move the basket again, this time without leaving behind a shadow.

1 On the Tools panel, click the Move Tool button to activate the Move Tool.

2 Drag the selection left and slightly up, as shown in Figure 2–22.

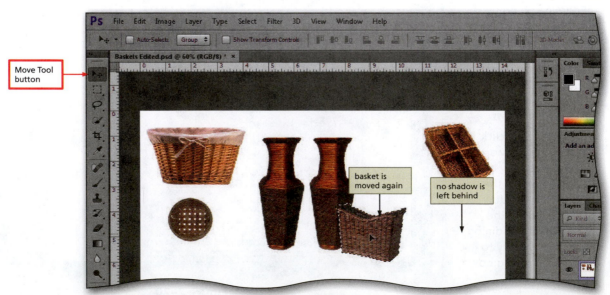

Figure 2–22

To Deselect Using a Shortcut Key

The following step deselects the selection using a shortcut key.

1 Press CTRL+D to deselect.

To Zoom

To facilitate selecting other baskets, the following steps zoom to the upper-left portion of the document window.

1 On the Tools panel, click the Zoom Tool button to select the tool.

2 Click the upper-left corner of the document window twice to zoom that portion of the window to 100% (Figure 2–23).

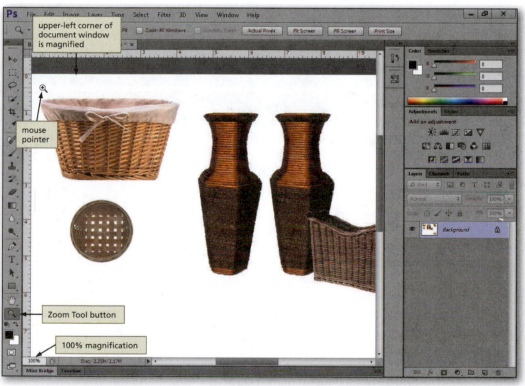

Figure 2–23

The Lasso Tools

The **lasso tools** draw freehand selection borders around objects. The lasso tools provide more flexibility than the marquee tools with their standardized shapes, and might be more suitable than the Quick Selection Tool when the object has a noncontrasting background. Photoshop provides three kinds of lasso tools. The first is the default Lasso Tool, which allows you to create a selection by using the mouse to drag around any object in the document window. You select the Lasso Tool button on the Tools panel. You then begin to drag around the desired area. When you release the mouse, Photoshop connects the selection border to the point where you began dragging, finishing the loop. The Lasso Tool is useful for a quick, rough selection.

BTW

Lasso Tool Selection
If you are using a different tool, and want to activate a lasso tool, you can click the Lasso Tool button on the Tools panel or press the L key on the keyboard to select the Lasso Tool. After selecting the Lasso Tool, pressing SHIFT+L cycles through the three lasso tools.

Completing Lassos

To complete a selection using the Lasso tool, simply release the mouse button. To complete a selection using the Polygonal Lasso or Magnetic Lasso, double-click. Alternatively, you can move the mouse pointer close to the starting point. When a small circle appears on the edge of the mouse pointer, single-click to complete the lasso.

The Polygonal Lasso Tool is similar to the Lasso Tool in that it draws irregular shapes in the image; however, the Polygonal Lasso Tool uses straight line segments. To use the Polygonal Lasso Tool, choose the tool, click in the document window, release the mouse button, and then move the mouse in straight lines, clicking each time you turn a corner. When you get back to the beginning of the polygon, double-click to complete the selection.

The Magnetic Lasso Tool allows you to click close to the edge of the object you want to select. The Magnetic Lasso Tool tries to find the edge of the object by looking for the nearest color change. It then attaches the marquee to the pixel on the edge of the color change. As you move the mouse, the Magnetic Lasso Tool follows that color change with a magnetic attraction. The Magnetic Lasso Tool's marquee displays fastening points on the edge of the object. You can create more fastening points by clicking as you move the mouse, to force a change in direction or to adjust the magnetic attraction. When you get all the way around the object, you click at the connection point to complete the loop, or double-click to have Photoshop connect the loop for you. Because the Magnetic Lasso Tool looks for changes in color to define the edges of an object, it might not be as effective to create selections in images with a busy background or images with low contrast. Each of the lasso tools displays its icon as the mouse pointer.

Table 2–3 describes the three lasso tools.

Table 2–3 The Lasso Tools

Tool	Purpose	Shortcut	Button
Lasso	Used to draw freeform loops, creating a selection border	L SHIFT+L toggles through all three lasso tools	
Polygonal Lasso	Used to draw straight lines, creating segments of a selection border	L SHIFT+L toggles through all three lasso tools	
Magnetic Lasso	Used to draw a selection border that snaps to the edge of contrasting color areas in the image	L SHIFT+L toggles through all three lasso tools	

Each of the lasso tools displays an options bar similar to the marquee options bar, with buttons to add to, subtract from, and intersect with the selection; the ability to feather the border; and, an Anti-alias check box to smooth the borders of a selection (Figure 2–24). Unique to the Magnetic Lasso Tool options bar, however, is a Contrast box to enter the **contrast**, or sensitivity of color that Photoshop evaluates in making the path selection. A higher value detects only edges that contrast sharply with their surroundings; a lower value detects lower-contrast edges. The Width box causes the Magnetic Lasso Tool to detect edges only within the specified distance from the mouse pointer. A Frequency box allows you to specify the rate at which the lasso sets fastening points. A higher value anchors the selection border in place more quickly. A tablet pressure button on the right changes the pen width when using a graphic drawing tablet instead of a mouse.

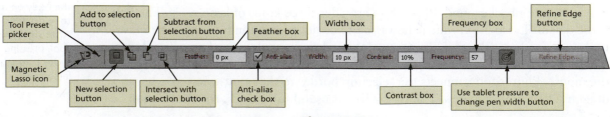

Figure 2–24

To Select using the Polygonal Lasso Tool

The following steps select the upper-left, lined basket by drawing lines around it with the Polygonal Lasso Tool. You will use the other lasso tools later in the chapter.

1

- In the document window, scroll as necessary to display the lined basket in the upper-left corner.

- Right-click the Lasso Tool button on the Tools panel to display the context menu (Figure 2–25).

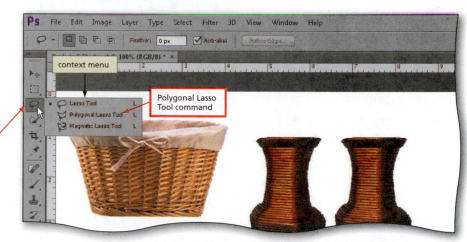

Figure 2–25

2

- Click Polygonal Lasso Tool to activate the lasso.

- If necessary, on the options bar, click the New selection button (Figure 2–26).

 **Experiment**

- Practice using the Polygonal Lasso Tool to draw a triangle by doing the following: in a blank area of the photo, click to begin; move the mouse pointer to the right; and then click to create one side. Move the mouse pointer up, and then click to create a second side. Move the mouse pointer to the beginning point, and then click to complete the lasso. When you are finished experimenting, press CTRL+D to deselect.

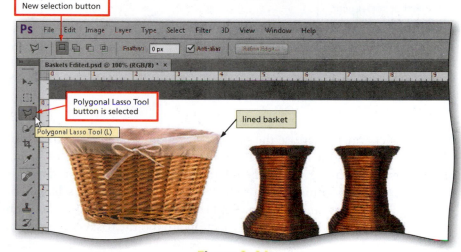

Figure 2–26

3

- Using the tip of the black arrow on the mouse pointer, click the top of the lined basket near the left side.

- Move the mouse pointer to the right to create the first line.

- Click the upper-right corner of the basket at a location before the basket's edge begins to curve downward (Figure 2–27).

Can I reposition the starting point if I make a mistake?

Yes. Press the ESC key and then start again.

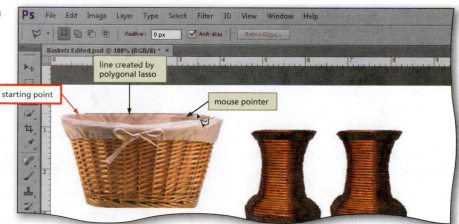

Figure 2–27

4

- Continue creating line segments by moving the mouse pointer and clicking each time you need to change direction.

- When you complete the lines all the way around the basket, move the mouse pointer until a small circle is visible, and then click to complete the selection (Figure 2–28).

Q&A What was the small circle that appeared when I moved close to the beginning of the polygonal lasso?

When the mouse pointer moves close to where you started the polygonal lasso, Photoshop displays a small circle, which means you can single-click to complete the lasso. Otherwise, you have to double-click to complete the lasso.

polygonal lasso lines are connected to create selection

Figure 2–28

Other Ways

1. Press L or SHIFT+L until Polygonal Lasso Tool is active, click photo, move mouse

BTW

The Similar Command
The Similar command increases the selection to include pixels throughout the selection, not just adjacent ones, which fall within the specified tolerance range. Choosing the Similar command more than once will increase the selection in increments.

To Grow the Selection

A quick way to increase the size of a selection without using the Refine Edge dialog box is to use the Grow command on the Select menu. The Grow command will increase, or grow, the selection border to include all adjacent pixels falling within the tolerance range as specified on the options bar of most selection tools. Choosing the Grow command more than once will increase the selection on increments. Similar to refining the edge, the Grow command helps to avoid leaving behind a shadow when you move the selection.

The following steps grow the selection around the basket, to prevent a shadow when moving.

1

- Click Select on the Application bar to display the Select menu (Figure 2–29).

Q&A Will I notice a big difference after I use the Grow command?

You might not see the subtle change in the selection marquee; however, growing the border helps ensure that you will not leave behind a shadow when you move the selection.

2

- Click Grow to increase the selection border.

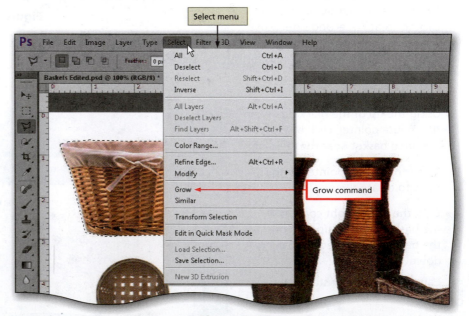

Select menu

Grow command

Figure 2–29

To Save using a Shortcut Key

The following step saves the image again, with the same file name, using a shortcut key.

 Press CTRL+S to save the Baskets Edited file with the same name.

Break Point: If you wish to take a break, this is a good place to do so. To resume at a later time, start Photoshop, open the file called Baskets Edited, select the upper-left basket, and continue following the steps from this location forward.

Grids, Guides, and Snapping

Photoshop can show a **grid** of lines that appears as an overlay on the image. The grid is useful for laying out elements symmetrically or positioning them precisely. The grid can appear as nonprinting lines or dots. To display the grid, click Show on the View menu and then click Grid.

BTW

Guides and Grids
You can change the color or style of guides and grids. On the Edit menu, point to Preferences, and then click Guides, Grid, & Slices.

Use grids and guides.
Showing grids in your document window gives you multiple horizontal and vertical lines with which you can align selections, copies, and new images. Grids also can help you match and adjust sizes and perspective.

Create guides when you have an exact margin, location, or size in mind. Because selections will snap to guides, you easily can create an upper-left corner to use as a boundary when you move and copy. Grids and guides do not print and are turned on and off without difficulty.

Plan Ahead

A **guide** is a nonprinting ruler line or dashed line that graphic designers use to align objects or mark key measurements. To create a guide, you turn on the ruler display and then drag from the horizontal ruler at the top of the document window or from the vertical ruler at the left side of the document window. When you release the mouse, a light, blue-green line appears across the image.

Table 2–4 displays various ways to manipulate guides.

Table 2–4 Manipulating Guides	
Action	**Steps**
Change color and style	Double-click guide.
Clear all guides	On the View menu, click Clear Guides.
Convert between horizontal and vertical guide	Select the Move Tool, ALT+click guide.
Create	Drag from ruler into document window, or, on the View menu, click New Guide, and then enter the orientation and position.
Lock in place	On the View menu, click Lock Guides.
Move	Select the Move Tool, and then drag the guide to a new location.
Remove	Select the Move Tool, and then drag the guide to the ruler.
Snap guide to ruler tick	SHIFT+drag the ruler.
Turn on/off display	On the Application bar, click View Extras, and then click Show Guides, or, on the View menu, point to Show, and then click Guides; or press CTRL+SEMICOLON (;).

Displaying Extras
On the View menu is an Extras command with which you can show or hide selection edges, guides, target paths, slices, annotations, layer borders, and smart guides. You also can use CTRL+H to show or hide those items.

The term **snapping** refers to the ability of objects to attach to, or automatically align with, a grid or guide. For example, if you select an object in your image and begin to move it, as you get close to a guide, the object's selection border will attach itself to the guide. It is not a permanent attachment. If you do not want to leave the object there, simply keep dragging. To turn on or off snapping, click Snap on the View menu.

In a later chapter, you will learn about smart guides that automatically appear when you draw a shape or move a layer. Smart guides further help align shapes, slices, selections, and layers. The Changing Screen Resolution appendix describes how to set guide and grid preferences using the Edit menu.

To Display a Grid

The following steps display the grid.

1

- On the Application bar, click View to display the View menu, and then point to Show to display the Show submenu (Figure 2–30).

Q&A

What does the Show Extras Options command do?

That command displays a dialog box where you can choose to display many different options such as grids, guides, layer edges, brush previews, and others. The choices you make then directly affect the Extras command on the View menu.

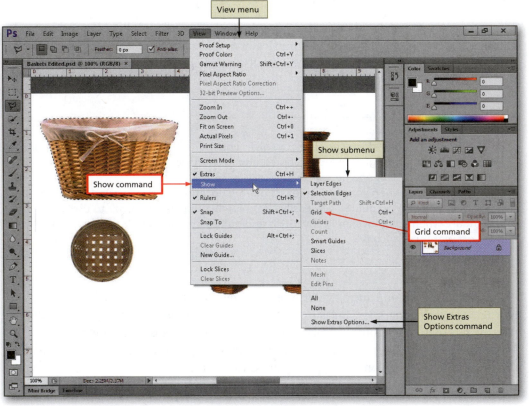

Figure 2–30

2

- Click the Grid command to display the grid (Figure 2–31).

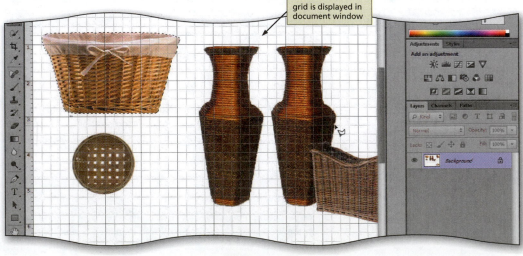

Figure 2–31

Other Ways

1. Press CTRL+APOSTROPHE (')

To Turn Off the Grid Display

The display of a grid is a **toggle**, which means that you turn it off in the same manner that you turned it on; in this case, with the same command.

1 On the Application bar, click View to display the View menu, and then point to Show to display the Show submenu.

2 Click Grid to remove the check mark and remove the grid from the display.

To Create a Guide

The following steps will create a guide to help you position the lined basket on the same horizontal plane as the previous basket.

- Position the mouse pointer in the horizontal ruler at the top of the document window.

- Drag down to create a guide, and stop at 6 inches as measured on the vertical ruler (Figure 2–32).

Q&A
What is the black box that appears as I drag?

It is a mouse pointer tool tip that shows the location as you drag.

- Release the mouse button.

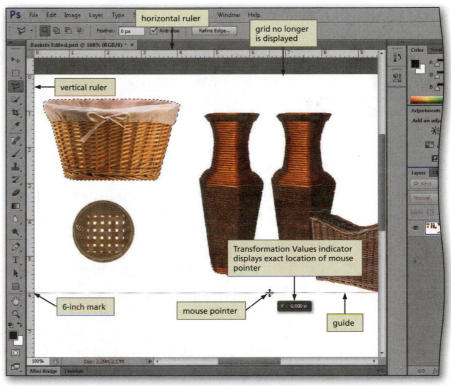

Figure 2–32

Other Ways

1. To show or hide guides, press CTRL+SEMICOLON (;)

2. To show or hide guides, point to Show on View menu, click Guides

3. To create guide, on View menu click New Guide, enter value, click OK button

BTW

Transformation Values Indicator
You can change the display of the Transformation Values indicator, or turn it off completely, by clicking Edit on the Application bar, pointing to Preferences, and then clicking Interface. In the Preferences dialog box, click the Show Transformation Values box arrow and then click the desired location of the indicator or click Never in the list.

To Snap a Selection to the Guide

The following steps move the selection, snapping it to the guide.

 1

- Press the V key to activate the Move Tool.

- Slowly drag the selection to a location in front of the tall baskets until the bottom of the selection snaps to the guide (Figure 2–33).

2

- Press CTRL+D to deselect.

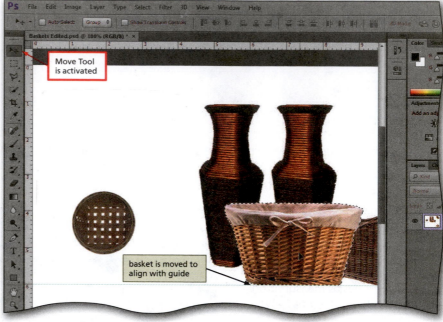

Figure 2–33

Other Ways

1. To turn on or off snapping, press SHIFT+CTRL+SEMICOLON (;)

To Reposition the Document Window

The following steps reposition the document window so that you can select the basket in the upper-right corner.

1 On the Tools panel, click the Hand Tool button.

2 Drag in the document window down and left until the basket in the upper-right corner is displayed, as shown in Figure 2–34.

Figure 2–34

To Select using the Magnetic Lasso Tool

The following steps use the Magnetic Lasso Tool to select the divided basket in the upper-right corner of the document window. Recall that the Magnetic Lasso Tool selects by finding the edge of a contrasting color and creating fastening points.

- Right-click the current lasso tool button, and then click Magnetic Lasso Tool to select it from the context menu.

- If necessary, on the options bar, click the New selection button to select the tool.

- Click the lower-left corner of the basket to start the selection (Figure 2–35).

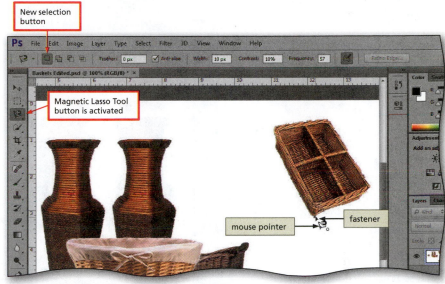

Figure 2–35

- Move, rather than drag, the mouse pointer slowly along the bottom edge of the basket to create a selection marquee (Figure 2–36).

Q&A How do I correct a mistake?

As you use the Magnetic Lasso Tool, if you make a mistake, press the ESC key and begin again.

Figure 2–36

- Continue moving the mouse pointer around the edge of the basket. Click the mouse when turning a corner to create an extra fastening point.

- When you get to the lower-left corner again, double-click to finish the lasso (Figure 2–37).

Q&A When I double-clicked, the selection disappeared. What did I do wrong?

If your mouse pointer is exactly on the fastening point, a small circle indicates you are back at the beginning. In that case, a single-click finishes the lasso. If your selection disappears, press CTRL+Z to undo the double-click; the selection then should appear as shown in Figure 2–37.

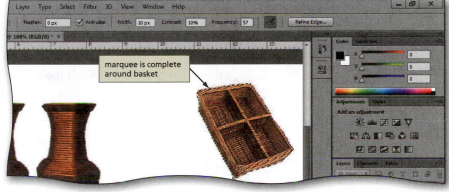

Figure 2–37

Other Ways

1. Press L or SHIFT+L until Magnetic Lasso Tool is active, click photo, move mouse

To Move a Selection using a Shortcut Key

The following steps move the selection.

 1

- Press the V key to activate the Move Tool.

- Slowly drag the selection to a location in front of the other baskets as shown in Figure 2–38.

Q&A

Should I redo the move if a shadow is left behind?

You can press CTRL+Z to undo the move and then use the Grow command on the Select menu; however, later in the chapter you will crop the photo, which will remove any shadows that are left behind.

2

- Press CTRL+D to deselect.

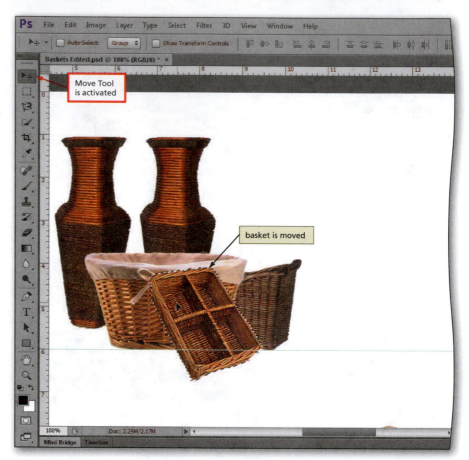

Figure 2–38

BTW

Nudging Selections
Instead of dragging to move a selection, you can use the arrow keys on the keyboard to move in small increments in a process called **nudging**.

To Navigate using a Shortcut Key

The following steps reposition the document window so that you can select the basket in the lower-right corner.

1 Press the H key to activate the Hand Tool.

2 Drag in the document window until the handled basket in the lower-right corner is displayed.

To Select using the Lasso Tool

The following steps use the Lasso Tool to create a selection by dragging around the object. As you will notice, the Lasso Tool leaves white space around the basket and inside the handle.

1
- Right-click the current lasso tool button on the Tools panel to display the context menu and then click Lasso Tool to select it.

- If necessary, on the options bar, click the New selection button to select the tool.

- Drag partway around the handled basket to start the lasso. Do not release the mouse button (Figure 2–39).

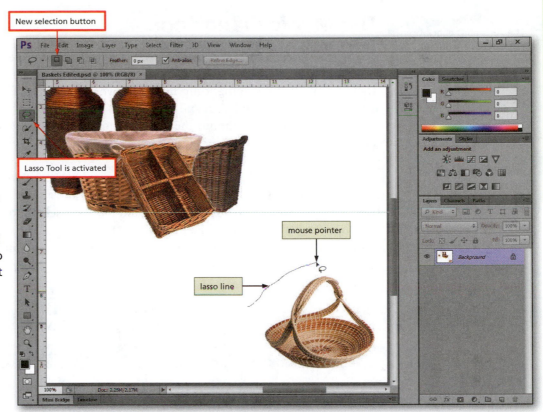

Figure 2–39

2
- Continue dragging around the basket to create a completed lasso, and then release the mouse button to finish the loop (Figure 2–40).

Q&A How will I know if the lasso is complete?

When you release the mouse button, Photoshop completes the Lasso Tool selection, no matter where you are in the image.

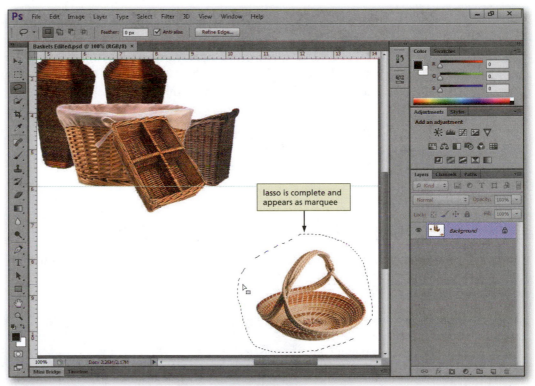

Figure 2–40

Other Ways

1. Press L or SHIFT+L until Lasso Tool is active, drag selection

BTW

Anti-Aliasing
The Anti-alias check box smooths the jagged edges of a selection by softening the color transition between edge pixels and background pixels. While anti-aliasing is useful when cutting, copying, and pasting selections to create composite images, it might leave behind a shadow after cutting or moving a selection.

The Magic Wand Tool

The Magic Wand Tool lets you select a consistently colored area with a single click. For example, if you wanted to select the blue sky in an image, clicking with the Magic Wand Tool would select it automatically, no matter what the shape of the blue area. When you use the Magic Wand Tool and click in the image or within a selection, Photoshop selects every pixel that contains the same or similar colors as the location you clicked. The Magic Wand Tool mouse pointer appears as a small line with a starburst on the end, similar to a magic wand.

The Magic Wand Tool options bar (Figure 2–41) contains the same selection adjustment buttons as the marquee tools, including the ability to create a new selection, add to or subtract from a selection, and intersect selections. The Magic Wand Tool options bar also has a Tolerance box that allows you to enter a value that determines the similarity or difference in the color of the selected pixels. A low value selects the few colors that are very similar to the pixel you click. A higher value selects a broader range of colors.

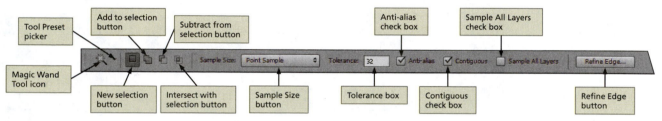

Figure 2–41

BTW

Cutting and Pasting
Just as you do in other applications, you can use the Cut, Copy, and Paste commands from the Edit menu or shortcut keys to make changes to selections. Unless you predefine a selection area by dragging a marquee, the Paste command pastes to the center of the document window. Both the commands and the shortcut keys create a new layer when they copy or paste.

When checked, the Contiguous check box selects only adjacent areas with the same color. Otherwise, Photoshop selects all pixels in the entire image that use the same color. Finally, the Sample All Layers check box selects colors using data from all visible layers. Otherwise, the Magic Wand Tool selects colors from the active layer only. You will learn about layers in a future chapter.

Besides using the options bar, the Magic Wand Tool can be used with many shortcut keys. Holding the SHIFT key while clicking adds to a Magic Wand Tool selection. Holding the ALT key while clicking subtracts from the selection. Holding the CTRL key while dragging with the Magic Wand Tool moves the selection.

To Subtract from a Selection using the Magic Wand Tool

The following steps use the Magic Wand Tool to eliminate the white background in the selection, leaving only the basket inside the marquee.

1
• With the basket still selected, right-click the Quick Selection Tool button on the Tools panel to display the context menu (Figure 2–42).

Figure 2–42

2

- Click Magic Wand Tool to activate it.

- On the options bar, click the 'Subtract from selection' button. Click the Anti-alias check box so it does not display a check mark.

- If necessary, type 32 in the Tolerance box, and, if necessary, click to display a check mark in the Contiguous check box (Figure 2–43).

Q&A Could I press the w key to choose the Magic Wand Tool?

Yes, if the Magic Wand Tool appears on the Tools panel, you can press the w key to activate it;

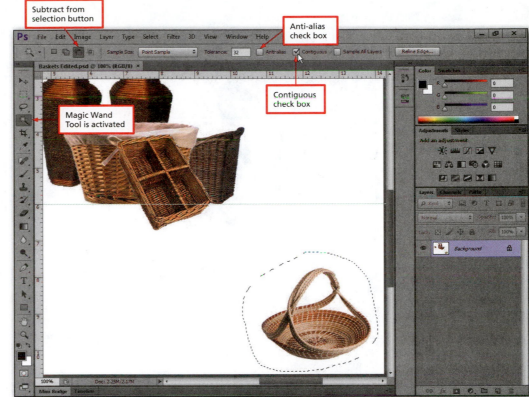

however, if the Quick Selection Tool appears on the Tools panel, you have to press SHIFT+W.

Figure 2–43

3

- Using the tip of the Magic Wand Tool mouse pointer, click the white space outside the basket, but inside the selection marquee, to remove the white color from the selection (Figure 2–44).

Q&A What is the minus sign next to the mouse pointer?

The minus sign appears whenever you choose to subtract from a selection. A plus sign would indicate an addition to the selection, and an X indicates an intersection. Photoshop displays

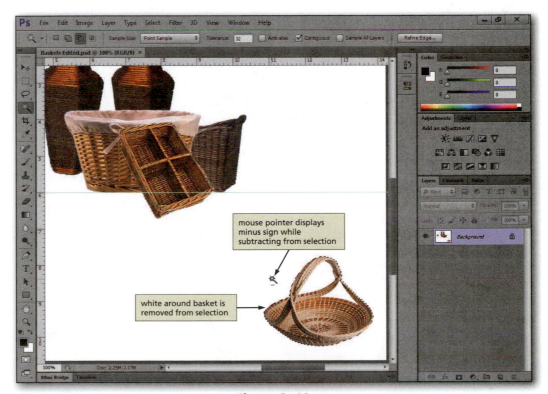

these signs so you do not have to glance up at the options bar to see which button you are using while you drag the selection.

Figure 2–44

- Click the white spaces inside the basket's handle to remove them from the selection (Figure 2–45).

Q&A

Could I have removed the Contiguous check mark and just clicked the white area to remove all white areas?

Yes, but doing so would remove pixels because there is some white on the basket itself. It was better to remove the contiguous white spaces around the basket and within the handles.

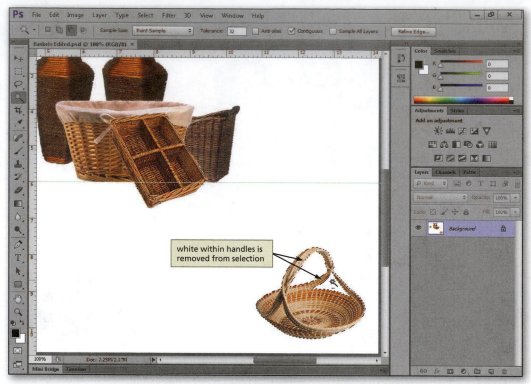

white within handles is removed from selection

Figure 2–45

Other Ways

1. Press W or SHIFT+W until Magic Wand Tool is active, click 'Subtract from selection' button, click selection

2. Select Magic Wand Tool, ALT+CLICK selection

3. Select Magic Wand Tool, right-click photo, click Subtract From Selection

To Move the Basket

The following steps move the basket.

1 Press the V key to activate the Move Tool.

2 Drag the basket to a location to the right of the previous selection, as shown in Figure 2–46.

3 Press CTRL+D to deselect.

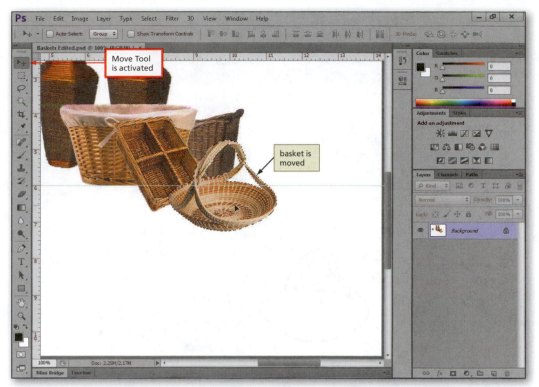

Figure 2–46

To Select using the Elliptical Marquee Tool

The following steps use the Elliptical Marquee Tool to draw a circle around the final basket to select it. Recall that SHIFT+dragging with a marquee tool maintains proportions, in this case creating a circle rather than an oval. In addition, you can press and hold the SPACEBAR key to move a selection while you create it.

1

● Scroll to the left until the entire round basket is displayed (Figure 2–47).

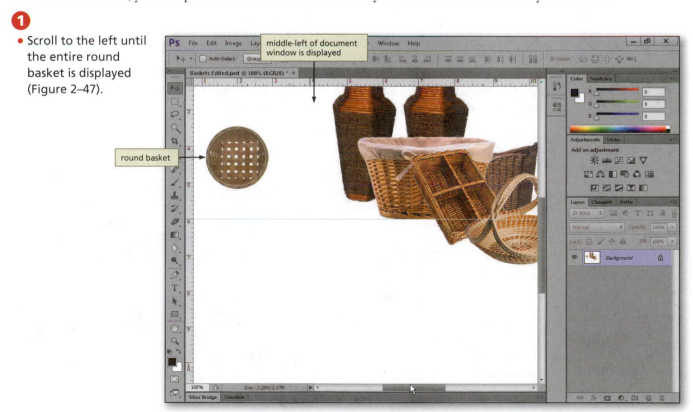

Figure 2–47

2

- Right-click the current marquee tool on the Tools panel to display the context menu (Figure 2–48).

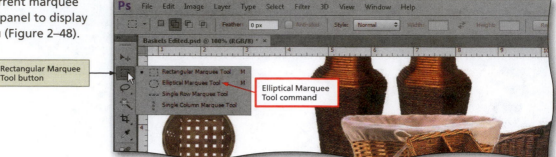

Figure 2–48

3

- Click Elliptical Marquee Tool to activate the tool.

- If necessary, click the New selection button on the options bar.

- Position the mouse pointer at the upper-left edge of the round basket and then SHIFT+drag down and to the right to create a circle selection. Do not release the SHIFT key or mouse button.

- If necessary, press and hold the SPACEBAR key and then drag the selection into position.

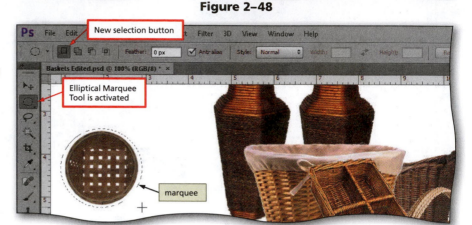

Figure 2–49

- Release the mouse button before releasing the SHIFT and SPACEBAR keys (Figure 2–49).

To Subtract Noncontiguous Pixels of the Same Color

The following step uses the Magic Wand Tool and the 'Subtract from selection' button to remove white pixels in the selection. Because there is white space around the edge of the basket and within the basket, you will subtract from the selection noncontiguously. You also will change the tolerance level.

1

- On the Tools panel, click the Magic Wand Tool button to select it.

- On the options bar, click the 'Subtract from selection' button if necessary. Double-click the Tolerance box and then type 10 to replace the current setting. Click the Contiguous check box to remove its check mark.

- Click the white area in the selection (Figure 2–50).

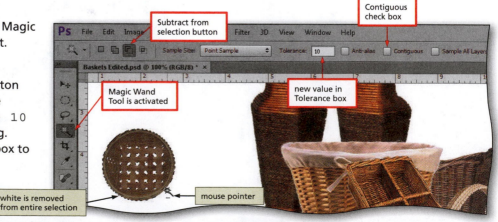

Figure 2–50

Q&A

How does the tolerance setting work?

In this selection, some of the edges of the basket are quite light. You do not want to leave them behind as a shadow when you move the basket; therefore, you are subtracting a more narrow range of color — the pixels that are closest in color to the strong white background.

To Move the Round Basket

The following steps move the round basket.

1 Press the V key to activate the Move Tool.

2 Drag the selection to a location in front of the lined basket as shown in Figure 2–51. Do not deselect.

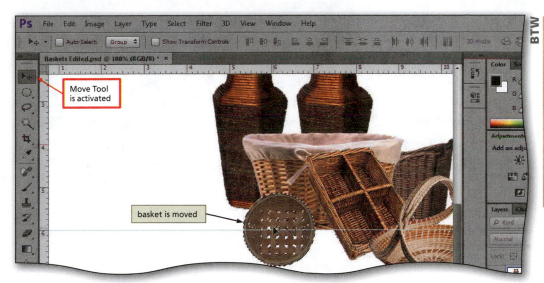

BTW

Resizing
Photoshop allows you to apply some transformations to entire images or photos, rather than just selections. For example, you can change the size of the photo or rotate the image using the Image menu. You then can enter dimensions or rotation percentages on the submenu and subsequent dialog boxes.

Figure 2–51

To Duplicate and Scale

The following steps create a smaller copy of the selected basket. When you click the Show Transform Controls check box on the Move Tool options bar, Photoshop displays a bounding box with sizing handles. To resize, drag one of the sizing handles. To resize proportionally, SHIFT+drag one of the sizing handles. When you change the size of a selection, it is called **scaling**.

1

- With the Move Tool still selected, ALT+drag the selection to a location slightly down and to the right of the original selection. The copy will overlap the original round basket slightly.

- On the options bar, click the Show Transform Controls check box to display a check mark (Figure 2–52).

Q&A
Could I just use the Copy and Paste commands?

Yes, however those commands create a new layer in the photo and increase the file size.

Figure 2–52

2

• SHIFT+drag a corner sizing handle toward the center of the basket to scale it down approximately 10 percent smaller (Figure 2–53).

Q&A

Why did the options bar change?

The options bar changed to the Transform options bar — an options bar not associated with any one specific tool. You will learn more about the Transform options bar in a future chapter.

Q&A

How do I know what 10 percent smaller is?

You can drag until the option bars display approximately 90% in the W and H boxes.

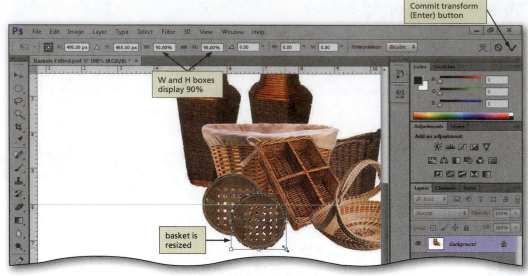

Figure 2–53

3

• On the options bar click the 'Commit transform (Enter)' button to accept the transformation.

• Press CTRL+D to deselect.

To Reselect

When you deselect on purpose or by accident, you can return to the previous selection by using the **Reselect** command. The following steps reselect the copy of the round basket.

1

• Click Select on the Application bar to display the Select menu (Figure 2–54).

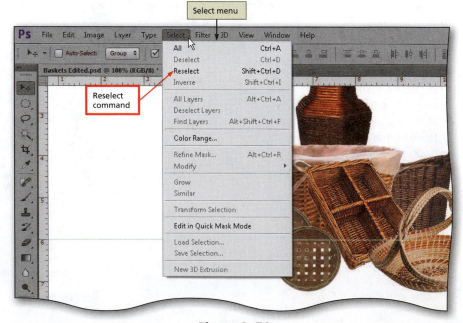

Figure 2–54

2

- Click Reselect to display the previous selection (Figure 2–55).

Figure 2–55

Other Ways

1. Press SHIFT+CTRL+D

To Create and Scale Another Copy

The following steps create another copy of the basket.

1 Select the Move Tool if necessary. ALT+drag the selection to a location slightly down and right of the previous selection. The copy will overlap slightly.

2 SHIFT+drag a corner sizing handle to scale the selection down by approximately 10 percent (Figure 2–56).

3 On the options bar, click the 'Commit transform (Enter)' button to accept the transformation, and then deselect.

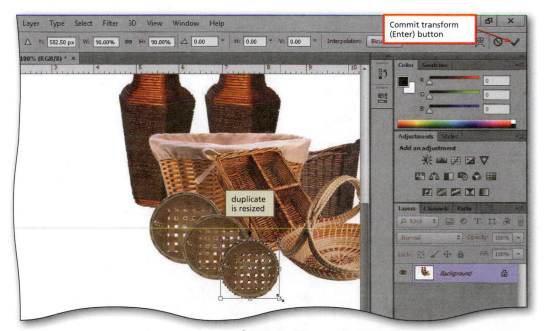

Figure 2–56

To Fit Screen

In moving around the screen in this project, you have zoomed, scrolled and used the Hand Tool. The following step uses the Fit Screen button on the Zoom Tool options bar to display the entire document window.

1

- Select the Zoom Tool.

- Click the Fit Screen button on the Zoom Tool options bar (Figure 2–57).

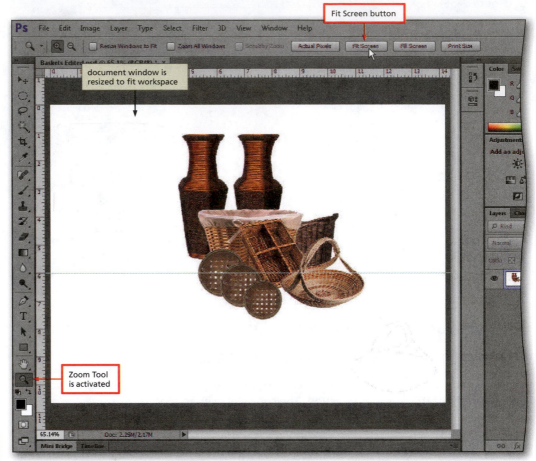

Figure 2–57

Other Ways

1. Press CTRL+0 (zero)
2. On View menu, click Fit on Screen

To Turn Off Guides using a Shortcut Key

The following step turns off the display of the green ruler guide.

1 Press CTRL+SEMICOLON (;) to turn off the display of guides.

To Crop a Selection

Finally, you will crop the advertisement to center the baskets, including a minimal amount of border space. In Chapter 1, you activated the Crop Tool and then adjusted the size of the selection. In the following steps, you will select first, and then crop.

- Press SHIFT+M to select the Rectangular Marquee Tool.

- Drag a rectangular marquee that leaves an even amount of white space on all four sides of the baskets.

- Press the C key to activate the Crop Tool (Figure 2–58).

Q&A

Why did I have to use SHIFT+M to activate the Rectangular Marquee Tool?

Previously, the Elliptical Marquee Tool had been selected. Pressing the M key would have activated it. Pressing SHIFT+M toggles through all of the marquee tools.

Figure 2–58

2

- On the options bar, click the Delete Cropped Pixels check box so it displays a check mark, if necessary.

- Press the ENTER key twice to accept the cropping selection and to complete the crop.

- Press the M key to return to the Rectangular Marquee Tool.

To Save Again

The following step saves the image again, with the same file name, using a shortcut key.

1 Press CTRL+S to save the Baskets Edited file with the same name.

Break Point: If you wish to take a break, this is a good place to do so. To resume at a later time, start Photoshop, open the file named Baskets Edited, and continue following the steps from this location forward.

Creating PDF Files

The final step is to create a PDF file of the advertising image for document exchange. **PDF** stands for **Portable Document Format**, a flexible file format based on the PostScript imaging model that is compatible across platforms and applications. PDF files accurately display and preserve fonts, page layouts, and graphics. There are two ways to create a PDF file in Photoshop. First, you can save the file in the PDF format. Alternatively, you can use the Print command to create the PDF format, allowing you to make some changes to the settings before saving.

Plan Ahead	**Create files in portable formats.**
	You might need to distribute your artwork in a variety of formats for customers, print shops, Webmasters, and e-mail attachments. The format you choose depends on how the file will be used, but portability is always a consideration. The document might need to be used with various operating systems, monitor resolutions, computing environments, and servers.
	It is a good idea to discuss with your customer the types of formats he or she might need. It usually is safe to begin work in the Photoshop PSD format and then use the Save as command or Print command to convert the files. PDF is a portable format that can be read by anyone on the Web with a free reader. The PDF format is platform and software independent. Commonly, PDF files are virus free and safe as e-mail attachments.

To Save a Photo in the PDF Format

The following steps save the photo in the PDF format for ease of distribution.

- Click File on the Application bar, and then click Save As to display the Save As dialog box.

- Click the Format button to display the various formats you can use to save Photoshop files (Figure 2–59).

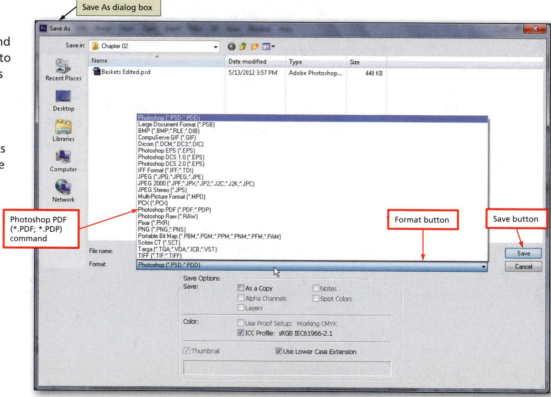

Figure 2–59

- Click Photoshop PDF (*.PDF;*.PDP) in the list to select the PDF format, and then click the Save button to continue the saving process (Figure 2–60).

Figure 2–60

3

- Click the OK button to display the Save Adobe PDF dialog box (Figure 2–61).

Q&A The Save Adobe PDF dialog box did not appear. What happened?

If you have multiple windows open on your system, the dialog box might be behind some of the other windows. In that case, minimize the other windows until the dialog box appears.

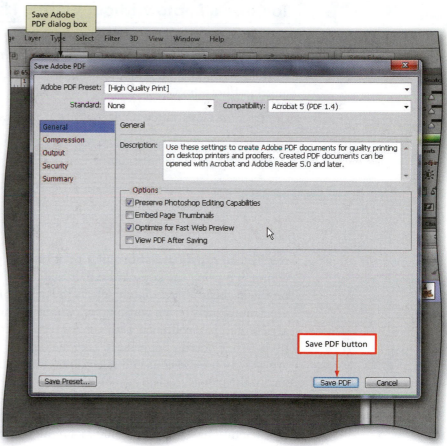

Figure 2–61

4

- Click the Save PDF button to continue the saving process and display a second Save Adobe PDF dialog box (Figure 2–62).

Q&A Will the PDF version have the same name?

Yes. After you save the file, you will see the name Baskets Edited.pdf on the document window tab because Photoshop can edit PDF files directly. The file also can be viewed with Adobe Acrobat or any PDF reader.

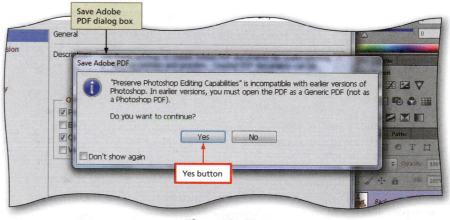

Figure 2–62

5

- Click the Yes button to finish saving.

Other Ways

1. Press CTRL+P, click Document box arrow, click Adobe PDF, click Print

To Close a Photo without Closing Photoshop

Recall that when you are finished editing a photo or file, you should close it to help save system resources. You can close a photo after you have saved it and continue working in Photoshop. The following steps close the Baskets Edited.pdf file without quitting Photoshop.

1 Click the Close button on the document window tab to close the Baskets Edited.pdf file.

2 If Photoshop displays a dialog box, click the No button to ignore the changes since the last time you saved the photo.

Keyboard Shortcuts

Recall that a **keyboard shortcut**, or **shortcut key**, is a way to activate menu or tool commands using the keyboard rather than the mouse. For example, pressing the L key on the keyboard immediately selects the current lasso tool without having to move your mouse away from working in the image. Shortcuts that combine two keystrokes are common as well, such as the use of CTRL+A to select an entire image. Shortcuts are useful when you do not want to take the time to traverse the menu system or when you are making precise edits and selections with the mouse and do not want to go back to any of the panels to change tools or settings. A Quick Reference summary describing Photoshop's keyboard shortcuts is included in the back of the book.

While many keyboard shortcuts already exist in Photoshop, there might be times when additional shortcuts would be useful. For instance, the Single Row and Single Column Marquee Tools have no shortcut key. If you frequently use those tools, adding the Single Row and Single Column Marquee Tools to the M keyboard shortcut might be helpful. Photoshop allows users to create, customize, and save keyboard shortcuts in one of three areas: menus, panels, and tools. When you create keyboard shortcuts, you can add them to Photoshop's default settings, save them in a personalized set for retrieval in future editing sessions, or delete them from your system.

Creating a Keyboard Shortcut

To create a new keyboard shortcut, Photoshop provides a dialog box interface, which is accessible from the Edit menu. Using that dialog box, you can select one of the three shortcut areas. Then you can assign a shortcut key or combination of keys. For menu commands, your shortcut keystrokes must include a combination of the CTRL key or a function key followed by a single keyboard character. When creating shortcuts for tools, you must use a single alphabetic character. To avoid conflicting duplications, Photoshop immediately warns you if you have chosen a keyboard shortcut used somewhere else in the program.

To Create a New Keyboard Shortcut

In the following steps, you will create a shortcut to display the Essentials workspace. While that command is accessible on the Window menu, a shortcut would save time when you need to choose the workspace.

- Click Edit on the Application bar to display the Edit menu, and then click Keyboard Shortcuts to display the Keyboard Shortcuts and Menus dialog box.

- Click the Shortcuts For box arrow, and then click Application Menus in the list, if necessary.

- In the Application Menu Command list, scroll down, and then click the triangle to the left of the Window command to display the list of Window menu commands (Figure 2–63).

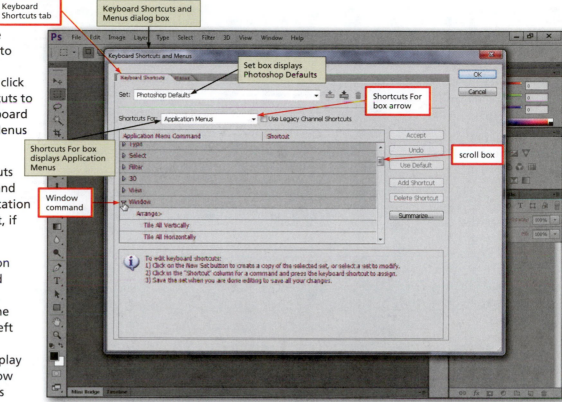

Figure 2–63

- Scroll down to display Workspace under the Window menu commands, and then click Essentials (Default) to display a shortcut key box (Figure 2–64).

Q&A

How are the buttons at the top of the dialog box used?

The 'Save all changes to the current set of shortcuts' button allows you to name the set for future retrieval. The 'Create a new set based on the current set of shortcuts' button creates a copy of the current keyboard shortcut settings. The 'Delete the current set of shortcuts' button deletes the set.

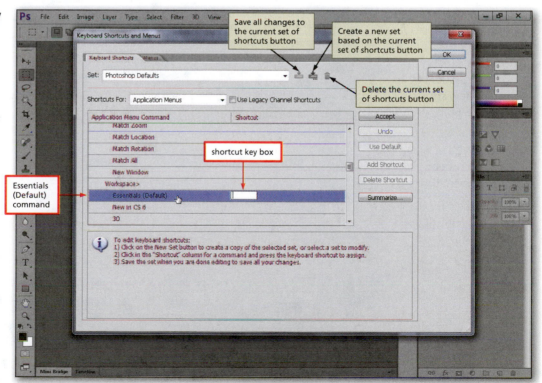

Figure 2–64

- Press the F12 key to enter a new shortcut keystroke for the Essentials (Default) command (Figure 2–65).

Q&A

How can I find out which shortcuts keys still are available?

When you click the Summarize button, Photoshop creates a Web page with all of the keyboard shortcuts in the set. You can save that file on your system or print it.

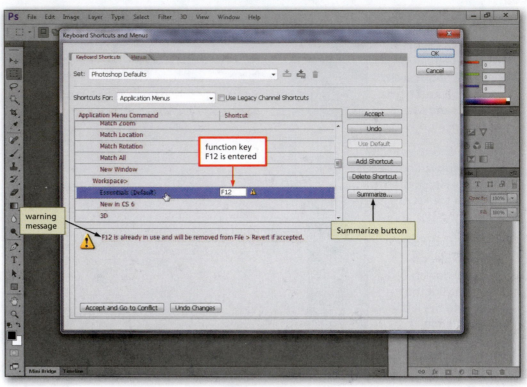

Figure 2–65

- Because Photoshop warns you that the F12 key already is being used as a shortcut for a different command, press CTRL+SLASH (/) to enter a new shortcut (Figure 2–66).

5

- Click the Accept button to set the shortcut key.

- Click the OK button to close the dialog box.

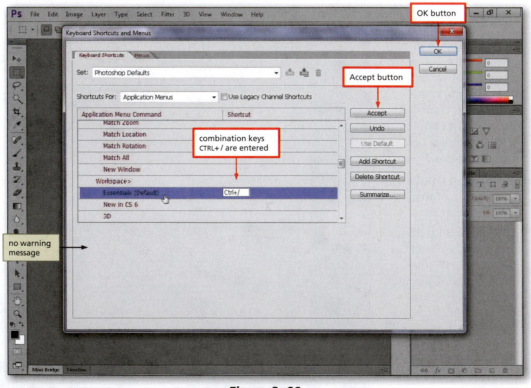

Figure 2–66

Other Ways

1. Press ALT+SHIFT+CTRL+K, edit settings, click OK button

To Test a New Keyboard Shortcut

The next steps test the new keyboard shortcut.

1

● Click Window on the Application bar and point to Workspace to verify the shortcut key assignment (Figure 2–67).

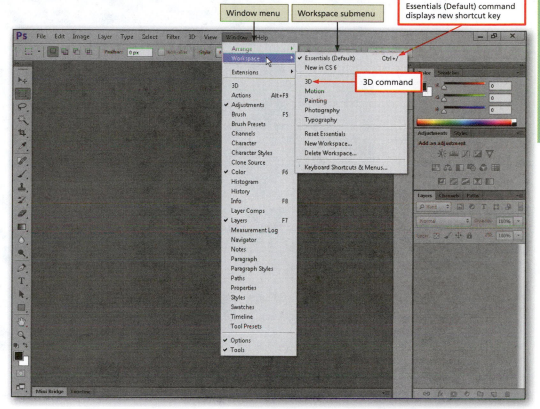

Figure 2–67

2

● Click the 3D command to change to the 3D workspace (Figure 2–68).

Q&A

Will the new shortcut become permanent?

The new shortcut will be saved on your system in the Photoshop Defaults (modified) set. That set will be in effect the next time you start Photoshop. If you want to remove it, you can edit that specific shortcut, or delete the set by clicking the 'Delete the current set of shortcuts' button.

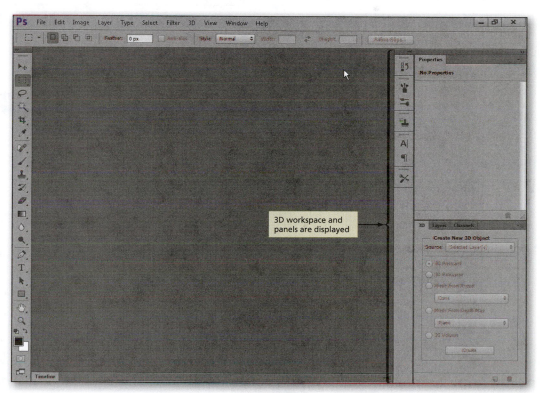

Figure 2–68

● Press CTRL+SLASH (/) to test the shortcut and display the Essentials workspace again (Figure 2–69).

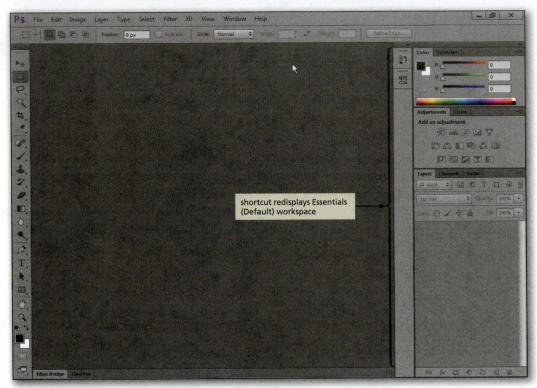

Figure 2–69

To Return to the Default Settings for Keyboard Shortcuts

It is a good idea, especially in a lab situation, to reset the keyboard shortcuts to their default settings. The following steps restore the default shortcut keys.

1

● On the Application bar, click Edit, and then click Keyboard Shortcuts to display the Keyboard Shortcuts and Menus dialog box.

● On the Keyboards Shortcuts tab, click the Set box arrow to display the list (Figure 2–70).

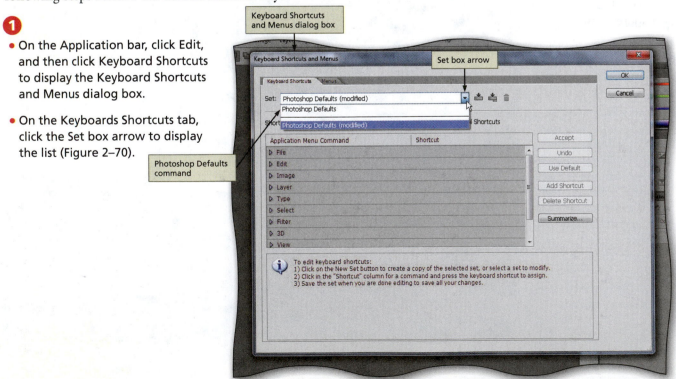

Figure 2–70

2

- Click Photoshop Defaults to choose the default settings for shortcuts (Figure 2–71).

3

- When Photoshop displays a message asking if you want to save your changes, click the No button so your previous changes are not saved.

- In the Keyboard Shortcuts and Menus dialog box, click the OK button to close the dialog box.

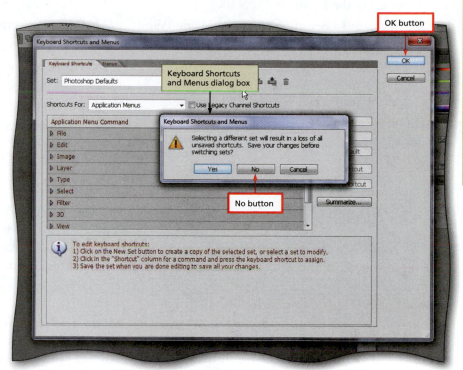

Figure 2–71

To Quit Photoshop using a Shortcut Key

The following step quits Photoshop and returns control to Windows.

1 Press CTRL+Q to quit Photoshop.

Chapter Summary

In this chapter, you learned how to use selection tools, including the marquee tools, the lasso tools, the Quick Selection Tool, and the Magic Wand Tool. You learned about the History panel and its states. You worked with the 'Subtract from selection' command, the Refine Edge dialog box, and the Grow command to edit the selection border. You used the Move Tool to move and copy selections and scaled them. Each of the tools and commands had its own options bar with settings to control how the tool or command worked. You used a guide to help align objects. Finally, you saved the photo as a PDF file, and you learned how to create and test a new keyboard shortcut.

The items listed below include all the new Photoshop skills you have learned in this chapter:

1. Use the Rectangular Marquee Tool (PS 79)
2. Use the Move Tool (PS 80)
3. Duplicate a Selection (PS 82)
4. Use the Quick Selection Tool (PS 83)
5. Display the History Panel (PS 86)
6. Undo Changes using the History Panel (PS 87)
7. Refine Edges (PS 89)
8. Select using the Polygonal Lasso Tool (PS 93)
9. Grow the Selection (PS 94)
10. Display a Grid (PS 96)
11. Create a Guide (PS 97)
12. Snap a Selection to the Guide (PS 98)
13. Select using the Magnetic Lasso Tool (PS 99)
14. Move a Selection using a Shortcut Key (PS 100)

Apply Your Knowledge

Reinforce the skills and apply the concepts you learned in this chapter.

Moving and Duplicating Selections

Instructions: Start Photoshop and perform the customization steps found on pages PS 6 through PS 10. Open the Apply 2-1 Bread file in the Chapter 02 folder from the Data Files for Students and save it, in the PSD file format, as Apply 2-1 Bread Edited. Visit www.cengage.com/ct/studentdownload for detailed instructions or contact your instructor for information about accessing the required files.

You will create a grocery advertisement featuring bakery items. First, you will select individual items from within the file, and then you will transform and move them so that the finished design looks like Figure 2–72. You will place the rest of the images from back to front.

Figure 2–72

Perform the following tasks:

1. Because the checkered tablecloth is in the very back of the arrangement, you will start with it. Use the Rectangular Marquee Tool to select the checkered tablecloth.

2. Use the Move Tool to move the tablecloth to the top-center portion of the page. Do not deselect the tablecloth.

3. With the Move Tool still selected, click the Show Transform Controls check box to display a check mark. To distort the tablecloth and make it appear in perspective, CTRL+drag each of the lower corner sizing handles down and outward. Do not overlap any of the bread items. The result should be a trapezoid shape, as shown in Figure 2–72. If you make a mistake, press the ESC key and start again. When you are satisfied with the shape, press the ENTER key to confirm the transformation. Do not deselect.

4. The croissant is the back-most item in the arrangement. Use the Polygonal Lasso Tool to select the croissant. (*Hint:* The croissant is the lower-right item in the Apply 2-1 Bread image.) Right-click the Quick Selection Tool button on the Tools panel, and then click Magic Wand Tool. On the options bar, click the 'Subtract from selection' button, then click the white area around the croissant to remove it.

5. Use the Move Tool to move the croissant to the upper-right portion of the tablecloth. ALT+drag a second croissant to a location below and to the left of the first, as shown in Figure 2–72. (*Hint:* Do not drag the center reference point.) Press CTRL+D to deselect it.

6. Repeat Steps 4 and 5 to select and move the French bread.

7. ALT+drag the French bread to the right to create a duplicate.

8. Select and move the remaining bread items until you are satisfied with the arrangement. For each bread item, use a selection tool that will approximate the shape of the bread. On the options bar, use the 'Add to selection' and 'Subtract from selection' buttons as necessary. Use the Magic Wand Tool to remove white space around the selection before moving it.

9. Right-click the Rectangular Marquee Tool button on the Tools panel, then click Elliptical Marquee Tool. Use the Elliptical Marquee Tool to select the Sale button. (*Hint:* Press and hold the SHIFT key as you select to maintain a perfect circle.)

10. Move the Sale button to the lower-right portion of the advertisement.

11. Use the Crop Tool to select the portion of the image to use for the final advertisement. (*Hint:* The remaining white space is unnecessary.)

12. Save the Apply 2-1 Bread Edited file, and then close Photoshop.

13. Submit the assignment in the format specified by your instructor.

Extend Your Knowledge

Extend the skills you learned in this chapter and experiment with new skills. You may need to use Help to complete the assignment.

Separating Objects from the Background

Instructions: Start Photoshop and perform the customization steps found on pages PS 6 through PS 10. Open the Extend 2-1 Flowers file in the Chapter 02 folder from the Data Files for Students and save it, in the PSD format, as Extend 2-1 Flowers Edited. Visit www.cengage.com/ct/studentdownload for detailed instructions or contact your instructor for information about accessing the required files.

The original flower image displays the flowers in their natural settings, with various colors in the background. After moving the frame and making a copy, you will select the flowers while preventing background colors from straying into the selection. Finally, you will position each flower in front of a frame, as shown in Figure 2–73.

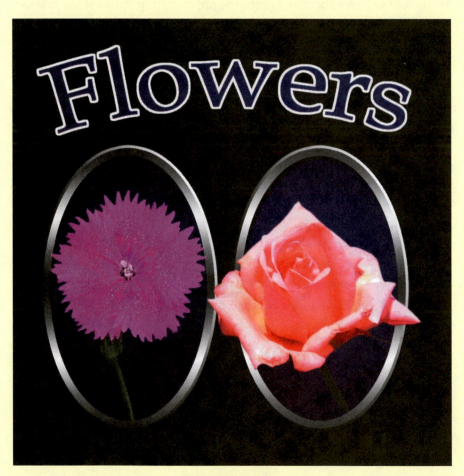

Figure 2–73

Perform the following tasks:

1. Use the Elliptical Marquee Tool to select the oval frame. (*Hint:* For more careful placement, while dragging to create the selection, you can press the SPACEBAR key to adjust the location of the drag and then release it to continue drawing the marquee.) Be careful to select only the frame, and eliminate any white around the edge of the selection using the Magic Wand Tool and the 'Subtract from selection' button.

2. Drag the selection to a location below the left side of the word, Flowers. Do not be concerned if you leave a slight shadow behind. On the Move Tool options bar, if necessary, click to display a check mark in the Show Transform Controls check box. SHIFT+drag a corner sizing handle to scale the selection approximately 10 percent bigger. (*Hint:* You also can increase the selection to 110 percent in both the Width and Height boxes.) Press the ENTER key to commit the transformation.

3. With the frame still selected, SHIFT+ALT+drag to create a duplicate and place it to the right of the original. (*Hint:* Recall that using the SHIFT key keeps the duplicate aligned with the original.)

4. Use appropriate selection tools to select the upper flower and its stem. (*Hint:* Use the Magic Wand Tool with a tolerance setting of 50 to select the contiguous pink and then add to the selection using other tools.) Click the 'Intersect with selection' button to combine selected areas, if necessary. Do not include the background.

5. To ensure that the selection does not have any stray pixels around its border, use the Refine Edge dialog box to refine the edge by increasing the radius to 7 px.

6. As you create the selection, if necessary, press CTRL+ALT+Z to step back through the editing history and return the image to an earlier state.

7. Move the selected flower onto the left frame and resize as necessary.

8. Repeat Steps 4 through 7 for the lower flower and the right frame. If you make an error, display the History panel and then click a previous state.

9. Crop the image to include only the word, Flowers, and the two framed flowers. Save the changes.

10. Use the Magic Wand Tool to select the blue color in the word, Flowers. (*Hint:* To select all of the letters, you will have to remove the check mark in the Contiguous box.) If parts of the image other than the word, Flowers, appear within the marquee, use the 'Subtract from selection' button to remove them.

11. Use Photoshop Help to investigate how to soften the edges of selections. Use the Refine Edge dialog box to soften the edges. Expand the selection and feather the edges.

12. Use Photoshop Help to investigate how to stroke a selection or layer with color. With the letters selected, use the Stroke command on the Edit menu to display the Stroke dialog box. Stroke the selection with a white color, 5 pixels wide, on the outside of the selection.

13. Save your changes, close the file, and then quit Photoshop. Send the revised photo to your instructor as an e-mail attachment.

Make It Right

Analyze a project and correct all errors and/or improve the design.

Correcting an Error in a Photo

Instructions: Start Photoshop and perform the customization steps found on pages PS 6 through PS 10. Open the Make It Right 2-1 Footballs file in the Chapter 02 folder from the Data Files for Students and save it as Make It Right 2-1 Footballs Edited. Visit www.cengage.com/ct/ studentdownload for detailed instructions or contact your instructor for information about accessing the required files.

A coworker has made an error when trying to make a duplicate of the football (Figure 2–74). The duplicate on the right included some white space around the football, which overlaps the football on the left. In addition, the football on the right should be bigger because it is closer in the picture. Use selection tools as necessary, along with the 'Add to selection' and 'Subtract from selection' buttons, to select only the football (and its shadow) on the right. Refine the edge. ALT+drag with the Move Tool to create a duplicate and place it over the top of the football on the left. Select the football on the right again. Display the transform controls and scale the selection to be approximately 10 percent bigger.

Save the project again. Submit the revised document in the format specified by your instructor.

Figure 2–74

In the Lab

Design and/or create a project using the guidelines, concepts, and skills presented in this chapter. Labs are listed in order of increasing difficulty.

Lab 1: Using Keyboard Shortcuts to Create a Logo

Problem: You are an intern with the Parks and Recreation department for the city. They are planning to create T-shirts for their summer youth program. Your supervisor has provided a file with some individual graphics about activities in the park. You are to move and place the graphics to form the logo shown in Figure 2–75. He reminds you that the T-shirt manufacturer needs a PDF file.

Figure 2–75

Note: To complete this assignment, you will required to use the Data Files for Students. Visit www.cengage.com/ct/studentdownload for detailed instructions or contact your instructor for information about accessing the required files.

Instructions: Perform the following tasks:

1. Start Photoshop. Set the default workspace, and reset all tools and colors.

2. Press CTRL+O to open the Lab 2-1 Park T-shirt file from the Chapter 02 folder of the Data Files for Students, or from a location specified by your instructor.

3. Press SHIFT+CTRL+S to display the Save As dialog box. Save the file on your storage device with the name, Lab 2-1 Park T-shirt Edited.

4. If the photo does not appear at 25% magnification, press CTRL+PLUS SIGN (+) or CTRL+HYPHEN (-) to zoom in or out as necessary.

5. Drag from the horizontal ruler to create a guide at 3.25 inches, which you will use to align the graphics.

6. To select and move the kite:

   a. Press SHIFT+L until the Polygonal Lasso Tool is selected.

   b. On the options bar, click the New selection button, if necessary.

Continued >

c. Click a corner of the kite to start the selection. Continue clicking corners to create straight line segments around the kite. When you are finished, double-click to finish the selection.

d. On the Select menu, click Grow to expand the selection slightly.

e. Press the v key to access the Move Tool. Drag the kite to a location in front of the red circle, snapping the bottom of the kite to the ruler guide. It is OK to leave behind a slight shadow, as the logo will be cropped later in the steps.

f. Press CTRL+D to deselect.

7. To select and move the bat:

a. Press SHIFT+L until the Lasso Tool is selected.

b. On the options bar, click the New selection button, if necessary.

c. Drag to create a selection around the bat.

d. Press SHIFT+W until the Magic Wand Tool is selected.

e. ALT+click the white area around the bat, within the selection. Recall that pressing the ALT key while clicking activates the 'Subtract from selection' button on the options bar; the mouse pointer displays a minus sign.

f. Press the v key to access the Move Tool. Drag the bat to a location in front of the kite, as shown in Figure 2–75 on the previous page, snapping the bottom of the bat to the ruler guide.

g. Press CTRL+D to deselect.

8. To select and move the ball:

a. Press SHIFT+M until the Elliptical Marquee Tool is selected.

b. On the options bar, click the New selection button, if necessary.

c. SHIFT+drag to create a circular selection around the ball. Avoid including any white space around the ball. If necessary, press the SPACEBAR key while dragging to position the selection marquee.

d. Press the v key to access the Move Tool. Drag the ball to a location in front of the kite as shown in Figure 2–75, snapping the ball to the ruler guide.

e. If you make a mistake while selecting or moving the ball, click the History button on the vertical dock of panels to display the History panel. Click a previous state and begin to select or move again.

f. Press CTRL+D to deselect.

9. To select and move the remote control airplane:

a. Press the z key to activate the Zoom Tool, and then click the airplane several times to zoom in.

b. Press SHIFT+L until the Magnetic Lasso Tool is selected.

c. On the options bar, click the New selection button, if necessary.

d. Click a corner of the airplane. Slowly move the mouse pointer around the airplane, creating fasteners along the edge. Click at each corner to create an extra fastener. When you get close to the beginning fastener, move your mouse pointer until a small circle appears, and then click to complete the lasso.

e. On the options bar, click the Refine Edge button to display the Refine Edge dialog box. Drag the Shift Edge slider to 75%, and then click the OK button to close the dialog box.

    f. Press the z key and then ALT+click to zoom out as necessary. Scroll to display the red circle and the remote control airplane.

    g. Press the v key to access the Move Tool. Drag the airplane to a location in front of the kite as shown in Figure 2–75 on page PS 125.

    h. Deselect.

10. To select and move the tennis racquet:

    a. Press CTRL+PLUS SIGN (+) several times to zoom in on the racquet, scrolling as necessary.

    b. Press SHIFT+W until the Quick Selection Tool is selected.

    c. On the options bar, click the New selection button, if necessary.

    d. Slowly drag from the handle, upward, to create a selection around the racquet. If you make a mistake, deselect and begin again.

    e. Press SHIFT+W until the Magic Wand Tool is selected. On the options bar, select the value in the Tolerance box and then type 10 to replace it. If necessary, click to remove the check mark in the Contiguous check box.

    f. ALT+click a white area within the selection. Be careful not to click the strings of the racquet.

    g. Press CTRL+ HYPHEN (–) to zoom out as necessary.

    h. Press the v key to access the Move Tool. Drag the racquet to a location in front of the kite as shown in Figure 2–75, snapping the bottom of the racquet to the ruler guide.

    i. Deselect.

11. Press CTRL+S to save the file with the same name. If Photoshop displays a Photoshop Format Options dialog box, click the OK button.

12. To crop:

    a. Press SHIFT+M until the Rectangular Marquee Tool is selected.

    b. SHIFT+drag around the red circle to create a square selection.

    c. Press the c key to crop. On the options bar, if necessary, click the Delete Cropped Pixels check box so it displays a check mark. Press the ENTER key twice to crop the selection.

13. To create the PDF file:

    a. Press SHIFT+CTRL+S to open the Save as dialog box.

    b. Click the Format button to display the various formats.

    c. Click Photoshop PDF (*.PDF;*.PDP) in the list to select the PDF format, and then click the Save button to continue the saving process, saving the file with the same name.

    d. When Photoshop displays a dialog box, click the OK button to display the Save Adobe PDF dialog box. Click the Save PDF button to continue the saving process.

    e. When Photoshop displays the Save Adobe PDF dialog box, click the Yes button to finish saving.

14. Quit Photoshop by pressing CTRL+Q.

15. Send the PDF file as an e-mail attachment to your instructor, or submit it in the format specified by your instructor.

Continued >

In the Lab

Lab 2: Creating a Graphic from Back to Front

Problem: A local author has asked for your help in creating a book cover graphic about clock collecting. He has several photos of clocks that he wants placed in specific locations and in varied sizes. The final graphic is shown in Figure 2–76.

Note: To complete this assignment, you will required to use the Data Files for Students. Visit www. cengage.com/ct/studentdownload for detailed instructions or contact your instructor for information about accessing the required files.

Figure 2–76

Instructions: Perform the following tasks:

1. Start Photoshop. Set the default workspace and reset all tools.

2. Open the file, Lab 2-2 Clocks, from the Chapter 02 folder of the Data Files for Students, or from a location specified by your instructor.

3. Use the Save As command to save the file on your storage device with the name Lab 2-2 Clocks Edited.

4. To select and transform the round clock:

   a. Use the Elliptical Marquee Tool to select the round clock (the lower-right clock). If necessary, use the Magic Wand Tool and the Subtract from selection button to remove any white from around the edge of the clock.

   b. Use the Move Tool to move it to a location in the center of the white area.

c. Show the transform controls and enlarge the selection approximately 500 percent as shown on the options bar. Do not let it overlap any of the other clocks. Drag a side handle to make the clock more round. When you are satisfied with the clock's appearance, deselect it.

5. To select and transform the mantle clock:

a. Use the Lasso Tool to select the mantle clock (the lower-left clock). Use the Magic Wand Tool and the 'Subtract from selection' button to remove the white areas from around the selection. Grow the selection to avoid leaving a shadow.

b. Use the Move Tool to move the mantle clock to a location just below the round clock face and slightly to the left.

c. Display the transform controls and enlarge the selection to match Figure 2–76.

6. To select and resize the grandfather clock:

a. Use the Rectangular Marquee Tool to select the grandfather clock. Use the Magic Wand Tool and the 'Subtract from selection' button to remove the white areas from around the selection.

b. Use the Move Tool to move the grandfather clock to a location in front of and on the right side of the round clock face.

c. Display the transform controls and enlarge the selection to match Figure 2–76. Notice that the clock is not perfectly straight. Move the mouse pointer to a location just outside the selection. When the mouse pointer changes to a curved double-arrow, drag to rotate the clock slightly to make it look like it is standing on a flat surface. (*Hint:* Turning on the grid display will help align the clock.) When you are satisfied with the transformation, deselect it.

7. To select and transform the wall clock:

a. Use the Lasso Tool to select the wall clock. Use the Magic Wand Tool and the 'Subtract from selection' button to remove any white from around the edge of the clock.

b. Use the Move Tool to move it to a location in the upper-left corner of the scene, as shown in Figure 2–76.

c. Display the bounding box and enlarge the selection, and then deselect it.

8. Save the file and then submit the document, shown in Figure 2–76, in the format specified by your instructor.

In the Lab

Lab 3: Creating a Money Graphic

Problem: Your local bank is starting an initiative to encourage children to open a savings account using their loose change. The bank would like a before and after picture showing how money can grow with interest.

Note: To complete this assignment, you will required to use the Data Files for Students. Visit www.cengage.com/ct/studentdownload for detailed instructions or contact your instructor for information about accessing the required files.

Instructions: Perform the following tasks:

1. Start Photoshop. Set the default workspace and reset all tools.

2. Open the file, Lab 2-3 Coins, from the Chapter 02 folder of the Data Files for Students, or from a location specified by your instructor.

3. Use the Save As command to save the file on your storage device with the name Lab 2-3 Coins Edited.

4. Use the Elliptical Marquee Tool to select the quarter. (*Hint:* While dragging, if your selection marquee does not match the quarter exactly, press and hold the SPACEBAR key to move the selection.) Once the quarter is selected, ALT+drag to create several duplicate copies. As you create the duplicates, display the transform controls on the options bar, and then right-click the selection to display the context menu. Use the context menu commands to distort, rotate 90° CW, and apply perspective.

5. Use the Magnetic Lasso tool to select the dime. ALT+drag to create several duplicate copies. As you create the duplicates, use the transform control sizing handle to move, scale, and drag a corner to create a slight distortion.

6. Use the Quick Selection Tool to select the nickel. ALT+drag to create several duplicate copies. As you create the duplicates, use the transform controls to change some of the copies.

7. Use the Magic Wand Tool to select the penny. Create several copies. Your document should resemble Figure 2–77.

8. Save the file again, and submit it in the format specified by your instructor.

Figure 2–77

Cases and Places

Apply your creative thinking and problem-solving skills to design and implement a solution.

Note: To complete this assignment, you will required to use the Data Files for Students. Visit www.cengage.com/ct/studentdownload for detailed instructions or contact your instructor for information about accessing the required files.

1: Design a Poster for the Computer Lab

Academic

The computer lab at your school wants a poster reminding students to save their work often. The department chair has asked you to create a graphic of a computer mouse that seems to be eating data. He has taken a picture of a mouse from the lab and started the poster for you. A file named Case 2-1 Poster is located in the Chapter 02 folder of the Data Files for Students. Start Photoshop and use the selection tools to select the mouse. Flip the mouse horizontally. Then, using the Subtract from selection button, remove the white part around the selection. Also, remove the dark gray bottom portion of the mouse from the selection. With the top portion of the mouse selected, warp the selection up and away from the bottom part of the mouse to simulate an open mouth. Move the selection close to the 0 and 1 data pattern. Save a copy of the poster as a PDF and send it as an e-mail attachment to your instructor.

2: Create a New Shortcut

Personal

You have decided to create a new keyboard shortcut to reset all tools, rather than having to move the mouse to the options bar, right-click, and then choose to reset all tools. Because other family members work on your computer system, you would like to save the new shortcut in a separate set for your personal use. You also would like to see a complete listing of the Photoshop shortcuts for your system. Access the Keyboard Shortcuts and Menus dialog box. Click the Shortcuts For box arrow, and then click Panel Menus in the list. Scroll down and double-click Tool Presets, and then click Reset All Tools in the list. Enter the shortcut, CTRL+SLASH (/). Click the 'Create a new set based on the current set of shortcuts' button, and save the shortcuts with your name. Click the Summarize button and save the summary as My Shortcut Summary. When the summary displays in the browser, print a copy for your records.

3: Create a Grocery Store Flyer

Professional

You have been hired to create an advertisement for a grocery store flyer about citrus fruits that are on sale. Search the Web for samples of fruit displays, noting the ones that look most appealing. A file named Case 2-3 Fruits is located in the Chapter 02 folder of the Data Files for Students. Start Photoshop and reset the workspace, tools, and colors. Use selection tools to select the various fruits and move them into an attractive display. Create duplicates of fruits and resize the copies as necessary. Keep in mind the horizon line and perspective.

3 | Working with Layers

Adobe product screenshots reprinted with permission from Adobe Systems Incorporated

Objectives

You will have mastered the material in this chapter when you can:

- Use the Layers panel and change options

- Create a layer via cut

- Rename layers and set identification colors

- Hide, view, and rearrange layers

- Arrange and consolidate document windows

- Create a new layer from another image or selection

- Transform selections and layers

- Use the Eraser, Magic Eraser, and Background Eraser Tools

- Create layer masks

- Make level adjustments and opacity changes

- Apply adjustments using the Adjustments panel

- Add a layer style

- Use the Clone Stamp Tool

- Flatten a composite image

3 | Working with Layers

Introduction

Whether it is adding a new person to a photograph, combining artistic effects from different genres, or creating 3D animation, the concept of layers in Photoshop allows you to work on one element of an image without disturbing the others. You might think of layers as sheets of clear film stacked one on top of another. You can see through transparent areas of a layer to the layers below. The nontransparent, or opaque, areas of a layer are solid and obscure the content of the layers beneath. You can change the composition of an image by changing the order and attributes of layers. In addition, special features, such as adjustment layers, layer masks, fill layers, and layer styles, allow you to create sophisticated effects.

Another tool that graphic designers use when they want to recreate a portion of another photo is the Clone Stamp Tool. As you will learn in this chapter, the Clone Stamp Tool takes a sample of an image and then applies, as you draw, an exact copy of that image to your document.

Graphic designers use layers and clones, along with other tools in Photoshop, to create **composite** images that combine or merge multiple images and drawings to create a new image, also referred to as a **montage**. Composite images illustrate the power of Photoshop to prepare documents for businesses, advertising, marketing, and media artwork. Composite images such as navigation bars can be created in Photoshop and used on the Web along with layered buttons, graphics, and background images.

Project — Room Furnishing

Chapter 3 uses Photoshop to create a composite image from several photographs by using layers. Specifically, it begins with a photo of an empty room and creates a composite image by inserting layers of furniture, a plant, a painting, and other decorative pieces to create a complete room design (Figure 3–1). The enhancements will show how the room will look when furnished. Wood flooring will replace the carpeting; a sofa, lamp, table, and other decorations will be added. Finally, adjustment layers will give the room eye appeal.

(a) Original image

(b) Edited image

Figure 3–1

Overview

As you read this chapter, you will learn how to create the composite room shown in Figure 3–1b by performing these general tasks:

- Create a layer via cut.
- Insert layers from new images.
- Use the eraser tools.
- Add a layer mask.
- Create layer adjustments and apply layer styles.
- Clone an image.
- Flatten the image.
- Save the photo with and without layers format.

**Plan
Ahead**

General Project Guidelines

When editing a photo, the actions you perform and decisions you make will affect the appearance and characteristics of the finished product. As you edit a photo, such as the one shown in Figure 3–1 on the previous page, you should follow these general guidelines:

1. **Gather your photos and plan your layers.** The graphics you choose should convey the overall message of your composite image. Choose high-quality photos with similar lighting characteristics. Create an ordered list of the layers you plan to include. Select images that are consistent with the visual effect you want to achieve as well as with customer requirements.

2. **Evaluate the best way to move outside images into the composite.** Sometimes it is easier to create a selection first and move the selection into the composite image as a layer. Other times, you may want to bring in the entire image and then erase or mask portions of the image. Once the layer exists, choose the correct tool for making edits and erasures.

3. **Create layer adjustments.** Fine-tune your layers by creating layer adjustments. Look at each layer and evaluate how it fits into the background scene. Experiment with different adjustment tools until the layer looks just right. Decide whether to use destructive or nondestructive edits. Keep in mind the standard tonal dimensions of brightness, saturation, and hue.

4. **Edit layer styles.** Add variety to your layers by including layer styles such as shadow, glow, emboss, bevel, overlay, and stroke. Make sure the layer style does not overwhelm the overall image or detract from previous layer adjustments.

When necessary, more specific details concerning the above guidelines are presented at appropriate points in the chapter. The chapter also will identify the actions performed and decisions made regarding these guidelines during the creation of the edited photo shown in Figure 3–1.

Creating a Composite

Creating a composite with visual layers is a powerful effect. Photographers sometimes try to achieve this effect by using a sharp focus on objects in the foreground against an out-of-focus background. Others stage their photos with three layers of visual action. For example, at a baseball game, a person in the stands (foreground) may be observing a close call at first base (middle ground), while outfielders watch from afar (background). When those kinds of photographic techniques cannot be achieved, graphic artists use **composition techniques,** the layering of images and actions. Not only can you make realistic changes to parts of a photo, but you also can add additional images and control their placement, blending, and special effects. In addition, you can make changes to a layer, independent of the layer itself, which is extremely helpful in composite production.

Simple layers may incorporate new objects or new people. Layer effects create adjustments, add blending modes, or edit the coloring, fill, and opacity of the layer. Masks conceal or reveal part of a layer. All of the layering techniques are **nondestructive**, which means that no pixels are changed in the process; the effect is applied over the image or layer to create the change. Adding layers increases the file size of a Photoshop document, but that increase is justified by the value and flexibility layers provide. When you are finished working with layers, you can flatten the Photoshop document to reduce the file size. You will learn about flattening later in this chapter.

When an image duplication is required and layering a new copy does not achieve the required effect, some graphic artists **clone**, or reproduce, an image by painting a copy into the scene. As with masks, cloning allows you to control exactly how much of the image you want to use — even down to the smallest pixel. You also can use cloning to remove minor imperfections in a photo or to clone over intricate elements that do not fit into the picture.

The steps in this chapter create a composite image with layers, layer effects, adjustments, masks, and cloning.

To Start Photoshop

If you are stepping through this project on a computer and you want your screen to match the figures in this book, then you should change your computer's resolution to 1024×768 and reset the panels, tools, and colors. For more information about how to change the resolution on your computer, and other advanced Photoshop settings, read the Changing Screen Resolution appendix.

The following steps, which assume Windows 7 is running, start Photoshop based on a typical installation. You may need to ask your instructor how to start Photoshop for your system.

1 Click the Start button on the Windows 7 taskbar to display the Start menu, and then type `Photoshop CS6` in the 'Search programs and files' box.

2 Click Adobe Photoshop CS6 in the list to start Photoshop.

3 If the Photoshop window is not maximized, click the Maximize button next to the Close button on the Application bar to maximize the window.

To Reset the Workspace

As discussed in Chapter 1, it is helpful to reset the workspace so that the tools and panels appear in their default positions. The following steps select the Essentials workspace.

1 Click Window on the Application bar to display the Window menu and then point to Workspace to display the Workspace submenu.

2 Click Essentials (Default) on the Workspace submenu to select the default workspace panels.

3 Click Window on the Application bar, and then point to Workspace again to display the list.

4 Click Reset Essentials to restore the workspace to its default settings and reposition any panels that may have been moved.

To Reset the Tools and the Options Bar

Recall that the Tools panel and the options bar retain their settings from previous Photoshop sessions. The following steps select the Rectangular Marquee Tool and reset all tool settings in the options bar.

1 If the tools in the Tools panel appear in two columns, click the double arrow at the top of the Tools panel.

2 If necessary, click the Rectangular Marquee Tool button on the Tools panel to select it.

3 Right-click the Rectangular Marquee Tool icon on the options bar to display the context menu, and then click Reset All Tools. When Photoshop displays a confirmation dialog box, click the OK button to restore the tools to their default settings.

To Set the Interface and Default Colors

Recall that Photoshop retains the interface color scheme, as well as the foreground and background colors, from session to session. The following steps set the interface to Medium Gray and the foreground and background colors to black over white.

1 Click Edit on the Application bar to display the Edit menu. Point to Preferences and then click Interface on the Preferences submenu to display the Preferences dialog box.

2 Click the third button, Medium Gray, to change the interface color scheme.

3 Click the OK button to close the Preferences dialog box.

4 Press the D key to reset the default foreground and background colors.

To Open a File

To open a file in Photoshop, it must be stored as a digital file on your computer system or on an external storage device. The photos used in this book are stored in the Data Files for Students. Visit www.cengage.com/ct/studentdownload for detailed instructions or contact your instructor for information about accessing the required files.

The following steps open the Room file from the Data Files for Students.

1 With the Photoshop window open, click File on the Application bar, and then click Open to display the Open dialog box.

2 In the Open dialog box, click the Look in box arrow to display the list of available locations, and then navigate to the storage location of the Data Files for Students.

3 Double-click the Photoshop folder and then double-click the Chapter 03 folder to open it. Double-click the file, Room, to open it.

4 When Photoshop displays the image in the document window, if the magnification shown on the status bar is not 33.33%, double-click the magnification box on the document window status bar, type 33.33 and then press the ENTER key to change the magnification (Figure 3–2).

file name is displayed on document window tab

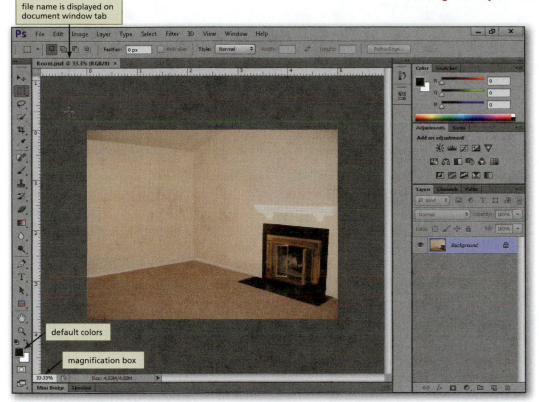

default colors

magnification box

Figure 3–2

To View Rulers

The following steps display the rulers in the document window to facilitate making precise measurements.

1 If the rulers are not shown on the top and left sides of the document window, press CTRL+R to display the rulers in the workspace.

2 If necessary, right-click the horizontal ruler and then click Inches on the context menu to display the rulers in inches.

To Save a Photo

Even though you have yet to edit the photo, it is a good practice to save the file on your personal storage device early in the process. The following steps save the photo with the name Room Edited in a new folder named Chapter 03.

1 With your USB flash drive connected to one of the computer's USB ports, click File on the Application bar to display the File menu and then click Save As to display the Save As dialog box.

2 In the File name text box, type `Room Edited` to rename the file. Do not press the ENTER key after typing the file name.

3 Click the Save in box arrow and then click Removable Disk (F:), or the location associated with your USB flash drive, in the list, if necessary.

BTW

Layer Comps
Graphic artists often create multiple versions, or compositions, of their work. A **layer comp** is a single view of the page layout with specific visible layers and attributes. You can use layer comps to demo versions of your composition to customers or colleagues, or simply to jump back and forth between different views and layers of your document. Similar to the History panel's snapshot, a layer comp takes a picture of the composite, using the Layers panel to show a particular stage of development.

④ On the Save As dialog box toolbar, click the Create New Folder button to create a new folder on the selected storage device.

⑤ When the new folder appears, type Chapter 03 to change the name of the folder, and then press the ENTER key. Double-click the new folder to open it.

⑥ Click the Save button in the Save As dialog box to save the file in the new folder.

Creating a Composite Image using Layers

Photoshop has many tools to help create composite images, photomontages, and collages. A composite, or composite image, is one that combines multiple photographs or images to display in a single combined file. Graphic artists use the newer term, **photomontage**, to refer to both the process and the result of creating a composite from photos.

Plan Ahead

> **Gather your photos and plan your layers.**
> One of the keys to successful image compositions is finding the best source material with similar lighting situations and tonal qualities. Choose high-quality photos and images that convey your overall message. Make sure you have permission to use the images if they are not original photographs taken by you or provided to you by a colleague or client. Obtain several versions of the same photo, if possible, including photos from different angles and with different lighting situations. Make two copies of each photo and store one as a backup. Crop unwanted portions of the photos before adding them as new layers.

BTW

Layer Comps vs. History Snapshots
Layer comps include the visibility, position, and appearance of layers, not the edited steps. In addition, layer comps are saved with the document, whereas History panel snapshots are not. You can export layer comps to separate graphic or PDF files for easy distribution.

BTW

Layer Comps Panel
The Layer Comps panel includes a status bar with buttons to move back and forth through the comps, to update comps from the current view, to create them, and to delete them. The Layer Comps menu has some of those same commands, as well as others to duplicate a layer comp and set its properties.

Layers

One of the most powerful tools in Photoshop is layering. A **layer** is a section within a Photoshop document that you can manipulate independently from the rest of the document. Layers can be stacked one on top of the other, resembling sheets of clear film, to form a composite image.

Layers have been used by business and industry for years. Cartoonists create layers of physical transparencies to help with animation. The medical field uses overlays to illustrate anatomical features. Virtual simulations use layers to display processes. With Photoshop, layers are easy to create and export for these kinds of applications.

Recall that you used selections in Chapter 2 to move, copy, and scale portions of a photo. Layers can perform all of the same functions performed by selecting, while providing added features. The most powerful feature of layers is the ability to revisit a portion of the image to make further changes, even after deselecting. Layers can be created, copied, deleted, displayed, hidden, merged, locked, grouped, repositioned, and flattened. Layers can be composed of images, patterns, text, shapes, colors, or filters. You can use layers to apply special effects, correct or colorize pictures, repair damaged photos, or import text elements. In previous chapters, you worked with images in a flat, single layer called the Background layer. In this chapter, you will create, name, and manipulate multiple layers on top of the Background layer.

Many layer manipulations are performed using the Layers panel, which lists all the layers, groups, and layer effects in an image (Figure 3–3). Each time you insert a layer onto an image, the new layer is added above the current layer, or to the top of the panel. The default display of a layer on the Layers panel includes a visibility

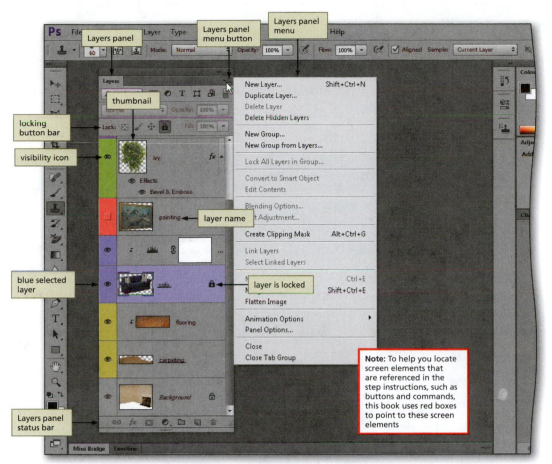

Figure 3–3

icon, a thumbnail of the layer, and the layer's name. To the right of the layer's name, a locking icon or other special effect notations might appear.

Photoshop allows you to **lock** three different components of layers. The 'Lock transparent pixels' button confines editing to opaque layer portions. The 'Lock image pixels' button prevents modification of the layer's pixels using paint tools. The Lock position button prevents the layer from being moved. The Lock all button enables all three ways of locking the layer. A lock icon appears to the right of the name on the Layers panel on locked layers.

The Layers panel is used in several different manners: to show and hide layers, create new layers, and work with groups of layers. You can access additional commands and attributes by clicking the Layers panel menu button or by right-clicking a layer. The Layers panel defines how layers interact. As you use the buttons and boxes on the Layers panel, each will be explained.

While Photoshop allows background editing, as you have done in previous chapters, the Background layer cannot be moved, nor can its transparency be changed. In other words, the Background layer fills the document window, and there is no layer behind the background. Partially locked by default, the Background layer displays a hollow lock (Figure 3–3). If you want to convert the Background layer into a fully editable layer, double-click the layer on the Layers panel, and then click the OK button in the New Layer dialog box.

When working with layers, it is important to make sure you know which layer you are editing by looking at the active layer on the Layers panel or by looking at the layer name, appended to the file name on the document window tab. Many other layer commands appear on the Layer menu, including those for making adjustments to the layer, creating layer masks, grouping layers, and other editing and placement commands.

To Change Layers Panel Options

The Panel Options command, accessible from the Layers panel menu, allows you to change the view and size of the thumbnail related to each layer. A thumbnail displays a small preview of the layer on the Layers panel. The Panel Options dialog box allows you to choose small, medium, large, or no thumbnails. The following steps select a medium-sized thumbnail of each layer.

1

- Click the Layers panel menu button to display the Layers panel menu (Figure 3–4).

Q&A Do I have to display thumbnails?

No, but displaying a thumbnail of each layer allows you to see easily what the layer looks like and helps you to be more efficient when editing a layer. To improve performance and save monitor space, however, some Photoshop users choose not to display thumbnails.

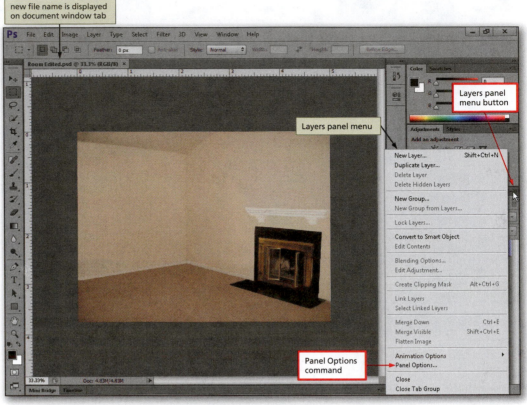

Figure 3–4

2

- Click Panel Options on the menu to display the Layers Panel Options dialog box.

- Click the medium thumbnail to select it.

- Click the Layer Bounds option button, if necessary, to change the look and feel of the Layers panel (Figure 3–5).

Q&A How does the Layer Bounds option change the interface?

The Layer Bounds option causes the Layers panel to display only the layer, restricting the thumbnail to the object's pixels on the layer.

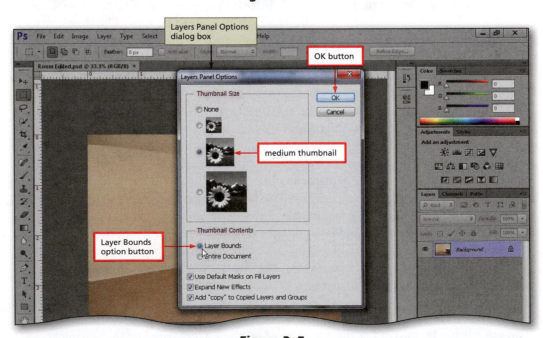

Figure 3–5

3

- Click the OK button to close the Layers Panel Options dialog box (Figure 3–6).

Q&A Should I see a difference on the Layers panel?

Yes. Unless a previous user had already changed it, the size of the thumbnail should have changed on the Layers panel. Layer bounds will not appear until you create a layer other than the Background layer.

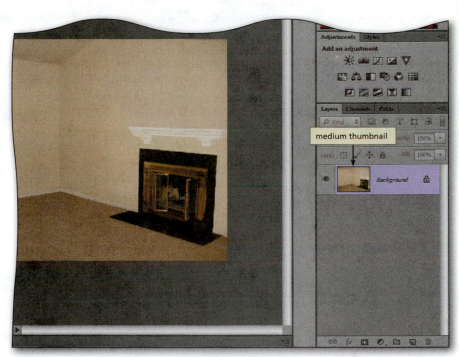

Figure 3–6

Creating a Layer via Cut

There are several ways to create a new layer. You can:

- Isolate a portion of the image and then cut or make a layer copy
- Create a new layer by copying from a different image
- Duplicate a layer that already exists
- Create a new, blank layer on which you can draw or create text

When you add a layer to an image, a new layer appears above, or on top of, the currently selected layer, creating a **stacking order**. By default, Photoshop names and numbers layers sequentially; however, you can rearrange the stacking order to change the appearance of the image. The final appearance of an edited Photoshop document is a view of the layer stack from the top down. In the document window, the layers at the top of the Layers panel appear in front of the layers at the bottom of the panel.

To Create a Layer via Cut

The steps on the next page create a new layer that includes only the carpeting on the floor. You will use the Quick Selection Tool to select the area and then use the Layer Via Cut command to isolate the floor from the rest of the photo, creating a new layer. You will manipulate the new layer, later in the chapter.

BTW

Deleting Layers
To delete a layer permanently, right-click the layer name and then click Delete Layer on the context menu, or activate the layer and press the DELETE key.

1

- On the Tools panel, select the Quick Selection Tool button. If the Magic Wand Tool is selected, press SHIFT+W to toggle to the Quick Selection Tool.

- If necessary, click the New selection button on the options bar to start a new selection.

- In the photo, drag slowly from the upper-left corner of the carpeting to the lower-right corner of the photo to select only the carpeting (Figure 3–7).

Q&A Why did Photoshop change to the 'Add to selection' button on the options bar?

Once you create a new selection, the most common task is to add more to the selection, so Photoshop selects that button automatically. If you want to start over, you can select the New selection button again.

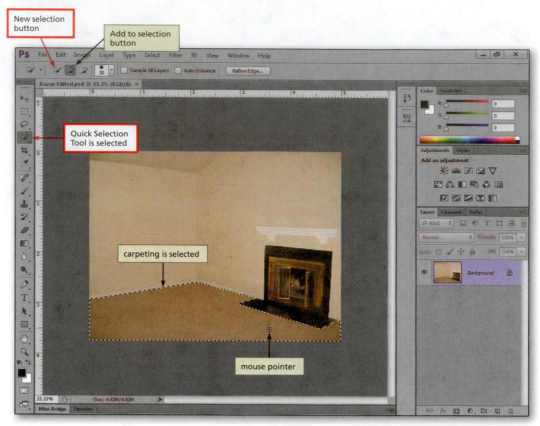

Figure 3–7

2

- Right-click the selection to display the context menu (Figure 3–8).

Q&A Could I use the New Layer command?

No. The New Layer command creates a blank layer.

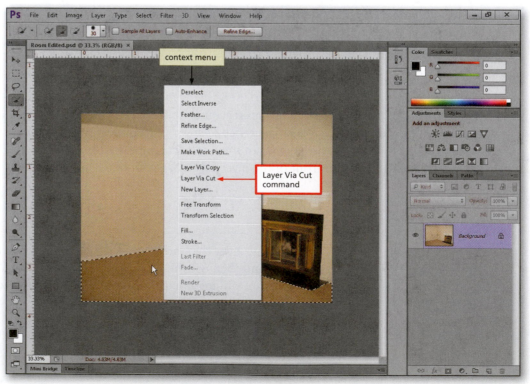

Figure 3–8

3

- Click Layer Via Cut on the context menu to create the new layer (Figure 3–9).

Q&A

What is the difference between Layer Via Cut and Layer Via Copy?

The Layer Via Cut command differs from the Layer Via Copy command in that it removes the selection from the background. Future edits to the Background, such as changing the color or lighting, will not affect the cut layer.

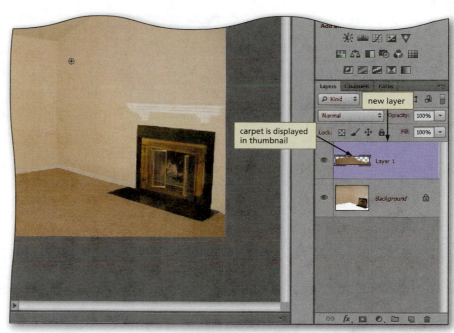

Figure 3–9

Other Ways
1. Create selection, on Layer menu, point to New, click Layer Via Cut   2. Create selection, press SHIFT+CTRL+J

To Rename a Layer

It is a good practice to give each layer a unique name so you can identify it more easily. The name of the active layer appears on the Layers panel and on the title bar of the document window. The following steps rename a layer.

1

- On the Layers panel, double-click the name of the layer you want to rename, in this case Layer 1 (Figure 3–10).

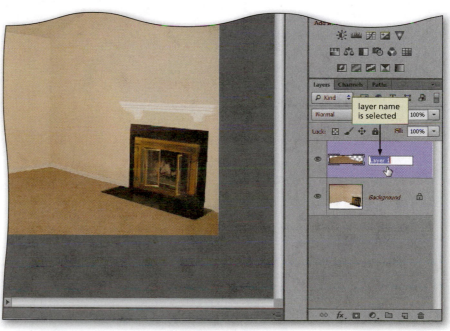

Figure 3–10

2

- Type carpeting to replace the current name of the layer, and then press the ENTER key to rename the layer (Figure 3–11).

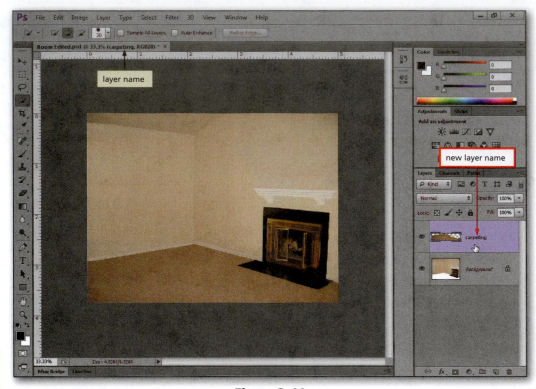

Other Ways

1. On Layer menu, click Rename Layer, enter new name, press ENTER key

Figure 3–11

To Assign a Color to a Layer

Photoshop allows you to give each layer its own color identification. Assigning a color helps you recognize relationships among layers. For example, if two of your layers display objects in the sky, you might assign those two layers a blue identification color so you quickly could see which layers were related to the sky. The color appears around the visibility icon on the left side of the layer. The following steps assign a color to a layer.

1

- Right-click the carpeting layer to display its context menu (Figure 3–12).

Q&A

Does it make any difference exactly where I right-click?

No. You can right-click anywhere on the layer. If you click the area around the visibility icon, Photoshop displays a shorter context menu with only color and hide/show options.

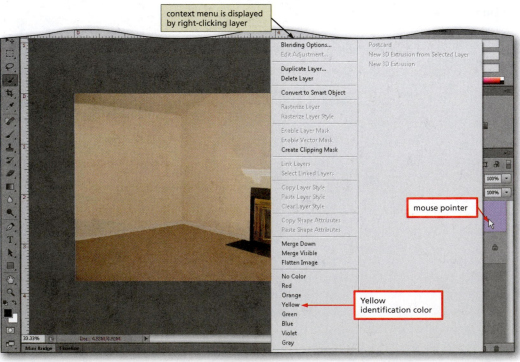

Figure 3–12

2

• Click Yellow in the list to choose a yellow identification color (Figure 3–13).

Figure 3–13

To Hide and Show a Layer

Sometimes you want to hide a layer to view other layers and make editing decisions. The visibility icon is a button that toggles the visibility of the layer on and off. The following steps hide and show the Background layer.

1

• Click the 'Indicates layer visibility' button to the left of the Background layer to hide the layer in the document window and hide the visibility icon (Figure 3–14).

Q&A

What is the checkerboard effect in the carpeting layer?

The checkerboard effect represents blank portions of the document window that are transparent.

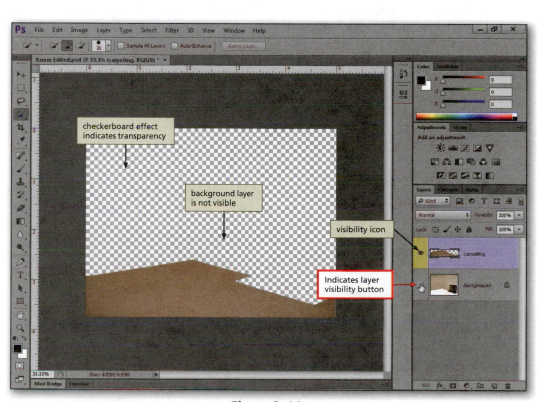

Figure 3–14

2

Q&A

- Click the 'Indicates layer visibility' button again to show the Background layer in the document window and display the visibility icon (Figure 3–15).

What is the white area on the Background layer thumbnail?

When you cut or delete from a locked layer, such as the Background layer, the default background color shows through; in this case, it is the default white color. Because other layers will eclipse the white, you do not have to remove it.

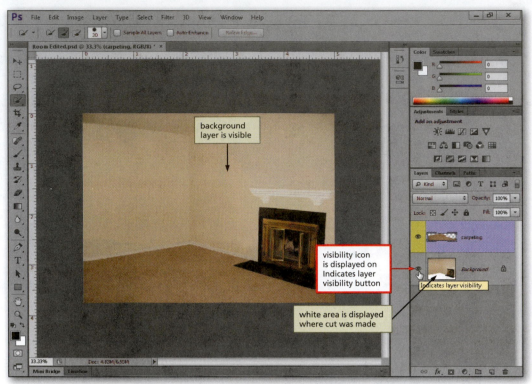

Figure 3–15

Other Ways

1. Right-click visibility icon, click Hide this layer or Show this layer
2. On Layer menu, click Hide Layers or Show Layers

BTW

Layer Selection
Sometimes a menu or panel will cover the Layers panel, or a layer might be scrolled out of sight. You always can identify which layer you are working with by looking at the document window tab. The name of the current layer appears in parentheses.

Creating a Layer from Another Image

When you create composite images, you might want to create layers from other images. It is important to choose images that closely match or complement color, lighting, size, and perspective if you want your image to look natural. While you can adjust disparate images to improve how well they match, it is easier to start with as close a match as possible, ideally with similar lighting situations and tonal qualities.

Many sources exist for composite images, and they come in many different file types and sizes. For example, you can use your own digital photos, scanned images, images from royalty-free Web sites, or you can draw your own. If you use a photo or image from the Web, make sure you have legal rights to use the image. Means of obtaining legal rights include getting permission from the photographer or artist to use the image or purchasing the rights, through a contract, from an online store.

Plan Ahead

Evaluate the best way to move outside images into the composite.
If the desired portion of the outside image is selected easily, such as a rectangle, oval or polygon, then select and copy it. Paste it in the composite image to create a layer. If the desired portion of the outside image is not easy to select, drag the entire image into the composite, creating a layer. Then, use eraser tools to eliminate the unwanted portion of the layer. That way, you have not changed the original image, should you need to return to it later.

The basic process of creating a new layer from another image involves opening a second image, selecting the area you want to use, and then moving it to the original photo in a drag-and-drop, or cut-and-paste, fashion. Once the layer exists in the destination photo, you might need to do some editing to remove portions of the layer, to resize it, or to make tonal adjustments.

To Open a Second Image

To add a sofa as a layer to the Room Edited image, you will need to open a new file, Sofa, from the Data Files for Students, or from a location specified by your instructor. The following steps open the Sofa file, which is stored in the PSD format.

1 Press CTRL+O to display the Open dialog box.

2 In the Open dialog box, if necessary, click the Look in box arrow, and then navigate to the Chapter 03 folder of the Data Files for Students or a location specified by your instructor.

3 Double-click the file named Sofa to open it (Figure 3–16).

BTW

Creating Layer Groups
Layer groups help you manage and organize layers in a logical manner. To create a layer group, click the Create New Group button on the Layers panel. A new layer will appear with a folder icon. You then can drag layers into the folder or use the Layers panel menu to insert a new layer. You can apply attributes and masks to the entire group.

Figure 3–16

Displaying Multiple Files

Photoshop offers many different ways to arrange and view document windows when more than one file is open. You also can create a custom workspace by moving and manipulating document windows manually.

For example, you might want to display two document windows, horizontally or vertically, in order to drag and drop from one image to another. You might want to compare different versions or views of photos beside each other in the document window. Or, when creating a panorama, you might want to preview how certain photos will look side by side.

When you are finished viewing multiple document windows in the workspace, you can **consolidate** them, or view only one window at a time.

BTW

2-Up vs. Tile
When you click Window on the Application bar, the Arrange submenu displays the 2-up Horizontal command, which arranges the more recently opened window on top. The Tile All Horizontally command puts the new window on the bottom.

To Arrange Document Windows

The following steps display the Room Edited and Sofa windows beside each other using the Arrange submenu on the Window menu.

1

- On the Application bar, click Window and then point to Arrange to display the Arrange submenu (Figure 3–17).

Q&A

Why are some of the arrangements grayed out?

Because you have only two document windows open, the only arrangements enabled are the ones that display two windows.

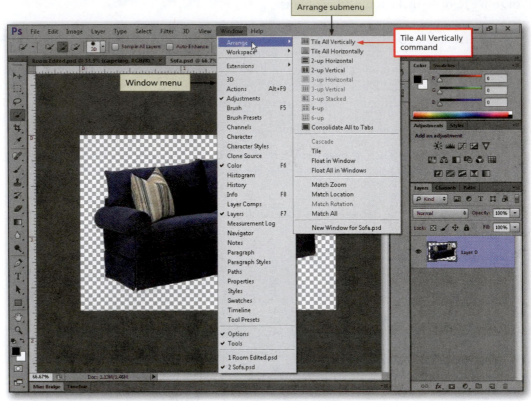

Figure 3–17

2

- Click Tile All Vertically in the submenu to display the windows beside each other (Figure 3–18).

Q&A

What is the difference between Tile All Vertically and 2-up Vertical?

When you have only two document windows open, there is no difference. If you have more than two document windows open, Tile All Vertically will open all the windows; 2-up Vertical will open only the two most recently used document windows.

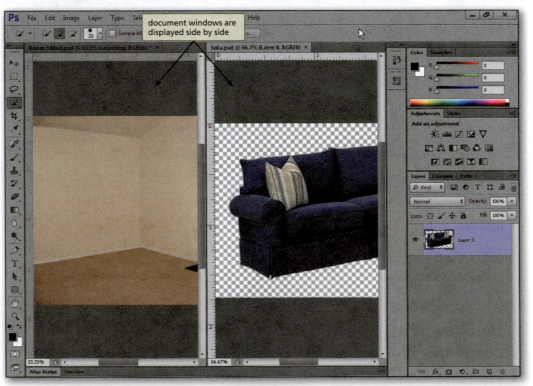

Figure 3–18

To Create a Layer by Dragging an Entire Image

When you drag a selection from one document window to the other, Photoshop creates a new layer in the destination document window, above the currently selected layer. If you want to include the entire image from the source window, use the Move Tool to drag from any location in the source window to the destination window. Dragging between document windows is an automatic duplication rather than a true move out of one window and into the other. The original, source image remains unchanged.

The following step moves the entire image from the source window, Sofa, to the destination window, Room Edited.

1

- Press the V key to activate the Move Tool.

- Drag the sofa image into the Room Edited window and drop it in the room (Figure 3–19).

Q&A Why is the sofa so much bigger in its own document window?

The sofa is the same size; the magnification of the windows is different.

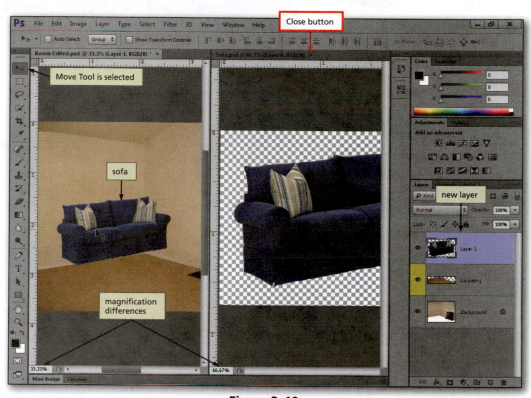

Figure 3–19

To Close the Sofa Document Window

Because you are finished with the Sofa image, the following step closes the Sofa window.

1 Click the Close button on the Sofa document window tab. If Photoshop asks you to save the file again, click the No button.

Other Ways

1. In source window, on Edit menu click Copy, in destination window on Edit menu click Paste

---

BTW

Consolidate Windows
Sometimes, after viewing multiple document windows, you might want to view only one window at a time. In that case, right-click the tab at the top of the Room Edited document window to display the context menu and then click Consolidate All to Here to view that document window alone. The Arrange submenu has a Consolidate All to Tabs command that has the same effect.

To Move a Layer in the Document Window

If there is no marquee selection, the Move Tool moves the entire current layer when you drag. The following step moves the sofa to a new location.

1

- With the new layer still selected on the Layers panel, and the Move Tool still selected on the Tools panel, drag the sofa to a position along the left wall, on the floor (Figure 3–20).

Q&A

Is it acceptable for some of the sofa to disappear off the edge of the document window?

Yes. Your goal is to make it look as natural as possible, as if it is sitting on the floor.

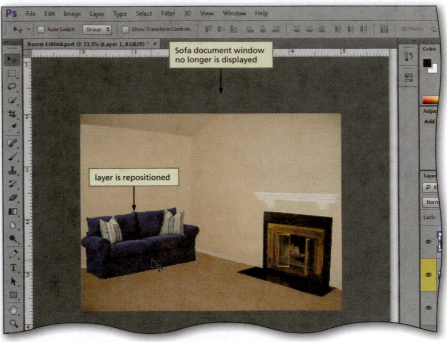

Figure 3–20

To Name and Color the Sofa Layer

The following steps rename the new layer and assign it a color.

1 On the Layers panel, double-click the name of the layer, Layer 1. Type `sofa` and then press the ENTER key to name the layer.

2 Right-click the layer to display the context menu, and then click Blue in the list to choose a blue identification color (Figure 3–21).

BTW

Layer Boundaries
The settings you chose in the Layer Panel Options dialog box appear in Figure 3-21. Only the portion of the layer that contains an image is displayed in the medium-sized thumbnails because of the Layer Bounds setting.

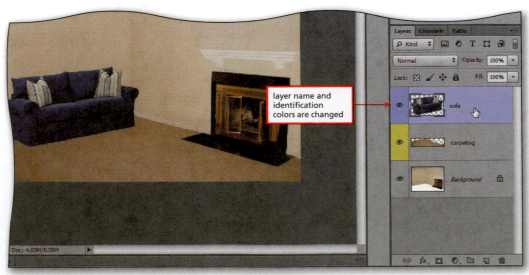

Figure 3–21

To Save the File

Because you have created layers and made changes to the image, it is a good idea to save the file again. The following step saves the file again.

1 Press CTRL+S to save the Room Edited file with the same name. If Photoshop displays a dialog box about compatibility, click the OK button.

Break Point: If you wish to stop working through the chapter at this point, you can quit Photoshop now and then resume the project at a later time by starting Photoshop, opening the file named Room Edited and continuing to follow the steps from this location forward.

Creating a Layer by Dragging a Selection

Sometimes you do not want to move an entire image from one window to another. When you want to move only a part of an image, you create a selection, as you learned in Chapter 2 and then move the selection to the destination window. Once the selection exists in the destination window, you might need to do some editing, such as scaling, erasing, or adjusting.

To Open the Painting Image

The following steps open a file named Painting.

1 Press CTRL+O to display the Open dialog box.

2 Click the Look in box arrow, and then navigate to the Chapter 03 folder of the Data Files for Students, or a location specified by your instructor.

3 Double-click the file named Painting to open it.

To Select the Painting

When adding the painting image to the Room Edited image, you will not need the surrounding wall. The following steps select the painting using the Rectangular Marquee Tool.

1 If necessary, right-click the current marquee tool and then click Rectangular Marquee Tool on the context menu to select it.

2 If necessary, click the New selection button on the options bar to start a new selection.

3 Drag around the painting, including the gold frame and matte. Avoid including the wall in the selection. If you make a mistake while selecting, press the ESC key and then begin again (Figure 3–22 on the next page).

BTW

Smart Objects
You can convert a layer into a smart object, which is a nondestructive layer that does not change the original pixels. Smart Objects are useful for warping, scaling, or rotating both raster and vector graphic layers. To convert a layer into a smart object, right-click the layer, and then click Convert to Smart Object on the context menu.

BTW

JPG File Type
The Painting image is stored as JPG file. Recall that JPG stands for Joint Photographic Experts Group and is the file type typically generated by digital cameras. JPG format supports many different color modes. JPG retains all color information in an RGB image, unlike GIF format.

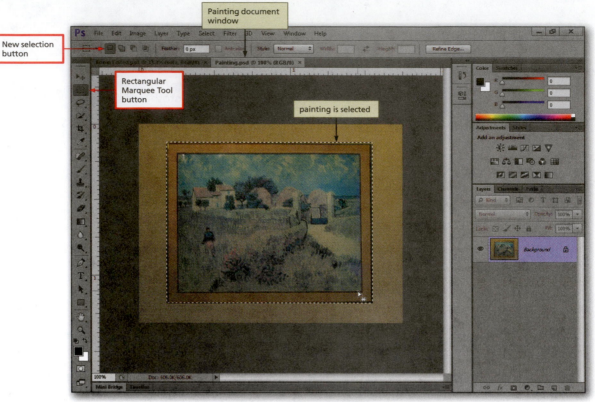

Figure 3–22

To Create a Layer by Dragging a Selection

The following steps move the selection. To facilitate dragging the selection between windows, you will view the windows above and below one another.

1

• On the Application bar, click Window, point to Arrange to display the submenu and click the Tile All Horizontally command to display the windows above and below one another (Figure 3–23).

 Experiment

• Open a third file and then try some of the other configurations on the Arrange submenu. When you are done, close the third file. Repeat Step 1.

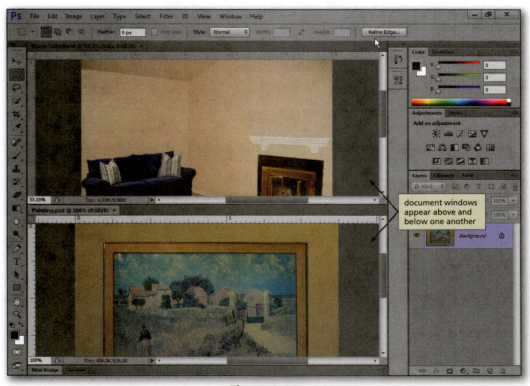

Figure 3–23

2

- Press the v key to activate the Move Tool.

- Drag the selection and drop it in the Room Edited window (Figure 3–24).

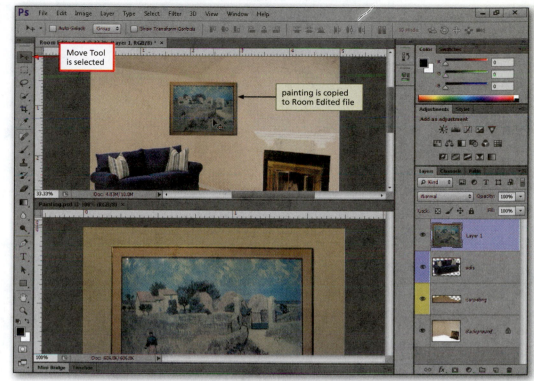

Figure 3–24

Other Ways

1. In source window, create selection, on Edit menu, click Copy, in destination window, on Edit menu, click Paste

To Close the Painting Window

The next step closes the Painting window.

1 Click the Close button on the Painting document window tab. If Photoshop displays a dialog box asking if you want to save the changes, click the No button.

To Name and Assign a Color to the Painting Layer

The following steps rename the new layer and assign an identification color.

1 Double-click the name, Layer 1, on the Layers panel and then type `painting` and press the ENTER key to rename the layer.

2 Right-click the layer and then click Red to assign an identification color.

To Position the Painting Layer

The following steps move the painting to a location above the sofa.

1 Press the v key to active the Move Tool, if necessary.

2 Drag the painting to a location above the sofa, as shown in Figure 3–25 on the next page.

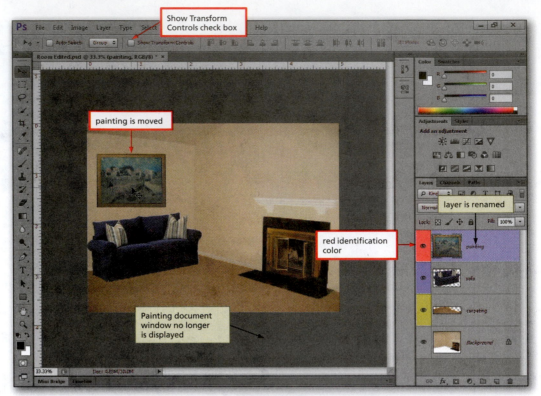

Figure 3–25

The Transformation Commands

In Photoshop, the word **transform** refers to changing the appearance of a selection by altering its shape, size, or other physical characteristics. To choose a transformation command, click the Edit menu, point to Transform, and then click the desired transformation. Alternatively, you can click Transform Selection on the context menu that is displayed when you right-click a selection.

Table 3–1 lists the types of transformations you can perform on a selection, the techniques used to perform a particular transformation, and the result of the transformation. Many of the commands also appear on the context menu when you right-click the bounding box. If you choose free transform, you must use the mouse techniques to perform the transformation.

Table 3–1 Transformation Commands

Using the Menu	Using the Mouse (Free Transform)	Using the Transform Options Bar	Result
Scale	Drag a sizing handle on the bounding box. SHIFT+drag to scale proportionately. ALT+drag to scale opposite sides at the same time.	To scale numerically, enter percentages in the Width and Height boxes, shown as W and H, on the options bar. Click the Link icon to maintain the aspect ratio.	Selection is displayed at a different size.
Rotate 180° Rotate 90° CW Rotate 90° CCW (CW stands for clockwise. CCW stands for counterclockwise.)	Move the mouse pointer outside the bounding box border. It becomes a curved, two-headed arrow. Drag in the direction you want to rotate. SHIFT+drag to constrain the rotation to 15° increments.	In the Set Rotation box, shown as a compass on the options bar, type a positive number for clockwise rotation or a negative number for counterclockwise rotation.	Selection is rotated or revolved around the reference point.

Table 3–1 Transformation Commands *(continued)*

Using the Menu	Using the Mouse (Free Transform)	Using the Transform Options Bar	Result
Skew	Right-click selection and then click Skew. Drag a side of the bounding box. ALT+drag to skew both vertically and horizontally.	To skew numerically, enter decimal values in the horizontal skew and vertical skew boxes, shown as H and V on the options bar.	Selection is tilted or slanted either horizontally or vertically.
Distort	Right-click selection and then click Distort. Drag a corner sizing handle to stretch the bounding box.	Enter new numbers in the location, size, rotation, and skew boxes.	Selection is larger on one edge than on the others.
Perspective	Right-click selection and then click Perspective. Drag a corner sizing handle to apply perspective to the bounding box.	Enter new numbers in the size, rotation, and skew boxes.	The selection appears larger on one edge than on the others, giving the larger edge the appearance of being closer to the viewer.
Warp	When the warp mesh is displayed, drag any line or point.	Click the Custom box arrow. Click a custom warp.	Selection is reshaped with a bulge, arch, warped corner, or twist.
Flip Horizontal Flip Vertical	Flipping is available only on the menu.	Flipping is available only on the menu.	Selection is turned upside down or mirrored.

Figure 3–26 displays a painting in its original state and with various transformation effects applied (Figure 3–26).

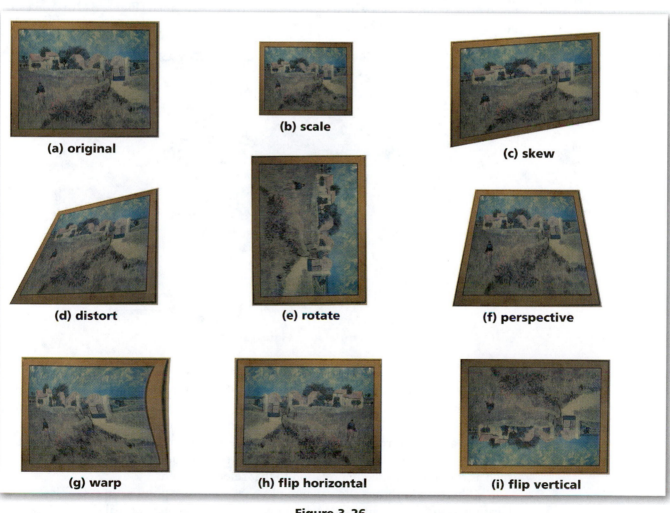

(a) original   **(b) scale**   **(c) skew**

(d) distort   **(e) rotate**   **(f) perspective**

(g) warp   **(h) flip horizontal**   **(i) flip vertical**

Figure 3–26

Transform is not a tool on the Tools panel; however, Photoshop displays a Transform options bar that contains boxes and buttons to help you with your transformation (Figure 3–27). To display the Transform options bar, create a selection and then do one of the following things: click Free Transform on the Edit menu, click a sizing handle, or press CTRL+T. Recall that if you are using the Move Tool, you also can click the Show Transform Controls check box. As you start to transform, Photoshop displays the Transform options bar.

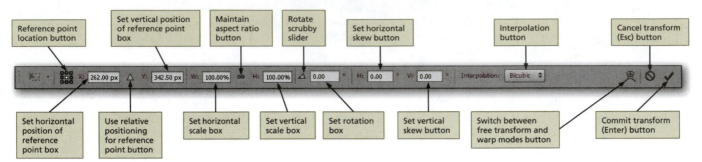

Reference point location button · Set vertical position of reference point box · Maintain aspect ratio button · Rotate scrubby slider · Set horizontal skew button · Interpolation button · Cancel transform (Esc) button

Set horizontal position of reference point box · Use relative positioning for reference point button · Set horizontal scale box · Set vertical scale box · Set rotation box · Set vertical skew button · Switch between free transform and warp modes button · Commit transform (Enter) button

Figure 3–27

BTW

Rotating
When the bounding box is displayed, you can rotate the selection by dragging just outside of the corner. The mouse pointer changes to a double-headed, curved arrow as shown in Figure 3-28.

When you choose to transform, Photoshop displays a **bounding box**, or border with eight sizing handles around the selection. A small reference point appears in the center of the selection as a small circle with a crosshair symbol. A **reference point** is a fixed pivot point around which transformations are performed (Figure 3–28). You can move a reference point by dragging it.

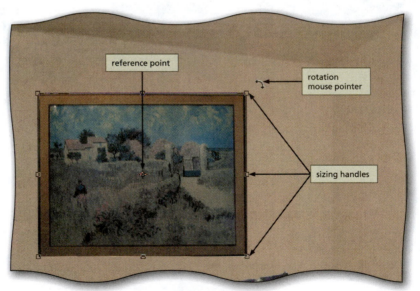

reference point · rotation mouse pointer · sizing handles

Figure 3–28

On the left side of the Transform options bar, Photoshop displays the 'Reference point location' button. Each of the nine squares on the button corresponds to a point on the bounding box. The default middle square represents the center reference point. To select a different reference point, click a different square on the 'Reference point location' button. By selecting one of the nine preset locations, any transformation, such as rotating, is applied in relation to that reference point.

The X and Y boxes allow you to place the reference point at an exact pixel location in the document window by entering horizontal and vertical values. When you enter a value in one of those boxes, Photoshop moves the entire selection. If you click the 'Use relative positioning for reference point' button, located between the X and Y boxes, the movement of the selection is relative to the current location.

The W and H boxes allow you to scale the width and height of the selection. When you click the 'Maintain aspect ratio' button between the W and H boxes, the aspect ratio of the selection is maintained.

To the right of the scale boxes is a Set rotation box. Entering a positive number rotates, or turns, the selection clockwise; a negative number rotates the selection counterclockwise.

The H and V boxes, to the right of the Set rotation box, set the horizontal and vertical skews of the selection, measured in degrees. A positive number skews the selection to the right; a negative number skews it to the left.

A unique feature is the ability to drag labels to change the box values. For example, if you drag the H, Y, W, or other labels, the values in the text boxes change. The interactive labels, called **scrubby sliders,** appear when you position the mouse pointer over the label. When you point to any of the scrubby sliders on the Transform options bar, the mouse pointer changes to a hand with a double-headed arrow, indicating the ability to drag. Dragging to the right increases the value; dragging to the left decreases the value. Holding the SHIFT key while dragging the scrubby slider accelerates the change by a factor of 10. Many options bars use scrubby sliders.

On the far right of the Transform options bar are three buttons. The first one switches between the Transform options bar and the Warp options bar. After you are finished making transformations, you commit changes, or apply the transformations by pressing the ENTER key or by clicking the Commit transform (Enter) button. **Committing** the transformation is the same as saving it. If you do not want to make the transformation, press the ESC key or click the Cancel transform (Esc) button.

After transforming a selection, you either must commit or cancel the transformation before you can perform any other action in Photoshop.

To Transform by Skewing

The following steps display the transformation controls and make the painting appear more natural in the setting by skewing the layer.

1

- Press CTRL+T to display the bounding box and the Transform options bar (Figure 3–29).

Q&A

Should I make a selection before pressing CTRL+T?

In this case, you are transforming the entire layer, so no selection is necessary. Photoshop displays the bounding box around the edges of the layer itself.

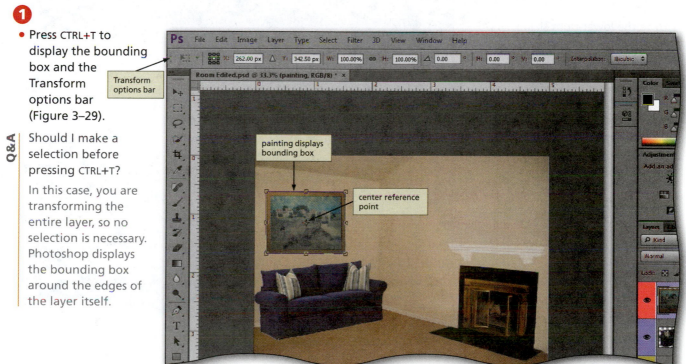

Figure 3–29

2

- Right-click the selection to display the context menu with the list of transformations (Figure 3–30).

Q&A

When should I use skew rather than perspective?

You should use skew when the selection or layer is titled or slanted either horizontally or vertically. Use perspective when you want the selection or layer to appear closer or further away in the setting.

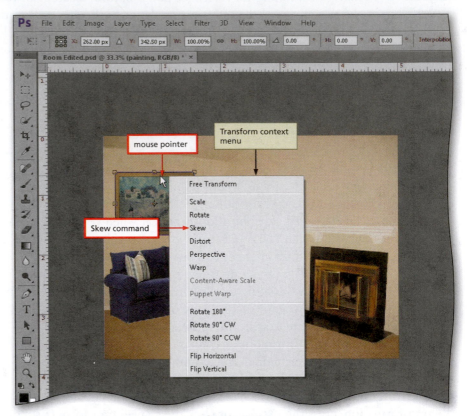

Figure 3–30

3

- Click Skew on the context menu to activate skewing.

- Drag the upper-left sizing handle up until the top of the painting is parallel with the top of the wall.

- Drag the lower-right sizing handle up until the bottom of the painting is parallel with the top of the sofa (Figure 3–31).

4

- Press the ENTER key to commit the transformation.

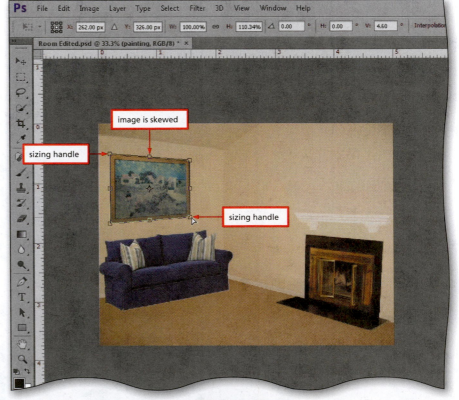

Other Ways

1. On Edit menu, point to Transform, click Skew, drag bounding box sizing handle

Figure 3–31

To Open the Coffee Table Image

The following step opens a file named Coffee Table in preparation for the next series of steps.

1 Open the Coffee Table file from the Chapter 03 folder of the Data Files for Students, or a location specified by your instructor.

To Create the Coffee Table Layer

The following steps create the coffee table layer.

1 On the Application bar, click Window, point to Arrange, and then click Tile All Horizontally to display the windows above and below one another.

2 With the Coffee Table window still active, click the Move Tool button on the Tools panel, if necessary.

3 Drag the entire coffee table image and drop it in the Room Edited window (Figure 3–32).

4 Close the Coffee Table document window. If Photoshop displays a dialog box asking if you want to save the changes, click the No button.

BTW

PNG File Type
The Coffee Table image is stored as PNG file. Recall that PNG stands for Portable Network Graphics and is a cross-platform file type similar to GIF. It differs in that you can control the opacity of transparent colors. PNG files **interlace**, or fill in, faster on Web pages.

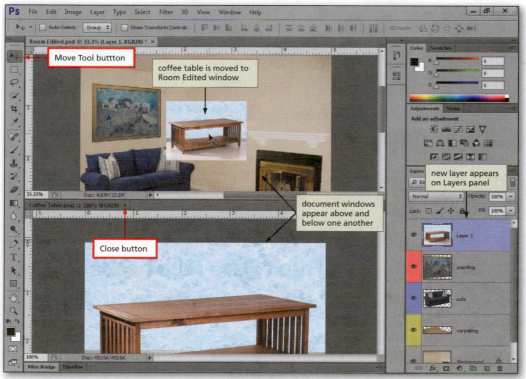

Figure 3–32

To Rename and Color the Coffee Table Layer

The following steps rename the new layer and assign an identification color.

1 Rename the layer `coffee table`.

2 Assign a Gray identification color to the layer.

3 With the Move Tool still selected, drag the layer to a location in front of the sofa (Figure 3–33).

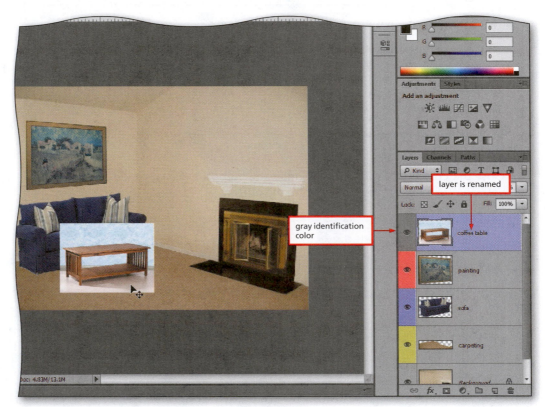

Figure 3–33

To Save the File

The following step saves the file again.

1 Press CTRL+S to save the Room Edited file with the same name. If Photoshop displays a dialog box about compatibility, click the OK button.

Break Point: If you wish to stop working through the chapter at this point, you can quit Photoshop now and then resume the project at a later time by starting Photoshop, opening the file named Room Edited and continuing to follow the steps from this location forward.

The Eraser Tools

In the painting layer, you eliminated the painting's background before moving it by using a selection technique. At other times, however, a new layer still might have extra color or objects that are not appropriate for the composite image. The image might be shaped oddly, making selecting tedious, or there might be other images in the background that come along with the selection and are not easily eliminated using the marquee selection technique you used previously. In those cases, dragging the image into a layer and then erasing part of that layer gives you more freedom and control in how the layer appears.

On the Tools panel, when you right-click the Eraser Tool button, Photoshop displays the three eraser tools. To alternate among the three eraser tools, press SHIFT+E. To access the eraser tools after using a different tool, press the E key.

The eraser tools are described in Table 3–2.

Table 3–2 Eraser Tools

Tool	Purpose	Shortcut	Button
Eraser Tool	Erases pixels beneath the cursor or brush tip	E SHIFT+E toggles through all three eraser tools	
Background Eraser Tool	Erases sample color from the center of the brush	E SHIFT+E toggles through all three eraser tools	
Magic Eraser Tool	Erases all similarly colored pixels	E SHIFT+E toggles through all three eraser tools	

When using the eraser tools, it is best to erase small portions at a time. That way each erasure is a separate state on the History panel. If you make mistakes, you can click earlier states on the panel. Small erasures also can be undone. To undo an erasure, press CTRL+Z, or click Edit on the Application bar, and then click Undo Eraser.

Using the Magic Eraser Tool

The Magic Eraser Tool erases all similarly colored pixels with one click. The Magic Eraser Tool options bar (Figure 3–34) gives you the choice of erasing contiguous or noncontiguous pixels and allows you to enter a tolerance value to define the range of erasable color. A lower tolerance erases pixels within a range of color values very similar to the pixel you click. A higher tolerance erases pixels within a broader range. Recall that the Anti-alias check box creates a smooth edge that can apply to both selecting and erasing. **Opacity** refers to the level at which you can see through a color to reveal the layer beneath it. When using the eraser tools, an opacity setting of 100% completely erases pixels. A lower opacity partially erases pixels.

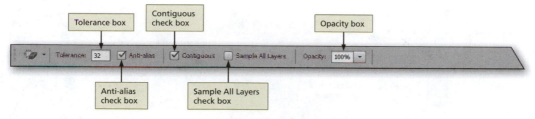

Figure 3–34

To Display Only the Current Layer

Some users find it easier to erase in a layer when only that layer appears in the document window. The following step hides all but the current layer by ALT+clicking the visibility icon.

 1

- On the Layers panel, ALT+click the coffee table layer visibility icon, so only the coffee table is displayed.

- Press the z key to activate the Zoom Tool, and then click the coffee table several times to zoom in (Figure 3–35).

- If necessary, scroll the document window so that the entire coffee table is visible.

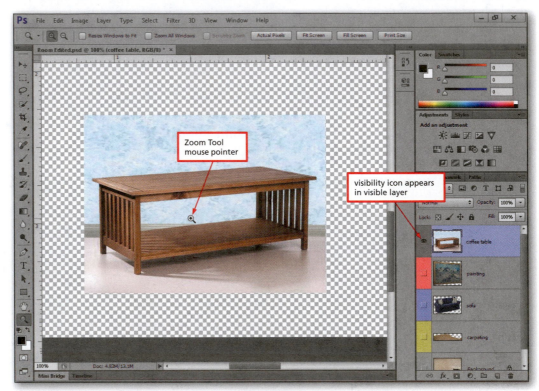

Figure 3–35

To Erase using the Magic Eraser Tool

The following steps use the Magic Eraser Tool to remove the blue wallpaper background from the coffee table image layer.

 1

- Right-click the Eraser Tool button on the Tools panel to display the context menu (Figure 3–36).

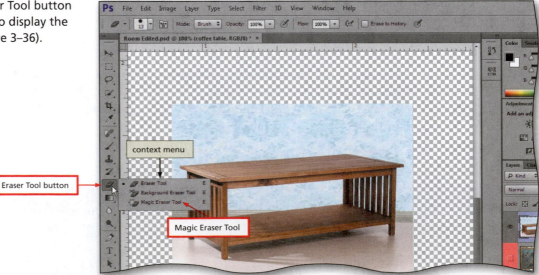

Figure 3–36

2

- Click Magic Eraser Tool to select it.

- If necessary, click the Anti-alias check box so it displays a check mark.

- Click the Contiguous check box so it does not display a check mark (Figure 3–37).

Q&A Why do I need to remove the Contiguous check mark?

You want to erase all occurrences of the wallpaper color, even those that are not connected continuously, such as those in between the slats of the coffee table.

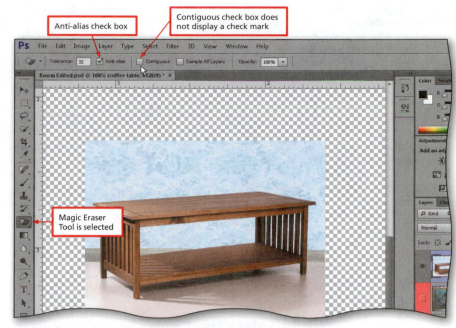

Figure 3–37

3
- Click the wallpaper to delete all of the blue color.

- If some blue remains in your layer, click it (Figure 3–38).

Q&A How should I position the Magic Eraser Tool mouse pointer?

Position the lower-left tip of the eraser over the pixel color to erase.

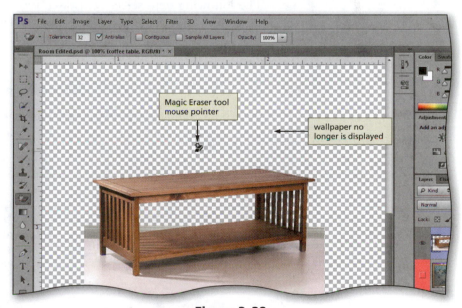

Figure 3–38

Other Ways

1. Press SHIFT+E until Magic Eraser Tool is selected, click photo

Using the Eraser Tool

The Eraser Tool changes pixels in the image as you drag through them. On most layers, the Eraser Tool simply erases the pixels or changes them to transparent, revealing the layer beneath. On a locked layer, such as the Background layer, the Eraser Tool changes the pixels to the current background color.

The Eraser Tool options bar (Figure 3–39 on the next page) displays a Mode box in which you can choose one of three shapes for erasure: brush, block, and pen. The brush shape gives you the most flexibility in size, and many different brush tips are available. The default brush tip is a circle. Block mode is a hard-edged, fixed-sized square with no options for changing the opacity or flow; however, it does give you quick access to a square to erase straight lines and corners. The pencil mode is similar to the brush mode, except that the pencil does not spread as much into adjacent pixels.

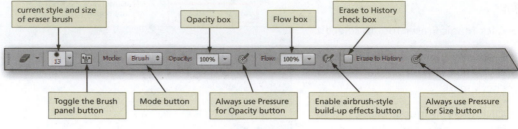

Figure 3–39

As with the Magic Eraser Tool options bar, an Opacity box allows you to specify the depth of the erasure. The Flow box specifies how quickly the erasure is performed. In addition, you can erase to a saved state or snapshot in the History panel.

As you erase with the brush shape, the RIGHT BRACKET (]) and LEFT BRACKET ([) keys increase and decrease the size of the eraser, respectively.

To Select the Eraser Tool and Resize the Mouse Pointer

The following steps select the Eraser Tool in preparation for erasing more of the layer.

1 Right-click the Magic Eraser Tool button on the Tools panel, and then click Eraser Tool on the context menu.

2 Move the mouse pointer into the document window.

3 If the mouse pointer is extremely small, press the RIGHT BRACKET (]) key several times to resize the eraser until the mouse pointer changes from a dot to a small circle (Figure 3–40).

Figure 3–40

To Erase using the Eraser Tool

The following steps erase the floor using the Eraser Tool.

1

• Drag the mouse across a portion of the floor to erase it. Do not drag across the coffee table (Figure 3–41).

Q&A

How should I position the Eraser Tool mouse pointer?

By default, the Eraser Tool mouse pointer appears as a circle. When you click or drag, Photoshop erases everything within the circle. You can change the size of the mouse pointer using the bracket keys.

molding

flooring

part of layer is erased

Figure 3–41

2

• Continue dragging to erase more of the floor and the molding, using the LEFT BRACKET ([) and RIGHT BRACKET (]) keys to change the size of your eraser. Do not erase completely along the very edge of the coffee table (Figure 3–42).

Experiment

• Drag a short erasure over the coffee table that creates an error. Then press CTRL+Z to undo the erasure.

floor, shadow, and molding are erased

some shadow remains

Figure 3–42

To Erase using the Block Mouse Pointer

The following steps delete flooring and shadows that are very close to the coffee table using a block mouse pointer.

- Click the Mode button on the options bar to display its list (Figure 3–43).

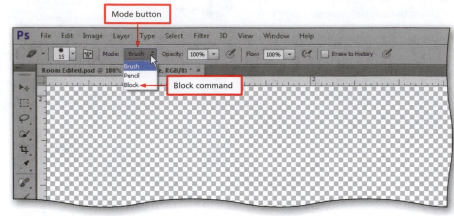

Figure 3–43

- Click Block to choose a block mouse pointer.

- Drag close to the coffee table to erase the rest of the flooring and shadows (Figure 3–44).

Q&A

I cannot get close enough to the edge to erase. What should I do?

You can zoom in to erase more closely, or use the Magic Eraser Tool, contiguously, with a high tolerance level. When you get close, you can press and hold the SHIFT key while dragging to create a straight line of erasure.

Figure 3–44

Other Ways

1. Press SHIFT+E until Eraser Tool is selected, click document

To View All Layers

The following steps show all of the layers.

1. ALT+click the visibility icon on the visible layer, in this case the coffee table, to show all of the layers.

2. If you see pixels that need to be erased, click them, zooming and scrolling as necessary.

To Transform by Changing the Perspective

The following steps transform the coffee table layer to make it fit the perspective of the room.

1

- With the coffee table layer still selected, press CTRL+T to turn on the bounding box.

- Right-click within the bounding box to display the context menu and then select Perspective.

- Drag the left-center sizing handle down to change the perspective so that the horizontal lines of the coffee table parallel the lines of the sofa (Figure 3–45).

2

- Press the ENTER key to confirm the transformation.

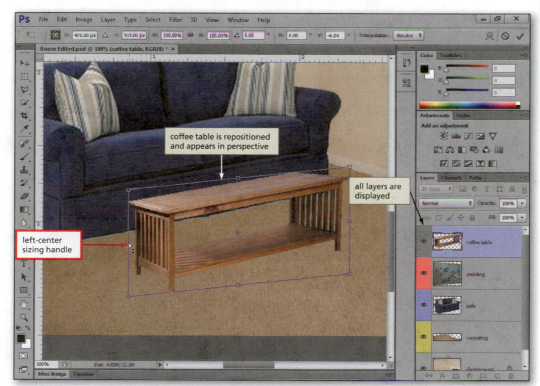

Figure 3–45

- If necessary, use the Move Tool to drag the coffee table to a location centered in front of the sofa.

Other Ways

1. On Edit menu, point to Transform, click Perspective, drag bounding box sizing handle

To Create the Ivy Layer

To create the ivy layer, you will open the file and then move the entire image into the Room Edited document window.

1 Open the Ivy file from the Chapter 03 folder of the Data Files for Students, or from a location specified by your instructor.

2 On the Application bar, click Window, point to Arrange, and then click Tile All Vertically to display the windows beside each other.

3 With the Ivy window still active, click the Move Tool button on the Tools panel, if necessary.

4 Drag the entire ivy image and drop it in the Room Edited window.

5 Close the Ivy document window. If Photoshop displays a dialog box asking if you want to save the changes, click the No button.

BTW

TIFF File Type
The Ivy file is stored as a TIF file. The TIF, or TIFF, is a flexible raster image format. A raster image is a digital image represented by a matrix of pixels. TIFF stands for Tagged Image File Format and is a common file format for images acquired from scanners and screen capture programs. Because TIF files are supported by virtually all paint, image-editing, and page-layout applications, it also is a versatile format for cross-platform applications.

To Rename and Color the Ivy Layer

The following steps rename the new layer and assign an identification color.

1 Rename the layer `ivy`.

2 Assign a Green identification color to the layer.

3 Zoom to 50 percent magnification and scroll to display the entire layer (Figure 3–46).

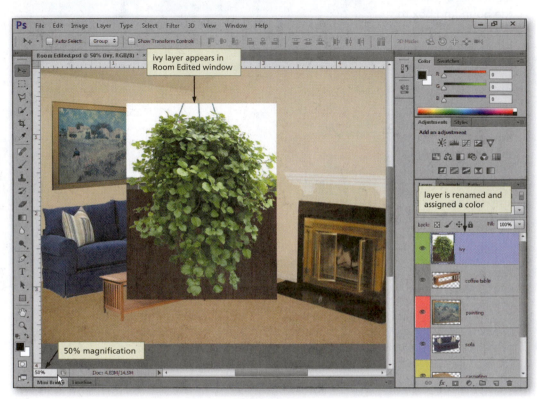

Figure 3–46

BTW

The Background Eraser Tool

The Background Eraser Tool samples the hot spot and then, as you drag, it deletes that color wherever it appears inside the brush. The Background Eraser Tool overrides the lock transparency setting of a layer.

Using the Background Eraser Tool

The Background Eraser Tool erases the background while maintaining the edges of an object in the foreground, based on a set color that you choose for the background. The Background Eraser Tool samples the color in the center of the mouse pointer, called the **hot spot**. As you drag, the tool erases that color, leaving the rest of the layer intact. You release the mouse button and drag again to sample a different color. On the Background Eraser Tool options bar (Figure 3–47), you can use the tolerance setting to control the range of colors that will be erased, sample the color selections, and adjust the sharpness of the boundaries by setting limits. The three sampling buttons on the Background Eraser Tool options bar sample in different ways. When you use the Sampling: Continuous button, it samples colors and erases continuously as you drag, the Sampling: Once button erases only the areas containing the color you first click, and the Sampling: Background Swatch button erases only areas containing the current color on the Tools panel, Color panel, or Swatches panel.

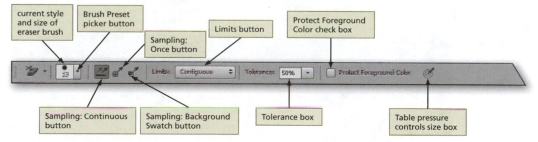

current style
and size of
eraser brush

Brush Preset
picker button

Sampling:
Once button

Limits button

Protect Foreground
Color check box

Sampling: Continuous
button

Sampling: Background
Swatch button

Tolerance box

Table pressure
controls size box

Figure 3–47

To Erase using the Background Eraser Tool

The following steps use the Background Eraser Tool to remove the paneling from behind the ivy plant. If you make a mistake while erasing, click the previous state on the History panel or press CTRL+Z and begin erasing again.

1

- With the ivy layer still selected, right-click the Eraser Tool button on the Tools panel and then click Background Eraser Tool on the context menu to select the tool.

- On the options bar, click the Sampling: Once button to erase only the areas containing the color you first click.

- Click the Limits button to display its list (Figure 3–48).

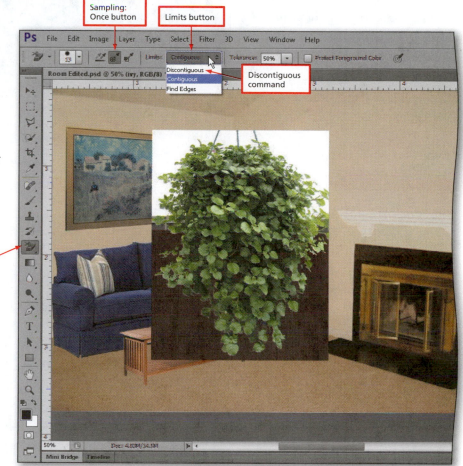

Sampling:
Once button

Limits button

Discontiguous
command

Background Eraser
Tool is selected

Figure 3–48

2

- Click Discontiguous to choose the setting.

- Enter 25 in the Tolerance box, and then press the ENTER key to lower the Tolerance setting, which will erase a more narrow range of color.

- Move the mouse pointer to the document window, and then press the RIGHT BRACKET (]) key several times to increase the size of the eraser, if necessary (Figure 3–49)

 Q&A

What does discontiguous mean?

Discontiguous refers to noncontiguous pixels, or pixels of the same color that are not physically located together. In the ivy layer, parts of the brown panel appear behind the ivy and are not adjacent to the other brown paneling.

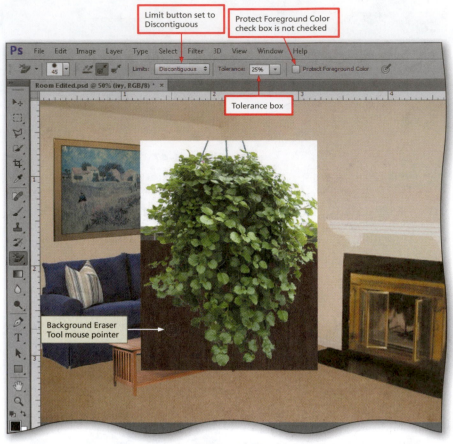

Figure 3–49

3

- Position the center of the mouse pointer directly over a portion of the paneling.

- Click and hold the mouse button. Drag across the layer, including the ivy, to erase some of the paneling (Figure 3–50).

Q&A

What is the purpose of the Protect Foreground Color check box?

When checked, the Protect Foreground Color check box gives you even more control of the background erasing. When colors are very similar, you can ALT+click the color you want to keep, then drag the color you want to erase.

Figure 3–50

4

- Position the mouse pointer directly over a portion of the paneling.

- Click and hold the mouse button. Drag to erase the rest of the paneling.

- If some color remains, zoom as necessary to position your mouse directly over any remaining shadow or color of the paneling. Click and drag to erase the rest of the color (Figure 3–51).

all paneling is erased

Figure 3–51

Other Ways

1. Press SHIFT+E until Background Eraser Tool is selected, set options bar, click document

To Finish the Ivy Layer

The following steps erase the rest of the background and resize the ivy layer.

1 With the ivy layer still selected on the Layers panel, use a combination of eraser tools and techniques in the document window to erase the white portion of the layer and the chair rail molding.

2 Press CTRL+T to display the Transform bounding box, and then SHIFT+drag a corner sizing handle to scale the size of the selection down to approximately 35 percent. Press the ENTER key to commit the transformation.

3 Move the layer to a location on the left side of the fireplace mantel (Figure 3–52).

background is removed and layer is scaled and repositioned

Figure 3–52

To Add a Pole Lamp to the Room

The following steps add a pole lamp layer to the room.

1 Open the file named Pole Lamp from the Chapter 03 folder of the Data Files for Students or from a location specified by your instructor.

2 Use the techniques you have learned to create a new layer and place the pole lamp in the Room Edited document window.

3 Name the new layer `pole lamp` and color the layer orange.

4 Close the Pole Lamp document window.

To Rearrange Layers

The following steps rearrange the layers on the Layers panel, moving the pole lamp layer below the sofa layer, so the pole lamp appears behind the end of the sofa.

 1

- Select the pole lamp layer on the Layers panel, if necessary.

- Press CTRL+LEFT BRACKET ([) several times to move the layer down and place it below the sofa layer on the Layers panel.

- In the document window, move the pole lamp to the right end of the sofa, in the corner of the room (Figure 3–53).

 Experiment

- Drag individual layers on the Layers panel to new locations in the stack, and watch how that changes the document window. When you are finished, rearrange the layers to appear as shown in Figure 3–53.

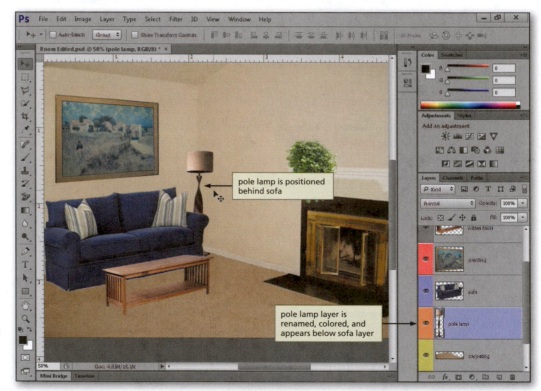

Figure 3–53

2

- Reposition the pole lamp layer as necessary.

Other Ways	
1. To move a layer up, press CTRL+RIGHT BRACKET (])	2. Drag layer on Layers panel, drop between other layers

BTW

Arranging Layers
To rearrange layers, change their visibility, or better organize them, drag the layer up or down on the Layers panel. The top layer on the Layers panel appears in front of any other layers in the document window. The Layer menu also contains an Arrange submenu to help you organize your layers.

To Add Mantel Decorations to the Room

The following steps add a mantel decoration layer to the room.

1 On the Layers panel, click the top layer to select it, so the new layer will appear on top.

2 Open the file named Mantel Decorations from the Chapter 03 folder of the Data Files for Students, or from a location specified by your instructor.

3 Use the techniques you have learned to create a new layer and edit it as necessary; you may want to scale to 50% and adjust the perspective.

4 Place the mantel decorations on the mantel in the Room Edited document window.

5 Name the new layer `mantel decorations` and color the layer violet.

6 Close the Mantel Decorations document window, and zoom to 33.33% magnification (Figure 3–54).

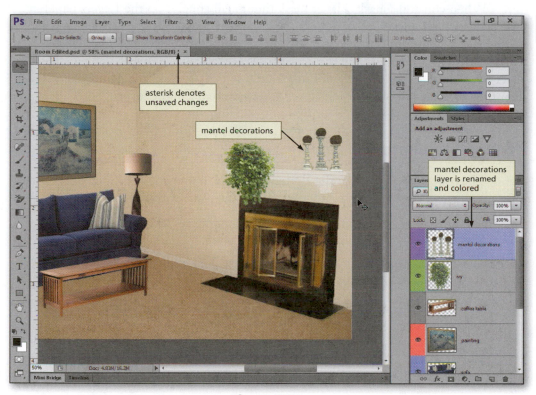

BTW

Saving Files
Photoshop displays an asterisk (*) on the document window tab to denote changes have been made to the file (Figure 3–54). Once you save the file, the asterisk no longer is displayed.

Figure 3–54

To Save the File

Many layers have been added to the composite image. The following step saves the file.

1 Save the Room Edited file with the same name.

Break Point: If you wish to stop working through the chapter at this point, you can quit Photoshop now and then resume the project at a later time by starting Photoshop, opening the file named Room Edited and continuing to follow the steps from this location forward.

Layer Masks

Default Colors and Layer Masks
When you apply a mask to a layer, or select a previously created mask on the Layers panel, Photoshop automatically inverts the default colors. White is used to reveal portions of the mask. Black is used to hide portions of the mask. Double-check the colors in the lower portion of the Tools panel when working with masks.

Manipulating Masks
Once you have created a mask, you might want to perform other manipulations on the mask. For example, if you want to unlink a mask to move it independently of its layer, click the link icon on the Layers panel. To unlink a mask temporarily, SHIFT+click the link icon. If you want to mask the entire layer completely, you can ALT+click the 'Add layer mask' button. In that case, you would paint with white in the mask to reveal portions of the mask. To make the mask permanent and reduce overall file size, apply the mask using a command on the mask's context menu.

Another way to edit layers is by creating a mask. A **mask** is an overlay that hides portions of a layer; it also can protect areas of the layer from inadvertent editing. For example, in a graphic of an exotic animal, you might want to mask all of the area except the animal, rather than permanently delete the background. Or, if you wanted to layer a musical score over the top of a piano graphic, you might mask the edges of the paper so the notes look like they blend into the piano. A mask does not alter the layer as the Eraser Tool does; it merely overlays a template to conceal a portion of the layer. That way, if you change your mind and need to display more of the layer, you can. Nothing has been erased permanently. With the Eraser Tool, you would have to delete the layer, open a backup copy, recreate the layer, and then begin to edit again. With masks, you simply edit the mask.

Photoshop provides two types of masks. **Layer masks** or **pixel masks** are resolution-dependent bitmap images, created with the painting or selection tools. **Vector masks** are resolution independent, created with a pen or shape tool. In this chapter, you will create a layer mask.

When you add a mask, a layer mask thumbnail appears on the Layers panel in **grayscale**, which means each pixel in the mask uses a single shade of gray on a scale from black to white. When selecting the layer mask thumbnail, the default colors change to white over black and the eraser tools are inactive. To mask, you paint on the layer with black. If you change your mind and want to unmask, you paint with white. Painting with gray displays various levels of transparency in the layer.

To Open the Potted Plant File

The following steps open the Potted Plant file in preparation for creating a layer mask, and uses a copy and paste process to place the plant in the room.

1 Open the file named Potted Plant from the Chapter 03 folder of the Data Files for Students or from a location specified by your instructor.

2 With the Potted Plant window active, press CTRL+A to select all, and then press CTRL+c to copy the entire image.

3 Click the Room Edited document window tab to make the window active. Press CTRL+V to paste the copied image from the Windows clipboard.

4 Name the new layer `potted plant` and color the layer green.

5 Close the Potted Plant document window.

To Create a Layer Mask

The following steps mask the plant in the potted plant layer to reveal only the pot. That way, potential decorators can see what the room would look like with and without the plant. As you create the layer mask, you will use the Brush Tool to brush over the parts of the image to mask.

Moving Masks
To move the mask, first click the link icon on the Layers panel to unlink the mask from the layer. Select the Move Tool. Then, in the document window, drag the layer to reposition it. When the mask is positioned correctly, click between the layer and layer mask on the Layers panel to relink them.

1

- With the potted plant layer selected, zoom to 100 percent.

- Click the 'Add layer mask' button on the Layers panel status bar to create a layer mask (Figure 3–55).

Q&A What is the new notation on the Layers panel?

Photoshop adds a layer mask thumbnail to the selected layer on the panel. The link icon **links**, or connects, the mask to the layer. A link icon appears between the layer thumbnail and the mask thumbnail. Also, notice that the default color swatches on the Tools panel are reversed.

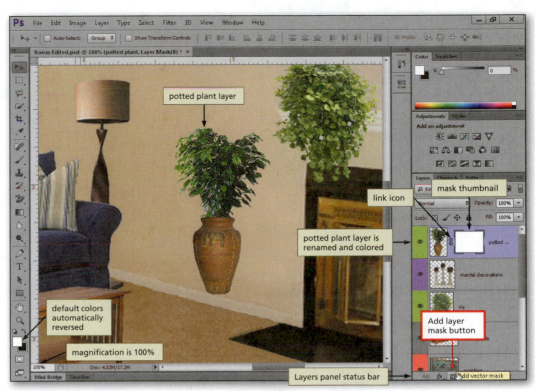

Figure 3–55

2

- Press the X key to choose black over white, which creates a mask.

- Press the B key to activate the brush and then move the mouse pointer into the document window.

- Press the RIGHT BRACKET (]) key to increase the size of the brush's circle, as necessary.

- Drag the mouse across the plant itself. Do not drag the pot (Figure 3–56).

Q&A Did I erase the plant?

No, you still can see the plant in the layer thumbnail on the Layers panel. You only masked the plant out of view.

Figure 3–56

- Continue dragging through the layer to remove everything except the pot. Zoom the magnification and adjust the size of the brush mouse pointer, as necessary (Figure 3–57).

Q&A

Why does the layer mask use a brush tip mouse pointer?

Layer masks use painting techniques to mask out portions of the image.

Figure 3–57

To Correct a Masking Error

The following steps create a masking error and then unmask the area by painting with white.

- Drag across the pot to mask a portion of the pot (Figure 3–58).

Figure 3–58

- Press the x key to switch the foreground and background colors so you are painting with white, which restores the image.

- Drag across the same portion of the pot to unmask it (Figure 3–59).

🔍 Experiment

- On the Layers panel, right-click the mask and then click Disable Layer Mask. Notice the entire potted plan appears and the mask has an X through it. Right-click the mask again and then click Enable Layer Mask.

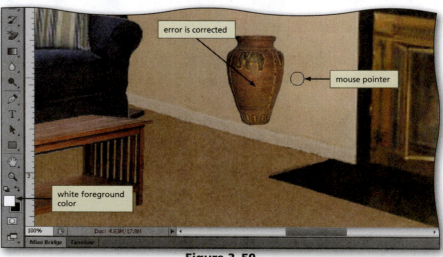

Figure 3–59

To Move the Potted Plant

The following step moves the potted plant to the right side of the fireplace.

1 Select the Move Tool and drag the potted plant to the floor on the right side of the fireplace. Scroll as necessary.

Fine-Tuning Layers

Sometimes layers need special adjustments to better fit into their new surroundings in the document window. This fine-tuning usually involves **tonal adjustments** that affect the color, lighting, opacity, level, or fill; **style adjustments** such as special effects or blends; or **filter adjustments** that let you apply pictures, tiles, or patterns. With the correct adjustment, a layer can be made to look like it was an original part of the image, maintaining a consistency of appearance for the overall composite image.

Create layer adjustments.
Layer adjustments allow you to fine-tune your layers. Evaluate layers to see if a change in levels, brightness, saturation, or hue would help them to fit more naturally into the background scene. Use nondestructive edits when possible, so that if you are not satisfied with the adjustment, you can remove it.

Plan Ahead

When you do not want to alter the pixels in an image permanently, you can create an extra layer in which to make changes while preserving the original pixels. An **adjustment layer** is a new layer added to the image to affect a large-scale tonal change. You can create adjustment layers for the entire composite image or just a specific layer.

Adjustment layers have several advantages. They are nondestructive, which means you can experiment with various settings and reedit the adjustment layer at any time. Adjustment layers reduce the amount of damage you do to an image by making direct edits. You can copy adjustments to other layers and images, saving time and maintaining consistency.

If you want to make permanent tonal, style, or filter changes to the pixels themselves, you can edit the layer directly. Features such as opacity, fill, and blending modes can be changed on the Layers panel. These changes can be undone using the History panel, but they become permanent when you save the image.

Making an Opacity Change to a Layer

Some adjustment tools specific to layers are located on the Layers panel. (See Figure 3-60 on the next page.) The Opacity box allows you to change the opacity or transparency of a layer. You can control exactly how solid the objects on a specific layer appear. For example, if you wanted to display an American flag superimposed over a memorial or monument, you might change the flag layer's opacity to 50 percent. The monument easily would be visible through the flag.

The Fill box changes the fill of a layer's opacity as well, but it only changes the pixels in the layer rather than changing any applied layer styles or blending modes. Adjusting the fill percentage sometimes is called changing the **interior opacity**. If you have no layer styles or blending modes, you can use either the Opacity or Fill box.

The Blending mode button displays a list of blending modes for the selected layer or layers. **Blending modes** define how an object interacts with other objects, such as the Background layer.

BTW

Pop-Up Sliders
If there is a triangle next to a text box in the Photoshop interface, you can click it to display a **pop-up slider**. Drag the slider to the desired value. Click outside the slider or press the ENTER key to close the slider box. To cancel the changes, press the ESC key.

BTW

Panel Boxes
The Opacity and Fill boxes can be changed in one of three ways. You can drag the scrubby slider label. When you click the box arrow, a pop-up slider is displayed to adjust the percentage. You also can type a percentage in either box.

To Make an Opacity Change to a Layer

The following step lightens the mantel decorations by lowering the opacity, to make them fit better into the room design.

- Zoom to display the mantel decorations in the document window at 100% magnification.

- On the Layers panel, click to select the mantel decorations layer.

- On the Layers panel, point to the word, Opacity, and then drag the scrubby slider to the left until the Opacity box displays 85% to lower the opacity (Figure 3–60).

 **Experiment**

- Click the Blending mode button and choose a blending mode such as Hard Light or Linear Burn. Experiment with other blending modes. When you are done, click the Blending mode button and then click Normal in the list.

Figure 3–60

Adjustments and Properties

Tools that nondestructively adjust image lighting and shading are located on the Adjustments panel (Figure 3–61).

Figure 3–61

Clicking an **adjustment icon**, or preset, also displays the Properties panel and its settings for the specific adjustment, including channel selectors, eyedroppers, sliders, and input boxes, among others. Buttons on the Properties panel status bar allow you to specify visibility, delete the adjustment, or create a **clip** that applies the adjustment to a layer rather than the entire image.

Some adjustments also can display their settings using a dialog box, if accessed from outside the Adjustments panel with a shortcut key or a menu command. Table 3–3 displays a list of the Adjustments available on the Adjustments panel. Many of the adjustments also are available through the Adjustments panel menu (Figure 3–61), through the Layers menu on the application bar, or through a button on the Layers panel.

Table 3–3 Adjustments Panel Icons

Adjustment	Description	Shortcut (if available)	Icon
Brightness/ Contrast	Changes general brightness (shadows and highlights) and overall contrast (tonal range)		
Levels	Adjusts color balance for shadows, midtones, highlights, and color channels	CTRL+L	
Curves	Adjusts individual points in the tonal range of black to white	CTRL+M	
Exposure	Changes exposure, which adjusts the highlights; changes offset, which darkens the shadows and midtones; changes gamma, which adjusts the midtones		
Vibrance	Adjusts vibrance and color saturation settings so shifting to primary colors, or clipping, is minimized		
Hue/Saturation	Changes hue, saturation, and lightness of entire image or specific colors	CTRL+U	
Color Balance	Adjusts the overall midtone of colors in an image	CTRL+B	
Black & White	Converts a color image to grayscale	ALT+SHIFT+CTRL+B	
Photo Filter	Simulates effects of using a filter in front of a camera lens		
Channel Mixer	Modifies and adjusts individual color channels		
Color Lookup	Remaps every color using a lookup table or predetermined style		
Invert	Converts every color to its inverse or opposite	CTRL+I	
Posterize	Specifies the number of tonal levels in each channel		
Threshold	Converts images to high-contrast black and white		
Selective Color	Changes the mixture of colors in each of the primary color components		
Gradient Map	Maps colors to a specified gradient fill		

Level Sliders

In the Levels dialog box, the Input Level sliders on each end map the black point (on the left) and white point (on the right) to the settings of the Output sliders. The middle Input slider adjusts the gamma or midtone in the image, changing the intensity values of the middle range of gray tones without dramatically altering the highlights and shadows. As you move any of the Input Level sliders, the black point, midtone, and white point change in the Output sliders; all the remaining levels are redistributed.

Level Adjustments

A **level adjustment** is one way to make tonal changes to shadows, midtones, and highlights. A **shadow** is a darkened shade in an image. A **midtone**, also called **gamma**, is the midpoint gray between shadows and highlights. A **highlight** is a portion of an image that is strongly illuminated and may appear as the lightest or whitest part of the image. To change levels, Photoshop uses black, gray, and white sliders to adjust any or all of the three tonal input levels. A **histogram**, or frequency distribution bar chart, indicates the amount of color in the tonal ranges. When adjusting levels using the histogram, a general guideline is to drag the black-and-white sliders to the first indication, or outlier, of strong tonal change in the histogram. Then, experiment with the gray slider to change the intensity value of the middle range of gray tones without dramatically altering the highlights and shadows. Becoming proficient at adjusting levels takes practice. Furthermore, adjustments are subjective; the impact of some effects is a matter of opinion.

To Make a Levels Adjustment

In the sofa layer of the image, you will adjust the levels to make the layer better fit into the picture. The following steps make level adjustments to the sofa.

1

- Select the sofa layer on the Layers panel and scroll the document window to display the sofa.

- Click the Levels icon on the Adjustments panel to display the level settings and options on the Properties panel.

- Click the Clip to Layer button on the Properties panel status bar to adjust only the sofa layer (Figure 3–62).

Experiment

- Drag the three Levels Input sliders below the histogram to see how they affect the appearance of the sofa layer.

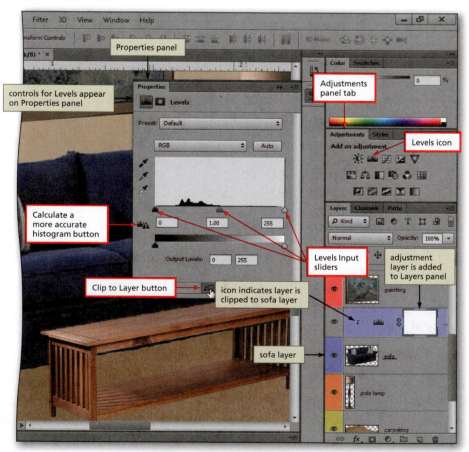

Figure 3–62

● Click the 'Calculate a more accurate histogram' button to make the level change more visible.

● Below the histogram display, drag the white Levels Input slider to approximately 223, aligning it with the first visible increase on the right side of the histogram to adjust the highlights.

● Drag the black Levels Input slider to approximately 30, aligning it with the first visible increase on the left side of the histogram to adjust the shadows.

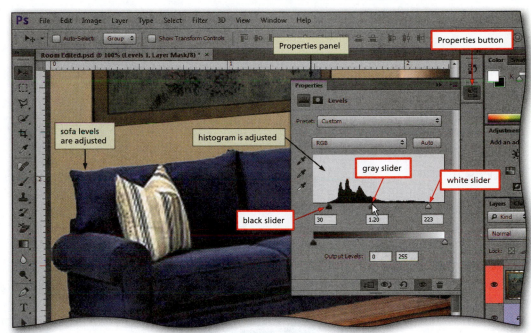

Figure 3–63

● Drag the gray Levels Input slider to 1.20 to adjust the midtone colors (Figure 3–63).

Q&A My visible changes were at different levels. Did I do something wrong?

No, your histogram might differ, depending on your previous erasures.

● Click the Properties button on the vertical dock to collapse the Properties panel and complete the adjustment.

Q&A Did the Layers panel change?

Yes, you will see an extra layer created just above the sofa layer, with a clipping symbol to imply the relationship (Figure 3-64 on the next page).

 Experiment

● Click the visibility icon of the new levels layer to notice the change in the sofa. Click it again to redisplay the level adjustment.

Other Ways

1. Press CTRL+L, adjust levels, click OK button

2. On Image menu, point to Adjustments, click Levels, adjust levels, click OK button

Hue and Saturation

Another way to adjust a layer or image is to change the hue or saturation. **Hue** is the shade of a color in an image. **Saturation** is the intensity of a hue and is highly dependent upon the chosen color model, but in general, pastels have low saturation, and bright colors have high saturation. You will learn more about color models and the color wheel in later chapters and by reading Appendix B, the Graphic Design Overview appendix.

BTW

Other Level Adjustments
The three eyedroppers in the Levels area allow you to select the values for shadow, midtone, and highlight from the image itself. To do so, click the eyedropper and then click the location in the image that you want use. Once selected, that color becomes the slider value.

To Adjust the Hue and Saturation

The following steps adjust the hue and saturation of the coffee table layer.

 1

- Select the coffee table layer and scroll to display the coffee table in the document window, if necessary.

- Click the Hue/ Saturation icon on the Adjustments panel.

- Click the Clip to Layer button on the Properties panel status bar to adjust only the selected layer.

- Drag the Hue slider to +5. Drag the Saturation slider to –5. Drag the Lightness slider to –10 (Figure 3–64).

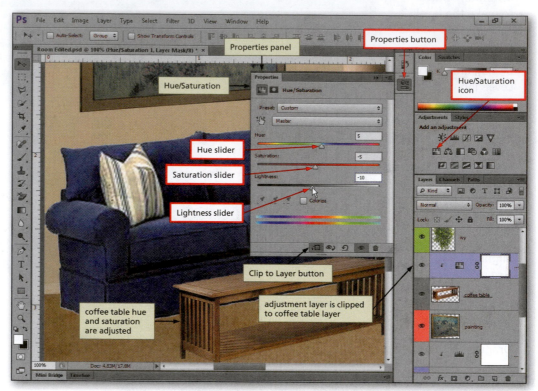

Figure 3–64

 **Experiment**

- Drag the sliders to view the effect of hue and saturation settings to the layer. When you are done experimenting, drag the sliders to the settings listed in the step.

 2

- Click the Properties button on the vertical dock to collapse the Properties panel and complete the adjustment.

Other Ways
1. Select layer, press CTRL+U, drag sliders, click OK button.   2. On Layer menu, point to New Adjustment Layer, click Hue/Saturation, edit settings

To Fit the Image on Screen

In previous chapters, you changed the magnification by using a box on the status bar and by using the Navigator panel. The View menu also offers several settings to change the magnification. The following steps use a command to change the magnification, to display the picture as large as possible while still fitting on the screen, in preparation for adjusting the Background layer.

1

• Click View on the Application bar to display the View menu (Figure 3–65).

Q&A

What does the Actual Pixels command do?

The Actual Pixels command displays the document window so that one image pixel equals exactly one monitor pixel, allowing you to see the maximum amount of detail available in your image.

Figure 3–65

2

• Click Fit on Screen to display the entire photo at the largest magnification (Figure 3–66).

Figure 3–66

Other Ways

1. Press CTRL+0 (zero)

Brightness and Contrast

Brightness refers to color luminance or intensity of a light source, perceived as lightness or darkness in an image. Photoshop measures brightness on a sliding scale from –150 to +150. Negative numbers move the brightness toward black. Positive numbers compress the highlights and expand the shadows. For example, the layer might be an image photographed on a cloudy day; conversely, the image might appear overexposed by having been too close to a photographer's flash. Either way, editing the brightness might enhance the image.

Contrast is the difference between the lightest and darkest tones in an image, involving mainly the midtones. When you increase contrast, the middle-to-dark areas become darker, and the middle-to-light areas become lighter. High-contrast images contain few color variations between the lightest and darkest parts of the image; low-contrast images contain more tonal gradations.

To Adjust the Brightness and Contrast

The following steps edit the brightness and contrast of the Background layer, this time creating the adjustment layer using the Layers panel.

1
- Scroll in the Layers panel as necessary to select the Background layer.

- On the Layers panel status bar, click the 'Create new fill or adjustment layer' button to display the list of adjustments (Figure 3–67).

Q&A

What is the difference between clicking the Brightness/Contrast button on the Adjustments panel and clicking the 'Create new fill or adjustment layer' button?

There is no difference when adjusting the brightness or contrast. The list of adjustments accessed from the Layers panel includes a few more settings than the Adjustments panel.

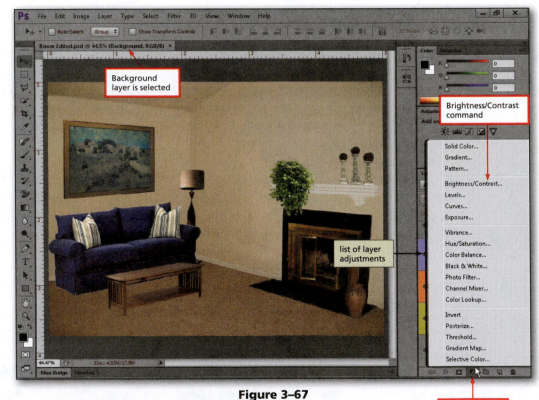

Figure 3–67

2

- Click Brightness/ Contrast in the list to display the settings on the Properties panel.

- Click the Clip to Layer button on the Properties panel status bar to adjust only the Background layer.

- Drag the Brightness slider to 10 and the Contrast slider to −10 to brighten the room (Figure 3–68).

 Experiment
Drag the sliders to various locations and note how the document window changes. When you are finished, drag the Brightness slider to +10 and the Contrast slider to −10.

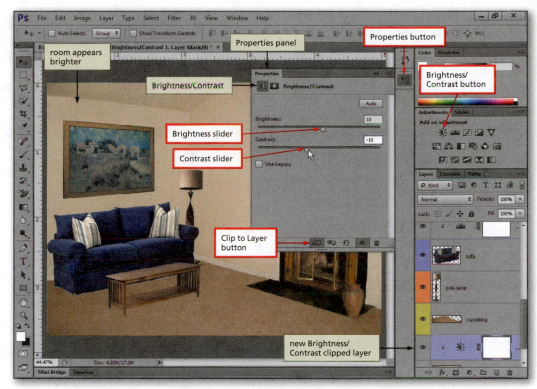

Figure 3–68

2

- Collapse the Properties panel.

Other Ways	
1. On Adjustments panel, click Brightness/ Contrast icon, adjust settings	2. On Layer menu, point to New Adjustment Layer, click Brightness/Contrast, click OK, adjust settings

Layer Styles

Similar to a layer adjustment, a **layer style** is applied to a layer rather than changing the layer's actual pixels. Layer styles, or layer effects, alter the appearance of the layer by adding depth, shadow, shading, texture, or overlay. A layer can display multiple styles or effects.

Edit layer styles.
Layer styles add dimension, texture, and definition to your layers. Styles such as shadow, glow, emboss, bevel, overlay, and stroke commonly distinguish the layer rather than making it fit in. Choose the settings carefully and think about direction, angle, distance, and spread. Make sure the layer style does not overwhelm the overall image or detract from previous layer adjustments.

Plan Ahead

Copying and Moving Layer Styles
To copy a layer style, right-click the source layer and then click Copy Layer Style on the context menu. Right-click the destination layer and then click Paste Layer Style. To move a layer style, drag the fx icon from one layer to another on the Layers panel.

BTW
Styles vs. Adjustments
Layer styles are special effects such as shadows, glows, and overlays. Styles appear attached to a layer on the Layers panel. An adjustment applies color, level, and tonal changes on its on layer.

BTW
Bevels
A bevel adds depth to an image by creating an angle between an edge and a shadow that softens the look. A bevel increases the 3D look of an image.

Table 3–4 lists the layer styles.

Table 3–4 Layer Styles	
Style	**Description**
Drop Shadow	Creates a shadow behind the layer
Inner Shadow	Creates a shadow inside the edges of the layer
Inner Glow	Adds a glow around the inside edge of the layer
Outer Glow	Adds a glow around the outside edge of the layer
Bevel and Emboss	Adds highlights and shading to a layer
Satin	Applies interior shading to create a satin finish
Color Overlay	Adds a color over the layer
Gradient Overlay	Inserts a gradient in front of the layer
Pattern Overlay	Fills the layer with a pattern
Stroke	Outlines the layer with a color, gradient, or pattern

Each of the layer styles has its own set of options and properties. Table 3–5 describes some of the layer style options. The options apply to many of the styles.

Table 3–5 Layer Style Options	
Option	**Description**
Angle	Sets a degree value for the lighting angle at which the effect is applied
Anti-alias	Blends the edge pixels of a contour or gloss contour
Blend Mode	Determines how a layer style blends with its underlying layers
Color	Assigns the color of a shadow, glow, or highlight
Contour	Allows you to create rings of transparency such as gradients, fades, beveling and embossing, and sculpting
Depth	Sets the depth of a bevel or pattern
Distance	Specifies the offset distance for a shadow or satin effect
Fill Type	Sets the content of a stroke
Global Light	Allows you to set an angle to simulate the direction of the light
Gloss Contour	Creates a glossy, metallic appearance on a bevel or emboss effect
Gradient	Indicates the gradient of a layer effect
Highlight or Shadow Mode	Specifies the blending mode of a bevel or emboss highlight or shadow
Jitter	Varies the color and opacity of a gradient
Layer Knocks Out Drop Shadow	Controls the drop shadow's visibility in a semitransparent layer
Noise	Assigns the number of random elements in the opacity of a glow or shadow
Opacity	Sets the opacity or transparency
Pattern	Specifies the pattern
Position	Sets the position of a stroke
Range	Controls which portion or range of the glow is targeted for the contour
Size	Specifies the amount of blur or the size of the shadow
Soften	Blurs the results of shading to reduce unwanted artifacts
Source	Specifies the source for an inner glow
Style	Specifies the style of a bevel or emboss

BTW
Hide Layer Styles
If you want to hide the notation of the Layer styles on the Layers panel, click the 'Reveals layer effects in the panel' button. To redisplay the style, click the button again.

BTW
Delete Layer Styles
If you want to delete a layer style, right-click the layer style, and then click Clear Layer Style on the context menu.

When a layer has a style applied to it, an fx icon appears to the right of the layer's name on the Layers panel. You can expand the icon on the Layers panel to view all of the applied effects and edit them when changing the style.

As you can tell from Table 3–4 and Table 3–5, there are a large number of layer styles and settings in Photoshop.

To Apply a Layer Style

The following steps apply a layer style to the ivy. You will create an inner bevel to give the ivy more depth.

1

- On the Layers panel, select the ivy layer.

- Click the 'Add a layer style' button on the Layers panel status bar to display the menu (Figure 3–69).

Will I see much change in the document window?

It depends on the magnification — at larger magnifications, you will see more change. The printed image will display more depth in the ivy.

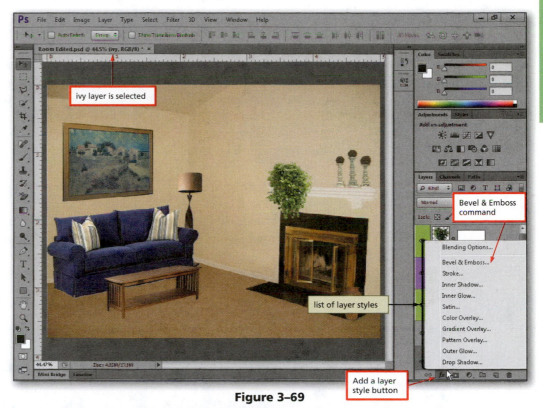

Figure 3–69

2

- Click Bevel & Emboss to display the Layer Style dialog box.

- In the Layer Style dialog box, enter 50 in the Depth box to decrease the strength of the shading.

- Enter 10 in the Size box and 5 in the Soften box to edit the bevel (Figure 3–70).

3

- Click the OK button to close the Layer Style dialog box.

 Experiment

- To view the difference that the adjustment has made, press CTRL+Z to undo the step and then press CTRL+Z again to redo the step.

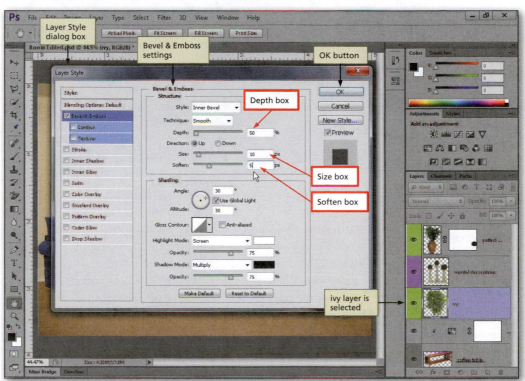

Figure 3–70

Other Ways
1. On Layer menu, point to Layer Style, click desired style, edit settings in Layer Style dialog box, click OK button

The Clone Stamp Tool

Color Modes
The color mode of an image appears on the document window tab.

The Clone Stamp Tool reproduces portions of an image, changing the pixels in a specific area. After clicking the Clone Stamp Tool button on the Tools panel, you press and hold the ALT key while clicking the portion of the picture that you want to copy. Photoshop takes a **sample** of the image, remembering where you clicked. You then move the mouse pointer to the position where you want to create the copy. As you drag with the brush, the image is applied. Each stroke of the tool applies more of the sample. The Clone Stamp Tool is useful for duplicating specific parts of an object or correcting defects in an image. You can clone from image to image, or clone locations within the same document window.

The Clone Source panel (Figure 3–71) appears when you click Clone Source on the Window menu. The panel has options to rotate or scale the sample, or specify the size and orientation. The Clone Source panel makes it easy to create variegated patterns using multiple sources. You can create up to five different clone sources to select the one you need quickly, without resampling each time. For example, if you are using the Clone Stamp Tool to repair several minor imperfections in an old photo, you can select your various samples first, and then use the sources as needed. The Clone Source panel also helps you create unique clones positioned at different angles and perspectives from the original.

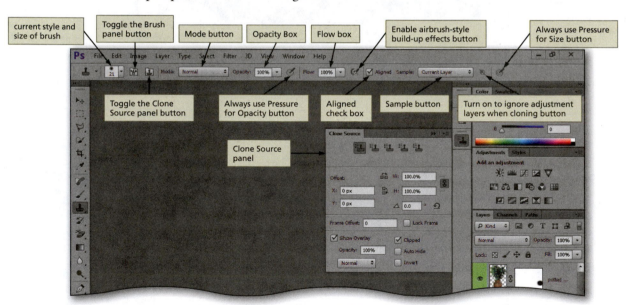

Figure 3–71

Clone Sampling
The size of the mouse pointer when you sample does not make any difference. It is the center point of the crosshair that is sampled. When you clone after making the sample, you can create larger or smaller strokes by adjusting the size of the mouse pointer.

The Clone Stamp Tool options bar (Figure 3–71) displays some of the same settings that you used with layer masks, along with an Aligned check box and Sample box. When you align, the sample point is not reset if you start dragging in a new location; in other words, the sampling moves to a relative point in the original image. Otherwise, the sample point begins again as you start a new clone. The default value is to sample only the current layer or background. When you select All Layers in the Sample box, the clone displays all layers. One restriction when using the Clone Stamp Tool from one image to another is that both images have to be in the same color mode, such as RGB or CMYK. The color mode of an image appears on the document window tab. You will learn more about color modes in a later chapter.

Grouped with the Clone Stamp Tool, a second kind of stamp, the Pattern Stamp Tool, allows you to paint with a pattern chosen from Photoshop's pattern library. A **pattern** is a repeated or tiled image, used to fill a layer or selection. On the Pattern Stamp Tool options bar, a Pattern Picker box arrow displays installed patterns. You can import additional patterns into the Pattern Picker box.

To Open the Flooring File and Arrange the Windows

To finish the composite image of the room, you will replace the carpeting with wood flooring. The following steps open the Flooring file.

1 Open the Flooring file from the Chapter 03 folder of the Data Files for Students or from a location specified by your instructor.

2 Tile All Horizontally to arrange the windows above and below one another.

3 Drag the border between the two document windows so more of the Room Edited window is displayed. Scroll in the Room Edited window to display the carpeting.

4 Select the carpeting layer.

To Create a New Blank Layer

The following steps create a new blank layer that clips the carpeting layer, in preparation for cloning.

1

- ALT+click the visibility icon on the carpeting layer to display only the carpeting.

- Press SHIFT+CTRL+N to display the New Layer dialog box.

- Name the layer, flooring.

- Click to display a check mark in the Use Previous Layer to Create Clipping Mask check box.

- Choose a yellow identification color. Do not change the mode or opacity (Figure 3–72).

2

- Click the OK button to close the New Layer dialog box.

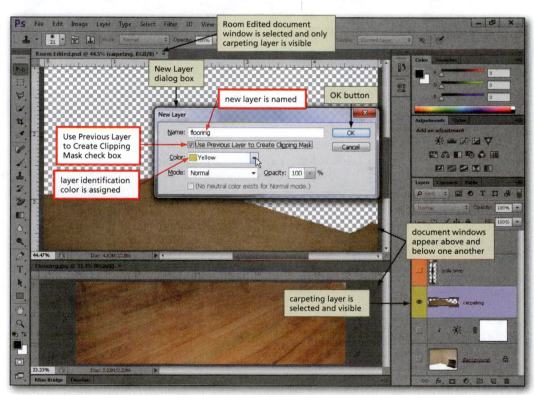

Figure 3–72

To Create a Clone

Using the Clone Stamp Tool, you will sample the Flooring image and then clone it to the carpeted area in the Room Edited image, as shown in the following steps. As you clone the flooring, adjust the magnification of the image to view the corners and small areas clearly. If you make a mistake while cloning, press CTRL+Z to undo the most recent clone stroke or access the History panel and click a previous state, then begin cloning again.

- Click the Flooring document window tab to make the window active.

- Click Window on the Application bar, and then click Clone Source to display the Clone Source panel.

- On the Clone Source panel, click the Invert check box to remove its check mark, if necessary.

- On the Tools panel, right-click the Clone Stamp Tool button to display its context menu (Figure 3–73).

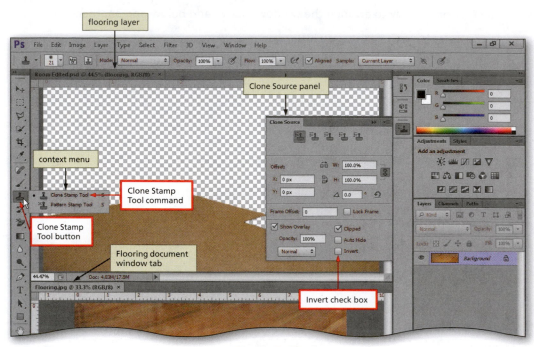

Figure 3–73

- Click Clone Stamp Tool to select it.

- On the options bar, click the Aligned check box so it displays a check mark, if necessary.

- Click the Clone Source button on the vertical dock to collapse the panel.

- Move the mouse pointer to the Flooring document window and ALT+click the left-middle edge of the flooring to select the sampling point (Figure 3–74).

Q&A How do I know if I indicated the clone source correctly?

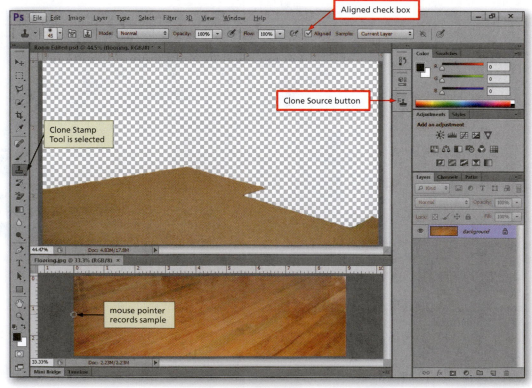

Figure 3–74

As you ALT+click, the Clone Stamp Tool displays a crosshair mouse pointer and the Clone Source panel displays the source of the clone.

3

- Click the Room Edited document window tab to make it active.

- With the flooring layer still selected, and the carpeting layer visible, move the mouse pointer into the document window. Adjust the size of the mouse pointer as necessary.

- Drag from the upper-left corner of the carpeting down to the lower-left corner to create the first stroke of the clone (Figure 3–75).

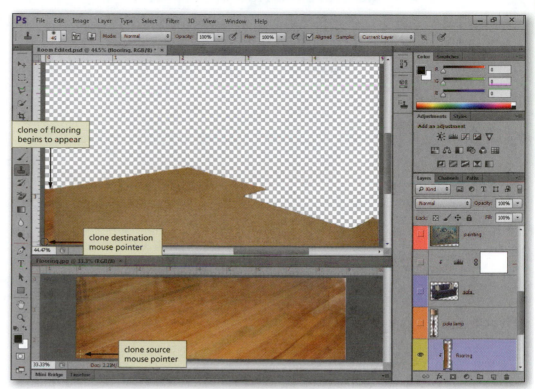

Figure 3–75

4

- Working from left to right, drag to replace the carpeting. Zoom, scroll, and adjust the pointer size as necessary to fill in corners. Use short strokes, so if you make a mistake, you can press CTRL+Z to undo the error. Do not resample (Figure 3–76).

Q&A

What is the purpose of the Aligned check box?

When checked, the Aligned check box allows you to use short strokes as you clone. The clone will not start over if you lift the mouse button to drag in another location. Aligning is good for cloning areas with a pattern.

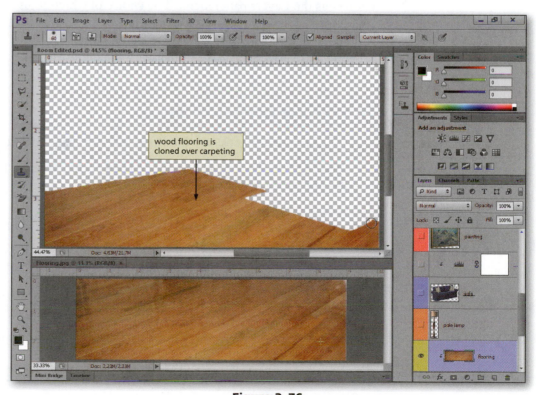

Figure 3–76

Other Ways

1. From another tool, press S key, ALT+click sample, drag clone

2. From Pattern Stamp Tool, press SHIFT+S, ALT+click sample, drag clone

To Close the Flooring Window

The following steps close the Flooring window and redisplay all the layers.

1 Close the Flooring document window. If Photoshop asks if you want to save changes to the document, click the No button.

2 Display all of the layers.

Flattening a Composite Image

When you **flatten** a composite image, Photoshop reduces the file size by merging all visible layers into the background, discarding hidden layers, and applying masks. A flattened file is easier to print, export, and display on the Web. It is a good practice, however, to save the layered version in PSD format before flattening in case you want to make further changes to the file. It is very important to remember that once a file is flattened and saved, no changes can be made to individual layers. If you flatten an image and then change your mind, if the file still is open, you can click the previous state on the History panel to restore all of the layers.

If you want to save each layer as a separate file, click File on the Application bar, point to Scripts, and then click Export Layers to Files. This script is useful if you think you might want to use your layers in other composite images.

The Layer menu displays a Flatten Image command and has many of the same choices as the Layers panel menu. The choice of which to use is a matter of personal preference and the location of your mouse pointer at the time. After saving the composite image, you will use the Layer menu to flatten the visible layers. Finally, you will save the flattened file in TIFF format with the name, Room TIFF.

To Save the Composite Image

The following steps save the Room Edited image with its layers.

1 With your USB flash drive connected to one of the computer's USB ports, click File on the Application bar and then click Save As.

2 When the Save As dialog box is displayed, type `Room Composite` in the File name text box. Do not press the ENTER key after typing the file name.

3 If necessary, click the Format box arrow and then choose Photoshop (*.PSD, *.PDD) in the list.

4 If necessary, click the Save in box arrow and then click Removable Disk (F:), or the location associated with your USB flash drive, in the list.

5 Click the Save button in the Save As dialog box. If Photoshop displays an options dialog box, click the OK button.

To Flatten a Composite Image

The following steps use the Layer menu to flatten the composite image.

1

- Click Layer on the Application bar to display the Layer menu (Figure 3–77).

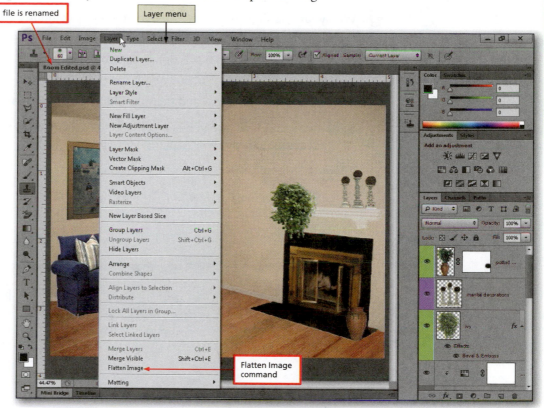

Figure 3–77

2

- Click Flatten Image on the Layer menu to combine all of the layers (Figure 3–78).

Q&A What is the difference between flatten and merge?

The Merge command flattens specific layers together. The Flatten command uses all of the layers and merges into a Background layer.

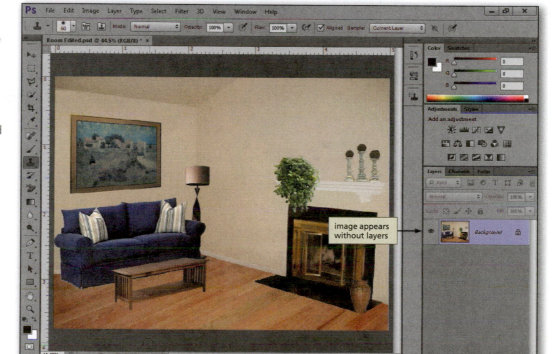

Figure 3–78

Other Ways	
1. Right-click any layer, click Flatten Image	2. Click Layers panel menu button, click Flatten Image

To Save a File in the TIFF Format

The following steps save the flattened image as a TIFF file.

1 With your USB flash drive connected to one of the computer's USB ports, click File on the Application bar and then click Save As.

2 When the Save As dialog box is displayed, type `Room TIFF` in the File name text box. Do not press the ENTER key after typing the file name.

3 Click the Format box arrow and then click TIFF (*.TIF, *TIFF) in the list.

4 If necessary, click the Save in box arrow and then click Removable Disk (F:), or the location associated with your USB flash drive, in the list.

5 Click the Save button in the Save As dialog box.

6 When Photoshop displays the TIFF Options dialog box, click the OK button to finish saving the file (Figure 3–79).

Figure 3–79

To Print the Room TIFF Image

The following steps print a copy of the Room TIFF image on the default printer. If you are unsure which printer is set as your default, use the Print command rather than the Print one Copy command so you can choose your printer.

1 Ready the printer according to the printer instructions.

2 Click File on the Application bar and then click Print One Copy on the File menu to print the image on the default printer.

To Close the Document Window and Quit Photoshop

The final steps close the document window and quit Photoshop.

1 Click the Close button in the document window.

2 If Photoshop displays a dialog box, click the No button to ignore the changes since the last time you saved the photo.

3 Quit Photoshop.

Chapter Summary

In virtually decorating a room, you gained a broad knowledge of Photoshop's layering capabilities. First, you were introduced to the concept of layers. You created a layer via cut, a layer from another image, and a layer from a selection, using the Layers panel to set options, select, rename, color, view, and hide layers. You then used the eraser tools to erase unneeded portions of a layer. You learned how to hide portions of layers and fine-tuned layers with layer masks, adjustments, and styles. Finally, you used the Clone Stamp Tool to add wood flooring into the composite image. The file was flattened and saved in the TIF format.

The items listed below include all the new Photoshop skills you have learned in this chapter:

1. Change Layers Panel Options (PS 142)
2. Create a Layer via Cut (PS 143)
3. Rename a Layer (PS 145)
4. Assign a Color to a Layer (PS 146)
5. Hide and Show a Layer (PS 147)
6. Arrange Document Windows (PS 150)
7. Create a Layer by Dragging an Entire Image (PS 151)
8. Move a Layer in the Document Window (PS 152)
9. Create a Layer by Dragging a Selection (PS 154)
10. Transform by Skewing (PS 159)
11. Display Only the Current Layer (PS 164)
12. Erase using the Magic Eraser Tool (PS 164)
13. Erase using the Eraser Tool (PS 167)
14. Erase using the Block Mouse Pointer (PS 168)
15. Transform by Changing the Perspective (PS 169)
16. Erase using the Background Eraser Tool (PS 171)
17. Rearrange Layers (PS 174)
18. Create a Layer Mask (PS 176)
19. Correct a Masking Error (PS 178)
20. Make an Opacity Change to a Layer (PS 180)
21. Make a Levels Adjustment (PS 182)
22. Adjust the Hue and Saturation (PS 184)
23. Fit the Image on Screen (PS 184)
24. Adjust the Brightness and Contrast (PS 186)
25. Apply a Layer Style (PS 189)
26. Create a New Blank Layer (PS 191)
27. Create a Clone (PS 192)
28. Flatten a Composite Image (PS 195)

Apply Your Knowledge

Reinforce the skills and apply the concepts you learned in this chapter.

Creating Layers in a Poster

Instructions: Start Photoshop and perform the customization steps found on pages PS 6 through PS 10. Open the file named Apply 3-1 Storage History from the Data Files for Students. Visit www.cengage.com/ct/studentdownload for detailed instructions or contact your instructor for information about accessing the required files.

The purpose of this exercise is to create a composite poster showing the history of external storage devices by creating layers. The edited photo is displayed in Figure 3–80.

Perform the following tasks:

1. Press SHIFT+CTRL+S to open the Save As dialog box. Enter the name, Apply 3-1 Storage History Composite. Do not press the ENTER key. Click the Format box arrow and then select the Photoshop PSD format, if necessary. Click the Save in box arrow and then select your USB flash drive location. Click the Save button to save the file in the PSD format. If Photoshop displays an Options dialog box, click the OK button.

Figure 3–80

Table 3–6 lists the other files, layer names, identification colors, and manipulations that you will use in this assignment.

Table 3–6 Storage Device Layers			
File Name	**Layer Name**	**Layer Color**	**Layer Manipulations**
Apply 3-1 CD	CD	Violet	Layer Style | Outer Glow
Apply 3-1 Flash Drive	flash drive	Green	Layer Style | Inner Glow Mask lid
Apply 3-1 Zip Disk	zip disk	Orange	Layer Style | Bevel and Emboss
Apply 3-1 Tape	tape	Yellow	Adjustments | Hue 10, –10, 0
Apply 3-1 Cassette Tape	cassette tape	Yellow	Adjustments | Brightness/Contrast
Apply 3-1 Small Floppy	small floppy	Blue	erase background and rotate
Apply 3-1 Medium Floppy	medium floppy	Blue	erase background and rotate
Apply 3-1 Large Floppy	large floppy	Blue	erase background and rotate
Apply 3-1 Punched Card	punched card	Red	clone

2. To create the CD layer:

    a. Press CTRL+O to display the Open dialog box. Navigate to the Data Files for Students and then double-click the file named Apply 3-1 CD to open it.

    b. On the Application bar, click Window, point to Arrange to display the Arrange submenu, and then click Tile All Horizontally to arrange the document windows. Press the v key to activate the Move Tool. Drag the image from the Apply 3-1 CD document window into the Apply 3-1 Storage History Composite document window. Close the Apply 3-1 CD file.

c. Name and color the layer as directed in Table 3–6.

d. Click the 'Add a layer style' button on the Layers panel status bar, and then click Outer Glow. Change the Opacity to 75% and the Size to 150 px. Use the default values for all other settings.

e. Resize the CD, if necessary, and position it as shown in Figure 3–80.

3. To create the flash drive layer:

a. Press CTRL+O to display the Open dialog box. Navigate to the Data Files for Students and then open the file named Apply 3-1 Flash Drive.

b. On the Application bar, click Window, point to Arrange and then click Tile All Horizontally to arrange the document windows.

c. Drag the flash drive image into the Apply 3-1 Storage History Composite document window. Close the Apply 3-1 Flash Drive file.

d. Name and color the layer.

e. Click the 'Add a layer style' button on the Layers panel status bar, and then click Inner Glow. Change the Opacity to 75% and the Size to 25 px. Use the default values for all other settings.

f. Resize the flash drive and position it as shown in Figure 3–80.

g. Click the 'Add a layer mask' button. Press the x key to switch the default colors to black over white, if necessary. Press the B key to access the brush and then paint over the lid to mask it.

4. To create the zip disk layer:

a. Open the file, Apply 3-1 Zip Disk.

b. Arrange the document windows side by side.

c. Drag the image from the new window into the Storage History Composite document window. Close the Apply 3-1 Zip Disk file.

d. Name and color the layer.

e. Click the 'Add a layer style' button on the Layers panel status bar, and then click Bevel & Emboss. Click the Style button and then click Inner Bevel, if necessary. Change the Size to 90 px. Use the default values for all other settings.

f. Resize the zip disk, if necessary, and position it as shown in Figure 3–80.

5. To create the tape layer:

a. Open the file, Apply 3-1 Tape. Press CTRL+A to select the entire image. Press CTRL+C to copy the image to the clipboard.

b. Paste the image into the Apply 3-1 Storage History Composite document window. Close the Apply 3-1 Tape file.

c. Name and color the layer.

d. Click the Hue/Saturation icon on the Adjustments panel to display the settings. On the panel's status bar, click the Clip to Layer button. Adjust the Hue to 10, the Saturation to –10 and the Lightness to 0. Click the Adjustments button in the vertical dock to collapse the Adjustments panel.

e. Resize the tape, if necessary, and position it as shown in Figure 3–80.

Continued >

6. To create the cassette tape layer:

   a. Open the file, Apply 3-1 Cassette Tape.

   b. Arrange the document windows and drag the image from the new window into the Apply 3-1 Storage History Composite document window. Close the Apply 3-1 Cassette Tape file.

   c. Name and color the layer.

   d. On the Adjustments panel, click the Brightness/Contrast icon and then click the Clip to Layer button. Adjust the Brightness to 35.

   e. Click the Adjustments button in the vertical dock to collapse the Adjustments panel.

7. To create the floppy disk layers:

   a. One at a time open each of the floppy disk files listed in Table 3–6 on page PS 198.

   b. Copy and paste each image into the Storage History Composite document window.

   c. Name and color each layer.

   d. Use the eraser tools to erase extraneous background.

   e. Position and rotate the images as shown in Figure 3–80 on page PS 198.

8. To clone the punched card:

   a. Select the Background layer. Create a new layer by pressing CTRL+SHIFT+N. Name the layer, punched card. Do not check the Use previous Layer to Create Clipping Mask check box. Choose a red identification color. Do not change the mode or opacity. Click the OK button to close the New Layer dialog box. Press CTRL+LEFT BRACKET ([) to move the punched card layer below the Background layer. ALT+click the visibility icon on the punched card layer to display only that layer.

   b. Open the file, Apply 3-1 Punched Card.

   c. Arrange the document windows above and below one another.

   d. Press the s key to activate the Clone Stamp Tool. On the options bar, click to display the Aligned check mark, if necessary.

   e. ALT+click in the punched card document window, close to the upper-left corner.

   f. Drag in the Apply 3-1 Storage History Composite document window to create a clone.

   g. Repeat Steps e and f to create four more clones at various locations in the window. (*Hint:* in this montage, it is okay for part of a cloned image to run off the edge of the document window.)

9. Close the Apply 3-1 Punched Card window.

10. On the Layers panel of the Apply 3-1 Storage History Composite window, click the 'Indicates layer visibility' button beside each layer to display the layers.

11. Save the file again by pressing CTRL+S.

12. On the Layers panel, click the Layers panel menu button to display the menu. Click Flatten Image on the menu to flatten all of the layers.

13. Press SHIFT+CTRL+S to open the Save As dialog box. Type Apply 3-1 Storage History Complete in the Name box. Click the Format box arrow and then click TIFF in the list. Click the Save button. If Photoshop displays a dialog box, click the OK button.

14. Turn in a hard copy of the photo to your instructor.

15. Quit Photoshop.

Extend Your Knowledge

Extend the skills you learned in this chapter and experiment with new skills. You may need to use Help to complete the assignment.

Exploring Layer Comps

Instructions: Start Photoshop. Set the default workspace, default colors, and reset all tools. To complete this assignment, you will be required to use the Data Files for Students. Visit www.cengage.com/ct/studentdownload for detailed instructions or contact your instructor for information about accessing the required files. Open the file Extend 3-1 Marketing Graphic from the Chapter 03 folder of the Data Files for Students.

The purpose of this exercise to create layer comps of a product box for client evaluation. The current graphic has layers for the background, inside, and outside of the box. You are to insert the trophy graphic and scale it to fit the box, then create layer comps showing the inside and the outside. The edited photo is shown in Figure 3–81.

Figure 3–81

Perform the following tasks:
1. Save the file with the name, Extend 3-1 Marketing Graphic Composite. If necessary, click the Format box arrow and then select the Photoshop PSD format. Click the Save in box arrow and then select your USB flash drive location. Click the Save button. If Photoshop displays a Format Options dialog box, click the OK button.

2. Show and hide the various layers using the visibility icon to gain familiarity with the graphic.

3. Make the Background layer and inside layer visible; hide all other layers. Select the inside layer.

4. Open the Extend 3-1 Trophy file from the Chapter 03 folder of the Data Files for Students. Use the Arrange Documents button to display the windows side by side.

5. Use the Move Tool to drag the trophy from its own window into the Extend 3-1 Marketing Graphic Composite document window. Scale the trophy to fit in the box. Make the outside

Continued >

Extend Your Knowledge *continued*

layer visible and make sure the trophy can be seen through the opening in the outer box. Name the layer, trophy.

6. Make the front panel layer visible and select it. At the top of the Layers panel, adjust the Fill setting so the layer looks more transparent, as if it were plastic.

7. Make the gleam layer visible. Adjust the Opacity and Fill settings as necessary. Save the file.

8. Use Photoshop Help to learn about Layer Comps. Also read the BTW boxes on page PS 140. Open the Layer Comps panel and create the layer comps described in Table 3–7.

Table 3–7 Marketing Graphic Layer Comps

Layer Comp Name	Visible Layers
Empty Box	Background, inside
Inner Box with Trophy	Background, inside, trophy
Outer Box with Trophy	Background, inside, trophy, outside, shadow
Complete Graphic	All layers

9. Save the file again.

10. For extra credit, copy the trophy layer and scale it to approximately 30 percent of its original size. In the Layers panel, move the layer above the outside layer. Position the trophy in the lower-middle portion of the box. Warp the layer to make it wrap around the corner of the box. Create a layer comp named Complete with Wrapped Logo and include all layers.

11. Submit this assignment in the format specified by your instructor.

Make It Right

Analyze a project and correct all errors and/or improve the design.

Correcting Layer Errors

Instructions: Start Photoshop and perform the customization steps found on pages PS 6 through PS 10. To complete this assignment, you will be required to use the Data Files for Students. Visit www.cengage.com/ct/studentdownload for detailed instructions or contact your instructor for information about accessing the required files. Open the Make It Right 3-1 Park file from the Chapter 03 folder of the Data Files for Students.

The photo has layers that are invisible, layers that need transformation, and layers that need to be moved, trimmed, and adjusted for levels (Figure 3–82).

Perform the following tasks:
Save the file on your storage device in the PSD format with the name, Make It Right 3-1 Park Composite. For each invisible layer, reveal the layer, correct any order problem by dragging the layer to an appropriate position on the Layers panel, erase or mask parts of the layer as necessary, and move the layer to a logical position.

Use the Adjustments panel and tools such as Levels, Brightness/Contrast, and Hue/Saturation to create adjustment layers. (*Hint:* Be sure to click the Clip to Layer button on the Adjustments panel status bar, so the adjustment will apply to that layer only.) Make any other adjustments or layer style changes that you deem necessary. Save the file again and submit it in the format specified by your instructor.

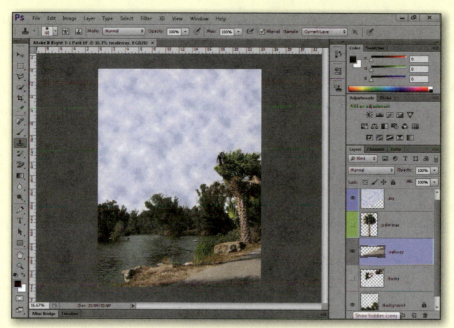

Figure 3–82

In the Lab

Design and/or create a project using the guidelines, concepts, and skills presented in this chapter. Labs are listed in order of increasing difficulty.

Lab 1: Using the Clone Stamp Tool and Creating a Layer with Outer Glow

Problem: The marketing agency that you work for has asked you to edit the latest advertisement for Qintara perfume. You decide to use Photoshop's layering capabilities to insert the image of the perfume bottle. You also decide to clone the Q of the logo multiple times to create a stylistic band of color across the advertisement. A sample of the advertisement is displayed in Figure 3–83.

Note: To complete this assignment, you will be required to use the Data Files for Students. Visit www.cengage.com/ct/studentdownload for detailed instructions or contact your instructor for information about accessing the required files.

Figure 3–83

Continued >

In the Lab *continued*

Instructions: Perform the following tasks:

1. Start Photoshop. Set the default workspace, default colors, and reset all tools.

2. Open the file Lab 3-1 Perfume from the Chapter 03 folder of the Data Files for Students.

3. Click View on the Application bar and then click Fit on Screen to view the entire image at the largest possible magnification.

4. Click the Save As command on the File menu. Type `Lab 3-1 Perfume Edited` as the file name. If necessary, click the Format box arrow and then click PSD in the list. Browse to your USB flash drive storage device. Click the Save button. If Photoshop displays a Format Options dialog box, click the OK button.

5. On the Layers panel, select the layer named, slogan. In the document window, use the Move Tool to move the layer to the lower portion of the image.

6. Open the Lab 3-1 Bottle file from the Chapter 03 folder from the Data Files for Students. Arrange the files horizontally. Select the entire bottle image and then drag a copy to the Lab 3-1 Perfume Edited window.

7. In the Lab 3-1 Perfume Edited window, name the new layer and set an identification color. Close the Lab 3-1 Bottle document window.

8. On the Layers panel status bar, use the 'Add layer mask' button to create a layer mask in the bottle layer. (*Hint:* Make sure you have black over white for the foreground and background colors.) Use the Brush Tool with black to mask the area around the bottle.

9. Click the 'Add a layer style' button on the Layers panel status bar, and then click Outer Glow. When the Layer Style dialog box is displayed, type `25` in the Size box, and then click the OK button.

10. Select the Background layer. Click the Clone Stamp Tool on the Tools panel. ALT+click the top of the letter Q in the logo. Move the mouse pointer down and to the right. Drag to create a clone of the Q.

11. Repeat Step 10, creating multiple, overlapped clones of the letter Q as shown in Figure 3–83 on the previous page. Use short strokes. If you make a mistake, press CTRL+Z and drag again.

12. When you are satisfied with your clones, flatten the image.

13. Save the file again and submit the assignment in the format specified by your instructor.

In the Lab

Lab 2: Creating a Toy Company Advertisement

Problem: You are to create a composite photo for a toy company by adding and adjusting layers, as shown in Figure 3–84.

Note: To complete this assignment, you will be required to use the Data Files for Students. Visit www.cengage.com/ct/studentdownload for detailed instructions or contact your instructor for information about accessing the required files.

Figure 3–84

Instructions: Perform the following tasks:

1. Start Photoshop. Perform the customization steps found on pages PS 6 through PS 10.

2. Open the Lab 3-2 Robot Background file from the Chapter 03 folder of the Data Files for Students and save it on your USB flash storage device with the file name Lab 3-2 Robot Composite.

3. To clone over the shadow on the right side of the image:

   a. Select the Clone Stamp Tool. On the options bar, click the Aligned check box so it does not display a check mark.

   b. ALT+click the ground approximately one inch below the shadow to create the sample for the clone. Drag over the shadowed area, including any rocks, to create a cloned area and hide the shadow. (*Hint*: Use the LEFT BRACKET ([) and RIGHT BRACKET (]) keys to adjust the size of the mouse pointer as needed.)

4. To create a sky layer:

   a. Use the Magic Wand Tool and the 'Add to selection' button to select all of the sky.

   b. On the Layer menu, point to New, and then click Layer Via Cut.

   c. On the Layers panel, double-click the new layer name and type sky to rename the layer. Right-click the visibility icon and select Blue in the list.

5. To add the robot body:

   a. Open the Lab 3-2 Robot Body file from the Chapter 03 folder of the Data Files for Students.

   b. Using the Window menu, arrange the windows side by side.

   c. Use the Move Tool to drag the robot body from the Lab 3-2 Robot Body document window to the Lab 3-2 Robot Composite document window. (*Hint:* Holding down the SHIFT key as you drag automatically centers the image and creates a new layer.) After creating the layer, close the Lab 3-2 Robot Body document window.

   d. Name the layer, robot, and use a violet identification color.

6. Repeat Step 4 to add the shadow graphic using the file, Lab 3-2 Robot Shadow file. Position it behind the robot near the feet, as shown in Figure 3–84. Name the layer, shadow, and use a gray identification color. Close the Lab 3-2 Robot Shadow document window.

Continued >

In the Lab *continued*

7. To move the shadow behind the robot, on the Layers panel, drag the shadow layer just below the robot layer.

8. Repeat Step 4 to add the earth graphic using the file, Lab 3-2 Robot Earth file. Position it in the upper-right corner of the scene. Name the layer, earth, and use a green identification color.

9. Repeat Step 4 to add the title graphic using the file, Lab 3-2 Robot Title file. Position the words centered above the robot's head. Name the layer, title, and use a yellow identification color.

10. To create an adjustment layer and make the background appear more like a moonscape:

    a. On the Layers panel, select the Background layer.

    b. On the Adjustments panel, click the Hue/Saturation icon to display the settings on the Properties panel.

    c. On the Properties panel status bar, click the Clip to Layer button to create a new adjustment layer for the background.

    d. Change the Hue to +20 and the Saturation to –80.

    e. Click the Properties button on the vertical dock of panels to collapse the panel.

11. To create an adjustment layer and make the sky layer appear black:

    a. Select the sky layer.

    b. On the Adjustments panel, click the Brightness/Contrast icon to display the settings on the Properties panel. Click the Clip to Layer button. Click the Use Legacy check box so it displays a check mark.

    c. Drag both the Brightness and Contrast sliders to the left to create a black sky.

    d. Click the Properties button on the vertical dock of panels to collapse the panel.

12. To add a layer effect to the title layer:

    a. Select the title layer.

    b. Click the 'Add a layer style' button on the Layers panel status bar, and then click Stroke to display the Layer Style dialog box. (*Hint:* You can read about the Stroke command in Photoshop Help.) Reposition the Layer Style dialog box title bar so you can view title in the document window.

    c. In the Layer Style dialog box, click the Color box to display the Color Picker (Stroke Color) dialog box. Reposition the dialog box so you can view the robot in the document window, if necessary.

    d. Click one of the yellow eyes of the robot to select the yellow color. (*Hint:* The mouse pointer looks like an eyedropper when selecting a color.)

    e. Click the OK button to close the dialog box and then click the OK button to close the Layer Style dialog box.

13. Save the composite file again with all the layers.

14. Right-click any layer on the Layers panel and then click Flatten Image.

15. Press SHIFT+CTRL+S to open the Save As dialog box. Type Lab 3-2 Robot Complete in the Name box. Click the Format box arrow and then click TIFF in the list. Click the Save in box arrow, and then click Removable Disk (F:) or the location associated with your USB flash drive, in the list. Click the Save button. If Photoshop displays a dialog box, click the OK button.

16. Quit Photoshop.

In the Lab

Lab 3: Creating a Contest Entry with Layers

Problem: You would like to enter your hamster in a creative pet photo contest. You decide to use Photoshop's layering capabilities to dress up your hamster, as shown in Figure 3–85.

Note: To complete this assignment, you will be required to use the Data Files for Students. Visit www.cengage.com/ct/studentdownload for detailed instructions or contact your instructor for information about accessing the required files.

Figure 3–85

Instructions: Perform the following tasks:

Start Photoshop. Set the default workspace, default colors, and reset all tools. Open the file Lab 3-3 Hamster from the Chapter 03 folder of the Data Files for Students. Rename the file, Lab 3-3 Hamster Composite and save it as a PSD file on your file storage device.

Open the Lab 3-3 Pipe file, arrange the windows, and then drag a copy to the Lab 3-3 Hamster Composite window. Set the layer properties. Close the Lab 3-3 Pipe document window. Remove the background around the pipe. Scale and position the layer as necessary. Adjust the perspective. Repeat the process for the Lab 3-3 Magnifying Glass file. Reposition the layers as necessary.

Repeat the process for the Lab 3-3 Hat file, scaling the layer as necessary, and place it on top of the hamster's head. Select the right third (back) of the hat and create a layer via cut. On the Layers panel, set the properties and move the back of hat layer, below the hamster layer, so that part of the hat appears behind the hamster's ear.

Make any other adjustments to the layers that you feel would enhance the photo. When you are satisfied with your layers, save the image again. Flatten the image, save it as a TIFF file, and submit a copy to your instructor.

Cases and Places

Apply your creative thinking and problem-solving skills to design and implement a solution.

Note: To complete this assignment, you will be required to use the Data Files for Students. Visit www.cengage.com/ct/studentdownload for detailed instructions or contact your instructor for information about accessing the required files.

1: Clone within the Same Document

Academic

Earlier in this chapter, a suggestion was made to create a flag with 50 percent opacity superimposed over a memorial. Open the files named Case 3-1 Memorial and Case 3-1 Flag, located in the Chapter 03 folder of the Data Files for Students. (Alternatively, locate or take a photo of a memorial in your city or a building on your campus. If necessary, obtain permission to use a digital photo or scan the image.) Arrange the windows. Select only the flag and then drag it as a new layer into the memorial photo. Resize the layer to fit across the memorial. Change the opacity to 50 percent. Make other corrections as necessary. Save the composite photo and print a copy.

2: Create a Graphic with Opacity Changes

Personal

You recently took a photo of a deer at the local forest preserve. To make the picture more interesting, you decide to create a layer and clone the deer. Open the photo named Case 3-1 Deer, located in the Chapter 03 folder of the Data Files for Students. Click the Layer command on the Application bar, point to New, and then click Layer. Click the Background layer, choose the Clone Stamp Tool, and take a sample of the middle of the deer. Click the new layer and clone the deer. On the Edit menu, click Free Transform and resize the cloned deer so it appears to be farther away. Flip the clone horizontally. Save the file as Case 3-2 Deer Cloned on your storage device.

3: Create a Greeting Card Graphic with Masking

Professional

You have been hired as an intern with a greeting card company. You were given several photos to use in preparing holiday cards. The file named Case 3-3 Santa Scene is located in the Chapter 03 folder of the Data Files for Students. You want to use only the figure of Santa Claus on the front of a card. Save the photo in the PSD format on your USB flash drive storage device as Case 3-3 Santa Layered. Create a rectangular marquee selection around the figure. Use the Layer Via Cut command and name the new layer, Santa. Hide the background. Create a layer mask, painting with black to display only the figure. Print the photo with the background hidden.

1 | Creating a Simple Animated Web Banner

Objectives

You will have mastered the material in this chapter when you can:

- Start Flash and customize the Flash workspace
- Create a Flash document
- Describe the Flash workspace
- Show and hide panels
- Import a bitmap image
- Convert a bitmap image to a vector image
- Modify the stage

- Insert keyframes
- Create a shape tween animation
- Run an animation
- Export a Flash document
- Write ActionScript code
- Publish a Flash animation
- Use Flash Help

1 | Creating a Simple Animated Web Banner

What Is Flash CS6?

Flash CS6 is a popular animation software program produced by Adobe Systems Incorporated. Designers use Flash to create movies that can run in Web pages or over a computer network. A Flash movie can be an animated greeting card; a banner advertisement for a Web page, game, cartoon, or stand-alone program; or any other animation intended for use on a Web site, mobile device such as a smartphone, kiosk, or computer. Flash movies are often categorized as **Rich Internet Applications (RIAs)**, which are Internet-accessed programs that incorporate a high level of user interactivity. Rich Internet Applications that are developed with Flash are known as **Flash movies**. Designers often use Flash CS6 to create audio and video players, which are software programs that contain buttons to control media actions such as play, pause, back, and forward. For example, video on YouTube plays in a Flash video player in a Web browser and music on Myspace plays with a Flash audio player.

Designers also use Flash CS6 to work with image files for tasks that can be performed in other Adobe software (such as Photoshop and Illustrator). Sometimes it is easier to perform basic image editing or conversion tasks in Flash rather than learning or using more specialized image-editing software.

Flash CS6 is part of the **Adobe Creative Suite 6** and is also sold and used independently as a stand-alone application. Flash CS6 is available for both the PC and Macintosh computer platforms. The chapters in this book use Flash CS6 on the PC platform, running the Windows 7 operating system.

To illustrate the features of Flash CS6, this book presents a series of chapters that use Flash to create visually exciting and interactive projects similar to those found on many Web sites.

Project Planning Guidelines

> The process of creating an animation or an RIA requires careful analysis and planning. After planning a project with a client and agreeing on the final outcome, begin a Flash project by drawing shapes and creating a background scene. Once the background is designed, create and animate the foreground objects. Then, adjust and perfect the animation as needed. Add interactivity, if it is desired, and then test the movie. Finally, export the movie to a format suitable for the project's use. Each chapter in this book provides practical applications of these planning considerations.

Project — Morphing Web Banner

A Web banner is a generic name for an advertisement on a Web site that encourages a user to click it. When clicked, the user's Web browser usually links to the advertiser's Web site. Many advertisers believe that an animated Web banner catches the attention of users and is more likely to be clicked than a nonanimated advertisement. Creating an animation with vector images rather than bitmap images provides more options to manipulate and control the animation.

A **vector image** is a graphic that you can resize with no loss of quality, unlike a **bitmap image**, which becomes blurry when enlarged. Organizations of all kinds, from large corporations to small businesses, schools, rock bands, and sports teams, all need to use images or logos in a variety of scenarios. Some of these usages include Web sites, letterhead, marketing materials, product packaging, and billboards. Often, an organization's logo is available only as a bitmap. Flash can convert a bitmap to a vector. Additionally, Flash has the ability to create morphing animations, in which one image appears to melt and turn into another image. This technique creates a highly visual and interesting animation perfect for use on a Web site.

The project in this chapter uses Flash to convert two bitmap images into vector images. After converting the images, you create an animation in which the first image, a guitar, blends, or **morphs** into the second image, the logo. Figure 1–1a displays the initial state of the vector animation. Figure 1–1b displays the animation partway through the morphing process. Figure 1–1c shows the final state of the animation. The conversion from bitmap to vector requires the use of many Flash CS6 skills, including importing and tracing bitmaps, making selections, working with color, working with layers, and exporting (or publishing) the final work. Creating a morphing animation requires a basic understanding of Flash objects, the Timeline, keyframes, and tweening.

Guitar image © Martijnmulder, Dreamstime LLC

(a) Original vector image

(b) Animation in process

(c) Final vector image

Logo courtesy of Asheville Rock Academy

Figure 1–1

Overview

As you read this chapter, you will learn how to create the project shown in Figure 1–1. Once you have converted the bitmap to vector artwork, you will add a morphing animation. The project will be completed by performing these general tasks:

- Customize the workspace.
- Import and trace a bitmap.
- Insert a keyframe.
- Insert a shape tween.
- Export a vector image.
- Publish a Web graphic.
- Use Flash Help.

Plan Ahead

BTW

By The Way Boxes
For a complete list of the BTWs found in the margins of this book, visit the BTW chapter resource on the student companion site located at www.cengagebrain.com.

General Project Guidelines

When converting a bitmap to a vector and creating a morphing animation, the actions you perform and decisions you make will affect the appearance and characteristics of the finished product. As you perform the conversion and create the animation, you should follow these general guidelines:

1. **Determine the best file format for the image.** If an image will need to be enlarged, it will need to be in a vector format. If the image is meant for use only on a computer screen without being animated, a bitmap format might be appropriate.

2. **Find an appropriate image or photo.** The more detail or color gradient in the original image, the more difficult it will be to convert it to a vector image with satisfying results. Keep in mind how the image will appear in a small format, like on a business card, and what it will look like in a larger version, such as on a banner or billboard.

3. **Determine an appropriate length of time for the animation.** Animation can occur in a fraction of a second or over several minutes. Make the animation long enough so your viewers have time for it to register, but not so long that it becomes tedious to watch.

4. **Plan keyframes.** With the length of the animation determined, plan the placement of keyframes accordingly. Typically, Flash animations run 24 frames per second with keyframes assigned at transitional parts of the animation.

5. **Plan export formats in preparation for publication.** Export the vector artwork in a format appropriate for use in dedicated vector artwork software. Publish the animation in a format appropriate for its delivery method, such as for use on a Web site, mobile device, or stand-alone desktop application.

When necessary, more specific details concerning the above guidelines are presented at appropriate points in the chapter. The chapter also will identify the actions performed and decisions made regarding these guidelines during the creation of the edited images shown in Figure 1–1.

Starting Flash

If you are using a computer to step through the project in this chapter, and you want your screen to match the figures in this book, you should change your screen's resolution to 1024×768. (Adobe recommends a minimum screen resolution of 1280×800 for Flash.) For information about how to change a screen's resolution, see the Changing Screen Resolution appendix at the back of this book.

To Start Flash

The following steps, which assume Windows 7 is running, start Flash, based on a typical installation. You may need to ask your instructor how to start Flash for your computer.

1

● Click the Start button on the Windows 7 taskbar to display the Start menu.

● Type `Flash CS6` as the search text in the 'Search programs and files' text box, and watch the search results appear on the Start menu (Figure 1–2).

Q&A Why do I have documents and files in my list of results?

Any documents containing the words, Flash CS6, and any files that have been opened with Flash CS6 might appear in your list.

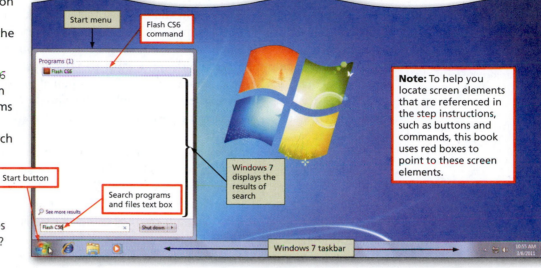

Note: To help you locate screen elements that are referenced in the step instructions, such as buttons and commands, this book uses red boxes to point to these screen elements.

Start menu • Flash CS6 command • Programs (1) Flash CS6 • Start button • Search programs and files text box • Windows 7 displays the results of search • See more results • Flash CS6 • Shut down • Windows 7 taskbar

Figure 1–2

2

● Click Adobe Flash Professional CS6 in the search results on the Start menu to start Flash.

● After a few moments, when the Flash window is displayed, if the window is not maximized, click the Maximize button next to the Close button on the title bar to maximize the window (Figure 1–3).

Q&A What is a maximized window?

A maximized window fills the entire screen. When you maximize a window, the Maximize button changes to a Restore Down button.

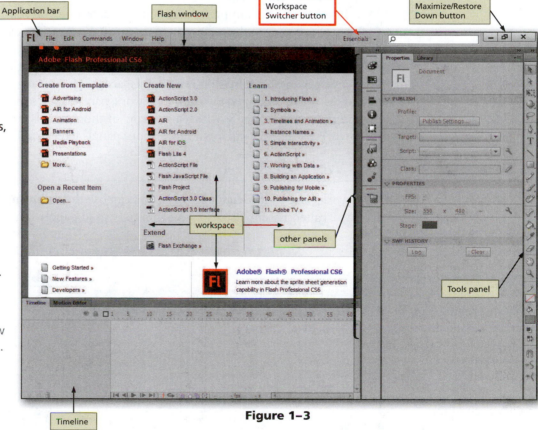

Application bar • Flash window • Workspace Switcher button • Maximize/Restore Down button • workspace • other panels • Tools panel • Timeline

Figure 1–3

Other Ways

1. Double-click Flash icon on desktop, if one is present
2. Click Adobe Flash Professional CS6 on Start menu

 For a detailed example of this procedure using the Mac operating system, refer to the steps in the For Mac Users appendix at the back of this book.

BTW

Q&A
For a complete list of the Q&As found in many of the step-by-step sequences in this book, visit the Q&A chapter resource on the student companion site located at www.cengagebrain.com.

Customizing the Flash Workspace

The screen in Figure 1–3 shows how the Flash workspace looks the first time you start Flash after installation on most computers. Flash does not open a blank or default file automatically; rather, the Application bar appears across the top of the screen with a gray work area below. By default, the gray work area displays a menu for creating new documents. This menu disappears when a file is opened or created. The Tools panel and other panels are displayed on the right. The Timeline is a panel that appears below the work area. The gray work area and panels are referred to collectively as the **workspace**.

The workspace can be customized to display only the panels you want. Panels, which are containers for various commands and tools, can also be moved from their default locations and positioned where you like. This is a good way to optimize your Flash environment so that you can work as efficiently as possible. You can save or reset altered workspaces to the default settings using the Workspace Switcher in the Application bar.

As you work in Flash, the panels and the selected tool might change in location and appearance from the default settings. Therefore, if you want your screen to match the figures in this book, you should restore the default workspace and select the default tool. For more information about how to change other advanced Flash settings, see the Using Flash CS6 Help appendix.

Because of a default preference setting, each time you start Flash, the Flash workspace is displayed the same way it appeared the last time you used Flash. If you or another user relocates the panels while working with Flash, then they will appear in their new locations the next time you start Flash. You can create and save your own workspaces, or use Flash's saved workspaces that show a group of panels used for certain tasks. For example, the Animator workspace displays the panels on both the left and right sides of the work area — many of those panels are hidden by default in other workspaces. You will learn more about panels later in this chapter.

To Select the Essentials Workspace

If you want to return the workspace to its default settings, you can use the following steps each time you start Flash. The default workspace, called Essentials, displays commonly used panels. The following steps select the Essentials workspace.

1

- Click the Workspace Switcher button on the Application bar to display the names of saved workspaces (Figure 1–4).

 Experiment

- Click each of the workspaces that are displayed in the list to view the different panel configurations. When you are finished, click the Workspace Switcher button again to display the list.

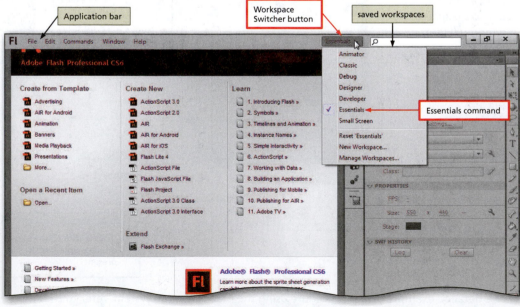

Figure 1–4

2

- If necessary, click Essentials to select the default workspace panels.

- Click the Workspace Switcher button again to display the list (Figure 1–5).

Q&A What does the New Workspace command do?

The New Workspace command displays a dialog box where you can create a new workspace based on the currently displayed panels. You also can add the current keyboard shortcuts and menus to the new workspace.

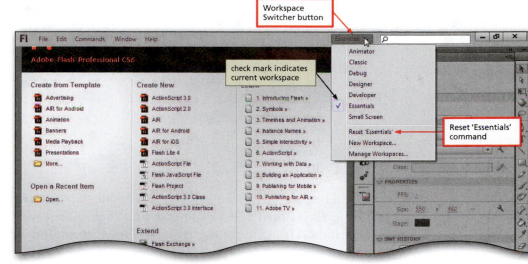

Figure 1–5

3

- Click Reset 'Essentials' to restore the workspace to its default settings and reposition any panels that might have been moved (Figure 1–6).

Q&A My screen did not change. Did I do something wrong?

If Flash is a new installation on your system, you might notice few changes, if any, on your screen.

Figure 1–6

> **Other Ways**
> 1. On Window menu, point to Workspace, click Reset 'Essentials'

Creating a New Document

Flash can create many different types of files, including ActionScript (for general use on Web sites), Adobe AIR (for developing desktop applications), iPhone OS (for creating Apple iPhone games and apps), and Flash Lite (for game and app development on non-Apple mobile devices). This book focuses on the use of Flash for general Web site use, so you will use the ActionScript file type throughout this book. Flash CS6 offers two different versions of ActionScript files: ActionScript 2.0, which is the older version used for backward compatibility, and ActionScript 3.0, which is the current version.

When you create an ActionScript file, Flash creates a file with an **.fla** file extension. This file is referred to as an FLA (pronounced "eff-el-ay") file. It is considered a **source file** because it is the file used to generate other files that are actually used on Web sites. The general workflow is this:

1. Develop movie.
2. Export movie.
3. Edit original movie.
4. Re-export movie.
5. Add exported movie to Web site.

The Flash developer works on an FLA file in Flash to develop the application. The developer then publishes, or exports, a Web-friendly version of the complete application. This exported file has a **.swf** file extension and is called a SWF (pronounced "swiff") file. If the developer must later make changes to the application on the Web site, the changes are made in the FLA file, and the developer generates a new SWF file and copies it to the Web site. If you have worked with Adobe Photoshop before, you will notice that an FLA file is similar to a PSD file (the native Photoshop file type) and the SWF is similar to a JPG or GIF (Web-friendly file).

To Create a New ActionScript 3.0 Document

The following steps create a new Flash document using the ActionScript 3.0 file type.

1
- Click File on the Application bar to display the File menu (Figure 1–7).

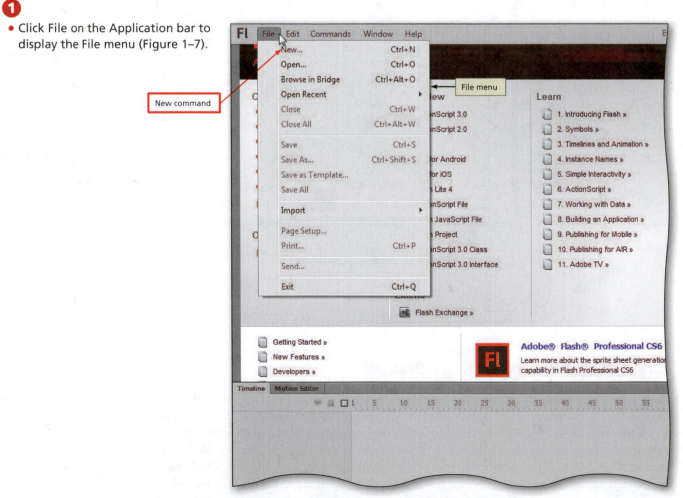

Figure 1–7

2

- Click New on the File menu to display the New Document dialog box (Figure 1–8).

Q&A

Can I just click one of the New options on the large menu that appears in the workspace's gray area?

Yes. However, using the File menu displays the New Document dialog box, which provides a description of each file type.

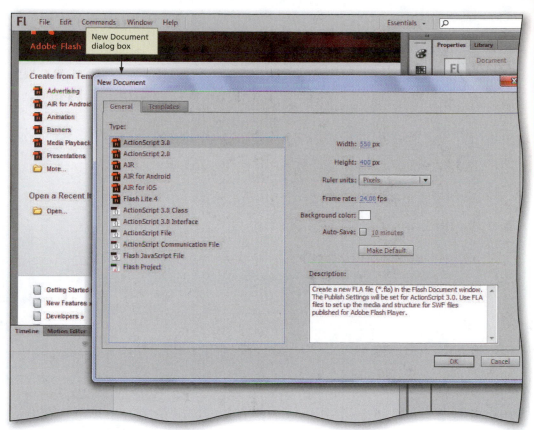

Figure 1–8

3

- If necessary, click ActionScript 3.0 in the New Document dialog box to select it and display its description (Figure 1–9).

Experiment

- Click each of the other file types that are listed in the Type menu to read their descriptions. When you are finished, click the ActionScript 3.0 file type again to select it.

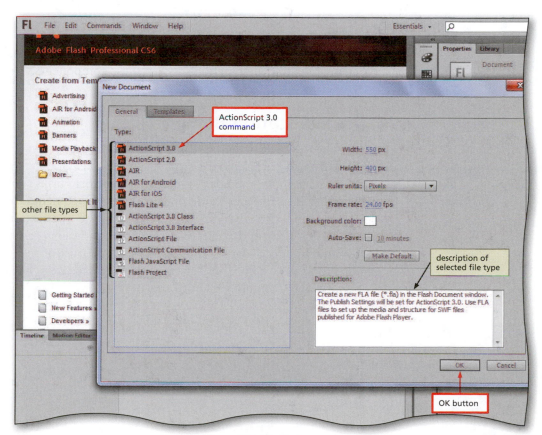

Figure 1–9

4

- Click the OK button to create a new ActionScript 3.0 document (Figure 1–10).

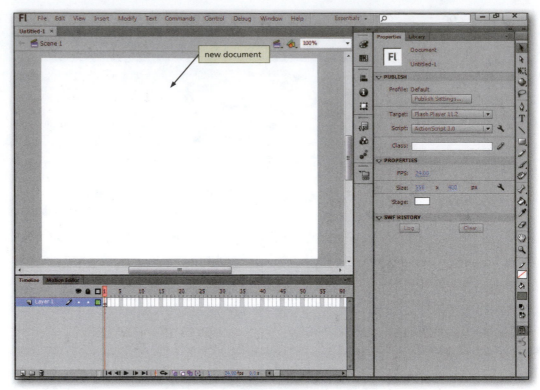

Figure 1–10

<table>
<tr><td>**Other Ways**</td></tr>
<tr><td>1. CTRL+N</td></tr>
</table>

The Flash Workspace

The Flash workspace consists of a variety of components to make your work more efficient. The following sections discuss these components.

The Application Bar

The Application bar appears at the top of the screen (Figure 1–11). The **Application bar** is a toolbar that displays the Flash menu names. Each **menu** contains a list of commands you can use to perform tasks such as opening, saving, and closing files and modifying objects in your document. To display a menu, such as the View menu, click the View menu name on the Application bar. If you point to a command on a menu that has an arrow on its right edge, as shown in Figure 1–11, a **submenu**, or secondary menu, displays another list of related commands. On the right side of the Application bar are the Workspace Switcher button and the Search box for Adobe Community Help.

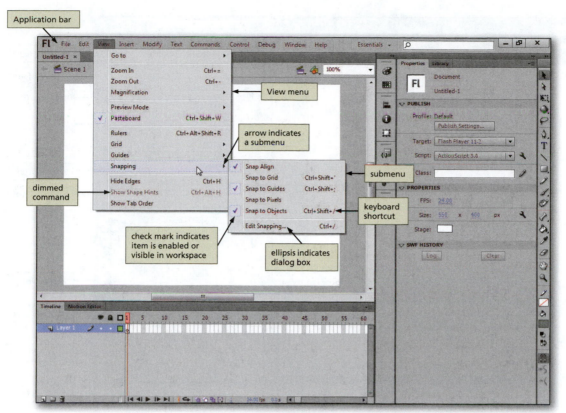

Figure 1–11

The Tools Panel

On the right side of the workspace is the Flash Tools panel. The Tools panel is a group of **tools**, or buttons, organized into a vertical toolbar. You can choose to hide or show the Tools panel, and you can drag it to a new location on your screen. Each tool on the Tools panel displays a **button**. When you point to the tool icon, a tool tip displays the name of the tool, including its shortcut key. You can expand some tools to show hidden tools beneath them. Expandable tools display a small triangle in the lower-right corner of the tool icon. Click and hold the tool button or right-click to see or select one of its hidden tools from the context menu. The default tool names and their corresponding shortcut keys are listed in Figure 1–12.

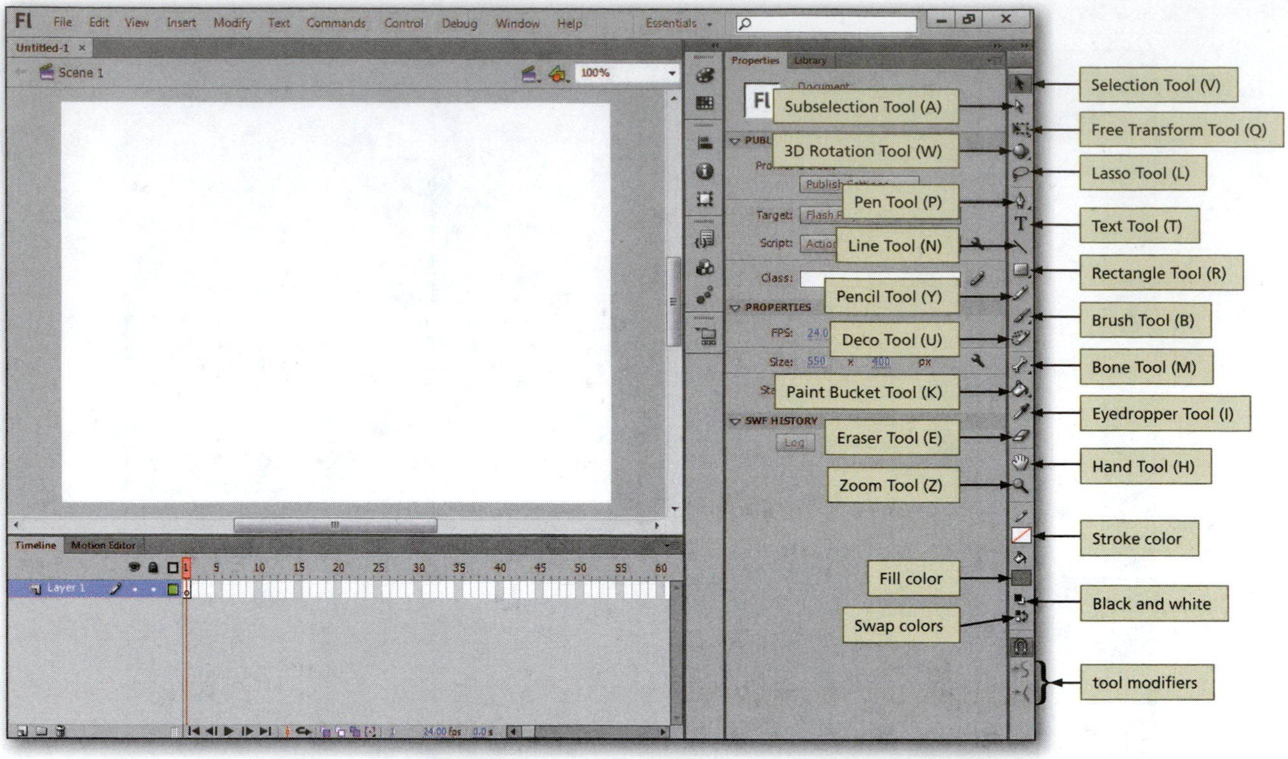

Figure 1–12

When you click a tool on the Tools panel to use it, Flash selects the button and displays the tool's options in the Properties panel, as shown in Figure 1–13. The Properties panel is where you set a tool's options or make modifications to an object selected on the stage. When using a tool from the Tools panel, the mouse pointer changes to reflect the selected tool.

The Tools panel is organized by purpose. At the top of the panel are the selection and transformation tools, followed by vector tools, then miscellaneous tools, and finally the navigation tools. At the bottom of the Tools panel are buttons to set colors, followed by tool modifier buttons that change depending on which tool is selected. Some tools do not display any additional buttons in this area.

As each tool is introduced throughout this book, its function and Properties panel options will be explained further.

BTW

Quick Reference
For a table that lists how to complete the tasks covered in this book using the mouse, menus, context menus, and keyboard, see the Quick Reference Summary at the back of the book or visit the student companion site located at www.cengagebrain.com.

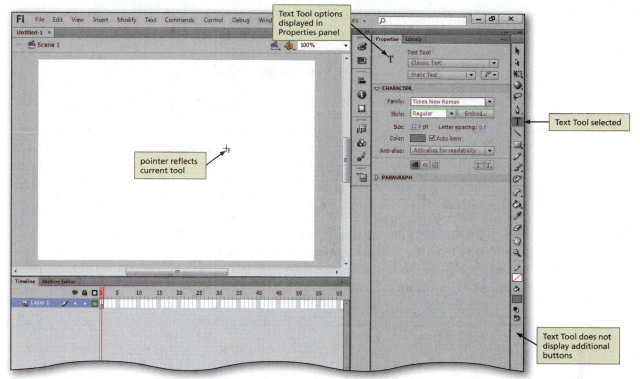

Figure 1–13

The Document Window

The **document window** is the area within the workspace that displays the active file. The document window contains the document window tab, edit bar, stage, work area, and scroll bars (Figure 1–14).

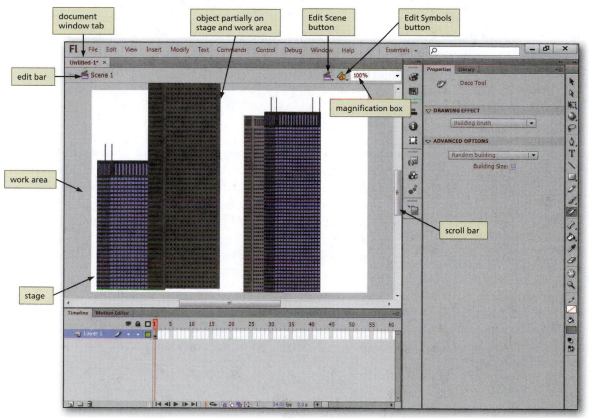

Figure 1–14

Document Window Tab Flash displays a **document window tab** at the top of the document window that shows the name of the file and a Close button. If you have multiple files open in Flash, each has its own document window tab. You can move the document window by dragging its document window tab, or dock it again by dragging it near the Application bar. When floating, the document tab expands across the top of the document window and displays Minimize, Restore Down, and Close buttons.

Edit Bar Just under the document window tab, Flash displays the document window edit bar. On the left side of the edit bar, Flash displays the name of the current scene. A complex Flash animation might contain multiple scenes; having the name of the current scene displayed in the edit bar indicates where you are in your Flash file.

The right side of the edit bar contains the Edit Scene button, which is used to switch between scenes; the Edit Symbols button, which is used to select a symbol for editing; and the magnification box. **Magnification** refers to the percentage of enlargement or reduction on the screen. For example, a 50% indication in the magnification box means the entire stage is displayed at 50 percent of its actual size. Changing the magnification does not change the physical size of the components on the stage; it merely displays it on the screen at a different size. You can type a new percentage in the magnification box to display a different view of the stage.

Stage The stage is the portion of the document window that displays what will be visible on the screen when users view your Flash movie. Think of it like a canvas or a piece of paper on which to draw. You perform most tool tasks and edit the shapes and objects in the stage. By default, the stage is white, but you can change it to any background color you desire.

Work Area The work area is the gray portion of the document window surrounding the stage. It is used as a storage area to place objects that might enter an animation from off-screen or completely exit the screen at the end of an animation. Additionally, you can place objects partially on the stage and partially on the work area so that they appear clipped in the final version of the project.

Scroll Bars **Scroll bars** appear on the right and bottom of the document window. When the stage is bigger than the document window, the scroll bars become active and display scroll arrows and scroll boxes to move the image up, down, left, and right.

Panels

A **panel** is a collection of graphically displayed choices and commands, which can include specific tool settings, colors, or animation details (Figure 1–15). Panels help you monitor and modify your work. Each panel displays a panel tab with the name of the panel and a panel menu button. By default, Flash displays the Library and Properties panels when you start the program. When you click the panel menu button, also called the panel menu icon, Flash displays a context-sensitive menu that allows you to make changes to the panel. Some panels have a status bar across the bottom. A panel can display buttons, boxes, sliders, scroll bars, or lists.

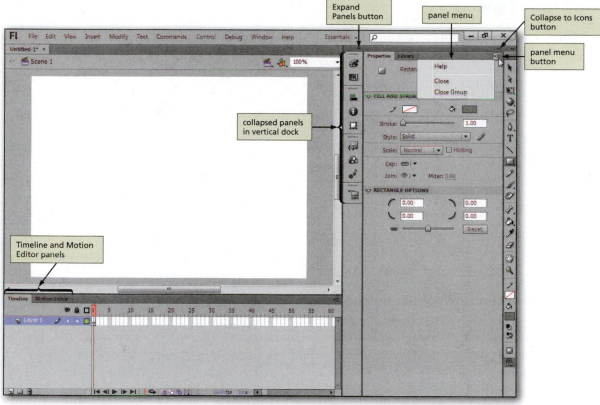

Figure 1–15

The Essentials workspace contains several panels. Some panels are expanded to display their contents and are grouped by general purpose. A **panel group** or **tab group** displays several panels horizontally, joined by a title bar. Panels are **collapsed** when they appear as a button or **expanded** when they display their contents. Panels are **minimized** when they display only their tab. To collapse or expand a panel, click the double arrow in the panel's title bar. To minimize a panel, double-click its tab. To close a panel, click Close on the panel menu. To redisplay the panel, click the panel name on the Window menu or use a panel shortcut key.

You can arrange and reposition panels either individually or in groups. To move them individually, drag their tabs; to move a group, drag the area to the right of the tabs. To float a panel in the workspace, drag its tab outside the vertical dock. You can create a **stack** of floating panels by dragging a panel tab to a location below another floating panel and docking it. Panels can be docked on any side of the stage, though the Essentials workspace only docks panels to the right and below the stage by default.

Flash comes with more than 30 panels, many of which are used to access advanced features. As each panel is introduced throughout this book, its function and characteristics will be explained further.

BTW

The Property Inspector
Previous versions of Flash used the term, Property inspector, to describe the Properties panel. You might also see the term used in the Adobe help system.

To Show and Hide Panels

The following steps show and hide panels.

- Double-click the Properties panel tab to collapse the Properties panel group.

- Click the Library panel tab to expand the Library panel group (Figure 1–16).

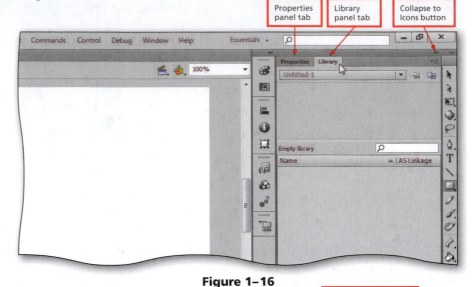

Figure 1–16

- Click the Collapse to Icons button to collapse the Properties panel group (Figure 1–17).

Figure 1–17

- Click the Expand Panels button to expand the Library panel group.

 Where did the Collapse to Icons button go?

The Collapse to Icons button and Expand Panels button are in the same location and are essentially the same button. They toggle back and forth depending on whether a panel group is collapsed or expanded.

- Click the Properties panel tab to redisplay the Properties panel (Figure 1–18).

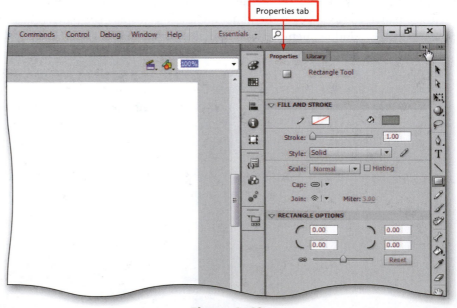

Figure 1–18

Saving Documents

The three most important rules of computing are save, save, and save! Do not wait until a movie is completely finished before saving. Save periodically as you work so if your computer crashes or the power goes out, you do not lose all of your progress. Flash has the ability to automatically save your file every few minutes, but this option is disabled by default. You might not want to save after performing certain steps if you are just experimenting, so saving manually rather than automatically gives you total control over when your progress is saved.

To Save a Flash Document

You have begun creating this movie and do not want to risk losing work completed thus far. Accordingly, you should save the file. The following steps save the movie on a USB flash drive using the file name, Rock Academy Vector Logo. Even though you have yet to edit the Flash movie, it is a good practice to save the file on your personal storage device early in the process.

1

- With a USB flash drive connected to one of the computer's USB ports, click File on the Application bar to display the File menu (Figure 1–19).

Q&A Do I have to save to a USB flash drive?

No. You can save to any device or folder. A **folder** is a specific location on a storage medium. You can save to the default folder or a different folder.

Q&A What if my USB flash drive has a different name or letter?

It is very likely that your USB flash drive will have a different name and drive letter and be connected to a different port. Verify that the device in your Computer list is correct.

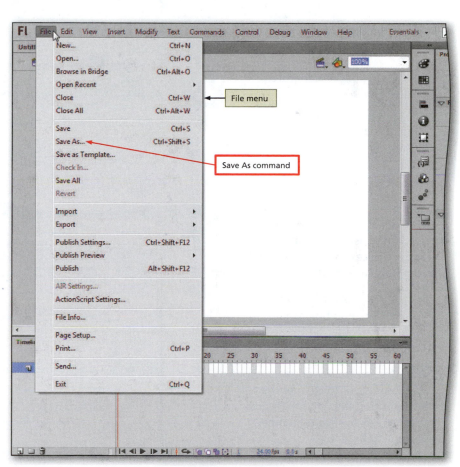

Figure 1–19

2

- Click Save As to display the Save As dialog box.

- Type `Rock Academy Vector Logo` in the File name text box to change the file name. Do not press the ENTER key after typing the file name.

- Click Computer in the left pane of the Save As dialog box to display the list of available drives. (Figure 1–20).

Q&A What if the Save As dialog box does not display a left pane?

The left pane might be hidden. Click the Browse Folders button (Save As dialog box) to display the left pane.

Q&A What if I do not see Computer in the left pane?

You might have to scroll down in the left pane to see the Computer button.

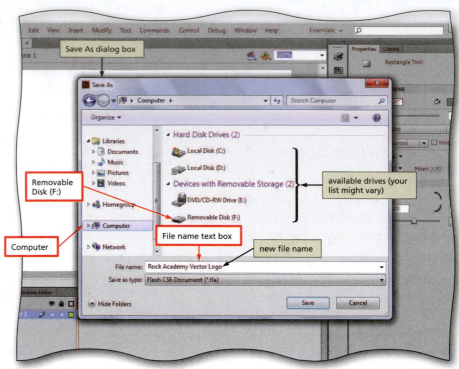

Figure 1–20

3

- Double-click Removable Disk (F:), or the name of your USB flash drive, in the list of available storage devices to select that drive as the new save location.

- Click the New folder button on the Save As dialog box toolbar to create a new folder on the selected storage device.

- When the new folder appears, type `Chapter 01` to change the name of the folder, and then press the ENTER key to save the name (Figure 1–21).

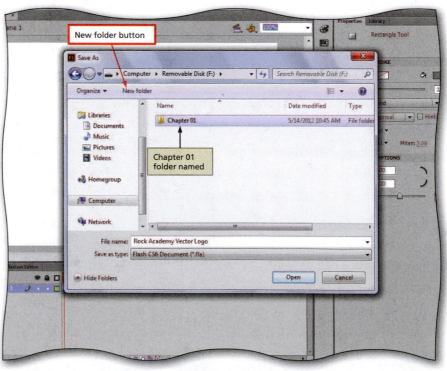

Figure 1–21

4

- Double-click the Chapter 01 folder to open it.

- Click the 'Save as type' box arrow to display the list of available file formats (Figure 1–22).

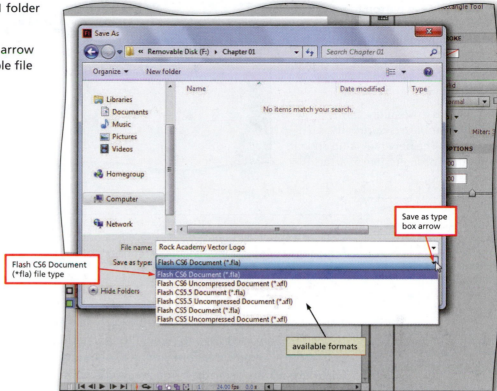

Figure 1–22

5

- If necessary, click Flash CS6 Document (*.fla) to select it (Figure 1–23).

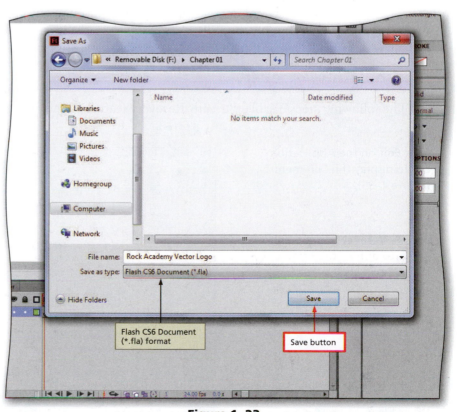

Figure 1–23

6

- Click the Save button to save the document on the selected drive with the new file name (Figure 1–24).

Q&A

How do I know that the project is saved?

Your USB drive might have a light that flashes during the save process. The new file name appears on the document window tab.

new file name displayed in document window tab

Figure 1–24

Other Ways

1. SHIFT+CTRL+S, choose settings, click Save button

MAC For a detailed example of this procedure using the Mac operating system, refer to the steps in the For Mac Users appendix at the back of this book.

Auto-Recovery

Flash can automatically save your file every few minutes as you work. The benefit to this is that you don't have to remember to continually save your work. If your computer crashes or loses power before you save, all unsaved work is lost. However, when the auto-save feature is enabled, you are no longer in control of the save points — the point at which your file was last saved. This can cause problems when trying to undo all changes in a file to the last saved state. You might want to undo all recent changes if you perform several steps and decide you don't like what you did. The Revert command is used to undo all changes and revert the file back to the last saved state. If you think there is ever a chance you might want to revert a document, you should disable the auto-save feature in Flash. This option, which is called Auto-Recovery, is part of the General preferences accessible from the Edit menu on the Application bar.

To Disable Auto-Recovery

The following steps disable the Auto-Recovery feature so that you can later use the Revert command.

1

- Click Edit on the Application bar to display the Edit menu (Figure 1–25).

2

- Click Preferences on the Edit menu to display the Preferences dialog box.

Other Ways

1. CTRL+U

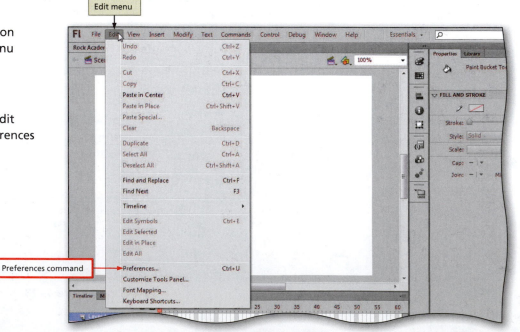

Edit menu

Preferences command

Figure 1–25

3

- Click the General category to select it, if necessary.

- Remove the check mark, if necessary, from the Auto-Recovery option (Figure 1-26).

 4

- Click the OK button to save your changes and close the Preferences dialog box.

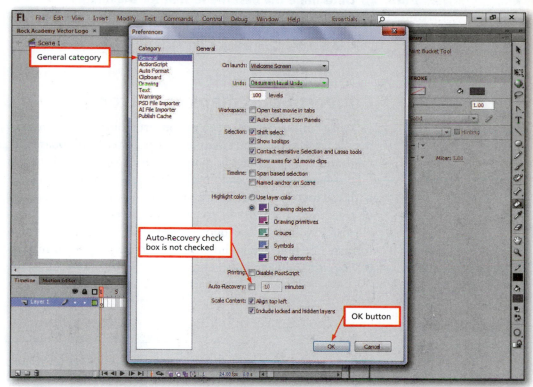

Figure 1–26

Computer Graphics

Computer graphics can be defined by two main categories — bitmap graphics and vector graphics. A bitmap graphic is composed of pixels, which are tiny dots of light that combine to form the image you see on a computer monitor. Photos from a digital camera or images copied to a computer from a scanner are examples of bitmap graphics. The bitmap format is an excellent choice for photos because it can reproduce the high level of detail needed by a photo. In fact, images from a digital camera or scanner always begin as bitmap graphics, or bitmaps. However, enlarging bitmap graphics results in significant loss of quality. As you enlarge a bitmap graphic, it becomes blurry and jagged. JPG, GIF, PNG, and TIF are all common bitmap formats. In comparison, a vector graphic is created with points and curves based on a mathematical formula. Points are placed a certain distance apart and Flash calculates a curve that connects the points. Logos, line drawings, or artwork with large areas of flat nongradient color are good choices for vector graphics. EPS, SVG, AI, and FXG are all common vector formats. Unlike bitmaps, vectors can be enlarged with no loss of quality. Enlarged vectors remain sharp, clean, and in focus. Flash is designed to work primarily with vector artwork.

<table>
<tr><td>**Plan
Ahead**</td><td>**Determine the best file format for the image.**
Vector graphics allow for more animated manipulation than bitmap graphics. Before drawing a vector graphic from scratch, you should import a bitmap version and convert it to a vector. Converting a bitmap is also called tracing.</td></tr>
</table>

Converting Bitmaps to Vectors

At times, you will need to convert a bitmap to a vector. For example, you might need a large version of a logo for a newsletter or billboard advertisement, or you just might need to animate a logo in Flash to have it grow from a small to a large size. If you do not have a vector version of the logo — instead you just have a client's letterhead with the logo — you can scan the logo, save it as a bitmap, and then convert the bitmap to a vector, which allows you to resize it as needed. If your client provides you an electronic version of the logo (a JPG or GIF file), you also will have to convert it to vector format. The first step in the process of converting the bitmap to a vector is to import the bitmap into a Flash document.

To Import a Bitmap

The following steps open the Rockacademy file from the Data Files for Students and import it to the Flash stage. Because the Rockacademy file is a bitmap, you will later need to convert it to a vector.

- Click File on the Application bar to display the File menu.

- Point to Import on the File menu to display the Import submenu (Figure 1–27).

Q&A

What if I do not have the Data Files for Students?

You will need the Data Files for Students to complete the activities and exercises in this book. Visit www.cengage.com/ct/student download for detailed instructions, or see your instructor for information about accessing the required files.

Q&A

Can I use a shortcut key to import the bitmap graphic?

Yes. The shortcut keys are displayed on the menu. In this textbook, the shortcut keys also are displayed at the end of each series of steps in the Other Ways box.

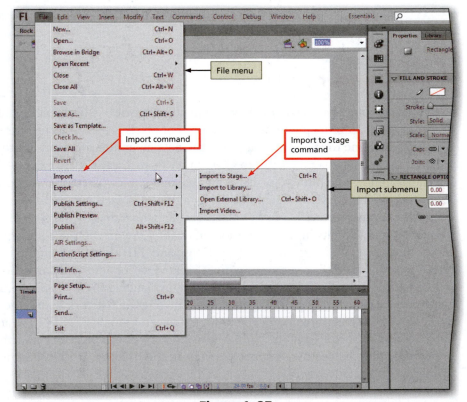

Figure 1–27

- Click Import to Stage on the Import submenu to display the Import dialog box.

- If necessary, scroll in the left side of the Import dialog box to display Computer.

- Click Computer to display a list of the available storage locations on your system (Figure 1–28).

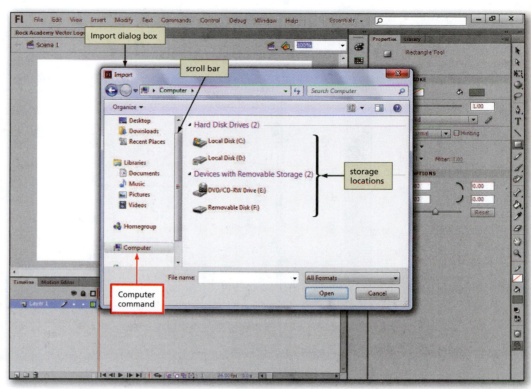

Figure 1–28

- Double-click the C: drive to open it.

- Double-click the Course Technology folder to open it.

- Double-click the Flash folder to open it.

- Double-click the Data Files for Students folder to open it so that the Chapter 01 folder is visible (Figure 1–29).

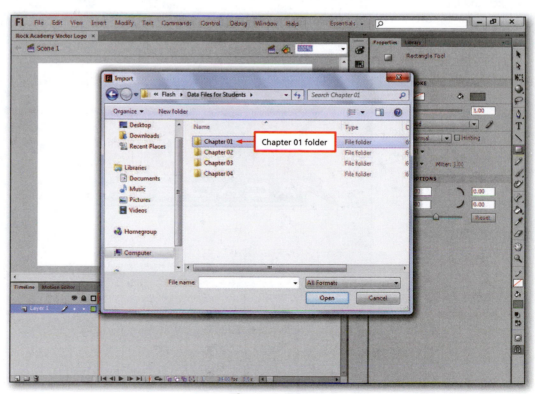

Figure 1–29

4

- Double-click the Chapter 01 folder to display its contents, and then click the file, Rockacademy, to select the file to be imported (Figure 1–30).

Q&A

Why does my file list look different?

Your list will vary. Also, the files in Figure 1–30 are displayed in List view. Click the View Menu button to verify your view.

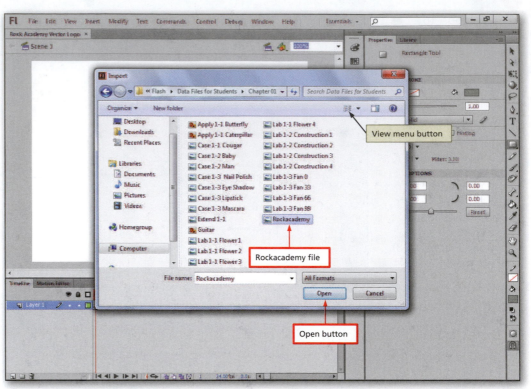

Figure 1–30

5

- Click the Open button to import the selected file and display the bitmap graphic on the Flash stage. The imported graphic is automatically selected on the stage.

- Notice the imported bitmap exceeds the dimensions of the stage and appears partially on the stage and partially in the work area. (Figure 1–31).

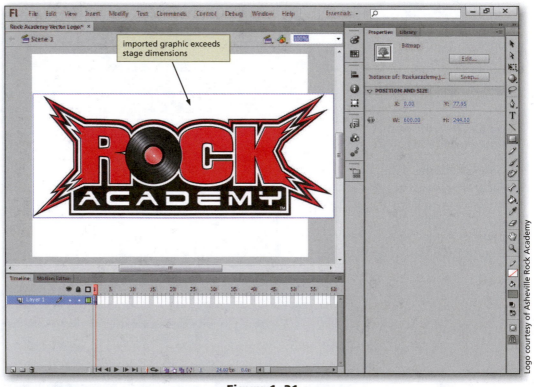

Logo courtesy of Asheville Rock Academy

Figure 1–31

MAC　For a detailed example of this procedure using the Mac operating system, refer to the steps in the For Mac Users appendix at the back of this book.

To Resize the Stage

By default, Flash creates new documents with a stage size of 550 × 400 pixels and a background color of white. You can view and change these characteristics using the Properties panel. You should set the stage size before you begin creating your movie because once the stage dimensions change, objects might no longer fit on the stage. Although you can change the stage dimensions at any time, it is more efficient to set it correctly the first time. You should know the dimensions of your target device or application ahead of time. For example, if you are developing a game to be played in a Web browser, you might set the stage dimensions to 800 × 600 pixels so that it will fit on most screens without having to use scroll bars. If you are developing an application for the iPhone, stage dimensions set to 480 × 320 are appropriate. If you are simply developing an animated greeting card, advertisement, or other Flash movie to display in a Web browser, you will have to know how the Flash movie fits into the overall Web page design. In the case of bitmap-to-vector conversion, it is a good practice to match the stage dimensions to that of the imported bitmap.

The following steps resize the stage to fit the imported bitmap.

1

• Look at the Properties panel and note the dimensions of the imported bitmap (Figure 1–32).

Q&A

How can I tell what the dimensions are?

The H and W in the Position and Size area of the Properties panel show the height and width dimensions.

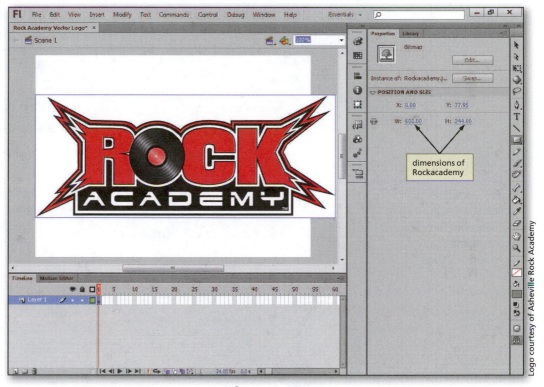

Logo courtesy of Asheville Rock Academy

Figure 1–32

- Click the Selection Tool button at the top of the Tools panel to select it.

- Click in the gray work area outside the stage to deselect the imported bitmap.

- Click the 'Edit document properties' button in the Properties area of the Properties panel to display the Document Settings dialog box (Figure 1–33).

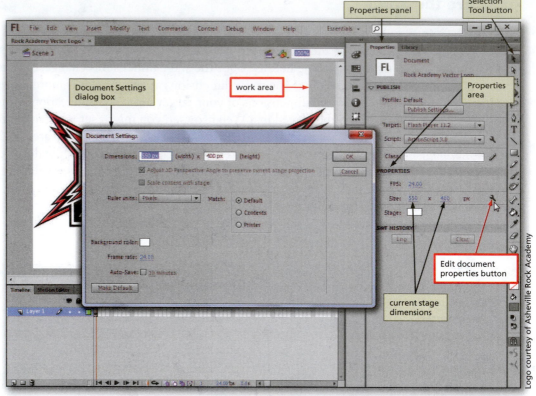

Figure 1–33

- Under Match, click the Contents option button to automatically resize the stage to fit its contents (Figure 1–34).

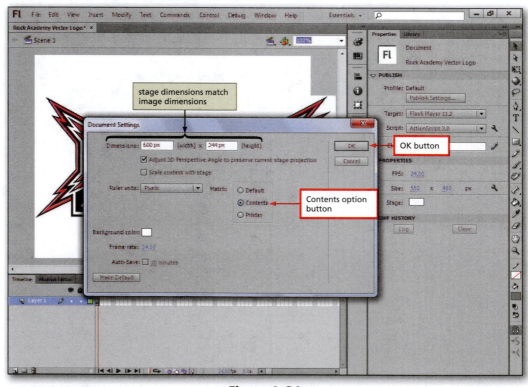

Figure 1–34

Logo courtesy of Asheville Rock Academy

4

- Click the OK button to apply the new settings and change the stage dimensions.

- Double-click the Hand Tool button on the Tools panel to center the stage and fit it to your screen (Figure 1–35).

Q&A

What if my magnification level does not match the figure in the book?

Your magnification level does not need to match. The magnification level is dependent on your screen size and resolution. As long as you double-clicked the Hand Tool to auto-fit the stage to your screen, you are fine.

Figure 1–35

Logo courtesy of Asheville Rock Academy

To Save the File with the Same Name

The following step saves the Flash document.

1 Press CTRL+S to save the file.

Tracing Bitmaps

The process of converting a bitmap to a vector is called **tracing**. Tracing a bitmap converts the pixel data into vector data (points, curves, and mathematical formulas). The quality of results can vary greatly from almost near-perfect photographic reproduction to a stylized pop art–type effect (Figure 1–36 on the next page). There is no scientific formula that you can apply to achieve your desired results. The process is very much trial and error. The settings in Table 1–1 are recommended for high-quality photographic reproduction. Flash has four settings that you can adjust when tracing a bitmap to achieve your results (Figure 1–37 on the next page).

(a) Original bitmap graphic   **(b) High-quality vector conversion**   **(c) Low-quality vector conversion**

Figure 1–36

Table 1–1 Bitmap Conversion Settings

Setting	Recommended Setting
Color threshold	10 or below
Minimum area	2 or below
Corner threshold	Many Corners
Curve fit	Pixels

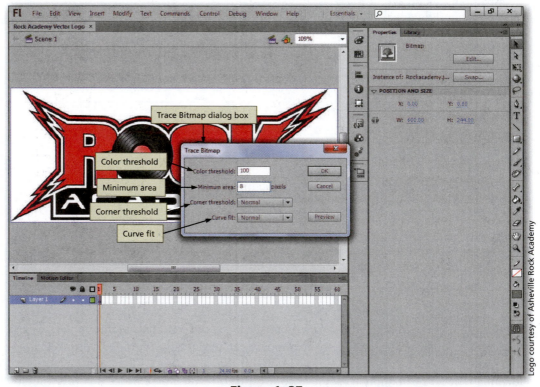

Figure 1–37

Color Threshold Color threshold determines how many colors are reproduced in your vector conversion. The lower the number, the more colors that are reproduced. However, lower numbers result in larger files and longer conversion times. Be careful not to set the number too low. If the original bitmap contains millions of colors, and you try to reproduce them all, Flash may display an error informing you there are too many colors and you will have to try again with a higher value. For photographic reproduction, use low numbers such as 10 or below if possible. For a pop-art or techno look, use high numbers.

Minimum Area The Minimum area setting determines how large of an area Flash examines when deciding which color to use when converting a pixel. For example, a setting of 8 tells Flash to start at the current pixel and use the colors of all pixels within an 8-pixel radius to determine the final color of the pixel. In other words, it is like telling Flash to ignore a pixel's neighbors or pay attention to them. For photographic reproduction, use a low number such as 1 so that neighboring pixels are ignored.

Corner Threshold The Corner threshold setting controls whether sharp edges are retained or smoothed out. For photographic reproduction, use the Many Corners option.

Curve Fit The Curve fit setting determines how smoothly outlines are drawn. For photographic reproduction, use the Pixels option.

Be warned! Using low values for both the Color threshold and Minimum area settings can result in Flash appearing to freeze as your computer's processor is being overworked trying to accomplish the conversion. If that happens, you need to either be patient as Flash finishes or force Flash to close using the Windows Task Manager. Depending on your computer's power, it might take up to 30 minutes to convert a large bitmap to a photographic-quality vector using very low settings.

To Trace a Bitmap

The following steps trace the Rockacademy bitmap graphic and convert it to vector artwork for use in the animation.

- If necessary, click the Selection Tool button on the Tools panel to select it.

- Click the imported Rockacademy bitmap on the stage to select it (Figure 1–38).

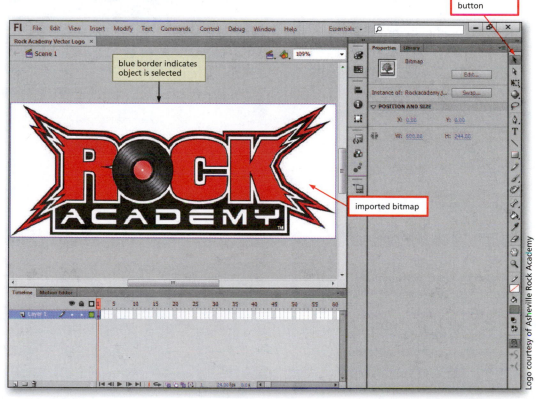

Figure 1–38

- Click Modify on the Application bar to display the Modify menu.

- Point to Bitmap on the Modify menu to display the Bitmap submenu (Figure 1–39).

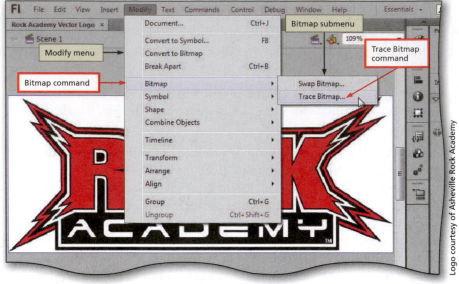

Figure 1–39

- Click Trace Bitmap on the Bitmap submenu to display the Trace Bitmap dialog box.

- Ensure the default settings match those shown in Figure 1–38 (Color threshold: 100, Minimum area: 8, Corner threshold: Normal, Curve fit: Normal).

- Click the Preview button to test the settings (Figure 1–40).

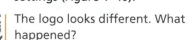 The logo looks different. What happened?

Converting to a vector reduces much of the image detail. You will correct this in the next step.

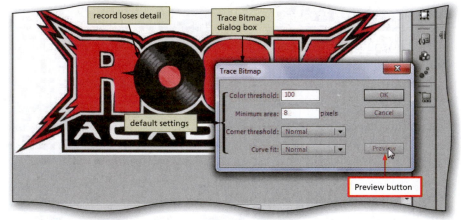

Figure 1–40

- Enter   50   in the Color threshold box.

- Enter   1   in the Minimum area box.

- Click the Preview button to test the new settings. Notice the record retains much of its detail (Figure 1–41).

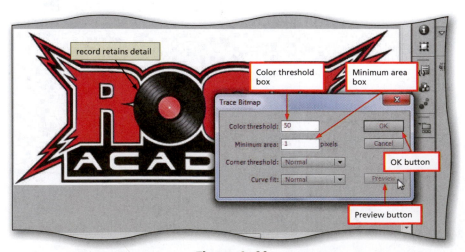

Figure 1–41

5

- Click the OK button to apply the settings and close the Trace Bitmap dialog box.

Q&A How do I know the bitmap was converted to a vector?

The logo no longer has a blue border. It is now covered in dots, indicating it has been converted to a vector.

- Click anywhere in the gray work area to deselect the logo.

- Press CTRL+S to save the document (Figure 1–42).

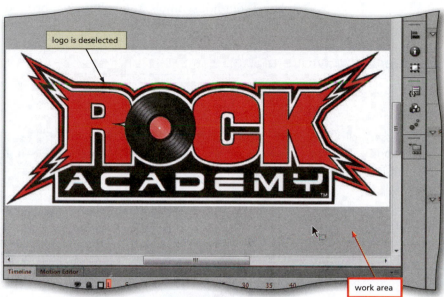

Figure 1–42

Flash Shapes and Symbols

Anything on the Flash stage is an **object**, including text, bitmaps, traced bitmaps, lines, circles, and rectangles. Objects are categorized as either **shapes** or **symbols**. Shapes and symbols each have different properties and capabilities, as you will learn in this book. In the remainder of this section, you will work with shapes. Symbols are covered in Chapter 3.

When you trace a bitmap, converting it to a vector, Flash interprets the result as a collection of shapes (rather than a symbol). One characteristic of a shape is that it is color-based. Simply clicking a shape selects all contiguous areas of the same color. Tiny gray dots covering a shape indicate it is selected (Figure 1–43). However, if you drag a shape to a new location on the stage and then deselect it, the shape merges with other shapes of the same color, destroying the underlying pixels. For this reason, you must be very careful when selecting and moving shapes. To deselect shapes, click the gray work area outside the stage.

(a) Clicking in the R selects contiguous pixels of the same color

(b) Selected shape in its new location

(c) Selecting and moving the R again leaves an R-shaped hole

Logo courtesy of Asheville Rock Academy

Figure 1–43

Shapes and symbols each support different types of animation. You can morph shapes, but not symbols. You will learn more about animation as you work with shapes and symbols throughout this book.

To Select and Move a Shape

The following steps select and move a shape.

 1

- If necessary, click the Selection Tool button on the Tools panel to select it.

- Click anywhere in the red letter K to select it.

Q&A What if I clicked in the wrong space?

Click the gray workspace to deselect your selection, and then click the red letter K to try again.

- While holding down the left mouse button, drag the K over the record (the letter O), and then release the mouse button (Figure 1–44).

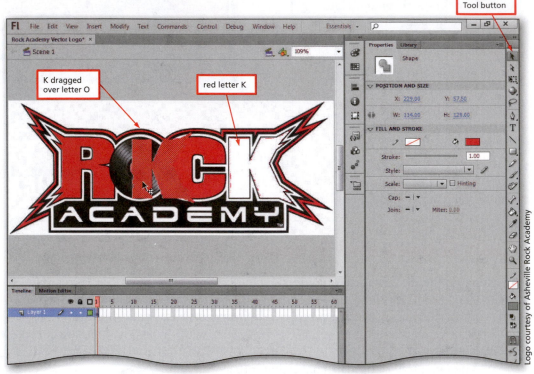

Figure 1–44

 2

- Click anywhere in the gray work area to deselect the shape.

- Click anywhere in the red letter K to select it again.

Q&A What if more than the K is selected?

If the red K is touching any part of the R or C, those letters might become selected. Remember that when you click a shape, all contiguous pixels of the same color are selected.

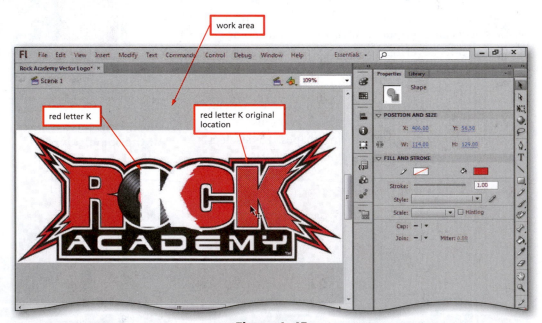

Figure 1–45

- Drag the selection to the right, dropping it near the K's original location (Figure 1–45).

3

• Click anywhere in the gray work area to deselect the shape. Notice that the original logo is now destroyed (Figure 1–46).

Figure 1–46

To Revert a Document

Flash allows you to undo a series of steps and **revert** the document to the state it was in the last time you saved it. If you never saved the document, it can be reverted immediately to the state it was in when it was initially opened, rather than undoing a step at a time. The following steps undo the actions performed in the previous exercise and revert the document to its last saved state.

1

• Click File on the Application bar to display the File menu (Figure 1–47).

Figure 1–47

Logo courtesy of Asheville Rock Academy

2
- Click Revert on the File menu to display the Revert? dialog box (Figure 1–48).

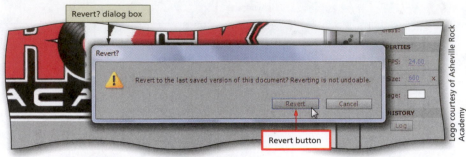

Figure 1–48

3
- Click the Revert button in the Revert? dialog box to confirm the reversion and return the logo to its previous undamaged state (Figure 1–49).

Q&A What if I change my mind and want to undo the reversion?

You cannot undo a reversion, so be sure you want to revert a document before using the Revert command.

Figure 1–49

Break Point: If you wish to take a break, this is a good place to do so. You can quit Flash now. To resume at a later time, start Flash, open the file called Rock Academy Vector Logo, and continue following the steps from this location forward.

The Timeline

Animation is a simulation of movement and is created by rapidly displaying a series of images. Imagine a pad of paper where the top sheet contains a drawing of a ball. The second sheet contains a similar drawing, but the ball is drawn slightly to the right. The third sheet contains a similar drawing with the ball drawn farther to the right. Continue this idea for the remaining sheets of paper. If you flipped through the pad, you would see an animation — a simulation of a ball rolling to the right. Flash is essentially the same as the pad of paper, but instead of having individual sheets, Flash uses frames. Each frame may contain a slightly different image, and when the frames appear one at a time in rapid succession, the result is an animation.

The **Timeline** is a panel at the bottom of the Flash window that is used to select frames and create specials kinds of frames called keyframes. Each numbered box in the Timeline represents a frame in the animation, similar to frames in a film reel or sheets of paper in a pad. Frames that display a dark solid circle (Figure 1–50) are called **keyframes**. A keyframe defines a frame that contains an important part of an animation and acts as a starting or ending point for an animation. When you place objects on the stage at specific keyframes, you are telling Flash that at these points in time, this is exactly how things should look in the animation. For example, an animated airplane flying across the stage might have a keyframe at Frame 1 (where the airplane starts its journey) and another keyframe at Frame 30 (where it ends its journey). All the frames between would show the airplane at various stages of its journey as it animates across the stage.

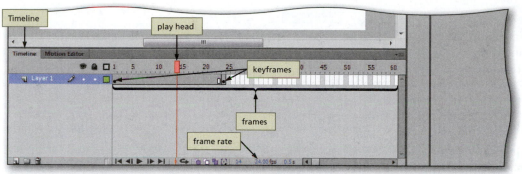

Figure 1–50

BTW

BTW
The standard frame rate for analog television and film in the United States is 23.976 fps, called the NTSC standard. Flash video is standardized at 24 fps to be roughly the same as the NTSC standard. Higher settings can cause stuttering playback on slower computers. Unless you have a specific need to use a faster or slower frame rate, use the standard of 24 fps.

By default, Flash creates movies that play 24 frames per second, indicated as 24.00 fps at the bottom of the Timeline. This measurement is called the **frame rate**. At a rate of 24 frames per second, a two-second animation contains 48 frames. Those 48 frames likely will include several keyframes that define important parts of the animation and can be located anywhere within the 48 frames. You will learn more about frames and keyframes later in this book.

Flash displays a red play head above the frames. The play head indicates which frame is currently shown on the stage. Drag the play head left or right to scroll through the animation, or press the ENTER key to have Flash play all frames on the Timeline.

Keyframes and Tweening

Keyframes define important, or key parts, of an animation. The frames between keyframes are simply called frames, or in-between frames. In the old days of animating by hand, a lead animator would draw the keyframes while lower-level animators would draw the remaining animation in the in-between frames. This process became known as tweening. When using Flash, you play the part of the lead animator as you define what the stage should look like at key points in time. Flash then creates the content for the in-between frames.

Plan keyframes.
Consider how long you want the animation to be and plan your keyframes accordingly. Because this involves some math, it is a good idea to have a pad of paper and a pencil nearby to help you determine which frames should contain keyframes. Typically, Flash animations run 24 frames per second with keyframes assigned at transitional parts of the animation. When planning keyframes, be sure to consider the placement of any tweens, morphs, or other transitions that your movie will include.

Plan Ahead

Developing an animation by creating in-between frames is called **tweening**. An animation created by tweening is called a tween. There are several different types of tweens. A motion tween creates an animation of something moving across the stage. A shape tween creates a morphing animation where one image appears to melt and turn into another image. You will learn more about working with the Timeline and tweening in Chapter 4.

To Create a Keyframe

You will create a morphing animation, called a shape tween, where an electric guitar morphs into the Rock Academy logo. The following steps create a keyframe to mark the end of the animation so that it will last one second.

1

- If necessary, click the Timeline tab to display the Timeline, and then click in Frame 24 on the Timeline to select that frame.

- Click Insert on the Application bar to display the Insert menu.

- Point to Timeline on the Insert menu to display the Timeline submenu (Figure 1–51).

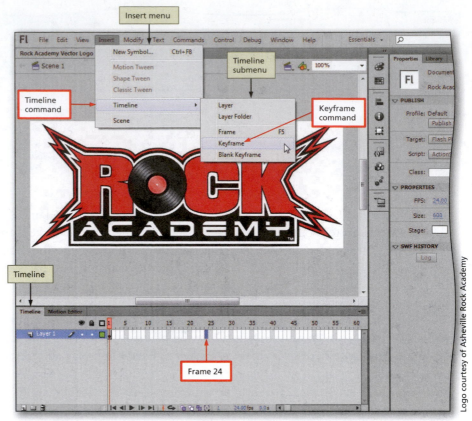

Figure 1–51

2

- Click Keyframe on the Timeline submenu to insert a new keyframe at Frame 24 (Figure 1–52).

Q&A

What does the white box at Frame 23 indicate?

It indicates the final frame in which the contents of the previous keyframe are displayed. Whatever is on the stage at Frame 1 (the previous keyframe) appears for a total length of time of 23 frames when the animation runs.

Other Ways

1. Right-click frame in Timeline, click Insert Keyframe

Figure 1–52

Removing Frame Contents

Because the stage can only display one frame at a time, you must remove any content from the frame before adding new content. The stage should only contain the Rock Academy logo at Frame 24, the final frame of the animation. At this point, the logo is present in every frame. To allow for the placement of the guitar in the earlier frames, you will need to remove the logo from those frames. The guitar image you will place at Frame 1 can then morph into the logo. Frames 2 through 23 will eventually contain the tweened frames.

To Delete Shapes

The following steps delete the shapes from Frame 1 so the stage is ready to accept the electric guitar image.

- Click Frame 1 on the Timeline to select that frame.

- Press the DELETE key to clear the stage (delete its contents) at Frame 1 (Figure 1–53).

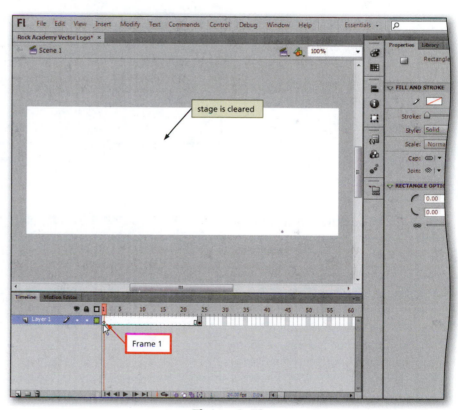

Figure 1–53

2

• Click Frame 24 on the Timeline to select that frame. Notice the stage contains shapes at Frame 24 (Figure 1–54).

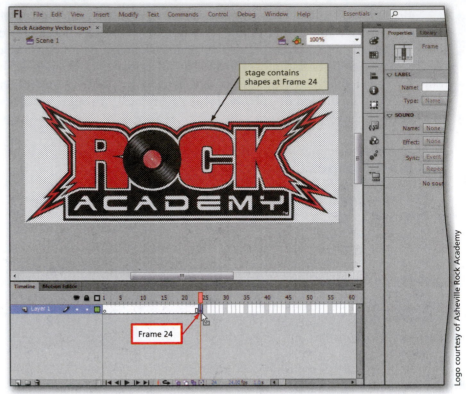

Figure 1–54

3

• Click Frame 1 on the Timeline to select that frame in preparation to insert a new image at Frame 1 (Figure 1–55).

Q&A

What does the white dot at Frame 1 indicate?

A white dot (empty keyframe) indicates the stage is empty. A solid dot (keyframe) indicates something is on the stage.

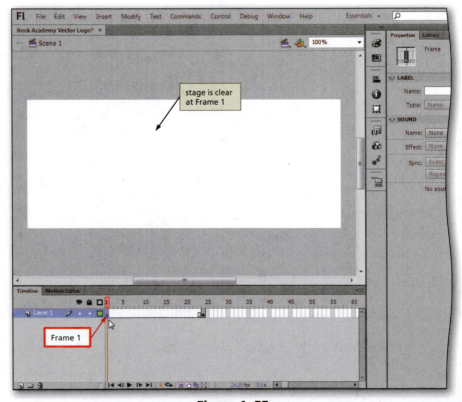

Figure 1–55

To Import and Trace the Guitar Bitmap

The next phase of the animation process involves importing an additional image and converting it to a vector. You will use this image of a guitar as the starting point for the animation. The following steps import and trace the guitar image.

1 Click File on the Application bar to display the File menu.

2 Point to Import to display the Import submenu.

3 Click Import to Stage to display the Import dialog box.

4 Click the Guitar image file to select it.

5 Click Open to import the image to Frame 1 of the stage.

6 Click Modify on the Application bar to display the Modify menu.

7 Point to Bitmap on the Modify menu to display the Bitmap submenu.

8 Click Trace Bitmap on the Bitmap submenu to display the Trace Bitmap dialog box.

9 Enter 75 in the Color threshold box, enter 1 in the Minimum area box, and confirm that Corner threshold and Curve fit options are both set to Normal.

10 Click the OK button to trace the bitmap.

11 Click in the gray work area to deselect the traced bitmap.

12 Press CTRL+S to save your changes.

To Create a Shape Tween

The following steps create a shape tween so that the guitar morphs into the Rock Academy logo over a period of one second.

1

• Click Insert on the Application bar to display the Insert menu (Figure 1–56).

Q&A

Why are all the tween commands disabled?

You cannot apply a tween to a keyframe. You must apply it to the frames that are between the keyframes.

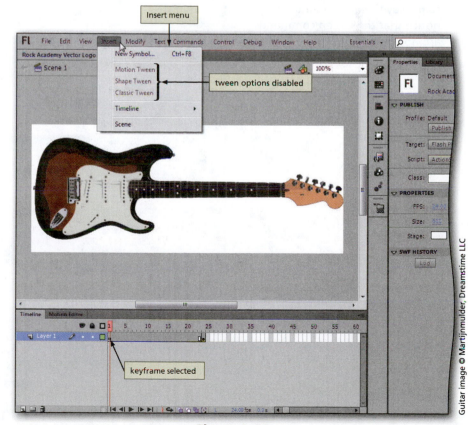

Guitar image © Martijnmulder, Dreamstime LLC

Figure 1–56

2

• Click anywhere along the gray area of the in-between frames on the Timeline to select a frame that is not a keyframe and move the play head to the selected frame (Figure 1–57).

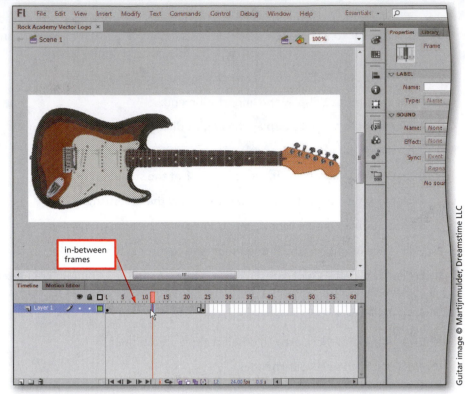

Figure 1–57

3

• Click Insert on the Application bar to display the Insert menu and notice that the tween commands are now available (Figure 1–58).

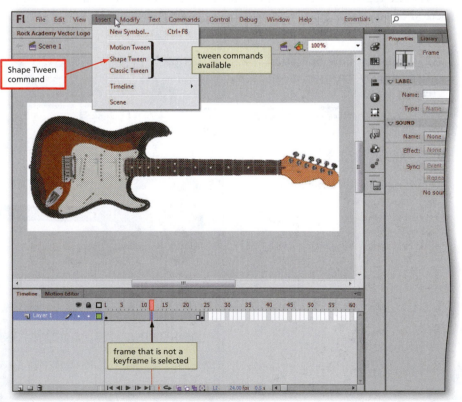

Figure 1–58

4

- Click Shape Tween on the Insert menu to create the tween (Figure 1–59).

Q&A

What is the green shading on the Timeline?

Flash displays the frames on the Timeline in green with an arrow to indicate the shape tween.

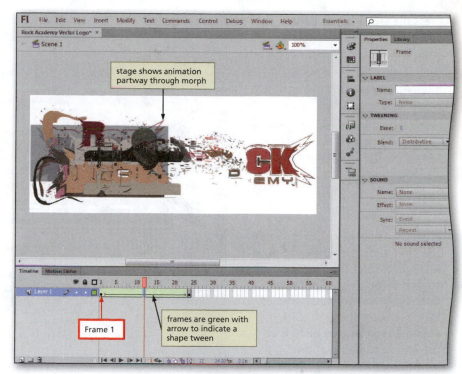

Figure 1–59

To Test an Animation

The following steps test the animation. As you develop a movie, it is a good idea to continually test it to ensure it animates and is displayed as intended. Testing a movie regularly helps you to identify and fix small errors as they occur rather than trying to identify and fix every issue at the very end of the movie development cycle.

1

- Click Frame 1 on the Timeline to select that frame and move the play head to Frame 1.

- Click anywhere in the work area to deselect the object (Figure 1–60).

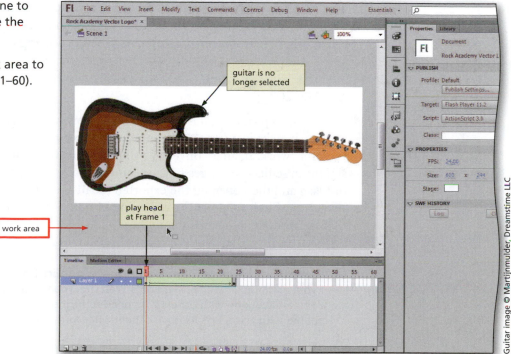

Figure 1–60

Guitar image © Martijnmulder, Dreamstime LLC

2

- Press the ENTER key to play the animation on the stage (Figure 1–61).

Q&A

Why does it take so long for the animation to begin?

Flash needs to prepare the animation. Depending on your computer's power, this could be instantaneous or it might take a few seconds.

 Experiment

- Press the ENTER key again to replay the animation. Drag the red play head across the Timeline manually to step through the animation or to examine individual frames. When you are through, click Frame 24 so the play head is at the end of the animation.

3

- Press CTRL+S to save your changes.

Figure 1–61

Logo courtesy of Asheville Rock Academy

Exporting and Publishing

Recall that the files you create for use in Flash documents use the FLA file type. The FLA file is not compatible with other software, nor can you use FLA files on a Web site. After creating an animation in Flash, you must convert the FLA files for use in other environments in a process called **exporting** or **publishing**.

Exporting

Flash's primary job is to create animations. Although it can convert bitmaps to vectors, it lacks many of the advanced tools necessary to edit and work efficiently with vector artwork. If, after converting a bitmap to a vector in Flash, you need to make significant edits or changes to the vector artwork, you are better off exporting it out of Flash and then opening the exported file in a dedicated vector program like Adobe Illustrator. Flash supports the exporting of frames as FXG files, which are vector files that Illustrator can open and modify.

Plan Ahead

Plan export formats in preparation for publication.
If your Flash movie will be used on a Web site, you will most likely export a SWF file. But if you are working with others who need to further modify the Flash movie or graphics created with Flash, be sure to ask them what format they prefer the file in.

To Export a File

The following steps export the logo to a format that can be opened and edited with Adobe Illustrator.

- If necessary, click Frame 24 on the Timeline to select the frame that contains the logo.

- Click File on the Application bar to display the File menu.

- Point to Export on the File menu to display the Export submenu (Figure 1–62).

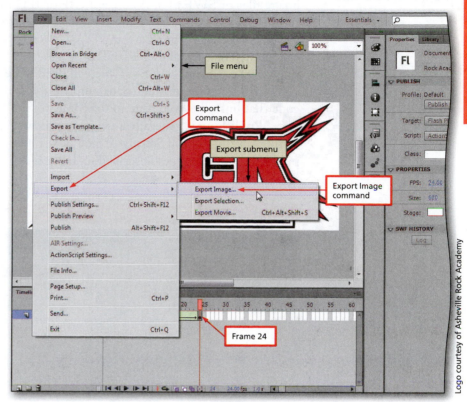

Figure 1–62

Logo courtesy of Asheville Rock Academy

2

- Click Export Image on the Export submenu to display the Export Image dialog box.

- Click the 'Save as type' box arrow to display the options for exporting.

- Click Adobe FXG (*.fxg) in the 'Save as type' list (Figure 1–63).

- If necessary, navigate to your file storage location, and then click the Save button to save the FXG version of the file.

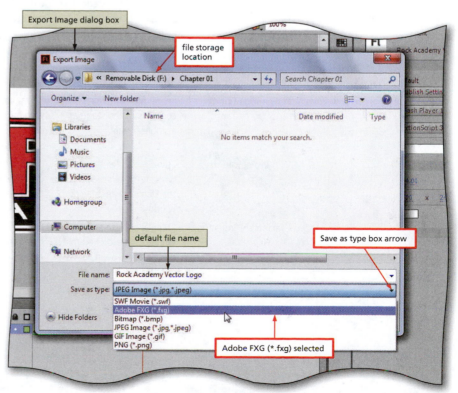

Figure 1–63

Publishing

The process of generating a Web version of a Flash file movie for use on a Web site is called **publishing**. Formats appropriate for publishing include GIF and JPG image files or SWF files. Whereas a GIF or JPG image file contains the stage contents from a single frame, a SWF file contains the entire animation.

Flash can also generate an HTML Web page that links to the SWF file — essentially creating all the HTML program code needed to create a valid Web page. However, it is likely your SWF file will need to be included on a Web page with other content. Therefore, it is better to simply publish the SWF file and write the HTML code that links the Web page to the SWF.

Publishing is generally a two-step process. First, you configure the publish settings in the Publish Settings dialog box. Then you publish your files. Flash supports publishing the file types described in Table 1–2.

Table 1–2 Flash-supported File Types			
Format Type	**Format Details**	**Usage**	**Additional Information**
Flash (.swf)	Contains complete animations	Used on Web sites	
SWC (.swc)	Compressed symbols and ActionScript	Used by advanced programmers	
HTML Wrapper (.html)	Web page written with HTML code, SWF, and JavaScript files	Used to create a Web page with the correct HTML code to link to a SWF	If HTML is selected, the SWF type is automatically selected.
GIF image (.gif)	Image file containing the contents of the stage at a single frame	Best suited for images with large areas of solid color	Adobe Photoshop is the industry standard software for working with GIFs.
JPEG image (.jpg)	Image file containing the contents of the stage at a single frame	Best suited for images with millions of colors or many gradients, like a photograph	Adobe Photoshop is the industry standard software for working with JPGs.
PNG image (.png)	Image file containing the contents of the stage at a single frame	Best suited for images with large areas of solid color; the PNG format also supports transparency	Adobe Photoshop and Adobe Fireworks are the industry standard software for working with PNGs.
Win Projector (.exe)	Stand-alone file that, when double-clicked, plays the Flash movie in its own window	Used for programming desktop applications or games	Plays on Windows computers
Macintosh Projector	Stand-alone file that, when double-clicked, plays the Flash movie in its own window	Used for programming desktop applications or games	Plays on Apple Macintosh computers

To Configure Publish Settings and Publish Files

Using Flash to create and publish an HTML file avoids the step of manually having to create an HTML file. The following steps configure the publish settings to create a SWF file and an HTML Web page in which the animation can run.

1

- Click File on the Application bar to display the File menu.

- Click Publish Settings on the File menu to display the Publish Settings dialog box (Figure 1–64).

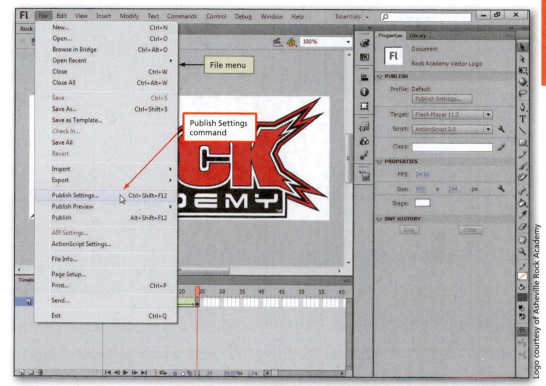

Figure 1–64

2

- Confirm that only the Flash (*swf) and HTML Wrapper check boxes are checked.

- Click the Flash (.swf) text to display the SWF options. Be careful not to click the check box itself or you will deselect the Flash (.swf) option (Figure 1–65).

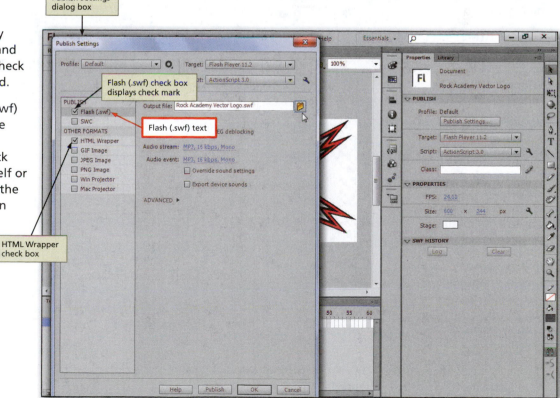

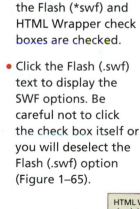

Figure 1–65

3

- Click the Select Publish Destination button to display the Select Publish Destination window.

- If necessary, navigate to your file storage location.

- Click in the File name text box, select the existing text, and type `RA Morph` as the new name for the SWF file (Figure 1–66).

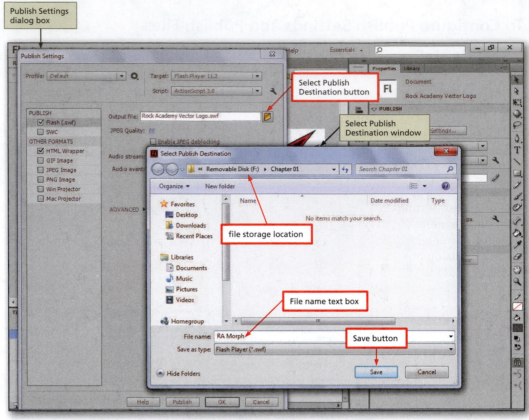

Figure 1–66

4

- Click the Save button to save the settings and return to the Publish Settings dialog box.

- Click the HTML Wrapper text to display the HTML Wrapper options. Be careful not to click the check box itself or you will deselect the HTML Wrapper option.

- Click the Select Publish Destination button to display the Select Publish Destination window.

- If necessary, navigate to your file storage location. Note that the file name and type already are specified.

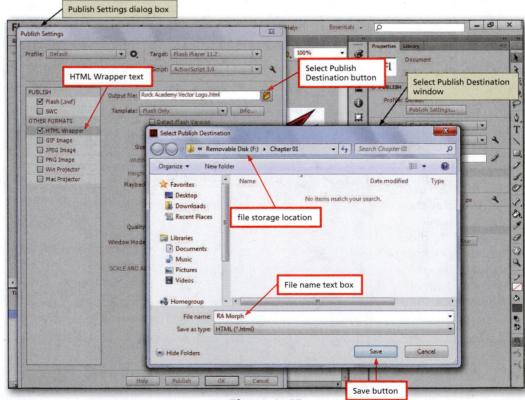

Figure 1–67

- Click in the File name text box, select the existing text, and type `RA Morph` as the new name for the HTML file (Figure 1–67).

5

- Click the Save button to save the settings and return to the Publish Settings dialog box (Figure 1–68).

Experiment

- Click the text for GIF Image, JPEG Image, or Win Projector to explore their various options. Be sure not to check their boxes.

- Confirm that only the Flash (.swf) and HTML Wrapper format check boxes are checked.

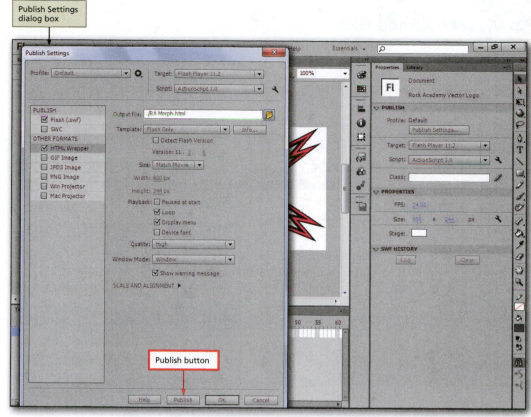

Figure 1–68

6

- Click the Publish button to save the publish settings and publish the files (Figure 1–69).

7

- Click the OK button to close the Publish Settings dialog box.

- Press CTRL+S to save the document.

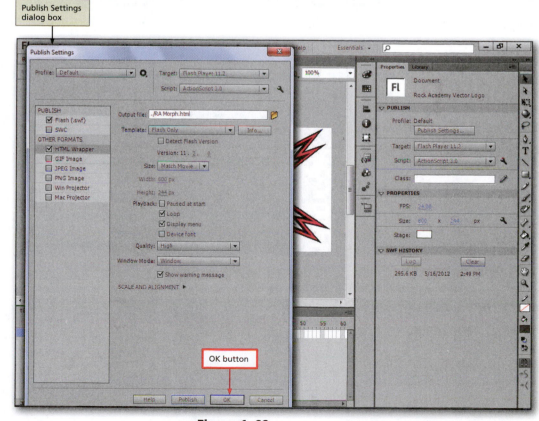

Figure 1–69

Other Ways
1. CTRL+SHIFT+F12

To View Published Files

So far, you have created a morphing animation and published the Flash movie as a SWF file. Flash has also published an HTML Web page with the correct code to load the SWF file. The following steps display the published SWF file as played in a Web page.

1

• Click the Start button on the Windows taskbar to display the Start menu (Figure 1–70).

Figure 1–70

2

• Click Computer on the Start menu to display the Computer window (your Computer window contents will differ) (Figure 1–71).

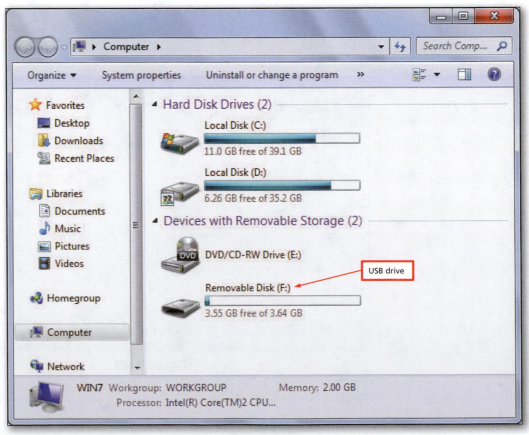

Figure 1–71

Logo courtesy of Asheville Rock Academy

3

• Navigate to Removable Disk (F:), or your file storage location, until you see the published files (Figure 1–72).

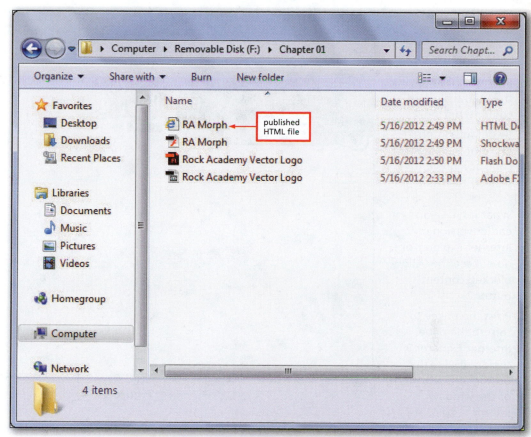

Figure 1–72

4

• Double-click the RA Morph HTML file to display the file in your Web browser (Figure 1–73).

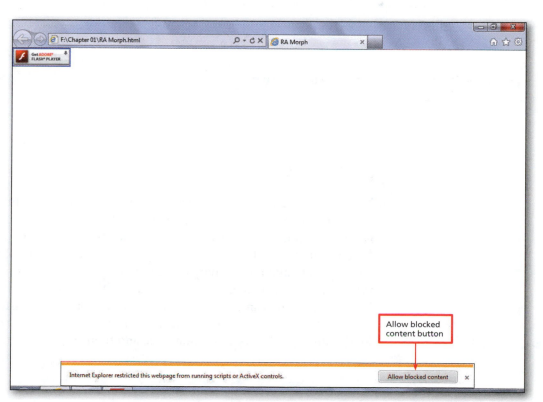

Figure 1–73

- Click the 'Allow blocked content' button to run the code (Figure 1–74).

Q&A Why do I have to click the 'Allow blocked content' button?

By default, Internet Explorer blocks active code as a preventive security measure.

Q&A What if I have an earlier version of Internet Explorer or I do not see the 'Allow blocked content' button?

Press the F5 key to refresh the page. Internet Explorer 9 should display the button at the bottom of the window. Internet Explorer 7 and 8 display a yellow warning bar across the top of the screen. Click that yellow bar, and then follow the on-screen instructions to allow the blocked content or ActiveX control.

Close button

Figure 1–74

Q&A The animation is repeating. Did I do something wrong?

You have not yet programmed the animation to stop. You will do so in a later step.

- Click the Close button to close the browser window.

Other Ways
1. ALT+F4

ActionScript

You created the Rock Academy animation in the ActionScript programming language. The current version is ActionScript 3.0. **ActionScript** is similar to JavaScript, which is a programming language for HTML Web pages. Whereas JavaScript allows Web programmers to add interactivity to a Web page, ActionScript allows Flash developers to add interactivity to a Flash movie. ActionScript code lets you perform tasks in a Flash document that are not available through Flash's standard interface. For example, you can write an ActionScript to connect a Flash movie to a database to display dynamic content. A simple implementation of ActionScript is to program the Flash movie to play its animation once and then stop, rather than looping endlessly.

You write ActionScript in the Actions panel (Figure 1–75). In addition to writing your own code from scratch, you can use any of the prebuilt code snippets in the panel.

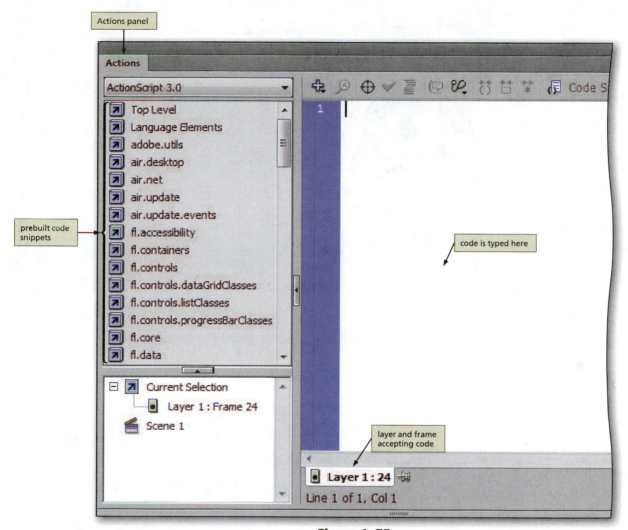

Figure 1–75

To Write ActionScript Code to Stop an Animation

The animation you created earlier runs in an endless loop. The following steps write the ActionScript 3.0 code necessary to stop the animation after it plays once.

1

- If necessary, click the Selection Tool button on the Tools panel to select it.

- Click Frame 24 on the Timeline to select the last frame of the animation.

- Click the gray work area to deselect the shape on the stage.

- Click Window on the Application bar to display the Window menu (Figure 1–76).

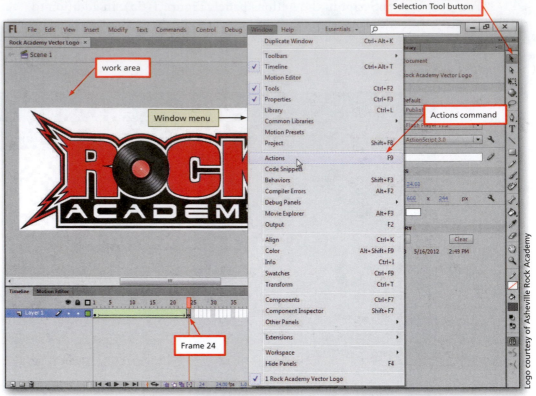

Figure 1–76

2

- Click Actions to display the Actions panel.

- If necessary, click the large white right column of the Actions panel.

- Type stop(); (be sure to include the semicolon) to enter the code that stops the animation from looping (Figure 1–77).

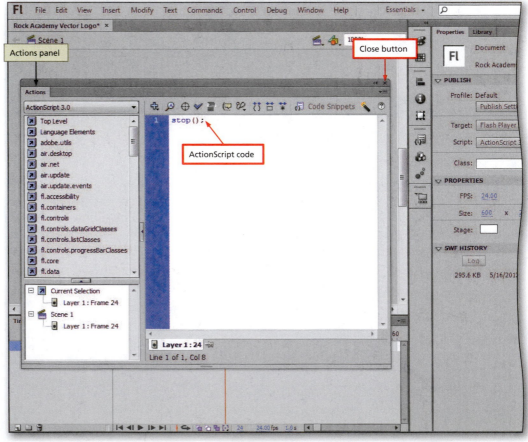

Figure 1–77

3

- Click the Close button on the Actions panel to close it.

- Press CTRL+S to save the file (Figure 1–78).

Figure 1–78

Other Ways

1. F9 to toggle Actions panel

To Publish an Animation

Because you previously configured publish settings, the following step publishes the animation with saved publish settings. The newly published HTML and SWF files will overwrite the existing previously published versions.

1

- Click File on the Application bar to display the File menu.

- Click Publish on the File menu to publish the animation with the current settings (Figure 1–79).

Publish command

Figure 1–79

Other Ways

1. ALT+SHIFT+F12 to publish with current settings

To View the Published Files

The following steps view the newly published file in a Web browser to ensure that the loop ends as intended and the animation plays only one time.

1 Click the Start button on the Windows 7 taskbar to display the Start menu.

2 Click the Computer button on the Start menu to display the Computer window.

3 Double-click Removable Drive (F:) or your file storage location and navigate until you see the published files.

4 Double-click the RA Morph HTML file to open it in your default browser.

5 If necessary, click the 'Allow blocked content' button at the bottom of the Internet Explorer 9 window to allow the code to run, playing the animation only once.

6 To view the animation again, reload the page by pressing the F5 key.

7 Click the Close button on the title bar to close the browser window and return to the Flash window.

BTW

Community Help
Community Help is an integrated Web environment that includes Flash Help and gives you access to community-generated content moderated by Adobe and industry experts. Comments from users help guide you to an answer.

Flash Help

At anytime while you are using Flash, you can get answers to questions using **Flash Help**. You activate Flash Help either by clicking Help on the Application bar or by pressing the F1 key. The Help menu includes commands to display more information about your copy of Flash as well as a list of how-to guides for common tasks. If you have an Internet connection, the Flash Help command opens your default Web browser and connects you to the Flash Professional Help area of the Adobe.com Web site. If you are not connected to the Internet, your Web browser displays the help files that were installed on your computer with Flash. The online help system is a better resource because it offers help from Adobe and other experts in addition to updated tutorials with detailed instructions accompanied by illustrations and video. Used properly, this form of online assistance can increase your productivity and reduce your frustration by minimizing the time you spend learning how to use Flash. Additional information about using Flash Help is available in the Using Flash CS6 Help appendix.

To Access Flash Help

The following step accesses Flash Help. You must be connected to the Web to complete this step.

1

- With Flash open on your system, press the F1 key to access Flash Professional Help online.

- If necessary, double-click the title bar to maximize the window (Figure 1–80).

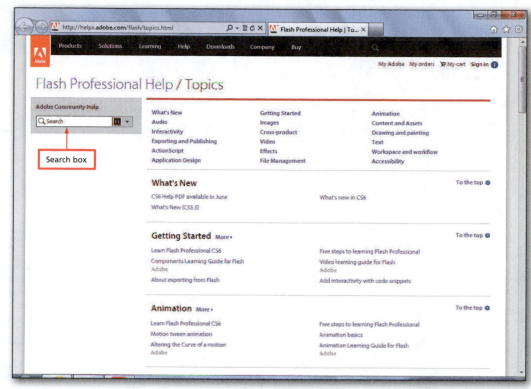

Figure 1–80

To Use the Help Search Box

The Search box allows you to type words or phrases about which you want additional information and help, such as tweening or keyframes. When you press the ENTER key, Flash Help responds by displaying a list of topics related to the word or phrase you typed. The following steps use the Search box to obtain information about the Timeline panel.

1

- Click the Search box and then type Timeline to enter the search topic (Figure 1–81).

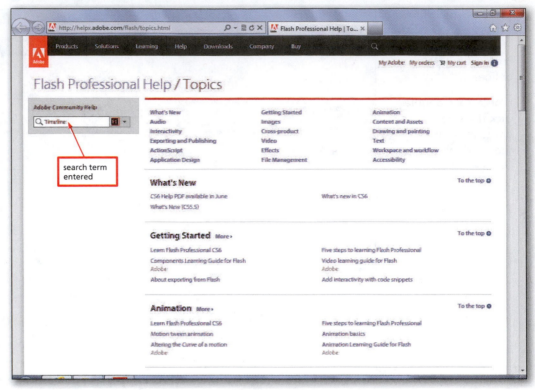

Figure 1–81

2

- Press the ENTER key to display the relevant links.

- Scroll down, if necessary, to display the link named Adobe Flash Professional* The Timeline (Figure 1–82).

Q&A

Why do my search results look different?

Adobe Flash Professional help is continually adding and changed pages, so your search results will likely differ. Click any link to explore the Help feature.

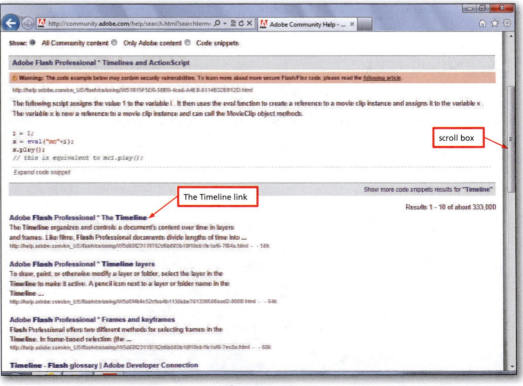

Figure 1–82

3

- Click Adobe Flash Professional * The Timeline to display the page (Figure 1–83).

- Scroll as necessary to read the information about tools.

 Experiment

- Click other links to view more information, or search for other topics using the Search box.

4

- In the browser title bar, click the Close button to close the window, and then, if necessary, click the Adobe Flash Professional CS6 button on the taskbar to return to Flash.

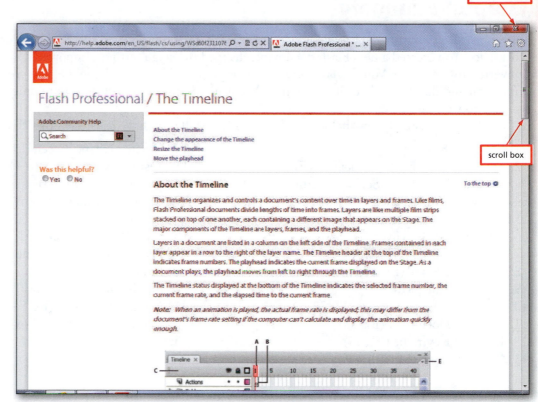

Figure 1–83

Close button

scroll box

Other Ways

1. On Help menu, click Flash Help, enter search topic

To Quit Flash

The following step quits Flash and returns control to Windows.

1

- Click the Close button on the right side of the Application bar to close the window.

- If Flash displays a dialog box asking you to save changes, click the No button.

Other Ways

1. On File menu, click Exit
2. CTRL+Q

 For a detailed example of this procedure using the Mac operating system, refer to the steps in the For Mac Users appendix at the back of this book.

Chapter Summary

In this chapter, you gained a broad knowledge of Flash. First, you started Flash and explored the Flash workspace. You created a new Flash document, changed the stage settings, imported a bitmap, and then converted it to a vector. You then exported a vector graphic. Using the Timeline, you created a shape tween animation and then published the animation. You learned how to use Adobe Community Help. Finally, you learned how to quit Flash.

The items listed below include all the new Flash skills you have learned in this chapter:

1. Start Flash (FL 4)
2. Select the Essentials Workspace (FL 6)
3. Create a New ActionScript 3.0 Document (FL 8)
4. Show and Hide Panels (FL 16)
5. Save a Flash Document (FL 17)
6. Disable Auto-Recovery (FL 20)
7. Import a Bitmap (FL 22)
8. Resize the Stage (FL 25)
9. Trace a Bitmap (FL 29)
10. Select and Move a Shape (FL 32)
11. Revert a Document (FL 33)
12. Create a Keyframe (FL 35)
13. Delete Shapes (FL 37)
14. Create a Shape Tween (FL 39)
15. Test the Animation (FL 41)
16. Export a File (FL 43)
17. Configure Publish Settings and Publish Files (FL 45)
18. View Published Files (FL 48)
19. Write ActionScript Code to Stop an Animation (FL 51)
20. Publish an Animation (FL 53)
21. Access Flash Help (FL 54)
22. Use the Help Search Box (FL 55)
23. Quit Flash (FL 57)

Apply Your Knowledge

Reinforce the skills and apply the concepts you learned in this chapter.

Creating and Publishing a Flash Animation

Instructions: Start Flash and perform the customization steps found on pages FL 6 through FL 7. You will create an animation as part of an advertisement for a preschool. In the animation, a caterpillar morphs into a butterfly, as shown in Figure 1–84. First, you will create a new ActionScript 3.0 document. Then you will import and trace two bitmaps at different keyframes. Next, you will create a shape tween to create a morphing animation. Finally, you will publish and view the HTML and SWF files.

(a)

(b)

(c)

Figure 1–84

Perform the following tasks:

1. On the File menu, click New. When Flash displays the New Document dialog box, select ActionScript 3.0, if necessary, and then click the OK button. On the File menu, click Save As. Navigate to your file storage location, type Apply 1-1 Butterfly Morph as the file name, and then click the Save button to save the file.

2. To import the first image:

   a. On the File menu, point to Import, and then click Import to Stage.

   b. If necessary, navigate to the Chapter 01 folder of the Data Files for Students folder, select the file named Apply 1-1 Caterpillar, and click the Open button. Visit www.cengage.com/ct/studentdownload for detailed instructions or contact your instructor for information about accessing the required files.

3. To resize the stage:

   a. Click in the gray workspace area to deselect the imported image.

   b. In the Properties panel, click the 'Edit document properties' button next to the document's size.

   c. In the Document Settings dialog box, click the Match Contents option button, and then click the OK button to resize the stage to match the imported image.

Continued >

Apply Your Knowledge *continued*

4. To trace the bitmap:

   a. Click the caterpillar to select it.

   b. On the Modify menu, point to Bitmap and then click Trace Bitmap.

   c. Type `50` for the Color threshold, `1` for the Minimum area, and then click the OK button.

5. To import and trace a second bitmap at a new keyframe:

   a. On the Timeline, click in Frame 24 to select it.

   b. On the Insert menu, point to Timeline and then click Keyframe to insert a new keyframe.

   c. Press the DELETE key to clear the stage at Frame 24.

   d. On the File menu, point to Import and then click Import to Stage.

   e. Select the file Apply 1-1 Butterfly and click the Open button.

   f. On the Modify menu, point to Bitmap and then click Trace Bitmap.

   g. Confirm that the Color threshold setting is set to 50 and the Minimum area setting is set to 1 and then click the OK button.

6. To create a shape tween:

   a. On the Timeline, click a frame between Frames 1 and 23.

   b. On the Insert menu, click Shape Tween.

   c. Press the ENTER key to preview the animation. It might take a moment for the animation to begin.

7. To stop the animation:

   a. On the Timeline, click Frame 24.

   b. In the Window menu, click Actions.

   c. In the right pane of the Actions – Frame panel, type `stop();` to enter the stop code.

   d. Close the Actions – Frame panel.

8. To publish the animation:

   a. On the File menu, click Publish Settings.

   b. Confirm that only the check boxes for the Flash (.swf) and HTML Wrapper types are checked.

   c. Click the Select Publish Destination button to the right of the Flash (.swf) file name, navigate to your file storage location, confirm that the file name is Apply 1-1 Butterfly Morph, and click the Save button to save this setting.

   d. Click the HTML Wrapper text, click the Select Publish Destination button to the right of the HTML Wrapper file name, navigate to your file storage location, confirm that the file name is Apply 1-1 Butterfly Morph, and click the Save button to save this setting.

   e. Click the Publish button to publish the HTML and SWF files.

   f. Click the OK button to close the Publish Settings dialog box.

9. Press CTRL+S to save the Flash document.

10. To view the published files:

   a. On the Windows 7 taskbar, click the Start button and then click the Computer button.

   b. Navigate to your file storage location and double-click the Apply 1-1 Butterfly Morph.html file.

   c. If your Web browser is Internet Explorer, click the 'Allow blocked content' button to allow the animation to run.

   d. If desired, press the F5 key to replay the animation.

   e. Close your Web browser.

11. Close Flash.

12. Submit the revised document in the format specified by your instructor.

Extend Your Knowledge

Extend the skills you learned in this chapter and experiment with new skills. You might need to use Help to complete the assignment.

Pausing an Animation at the Beginning

Instructions: Start Flash and perform the customization steps found on pages FL 6 through FL 7. You will morph a photograph of a musician into a stylized version (Figure 1–85 on the next page) for use on the biography section of a band Web site. The original photo must remain visible for one second before the animation begins. To delay the start of the animation, you will need to insert an additional keyframe.

Perform the following tasks:

1. Create a new ActionScript 3.0 document, import Extend 1-1 Guitarist from the Data Files for Students to the stage, and resize the stage to match the contents. Visit www.cengage.com/ct/ studentdownload for detailed instructions or contact your instructor for information about accessing the required files.

2. Trace the bitmap with low settings to retain maximum detail. Try a Color threshold of 25 and a Minimum area of 1. If your Color threshold is too low, you might have to wait a long time as your computer processes the image data.

3. Insert keyframes at Frame 24 and at Frame 72.

Continued >

STUDENT ASSIGNMENTS

Extend Your Knowledge *continued*

(a)

(b)

Figure 1–85

4. Clear the stage at Frame 72 and import a second copy of Extend 1-1 Guitarist. If you are prompted about a library conflict, click the 'Don't replace existing items' option button, if necessary, and then click the OK button.

5. Trace the second copy of the image. Set the Color threshold to 200 and set the Minimum area to 3.

6. Create a shape tween between Frames 25 and 72.

7. Add an action at Frame 72 to stop the animation.

8. Publish the HTML and SWF files with the name Extend 1-1 Guitarist Morph.

9. Navigate to your file storage location and save the Flash document as Extend 1-1 Guitarist Source.

10. Test the published HTML file and verify the animation begins after one second and stops after playing once.

11. Close Flash.

12. Submit the revised document in the format specified by your instructor.

Make It Right

Analyze a project and correct all errors and/or improve the design.

Fixing a Shape Tween

Instructions: Start Flash and perform the customization steps found on pages FL 6 through FL 7. Open the file Make It Right 1-1 Eggs from the Data Files for Students and save it in your file storage location as Make It Right 1-1 Eggs Fixed. Visit www.cengage.com/ct/studentdownload for detailed instructions or contact your instructor for information about accessing the required files.

A local diner is advertising a breakfast special with a Flash banner on its Web site. With the Flash file open, press the ENTER key to play the animation. Note the animation does not work (it simply switches from the egg to the fried egg with no morphing) and there is a broken line in the green area of the Timeline, indicating the shape tween is broken.

Remembering that bitmaps must be traced (and converted to shapes) before a shape tween can be applied, check Frames 1 and 24 and ensure both contain traced bitmaps. (*Hint*: A converted shape appears with a gray dotted overlay.)

Change the document properties, as specified by your instructor. Save the file as Make It Right 1-1 Eggs Fixed and publish the HTML and SWF files with the name, Make it Right 1-1 Eggs Fixed. Submit the revised document in the format specified by your instructor.

In the Lab

Design and/or create a project using the guidelines, concepts, and skills presented in this chapter. Labs are listed in order of increasing difficulty.

Lab 1: Creating a Slide Show

Problem: A florist has asked you to create a slide show for his Web site. Using Flash, you create a slide show where each image appears for three seconds and loops endlessly. One frame from the slide show is displayed in Figure 1–86.

Note: To complete this assignment, you will be required to use the Data Files for Students. Visit www.cengage.com/ct/studentdownload for detailed instructions or contact your instructor for information about accessing the required files.

Figure 1–86

Continued >

In the Lab *continued*

Instructions: Perform the following tasks:

1. Start Flash and create a new ActionScript 3.0 document.

2. Import Lab 1-1 Flower 1 from the Data Files for Students to the stage and resize the stage to match the contents. If you are prompted to import a sequence of images, click the No button.

3. Add a keyframe at Frame 72 and delete the contents of the stage at that frame.

4. Import Lab 1-1 Flower 2 to the stage at Frame 72. If you are prompted to import a sequence of images, click the No button.

5. Add a keyframe at Frame 144 and delete the contents of the stage at that frame.

6. Import Lab 1-1 Flower 3 to the stage at Frame 144. If you are prompted to import a sequence of images, click the No button.

7. Add a keyframe at Frame 216 and delete the contents of the stage at that frame.

8. Import Lab 1-1 Flower 4 to the stage at Frame 216.

9. Add a keyframe at Frame 288.

10. Navigate to your file storage location and save the Flash document with the name Lab 1-1 Slideshow.

11. Publish the HTML and SWF files with the name Lab 1-1 Flowers and save the document again.

12. Test the published HTML file in a Web browser.

13. Close your Web browser and quit Flash.

In the Lab

Lab 2: Creating an Animated Record of Construction

Problem: A local architect has asked you to create an animation for her Web site that shows the progress of one of her buildings being constructed. You will create the animation so that each of the four images appears for one second before morphing into the next. One frame from the slide show is displayed in Figure 1–87 on the next page.

Note: To complete this assignment, you will be required to use the Data Files for Students. Visit "http://www.cengage.com/ct/studentdownload" www.cengage.com/ct/studentdownload for detailed instructions or contact your instructor for information about accessing the required files.

Instructions: Perform the following tasks:

1. Start Flash and perform the customization steps found on pages FL 6 through FL 7. Create a new ActionScript 3.0 document.

2. At Frame 1, import Lab 1-2 Construction 1 to the stage. Do not import the sequence of images.

3. Resize the stage to match its contents.

4. Trace the bitmap with a Color threshold of 25 and a Minimum area of 1.

5. Create a keyframe at Frame 12.

6. Create a keyframe at Frame 24 and delete the contents of the stage at that frame.

7. At Frame 24, import Lab 1-2 Construction 2 to the stage. Do not import the sequence of images.

8. Trace the bitmap with a Color threshold of 25 and a Minimum area of 1.

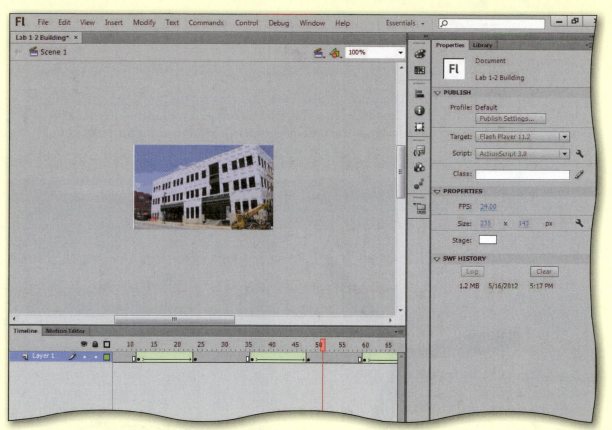

Figure 1–87

9. Create a shape tween between Frames 13 and 24.

10. Create a keyframe at Frame 36.

11. Create a keyframe at Frame 48 and delete the contents of the stage at that frame.

12. At Frame 48, import Lab 1-2 Construction 3 to the stage. Do not import the sequence of images.

13. Trace the bitmap with a Color threshold of 25 and a Minimum area of 1.

14. Create a shape tween between Frames 36 and 48.

15. Create a keyframe at Frame 60.

16. Create a keyframe at Frame 72 and delete the contents of the stage at that frame.

17. At Frame 72, import Lab 1-2 Construction 4 to the stage.

18. Trace the bitmap with a Color threshold of 25 and a Minimum area of 1.

19. Create a shape tween between Frames 61 and 72.

20. Add a stop action at Frame 72.

21. Navigate to your file storage location and save the file as Lab 1-2 Building.

22. Publish the HTML and SWF files with the name Lab 1-2 Building Morph and then save the document.

23. Test the HTML file in a Web browser and then close the browser and Flash. Submit the revised animation in the format specified by your instructor.

In the Lab

Lab 3: Preparing an Animated Logo

Problem: An alternative energy company has asked that you create a portion of a logo to be used on its Web site. Another designer will be responsible for designing the company site; your job is to create a spinning fan as it would appear on a wind turbine. One frame from the animation is displayed in Figure 1–88.

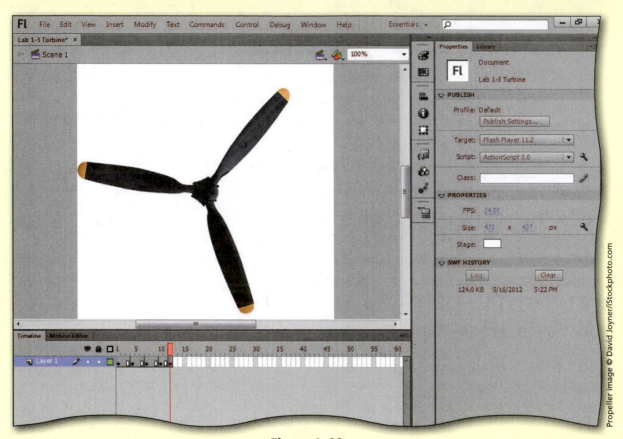

Figure 1–88

Propeller image © David Joyner/iStockphoto.com

Note: To complete this assignment, you will be required to use the Data Files for Students. Visit "http://www.cengage.com/ct/studentdownload" www.cengage.com/ct/studentdownload for detailed instructions or contact your instructor for information about accessing the required files.

Instructions: Perform the following tasks:
Start Flash and perform the customization steps found on pages FL 6 through FL 7 and create a new ActionScript 3.0 file. Import Lab 1-3 Fan 0, Lab 1-3 Fan 33, Lab 1-3 Fan 66, and Lab 1-3 Fan 99 to Frames 1, 4, 7, and 10, respectively. Create a keyframe and then clear the keyframe before adding the images to Frames 4, 7, and 10. Add another keyframe at Frame 12, which allows the last image to appear for the same amount of time as the other images do before the animation loops. Match the size of the stage to the contents.

Navigate to your file storage location and save the Flash file as Lab 1-3 Turbine. Publish the HTML and SWF files with the name Lab 1-3 Turbine Animation. Test the animation. Save the file again, and then quit Flash. Submit the revised animation in the format specified by your instructor.

Cases and Places

Apply your creative thinking and problem-solving skills to design and implement a solution.

Note: To complete these assignments, you will be required to use the Data Files for Students. Visit www.cengage.com/ct/studentdownload for detailed instructions or contact your instructor for information about accessing the required files.

1: Convert a Bitmap to a Vector for Use in Vector Image-Editing Software

Academic

As a member of your high school yearbook committee, it is your task to find an appropriate image for the yearbook cover and deliver it to the print company in the proper format. After starting Flash and creating a new ActionScript 3.0 document, import the photo, Case 1-1 Cougar, from the Data Files for Students. Trace the bitmap and retain as much detail as you can. Export the image as an Adobe FXG file with the name Case 1-1 Vector Cougar.

2: Create a Morph Animation for a Family Tree

Personal

You would like to create an animation of your grandfather changing from a baby to his current age. After starting Flash and creating a new ActionScript 3.0 document, you use the photos, Case 1-2 Baby and Case 1-2 Man, from the Data Files for Students. Create an animation that displays the baby photo for two seconds before beginning the morph. The animation itself should last two seconds and should not loop. Save the Flash document as Case 1-2 Man. Publish the HTML and SWF files with the name Case 1-2 Man Morph.

3: Create a Home Page Animation

Professional

You have landed a design contract with a cosmetics company. The company is planning a new line of makeup to be featured on the home page of its Web site. Use the photos named Case 1-3 Nail Polish, Case 1-3 Eye Shadow, Case 1-3 Lipstick, and Case 1-3 Mascara from the Data Files for Students to create an animated slide show where each product is displayed for four seconds before looping and repeating indefinitely. Save the Flash file as Case 1-3 Makeup. Save the published HTML and SWF files as Case 1-3 Makeup Animation.

2 | Drawing with Flash

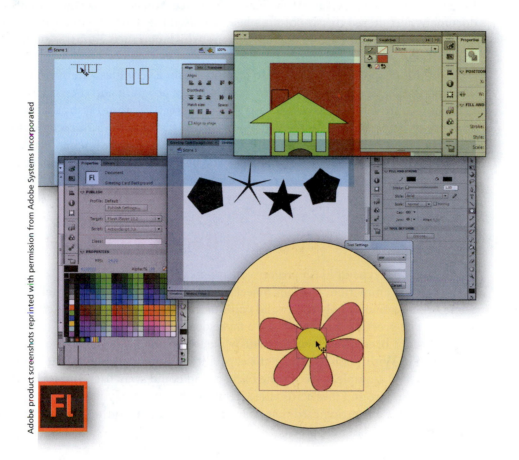

Objectives

You will have mastered the material in this chapter when you can:

- Edit strokes and fills
- Select shapes, fills, outlines, and segments
- Draw rectangles and ovals in merge and object drawing modes
- Draw lines and curves
- Align objects
- Transform shapes
- Draw polygons

- Convert objects to shapes
- Work with layers
- Create gradients
- Manage color stops
- Draw with free-form tools
- Modify anchor points
- Group objects
- Use the Deco Tool

2 | Drawing with Flash

Introduction

In Chapter 1, you learned about the Flash workspace. You created a new ActionScript 3.0 document and altered the size of the stage. You used the Timeline to create keyframes. You also created vector art by tracing bitmaps, which you then animated with a shape tween.

In this chapter, you will learn to draw in Flash. Every Flash animation contains artwork. Rather than create that artwork in another program and then import it into Flash, it is more efficient to create your artwork directly within Flash. You will use a variety of shape tools in merge and object drawing modes to draw recognizable everyday objects. You will use the Pencil and Pen Tools to draw lines and curves and the Brush Tool to selectively color objects. You also will learn to use layers to help manage all your objects. Finally, you will create and edit custom gradient fills.

BTW

Gradients
A gradient is a blending of colors into each other. A simple two-color gradient blends one color into the next, while a more complex gradient may blend one color into a second, then the second color into a third, and so on. Gradients add depth and visual interest when compared to solid colors.

Project — Greeting Card Background Scene

No matter what type of Flash project you are creating — a Web banner, application, game, cartoon animation, or other object — you will need to create a background. Some Web banners simply use a solid color or gradient background, whereas a cartoon animation or greeting card might use a more detailed background.

Often, a background will be static while foreground objects move and animate in front of it. With Flash, you have the capability to animate any element in the document. For example, a tree in the background could sway back and forth while a bird in the foreground flies across the screen. In this chapter, you will create a static background for a greeting card that later can be animated. You will learn to add text and animations in later chapters.

Overview

As you read this chapter, you will learn how to create the background scene shown in Figure 2–1 on page FL 71 by performing these general tasks:

• Draw shapes with the Rectangle, Oval, Line, Pencil, Brush, Pen, and Deco Tools.
• Align objects.
• Convert objects to shapes.
• Organize shapes with layers.
• Create a gradient fill.

Figure 2–1

General Project Guidelines

When drawing with Flash, the actions you perform and decisions you make will affect the appearance and characteristics of the finished product. As you become familiar with the various drawing methods, you should follow these general guidelines:

1. **Plan the scene.** Know what you are going to draw before you draw it. You are likely to add things as you build the background and will be inspired by moments of creativity. Having a basic idea of how to start will save a lot of wasted time.

2. **Choose the appropriate tool.** You can draw a shape many different ways. For example, you can use the Rectangle Tool, Pencil Tool, Line Tool, or Pen Tool to draw a rectangle, but you cannot do so using the Oval Tool. You will need to choose the best tool for the job. Sometimes the best tool is not necessarily the most efficient, but rather the one with which you are the most comfortable.

3. **Use layers to organize objects.** Organize your objects with layers to make them easier to arrange, stack, and align.

4. **Apply gradients appropriately.** Consider using gradient fills rather than solid fills to add depth and visual interest to your objects. Overuse of gradients can make your drawing look unprofessional, so use restraint.

When necessary, more specific details concerning the above guidelines are presented at appropriate points in the chapter. The chapter also will identify the actions performed and decisions made regarding these guidelines during the creation of the scene shown in Figure 2–1.

Plan Ahead

Creating a Greeting Card Background Scene

Although greeting cards can be traced back to ancient times, Judith Donath created the first electronic postcard, or **e-card**, Web site in 1994 at the MIT Media Lab. Since then, thousands of e-card Web sites have opened for business. In fact, a Web search of the term, e-cards, currently returns over 110,000,000 results. Internet users send approximately 500 million e-cards each year. The advent of Flash has allowed e-card developers to create more robust e-cards that can contain animation, sound, or video.

A background scene typically includes objects that remain visible or unchanged as other objects appear, disappear, move, or otherwise animate. A background should support, but not overwhelm, the overall design.

To Start Flash

The following steps, which assume Windows 7 is running, start Flash based on a typical installation.

1 Click the Start button on the Windows 7 taskbar to display the Start menu.

2 Type `Flash Professional CS6` as the search text in the 'Search programs and files' text box, and watch the search results appear on the Start menu.

3 Click Adobe Flash Professional CS6 in the search results on the Start menu to start Flash.

4 After a few moments, when the Flash window is displayed, if the window is not maximized, click the Maximize button next to the Close button on the title bar to maximize the window.

To Reset the Workspace

It is helpful to reset the workspace so that the tools and panels appear in their default positions. The following steps select the Essentials workspace.

1 Click the Workspace Switcher button in the upper-right area of the Application bar to display the Workspace menu.

2 If necessary, click Essentials to choose the Essentials workspace.

3 Click the Workspace Switcher button in the upper-right area of the Application bar to display the Workspace menu.

4 Click Reset 'Essentials' to reset the Essentials workspace.

To Disable Auto-Recovery

The following steps disable the Auto-Recovery feature so that you can use the Revert command later.

1 Click Edit on the Application bar to display the Edit menu.

2 Click Preferences on the Edit menu to display the Preferences dialog box.

3 Click the General category to select it, if necessary.

4 Remove the check mark, if necessary, from the Auto-Recovery option.

5 Click the OK button to save your changes and close the Preferences dialog box.

Drawing Tools

Flash supports drawing shapes in two modes — merge mode and object drawing mode. Using **merge mode**, you can create complex shapes by merging together simpler shapes. Additionally, shapes drawn in merge mode can be used to destroy the underlying pixels, effectively creating holes in the underlying shapes. **Object drawing mode** is useful when you want to overlap objects without altering them. Items drawn in merge mode are called **shapes**, whereas items drawn in object drawing mode are called **drawing objects**. After choosing a shape tool from the Tools panel (such as the Rectangle or Oval Tool), use the Object Drawing button at the bottom of the Tools panel to select the mode. When this button is selected and displays a gray box around it, you are in object drawing mode. When it is not selected, you are in merge mode (Figure 2–2).

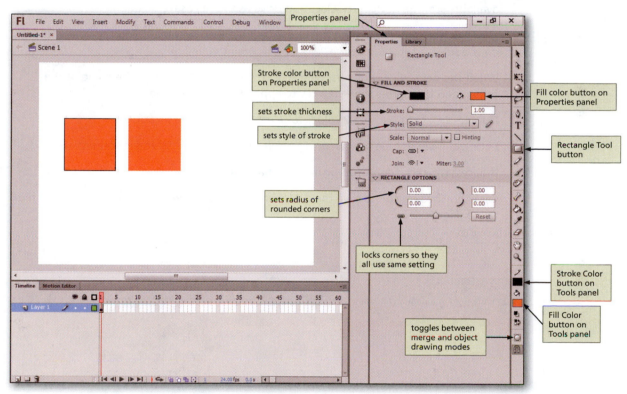

Figure 2–2

It is generally easier to draw in object drawing mode because you do not have to worry about objects touching, or overlapping and merging into a single shape. You can convert drawing objects that you created in object drawing mode to shapes as if you had drawn them in merge mode. One common workflow is to draw objects in object drawing mode; position, align, and overlap them as desired; then convert them to shapes so they merge together. Recall from Chapter 1 that to determine whether an object on the stage was drawn in merge or object drawing mode, you click it with the Selection Tool. Shapes drawn in merge mode display small dots when selected, whereas drawing objects drawn in object drawing mode display a blue border.

To Create and Save a New Document

The following steps create and save a new blank document.

1 Press CTRL+N to open the New Document dialog box.

2 Double-click the ActionScript 3.0 type to create a new blank ActionScript 3.0 document.

3 Press CTRL+S to open the Save As dialog box.

4 Type `Greeting Card Background` in the File name text box to change the file name. Do not press the ENTER key after typing the file name.

5 Click Computer in the left pane of the Save As dialog box to display the list of available drives.

6 Double-click Removable Disk (F:), or the name of your USB flash drive, in the list of available storage devices to select that drive as the new save location.

7 Click the New Folder button on the Save As dialog box toolbar to create a new folder on the selected storage device.

8 When the new folder appears, type `Chapter 02` to change the name of the folder, and then press the ENTER key to apply the name change.

9 Double-click the Chapter 02 folder to select it as your save location.

10 Click the 'Save as type' box arrow to display the list of available file formats.

11 If necessary, click Flash CS6 Document (*.fla) to select it.

12 Click the Save button to save the document in the Chapter 02 folder with the new file name (Figure 2–3).

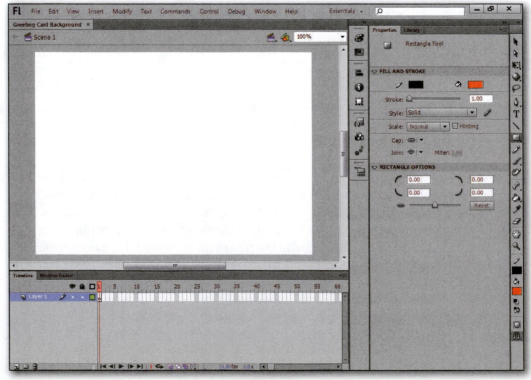

Figure 2–3

The Rectangle Tool

You use the Rectangle Tool to draw rectangles and squares. Hold the SHIFT key as you drag to constrain the shape to a square. Rectangles have two parts — a **stroke** (the outline) and a **fill** (the inside). It is a good idea to use the Tools panel buttons or the Properties panel to set the colors for the stroke and fill before you start drawing (refer to Figure 2–4 on page FL 70). However, you can change these colors at any time after drawing the rectangle. You will learn to do this later in this chapter.

The Properties Panel

Chapter 1 introduced you to the Properties panel (Figure 2–2), where you set various tool options not available on the Tools panel. Although the stroke and fill colors can be set on the Tools panel, they also can be set on the Properties panel — along with other tool settings. The settings displayed in the Properties panel vary from tool to tool. Three useful options for the Rectangle Tool include the Stroke, which sets the thickness of the stroke; the Style, which determines if the stroke is solid, dashed, dotted, or other; and the Rectangle Options area, which configures rounded corners on the rectangles.

Plan the scene.

Before you start working in Flash, you should plan the scene.

- Sketch it out with paper and pencil, or at least develop a clear picture of it in your mind.

- Decide how objects should overlap in the final scene to help you determine the best order in which to draw objects. Draw background objects first, and overlapping foreground objects last.

Plan Ahead

To Set the Stroke and Fill Colors

The following steps set the stroke and fill colors before you start drawing objects. You will select the colors by clicking color selections, called swatches, in the Color picker dialog box.

1

- Click the Stroke Color button on the Tools panel to display the Color picker (Figure 2–4).

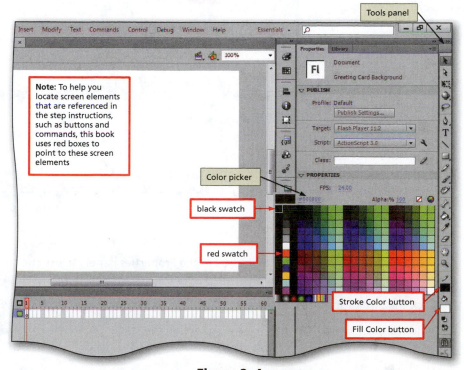

Figure 2–4

2

- Click a black swatch from the first column to set the stroke color. The Color picker will close automatically.

- Click the Fill Color button in the Tools panel to display the Color picker.

- Click the red swatch from the second column to set the stroke color (Figure 2–5).

Q&A   What happened to the Color picker?

The Color picker closes automatically after you select a color.

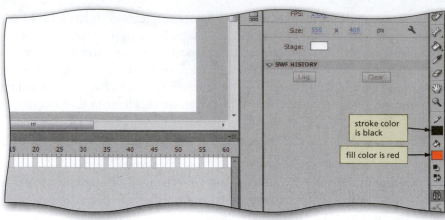

Figure 2–5

To Draw Rectangles and Squares in Object Drawing Mode

The following steps create rectangles and squares that you will use to draw a house and windows.

1

- Click the Rectangle Tool button on the Tools panel.

- If necessary, click the Object Drawing button at the bottom of the Tools panel to enable object drawing mode.

Q&A   How can I tell if object drawing mode is enabled?

When object drawing mode is enabled, the Object Drawing button at the bottom of the Tools panel has a gray background and appears to be selected. When object drawing mode is disabled, the button does not display a gray background and appears deselected.

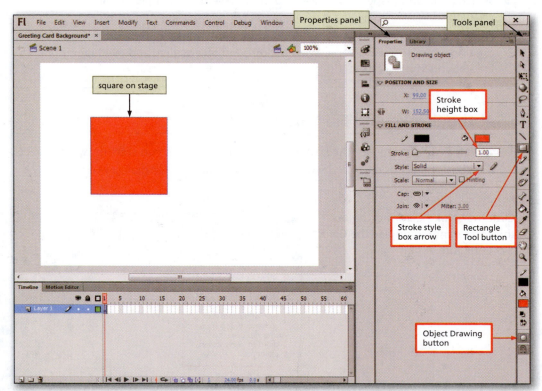

Figure 2–6

- If necessary, click the Stroke height box in the Properties panel, delete the current value, and type 1.00 to set the new stroke thickness.

- Click the Stroke style box arrow and select Solid, if necessary, to set the stroke style.

- Hold the SHIFT key as you drag a large square on the stage. Do not be concerned with the exact size because you will resize it later (Figure 2–6).

2

- SHIFT+drag on the stage to draw two smaller squares above the large square. You will resize and position them later.

- Drag (without pressing the SHIFT key) on the stage to draw two tall rectangles. You will resize and position them later (Figure 2–7).

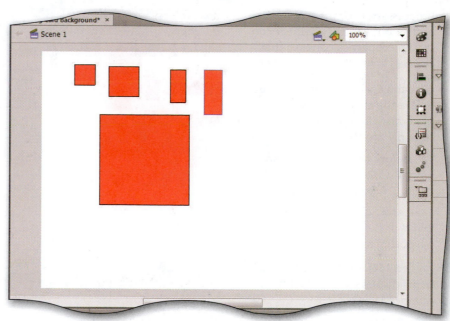

Figure 2–7

Modifying Drawing Objects

Once drawn, you can modify drawing objects by first selecting them on the stage and then adjusting various properties in the Properties panel. You modify multiple drawing objects at once by pressing the SHIFT key as you click or select objects on the stage.

To Resize Drawing Objects using the Properties Panel

The following steps resize the rectangles.

- Click the Selection Tool button on the Tools panel.

- Click the large square on the stage to select it (Figure 2–8).

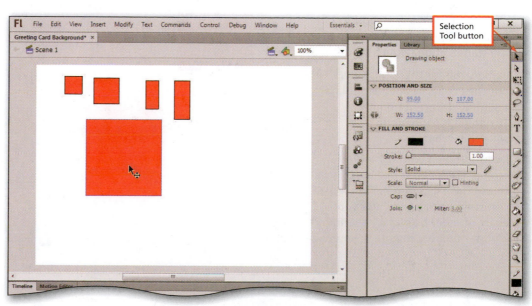

Figure 2–8

- If necessary, click the 'Lock width and height values together' icon on the Properties panel so that it appears linked (and not broken).

- Click the Selection width number, delete the current value, type 150, and then press the ENTER key to apply the change (Figure 2–9).

Q&A What does the 'Lock width and height values together' icon do?

Locking the width and height values causes changes to the width or height to maintain their proportions.

Q&A I typed 150, but the Properties panel displays a slightly different number. Why?

Depending on your computer screen, Flash might not be able to use the exact number you typed. It is fine if your number is off by a few decimal places.

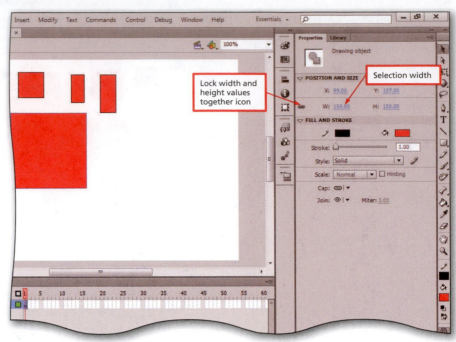

Figure 2–9

❸

- Click the Selection X position number to select it, delete the current value, type 180, and then press the ENTER key to position the square 180 pixels from the left of the stage's edge.

- Click the Selection Y position number to select it, delete the current value, type 170, and then press the ENTER key to position the square 170 pixels from the top of the stage's edge (Figure 2–10).

Q&A I typed 180 for the X position, but the Properties panel displays a slightly different number. The value for the width also changed. Why?

Depending on your computer screen, Flash might not be able to use the exact number you typed. Other times, Flash will use your exact number by slightly changing other values. It is fine if your numbers change by a few decimal places.

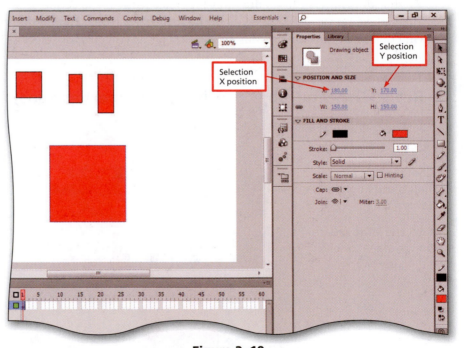

Figure 2–10

4

- Click the leftmost small square on the stage to select it.

- Click the Selection width number, type 25, and then press the ENTER key to apply the change.

- Click the rightmost small square on the stage to select it.

- Click the Selection width number, type 25, and then press the ENTER key to apply the change (Figure 2–11).

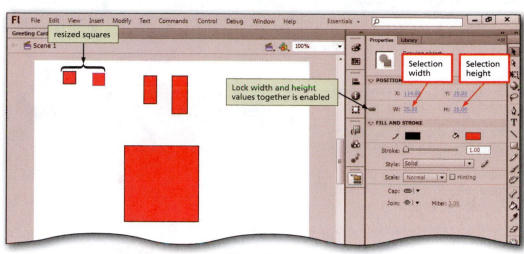

Figure 2–11

Q&A | Can I select both squares and apply the size changes simultaneously?

No, selecting both squares and then entering a width setting applies that setting to the total width spanned by the two squares, including the space between.

5

- Click the leftmost tall rectangle on the stage to select it.

- Click the 'Lock width and height values together' icon so that it appears broken.

- Click the Selection width number, type 25, and then press the ENTER key to apply the change.

- Click the Selection height number, type 50, and then press the ENTER key to apply the change (Figure 2–12).

- Click the rightmost tall rectangle on the stage.

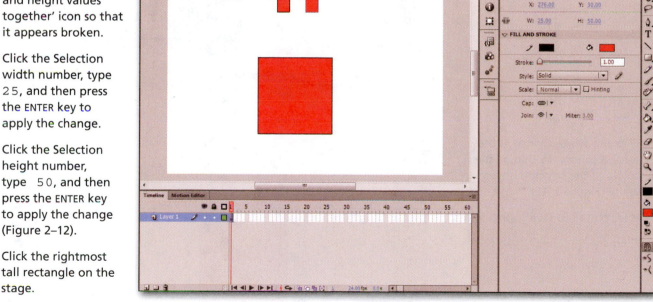

Figure 2–12

- Click the 'Lock width and height values together' icon so that it appears broken.

- Click the Selection width number, type 25, and then press the ENTER key to apply the change.

- Click the Selection height number, type 50, and then press the ENTER key to apply the change (Figure 2–12).

To Edit Multiple Objects

The two squares and two rectangles will become the windows in the drawing. The following steps select and change the fill color of all the windows.

- On the stage, click the leftmost small square to select it.

- SHIFT+click the rightmost small square to add it to the selection.

- SHIFT+click both of the tall rectangles so that all four windows are selected (Figure 2–13).

Q&A How can I tell that all four are selected?

A thin blue border appears around each selected object.

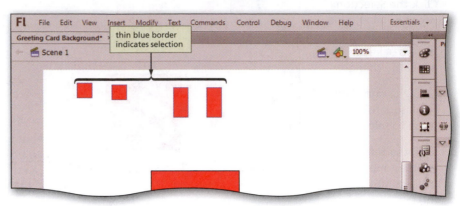

Figure 2–13

- Click the Fill color button on the Properties panel to display the Color picker (Figure 2–14).

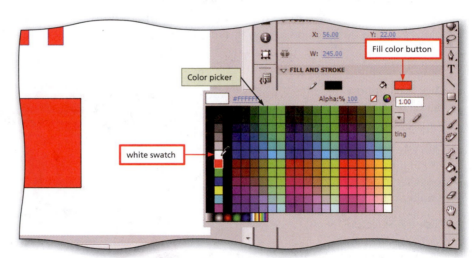

Figure 2–14

- Click the white swatch in the second column to change the fill colors of the selected objects to white (Figure 2–15).

- Press CTRL+S to save your changes.

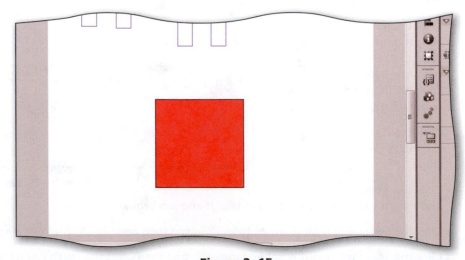

Figure 2–15

Aligning Objects

Flash offers two ways to align objects with each other. **Snap Align** displays dashed guides or lines on the stage as the edges of objects get close to being aligned (Figure 2–16). Snap Align causes objects to move into place as though attracted by a magnet. Alternatively, you can select and align multiple objects using the **Align panel** (Figure 2–16). The Align panel also offers an option to align objects to the stage rather than to each other.

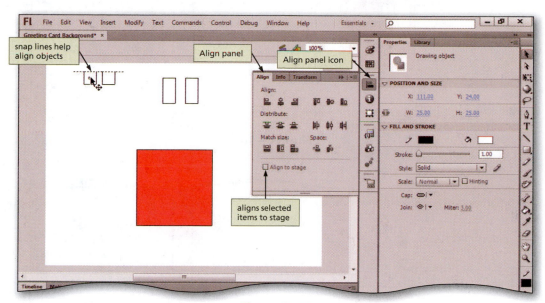

Figure 2–16

To Align Objects using the Align Panel

The following steps align the windows inside the house. First you will use the Snap Align guides, then you will use the Align panel.

- Click the gray work area outside the stage to deselect the currently selected objects.

- Click the Selection Tool button, if necessary, and then drag one of the tall rectangles onto the red square and position it as shown in Figure 2–17.

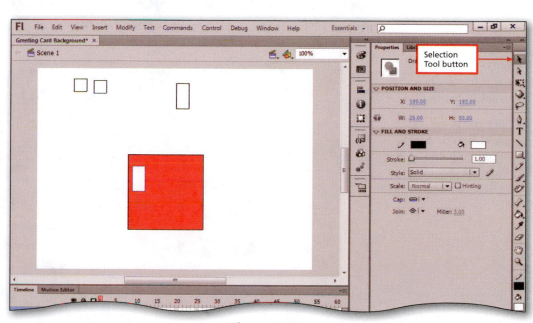

Figure 2–17

2

• Drag one of the small square windows to the right of the tall window and use the Snap Align guide to help you top-align the windows (Figure 2–18).

Q&A

How do I activate the Snap Align guide?

The Snap Align guide appears automatically when objects are close to being aligned.

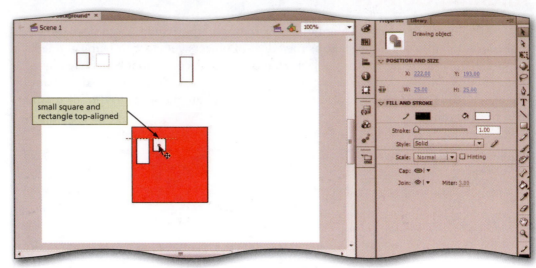

Figure 2–18

3

• Drag the remaining windows so that your screen resembles Figure 2–19.

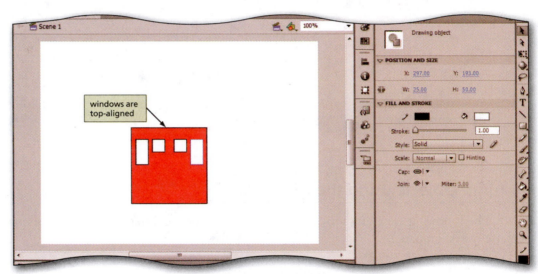

Figure 2–19

4

• SHIFT+click each of the four windows to select them all.

• Click the Align panel icon to display the Align panel (Figure 2–20).

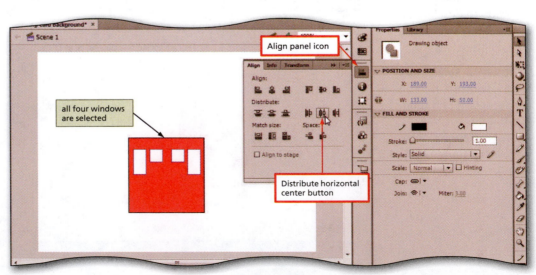

Figure 2–20

5

- Click the 'Distribute horizontal center' button to evenly space the objects horizontally (Figure 2–21).

- Click the stage to collapse the Align panel.

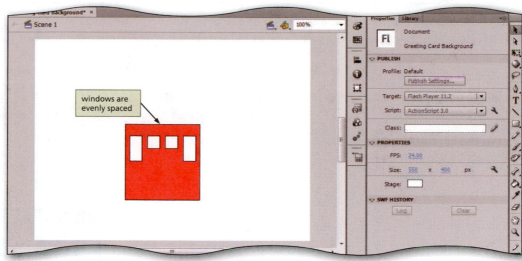

Figure 2–21

Changing a Drawing Object's Shape

Often you will want to change the shape of a drawing object once it has been drawn. To do so, double-click a drawing object with the Selection Tool to enter edit mode, then drag an object's border to reshape it. When in edit mode, you can select the stroke on each side of a drawing object as a separate line segment so you can color or delete the segments individually. You can drag a stroke to create a curved segment, changing the shape of the drawing object. Double-clicking the stroke selects all segments, and thus the entire outline. You also can change the color of the fill or delete the fill completely, leaving only the strokes (Figure 2–22). When you are done editing the drawing object, you can double-click the stage to return to normal mode.

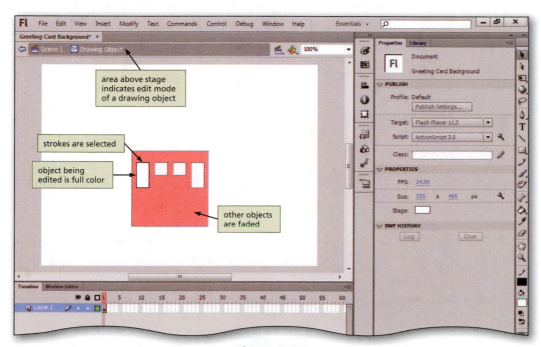

Figure 2–22

To Change the Rectangle's Shape

The following steps create a rectangle to use as a front door. You then will change the shape of the rectangle by arching its top to create a door with a rounded top. Finally, you remove the bottom stroke from the door shape so that it blends with the house.

- On the Tools panel, click the Rectangle Tool button.

- Click the Fill color button on the Properties panel to display the Color picker (Figure 2–23).

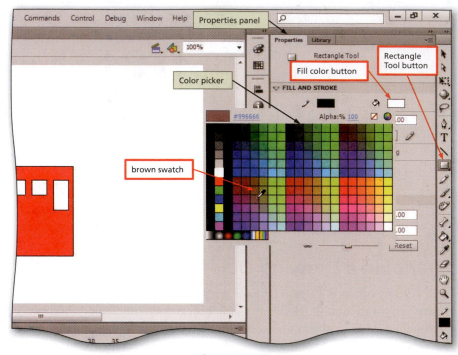

Figure 2–23

- Click the third brown swatch in the sixth column to select the fill color.

- Draw a rectangle on the stage to serve as the door. Do not be concerned with size; you will resize it in a later step (Figure 2–24).

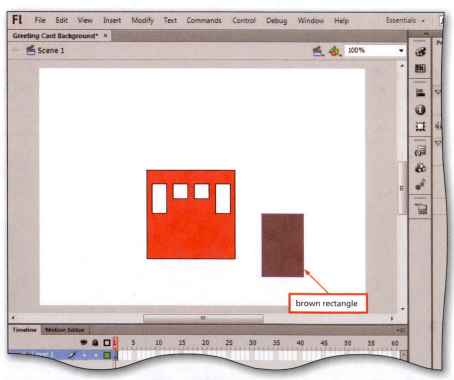

Figure 2–24

3

- On the Tools panel, click the Selection Tool button.

- Double-click the door on the stage to enter edit mode (Figure 2–25).

Q&A

How do I know if I am in edit mode?

The drawing object you click remains bright, while the rest of the objects on the stage are dimmed. The toolbar above the stage indicates you are inside a drawing object.

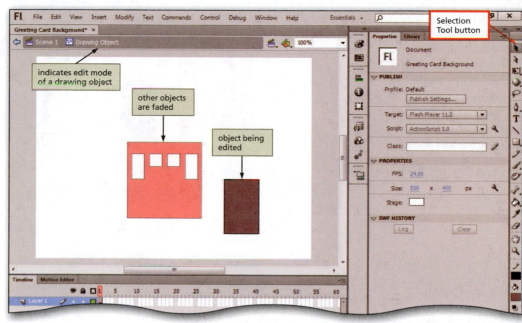

Figure 2–25

4

- Point to the top of the door until the mouse pointer changes to display a curved line (Figure 2–26).

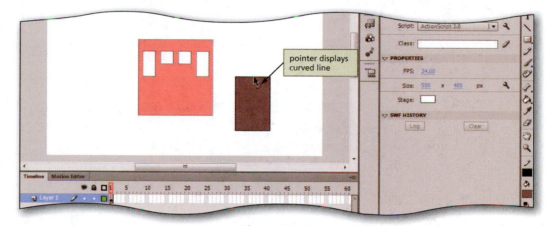

Figure 2–26

5

- Click and drag up to curve the top segment (Figure 2–27).

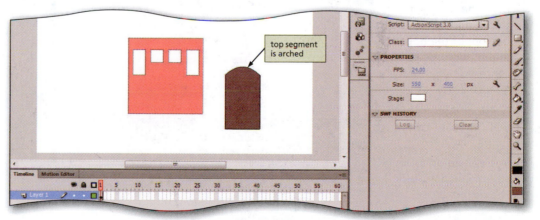

Figure 2–27

6

• Point to the bottom stroke of the door until the mouse pointer changes to display a curved line, and then click to select only that segment (Figure 2–28).

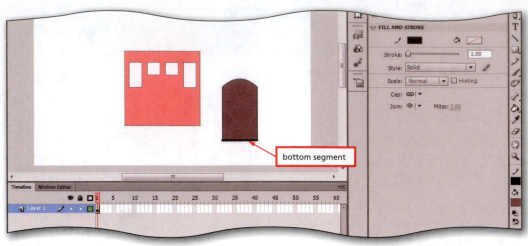

Figure 2–28

7

• Press the DELETE key to remove the bottom stroke from the door (Figure 2–29).

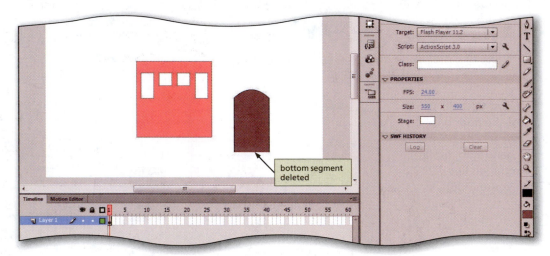

Figure 2–29

8

• Double-click the stage to exit edit mode.

• Drag the door so that it appears at the bottom of the house and is approximately centered horizontally (Figure 2–30).

Q&A

My door does not fit well. Should I try to fix it?

You will adjust the size of the door in the next exercise.

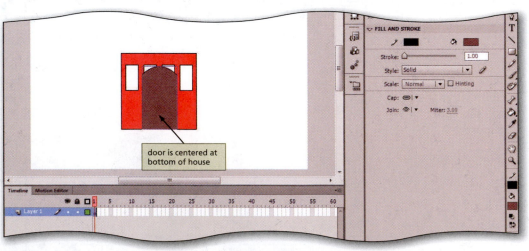

Figure 2–30

The Transform Panel

You use the Transform panel (Figure 2–31) to adjust the size, rotation, or skew of a selected object. To display the Transform panel, you press CTRL+T. You change values in the panel by clicking them and typing new values or by pointing to them and then dragging the mouse left or right. Changes are reflected on the stage.

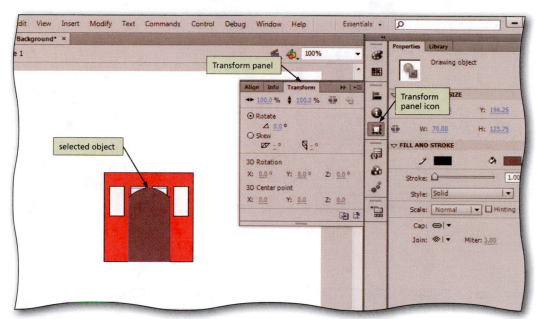

Figure 2–31

To Resize using the Transform Panel

The following steps resize the door using the Transform panel.

- Press CTRL+T to display the Transform panel.

- Point to the Scale Width value and then drag left (to narrow the door) or right (to widen the door) until the door is approximately the width of the two small windows (Figure 2–32).

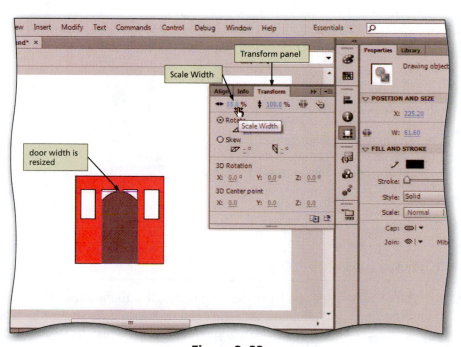

Figure 2–32

2

- Point to the Scale Height value and then drag left (to shorten the door) or right (to lengthen the door) until your door appears as if it will fit in the space beneath the windows (Figure 2–33).

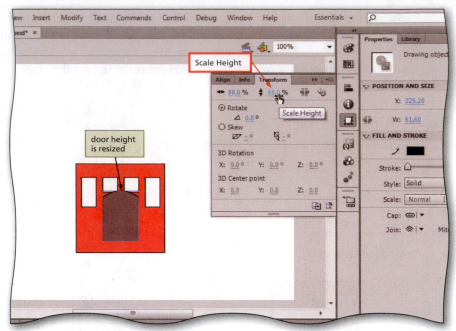

Figure 2–33

3

- Drag the door so that the bottom of the door aligns with the bottom of the house (Figure 2–34).

- Press CTRL+S to save your changes.

Q&A What if my door does not fit in the space?

Repeat Steps 1 through 3 to resize the door and drag it into position. It might take several tries before you get it sized perfectly.

🔍 **Experiment**

- Point to the other values in the Transformation panel, drag to change their values, and take note of how the changes affect the objects on the canvas. Press CTRL+Z after each transformation to undo it.

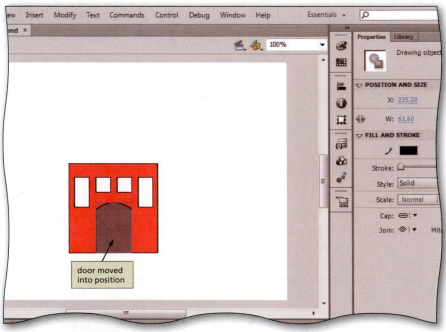

Figure 2–34

To Draw using the Oval Tool

Drawing ovals is similar to drawing rectangles. You use the Oval Tool to draw ovals and circles. Similar to the Rectangle Tool, holding the SHIFT key as you drag constrains the shape to a perfect circle. The following steps create a circle to use as the doorknob. You will remove the stroke from the circle, leaving only the fill.

1

- Click and hold the Rectangle Tool button on the Tools panel to display the menu of related tools (Figure 2–35).

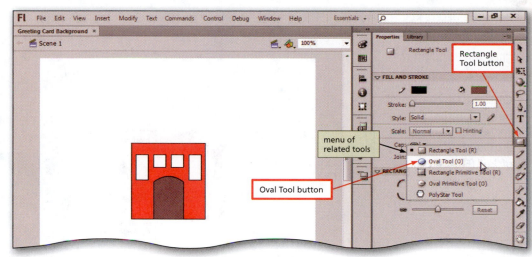

Figure 2–35

2

- Click the Oval Tool button to select it.

- SHIFT+drag on the stage to draw a perfect circle. Do not be concerned with the size because you will resize it in a later step. Draw it fairly large so that it is easier to select.

- Click the Selection Tool button on the Tools panel to select it (Figure 2–36).

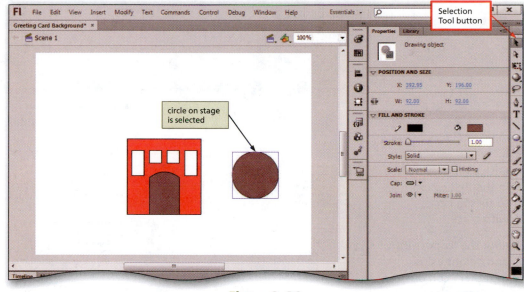

Figure 2–36

3

- Double-click the circle to enter edit mode.

- Click the stroke to select it (Figure 2–37).

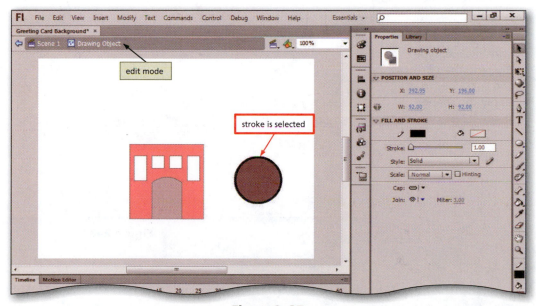

Figure 2–37

4

- Press the DELETE key to delete the stroke.

- Click the circle fill to select it.

- Click the Fill color button on the Properties panel to display the Color picker (Figure 2–38).

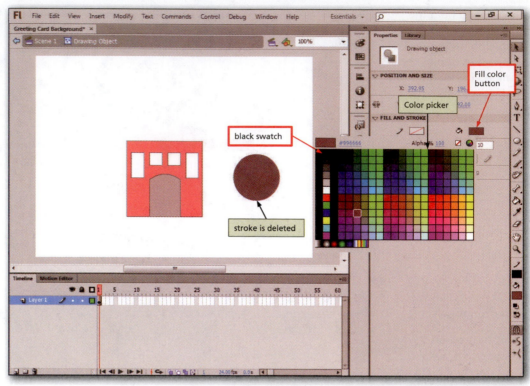

Figure 2–38

5

- Click a black swatch in the first column to fill the circle with black.

- Click the 'Lock width and height values together' icon on the Properties panel so it appears as a linked chain.

- Click the Selection width value, type 10, and then press the ENTER key to apply the change (Figure 2–39).

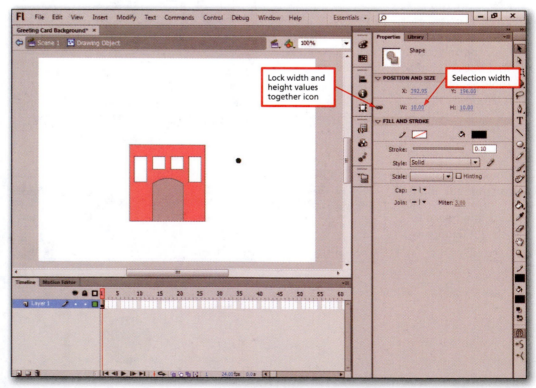

Figure 2–39

6

- Double-click the stage to exit edit mode.

- Drag the doorknob into position on the door.

- Use the arrow keys on the keyboard to nudge the doorknob into its final position.

- Click the stage to deselect the doorknob (Figure 2–40).

- Press CTRL+S to save your changes.

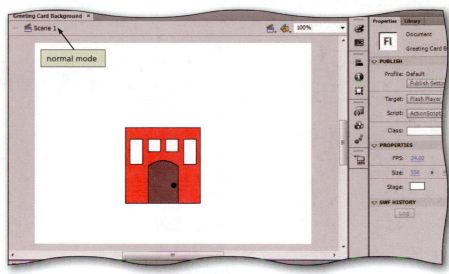

Figure 2–40

Other Ways

1. O key to toggle between Oval Tool and Oval Primitive Tool

The PolyStar Tool

The PolyStar Tool creates polygons or stars. Using the Tool Settings option on the Properties panel lets you configure the tool before you use it (Figure 2–41). Table 2–1 describes the tool settings.

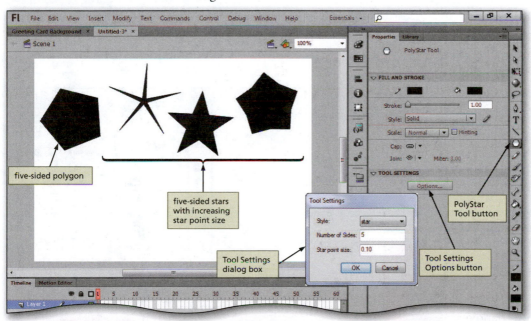

Figure 2–41

Table 2–1 PolyStar Tool Options and Settings

Setting	Value	What it controls
Style	N/A	Choose between polygon and star.
Number of Sides	An integer between 3 and 32	Set the number of sides for the polygon or star. Valid values are between 3 and 32.
Star point size	A decimal between 0 and 1	Has no effect on polygons. A smaller value creates deeper angles between star points. A larger value creates a thicker star.

To Draw using the PolyStar Tool

The following steps use the PolyStar Tool to create a triangle to be used as a roof.

- Click and hold the Oval Tool button on the Tools panel to display the menu of related tools (Figure 2–42).

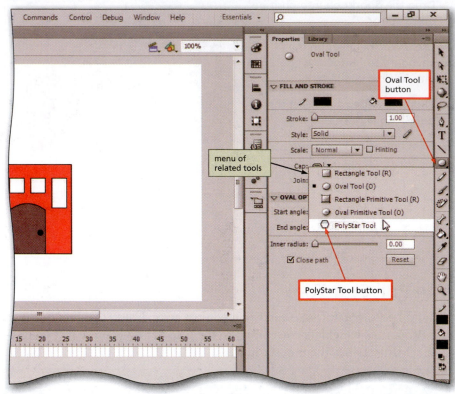

Figure 2–42

2

- Click the PolyStar Tool button to select it.

- In the Tool Settings area of the Properties panel, click the Tool Settings Options button to display the Tool Settings dialog box.

- Click the Style box arrow and then click polygon, if necessary, to specify that you are creating a polygon and not a star.

- Click the Number of Sides text box, delete the current value, and then type 3 to specify a triangle (Figure 2–43).

Q&A Do I have to enter a value for the Star point size?

No. Because you selected polygon from the Style menu, and not star, the Star point size setting has no effect.

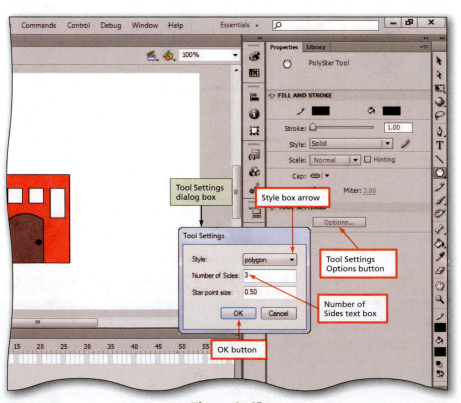

Figure 2–43

3

- Click the OK button to accept the settings and close the Tool Settings dialog box.

- SHIFT+drag on the stage to draw the triangle. Drag up or down while dragging to rotate the triangle so that the bottom is horizontal. Do not be concerned with the size or placement because you will adjust these later.

- Click the Selection Tool button on the Tools panel to select it.

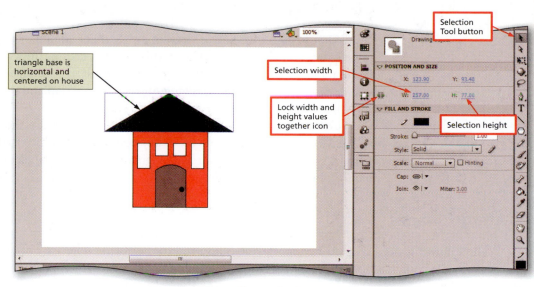

Figure 2–44

- Drag the triangle so that it is approximately centered on top of the house.

- Click the 'Lock width and height values together' icon on the Properties panel so it is displayed as a broken link, allowing you to adjust the triangle width and the height independently.

- Point to the Selection width value until the mouse pointer displays a double arrow, then drag left or right to adjust the value until the triangle is wider than the house.

- If necessary, point to the Selection height value until the mouse pointer displays a double arrow, then drag left or right to adjust the height of the triangle to your liking.

- If necessary, drag the triangle so that it slightly overlaps the top of the house and is once again centered (Figure 2–44).

4

- Click the Fill color button on the Tools panel to display the Color picker.

- Click anywhere on the red house to select the red color from the house on the stage and apply the red color to the roof (Figure 2–45).

Q&A

Why did I not click a swatch from the Color picker as the roof color?

Clicking the house sets the house's color as the source color and ensures that the

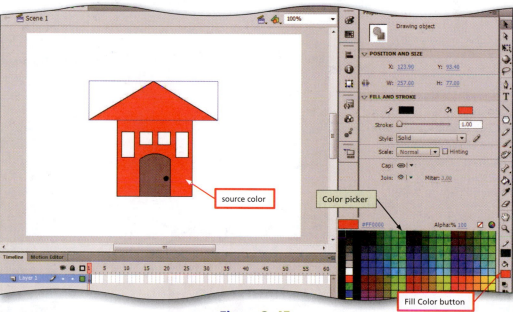

Figure 2–45

two shapes are the same color, which is important because the two shapes will be merged into one. When selecting colors using an existing object on the stage, the mouse pointer displays an eyedropper.

5

- Press CTRL+S to save your changes.

Converting Drawing Objects to Shapes

Recall that Flash allows you to draw in either object mode or merge mode. Object mode, which you have used so far in this chapter, creates drawing objects, whereas merge mode creates shapes. Drawing objects differ from shapes in that they interact with each other differently. Drawing objects can overlap and remain separate objects. If shapes overlap, they merge into a single shape.

To convert a drawing object into a shape, you can use the Break Apart command on the Modify menu or the CTRL+B key combination. Once a drawing object is converted to a shape, it is as if you had originally drawn the object in merge mode rather than in object drawing mode.

To Merge Shapes

The following steps convert and merge the house and roof drawing objects. This allows you to delete the line between the roof and house and to treat them as a single shape.

- If necessary, click the Selection Tool button to select it.

- If necessary, click the roof on the stage to select it.

- Click Modify on the Application bar to display the Modify menu (Figure 2–46).

Figure 2–46

2
- Click Break Apart on the Modify menu to convert the selected drawing object into a shape (Figure 2–47).

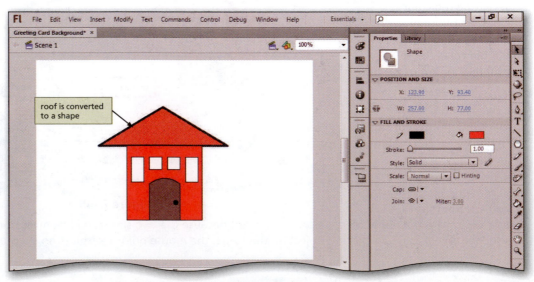

Figure 2–47

3

- Click the house to select it.

- Press CTRL+B to break it apart and convert it to a shape.

- Click the stage to deselect the house.

- Click the stroke segment between the roof and the house to select it (Figure 2–48).

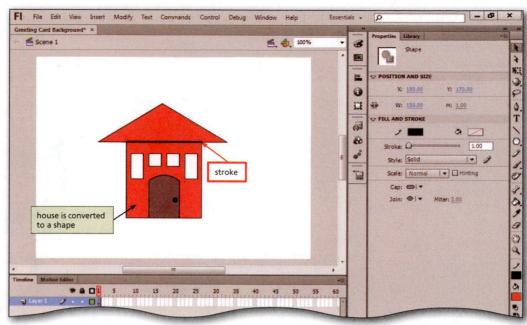

Figure 2–48

4

- Press the DELETE key to delete the segment.

- Click the red roof to select it (Figure 2–49).

Q&A

I clicked just the roof. Why is the house selected also?

The roof and the house were converted to shapes. Because the shapes overlapped each other, they were merged into a single shape.

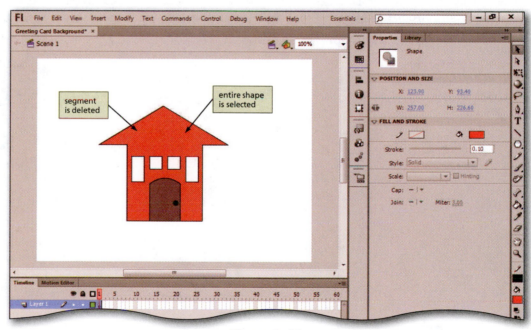

Figure 2–49

To Recolor a Merged Shape

With the roof and house converted to a merged shape, you can change the roof and house color together, as in the following steps.

1

 Click the Fill Color button on the Properties panel to display the Color picker (Figure 2–50).

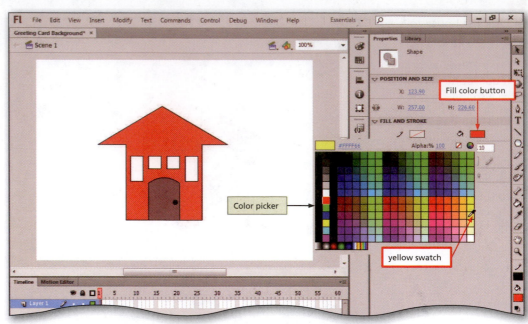

Figure 2–50

2

• Click the yellow swatch, fourth from the bottom of the last column, to change the fill color of the selected shape (Figure 2–51).

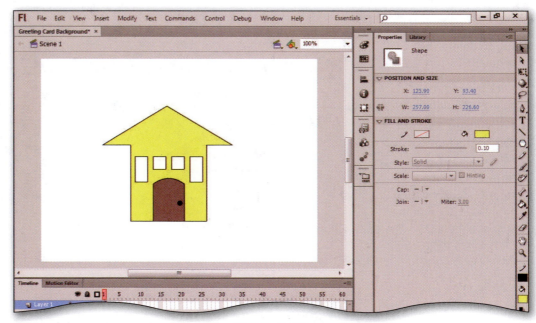

Figure 2–51

BTW

Overlapping Segments
Because strokes drawn in merge mode are treated as segments based on where they overlap, it is easy to trim off any overlapping ends.

The Line and Paint Bucket Tools

The Line Tool is used to draw straight lines. Holding the SHIFT key as you draw constrains the line to 45-degree angles. By drawing overlapping lines in merge mode, you can create your own odd-shaped polygon. To create a fill for a shape created with merged lines, click the inside of the shape with the Paint Bucket Tool; if you do not create a fill, the shape has no fill color.

To Create the Lawn Outline Using the Line Tool

The following steps create a lawn shape out of overlapping lines. You will delete the overlapping ends of the strokes, giving the outline four clean corners. You will deselect the Object Drawing button to draw in merge mode.

1

• Click the Line Tool button on the Tools panel to select it.

• Click the Object Drawing button at the bottom of the Tools panel to deselect it.

• Draw a diagonal line to the right of the house as shown in Figure 2–52. Be sure that your lines do not touch the house.

• SHIFT+drag to draw a horizontal line that overlaps the first.

• Draw a third line that overlaps the second.

• Draw the final horizontal line that overlaps the others to complete the outline of the lawn (Figure 2–52).

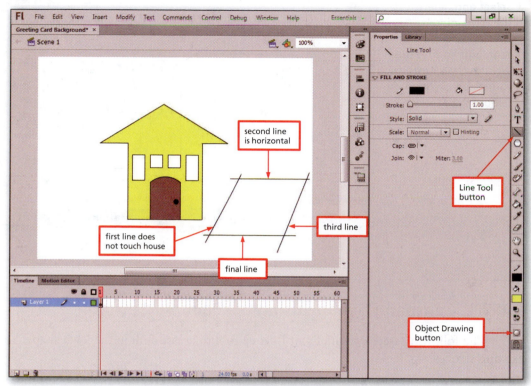

Figure 2–52

Q&A Why should I avoid drawing on the house?

Because the house is a shape (and not a drawing object), drawing a line on it in merge mode will merge the line and the house. For this scene, the house and the lines (which eventually will become the lawn) should not be merged.

2

• Click the Selection Tool button on the Tools panel to select it.

• Click the upper-left piece of overlapping line segment to select it (Figure 2–53).

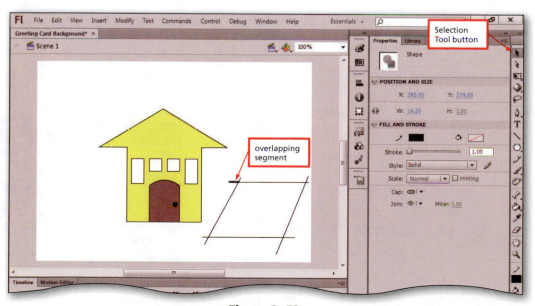

Figure 2–53

- Press the DELETE key to delete the selected segment.

- Select and delete the remaining overlapping segments so that the lawn outline contains four clean corners (Figure 2–54).

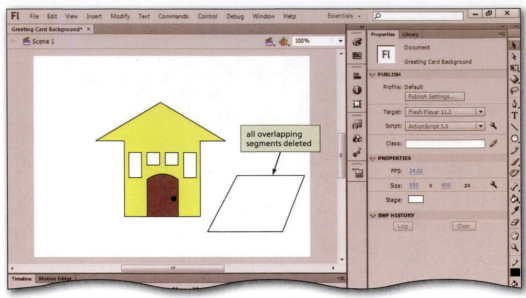

Figure 2–54

To Fill a Transparent Shape using the Paint Bucket Tool

The following steps use the Paint Bucket Tool to create a fill in the lawn shape. You will then delete the existing strokes.

- Click the Paint Bucket Tool button on the Tools panel to select it.

- Click the Fill Color button on the Tools panel to display the Color picker (Figure 2–55).

Q&A

What is in a transparent shape?

A shape is considered transparent if it does not have a fill; in other words, it contains no pixels.

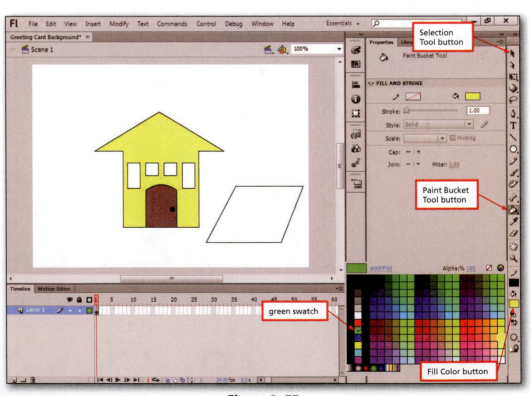

Figure 2–55

2

- Click the green swatch in the second column to set the fill color.

- Click the lawn shape on the stage to create a fill for the transparent shape.

- Click the Selection Tool button on the Tools panel to select it.

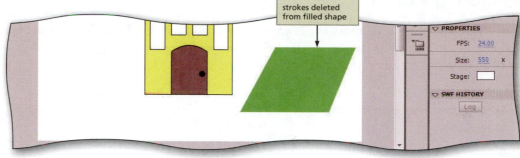

Figure 2–56

- Double-click the lawn's stroke to select the entire outline.

- Press the DELETE key to delete the stroke around the lawn.

- Press CTRL+S to save your changes (Figure 2–56).

Moving Shapes

Recall that overlapped drawing objects do not affect each other. When shapes of the same color overlap, they merge into a single shape. When shapes of different colors overlap, they punch holes in each other, with the top shape overriding the underlying shape. Overlapped shapes do not merge or create holes until the shape is deselected (Figure 2–57). Therefore, you must be careful not to deselect a moved shape until you are sure it is positioned exactly where you want.

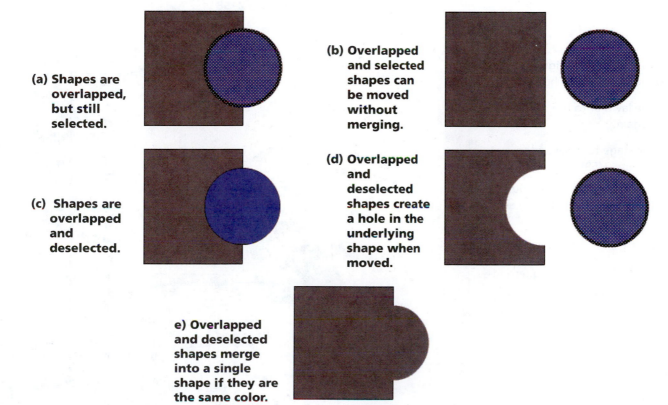

(a) Shapes are overlapped, but still selected.

(b) Overlapped and selected shapes can be moved without merging.

(c) Shapes are overlapped and deselected.

(d) Overlapped and deselected shapes create a hole in the underlying shape when moved.

e) Overlapped and deselected shapes merge into a single shape if they are the same color.

Figure 2–57

To Move the Lawn

The following steps move the lawn shape into position. However, because the lawn and house are both shapes, they will merge when overlapped. Merging problems are common when using Flash. You will learn how to overcome this common problem in a later exercise.

- Click the lawn shape on the stage to select it.

- Drag the lawn shape onto the house shape, toward the bottom of the house (Figure 2–58).

Q&A Why does the lawn appear sandwiched between the house and the door?

The lawn is a shape. When selected and moved, it is placed on top of other shapes but below drawing objects. The house is a shape, whereas the door, doorknob, and windows are drawing objects.

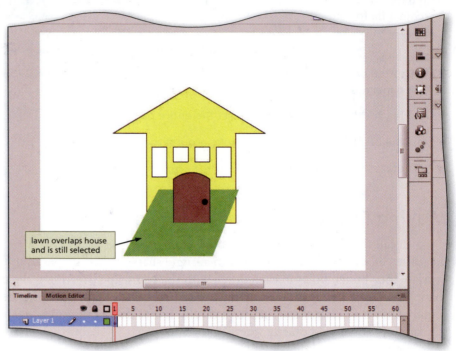

lawn overlaps house and is still selected

Figure 2–58

- Drag the lawn to the right so it no longer touches the house.

- Drag the lawn onto the house again.

- Click the stage to deselect the lawn (Figure 2–59).

Q&A Why did the lawn and the house not merge, even though they are both shapes?

Shapes do not merge until they are deselected. Because the lawn was never deselected, it never merged with the house.

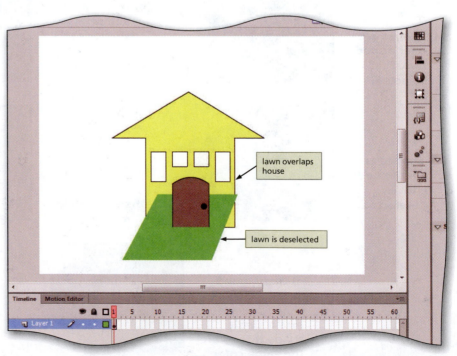

lawn overlaps house

lawn is deselected

Figure 2–59

3

- Click the lawn to select it again.

- Drag the lawn away from the house so they no longer touch (Figure 2–60).

Q&A

Why is the bottom portion of the house missing?

Because the lawn was deselected, it merged with the house. The lawn and house are different colors, so the lawn shape destroyed the underlying pixels of the house shape, effectively creating a lawn-shaped hole in the house.

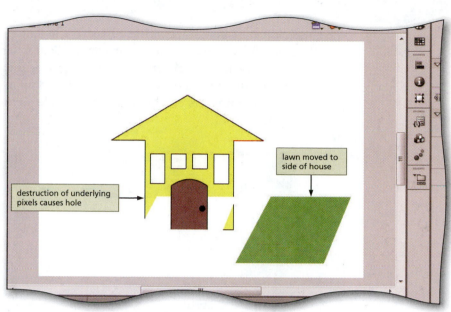

destruction of underlying pixels causes hole

lawn moved to side of house

Figure 2–60

To Revert the Document to Its Last Saved State

The following steps undo the damage to the house. Because the document was last saved after creating the fill for the lawn, the Revert command will return the document to that point.

1 Click File on the Application bar to display the File menu.

2 Click Revert on the File menu to display the Revert? dialog box.

3 Click the Revert button in the Revert? dialog box to revert the document to its last saved state (Figure 2–61).

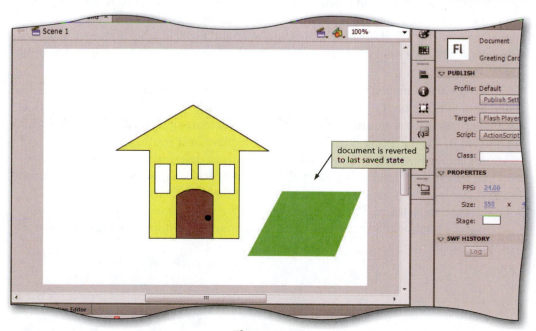

document is reverted to last saved state

Figure 2–61

Layers

A **layer** is a container within a Flash document. A layer holds drawing objects, shapes, and others items, which you will learn about in later chapters. In fact, everything you have drawn in this chapter's exercises thus far is contained within a single layer. Layers are like sheets of transparent plastic stacked upon one another. Different pictures on different layers combine to form a single picture when the layers are stacked (Figure 2–62).

Figure 2–62

Layers solve the problem of overlapping shapes without merging them. If you place one shape in one layer and a second shape in a different layer, the shapes do not merge or interact with each other because they are on different layers. You can control which shape appears on top by changing the **stacking order** of the layers.

In addition to controlling shape merging, layers are important organizational tools. You can store all the independent objects that make up one image. For example, you can store the roof, windows, and door that make up the house within a single layer named, house. You can then store clouds, the sun, and birds in a layer named, sky. This approach allows you to work with a set of related objects easily without disturbing the objects on other layers.

Layers are managed in the Timeline (Figure 2–63 on the following page). A pencil icon appears on the layer containing the currently selected object or shape. Each layer has three columns of clickable icons, which are described in Table 2–2. At the bottom of the Timeline is a status bar that displays buttons for creating a new layer, creating a folder in which to store multiple layers, and deleting layers. You can click a layer's name on the Timeline to select all the objects and shapes residing on that layer. To rename a layer, double-click the layer name in the Timeline, type a new name, and then press the ENTER key. To rearrange the stacking order of layers, drag them up or down in the Timeline. Flash assigns a color, shown in the Outline column, to each new layer you create.

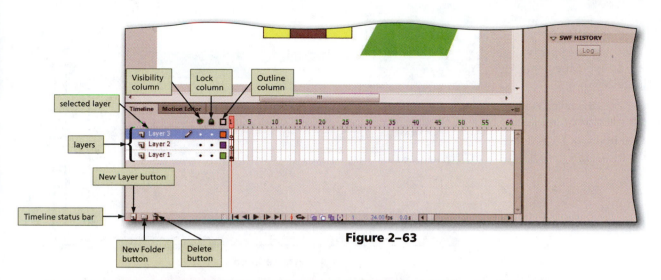

Figure 2–63

Table 2–2 Layer Icons

Column description	Visibility column	Lock Column	Outline Column
Icon in column header	👁	🔒	◻
State	A dot means the layer is visible. A red X means the layer is hidden.	A dot means the layer contents can be edited. A red X means the layer contents cannot be edited.	A colored square indicates the layer contents are displayed in full. A white square with a colored outline indicates the layer contents are displayed as outlines where the outline color matches the square icon's color.

Use layers to organize objects.
Consider placing multiple shapes that form a single object on the same layer. For example, if several rectangles arranged in a certain way form a house, place all those rectangles on the same layer, named House, to help keep your document organized. This makes it easier to locate and manipulate shapes during editing. Keep on separate layers objects that you want to prevent from merging.

Plan Ahead

To Rename a Layer

The following steps rename the existing layer to indicate its contents.

1
- Double-click the layer name in the Timeline to select it (Figure 2–64).

Q&A

Why is everything on the stage covered in dots?

When you click a layer in the Timeline, all shapes and objects residing on that layer are selected. Recall that selected shapes appear to be covered with dots and selected drawing objects are outlined in blue.

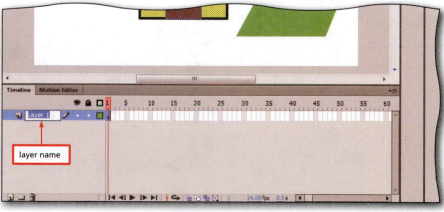

Figure 2–64

- Type `House` and then press the ENTER key to apply the name change (Figure 2–65).

Q&A

Why did we name the layer, House, if the lawn is still part of this layer?

You will move the lawn to its own layer later in the chapter.

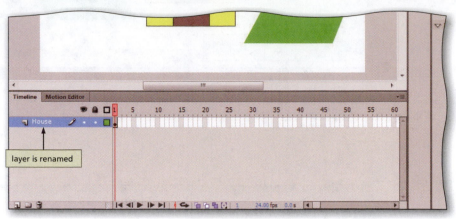

Figure 2–65

To Create a New Layer

The following steps create a new layer for the lawn.

- Click the New Layer button on the Timeline status bar to create a new layer, Layer 2, above the House layer (Figure 2–66).

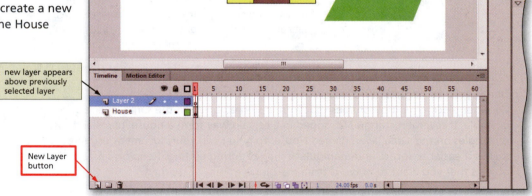

Figure 2–66

- Double-click the name of the new layer, type `Lawn` and press the ENTER key to apply the change (Figure 2–67).

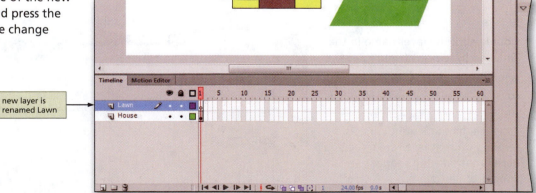

Figure 2–67

Moving Items between Layers

To move an item from one layer to another, you would cut the item from its current layer and paste it to the new layer. To **cut** an item, you select it and then choose the Cut command from the Edit menu, or press CTRL+X. To **paste** it to the new layer, you first select the desired layer in the Timeline, and then choose one of the Paste options from the Edit menu. Flash offers two useful paste options: Paste in Center and Paste in Place.

Paste in Center (CTRL+V) pastes the item in the center of the stage. Paste in Place (CTRL+SHIFT+V) pastes the item in its original location. This is helpful for moving an item from one layer to another while maintaining the exact position of the item.

To Move a Shape using Paste in Place

The following steps cut the lawn from the House layer and move it to the Lawn layer.

1
- Click the lawn shape on the stage to select it.
- Press CTRL+X to cut the lawn from the stage.
- Click the Lawn layer in the Timeline to select it (Figure 2–68).

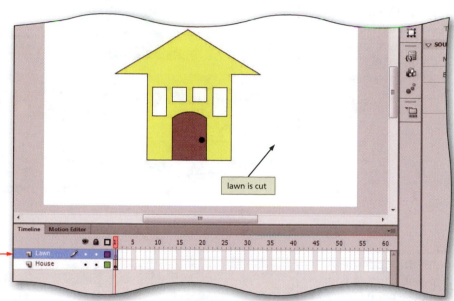

Figure 2–68

2
- Press CTRL+SHIFT+V to paste the lawn in place on the new layer (Figure 2–69).
- Press CTRL+S to save your changes.

Q&A

What happened? Nothing looks different.

The lawn was just moved from the House layer to the Lawn layer. Also, the Lawn layer is selected in the Timeline.

Experiment

- Click the Visibility column (the first column) of each layer to toggle the layer visibility. Click the Outline column (the third column) of each layer to toggle the layer outlines. When you are through, confirm that both layers are visible and display their contents in full view.

Figure 2–69

To Move the Lawn into Position

The following steps move the lawn into position in relation to the house. Because the lawn shape and the house shape are on different layers, they will not merge.

- Drag the lawn to the left so it overlaps the house (Figure 2–70).

Q&A

Why is the lawn no longer sandwiched between the house and the door like before?

The lawn is now on its own layer. Everything on the Lawn layer appears on top of everything on the House layer.

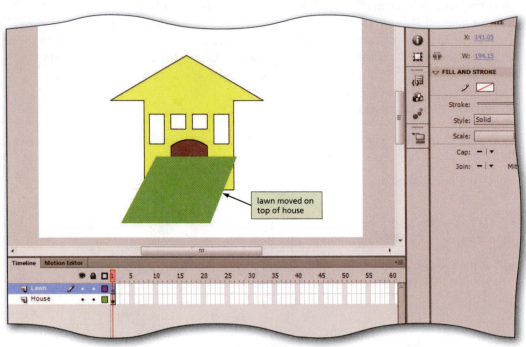

Figure 2–70

- On the Properties panel, position your mouse pointer over the Selection width value and then drag left or right over the value to resize the lawn so that it resembles the width in the figure.

- In the Properties panel, drag left or right over the Selection height value to resize the lawn so that it resembles the height in the figure (Figure 2–71).

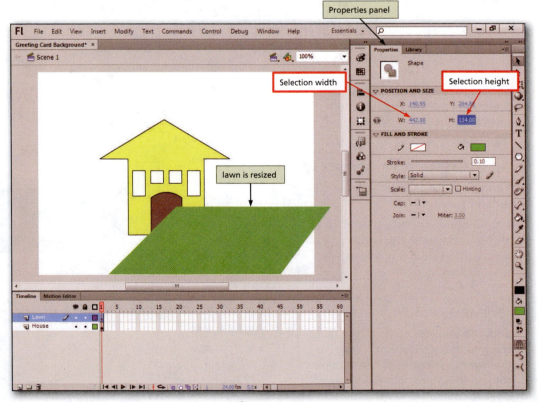

Figure 2–71

❸

- Click the stage to deselect the lawn shape.

- On the Timeline, click the Lawn layer and drag it below the House layer to change the layer stacking order and move the lawn behind the house.

- If necessary, drag the lawn shape on the stage to move it into its final position. You might need to use the Properties panel to adjust its width and height. It should resemble Figure 2–72 when you are finished.

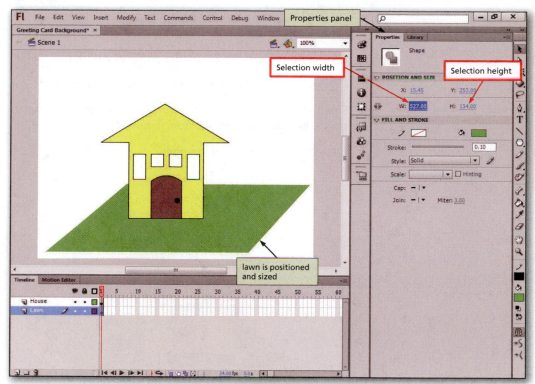

Figure 2–72

Arranging Objects and Shapes

Many times, multiple items reside on a single layer. Just as you can rearrange layers to adjust their stacking order, you can adjust the stacking order of individual items within a single layer. The Arrange submenu of the Modify menu contains options to move a selected object or shape forward or backward in relation to other items on the same layer. Forward means to bring it in front of other items on the same layer, whereas backward means to send it behind other items. This feature is helpful if you want to keep items on a single layer but need to change their stacking order so that a specific object is on top, or in front, of another object, such as the door being on top of the house.

Flash treats drawing objects and shapes differently when it comes to arranging. Drawing objects always appear on top of shapes. If you want a drawing object to appear behind a shape, you would move the object to a different layer and then adjust the layer stacking order.

To Create a Chimney using the Rectangle Tool

The following steps create a chimney on the House layer.

❶ Click the House layer on the Timeline to select it.

❷ Click and hold the PolyStar Tool in the Tools panel to display the menu of related tools, and then click the Rectangle Tool command to select the Rectangle Tool.

3 Click the Object Drawing button at the bottom of the Tools panel to enable object drawing mode.

4 Set the stroke color in the Properties panel to black.

5 Set the fill color in the Properties panel to a dark red.

6 Draw a tall rectangle to use as a chimney. Refer to Figure 2–73 for the approximate size.

7 Select the chimney using the Selection Tool and drag it to the left side of the house so that it overlaps the first window (Figure 2–73).

8 Press CTRL+S to save your changes.

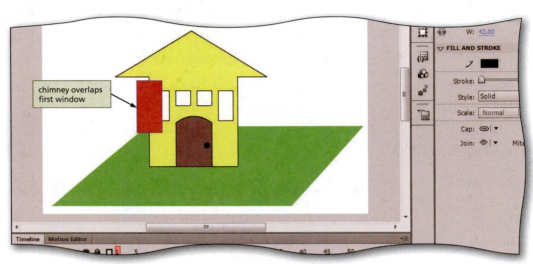

chimney overlaps first window

Figure 2–73

To Change the Stacking Order of Objects on the Same Layer

The following steps change the stacking order of the objects on the House layer so that the chimney is in the back.

- Click Modify on the Application bar to display the Modify menu.

- Point to Arrange on the Modify menu to display the Arrange submenu (Figure 2–74).

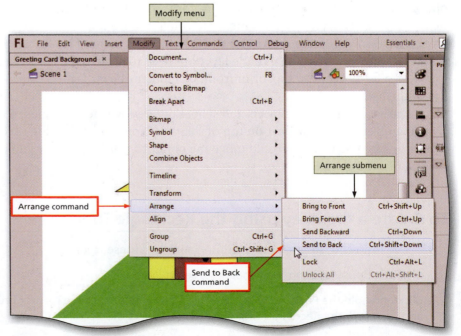

Modify menu

Arrange submenu

Arrange command

Send to Back command

Figure 2–74

2

- Click Send to Back on the Arrange submenu to send the chimney to the back of the layer (Figure 2–75).

Experiment

- Experiment with sending other objects on this layer to the front and back. Return all objects to their correct position when you are through.

Q&A

What is the difference between Send Backward and Send to Back?

Send Backward moves the selected object back one step at a time so that you can arrange it between any other objects on the layer. Send to Back moves the selected object all the way to the back so it immediately appears behind all other objects on the layer.

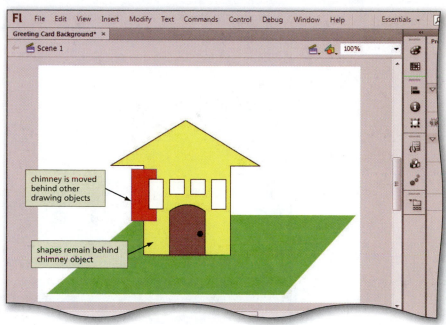

chimney is moved behind other drawing objects

shapes remain behind chimney object

Figure 2–75

Q&A

Why is the chimney still in front of the house?

The chimney, like the windows and door, is a drawing object. The house itself is a shape. Drawing objects always appear on top of shapes when they reside on the same layer. The chimney was moved to the back of the layer's drawing objects, so it appears behind the window. To place it behind the house, you must move it to a different layer.

To Move the Chimney to a New Layer

The following steps move the chimney to its own layer so that it can be positioned behind the house.

1 Click the New Layer button on the Timeline status bar to create a new blank layer.

2 Double-click the new layer name, type `Chimney`, and press the ENTER key to rename the layer.

3 Click the chimney on the stage to select it, then press CTRL+X to cut it from its location on the House layer.

4 Click the Chimney layer in the Timeline to select it.

5 Press CTRL+V to paste the chimney to the center of the Chimney layer.

6 Drag the chimney into position on the left side of the roof.

7 In the Timeline, drag the Chimney layer below the House layer so that your screen resembles Figure 2–76.

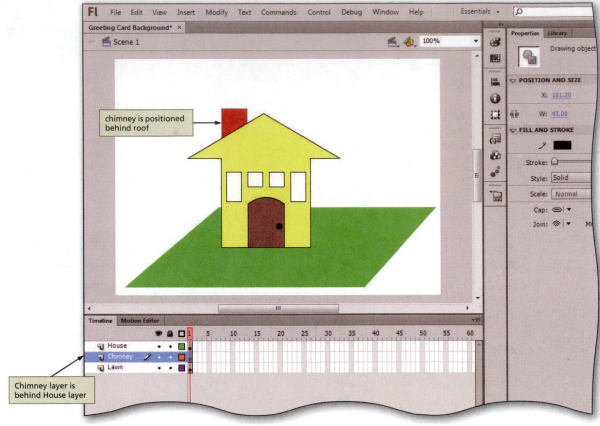

Figure 2–76

Grouping Layers

It is common to have several layers that form a single item, such as the Chimney and House layers that, when combined, form the completed house. In these situations, it is helpful to group the related layers together into a layer folder. A **layer folder** is a container that stores multiple layers (Figure 2–77). The names of layers inside a folder are indented to indicate they are subelements of the folder. Once folders contain layers, you can click the small triangle to the left of the folder name to expand or collapse the folder. As with regular layers, you can click the Visibility, Lock, or Outline buttons on a layer folder and the action affects all the layers nested within. You can select a layer folder in the Timeline to quickly select all the objects and shapes residing on the nested layers. Moving a layer folder within the Timeline moves its contained layers.

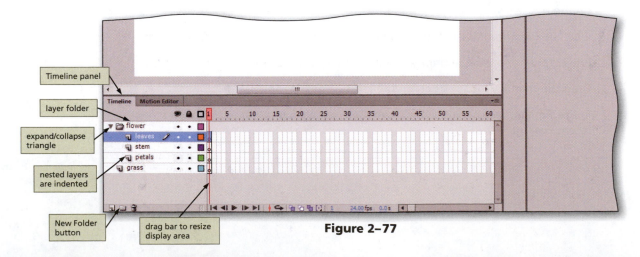

Figure 2–77

To Create a Layer Folder

The following steps create a layer folder and move the House and Chimney layers inside it.

- Click the New Folder button to create a new empty folder (Figure 2–78).

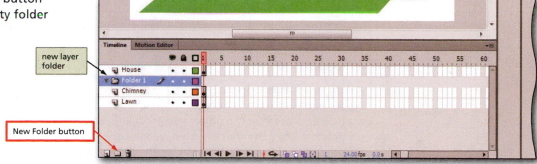

Figure 2–78

- Double-click the name of the new folder, type `House Complete`, and press the ENTER key to change the folder's name.

- Point to the bar separating the layer names from the frames until the mouse pointer becomes a double-headed arrow, and then drag the bar to the right until all layer names are visible (Figure 2–79).

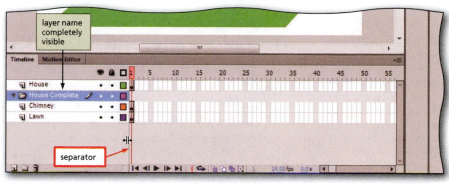

Figure 2–79

- Drag the House layer below the House Complete folder on the Timeline so that a thick black line appears under the folder, then release the mouse button to move the House layer into the folder.

- Drag the Chimney layer below the House layer in the Timeline so that a thick black line appears under the House layer, then release the mouse button to move the Chimney layer into the folder (Figure 2–80).

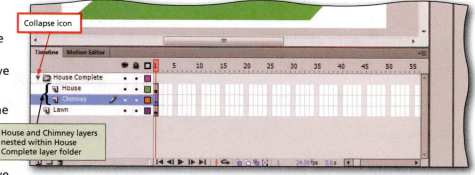

Figure 2–80

- Click the triangle to the left of the folder name to collapse the folder and reduce the clutter in the Timeline.

- Press CTRL+S to save your changes.

🔍 Experiment

- Click the layer folder to select all the objects and shapes within, then drag on the stage to move the house and chimney together. Drag the house and chimney back to their original location, or press CTRL+Z to undo your changes. Toggle the Visibility and Outline icons for the House Complete layer folder to see the effect on the stage. When you are done, make sure the layer is visible and is not in Outline view. Save your changes again, if necessary.

Break Point: If you wish to take a break, this is a good place to do so. To resume at a later time, start Flash and continue following the steps from this location forward.

Gradients

A **gradient** is a blend of two colors. Gradients add dimension and interest to a drawing. In Flash, you create gradients using the Color panel.

Plan Ahead

Apply gradients appropriately.
Before applying a gradient fill, consider the colors. Be sure to specify colors that would actually be present in the object you are filling. For example, to fill an apple, you would most likely use shades of red, yellow, or green rather than blue or orange. Also, consider the light source. If a light (or the sun) were shining on your object in the real world, would the shaded areas be at the top or the bottom? The left or the right? Try to arrange your gradient colors so they simulate real-world conditions.

BTW

Adding Realism
Few things in the physical world are a single solid color. Light sources and other environmental factors cause highlights and shadows on objects. Although Flash is not used for detailed drawings, even the simplest drawing can benefit from the varied color and the depth implied by a gradient.

The Color Panel and Gradients

The Color panel allows you to create colors and gradients to use on strokes and fills (Figure 2–81). To use the panel, you would first select a fill type from the Color Type menu. You can click an option button to select Hue, Saturation, Bright (HSB) mode or Red, Green, Blue (RGB) mode. Use the sliders or click in the large colored box to set a color. Adjusting the Alpha value sets the transparency of the color. An alpha value of 0% is transparent, while 100% is opaque. In the case of a gradient, a gradient bar appears at the bottom of the Color panel and displays the gradient. Color stops are located below the gradient bar. A **color stop** marks the location along the gradient where a new color starts. A gradient requires at least two color stops. You can click a color stop to set its color. To add a new color stop, click a blank area below the gradient bar. To delete a color stop, you would drag it down away from the gradient bar. Finally, you drag across a shape or object on the stage with the Paint Bucket Tool to apply the gradient.

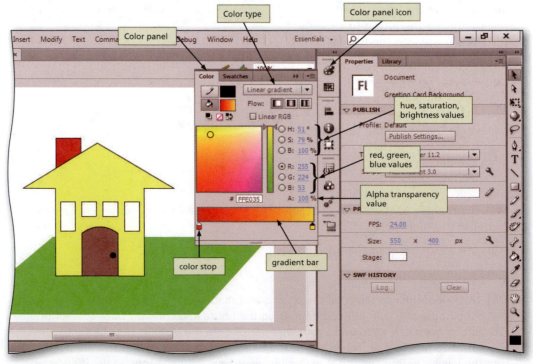

Figure 2–81

To Create a Sky

The following steps create a shape for the sky. You will change the shape to a gradient in a later step.

1 Click the Lawn layer on the Timeline to select it.

2 Click the New Layer button at the bottom of the Timeline to create a new blank layer above the Lawn layer.

3 Double-click the new layer name, type Sky, and then press the ENTER key to rename the layer.

4 Click the Rectangle Tool button to select it.

5 Click the upper-left corner of the lawn and drag up and to the right to create a rectangle for the sky. Drag to the right until the right edge of the rectangle lines up with the upper-right corner of the lawn. Drag up until a little space is left at the top of the stage (Figure 2–82).

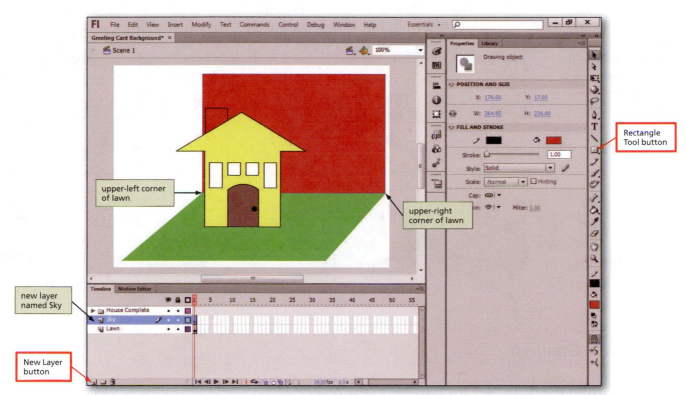

Figure 2–82

To Remove a Stroke Using the Color Panel

Flash often provides more than one way to accomplish a task. The following steps remove the stroke around the sky rectangle using the Color panel, rather than using the DELETE key as you did in an earlier step.

1

- Click the Color panel button to display the Color panel.

- Click the Stroke color button to display the Color picker (Figure 2–83).

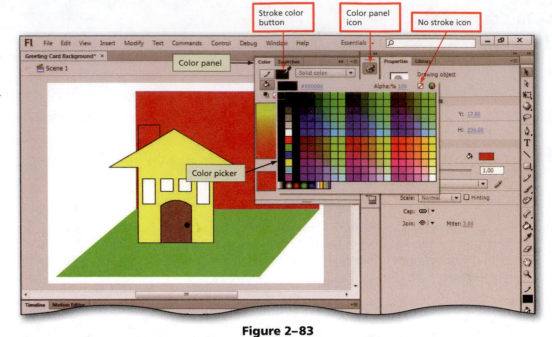

Figure 2–83

2

- Click the No Stroke icon to remove the stroke and close the Color picker (Figure 2–84).

Q&A

Why does there still appear to be a thin border?

The rectangle is still selected. You are seeing the selection border, not a stroke. Remember that selected objects display a thin border.

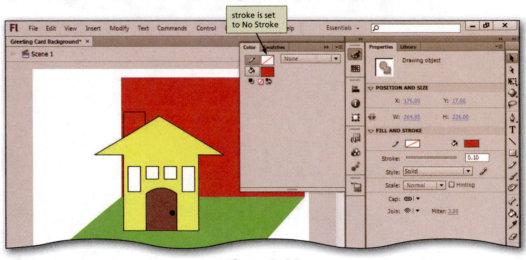

Figure 2–84

To Create a Gradient

The following steps create and apply a gradient fill to the sky.

1

- Click the Fill color button on the Color panel so that the options pertain to the fill rather than the stroke.

- Click the Color Type menu arrow to display the menu of fill options (Figure 2–85).

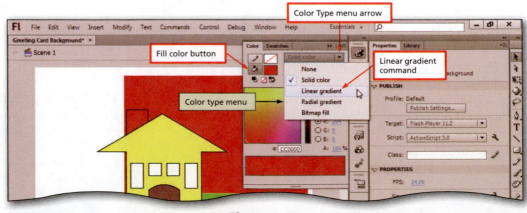

Figure 2–85

2

- Click Linear gradient so the gradient colors will blend together along a straight path.

- Click the H option button to select Hue, Saturation, Brightness mode.

- Click the left color stop below the gradient bar to select it.

- Click the color bar where the dark and light blues meet to set the base color for the large color field.

- In the color field, click to select a medium blue for the first color stop, as shown in Figure 2–86.

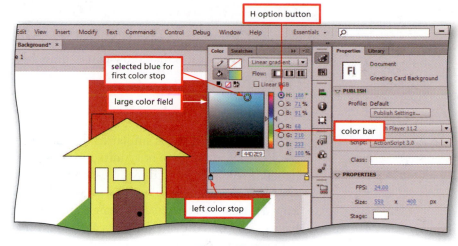

Figure 2–86

3

- Click the right color stop below the gradient bar to set the second gradient color.

- Click the color bar where the dark and light blues meet to set the base color for the large color field.

- In the color field, click to select a light blue for the second color stop, as shown in Figure 2–87.

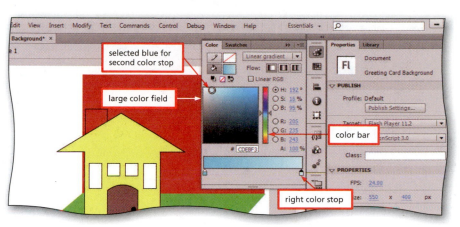

Figure 2–87

4

- Click the Paint Bucket Tool button on the Tools panel to select it.

- On the stage, drag from the bottom to the top of the sky rectangle to apply the gradient from bottom to top.

- In the Timeline, drag the Sky layer to the bottom of the layer stack so the sky is behind the other items on the stage (Figure 2–88).

- Press CTRL+S to save your changes.

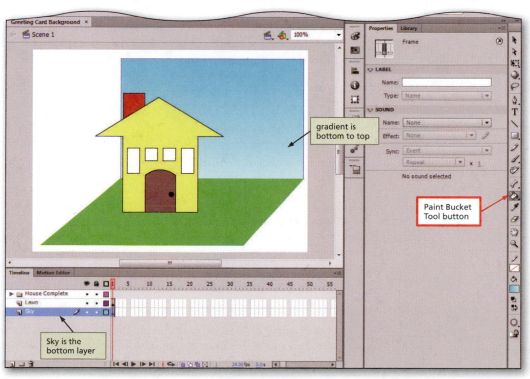

Figure 2–88

Drawing with Free-Form Tools

Whereas the Rectangle, Oval, PolyStar, and Line Tools all create regular shapes, Flash includes several tools that allow you to draw free-form shapes, including the Pencil, Brush, and Pen Tools.

The Pencil Tool

The Pencil Tool is similar to the Line Tool in that it draws only strokes, but with the Pencil Tool, you are not limited to straight lines. The Pencil Tool works like a real pencil. You can use it to draw free-form curves. When using the Pencil Tool, you can choose from three Pencil modes — Straighten, Smooth, or Ink — which determine how the final stroke appears. Straighten mode attempts to straighten any curves you have drawn, and the final result is a line with sharp corners. Smooth mode attempts to smooth curves for a neater appearance. Ink mode leaves your drawing exactly as you have drawn it (Figure 2–89).

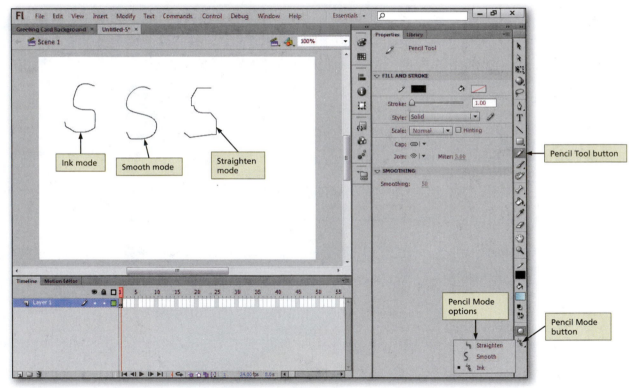

Figure 2–89

Plan Ahead	**Choose the appropriate tool.**
	Many shapes can be drawn with a variety of tools. The appropriate tool might not always be the obvious choice, but instead the one with which you are most comfortable. Use the tool that best combines your expertise with efficiency.

- To draw a rectangle, use the Rectangle Tool or the Line Tool.

- Use either the Oval Tool or Pen Tool to draw an oval.

At times, you will need to use a combination of tools, or use the same tool repeatedly, to create a shape. For example, clouds can be created by overlapping ovals or by drawing them freehand with the Pencil Tool.

To Draw using the Pencil Tool

The following steps use the Pencil Tool to draw clouds and chimney smoke.

- Click the Lawn layer on the Timeline to select it.

- Click the New Layer button to create a new blank layer above the Lawn layer.

- Double-click the new layer name, type Clouds & Smoke, and then press the ENTER key to change the layer name.

- Click the Pencil Tool button on the Tools panel to select it.

- Click the Pencil Mode button at the bottom of the Tools panel to display the Pencil Mode menu, and then click Smooth.

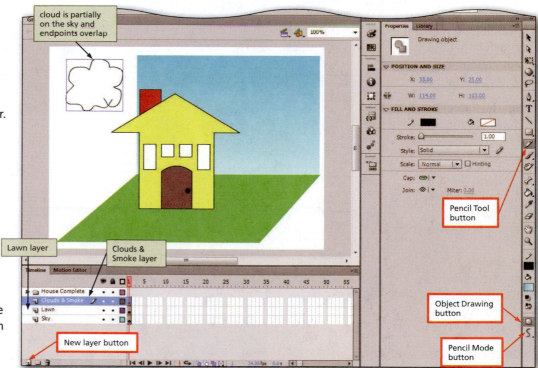

Figure 2–90

- Draw a cloud shape in the upper-left area of the stage. Be sure to overlap the starting and ending points (Figure 2–90).

- Click the Selection Tool button to select it.

- Double-click the stroke of the cloud on the stage to enter edit mode.

- Click one of the overlapped segments inside the cloud to select it (Figure 2–91).

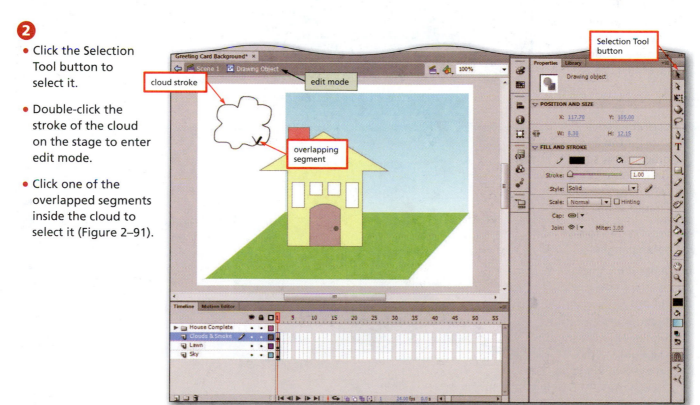

Figure 2–91

3

- Press the DELETE key to delete the selected segment.

- Select the remaining overlapping segment and delete it.

- Click the Paint Bucket Tool to select it.

- Set the Fill color button in the Properties panel to white.

- Click the cloud to fill it with white (Figure 2–92).

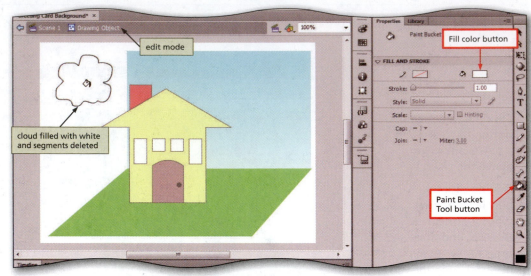

Figure 2–92

4

- Click the Selection Tool button on the Tools panel to select it.

- Double-click the stage to exit edit mode.

- Repeat Steps 1 through 4 to draw a second cloud on the right side of the stage; however, do not create any additional layers (Figure 2–93).

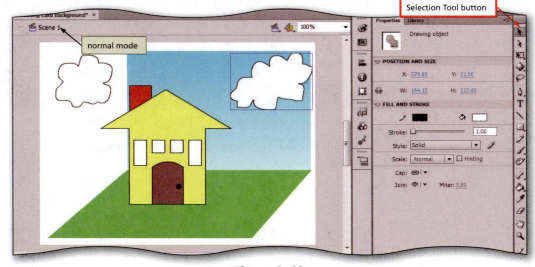

Figure 2–93

5

- Click the Pencil Tool button and draw a curly spiral for smoke coming out of the chimney (Figure 2–94).

- Press CTRL+S to save your changes.

Q&A

What if my smoke overlaps the chimney?

Because the Clouds & Smoke layer is behind the House Complete layer, anything you draw will be displayed behind the house and chimney.

Figure 2–94

The Brush Tool

Whereas you use the Pencil Tool to draw strokes, the Brush Tool is used to draw fills. The Brush Tool has three useful options that you can use: Brush Mode, Brush Size, and Brush Shape. The Brush Mode setting controls how the brush interacts with existing shapes, whereas the Brush Size and Brush Shape settings control exactly what they imply — the size and shape of the brush (Figure 2–95 shows the Brush Size button; the Brush Shape button is located below the Brush Size button but does not appear in the figure because of a bug in Flash).

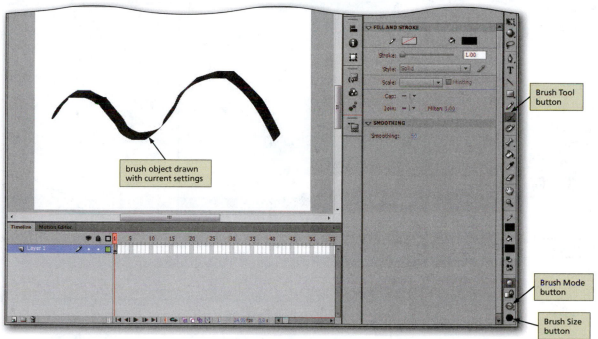

Figure 2–95

Working effectively with the Brush Mode setting can take some trial and error. Some of the Brush Mode settings force the Brush Tool to draw in merge mode only — even if you have enabled object drawing mode. When the Brush Tool is used in merge mode, the Brush Mode settings controls how your brush drawing interacts with existing shapes on the same layer. Table 2–3 describes the various Brush Mode settings.

Brush Mode	Icon	Behavior in Merge Mode	Behavior in Object Drawing Mode
Paint Normal		Draws on top of existing strokes and fills; merges into shapes of the same color; punches holes into shapes of differing color.	Creates a normal drawing object that can be moved in front of or behind other drawing objects on the same layer.
Paint Fills		Draws on top of shape fills only; does not interact with shape strokes.	Not supported. Always draws in merge mode.
Paint Behind		Draws on blank areas of the stage behind existing shapes; existing shapes cut holes in the shape drawn by the brush.	Not supported. Always draws in merge mode.
Paint Selection		Only draws on selected fills.	Not supported. Always draws in merge mode.
Paint Inside		Only draws on the fill in which you start a brush stroke. If you start on a blank area of the stage, Paint Inside works like Paint Behind.	Not supported. Always draws in merge mode.

Table 2–3 Brush Mode Settings

To Draw using the Brush Tool

The following steps use the Brush Tool to draw a flower bed behind the house. Later, you will add a flower to the flower bed. You will draw the flower bed on the House layer so that it interacts with the existing house shape.

- Click the triangle to the left of the House Complete folder to expand the folder.

- Click the House layer to select it and its contents.

- Click the Selection Tool button to select it.

- Click the gray work area outside the stage so all items on the House layer are deselected (Figure 2–96).

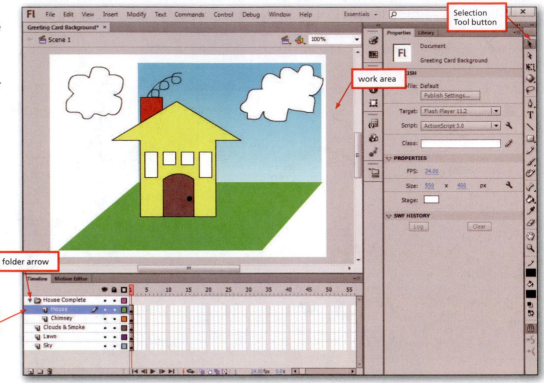

Figure 2–96

- Click the Brush Tool button to select it.

- Click the Fill color button on the Properties panel to display the Color picker, and click a dark brown of your choice.

- Click the Brush Mode button to display the Brush Mode menu (Figure 2–97).

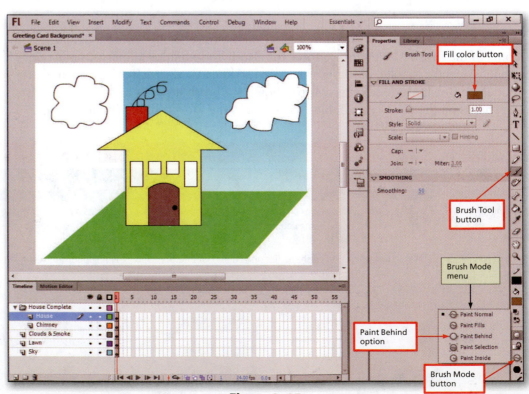

Figure 2–97

3

- Click Paint Behind to set the brush mode.

- Click the Brush Size button to display the Brush Size menu (Figure 2–98).

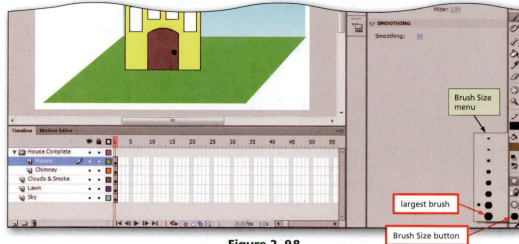

Figure 2–98

4

- Click the largest size on the Brush Size menu to select it.

- Click the Brush Shape button to display the Brush Shape menu (Figure 2–99).

Q&A

Why does the Brush Shape button appear to be cut off at the bottom?

This appears to be a software glitch.

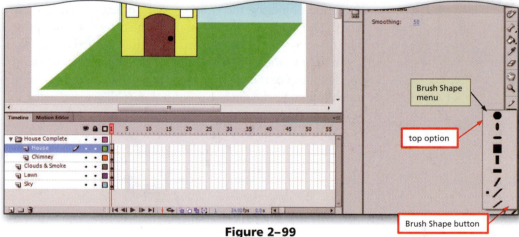

Figure 2–99

5

- Click the first brush shape, if necessary, so the brush shape is a large circle.

- Starting inside the house, draw a large section of brown dirt for the flower bed so that your stage resembles Figure 2–100.

 **Experiment**

- Click the Brush Size button, choose a different size, and try drawing different areas of the flower bed with different brush sizes.

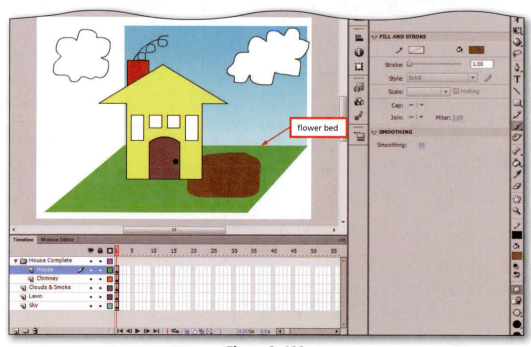

Figure 2–100

Q&A Why is there no brown dirt covering the house when I release the mouse button?

Because the brush mode is set to Paint Behind, only blank areas of the layer are painted.

6
• Press CTRL+S to save your changes.

Anchor Points
An anchor point is displayed as a small circle. The current or most recent anchor point is always a solid circle, indicating that it is selected. Nonselected anchor points are displayed as hollow squares.

The Pen Tool

The Pen Tool, like the Pencil Tool, draws strokes in both merge and object drawing modes but differs in that it is meant to draw curves. Each click on the stage with the Pen Tool creates an **anchor point**, and consecutive anchor points are connected by lines or curves. The anchor points and connecting lines combine to create a shape. To create a straight line, click the stage with the Pen Tool to create an anchor point, and then click again to create a second anchor point. Flash connects the two anchor points with a straight line.

When you want to create curved lines, you drag with the Pen Tool. Flash will display an anchor point and two **direction lines** with **direction points** (Figure 2–101). Direction points are the endpoints of a direction line and are used to change the length and angle of a direction line. The direction lines move outward as you drag. The direction of the drag determines the eventual direction of the curve. For instance, if you drag to the right, the bump of the curve expands out to the left. If you drag up, the bump of the curve extends down. The length of the drag determines how much influence the anchor point has over the curve — the longer the drag, the more exaggerated the curve.

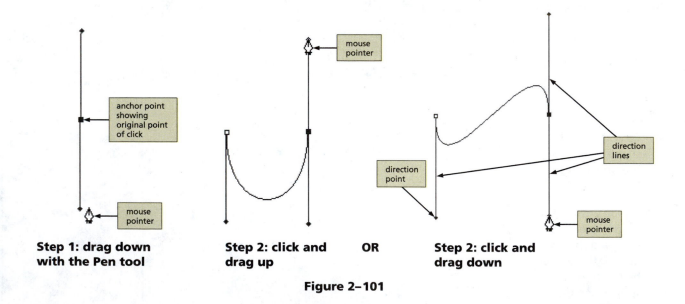

Step 1: drag down with the Pen tool   **Step 2: click and drag up**   **OR**   **Step 2: click and drag down**

Figure 2–101

When you are finished drawing the outline, you have two choices: Close the shape or leave it open. The ends of an open outline do not connect, creating a curve. The ends of a closed outline do connect, creating a polygon, ellipse, or other organic shape. To close the outline, click the first anchor point. Your mouse pointer will display a small open circle to indicate the outline will be closed. Table 2–4 displays some of the possible tasks when working with the Pen Tool.

Table 2–4 Pen Tool Actions

Task	Steps	Result
Create a straight line.	Click a beginning point. Click an ending point.	
Create an arc.	Drag the first anchor point in the direction of the bump of the curve. Drag the second anchor point in the opposite direction.	
Create an S-curve.	Drag both anchor points in the same direction.	
Create a polygon.	Click at least three times without dragging, and then click the first anchor point to close the outline.	
Create an ellipse.	Drag the first anchor point up. Drag the second anchor point down. Click the first anchor point and drag up.	

Corner Points

It can be difficult to draw the curve you want because each curve is affected by its preceding anchor point. For example, if you drag the first anchor point up, then no matter which direction you drag the second anchor point, the curve will start by curving up and then continuing in the direction in which the second anchor point was dragged (Figure 2–102). To avoid that, you can convert an anchor point into a **corner point** by clicking it before starting the next anchor point. Corner points allow you to create sharp angles within your outline.

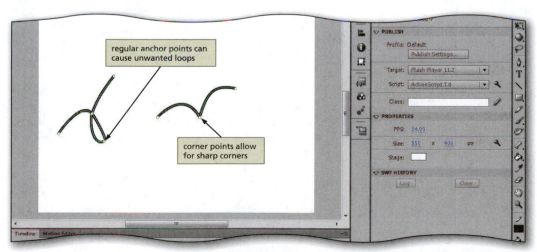

regular anchor points can cause unwanted loops

corner points allow for sharp corners

Figure 2–102

To Ready the Stage

The following steps ready the layers so that you can draw a flower on an uncluttered stage.

1 Click the House Complete folder in the Timeline to select it.

2 Click the New Layer button at the bottom of the Timeline to create a new blank layer above the House Complete folder.

3 Name the new layer, Flower.

4 Click the expand/collapse triangle on the House Complete folder to collapse it.

5 Click the Visibility icon on all layers except the Flower layer so that only the blank Flower layer is visible.

6 Click the Flower layer in the Timeline to select it.

To Draw using the Pen Tool

The following steps draw flower petals with the Pen Tool. You will experiment with anchor points and corner points as you work with the Pen Tool.

- Click the Pen Tool button to select it.

- If necessary, set the stroke color to black.

- If necessary, click the Object Drawing button to enable object drawing mode.

- Click the center of the stage to create the first anchor point (Figure 2–103).

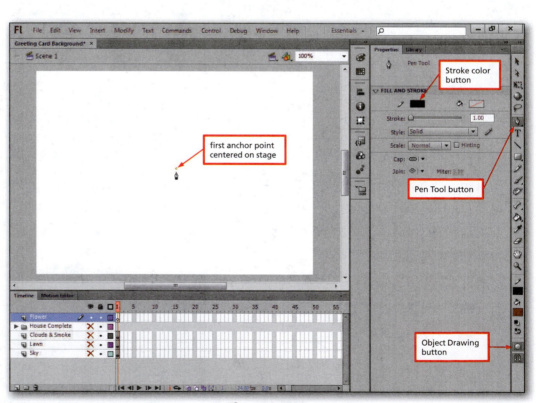

Figure 2–103

2

• Click approximately 1 inch above the first anchor point and then drag up and to the right to create the second anchor point and the first curve (Figure 2–104).

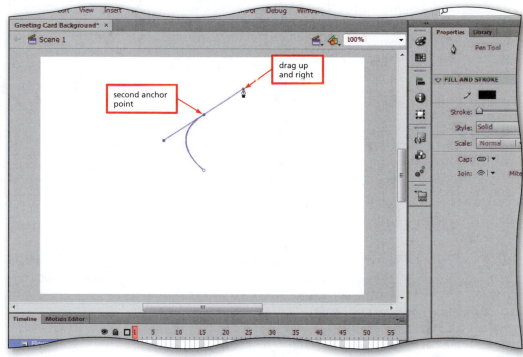

Figure 2–104

3

• Click slightly to the right of the first anchor point without dragging to create the third anchor point and curve (Figure 2–105).

Q&A

Why did I only click and not drag this anchor point?

Because you dragged the previous anchor point up and to the right, the curve following it curves in the direction of the anchor point. The curve you just created starts curving up and to the right to follow the previous direction line, and then continues down to the new anchor point. There is no need to drag.

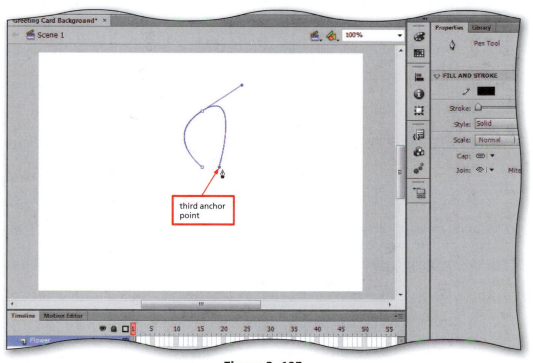

Figure 2–105

4

- Click to create a fourth anchor point at the tip of the next petal and drag slightly down and to the right to create the left curve of the petal (Figure 2–106).

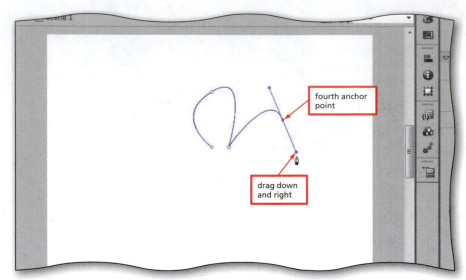

Figure 2–106

 5

- Click and drag down and to the left to create an anchor point at the base of the petal (Figure 2–107).

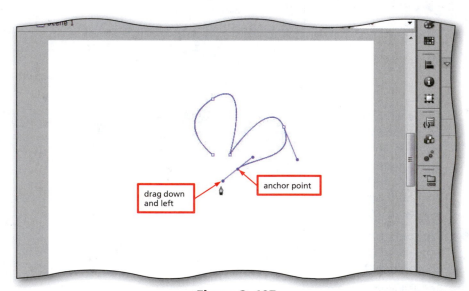

Figure 2–107

 6

- Click at the tip of the next petal and drag slightly to the right (Figure 2–108).

 Q&A

Why does the shape have a strange curve at the bottom?

Because the previous anchor point was dragged to the right, the new curve starts by following that direction. You will fix this in the next few steps.

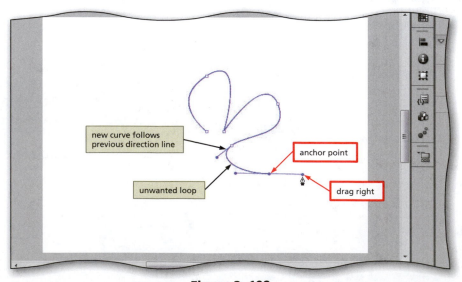

Figure 2–108

7

- Press CTRL+Z to undo the last anchor point.

- Point to the previous anchor point until your mouse pointer displays a small arrow shape.

- Click the anchor point to remove the direction line and convert it to a corner point (Figure 2–109).

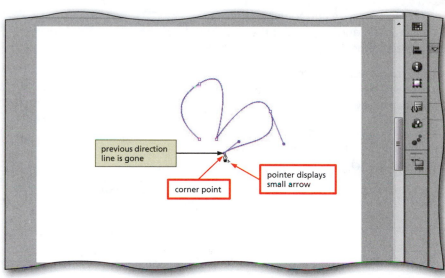

Figure 2–109

8

- Click and drag down and to the right to create an anchor point at the tip of the next petal.

- Click and drag left to create an anchor point at the base of the petal.

- Click the last anchor point to convert it to a corner point (Figure 2–110).

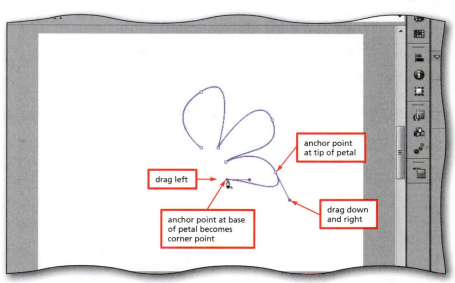

Figure 2–110

9

- Click and drag down and to the left to create an anchor point at the tip of the next petal.

- Click and drag right to create an anchor point at the base of the petal.

- Click the last anchor point to convert it to a corner point (Figure 2–111).

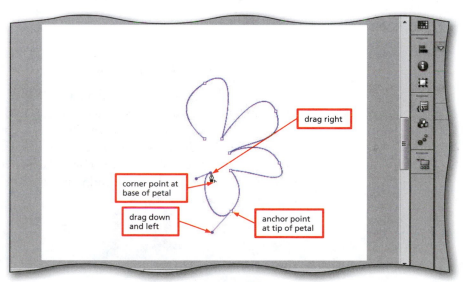

Figure 2–111

10

- Click and drag up and to the left to create an anchor point at the tip of the next petal.

- Click and drag up and right to create an anchor point at the base of the petal.

- Click the last anchor point to convert it to a corner point (Figure 2–112).

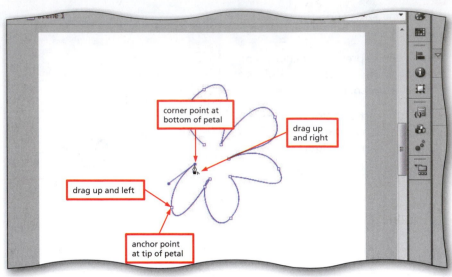

Figure 2–112

11

- Click and drag up to create an anchor point at the tip of the last petal.

- Click the first anchor point to close the outline and complete the flower outline (Figure 2–113).

- Press CTRL+S to save your changes.

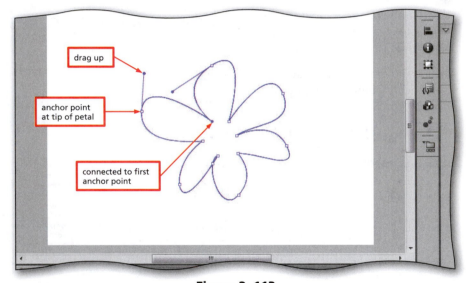

Figure 2–113

The Subselection Tool

With the Subselection Tool, you can adjust anchor points and direction lines. With the Subselection Tool selected, you can click a drawing object or shape that was created with the Pen Tool to display its anchor points. Clicking an anchor point with the Subselection Tool displays its direction lines. Dragging an anchor point or direction point adjusts the shape of the curve. A solid circle represents a selected anchor point and its direction handle's endpoints, whereas a hollow square represents an unselected anchor point.

To Edit Curves using the Subselection Tool

The following steps use the Subselection Tool to adjust the curvature of the petals.

1

- Click the Subselection Tool button to select it.

- Click an anchor point at the tip of one of the petals to display the direction lines affecting its curvature (Figure 2–114).

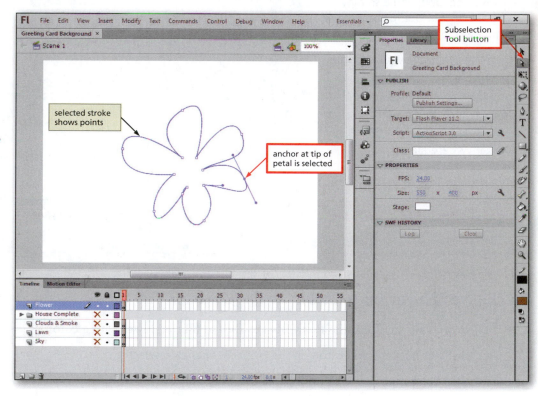

Figure 2–114

2

- Drag the direction points (the endpoints of the direction lines) to adjust the petal's curve. Experiment until you are satisfied with the curvature (Figure 2–115).

Q&A

How do I experiment?

Drag the direction points. If you do not like the result, press CTRL+Z to undo and try again. Use CTRL+Z repeatedly as needed.

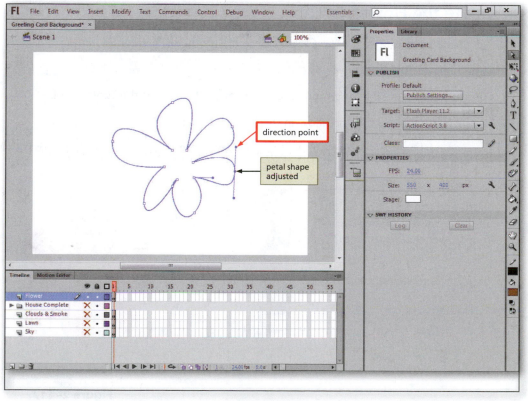

Figure 2–115

- Continue clicking the remaining anchor points and adjusting the curves as needed. You also may drag the anchor points themselves (Figure 2–116).

- Press CTRL+S to save your changes.

Q&A

I accidently clicked the stage instead of an anchor point and now the outline is deselected. How do I access the anchor point again?

Click anywhere along the stroke of the flower with the Subselection Tool to display its anchor points again.

final petals

Figure 2–116

To Fill the Flower with Color

The following steps use the Paint Bucket Tool to fill the flower with a color.

1 Click the Paint Bucket Tool button on the Properties panel to select it.

2 Set the Fill Color button on the Tools panel to a bright pink.

3 Click the flower to create a fill.

To Create the Flower Center

The following steps use the Oval Tool to create the flower center.

1 Click the Oval Tool button to select it.

2 Confirm that object drawing mode is enabled at the bottom of the Tools panel.

3 Set the Fill Color to a bright yellow in the Properties panel.

4 Draw an oval over the center of the flower.

5 If desired, adjust the Selection width and the Selection height on the Properties panel. Your flower should resemble Figure 2–117.

6 Press CTRL+S to save your changes.

Figure 2–117

Grouping Objects

Whereas shapes of the same color combine into a single merged shape when overlapped, drawing objects do not automatically become single objects. However, you can combine drawing objects into single objects, making it easier to resize or move items composed of several objects. To group drawing objects, SHIFT+click each object with the Selection Tool, click the Modify menu, and then click the Group command. To ungroup objects, use the Ungroup command on the Modify menu.

To Group Drawing Objects

The following steps group the flower center and petals into a single object so that it can be more easily resized and moved.

1
- Click the Selection Tool button to select it.

- Click any of the pink petals to select the outer portion of the flower.

- SHIFT+click the yellow center of the flower to add it to the selection (Figure 2–118).

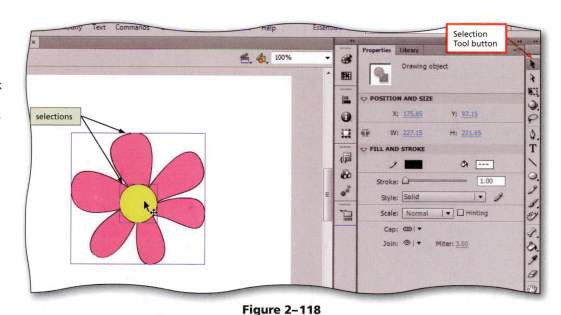

Figure 2–118

2
- Click Modify on the Application bar to display the Modify menu (Figure 2–119).

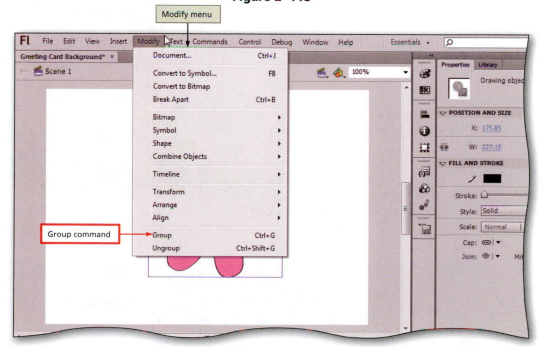

Figure 2–119

3

• Click Group on the Modify menu to group the selected objects into a single object (Figure 2–120).

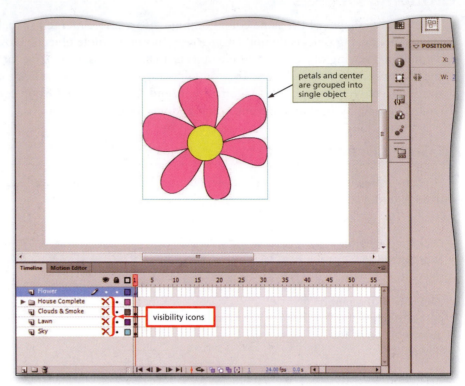

Figure 2–120

4

• Click the red X in the Visibility column of each layer in the Timeline so all layers are visible (Figure 2–121).

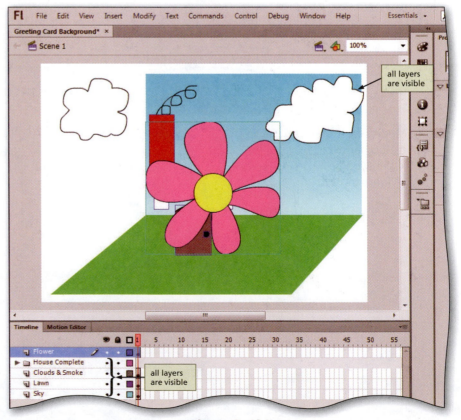

Figure 2–121

Other Ways

1. CTRL+G

To Resize and Position the Flower

Because the petals and flower center are grouped into a single object, you will resize the entire flower and move it into position so that it appears to be growing out of the flower bed.

1 Click the flower on the stage to select it.

2 Click the 'Lock width and height values together' icon so it appears as a linked chain and allows you to adjust the width and height proportionally.

3 Drag the Selection width value to the left to reduce the size of the flower until you are satisfied with its appearance.

4 Drag the flower into position above the flower bed, as shown in Figure 2–122.

Figure 2–122

To Create the Flower Stem

The following steps use the Pencil Tool to create the flower stem.

1 Click the gray work area outside the stage to deselect any selected objects and shapes.

2 Click the Pencil Tool button on the Tools panel to select it.

3 In the Properties panel, set the stroke color to a medium green.

4 In the Properties panel, set the stroke height to 5.

5 At the bottom of the Tools panel, set the pencil mode to Smooth.

6 If necessary, click the Object Drawing button to enable object drawing mode.

7 Draw a curving stem on the stage that overlaps the flower and the flower bed, as shown in Figure 2–123.

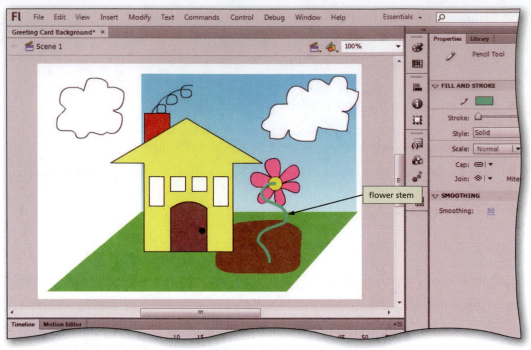

Figure 2–123

To Arrange the Flower Stem

The following steps move the stem behind the flower.

1 Click Modify on the Application bar.

2 Point to Arrange on the Modify menu.

3 Click Send to Back on the Arrange submenu to send the stem behind the flower.

4 If necessary, drag the stem or use the arrow keys on your keyboard to nudge it into a position of your liking.

5 Press CTRL+S to save your changes.

The Deco Tool

Flash provides an assortment of preloaded images, including trees, buildings, flowers, vines, fire, and lightning, among others, which you can access using the Deco Tool. You can drag with the Deco Tool to create a line of deco symbols. The Deco Tool provides a quick and convenient way to bring professional-looking imagery into your project.

The image you select determines the options that are available in the Properties panel. There is no wrong way to use the Deco Tool. The best way to become familiar with the Deco Tool is to start a new Flash document and experiment with it.

To Create Trees using the Deco Tool

The following steps use the Deco Tool to create trees on the left side of the lawn. You will create a new layer for the trees above the Lawn layer.

1
- Click the Lawn layer on the Timeline to select it.
- Click the New Layer button to create a new blank layer.
- Double-click the new layer name, type Trees, and press the ENTER key to apply the name change.
- Click the Deco Tool button on the Tools panel to select it.
- On the Properties panel, click the Drawing Effect box arrow to display the Drawing Effect menu (Figure 2–124).

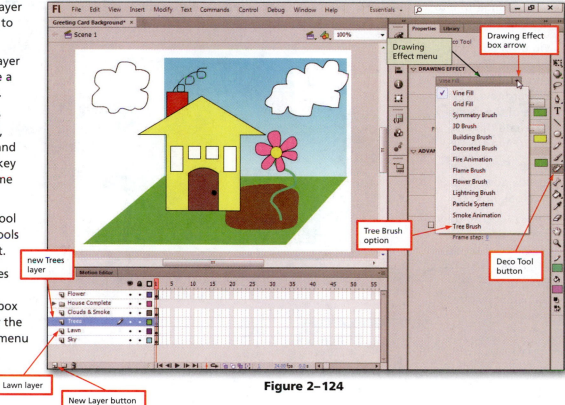

Figure 2–124

2
- Click Tree Brush at the bottom of the menu to select it.
- Click the triangle to the left of Advanced Options to display the Advanced Options menu, if necessary.
- Click the Advanced Options menu button to display the options (Figure 2–125).

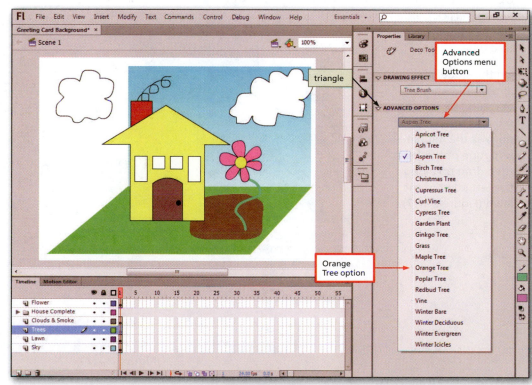

Figure 2–125

3

- Click Orange Tree to select it.

- On the stage, drag from the lower-left corner of the lawn upward toward the base of the chimney to create the first tree (Figure 2–126).

Q&A

What if my tree is upside down or does not look right?

Press CTRL+Z to undo and try drawing it again. Do not pause after your initial click. Drag quickly and immediately after you click.

Figure 2–126

4

- Click the Advanced Options menu button and then click Garden Plant to change the tree type.

- On the stage, click and hold without dragging for a few seconds to start a bush at the middle-left edge of the lawn, then drag up along the left edge of the lawn (Figure 2–127).

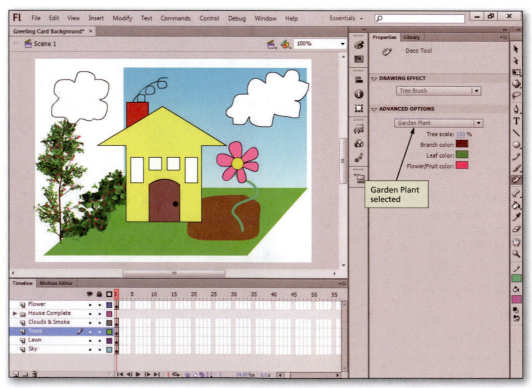

Figure 2–127

5

● On the Timeline, drag the Clouds & Smoke layer below the Lawn layer so the clouds appear behind the tree (Figure 2–128).

● Press CTRL+S to save your changes.

Clouds & Smoke layer below Lawn layer

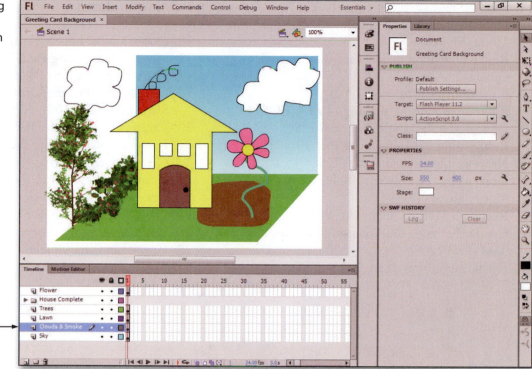

Figure 2–128

To Quit Flash

You have completed the greeting card background project. The following steps quit Flash.

1 Click the Flash Close button.

2 If Flash displays a dialog box asking you to save changes, click the No button.

Chapter Summary

In this chapter, you learned to draw with Flash. First, you learned the differences between merge mode and object drawing mode. You learned to use the Properties panel to set various tool options and both the Properties and Transform panels to edit shapes and objects on the stage after they are drawn. You learned to set and edit stroke and fill colors and gradients, how to delete strokes completely, and how to create fills. You learned to use the Rectangle, Oval, PolyStar, Pencil, Pen, Subselection, Brush, Line, Paint Bucket, and Deco Tools and used the Align panel to align and distribute shapes and objects. You also made use of Flash's Snap Align feature to align items. You learned to convert drawing objects to shapes and then merge the shapes. You grouped drawing objects together to make them easier to work with. You also learned how to use layers to help organize elements on the stage and used the Revert command to undo a series of changes.

The items listed below include all the new Flash skills you have learned in this chapter:

1. Set the Stroke and Fill Colors (FL 75)
2. Draw Rectangles and Squares in Object Drawing Mode (FL 76)
3. Resize Drawing Objects with the Properties Panel (FL 77)
4. Edit Multiple Objects (FL 80)
5. Align Objects using the Align Panel (FL 81)
6. Change the Rectangle's Shape (FL 84)
7. Resize using the Transform Panel (FL 87)
8. Draw using the Oval Tool (FL 88)
9. Draw using the PolyStar Tool (FL 92)
10. Merge Shapes (FL 94)
11. Recolor a Merged Shape (FL 95)
12. Create the Lawn Outline using the Line Tool (FL 97)
13. Fill a Transparent Shape using the Paint Bucket Tool (FL 98)
14. Move the Lawn (FL 100)
15. Rename a Layer (FL 103)
16. Create a New Layer (FL 104)
17. Move a Shape using Paste in Place (FL 105)
18. Move the Lawn into Position (FL 106)
19. Change the Stacking Order of Objects on the Same Layer (FL 108)
20. Create a Layer Folder (FL 111)
21. Remove a Stroke using the Color Panel (FL 113)
22. Create a Gradient (FL 114)
23. Draw using the Pencil Tool (FL 117)
24. Draw using the Brush Tool (FL 120)
25. Draw using the Pen Tool (FL 124)
26. Edit Curves using the Subselection Tool (FL 129)
27. Group Drawing Objects (FL 131)
28. Create Trees using the Deco Tool (FL 134)

Apply Your Knowledge

Reinforce the skills and apply the concepts you learned in this chapter.

Animating Card Suits

You will create a scene displaying a magic wand and the four suits of playing cards for an ad on a magic trick distributor's Web site. A programmer or advanced Flash developer can later animate the objects. You will create the magic wand, diamond, heart, spade, and club. Figure 2–129 shows the final drawing.

Figure 2–129

Perform the following tasks:

1. Start Flash and create a new ActionScript 3.0 document. Save the file to the Chapter 02 folder as `Apply 2-1 Magic Complete`.

2. To draw the magic wand:

   a. On the Tools panel, click the Rectangle Tool button and ensure object drawing mode is enabled so that you create drawing objects rather than shapes.

   b. On the Properties panel, set both the stroke color and the fill color to black. Set the stroke style to Solid and the stroke height to 1.00.

   c. Draw a rectangle on the stage, then use the Properties panel to set the size as follows: 'Lock width and height values together' = disabled, Selection width = 10, Selection height = 110.

   d. Draw a second rectangle and change its fill color to white. Set its size as follows: 'Lock width and height values together' = disabled, Selection width = 10, Selection height = 20.

   e. Drag the small white rectangle on top of the larger one so that it creates a white tip of the magic wand.

3. To draw magic sparks:

   a. On the Tools panel, select the Pencil Tool and set the Pencil mode to Smooth, if necessary.

   b. On the Properties panel, set the stroke color to black, if necessary, and set the stroke style to Dotted.

   c. Draw four curved lines near the tip of the magic wand, as shown in Figure 2–129.

4. To position the wand:

   a. On the Timeline, click Frame 1 to select everything on the stage at that frame.

   b. Press CTRL+T to display the Transform panel.

   c. Set the Rotate angle to 45.

   d. Click the Selection Tool button and drag the wand and sparks roughly to the center of the stage.

5. To draw the diamond:

   a. Select the Rectangle Tool.

   b. On the Properties panel, set the stroke color to No Stroke and the fill color to a bright red.

   c. Hold the SHIFT key as you draw a square on the stage, then use the Properties panel to size and position it as follows: 'Lock width and height values together' = enabled, Selection width = 50, Selection X position = 470, Selection Y position = 325.

   d. Press CTRL+T to display the Transform panel and set the Rotate angle to 45.

6. To draw the heart:

   a. On the Tools panel, select the Oval Tool.

   b. Hold the SHIFT key as you draw a perfect circle, then use the Properties panel to size and position it as follows: 'Lock width and height values together' = enabled, Selection width = 35, Selection X position = 8, Selection Y position = 16.

   c. Press CTRL+C to copy the circle, then press CTRL+V to paste a copy in the middle of the stage. Use the Selection Tool to drag the second circle to the right of the first circle so they are top-aligned and touch. Flash will help guide you with Snap Align.

   d. Press CTRL+V to create another copy of the circle and drag it to the lower-left area of the stage. You will use this later to create the club.

   e. Click the PolyStar Tool button.

   f. On the Properties panel, set the Tool Settings options as follows: Style = polygon and Number of Sides = 3 (*Hint:* Star point size is ignored for polygons.)

Continued >

Apply Your Knowledge *continued*

   g. Hold the SHIFT key as you draw a triangle on the stage, making sure the triangle points down and the top is perfectly horizontal. Use the Properties panel to set the position and size as follows: 'Lock width and height values together' = disabled, Selection width = 70, Selection height = 35, Selection X position = 8, Selection Y position = 36.

   h. SHIFT+click the two circles with the Selection Tool so that all three parts of the heart are selected, then press CTRL+B to convert the objects to merged shapes.

   i. Click the gray work area outside the stage to deselect the heart.

   j. Point to the lower sides of the heart with the Selection Tool and drag inward to shape the heart, as shown in Figure 2–129.

7. To draw the spade:

   a. Click the heart to select it, press CTRL+C to copy it, and press CTRL+V to paste it to the middle of the stage. Drag the copied heart to the right so it no longer touches the magic wand.

   b. Use the Properties panel to change its fill color to black.

   c. Press CTRL+T to display the Transform panel and set the Rotate angle to 180.

   d. Use the Rectangle Tool to draw a rectangle and then use the Properties panel to set its width to 15 and its height to 45.

   e. Use the Selection Tool to drag the rectangle into position so it becomes the stem of the spade.

   f. Click the gray work area to deselect the rectangle, and then point to its sides and drag inward to shape the stem of the spade, as shown in Figure 2–129.

   g. Copy the rectangle, paste a copy to the center of the stage, and then drag the copy to the lower-left area of the stage. You will use this later to create the club.

   h. Click the spade's stem and then press CTRL+B to break apart the stem and convert it to a shape so that it merges with the rest of the spade.

   i. Click the gray work area to deselect the stem.

   j. Click the spade to select all of it and drag it to the upper right of the stage. Use Snap Align to help you align it to the top of the heart and the right of the diamond.

8. To create the club:

   a. With the Selection Tool, click the red circle in the lower-left area of the stage, then use the Properties panel to change its fill color to black and position it at X = 26 and Y = 315.

   b. Copy and paste the circle to the stage and drag the copy under and to the left of the original circle so they touch. Let Snap Align help you position it.

   c. Paste a final copy of the circle to the stage and drag it into position on the right side of the club. Do not be concerned if there is a white spot in the middle of the club. You will fix that later.

   d. Drag the club's stem into position. You may have to use the arrow keys on the keyboard to nudge it into its final position. It should cover up any white areas in the middle of the club so that the club is entirely black.

   e. SHIFT+click the three circles and the stem of the club and press CTRL+B to break it apart and convert it to a shape.

9. Press CTRL+S to save the Flash document.

10. Close Flash.

Extend Your Knowledge

Extend the skills you learned in this chapter and experiment with new skills. You may need to use Help to complete the assignment.

Drawing an Ice Cream Cone

Instructions: Start Flash. You will draw an ice cream cone complete with sprinkles and a cherry on top (Figure 2–130) for use in a Flash mobile phone application where users design and create their own desserts.

Figure 2–130

Perform the following tasks:

1. Create a new ActionScript 3.0 document and save it as `Extend 2-1 Ice Cream`.

2. Draw a triangle (pointing down) with a width of about 115, a height of about 225, and colored brown. Rename the layer Cone.

3. Create a new layer on top of Cone called Ice Cream. On the Ice Cream layer, draw a pink circle (no stroke) with a diameter of about 175. Use the Pencil Tool to draw the bottom of the ice cream scoop so that it is not perfectly round. Be sure to draw a closed shape with the Pencil Tool so that you can fill it with pink and remove the stroke. Position the ice cream scoop on top of the cone.

4. Create a new layer on top of Ice Cream and name this new layer, Sprinkles. Use the Spray Brush Tool (which is located on the Tools panel with the Brush Tool) to create candy dots in at least three different colors. Position the sprinkles on the ice cream.

5. Create a new layer on top of Sprinkles called Cherry. Use the Oval Tool to create a dark red cherry on top of the ice cream scoop. Use the Pencil Tool to create a cherry stem with the same color.

6. Save your changes.

Make It Right

Analyze a project and correct all errors and/or improve the design.

Improving a Halloween Scene

Instructions: To complete this assignment, you will be required to use the Data Files for Students. Visit www.cengage.com/ct/studentdownload for detailed instructions or contact your instructor for information about accessing the required files. Start Flash and open the Make It Right 2-1 Halloween file from the Chapter 02 folder of the Data Files for Students. Save the file on your USB flash drive with the name, Make It Right 2-1 Halloween Fixed.

You would like to use a Halloween-themed background scene for a Flash animation, but the scene needs some improvement (Figure 2–131). In the original file, the cat's eyes are red, the pumpkin is too perfectly round, the moon is too large, the sky is a dull solid color, and the lightning just doesn't look good.

Select the cat's eyes and change them to a dark green fill color. Select the moon and make it significantly smaller. Delete the lightning and on the Lightning layer, use the Deco Tool to create better lightning. (*Hint*: Click and hold with the Deco Tool rather than dragging when creating lightning.) Point to the sides of the pumpkin with the Selection Tool (be careful not to actually click and select the pumpkin) and reshape the stroke to make the pumpkin less perfectly circular. Apply a gradient fill to the background so it blends from a dark blue at the top to a medium gray at the bottom. Finally, save your changes.

Figure 2–131

In the Lab

Design and/or create a project using the guidelines, concepts, and skills presented in this chapter. Labs are listed in order of increasing difficulty.

Lab 1: Creating a Music Player Interface

Problem: A programmer has asked you to create an interface for a music player that will be used on a Web site. The player's interface is shown in Figure 2–132.

Figure 2–132

Instructions: Perform the following tasks:

1. Start Flash, create a new ActionScript 3.0 document, and save it as Lab 2-1 Player.

2. Choose the Rectangle Tool and set the following options in the Properties panel:

   a. Stroke Color: No Stroke

   b. Fill Color: dark gray

   c. Rectangle Options: corner radius of 10

3. Draw a rectangle, then use the Properties panel to size and position it as follows:

   a. Width: 152

   b. Height: 275

   c. X Position: 195

   d. Y Position: 60

4. Draw another rectangle, fill it with white, and size and position it as follows:

   a. Width: 128

   b. Height: 107

   c. X Position: 206

   d. Y Position: 73

Continued >

In the Lab *continued*

5. Use the Oval Tool to draw an oval with a light gray stroke and a black fill. Size and position it as follows:

   a. Width and Height: 120

   b. X Position: 210

   c. Y Position: 200

6. Fill the circle with a gradient that blends from a dark gray at the top to a light gray at the bottom.

7. Draw a circle with a light gray stroke and black fill. Size and position it as follows:

   a. Width and Height: 21

   b. X Position: 260

   c. Y Position: 202

8. Draw a rectangle with the same stroke and fill colors as the small circle. Set the corner radius to 0, if necessary, before drawing. Size and position it as follows:

   a. Width: 7

   b. Height: 25

   c. X Position: 263

   d. Y Position: 290

9. Copy the small rectangle and paste a copy of it in the middle of the stage. Then position it at an X Position of 273 and a Y Position of 290.

10. Use the PolyStar Tool to draw a triangle with the same stroke and fill colors as the small circle. Draw it so it points to the right and its left side is perfectly vertical. Set its size and position as follows:

    a. Width: 16

    b. Height: 33

    c. X Position: 308

    d. Y Position: 240

11. Copy the triangle and paste it to the center of the stage. Click Modify, point to Transform, and then click Flip Horizontal so that the duplicated triangle points to the left. Position it at an X Position of 215 and a Y Position of 240.

12. Save your changes.

In the Lab

Lab 2: Creating an Animated Lamp

Problem: A local lighting store has asked you to create an animation for its Web site that shows a floor lamp turning on. You will draw the lamp and create the animation so that the lightbulbs change from white to yellow. The final frame from the animation is displayed in Figure 2–133.

Figure 2–133

Instructions: Perform the following tasks:

1. Start Flash, create a new ActionScript 3.0 document, and save it as Lab 2-2 Lamp.

2. Rename the layer, Stand.

3. Draw a rectangle in object drawing mode with no stroke and a medium gray fill to become the lamp's base. Set its width to 84 and its height to 30. Drag the top of the rectangle up to create a slight curve.

4. Use the Line Tool to draw a line the same color as the rectangular base with a stroke height of 10 to become the main stem of the lamp. Make the line a height of about 210 and center-align its bottom with the rectangular base so that it resembles Figure 2–133.

5. Use the Pencil Tool to draw three curves to act as the lightbulb stems. The pencil stroke should be the same color as the other lamp pieces, have a stroke height of 5, and use a pencil mode of Smooth. Draw the curves to roughly match Figure 2–133.

6. Draw a square with no stroke and use the same fill color as the other parts of the lamp. The square should have a width and height of about 25.

7. Position the square at the end of the first curved lightbulb stem and use the Transform panel to rotate it slightly.

8. Copy and paste the small square, rotate the copy, and position it at the end of one of the remaining curved lightbulb stems.

Continued >

9. Copy and paste the small square, rotate the copy, and position it at the end of the final curved lightbulb stem.

10. Create a new layer above the Stand layer. Type `Bulbs` as the new layer name.

11. On the Bulbs layer, use the Oval Tool to draw a perfect circle with a stroke color one shade darker than the rest of the lamp and a fill color of white. Set the stroke height to 2 and the width and height to 24. Position the lightbulb on top of the first small square so it resembles Figure 2–133.

12. Copy and paste two copies of the lightbulb. Position the copies over the remaining small squares so that all three lightbulbs are in place.

13. SHIFT+click to select all three lightbulbs and press CTRL+B to break them apart and convert them into shapes.

14. Create a keyframe at Frame 24 of the Bulbs layer.

15. Create a second keyframe at Frame 48 of the Bulbs layer.

16. Create a final keyframe at Frame 48 of the Stand layer.

17. In the Timeline, click Frame 48 on the Bulbs layer to select the three lightbulbs at that frame. Use the Tools panel to change the fill color to a bright yellow.

18. Right-click any part of the gray bar in the Timeline between Frames 25 and 47 of the Bulbs layer and click Create Shape Tween from the pop-up menu.

19. Click the keyframe at Frame 48 in the Bulbs layer and then click the gray work area outside the stage to deselect everything at that frame.

20. Click the keyframe at Frame 24 in the Bulbs layer and then click the gray work area outside the stage to deselect everything at that frame.

21. Click the keyframe at Frame 1 in the Bulbs layer and then click the gray work area outside the stage to deselect everything at that frame.

22. Press the ENTER key to view the animation.

23. Save your changes.

In the Lab

Lab 3: Creating an Archery Club Ad

Problem: A local archery club has asked you to create an ad to use on its Web site. Knowing that eventually the ad will be animated, you decide to use Flash to draw the initial target and arrow. The final image is displayed in Figure 2–134.

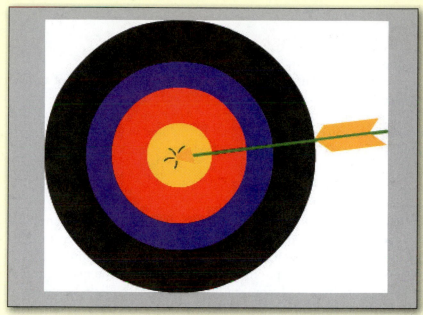

Figure 2–134

Instructions: Perform the following tasks:
Start Flash and create a new ActionScript 3.0 file. Create a circle with a blue fill and black stroke. The stroke height should be about 40. Create a second smaller circle with a red stroke and a yellow fill. Align the circles so the smaller one is centered inside the larger one. Adjust the sizes and stroke heights until the black, blue, and red areas are roughly the same widths and the center yellow area is small and adequately sized for the center of a target.

Create an arrow from a triangle and a line. Then add feathers to the other end of the arrow with rectangles that have been skewed with the Transform panel. Use the Pencil Tool to draw the impact lines where the arrowhead contacts the target. Fit the canvas to its contents.

Save the Flash file as Lab 2-3 Archery. Publish GIF and JPG files with the name Lab 2-3 Archery Web.

Cases and Places

Apply your creative thinking and problem-solving skills to design and implement a solution.

1: Create a Polygon Slide Show

Academic

As a member of your high school math club, you have been asked to create a simple slide show of polygons with increasing sides as part of an end-of-year celebration. After starting Flash and creating a new ActionScript 3.0 document, create a triangle with different colors for the stroke and fill at Frame 1. Center it on the stage. Create a keyframe at Frame 24, delete the triangle at that frame, and draw a square with the same colors as the triangle. Center it on the stage. Create a keyframe at Frame 48, delete the square at that frame, and draw a pentagon (five-sided polygon) with the same colors as the triangle. Center it on the stage. Continue to create keyframes every 24 frames, delete the content at each keyframe, and draw a new polygon, centered on the stage, with one more side than the previous polygon until you have drawn an octagon (eight-sided figure). Add a stop action at the final frame so the animation halts when the octagon is displayed. Save the file with the name Case 2-1 Polygons.

Continued >

Cases and Places *continued*

2: Draw a Monster Truck for a Personal Web Site

Personal

As a monster truck fan, you would like to create an animation of a monster truck to include on your personal Web site. Before animating the truck, you need to draw it. Search the Internet for a photo of a monster truck to use as a reference. After starting Flash and creating a new ActionScript 3.0 document, use any of the drawing tools you used in this chapter to draw a version of the truck. Save the Flash file with the name Case 2-2 Monster Truck.

3: Draw a Bedroom Dresser

Professional

You have landed a development contract with a furniture company. They are planning to develop an application for mobile phones where users can open drawers in a variety of furniture the store sells to find coupons for instant savings on purchases. A programmer will be responsible for animating the drawers, but you need to first draw the furniture. You may want to research photos of bedroom dressers on the Internet before starting to draw with Flash. Using only the Rectangle and Oval Tools, draw a bedroom dresser with five drawers. Give the drawers handles and draw legs on the dresser. Use the Transform panel to skew and rotate rectangles so your dresser is three-dimensional and shows a front, side, and top. Use the Deco Tool to create a Curl Vine (within the Tree Brush) design on the side and top of the dresser. Save the file as Case 2-3 Dresser.

3 | Creating Symbols, Instances, and Text

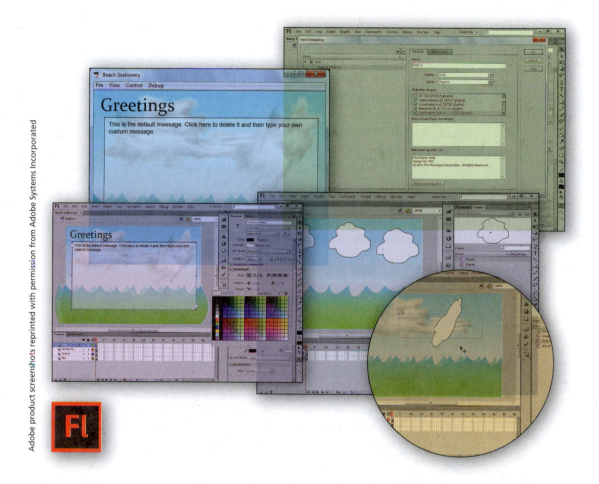

Objectives

You will have mastered the material in this chapter when you can:

- Describe symbols
- Explain instances
- Create graphic symbols
- Transform gradients
- Use the Library panel
- Create and modify instances
- Swap symbols

- Create text fields
- Format text
- Create read-only and editable text
- Embed fonts
- create a classic tween animation
- Test a movie
- Purge the library

3 | Creating Symbols, Instances, and Text

Introduction

In Chapter 2, you learned about the Flash drawing tools. You used a variety of shape and free-form tools to create a background scene for an online greeting card. You also used layers to organize and manage your content.

In this chapter, you will learn to use symbols and instances to make your work flow more efficient and minimize the size of your document files. You also will learn to create a variety of text boxes and format both editable and noneditable text. You will embed fonts so that any font used in your Flash movie appears properly — even on computers that do not have the fonts you used. Finally, you will create a simple classic tween animation.

As you work through the project in this chapter, you might think a drawing program would be a better tool to use. Do not be fooled by the apparent simplicity of the project, which could form the basis for a more complex Flash project, should the need arise. Objects must be drawn on the stage before they can be animated. This chapter expands on the drawing skills you learned in Chapter 2.

Project — Editable Animated Stationery

In this chapter, you will create a Flash movie consisting of a sheet of stationery with a beach theme (Figure 3–1). Rather than use copies of drawing objects and shapes, which increase file size and pose management issues when trying to edit multiple objects, you will create symbols and use instances, or copies, of those symbols on the stage. You will also create both editable and noneditable text areas so that some text becomes part of the stationery design while other text is editable by the user. Furthermore, you will animate the stationery to increase the visual appeal when viewed on the Web. Although the animation will not print, it will be more interesting to look at in a Web browser compared with nonanimated stationery.

Electronic stationery is almost exactly the same as its physical counterpart — a sheet of paper with a themed design on which you can write a letter. The only difference is that online stationery is virtual paper that exists on a computer rather than being a physical sheet of paper. Just as with physical stationery, online stationery allows users to add visual appeal to letters, e-mails, and other messages.

Electronic stationery is used in Web mail systems, electronic greeting cards, messaging systems, mobile phone games, and other Web-based applications where users type their own messages. Some stationery has text that a user cannot edit; for example, the header or footer on a Web page. Other sections of the stationery are editable.

Stationery designs are available on many Web sites; a user might use such a design as a template for his or her own electronic communications. Once a user selects and downloads (and purchases, if necessary) stationery, he or she then types a message, and saves, prints, or e-mails the message to a recipient. Many desktop applications, such as Microsoft Word, offer similar functionality.

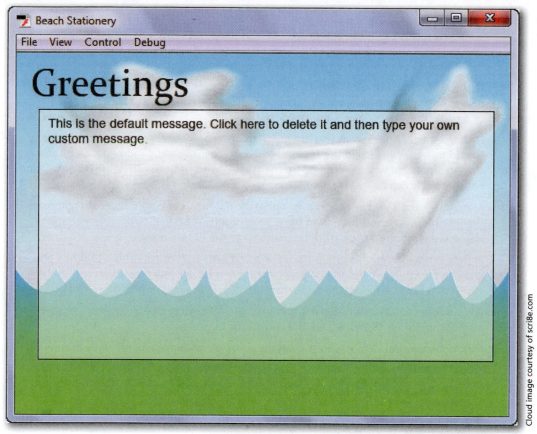

Cloud image courtesy of scri8e.com

Figure 3–1

Overview

As you read this chapter, you will learn how to create the stationery shown in Figure 3–1 by performing these general tasks:

- Create and edit graphic symbols.
- Add symbols to the library.
- Organize symbols using the Library panel.
- Create and edit instances of symbols.
- Create text boxes.
- Create editable text areas.
- Format text.
- Embed fonts.
- Create a classic tween.
- Test a movie.

**Plan
Ahead**

General Project Guidelines

When creating a project, the actions you perform and decisions you make will affect the appearance and characteristics of the finished product. As you create a movie, such as the one shown in Figure 3–1, you should follow these general guidelines:

1. **Use symbols and instances.** When creating documents that contain repeated or similar objects, determine which objects on the stage can be instances, or copies, of a master.

2. **Plan the scene.** Know what you are going to draw before you draw it. You are likely to add things as you build the background and are inspired by moments of creativity. Having a sense of what should be on the stage ahead of time will help you determine which objects can be instances of symbols.

3. **Manage symbols and instances appropriately.** Rather than create several versions of similar objects, use instances that have been slightly modified to achieve variation. Name the symbols to keep track of elements as the library grows.

4. **Plan text boxes.** Consider the purpose of a text area before creating a text box and assign a text style accordingly. When creating text boxes, pay careful attention to which text boxes are editable and which are not. Make text editable only if necessary.

5. **Embed fonts.** Embed fonts before publishing so all devices display the text properly, even if the device does not have the correct font installed.

6. **Plan the animation.** Think about what objects will be animated and place them on their own layers so that you have maximum control over animating them independently of each other.

7. **Purge the library.** Before publishing your final project, clear the library of unused items and embed the fonts. Deleting unused objects helps minimize the size of your Flash documents.

When necessary, more specific details concerning the above guidelines are presented at appropriate points in the chapter. The chapter also will identify the actions performed and decisions made regarding these guidelines during the creation of the stationery shown in Figure 3–1.

Symbols and Instances

Every drawing object or shape on the stage increases the file size of a published Flash project, leading to increased download times for users accessing Flash movies over the Internet. Using symbols and instances greatly reduces file size and also simplifies the work of making similar edits to a group of drawing objects or shapes.

A **symbol** in Flash is like a template. It is a master copy of an object that is stored in the library and is accessed through the Library panel. Flash supports three types of symbols: graphic, button, and movie. In this chapter, you will work with graphic symbols. A **graphic symbol** is simply an image (object or shape) that you can reuse multiple times on the stage.

An **instance** is a copy of a symbol on the stage. Symbols themselves are never on the stage — they reside in the library and are accessed through the Library panel. The Flash Library is similar to a physical library. Whereas a physical library stores books, the Flash Library stores symbols and imported items. When a symbol is copied to the stage, it is called an instance. You can have as many instances of a specific symbol on the stage as you like. Any changes to the original symbol apply immediately to every instance on the stage. Instances can be modified in shape, size, color, rotation, and opacity while maintaining their link to the original symbol.

By using symbols and instances, you reduce file size. For example, in a design that requires birds, rather than drawing six unique birds on the stage — each increasing the file size — you would create a single bird symbol, and then create six instances of that bird on the stage. File size is not increased because Flash treats the seven birds (six instances and one symbol) as a single symbol. Your work flow also is made more efficient by symbols and instances. If you realize later that you need to edit the six birds to add feet, it would be tedious to edit each of the six objects on the stage. Instead, you can edit the single bird symbol in the library to add the feet. Flash automatically makes the edit to each instance of the bird on the stage. You still can achieve variation in the birds by modifying certain characteristics of each individual instance.

To Start Flash

The following steps, which assume Windows 7 is running, start Flash based on a typical installation.

1 Click the Start button on the Windows 7 taskbar to display the Start menu.

2 Type `Flash Professional CS6` as the search text in the 'Search programs and files' text box, and watch the search results appear on the Start menu.

3 Click Adobe Flash Professional CS6 in the search results on the Start menu to start Flash.

4 After a few moments, when the Flash window is displayed, if the window is not maximized, click the Maximize button next to the Close button on the title bar to maximize the window.

To Reset the Workspace

It is helpful to reset the workspace so that the tools and panels appear in their default positions. The following steps select the Essentials workspace.

1 Click the Workspace Switcher button in the upper-right area of the Application bar to display the Workspace menu.

2 If necessary, click Essentials to choose the Essentials workspace.

3 Click the Workspace Switcher button in the upper-right area of the Application bar to display the Workspace menu.

4 Click Reset 'Essentials' to reset the Essentials workspace.

To Disable Auto-Recovery

The following steps disable the Auto-Recovery feature.

1 Click Edit on the Application bar to display the Edit menu.

2 Click Preferences on the Edit menu to display the Preferences dialog box.

3 Click the General category to select it, if necessary.

4 Remove the check mark, if necessary, from the Auto-Recovery check box.

5 Click the OK button to save your changes and close the Preferences dialog box.

To Create and Save a New Document

You will begin the stationery project by creating a new Flash movie. Within the file, you will create a background using a gradient. Recall that you worked with gradients in Chapter 2. The following steps create and save a new blank document.

1 Press CTRL+N to display the New Document dialog box.

2 Double-click the ActionScript 3.0 type to create a new blank ActionScript 3.0 document.

3 Press CTRL+S to display the Save As dialog box.

4 Type Beach Stationery in the File name text box to change the file name. Do not press the ENTER key after typing the file name.

5 Click the Save in box arrow to display the list of available drives.

6 Click Removable Disk (F:), or the name of your USB flash drive, in the list of available storage devices to select that drive as the new save location.

7 On the Save As dialog box toolbar, click the New Folder button to create a new folder on the selected storage device.

8 When the new folder appears, type Chapter 03 to change the name of the folder, and then press the ENTER key to apply the name change.

9 Double-click the Chapter 03 folder to select it as your save location.

10 Click the 'Save as type' box arrow to display the list of available file formats.

11 If necessary, click Flash CS6 Document (*.fla) to select it.

12 Click the Save button to save the document in the Chapter 03 folder with the new file name.

Transforming Gradients

Recall that a gradient is a transition from one color to another. Many times a gradient, when initially applied, does not create the look you want. You can use the Gradient Transform Tool, which is grouped with the Free Transform Tool on the Tools panel, to alter three characteristics of a gradient (Figure 3–2). All adjustments to a gradient are based on the transition between the first and last color stops.

When you click an object on the stage with the Gradient Transform Tool, the gradient's transition displays a border with editing handles. Dragging any of these handles with the Gradient Transform Tool changes the size, position, or direction of the gradient's transition. By default, the transition from the first color stop to the last color stop appears centered in the object. You can drag the center point editing handle in the middle of the transition border to reposition the location of the transition so that the transition starts at a different point, resulting in one color being more prominent than the other.

By default, the transition spans the full width or height of the object, resulting in a gradual transition. You can drag the resize editing handle to resize the transition, varying the shading and location of the transition.

When first applying a gradient, you can drag with the Paint Bucket Tool to set the initial direction of a gradient's transition so that the colors blend side to side, top to bottom, or diagonally. Dragging the rotate editing handle rotates the transition, changing the direction of the gradient.

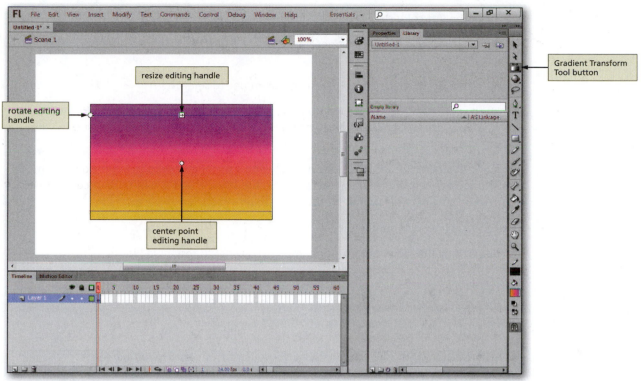

Figure 3–2

To Create a Rectangle for the Sky Background

The following steps create a background for a sky.

1 Click the Rectangle Tool button on the Tools panel and ensure object drawing mode is enabled.

2 Draw a rectangle on the stage and then use the Properties panel to set its width to 550, its height to 400, its X position to 0, and its Y position to 0 so that it completely fills the stage.

3 Click the Stroke color button on the Properties panel and click the No Stroke button in the upper-right corner of the Color picker to remove the stroke.

To Create a Gradient Fill for the Sky Background

The following steps add a gradient to give the sky background interest and depth.

1 Click the Color panel button at the top of the collapsed docking of panels to display the Color panel.

2 Click the Color type button and then click Linear Gradient in the menu to set the gradient style.

3 Click the H option button to choose Hue, Saturation, Brightness mode.

4 Click the left color stop below the gradient bar to select it.

5 In the color field, click the upper-left corner to select a white or very light gray as the color for the first color stop.

6 Click the right color stop below the gradient bar to select it.

7 In the thin color bar, click a medium blue to set the tonal range of the color field, and then click the upper-right corner of the color field to choose a medium blue for the right color stop.

8 Click the Paint Bucket Tool button on the Tools panel and drag straight down from the top to the bottom of the rectangle on the stage to set the initial direction of the transition and apply the gradient.

9 On the Timeline, rename the layer, Sky.

10 Press CTRL+S to save your changes. Your screen should resemble Figure 3–3.

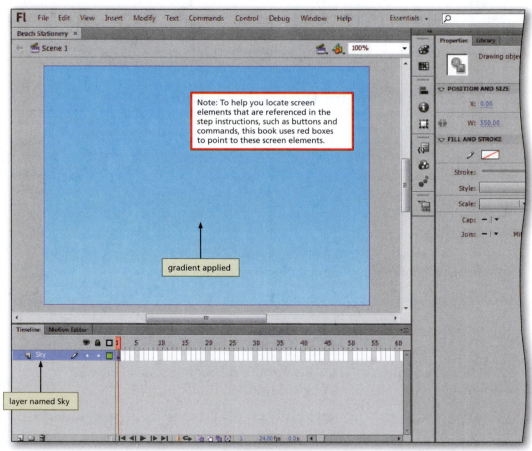

Figure 3–3

To Transform a Gradient Transition

The following steps transform the gradient to achieve a gradual transition from blue to white.

1

- Click and hold the Free Transform Tool on the Tools panel to display the menu of related tools (Figure 3–4).

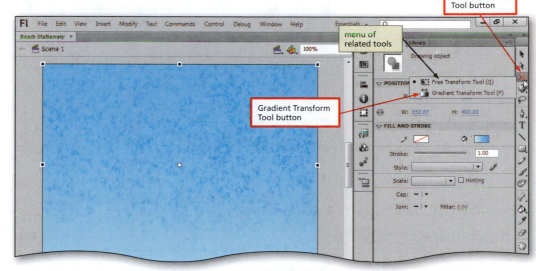

Figure 3–4

2

- Click the Gradient Transform Tool button to select it.

- If necessary, click the sky rectangle on the stage to select it and to display the gradient transition's border (Figure 3–5).

Q&A

Why do I only see the center point handle? Where is the square with an arrow in it that should be on the border? Where is the rotate handle that should be in the corner?

Depending on how the initial gradient

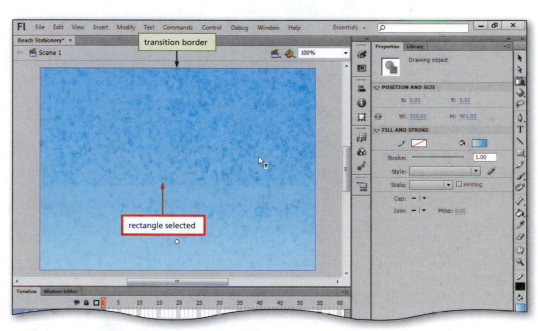

Figure 3–5

was drawn with the Paint Bucket Tool, the transition's borders could extend beyond the stage or computer screen so that the editing handles appearing on the transition border are not visible. This can be fixed easily by using the Paint Bucket Tool to draw a shorter line across the rectangle, which defines a quicker and smaller transition. You will do this in the next step.

3

- Click the Paint Bucket Tool button on the Tools panel to select it.

- Drag a short vertical line in the center of the rectangle on the stage to redefine a smaller gradient transition (Figure 3–6).

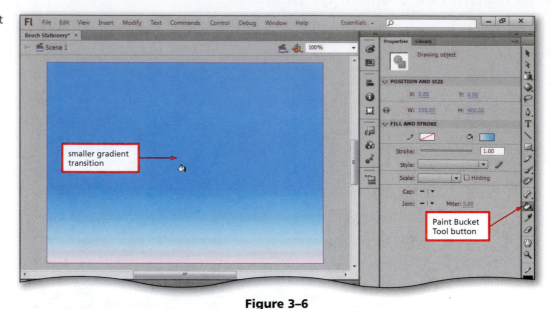

Figure 3–6

4

- Press the F key to select the Gradient Transform Tool.

- Click the rectangle on the stage to select it and display the gradient transition border with its three editing handles (Figure 3–7).

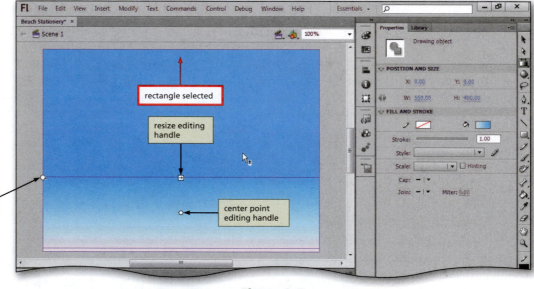

Figure 3–7

5

- Point to the center point until your mouse pointer displays a four-headed arrow.

- Drag the center point editing handle approximately to the center of the rectangle to center the transition within the rectangle (Figure 3–8).

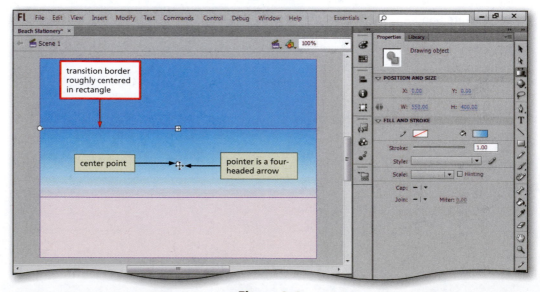

Figure 3–8

6

- Point to the resize editing handle along the top border of the transition until your mouse pointer displays a double-headed arrow.

- Drag the resize editing handle up or down to resize the transition until your screen resembles Figure 3–9.

 **Experiment**

- Drag the rotate editing handle in the corner of the transition border to rotate the transition. Experiment by dragging all three of the transition border's editing handles to resize, reposition, and rotate the transition. When you are through, your screen should resemble Figure 3–9.

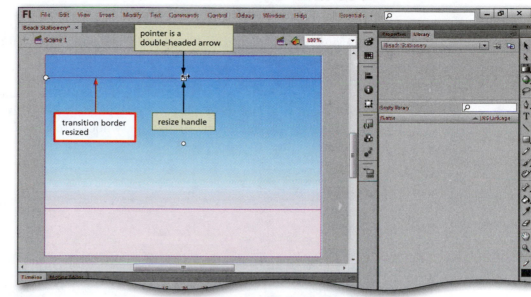

Figure 3–9

Other Ways
1. Press F

To Lock a Layer

The following step locks the Sky layer to prevent accidental editing of the sky.

1

- Click the white dot on the Sky layer under the Lock or Unlock All Layers icon to lock the Sky layer.

- Press CTRL+S to save your changes (Figure 3–10).

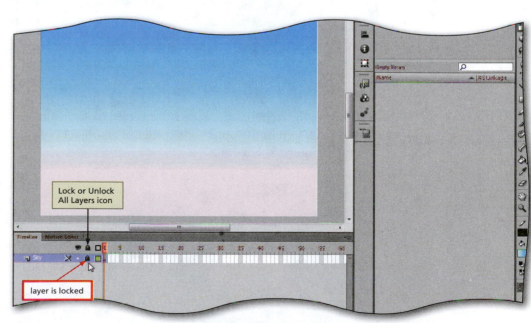

Figure 3–10

Creating Symbols

Symbols begin as shapes or drawing objects on the stage. Once you create a shape or drawing object, you can click it and use the Convert to Symbol command on the Modify menu to convert it to a symbol, or press the F8 key for the same result. When you initiate a conversion, Flash displays the Convert to Symbol dialog box, where you can select the symbol type, enter a name for the new symbol, and set other advanced options (Figure 3–11). The graphic symbol type is the most basic kind of symbol and is used for static images. Movie and button symbols are advanced symbol types with unique capabilities.

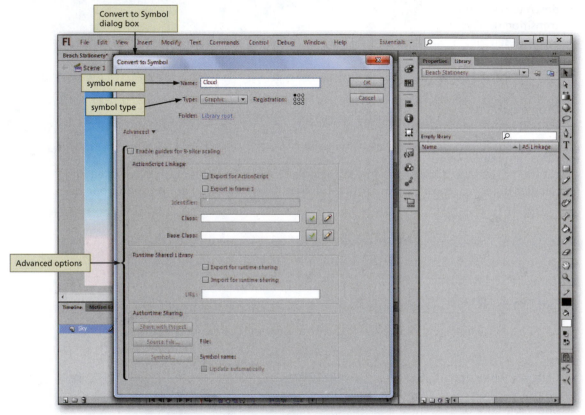

Figure 3–11

When you convert an item on the stage into a symbol, Flash adds the symbol to the library; the item on the stage is converted to an instance of the symbol at the same time. A plus sign in the upper-left corner of an object's border identifies it as a selected instance (Figure 3–12).

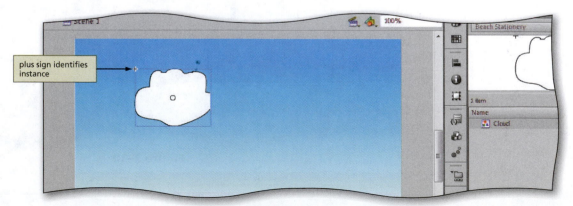

Figure 3–12

After creating a gradient rectangle, you will use the Subselection, Pen, and Selection Tools to modify the top of the rectangle and create ocean waves. First, you will use the Subselection Tool to select the rectangle and display its anchor points. Then you will use the Pen Tool to add more anchor points. Finally, you will use the Selection Tool to curve the segments between the anchor points, creating a series of waves.

Use symbols and instances.

Decide which components of your Flash movie should be created as copies (instances) of an original (symbol). If an object on the stage is used multiple times, such as birds in a sky, you should convert the object to a symbol so that multiple instances can be used on the stage. Using instances of a symbol that exists in the library saves time and effort and reduces the file size of your Flash movie.

Plan Ahead

To Create a Gradient Rectangle for the Waves

The following steps create a rectangle filled with a gradient, which you later will modify to look like ocean waves.

1 Click the New Layer button on the Timeline status bar to create a new layer above the Sky layer.

2 Double-click the new layer, type Waves, and then press the ENTER key to name the new layer.

3 Click the Rectangle Tool button on the Tools panel and confirm that object drawing mode is enabled.

4 Draw a rectangle on the stage and then use the Properties panel to set its width to 550, its height to 160, its X position to 0, and its Y position to 240 so that it sits at the bottom of the stage.

5 Use the Properties panel to remove the stroke, if necessary.

6 Display the Color panel and create a linear gradient fill with a medium blue color stop on the right and a medium green color stop on the left.

7 Click the Paint Bucket Tool on the Tools panel.

8 On the stage, drag from the top to the bottom of the Waves rectangle to set the gradient direction.

9 Click the Gradient Transform Tool button on the Tools panel.

10 Click the Waves rectangle on the stage to display the transition's border and drag the three editing handles so that your screen resembles Figure 3–13 on the next page.

11 Press CTRL+S to save your changes.

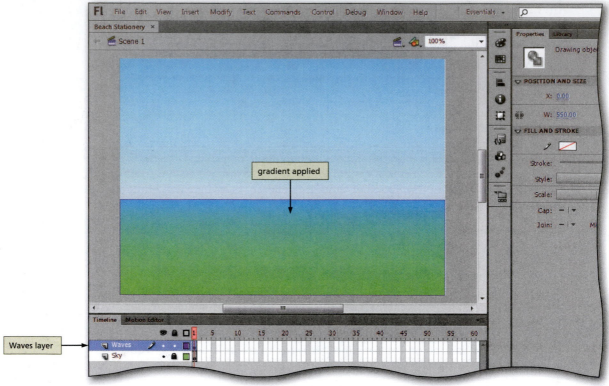

Figure 3–13

To Use the Subselection Tool to Display Anchor Points

The following step selects the Subselection Tool and uses it to display anchor points on the Waves rectangle.

- Click the Subselection Tool button on the Tools panel to select it.

- Point to the top edge of the Waves rectangle until the mouse pointer displays a solid square.

- Click the Waves rectangle to select it and to display its anchor points (Figure 3–14).

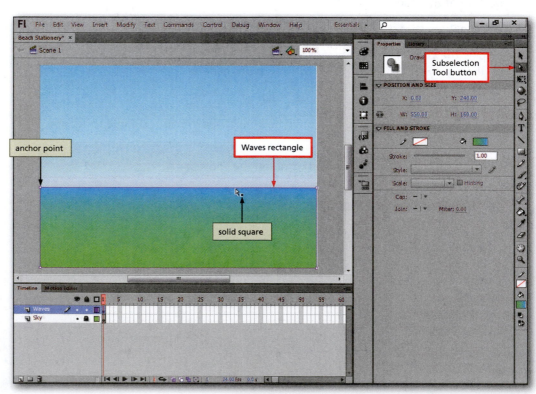

Figure 3–14

To Add Anchor Points using the Add Anchor Point Tool

The following steps add anchor points to the top of the Waves rectangle so that multiple line segments across the top of the rectangle are created. These segments will then be reshaped into waves.

1

- Click and hold the Pen Tool button on the Tools panel to display the menu of related tools (Figure 3–15).

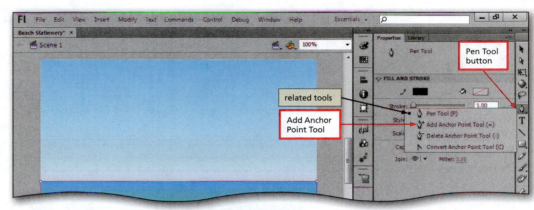

Figure 3–15

2
- Click the Add Anchor Point Tool to select it.

- Click the upper-center of the Waves rectangle border to add an anchor point and split the top border into two similarly sized segments.

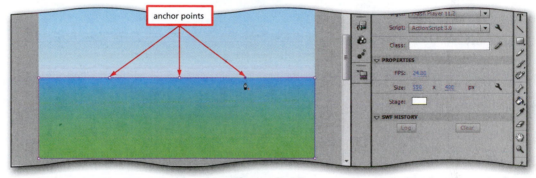

Figure 3–16

- Click the center of the upper-left half of the border to add an anchor point.

- Click the center of the upper-right half of the border to add an anchor point and divide the top border into fourths (Figure 3–16).

3

- Click the center of each segment along the top border, adding anchor points to each of the four segments you created in Step 3, so that there are eight segments (Figure 3–17).

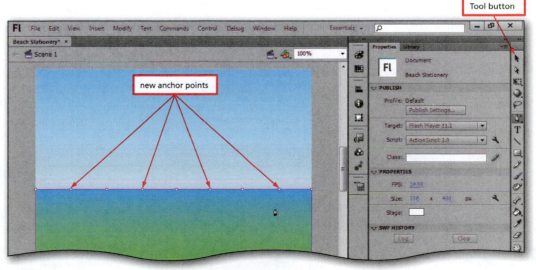

Figure 3–17

To Reshape Line Segments using the Selection Tool

The following steps use the Selection Tool to reshape the line segments at the top of the rectangle into waves.

• Click the Selection Tool button on the Tools panel to select it (Figure 3–18).

Q&A Why did the anchor points disappear?

Anchor points are visible only when using the Subselection or Pen Tools. Because you just activated the Selection Tool, the anchor points are no longer visible. However, the top edge of the Waves rectangle is still split into eight segments.

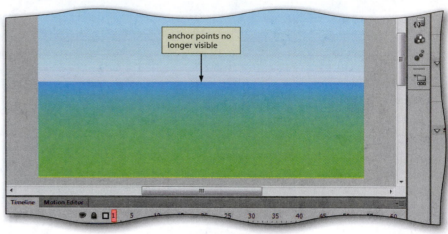

Figure 3–18

• Point to where you estimate the leftmost segment to be so that the mouse pointer displays a curved line (Figure 3–19).

Q&A What if my mouse pointer will not display a curved line?

This is a bug in Flash. If you cannot get the mouse pointer to display a curved line, then double-click the rectangle to enter edit mode, double-click the stage to exit edit mode, and then point to the upper-left area of the border again to see if the mouse pointer displays a curved line.

Figure 3–19

• Drag down to create a curve with the first segment between its two anchor points.

Q&A The whole rectangle moved and the segment did not curve. What happened?

Be very careful not to drag until your mouse pointer displays the curved line. If the mouse pointer does not display the curved line, you will drag the entire object rather than reshape the segment. If this happens, press CTRL+Z to undo the move, click the work area to select the rectangle, and then try again.

• Point to the approximate position of the second segment so that your mouse pointer displays a curved line (Figure 3–20).

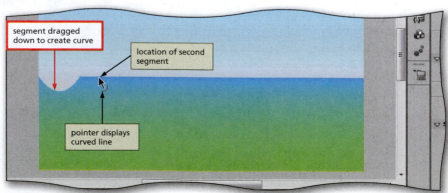

Figure 3–20

4

- Drag down to create a curve in the second segment between the second and third anchor points.

- Continue dragging the remaining segments until you have created waves similar to Figure 3–21. Vary the shape of the curves to add visual interest.

- Press CTRL+S to save your changes.

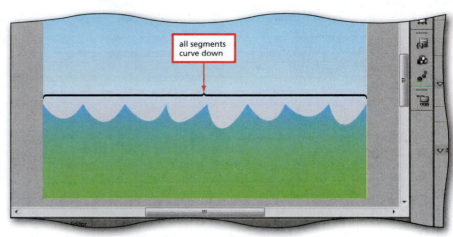

all segments curve down

Figure 3–21

To Create a Symbol from the Stage

The following steps convert the drawing object on the stage to a symbol. When the symbol is created, the drawing object on the stage becomes an instance of the symbol.

1

- Click the Waves rectangle on the stage to select it.

- Click Modify on the Application bar to display the Modify menu (Figure 3–22).

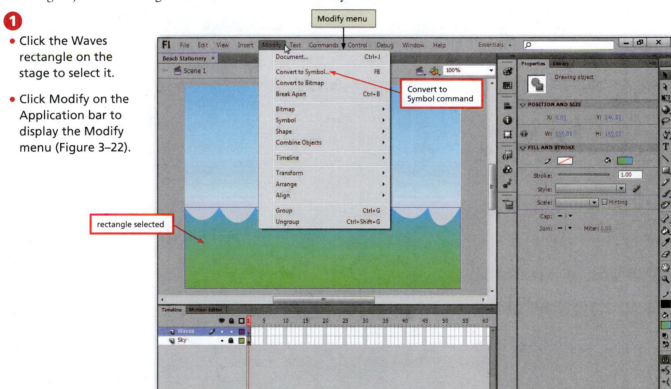

Modify menu

Convert to Symbol command

rectangle selected

Figure 3–22

2

- Click Convert to Symbol on the Modify menu to display the Convert to Symbol dialog box (Figure 3–23).

Q&A

My Convert to Symbol dialog box is much larger than the one shown in the figure. Did I do something wrong?

You probably are seeing the advanced options. Click the Advanced button to close the advanced view.

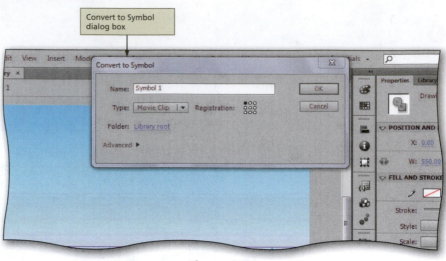

Figure 3–23

3

- Type Waves in the Name text box.
- Click the Type box arrow to display its menu (Figure 3–24).

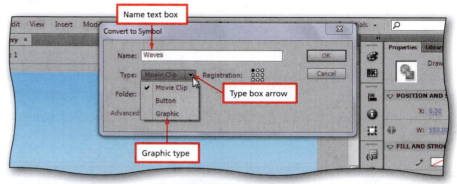

Figure 3–24

4

- Click Graphic to specify a graphic symbol (Figure 3–25).

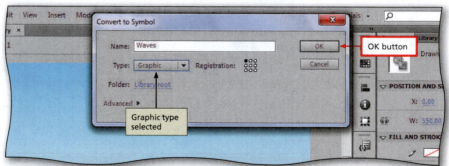

Figure 3–25

5

- Click the OK button to convert the drawing object to a symbol and to close the Convert to Symbol dialog box (Figure 3–26).
- Press CTRL+S to save your changes.

Q&A

How do I know whether the symbol was created?

The upper-left corner of the wave border displays a plus sign. Also, there is an open circle in the center of the wave rectangle.

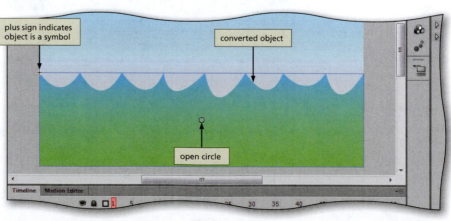

Figure 3–26

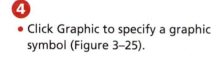

Other Ways

1. Press F8, enter settings, click OK

The Library

Flash stores the symbols you create, in addition to imported images, audio, and video, in a storage area called the library. Each document you create with Flash contains its own unique library, so adding or deleting symbols from the library has no effect on other Flash documents.

Library items are accessed through the Library panel (Figure 3–27). Clicking a symbol in the Library panel selects it and displays a preview of the symbol at the top of the panel. The status bar on the Library panel includes buttons to create new symbols, to create folders in which to store and organize symbols, to delete symbols, and to edit a symbol's properties. You can double-click a symbol in the library to enter edit mode to edit the original drawing object or shape, or double-click a symbol's name to rename it. Dragging a symbol from the Library panel to the stage creates an instance of it on the stage.

Large projects commonly have hundreds of symbols. A Search box near the top of the Library panel lets you search by name for symbols within a document.

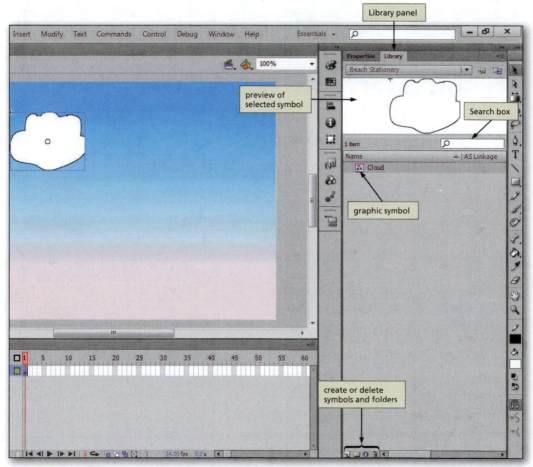

Figure 3–27

To View the Library Panel and Create a New Symbol

The following steps create a new symbol directly in the Library panel without initially displaying the symbol on the stage.

1
- Click the Library panel tab to display it (Figure 3–28).

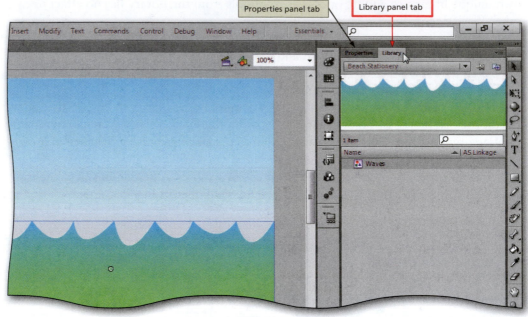

Figure 3–28

2
- Click the New Symbol button on the Library panel status bar to display the Create New Symbol dialog box (Figure 3–29).

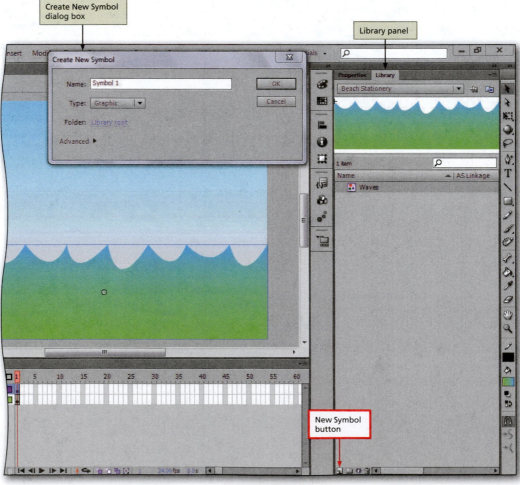

Figure 3–29

- Type `Clouds` in the Name text box.

- If necessary, click the Type box arrow and then click Graphic in the menu (Figure 3–30).

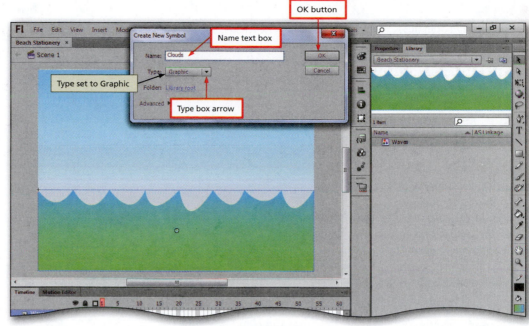

Figure 3–30

4

- Click the OK button to create a new blank symbol, close the Create New Symbol dialog box, and place the stage in symbol editing mode.

- On the Tools panel, click the Pencil Tool button to select it.

- Click the Pencil Mode button, and then click Smooth, if necessary, to set the pencil mode to Smooth.

- Click the Object Drawing button to deselect it and disable object drawing mode, which will allow you to draw a shape instead of a drawing object (Figure 3–31).

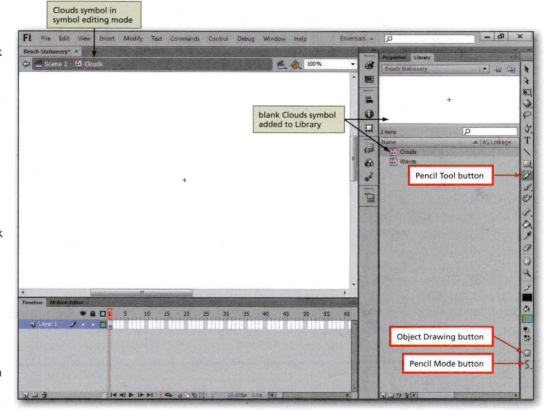

Figure 3–31

Q&A How do I know if I am in symbol editing mode?

The toolbar at the top of the stage indicates you are viewing the Clouds symbol. Also, there is a plus sign in the middle of the stage and the sky and waves no longer appear.

5

- Click the Properties panel tab to display the Properties panel.

- If necessary, set the stroke color to black.

- If necessary, set the stroke height to 1.00.

- On the stage, draw a cloud shape, trying to keep the plus sign in the middle of the cloud. Make sure to overlap the start and end points (Figure 3–32).

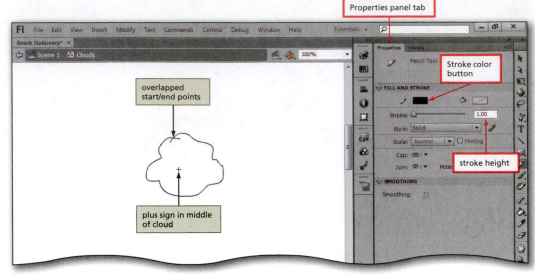

Figure 3–32

Q&A

Why do I need to overlap the start and end points?

Overlapping the endpoints ensures that the cloud is a closed shape and makes it easier to fill with a color later.

6

- Click the Selection Tool button on the Tools panel to select it.

- Click one of the overlapping segments on the inside of the cloud to select it (Figure 3–33).

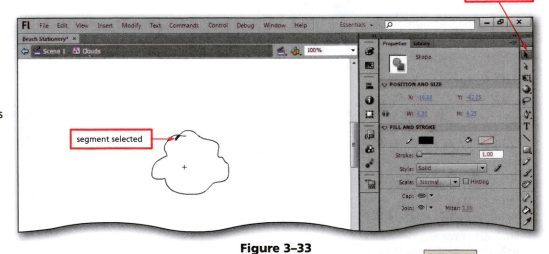

Figure 3–33

7

- Press the DELETE key to delete the extraneous segment.

- Click the remaining segment inside the cloud to select it.

- Press the DELETE key to delete the extraneous segment.

- On the Tools panel, click the Paint Bucket Tool button to select it.

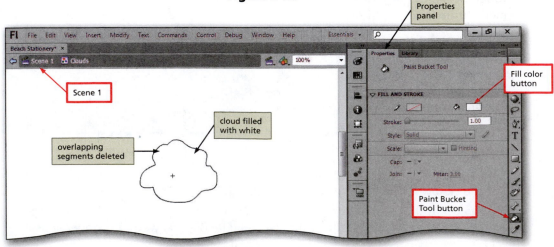

Figure 3–34

- On the Properties panel, set the fill color to white.

- Click inside the cloud to fill it with white (Figure 3–34).

Q&A How do I know the cloud has been filled with white?

Because the cloud is on a white background, the white fill is not visible. To ensure that the fill is white, select a different fill color, such as red, to fill the cloud. Then change the fill color to white. The white fill will be visible on the blue sky when you later add it to the scene.

8

• Click Scene 1 on the toolbar above the stage to exit symbol editing mode and return to the scene.

• Click the Library panel tab to select it (Figure 3–35).

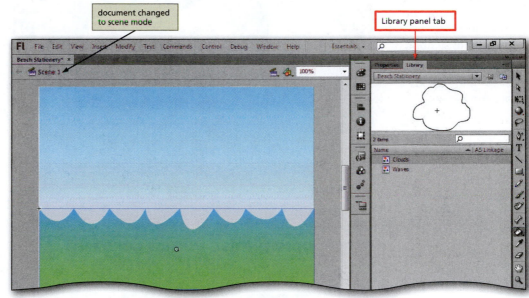

Figure 3–35

To Add Instances to the Stage

The following steps create multiple instances of the Clouds symbol on the stage.

1

• Click the Selection Tool button to select it.

• Click the Sky layer on the Timeline to select it, if necessary.

• Click the Lock button on the Timeline's Sky layer to unlock it so that you can add instances to the layer.

• Drag the Clouds symbol from the Library panel to the upper-left area of the stage (Figure 3–36).

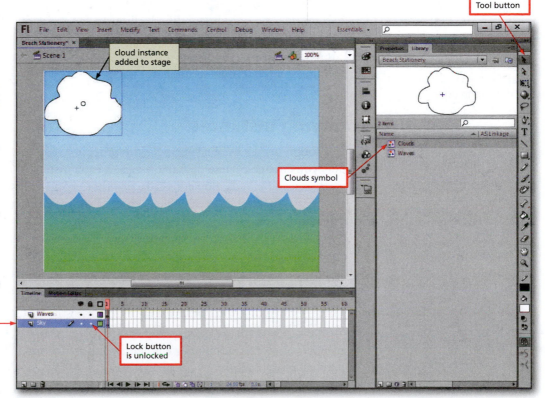

Figure 3–36

2

- Drag the Clouds symbol from the Library panel to the stage two more times to create two more instances of the Clouds symbol on the stage.

Q&A What if my clouds are too big?

You will resize the clouds in a later exercise.

- Click the gray work area to deselect the last cloud (Figure 3–37).

- Press CTRL+S to save your changes.

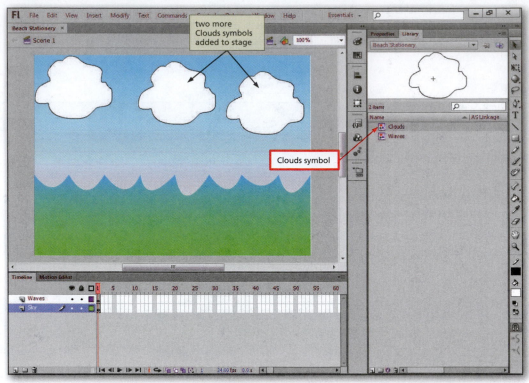

Figure 3–37

Modifying Symbols and Instances

Instances on the stage can be modified, allowing for variation among otherwise identical objects. As instances are linked to their parent symbol, changes to a symbol affect all its instances in the same way; and as you will see later, changes to an instance have no effect on the parent symbol.

Modifying Instances

Although instances of a specific symbol begin as identical objects on the stage, Flash lets you change certain characteristics of each instance. This is an efficient way to produce a series of clouds, flowers, birds, or other group of instances with some variety and, thus, visual interest. You can change the following characteristics of instances: size, rotation, color, transparency, and brightness.

You can use the Properties panel, Transform panel, or Free Transform Tool to alter the size of an instance. Using the Transform panel or Free Transform Tool alters an instance's rotation. The following characteristics of an instance can be modified from the Style menu in the Color Effect area of the Properties panel (Figure 3–38):

- **Tint** — Changing the tint changes the color of the instance.
- **Alpha** — The alpha controls the instance's transparency. A low value fades the instance, allowing underlying elements to show through. A high value makes the instance more opaque.
- **Brightness** — The brightness control adjusts the overall brightness and darkness of an element. A low value darkens it, whereas a high value lightens it.

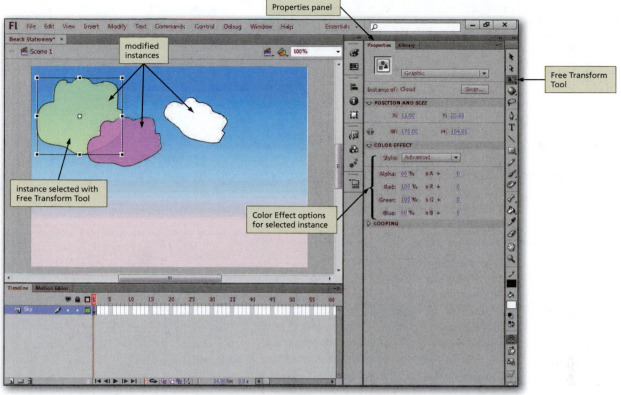

Figure 3–38

The Free Transform Tool

Although the Properties and Transform panels can be used to modify an object selected from the stage, it is often more efficient to make changes with the Free Transform Tool because you simply can click and drag an object on the stage rather than switch panels and enter a variety of values. The Free Transform Tool lets you change the width, height, rotation, or skew of the selected object. The Free Transform Tool will alter the selected object differently based on which part of the object's border is dragged. Table 3–1 describes possible uses of the Free Transform Tool.

Table 3–1 Transform Tool Characteristics				
Free Transform Tool Icon	**Drag Location on Border**	**Transformation Description**	**Original Object**	**Transformed Object**
↕	Directly on a square handle	Drag top or bottom handle to change height. Drag left or right handle to change width. Drag corner handle to change both width and height. SHIFT+DRAG a corner to maintain aspect ratio. CTRL+DRAG a corner to adjust just that corner.		
⇄	Directly on border outline	Drag to skew the selected object.		
↶	Next to, but not on, a corner handle	Drag to rotate. SHIFT+DRAG to rotate in 45-degree increments.		

<table>
<tr><td>Plan
Ahead</td><td>**Manage symbols and instances appropriately.**
Rather than create multiple similar symbols, consider modifying instances of a single symbol instead. Instances can vary in size, rotation, and color characteristics, creating a variety of unique items on the stage all tied to the same parent symbol.</td></tr>
</table>

To Modify Instances using the Free Transform Tool

The following steps use the Free Transform Tool to adjust the size and rotation of two of the cloud instances.

- Click the Free Transform Tool button on the Tools panel to select it.

- Click the middle cloud on the stage so that it displays the transformation border.

- Point to the lower-center sizing handle of the cloud until your mouse pointer displays a double-headed arrow (Figure 3–39).

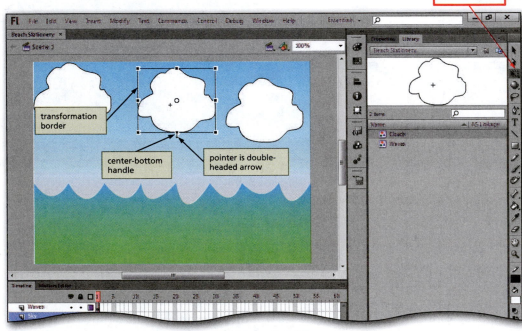

Figure 3–39

- Drag the sizing handle up to reduce the height of the cloud, similar to Figure 3–40.

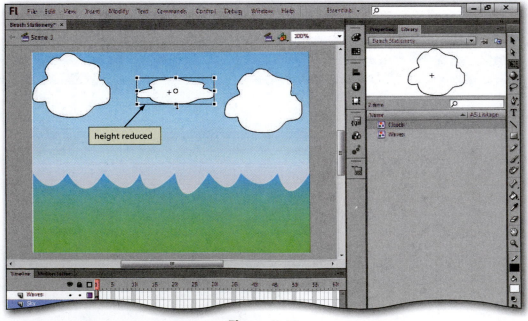

Figure 3–40

- Click the rightmost cloud to select it.

- Point to the lower-right sizing handle until the mouse pointer displays a double-headed arrow, and then drag down and to the left to increase the height and reduce the width (Figure 3–41).

Q&A

Can I change the size of an instance while maintaining the width-to-height proportion?

Yes. Hold the SHIFT key as you drag a corner handle to maintain the aspect ratio.

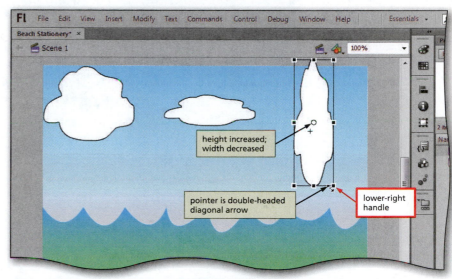

Figure 3–41

- Point to the lower-right corner of the cloud, not the sizing handle, until the mouse pointer changes to a circular arrow, then drag to the left to rotate the cloud to your liking.

- Drag the rightmost cloud to the left, overlapping the middle cloud as in Figure 3–42.

Q&A

If I overlap the clouds, will they merge?

No. The clouds are instances. Instances do not merge when overlapped.

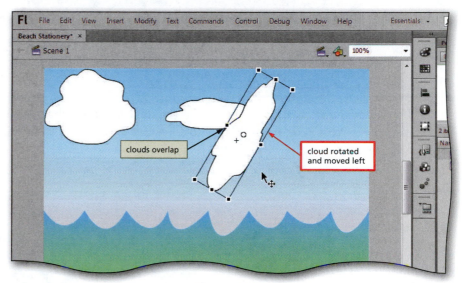

Figure 3–42

Modifying the Color Properties of an Instance

The Style menu in the Color Effect area of the Properties panel lets you alter the color of an instance (Figure 3–43 on the following page). For changes to a single characteristic, select Brightness, Tint, or Alpha from the Style menu. Brightness adjusts the overall lightness/darkness of the instance and offers a single Bright setting. Lowering the value in the Properties panel approaches black, whereas raising the value approaches white. Tint is used to change the color. Use the Red, Green, and Blue sliders to create the new color and then use the Tint slider to determine the amount of color added to the instance. A low Tint value adds less color than a high Tint value. The Alpha setting adjusts the overall opacity with a single Alpha slider. **Opacity** refers to the level at which you can see through a color to reveal the objects or layers behind it. A value of 0 fades the instance completely, whereas a value of 100 makes it completely opaque. For the most versatility, use the Advanced option from the Style menu because it allows you to change both the color and the opacity.

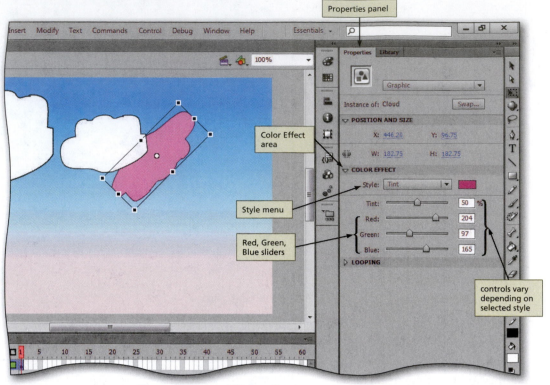

Figure 3–43

To Change the Opacity of an Instance

The following steps add more waves to the stage and then change the opacity of the new instances. The waves instance is created on its own layer to allow the waves layers to be animated independently of each other later in the chapter.

- Click the Selection Tool button on the Tools panel to select it.

- Click the Waves layer on the Timeline to select it.

- Click the New Layer button on the Timeline status bar to create a new layer above the Waves layer.

- Name the new layer Waves Front.

- Drag the Waves symbol from the Library panel to the stage, to add another instance of the wave to the Waves Front layer (Figure 3–44).

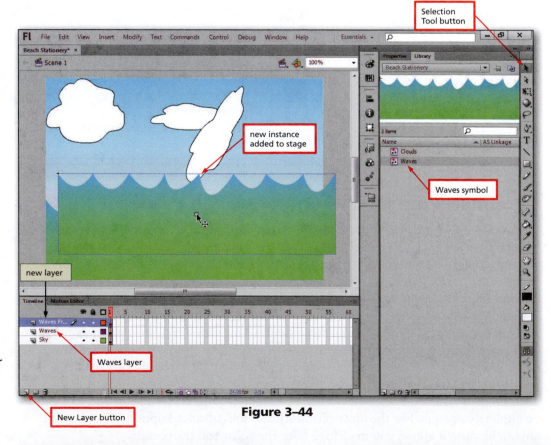

Figure 3–44

2

- Click the Properties panel tab to select it.

- Set the X position to -23 and the Y position to 240 to position the new instance.

- Click Color Effect on the Properties panel to expand the Color Effect area, if necessary.

- Click the Style box arrow to display the list of Style options (Figure 3–45).

Q&A Is it a problem that part of the new Waves instance is off the stage?

The left side of the Waves instance is in the gray work area outside the stage. When the final project is published, only the areas on the stage will be visible, so this is not a problem.

Q&A The right side of the new Waves instance looks bad because its right edge is completely straight. It does not look natural. Can it be fixed?

Yes. You will adjust the right edge of the wave in a later step.

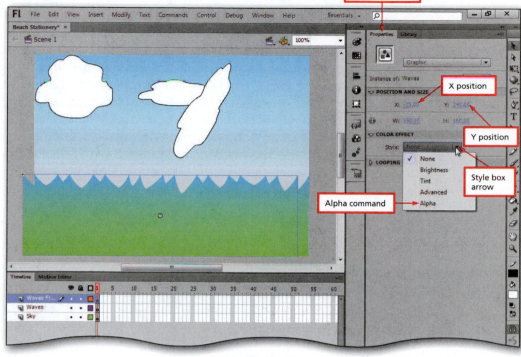

Figure 3–45

3

- Click Alpha on the Style list to select it.

- Drag the Alpha slider to the left until the new value reads 60, reducing the opacity of the new instance to give it a faded appearance (Figure 3–46).

- Press CTRL+S to save your changes.

Experiment

- Select Tint from the Color Effect Style menu and experiment with the Tint, Red, Green, and Blue sliders to change the color of the second Waves instance. When you are done experimenting, select Alpha from the Style menu again to apply the Alpha effect.

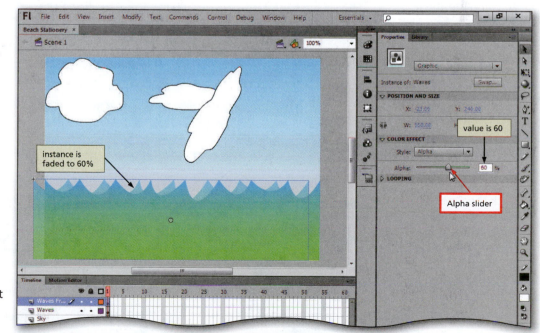

Figure 3–46

Swapping Instances

In some situations, you will create a symbol, add instances to the stage, modify the instances, and then decide you do not like the original symbol at all. Or, you might decide you need a completely different symbol; for example, instead of having created clouds, you realize you should have made balloons instead. Rather than deleting all instances on the stage, creating a brand-new symbol, adding instances of the new symbol on the stage in the exact location of the original deleted instances, and then trying to re-create the same modifications for the instances, it is much more efficient to simply swap symbols.

To swap symbols, you create a new symbol, select the instance on the stage you would like to swap, click Modify, Symbol, Swap Symbol on the Application bar, select the new symbol, and click the OK button. A quicker way is to right-click the instance on the stage and choose Swap Symbol from the context menu.

To Create a New Symbol from an Imported Image

The following steps import an image file to use as a replacement for the Clouds symbol.

- Click the Library panel tab to select it.

- Press CTRL+R to open the Import dialog box.

- Navigate to the Chapter 03 folder of the Data Files for Students.

Q&A

What if I do not have the Data Files for Students?

To complete this assignment, you will be required to use the Data Files for Students. Visit www.cengage.com/ct/studentdownload for detailed instructions or contact your instructor for information about accessing the required files.

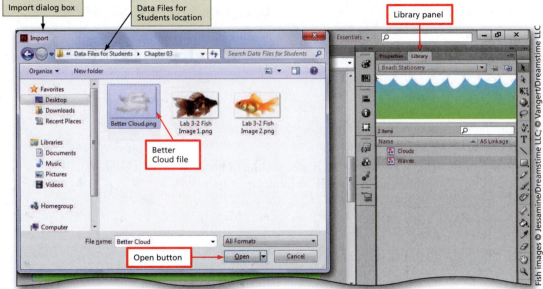

Figure 3–47

- Click the Better Cloud file to select it (Figure 3–47).

- Click the Open button to import the Better Cloud image to the stage and to the library (Figure 3–48).

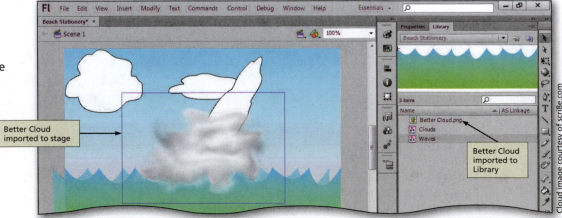

Figure 3–48

3

- Press the F8 key to display the Convert to Symbol dialog box (Figure 3–49).

- Type `Real Cloud` for the symbol name.

- Ensure the Type is set to Graphic.

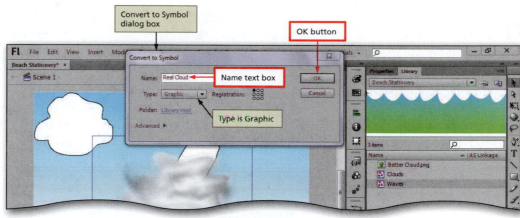

Figure 3–49

4

- Click the OK button to convert the image on the stage to a symbol.

- Press DELETE to delete the new cloud instance from the stage but leave both the new symbol and the imported image in the library (Figure 3–50).

- Press CTRL+S to save your changes.

Figure 3–50

To Swap a Symbol

The following steps swap the symbol used by the three cloud instances on the stage so that they all become instances of the new Real Cloud symbol.

1

- Click the Selection Tool button to select it, if necessary.

- Click the leftmost cloud on the stage to select it.

- Click Modify on the Application bar and then point to Symbol to display the Symbol submenu (Figure 3–51).

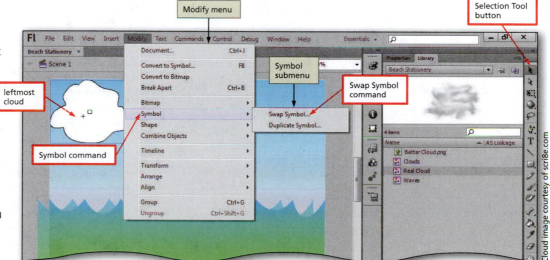

Figure 3–51

2

- Click Swap Symbol to display the Swap Symbol dialog box.

- Click Real Cloud to select the new symbol on which the cloud instances are based (Figure 3–52).

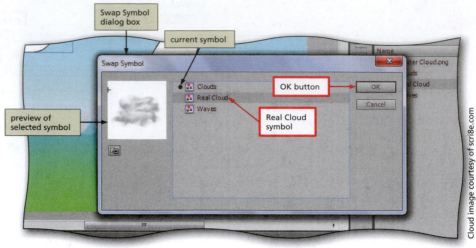

Figure 3–52

3

- Click the OK button to swap the symbol.

- If necessary, drag the instance so it fits in the upper-left area of the stage (Figure 3–53).

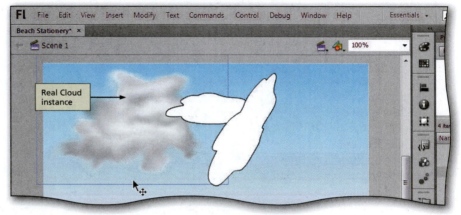

Figure 3–53

4

- Right-click the middle cloud to display the context menu (Figure 3–54).

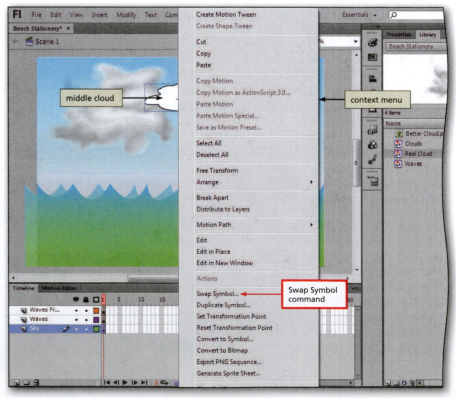

Figure 3–54

5

- Click Swap Symbol to display the Swap Symbol dialog box.

- Click Real Cloud to select it (Figure 3–55).

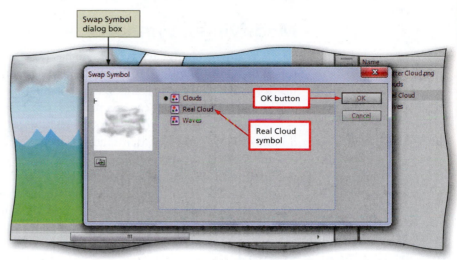

Figure 3–55

6

- Click the OK button to swap the symbol.

- Move and resize the middle cloud to your liking (Figure 3–56).

Q&A

Why does the middle cloud look different from the left cloud?

Earlier, you modified the shape of the middle and right clouds. Swapping a symbol changes the symbol that is used, but any modifications to the instance remain in effect. The middle cloud is shorter than the left cloud because previously you reduced the height of the middle cloud instance.

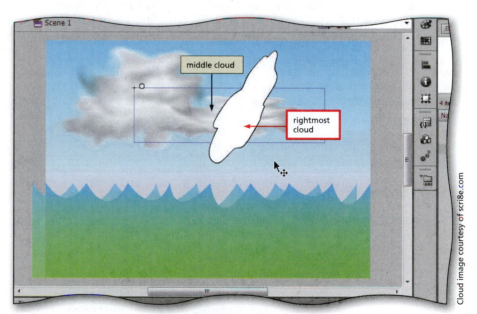

Cloud image courtesy of scri8e.com

Figure 3–56

7

- Repeat Steps 4–6 on the rightmost cloud so that all three clouds use the new symbol (Figure 3–57).

- Press CTRL+S to save your changes.

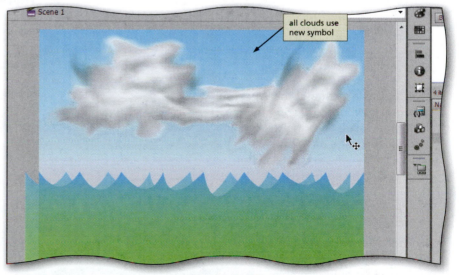

Figure 3–57

Modifying a Symbol

Making a change to an instance has no effect on other instances generated from the same parent symbol. However, making a change to a symbol does cascade its modification down to all its instances, which is helpful when you want to adjust the shape, stroke, or fill of all instances of a particular symbol.

To edit a symbol, you can locate the symbol in the Library panel and then double-click it. However, that method shows only the symbol being edited and nothing else on the stage. A more desirable way to edit a symbol is to use **edit in place**. With this method, you simply double-click any instance on the stage. The symbol becomes editable, but all other items on the stage remain visible, allowing you to see how your changes interact with the rest of the design. When you are finished editing the symbol, double-click the stage or use the toolbar above the stage to exit edit mode.

To Edit the Waves Symbol

The following steps edit the Waves symbol to curve the two side edges; this will improve the appearance of the waves so that when you animate them later, there will not be a gap on the side. Using edit in place to modify one of the Waves instances applies the changes to both of the Waves instances.

- Double-click either of the Waves instances on the stage to edit the symbol in place.

- Click the gray work area outside the stage to deselect the symbol.

- Point to the right edge of the Waves symbol until your mouse pointer displays a curved line (Figure 3–58).

Figure 3–58

- Drag the right edge of the Waves symbol to the right, to create a large curve down the entire right side.

- Point to the left edge of the Waves symbol until your mouse pointer displays a curved line, and then drag the left edge of the Waves symbol to the left, to create a large curve down the entire left side.

- Double-click the stage above the waves to exit edit mode.

- Click the gray work area outside the stage to deselect the waves. Your screen should resemble Figure 3–59.

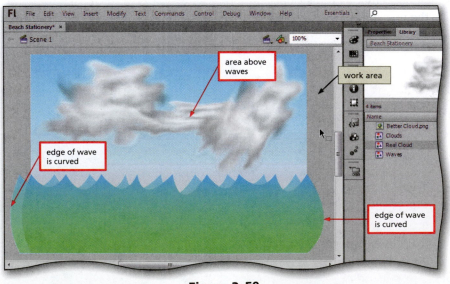

Figure 3–59

Hiding the Work Area

Flash refers to the work area (the gray area outside the stage) by two terms. You already know the term, work area, but Flash also calls it the **pasteboard**. Having items partially on the stage and partially in the work area can be distracting as you work. You can hide the portions of items in the work area by using the Pasteboard command on the View menu.

To Hide the Pasteboard

The following steps hide the portions of items in the pasteboard so that you get a better idea of what the design looks like. You then will show the pasteboard contents again so that you have access to the work area.

1
- Click View on the Application bar to display the View menu (Figure 3–60).

Figure 3–60

2
- Click Pasteboard on the View menu to hide the pasteboard contents (Figure 3–61).

 **Experiment**

- Click the waves on the stage to select a Waves instance and notice the portion of the border residing in the work area is not visible. Try to deselect the Waves instance by clicking the gray work area outside the stage. Notice that because the pasteboard is hidden, the work area is not available and you cannot deselect the waves.

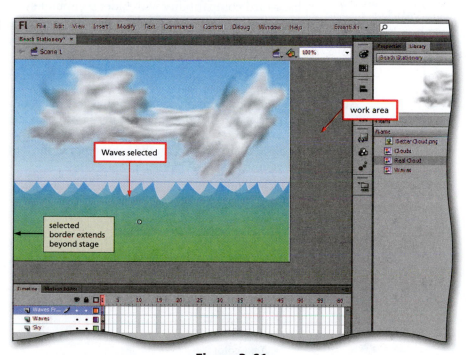

Figure 3–61

3

- Press CTRL+SHIFT+W to toggle the pasteboard and make the work area accessible.

- Click the gray work area outside the stage to deselect the waves (Figure 3–62).

- Press CTRL+S to save your changes.

Figure 3–62

Break Point: If you wish to take a break, this is a good place to do so. To resume at a later time, start Flash, open the file called Beach Stationery, and continue following the steps from this location forward.

Cloud image courtesy of scri8e.com

Classic or TLF?
The only reason to ever use Classic text is when you know your users have a very old version of the Flash Web browser plug-in. If you do not know which Flash plug-in your users have installed, use TLF text.

Using Text

Many Flash movies include text to support the document's graphics. You add text to a Flash project using the Text Tool on the Tools panel. Flash supports two main types of text: Classic text and TLF (Text Layout Framework) text. Classic text provides backward compatibility with older computer systems. You are more likely to use TLF text, which offers everything Classic text does plus more. TLF is the default in Flash, but you can switch between Classic and TLF using the Properties panel.

Plan Ahead

Plan text boxes.
Text adds information and functionality to your Flash movies. As part of planning the movie, determine the placement of text boxes and decide whether to use point or area text boxes or a combination of the two types. The size and style of the text box fonts have a large impact on the appearance of the movie. Text can be used in many ways in your movies, including:

- Headings
- Body text
- Labels
- Input fields for user responses, such as a form

Think about keeping the text readable. This can be achieved by carefully formatting the text and its container. Consider the following:

- Font family
- Text size
- Italic or bold
- Text color
- Contrast with text background

Point Text and Area Text Boxes

Before typing text on the stage, you must create a text container — a box in which the text resides. There are two kinds of text boxes in Flash: **point text boxes** and **area text boxes** (Figure 3–63).

A point text box automatically expands horizontally as text is typed; pressing the ENTER key expands a point text box vertically. Point text boxes do not wrap to the next line automatically when the text reaches the right edge of the stage (as word processors do). It is possible, therefore, to create a point text box and type so much text that you have a single long line that is wider than the stage. When using point text boxes, you must press the ENTER key to create new lines. You create a point text box by selecting the Text Tool button from the Tools panel and clicking the stage with the Text Tool. Point text boxes are identified by a white circular handle in the lower-right corner; the circle only appears when the text box is selected with the Text Tool.

An area text box, unlike a point text box, is a static size. You create an area text box by dragging the Text Tool on the stage to create a rectangular container. Text automatically wraps to the next line (like a word processor) in an area text box, but the box will not expand in either direction. It is possible to type more text than the container can show. In this case, the extra text is called **overflow text** because it overflows the container. You either can drag the borders of the area text box with the Text Tool to expand it or you can move the overflowing text into another text box. Area text boxes are identified by white squares in their upper-left and lower-right corners, which only appear when the text box is selected with the Text Tool. A red border with a red plus sign in the lower-right corner of the text box indicates that the box contains overflow text.

Point text boxes are best for headlines or other areas of single-line text. Area text boxes are required for multiline text.

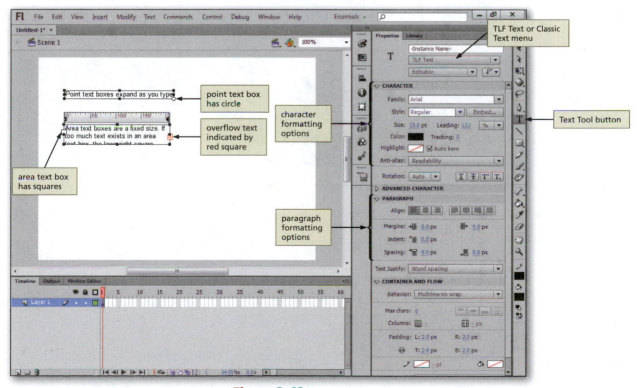

Figure 3–63

To Create a Point Text Box

The following steps create a point text box to use as the stationery heading.

• If necessary, click the Waves Front layer on the Timeline to select it.

• Click the New Layer button to create a new layer above the Waves Front layer.

• Double-click the new layer name on the Timeline, type Text, and press the ENTER key to rename the layer (Figure 3–64).

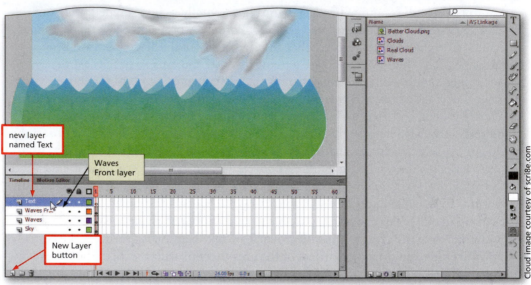

Figure 3–64

• Click the Text Tool button on the Tools panel to select it.

• Click the Properties panel tab to display it, if necessary.

• Click the Text engine box arrow, and then click TLF Text, if necessary.

• Click the upper-left corner of the stage to create a point text box (Figure 3–65).

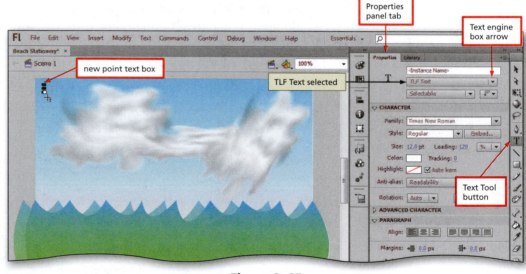

Figure 3–65

Q&A

How do I know I have created a point text box and not an area text box?

A single click creates a point text box. You can identify a point text box by the white circle in the lower-right corner. If your text box does not display a circle, press CTRL+Z to undo and try again.

Character Formatting

Character formatting specifies the font, size, color, and other basic characteristics of text. You can apply formatting to entire paragraphs, words, or individual letters. Formatting options can be set after selecting the Text Tool from the Tools panel, but before clicking on the stage or typing any text. This method allows you to set the formatting characteristics first and then type with the formatting already in place.

Alternatively, you may prefer to type your text first and then set the formatting characteristics afterward. To do this, use the Selection Tool to select a text box on the stage. Flash displays character formatting options in the Properties panel when text is selected with either the Selection Tool or the Text Tool. Selecting the text box applies formatting to all text within the box; you also can select specific words or characters to apply formatting to only the selected characters. Basic character formatting options are described in Table 3–2.

Table 3–2 Text Formatting Options	
Option	**Description**
Family	Selects the font family, such as Arial, Times New Roman, and so on.
Style	Specifies regular, bold, or italic.
Embed	Displays an additional dialog box to embed fonts in the published Flash movie so that fonts are displayed as expected on all devices, even those without the specified fonts installed.
Size	Sets the size of the font.
Leading	Controls the vertical spacing between lines of multiline text.
Color	Sets the color of the text.
Tracking	Controls the horizontal spacing between characters. A small or negative value brings characters closer together, whereas values over 0 spread the characters apart.
Highlight	Sets a highlight color for the text.
Auto kern	Automatically adjusts the horizontal spacing between characters that benefit from it.
Anti-alias	Controls how the text is smoothed to avoid jagged curves and increase overall readability.

To Set Character Formatting and Type Text in a Point Text Box

The following steps set basic character formatting and create the first line of text for the editable stationery. This text will serve as the stationery greeting.

- On the Properties panel, click the Family box arrow to display the available fonts and select Constantia to specify the font family.

- Click the Size value to highlight the existing size, type 42, and press the ENTER key to set a new font size of 42.

- If necessary, click the Text (fill) color button and then click a black swatch to set the font color to black.

- If necessary, change the remaining settings to the following values: Style = Regular, Leading = 120, Tracking = 0, Anti-alias = Readability (Figure 3–66).

Figure 3–66

Cloud image courtesy of scri8e.com

Q&A I do not see the Constantia font in the list. What should I do?

Use the scroll box to review the list of installed fonts. If your computer does not have the Constantia font, select a font of your choice.

- Type Greetings and notice that the point text box automatically expands horizontally as you type.

- Click the Selection Tool button to select it.

- If necessary, drag the text box to the upper-left corner of the stage, but leave some space between the text box and the edge of the stage.

- Click the gray work area outside the stage to deselect the text box (Figure 3–67).

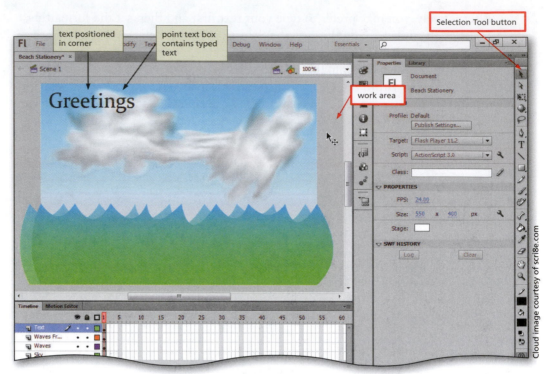

Figure 3–67

To Create an Area Text Box

The following steps create an area text box with a fixed width and height. This text box will be used as the editable text area of the stationery. In the previous steps, you created a point text box on the stage before setting text formatting. In this exercise, you will set the formatting options before creating a text box.

- Click the Text Tool button on the Tools panel to select it.

- On the Properties panel, click the Family box arrow, scroll as needed, and then select Arial (or a different font of your choice) from the list to specify the font family.

- Set the size to 14.

- On the stage, position the mouse pointer under the G in the word Greetings so that the mouse pointer displays the Text Tool icon (Figure 3–68).

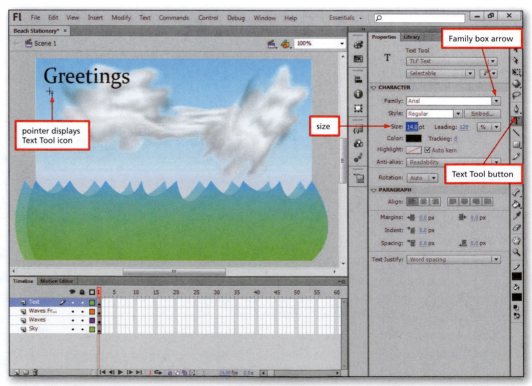

Figure 3–68

2

• Drag down and to the right to create an area text box that is centered horizontally on the stage and that extends vertically, approximately halfway down the waves.

• Type the following: This is the default message. Click here to delete it and then type your own custom message. (Figure 3–69).

How do I know I created an area text box and not a point text box?

Area text boxes display white squares in the upper-left and lower-right corners.

Figure 3–69

3

• Click the gray work area outside the stage to deselect the text box (Figure 3–70).

Figure 3–70

Cloud image courtesy of scri8e.com

Formatting Text Boxes

By default, text boxes are transparent, which is appropriate if you want the text to appear directly on the background elements. Sometimes, however, you might want a border or background color so that the text stands apart from the rest of the design. The Container and Flow area of the Properties panel (Figure 3–71 on the following page) has settings to control various aspects of the text box, such as its border, fill color and opacity, padding or spacing between the text and the text box border, vertical alignment, and the number of columns.

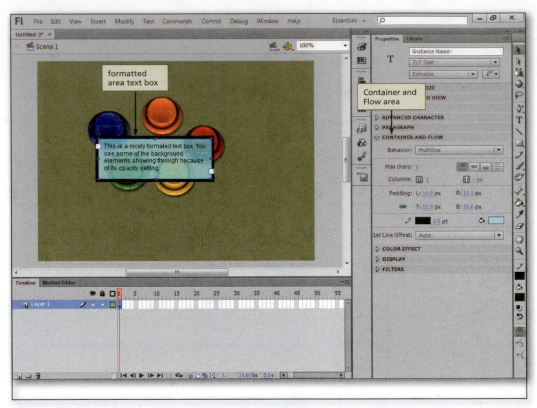

Figure 3–71

To Format a Text Box

The following steps add a border and color to the area text box. The opacity of the text box is reduced so the waves and clouds show through.

- Click the Selection Tool button to select it.

- Click the text in the area text box to select the text box and display its options on the Properties panel.

- If necessary, scroll down in the Properties panel until you see the Container and Flow area.

- If necessary, click the Container and Flow button to expand the area. Scroll as needed to display the Container and Flow settings (Figure 3–72).

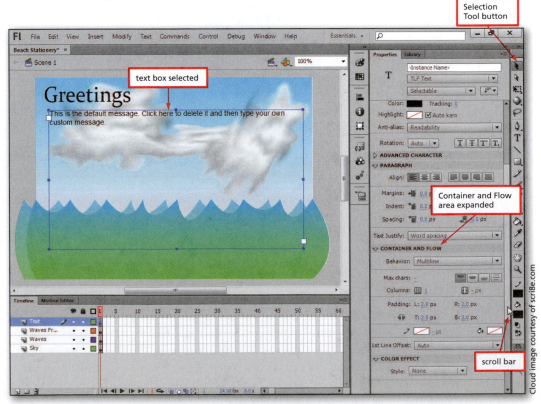

Figure 3–72

2

- If necessary, click the 'Lock the four padding values together' button so that it appears as a solid chain link and the four values can be adjusted as one.

- Click the Left padding value to select it, type 10, and press the ENTER key to create 10 pixels of space, or padding, on all sides of the text box (Figure 3–73).

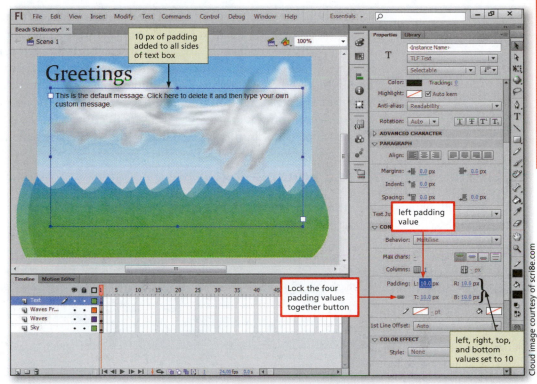

Figure 3–73

3

- Click the 'Container border color' button to display the Color picker, and then click a black swatch to change the border color to black.

- Click the 'Container background color' button and change the background color to white.

- Click the 'Container background color' button again to display the Color picker, click the Alpha value, type 50, and then press the ENTER key to set the new alpha value to 50% opacity (Figure 3–74).

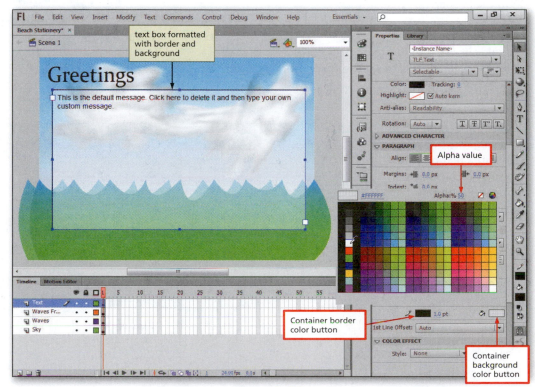

Figure 3–74

Kinds of Flash Text

Users can interact with text in a published movie, or completed Flash document, in one of three ways. The text can be Read Only, Selectable, or Editable. **Read-only** text is just that — readable. A user cannot select it for copying, nor can he or she edit it. If text is set to be **selectable**, a user can use the mouse to drag across the text to highlight it and then copy the text to their system's Clipboard and paste it into another program or document. **Editable** text is selectable, and the user can also edit it. This is helpful when you want to allow your users to create their own messages. You choose the text type from the Text type menu on the Properties panel.

To Create Read-Only and Editable Text

The following steps set the text in the point text box to be read-only and the text in the area text box to be Editable.

1

- If necessary, click the Selection Tool button on the Tools panel to select it.

- Click the Greetings text to select the point text box and display its properties on the Properties panel.

- On the Properties panel, click the Text type box arrow to display its list, and then click Read Only to set the text property (Figure 3–75).

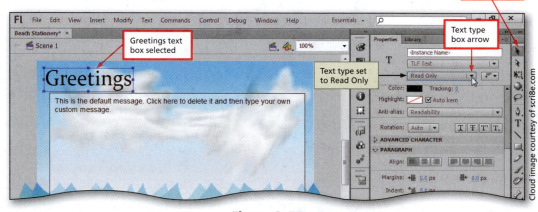

Figure 3–75

2

- Click the default message text to select the area text box and display its properties on the Properties panel.

- Click the Text type box arrow and then click Editable to set the text property (Figure 3–76).

- Press CTRL+S to save your changes.

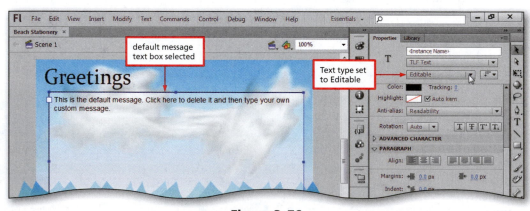

Figure 3–76

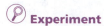 **Experiment**

- With the default message still selected, experiment with changing the container background color and Alpha (opacity) from 50% white to other colors and Alpha values. Set a different font for the message text. When you are done experimenting, set the message text back to the Arial font and its background back to 50% white.

Plan
Ahead

> **Embed fonts.**
> Embed fonts used in editable text regions. Doing so ensures that your text box will look and function as you intend.
>
> - At a minimum, embed uppercase, lowercase, numerals, and punctuation.
>
> - Embed additional characters according to your personal preference and your audience. Because many complete font families contain non-English characters, you often will not need to embed all of the characters available within a certain font.
>
> - Embedded fonts increase the file size of your Flash movie, so be selective when making choices about which characters to embed.

Embedding Fonts

Although most computer users have a wide variety of fonts installed on their systems, discrepancies do occur and can cause problems with the look of your Flash movie. If you use a specific font in a Flash project, publish the Flash movie, and then view the Flash movie on another computer, it might not look the same if the other computer does not have those fonts installed. In that case, the second computer will substitute a default font, which can affect the spacing or the look and feel of your Flash movie. To prevent this problem, you should embed your fonts.

To **embed fonts** means to incorporate the fonts used in a Flash project in the project itself. The font becomes part of the Flash project, so when the published file is viewed on different computers, the fonts are available.

Flash automatically embeds some of the fonts; characters that are used in a noneditable text box are automatically embedded by Flash. However, in situations where your project includes a default message in an editable text box, only the specific characters included in the default message are embedded automatically. A user who views the published movie and types his or her own message might type characters that were not in the original default message, and thus were not embedded. Having some font characters that are embedded and some that are not can lead to undesirable results when the published movie is viewed, such as squares or other strange characters appearing in place of the desired characters.

Flash lets you embed extra characters — in addition to those automatically embedded — so that users can display all letters, numbers, and/or punctuation from a specific font. Font embedding preferences are set using the Font Embedding dialog box, which is launched from the Embed button in the Character area on the Properties panel (Figure 3–77 on the next page).

Embedding fonts increases the size of the published file, so you only should embed additional characters when your movie includes editable text.

BTW

Corporate Fonts
Some companies require specific fonts for branding (name recognition) purposes. You might work on a project that requires you to install a custom font on your computer so that it can be integrated into a Flash movie. This is a perfect example of when to embed a font because the general public viewing your Flash movie is unlikely to have that custom font installed on their computer.

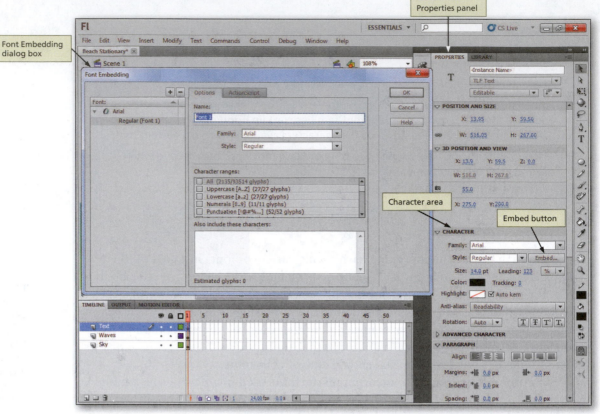

Figure 3–77

To Embed a Font

The following steps embed the complete character set for the Arial font used in the editable text box.

1

- If necessary, select the Selection Tool.

- If necessary, click the message text to select the area text box.

- If necessary, scroll up in the Properties panel to the Character area (Figure 3–78).

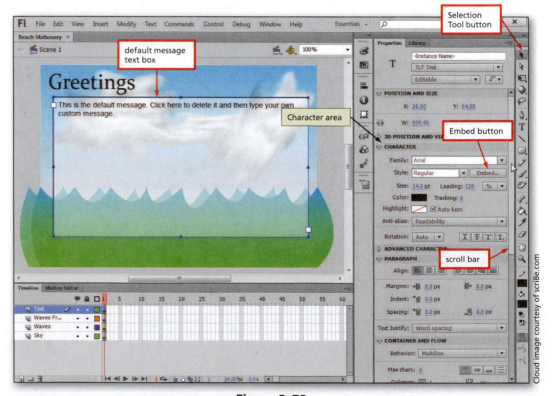

Figure 3–78

2
- Click the Embed button to display the Font Embedding dialog box.

- Click to display check marks in the boxes for Uppercase, Lowercase, Numerals, and Punctuation (Figure 3–79).

Q&A

Why do only these four check boxes get checked?

Your users are unlikely to type Latin, Japanese Kanji, Cyrillic, or the other characters specified by the different check boxes. However, if there is a chance that users might need these characters, you should check the boxes to include them.

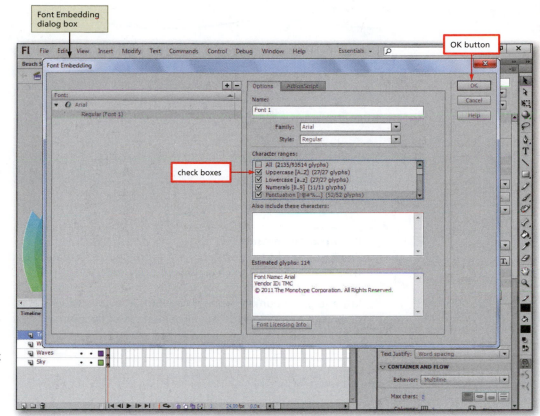

Figure 3–79

3
- Click the OK button to close the Font Embedding dialog box and save your embedding preferences.

- Press CTRL+S to save your changes.

Animating with Classic Tweens

Recall from Chapter 1 that a tween in Flash is an animation in which Flash automatically creates the in-between frames — that is, the frames between keyframes. As you learned, Flash can create three types of tween animation: shape tweens, motion tweens, and classic tweens. This section covers classic tweens.

Using a classic tween is a quick and easy way to animate a symbol's movement across the stage. It requires a single symbol on the layer you wish to animate, and also requires a beginning and ending keyframe.

You always can identify the presence of a classic tween by looking at the Timeline panel. Regular (nontweened) frames are gray. If a layer has a classic tween applied, the tweened frames will be blue and will display a right-pointing arrow across the frames (Figure 3–80 on the next page). If the frames are blue but there is no arrow, there are problems with your tween and the animation will fail.

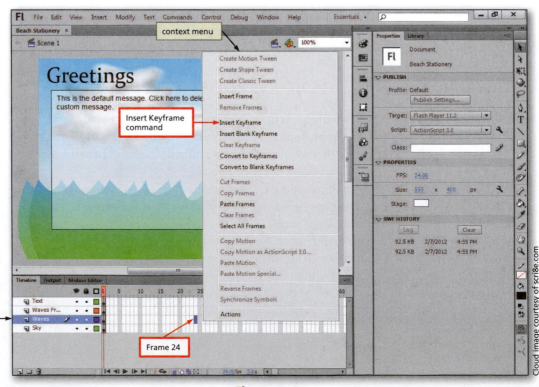

Figure 3–80

Cloud image courtesy of scri8e.com

Plan Ahead

Plan the animation.
Think about which objects on the stage might be animated. Place these objects on their own individual layers so that you can apply separate animations to each object individually without conflicts. Also determine how long you want the animation to last and plan your keyframes accordingly. Lastly, consider staggering the animation of objects so that objects do not all animate in perfect synchronicity, creating an unnatural robotic look.

To Create a Classic Tween Animation

Before creating a classic tween, be sure that the symbols you want to animate reside on their own layers; this is necessary because classic tweens only can animate a single symbol per layer. You also need to ensure that starting and ending keyframes exist. Take the time to position both the start and end states of the symbols carefully, so that Flash can create all the in-between frames.

The following steps animate the waves using a classic tween. First, you will add keyframes. Then you will alter the position of the waves on the stage at each keyframe. Finally, you will tween the frames between the keyframes.

- On the Timeline, click the Waves layer to select it.

- Right-click Frame 24 of the Waves layer on the Timeline to display a context menu (Figure 3–81).

Figure 3–81

2

- Click Insert Keyframe on the context menu to insert a keyframe at Frame 24 of the Waves layer.

- Right-click Frame 48 of the Waves layer and then click Insert Keyframe on the context menu to insert a final keyframe on the Waves layer (Figure 3–82).

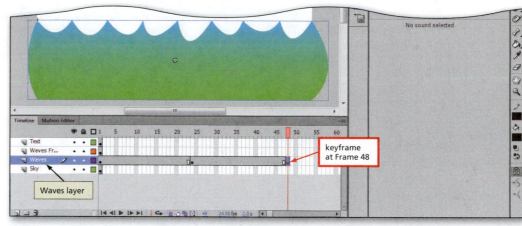

Figure 3–82

3

- Click the keyframe at Frame 24 to select it.

- Select the Free Transform Tool.

- Point to the upper-right corner of the waves on the stage until your mouse pointer displays a curved arrow.

- Drag up and to the left to rotate the waves slightly (Figure 3–83).

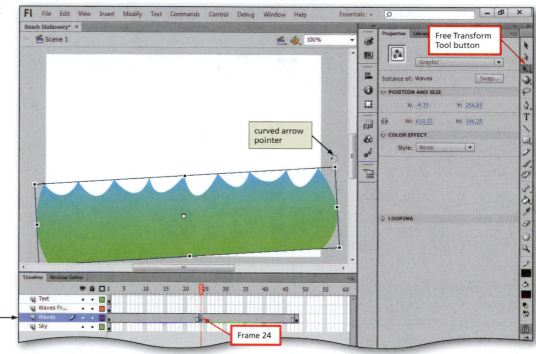

Figure 3–83

4

- Point to the lower-center sizing handle on the wave's border until your mouse pointer displays a double-headed arrow.

- Drag down to eliminate the gap below the lower-right area of the waves. The bottom of the waves should cover the stage completely (Figure 3–84).

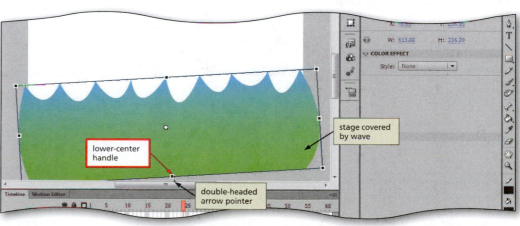

Figure 3–84

Q&A | What if I cannot see the bottom of the stage?

Use the scroll bar to the right of the stage as necessary to scroll up or down.

5

- On the Timeline, click anywhere within the gray frames between Frames 1 and 24 of the Waves layer, so you can create a tween for the first half of the wave.

- Click Insert on the Application bar to display the Insert menu (Figure 3–85).

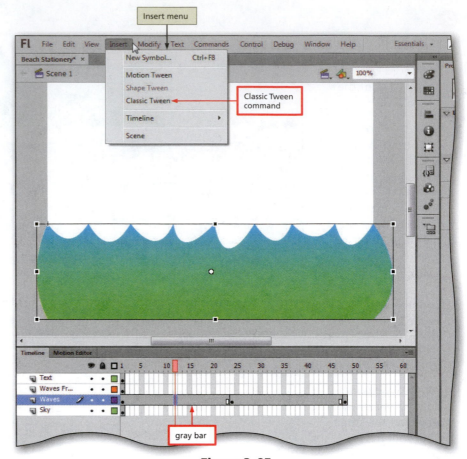

Figure 3–85

6

- Click Classic Tween on the Insert menu to create a classic tween in the first half of the Wave layer.

- Click anywhere within the gray bar between Frames 25 and 48 of the Waves layer on the Timeline, so you can create a tween between the keyframes at Frames 25 and 48.

- Click Insert on the Application bar and then click Classic Tween to create a classic tween in the second half of the Wave layer (Figure 3–86).

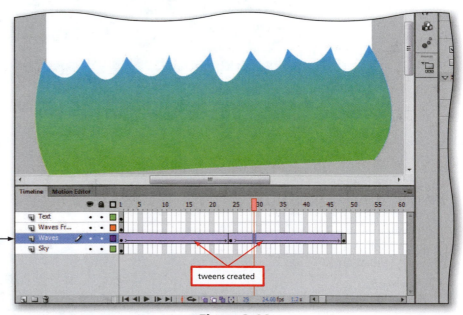

Figure 3–86

Other Ways

1. Right-click gray barred frames on Timeline, click Create Classic Tween on context menu

To Animate the Front Waves

The following steps animate the other layer of waves using classic tweens. Keyframes are placed at different locations than those of the previous Waves layer so that the final animation looks natural. Each layer of waves will move at different intervals.

1 Click the Waves Front layer on the Timeline to select it.

2 Right-click Frame 16 of the Waves Front layer on the Timeline and then click Insert Keyframe to insert a keyframe at Frame 16.

3 Repeat Step 2 to create keyframes at Frames 32 and 48 of the Waves Front layer.

4 Select the keyframe at Frame 16 of the Waves Front layer.

5 Select the Free Transform Tool on the Tools Panel, if necessary, and rotate the waves on the Waves Front layer slightly down and to the right.

6 Drag the bottom-center sizing handle of the wave's border down, to stretch the wave taller so that the lower-left corner of the wave is even with the bottom edge of the waves from the Waves layer.

7 Select the keyframe at Frame 32 of the Waves Front layer and rotate the waves up and to the left.

8 Drag the bottom-center sizing handle of the wave's border down, to stretch the wave taller so that the lower-right corner of the wave is even with the bottom edge of the waves from the Waves layer.

9 One at a time, right-click each of the three gray sections of the Waves Front layer, and then click Create Classic Tween on the context menu so that the entire layer is animated. Your screen should resemble Figure 3–87.

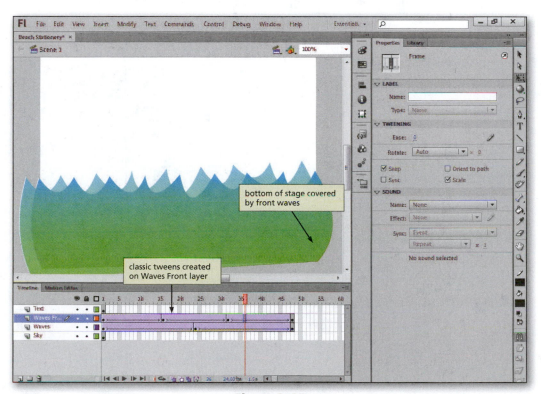

Figure 3–87

To Extend the Remaining Layers

Currently, the Text and Sky layers only appear at Frame 1, but the tweened animation extends through Frame 48. The following steps extend the Text and Sky layers to Frame 48 so that they are visible for the duration of the animation.

1
• Right-click Frame 48 of the Text layer to display the context menu (Figure 3–88).

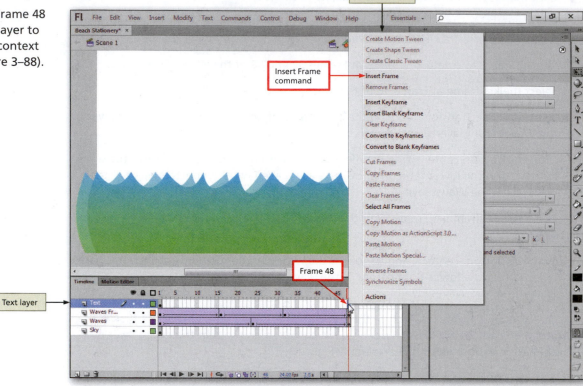

Figure 3–88

2
• Click Insert Frame on the context menu to insert a frame and extend the Text layer, making it visible throughout all 48 frames (Figure 3–89).

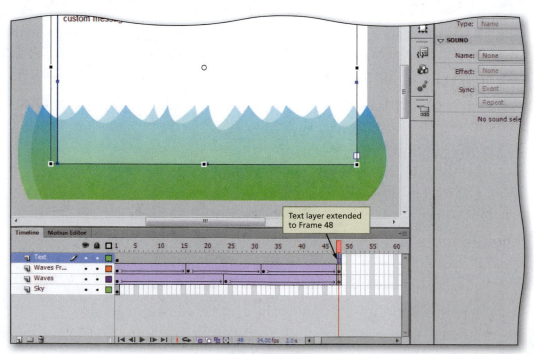

Figure 3–89

3

- Right-click Frame 48 of the Sky layer to display the context menu.

- Click Insert Frame on the context menu to insert a frame and extend the Sky layer so that it is visible throughout all 48 frames.

- Click the gray work area to deselect all objects.

- Press CTRL+S to save your changes (Figure 3–90).

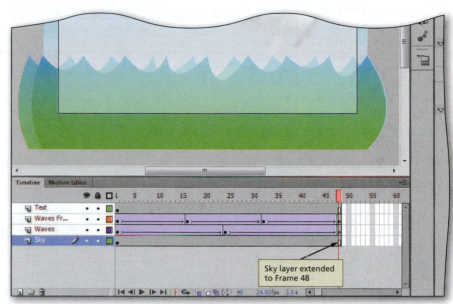

Sky layer extended to Frame 48

Figure 3–90

Testing Movies

Recall from Chapter 1 that the process of generating a Web version of a Flash file for use on a Web site is called publishing. Viewing a Flash project in Flash is not the same as viewing the published movie in a Web browser or mobile device. As you work on your movie, you will need to test it along the way to ensure that it works as you intend. Publishing a movie simply to test it is not efficient because you have to configure the publish settings, publish the movie, browse on your hard drive to the published files, open the published files, and then close the published files to return to Flash. It is more efficient to simply test the movie from within Flash.

The Test Movie command, available from the Control menu on the Application bar, displays the movie in a Flash player window, allowing you to see a preview of how your movie will look and act when published. This command also creates a SWF file with the same name as the Flash movie in the same file storage location as the Flash movie. Every time you issue the Test Movie command, that SWF file is overwritten with a fresh copy. Flash then displays the current SWF file in the Flash player window. If your Flash movie includes text, Flash also creates a text layout file in the same storage location, which helps Flash load the movie faster. Because Flash re-creates the SWF and text layout files as necessary each time you run the Test Movie command, you safely can delete either of the two files at any time. When you are done testing your movie, you can close the player window to return to Flash.

To Test a Movie

The stationery movie is complete. As you learn more about Flash animation, you might decide to animate the greeting or message text boxes to fade in or out, or add other animation features. The following steps test the movie so that you can check the functionality and display before publishing.

1

• Click Control on the Application bar to display the Control menu.

• Point to Test Movie on the Control menu to display the Test Movie submenu (Figure 3–91).

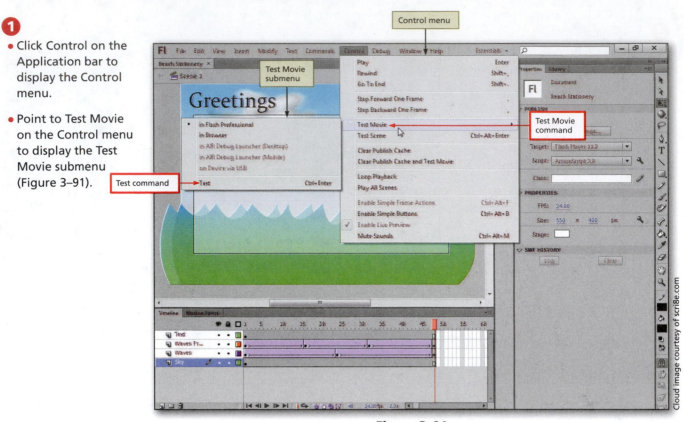

Figure 3–91

Cloud image courtesy of scri8e.com

2

• Click Test on the Test Movie submenu to test the movie in a player window (Figure 3–92).

🔍 **Experiment**

• Try to select the Greetings text in the Beach Stationery player window and notice that because the greeting is read-only, you cannot do so.

Figure 3–92

3

- Click the default message text box.

- Drag to select all of the default message text (Figure 3–93).

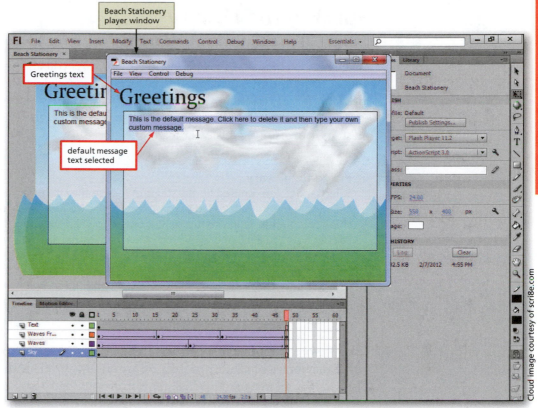

Figure 3–93

4

- Press the DELETE key to delete the editable text.

- Type Welcome back! Hope you had a wonderful time at the beach. It's back to reality now! or a message of your choice (Figure 3–94).

5

- Close the Beach Stationery player window to return to Flash.

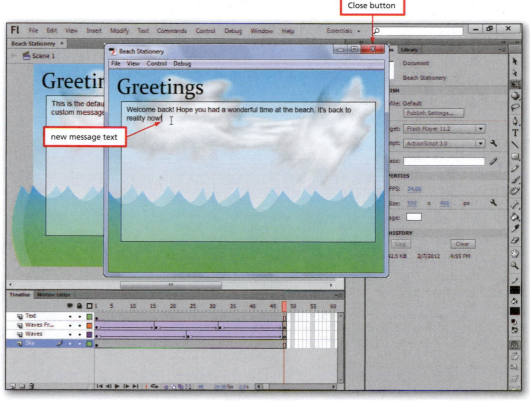

Figure 3–94

Other Ways

1. Press CTRL+ENTER

Purging the Library

In developing Flash movies, many designers find it useful to experiment with various images and elements as they perfect the project. As you add and swap symbols or import images to the stage, the library grows. If you delete an imported image from the stage, it still resides in the library. Similarly, symbols that have no instances on the stage also reside in the library. These unused items increase the overall size of your Flash movie, resulting in slower load times for users.

Before publishing a movie for distribution and general use, it is a good idea to purge the library of all unused items. **Purging** helps reduce the overall size of the Flash movie. To delete individual items from the library, you can select them in the Library panel and click the Delete button on the Library panel status bar. The benefit to this technique is that you can choose which items to delete selectively. For example, the library might contain some symbols that are not currently being used but that you want to save for possible future use if the movie ever has to be edited. The downside to this technique is that you may accidentally delete an item that is in use on the stage — deleting it from the library will remove it from the stage.

Flash offers a Select Unused Items command available on the Library panel's menu. You can use this command to select all unused items, then click the Delete button to purge the library.

To Purge the Library

The following steps select and delete unused library items, reducing the size of the movie.

1
- Click the Library panel tab to select the Library panel.

- Click the Waves symbol on the Library panel to select it (Figure 3–95).

Q&A
There are items in the library that I did not add. What are they?

You will see all the symbols you created, in addition to other items Flash created automatically. When you imported the Better Cloud image, Flash added the image itself to the library. You later used that image to create a symbol, which is also stored in the library. Additionally, Flash stored the embedded font in the library.

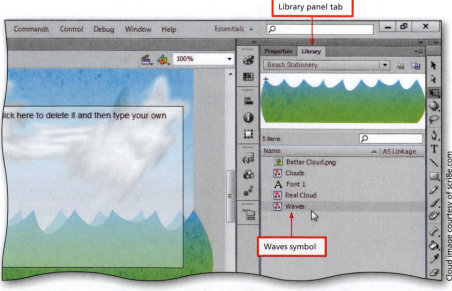

Figure 3–95

2

- Click the Delete button on the Library panel status bar to delete the Waves symbol from the stage (Figure 3–96).

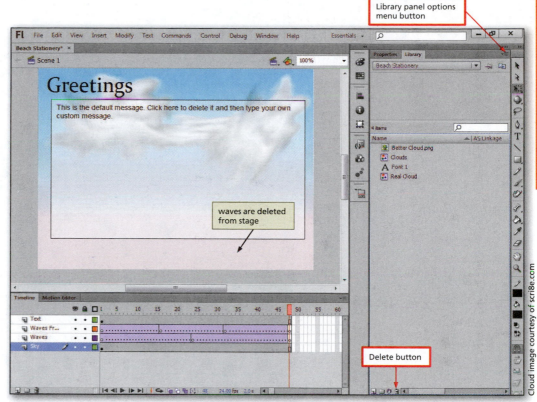

Figure 3–96

3

- Press CTRL+Z to undo the deletion and redisplay the waves on the stage and in the library.

- Click the Library panel options menu button to display the panel menu (Figure 3–97).

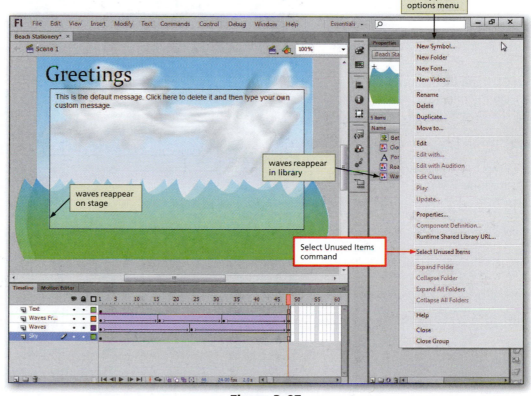

Figure 3–97

• Click the Select Unused Items command in the menu to select unused library items (Figure 3–98).

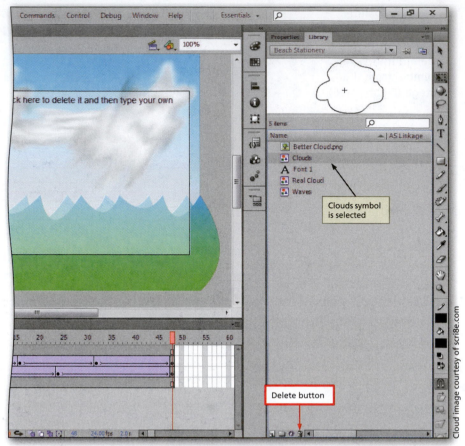

Figure 3–98

• Click the Delete button on the Library panel status bar to delete the Clouds symbol (Figure 3–99).

• Press CTRL+S to save the Beach Stationery file.

Figure 3–99

To Quit Flash

The stationery and its movie are complete. The following step quits Flash.

 1 Click the Close button on the Application bar to quit Flash.

Chapter Summary

In this chapter, you learned about the benefits of using symbols and instances. You created symbols from an existing object on the stage and from scratch using the Library panel. You learned to add instances to the stage using the Library panel. You also learned to achieve variety in instances by modifying their shape and rotation with the Free Transform Tool and by modifying their color properties with the Properties panel. You then learned to apply the same modification to all instances by editing the original parent symbol and you swapped symbols used by instances on the stage. You learned to hide the pasteboard to give you a better idea of how the final published movie will look. You learned to add two types of text boxes and specify whether text is read-only or can be edited by the user. You also learned to format both the text and the text box itself. You learned how to test a movie to see how the published movie will function. Finally, you learned how to purge the library of unused items to minimize the movie's file size.

The items listed below include all the new Flash skills you have learned in this chapter:

1. Transform a Gradient Transition (FL 157)
2. Lock a Layer (FL 159)
3. Use the Subselection Tool to Display Anchor Points (FL 162)
4. Add Anchor Points using the Add Anchor Point Tool (FL 163)
5. Reshape Line Segments using the Selection Tool (FL 164)
6. Create a Symbol from the Stage (FL 165)
7. View the Library Panel and Create a New Symbol (FL 168)
8. Add Instances to the Stage (FL 171)
9. Modify Instances using the Free Transform Tool (FL 174)
10. Change the Opacity of an Instance (FL 176)
11. Create a New Symbol from an Imported Image (FL 178)
12. Swap a Symbol (FL 179)
13. Edit the Waves Symbol (FL 182)
14. Hide the Pasteboard (FL 183)
15. Create a Point Text Box (FL 186)
16. Set Character Formatting and Type Text in a Point Text Box (FL 187)
17. Create an Area Text Box (FL 188)
18. Format a Text Box (FL 190)
19. Create Read-Only and Editable Text (FL 192)
20. Embed a Font (FL 194)
21. Create a Classic Tween Animation (FL 196)
22. Extend the Remaining Layers (FL 200)
23. Test a Movie (FL 201)
24. Purge the Library (FL 204)

Apply Your Knowledge

Reinforce the skills and apply the concepts you learned in this chapter.

Creating a Pest Control Banner

Instructions: To complete this assignment, you will be required to use the Data Files for Students. Visit www.cengage.com/ct/studentdownload for detailed instructions or contact your instructor for information about accessing the required files. Start Flash and perform the customization steps on pages FL 153 through FL 154. Open the Apply 3-1 Pest file from the Chapter 03 folder of the Data Files for Students.

In this exercise, you will create a Web banner for a pest control company. Rather than drawing and duplicating ants, you will draw a single ant, convert it to a symbol, and then add multiple instances to the stage. Figure 3–100 shows the final drawing.

Figure 3–100

Perform the following tasks:

1. Click File, click Save As, navigate to your file storage location, and save a copy of the file as Apply 3-1 Pest Complete.

2. To draw the ant:

   a. Click the Text layer on the Timeline, then click the New Layer button on the Timeline status bar to create a new layer above Text.

   b. Name the new layer, Ants.

   c. Click the Oval Tool button on the Tools panel and ensure object drawing mode is enabled.

   d. On the Properties panel, set the stroke color to No Stroke and the fill color to black.

   e. Draw an oval on the stage and then use the Properties panel to set its dimensions and position as follows: Width: 44, Height: 35, X position: 78, Y position: 96.

   f. Draw a second oval on the stage and then use the Properties panel to set its dimensions and position as follows: Width: 71, Height: 27, X position: 116, Y position: 100.

   g. Draw a third oval on the stage and then use the Properties panel to set its dimensions and position as follows: Width: 44, Height: 35, X position: 182, Y position: 96.

   h. Click the Pencil Tool button on the Tools panel and ensure object drawing mode is enabled. Set the pencil mode to Straighten.

   i. On the Properties panel, set the stroke color to black and the stroke height to 2. Draw six legs and antennae, as shown in Figure 3–100. Do not draw the small pincers at the head. You will draw those later.

3. To convert the drawing to a symbol:

   a. Click the Ants layer on the Timeline to select all objects on the layer.

   b. Click Modify on the Application bar and then click Convert to Symbol.

   c. Name the symbol, Ant, and ensure the Type is set to Graphic. Click the OK button to complete the conversion.

4. To add instances:

   a. Click the Library panel.

   b. Drag the Ant symbol from the Library panel to the stage to create a second instance.

   c. Drag two more instances onto the stage so that there are four ants.

5. To modify instances:

   a. Click the Free Transform Tool button on the Tools panel.

   b. Click one of the ants to select it.

   c. Hold the SHIFT key as you drag a corner handle in toward the center to reduce the size of the ant proportionally.

   d. Point to the transformation border until the mouse pointer displays the circular rotation arrow, then drag to rotate the ant to your liking.

   e. Point to the inside of the transformation border and drag the ant to a location of your liking.

   f. Resize, rotate, and position the remaining ants until your screen resembles Figure 3–100.

6. To modify the symbol:

   a. Double-click any ant to edit the symbol in place.

   b. Click the Zoom Tool button on the Tools panel and then click the ant several times to zoom in to your liking, or ALT+CLICK the ant to zoom out.

   c. If necessary, use the scroll bars at the bottom and right of the stage to center the ant being edited.

   d. Click the Pencil Tool button and set the pencil mode to Smooth.

   e. Draw two small pincers at the head, as shown in Figure 3–100.

   f. Click Scene 1 at the upper-left area of the toolbar above the stage to exit symbol editing mode.

   g. Double-click the Zoom Tool button to zoom back to 100%. Use the scroll bars, if necessary, to center the stage on your screen.

7. Press CTRL+S to save the Flash movie.

8. Close Flash.

9. Submit the file in the format specified by your instructor.

Extend Your Knowledge

Extend the skills you learned in this chapter and experiment with new skills. You may need to use Help to complete the assignment.

Creating a Band Bio

Instructions: To complete this assignment, you will be required to use the Data Files for Students. Visit www.cengage.com/ct/studentdownload for detailed instructions or contact your instructor for information about accessing the required files. Start Flash and perform the customization steps on pages FL 153 through FL 154. Open the Extend 3-1 Bio file from the Chapter 03 folder of the Data Files for Students.

Continued >

Extend Your Knowledge *continued*

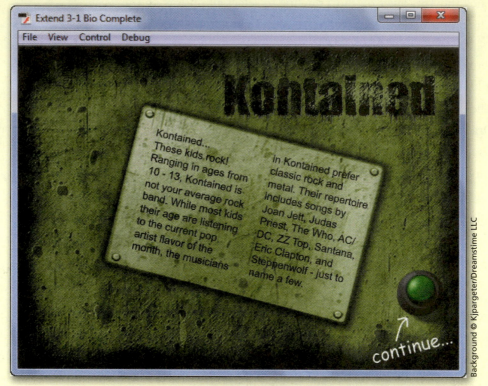

Figure 3–101

Perform the following tasks:

1. Navigate to your file storage location and save the Extend 3-1 Bio document as Extend 3-1 Bio Complete.

2. Minimize Flash, navigate to the Chapter 03 folder of the Data Files for Students, and double-click the Extend 3-1 Text file to open it in your default text editor.

3. Press CTRL+A to select all the text, press CTRL+C to copy the selected text, close your text editor, and then click the Flash button on the Windows taskbar to return to Flash.

4. Click the Text Tool button on the Tools panel and set the following properties in the Properties panel: Family = Arial, Style = Regular, Size = 13, Color = black.

5. Click Frame 1 on the Text layer on the Timeline, and then drag on the stage to create an area text box. You will resize it later.

6. Press CTRL+V to paste the copied text into the text box.

7. Click the Free Transform Tool button on the Tools panel.

8. Use the Free Transform Tool to rotate the text box so that its top edge is roughly parallel to the top edge of the rectangular design on the background.

9. Use the Type Tool to resize the text box so that it almost fills the rectangular design on the background, but still leaves appropriate space around the outside of the text. You might have to switch between the Free Transform Tool to rotate the text box and the Text Tool to resize the text box. Refer to Figure 3–101 (though your text will not yet appear in multiple columns).

10. If necessary, scroll down the Properties panel until you locate the Container and Flow area. Change the Columns value to 2.

11. Click the Text Tool button on the Tools panel, click Frame 5 on the Text layer on the Timeline, and drag a second area text box on the stage.

12. Use the Free Transform Tool to rotate the text box and position it in approximately the same position as the previous text box. Use the Text Tool to resize the text box so it almost fills the rectangular design on the background.

13. Switch to the Selection Tool and click Frame 1 on the Text layer on the Timeline.

14. Click the red square on the lower-right border of the text box to load the mouse pointer with the overflow text.

15. Click Frame 5 on the Text layer on the Timeline and then click inside the empty text box to move the overflow text into it.

16. If necessary, scroll down the Properties panel until you locate the Container and Flow area. Change the Columns value to 2.

17. Press CTRL+ENTER to test the movie. Click the green button in the player window to move back and forth between the two frames containing text. When you are through testing the movie, close the player window.

18. Save your changes and submit the file in the format specified by your instructor.

Make It Right

Analyze a project and correct all errors and/or improve the design.

Optimizing a Document with Symbols

Instructions: To complete this assignment, you will be required to use the Data Files for Students. Visit www.cengage.com/ct/studentdownload for detailed instructions or contact your instructor for information about accessing the required files. Start Flash and perform the customization steps on pages FL 153 through FL 154. Open the Make It Right 3-1 Cars file from the Chapter 03 folder of the Data Files for Students. Navigate to your file storage location and save the file with the name, Make It Right 3-1 Cars Complete.

You are developing the opening screen for a Flash game, but the scene needs some improvement (Figure 3–102). In the original file, each car, yellow line, and white parking block is a unique shape, which adds to the overall size of the file. Additionally, the yellow lines are not of equal height, nor are they aligned. Lastly, the text at the top is cramped inside its white container and would look better with some padding.

1. Delete all but one white parking block. Convert the remaining parking block into a graphic symbol. Add parking block instances to the stage to re-create the scene. Use the Align panel to align and evenly space the parking blocks. (*Hint*: Use one of the two Space options on the Align panel.)

2. Delete all but one yellow parking line, convert the remaining yellow line into a graphic symbol, and replace the deleted lines with instances. Ensure all the yellow lines are aligned and are the same size.

3. Delete all but one car, convert the remaining car into a graphic symbol, and replace the deleted cars with instances, making sure they are aligned and evenly spaced. (*Hint*: Lock the other layers to make selecting the cars easier. You might want to keep the white car and delete all others to make changing the colors of the instances easier.) Modify the tint of the instances so that each car is a different color of your choice.

4. Add 10 pixels of padding around all four sides of the text. Save your changes and submit the file in the format specified by your instructor.

Continued >

Make It Right *continued*

Figure 3–102

In the Lab

Design and/or create a project using the guidelines, concepts, and skills presented in this chapter. Labs are listed in order of increasing difficulty.

Lab 1: Creating a Piano Keyboard

Problem: As part of a group project to create a piano keyboard for use on a music store's Web site, your task is to create the initial keyboard layout, as shown in Figure 3–103. The group's programmer will make the keys playable later. Because the program code will add to the file size, you need to minimize the impact of the graphics on the overall file size. Use symbols and instances to achieve this optimization.

Figure 3–103

Instructions: Perform the following tasks:

1. Start Flash, create a new ActionScript 3.0 document, and save it in your file storage location with the file name Lab 3-1 Keyboard Complete.

2. Use the Rectangle Tool to draw a rectangle that covers the stage. Fill the rectangle with a dark gray color. Name the layer Background and lock it so you do not accidentally edit the background rectangle. Create a new layer above the Background layer.

3. With the Rectangle Tool still selected, set the following options in the Properties panel:
   a. Stroke color: black
   b. Fill color: white
   c. Stroke height: 1
   d. Rectangle options — corner radius of 3

4. Draw a rectangle and use the Properties panel to size it as follows:
   a. Width: 40
   b. Height: 200

5. Convert the rectangle to a graphic symbol named White Key.

6. Add White Key instances to the stage until you have a total of 14 keys. SHIFT+click all the keys, and then use the Align panel to align and evenly space the keys.

7. Click the gray work area to deselect the keys.

8. Rename the layer White Keys.

9. Create a new layer above White Keys and name the new layer Black Keys.

10. Select the Rectangle Tool and set the following options in the Properties panel:
    a. Stroke color: No Stroke
    b. Fill color: black
    c. Stroke height: 1
    d. Rectangle Options — corner radius of 3

11. Draw a rectangle on the Black Keys layer and use the Properties panel to size it as follows:
    a. Width: 32
    b. Height: 125

12. Convert the rectangle to a graphic symbol named Black Key.

13. Add Black Key instances to the stage until you have a total of 10 black keys. Move the black keys into position and use the Align panel to align them, if necessary. It is fine if the keys extend beyond the stage into the work area. Refer to Figure 3–103 if you are unfamiliar with the layout of black keys on a piano keyboard.

14. Save your changes.

15. Submit the file in the format specified by your instructor.

In the Lab

Lab 2: Creating an Aquarium Scene

Problem: A local pet store has asked you to create an animation for its Web site. The movie will be used to promote an upcoming sale on fish. A programmer will be responsible for the actual animation. Your task is to provide a starting screen with gravel, plants, and a few fish that the programmer can later animate. You will use symbols to minimize the file size and to make editing objects more efficient. The final scene is displayed in Figure 3–104.

Continued >

In the Lab *continued*

Figure 3–104

Note: To complete this assignment, you will be required to use the Data Files for Students. Visit www.cengage.com/ct/studentdownload for detailed instructions or contact your instructor for information about accessing the required files.

Instructions: Perform the following tasks:

1. Start Flash, open the Lab 3-2 Fish file from the Chapter 03 folder of the Data Files for Students, and save it in your file storage location as Lab 3-2 Fish Complete.

2. Create a new layer above the Water layer and name it Gravel Bottom.

3. Drag instances of the Rock symbol from the Library panel to the stage. Resize and rotate the instances to achieve variety. Cover about the bottom one-fourth of the stage with the rocks. (*Hint:* Lock each layer as you complete it to avoid accidental editing.)

4. Create a new layer above Gravel Bottom and name it Plants.

5. Drag instances of the Plant symbol from the Library panel to the stage. Resize and rotate the instances to achieve variety. Use the Properties panel to apply a Color Effect (Tint or Brightness) to a few of the instances to vary the color between yellows and greens. Refer to Figure 3–104 as a guide.

6. Create a new layer above the Plants layer and name it Gravel Top.

7. Drag a few instances of the Rock symbol to the Gravel Top layer and arrange them around the bottom of the plants so it appears the plants are growing out of the gravel. Resize and rotate the top gravel to your liking.

8. Create a final layer above the Gravel Top layer and name it Fish.

9. Import the Lab 3-2 Fish Image 1 from the Chapter 03 folder to the stage. Convert the image on the stage to a graphic symbol named Fish 1. Import the Lab 3-2 Fish Image 2 from the Chapter 03 folder to the stage. Convert the image on the stage to a graphic symbol named Fish 2.

10. Use the Free Transform Tool to resize the fish to your liking.

11. Drag more instances of each Fish symbol onto the Fish layer. Resize and rotate them to your liking. Apply a Color Effect (Tint or Brightness) to the instances to vary them. Arrange them to your liking. If necessary, refer to Figure 3–104 for placement.

12. Save your changes and submit the file in the format specified by your instructor.

In the Lab

Lab 3: Creating a Gym Web Banner

Problem: A local gym has asked you to create a banner for its Web site. The graphic needs to feature a stack of weights next to a barbell. The final image is displayed in Figure 3–105.

Figure 3–105

Instructions: Perform the following tasks:

Start Flash and create a new ActionScript 3.0 file. Create a bar for the barbell with the Line Tool with a medium gray stroke color and a stroke height of 10. Create a rectangle with a black fill, no stroke, and rounded corners with a corner radius of about 5 to use as a weight for the barbell. Position the weight on the bar and adjust the size of each until the proportions are to your liking.

Convert the rectangular weight to a graphic symbol named Plate. Drag additional Plate instances to the stage and arrange them on the bar. Drag three more Plate instances to the stage to arrange in a stack next to the barbell. Resize and rotate the plates to match Figure 3–105.

Create a point text box with light gray text and the Arial font family. Type 45, position it in the middle of the large plate on the right of the barbell, make the text bold, and adjust the font size so that it fits on the plate. Duplicate the text box and position it over the large plate on the left of the barbell. Duplicate the text again, rotate it 90 degrees counterclockwise, and position it in the center of the large plate at the bottom of the stack. Label the remaining plates 25 and 10.

Create additional text boxes above and below the weights with the gym name and tagline (make up your own text). Use your best judgment when formatting the text and container.

Save the file in your file storage location with the file name Lab 3-3 Gym Complete. Submit it in the format specified by your instructor.

Cases and Places

Apply your creative thinking and problem-solving skills to design and implement a solution.

Note: To complete these assignments, you will be required to use the Data Files for Students. Visit www.cengage.com/ct/studentdownload for detailed instructions or contact your instructor for information about accessing the required files.

Continued >

Cases and Places *continued*

1: Create a Book

Academic

A neighborhood preschool has asked you to create a section of their Web site that will include a book with animated pages. Children will be able to click the book pages to flip through the book. Before animating the pages, you need to create the text boxes to hold the text. Open the file Case 3-1 Book from the Chapter 03 folder of the Data Files for Students and save it in your file storage location as Case 3-1 Book Complete. Create a new layer named Text. Use the Text layer for the remainder of this project. Create a point text box at the upper-left of the book, type Storybook Tales, and format the text to your liking so that it acts as a title to the story. Create an area text box on the left page, under the title, that fills the page but still leaves appropriate space around the outside so that the text is not up against the edge of the page. Minimize Flash, open the Case 3-1 Storybook Text file from your Chapter 03 folder, copy all the text, and then close the text file. Paste the copied text into the area text block on the stage. Format the text with the Times New Roman font family, regular style, size 14, and color black. Display the text in two columns. Create a second area text block on the right side of the book with the same settings. Paste any overflow text into the new text box. Resize the text boxes, if necessary, so there is no more overflow text. Save your changes.

2: Draw Picture Frames for a Family Tree

Personal

As part of your personal Web site, you would like to have a page displaying framed pictures of family members. Your first step is to draw the picture frames. Use the Rectangle Tool to draw a large rectangle on the stage. Use a stroke height of at least 30 so that you can later add text to the frame. Experiment with positive and negative values for the rounded corner radius to achieve an appealing frame. Use the Selection Tool to reshape the sides of the rectangle so that each side is slightly curved. Use the Oval or PolyStar Tools to create additional shapes to use as ornamental decorations around the frame. Convert the frame to a graphic symbol named Frame. Create a total of three instances of the frame on the stage and vary their size, angle of rotation, and color. Create one point text box for each frame and use a font family, style, color, and size of your choice for each. Use text boxes to give each frame a label using names of your family members. Format the text boxes so that the text box container has both stroke and fill colors and appropriate padding around the text. Position each text box at the lower-center of a frame. Save the Flash file in your file storage location with the name Case 3-2 Frames Complete.

3: Create a Weather Forecast

Professional

The local Chamber of Commerce has hired you to create a Flash movie that displays projected local weather conditions on its Web site. Start a new blank ActionScript 3.0 file and save it in your file storage location as Case 3-3 Weather Complete. Resize the stage to 300 pixels wide by 250 pixels tall and give it a light blue background. Create a new graphic symbol for the sun and name it appropriately. Use the PolyStar Tool to create a sun shape on the stage with an appropriate color. Create another graphic symbol that includes a cloud with a few raindrops. Create a final graphic symbol that includes several clouds, but no rain. Name the weather symbols to represent their meaning. When you are through, exit symbol editing mode and return to Scene 1. Create a point text box at the top of the stage and type Weekly Outlook in the text box, formatting the text to your liking. Create an area text box and type the days of the week, one day per line. Increase the Leading so that there is ample space between each word. Format the text box to include a stroke color, a fill color, equal padding on the top, right, and bottom sides, and significantly more padding on the left side. (The space to the left of each word is where the weather icon will be displayed.) Center the text box horizontally on the stage and drag a sunny, rainy, or cloudy instance to the left of each day to indicate the projected weather. Resize the instances as needed. Save your changes.

Importing Files between Photoshop and Flash

Objectives

You will have mastered the material in this project when you can:

- Describe the need to integrate Photoshop and Flash
- Prepare images for roundtripping
- Import Photoshop documents to the Flash stage
- Import Photoshop layers to Flash layers
- Edit destructively in Photoshop from Flash
- Send an edited image from Photoshop back to Flash

Importing Files between Photoshop and Flash

Introduction

In the Photoshop and Flash sections of this book, you learned to work with layers in both programs. You also learned basic Photoshop editing techniques and Flash animation techniques using keyframes, shape tweens, and classic tweens.

From working with the two programs, you have seen the strengths of both applications: Photoshop excels at editing images while Flash excels at creating animations. Because many animation projects require images, it is natural to use both programs to create a single project.

In this chapter, you will employ features and techniques you learned in earlier chapters as you integrate Photoshop and Flash, using them together to create an animated product showcase slide show for the Web.

Project — Animated Slide Show

Retailers know that using imagery to sell a product is more desirable than using only words. Although a description or explanation of a product is helpful, users browsing Web stores are more likely to glance at product thumbnails before making a decision to read about a product. Using high-quality images in an animated slide show is an excellent way to grab your user's attention and showcase sale items.

In this project, you will create an animated Flash slide show for a food Web site promoting gourmet olive oil (Figure 1). You will start by organizing the images in Photoshop layers. You then will import the Photoshop document into Flash, where you will create the slide show animation. Throughout the process, you will switch between Photoshop and Flash as you use these two programs together to create one cohesive project.

© Pawel Kryj, Gunnar Brink/Stock.xchng

Figure 1

Overview

As you read this chapter, you will learn how to create the animated slide show shown in Figure 1 by performing these general tasks:

- Edit images in Photoshop.
- Organize images in Photoshop layers.
- Import Photoshop files into Flash.
- Animate images in Flash.
- Transfer an image from Flash to Photoshop for editing.
- Roundtrip between Photoshop and Flash.

General Project Guidelines

When creating a project, the actions you perform and decisions you make will affect the appearance and characteristics of the finished product. As you create a movie, such as the one shown in Figure 1, you should follow these general guidelines:

1. **Plan the animation.** Although creating a Flash animation is very much an organic process, requiring trial and error, it is helpful to have an idea of the overall length of the animation. Sometimes the overall length is determined by the time you want certain smaller parts of the animation to last.

2. **Organize images in Photoshop layers.** Before importing images into Flash, perform all edits and touch-ups in Photoshop. If possible, keep individual images on separate layers within a single Photoshop document as it is easier to keep track of a single file.

3. **Use the right tool for the right job.** As any project progresses, unexpected problems will arise. You might need to edit images or change the length of animations. Use the right software for a task. If a bitmap image needs to be edited, use Photoshop. Do not hesitate to use multiple programs to complete a single project.

When necessary, more specific details concerning the above guidelines are presented at appropriate points in the chapter. The chapter also will identify the actions performed and decisions made regarding these guidelines during the creation of the edited photo shown in Figure 1.

Roundtripping

The term **roundtripping** refers to moving back and forth between multiple programs to complete a single project or a series of related projects. For example, multiple programs can be used to create a Web site where one program is used to edit images and a different program is used to create HTML code. In a more complex project, a designer might use one program to edit images, a second program to animate the images, and a third program to create a Web page that incorporates the animation. Additionally, a fourth program can be used to create a brochure for print using the edited images, while a fifth program can use the images to create an e-book.

The Adobe Creative Suite programs, including Photoshop, Flash, and Dreamweaver, are designed to work together. Rather than doing work in one program, closing it, and importing the file in a second, seemingly unrelated program, Adobe makes the process of roundtripping more efficient by integrating programs so that you can move files back and forth from one program to another. This feature, combined with the similar workspaces of each program, creates a consistent work experience.

**Plan
Ahead**

> **Organize images in Photoshop layers.**
> Name your Photoshop layers so that the layer names describe the layer contents. The default names of Layer 0, Layer 1, Shape 1, and so on will not be helpful in identifying what is on a layer once the Photoshop file is imported to Flash. Because each Photoshop layer is imported as a Flash layer, naming the layer in Photoshop ensures consistency across both the original Photoshop file and the Flash file.

Preparing Images

If you want to animate a layered Photoshop image, Flash can place each Photoshop layer automatically into a Flash layer on the main Timeline. It is important to think about the size of the Photoshop image and its layers. For example, if you want your animation to run in a 300 × 300 pixel window, you need to resize the Photoshop image to match. The layer names are maintained across applications, so it is a good idea to name the layers in Photoshop for easy identification when imported to Flash (Figure 2).

(a) Photoshop layers   **(b) Flash layers on the Timeline**

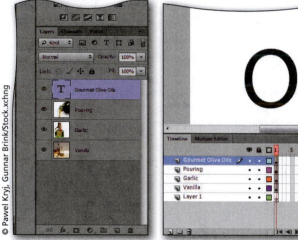

© Pawel Kryj, Gunnar Brink/Stock.xchng

Figure 2

To Start Photoshop and Open a File

To complete this assignment, you will be required to use the Data Files for Students. Visit www.cengage.com/ct/studentdownload for detailed instructions or contact your instructor for information about accessing the required files. The following steps start Photoshop and open the Photos file from the Data Files for Students.

1 Start Photoshop.

2 Press CTRL+O to display the Open File dialog box. Navigate to the storage location of the Data Files for Students and the Integration 01 folder.

3 Double-click the Photos.psd file to open it.

To Resize Images

You will begin this integration project by examining a Photoshop file containing multiple layers of photos. You will resize the Photoshop file so that each image is sized at 300 pixels by 300 pixels — an appropriate size for a Web page slide show. The following steps change the size of the image.

1 Click Image on the Photoshop Application bar and then click Image Size to open the Image Size window.

2 In the Pixel Dimensions area, change the units to Pixels if necessary.

3 In the Pixel Dimensions area, change both the Width and Height to 300 and then click the OK button to resize the Photoshop document.

4 If necessary, double-click the Zoom Tool button to zoom the canvas to 100%.

To Name Photoshop Layers

The following steps rename the layers so they can be identified easily when imported to Flash.

1 On the Layers panel, double-click the layer name Layer 2, type `Pouring,` and press the ENTER key to rename the layer.

2 Rename Layer 1 as Garlic.

3 Rename Layer 0 as Vanilla.

To Save and Close the File

The following steps save the Photoshop file and close it without quitting the application.

1 Press SHIFT+CTRL+S to open the Save As dialog box. Navigate to Removable Drive (F:) or the location of your storage device.

2 Click the Create New Folder button on the Save As dialog box toolbar to create a new folder on the selected storage device.

3 When the new folder appears, type `Integration 01` to change the name of the folder, and then press the ENTER key to apply the name change.

4 Double-click the Integration 01 folder to set it as the save location.

5 Click the Save button to save the file in the new location.

6 Press CTRL+W to close the file but leave Photoshop open.

Importing Photoshop to Flash

Once you have modified the Photoshop file's characteristics and layer names, you are ready to import the PSD file to Flash. The Import command on the File menu in Flash displays the Import to Stage dialog box where you can set import options. The Import to Stage dialog box lets you choose whether to import all layers or only specific layers of the Photoshop document. You can choose to import each Photoshop layer as a separate Flash layer. Alternatively, you can import each Photoshop layer as a keyframe on a single Flash layer, which is helpful if you are creating a frame-by-frame animation based on the contents of the Photoshop layers. Another helpful option in the Import to Stage dialog box is the ability to resize the Flash canvas automatically to match the dimensions of the Photoshop file, which ensures that the Flash canvas is large enough to display all of the imagery from the Photoshop file without being larger than necessary (Figure 3).

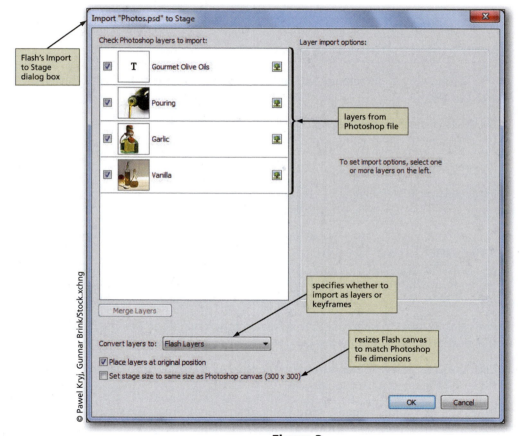

Figure 3

To Start Flash and Save a New Document

The following steps start Flash and create and save a new blank Flash document.

1 Start Flash and then press CTRL+N to display the New Document dialog box, if necessary.

2 In the Create New area, double-click ActionScript 3.0 to create a new blank ActionScript 3.0 document.

3 Press CTRL+S to open the Save As dialog box.

4 Type `Product Showcase` in the File name text box to change the file name. Do not press the ENTER key after typing the file name.

5 Click the Previous Locations box arrow to display the list of available drives.

6 Click Removable Disk (F:), or the name of your USB flash drive, in the list of available storage devices to select that drive as the new save location.

7 Double-click the Integration 01 folder to open it.

8 Click the Save as type box arrow to display the list of available file formats.

9 If necessary, click Flash CS6 Document (*.FLA) to select it.

10 Click the Save button to save the document in the Integration 01 folder with the new file name.

Library Additions

When Photoshop files are imported to Flash, Flash creates a folder in the library with the name of the imported Photoshop file. Each Photoshop layer is imported as a separate JPG image and is stored in this folder in the library, regardless of whether the layers will be used as individual layers in Flash or as keyframes (Figure 4).

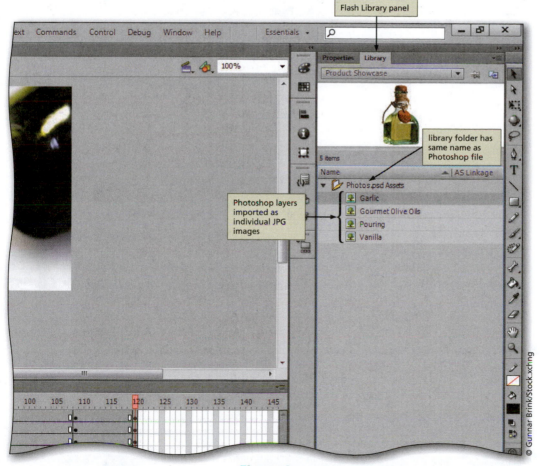

Figure 4

© Gunnar Brink/Stock.xchng

To Import a Photoshop Document to Flash

The following steps import the Photos.psd file into Flash.

- Click File on the Flash Application bar to display the File menu and then point to Import to display the Import submenu (Figure 5).

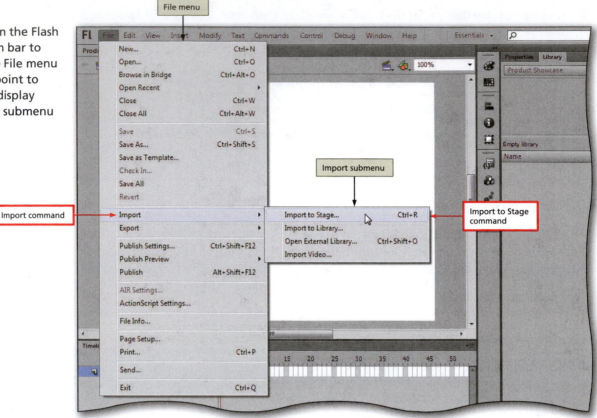

Figure 5

❷

- Click Import to Stage on the Import submenu to open the Import dialog box.

- Navigate to the Integration 01 folder of the Data Files for Students folder.

- Click the Photos file to select it (Figure 6).

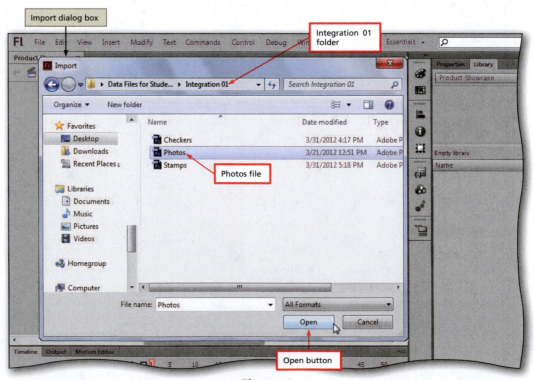

Figure 6

3

- Click the Open button to display the Import "Photos.psd" to Stage dialog box.

- Select the 'Place layers at original position' check box, if necessary.

- Select the 'Set stage size…' check box to resize the Flash canvas to match the dimensions of the Photoshop file automatically (Figure 7).

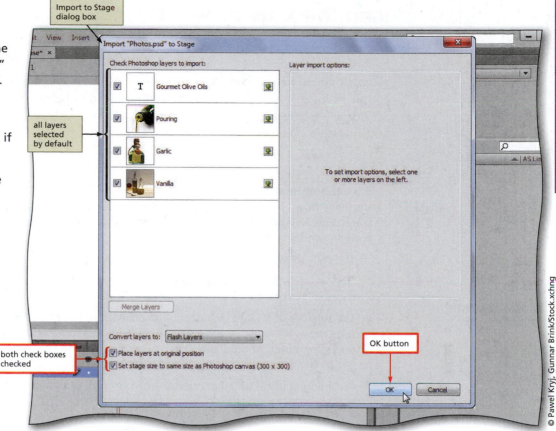

Import to Stage dialog box

all layers selected by default

both check boxes checked

OK button

© Pawel Kryj, Gunnar Brink/Stock.xchng

Figure 7

4

- Click the OK button to import the Photoshop file to Flash.

- Press CTRL+S to save your changes to the Flash document (Figure 8).

Q&A

What is on Layer 1?

Layer 1 was the original Flash layer. It is currently empty. You either can delete this layer or save it for possible future use.

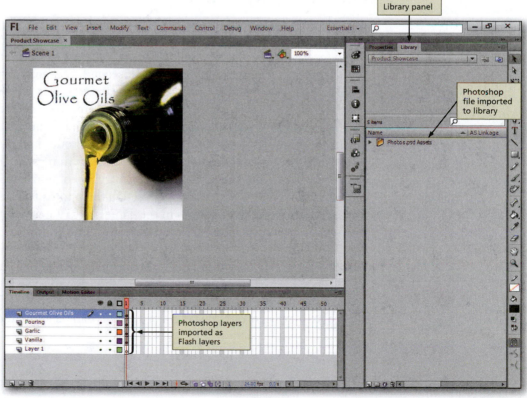

Library panel

Photoshop file imported to library

Photoshop layers imported as Flash layers

Figure 8

Other Ways

1. Press CTRL+R, select file and settings, click OK button

Plan the Animation

The product showcase animation you create in this chapter will feature three images. Each should appear for 4 seconds, resulting in a 12-second total animation. When planning an animation, consider the dimensions of the animation in addition to the length. Web page banners and advertisements need to be smaller than slide shows or other Flash movies. A slide show such as the one you will create in this chapter would fit nicely on a Web page at a size of 300 pixels by 300 pixels.

Plan Ahead

Plan the animation.
Visualize how you want the final animation to look because the desired timing of transitions will guide the placement of keyframes. Consider the following aspects when planning the animation:

- The style of animation, such as retro and choppy or modern and smooth.
- The desired effect of the animation. Slide shows require slower transitions than other styles of morphing.
- The number of images included in the animation. The more images you include in a slide show, the larger the file size will be and the longer it will take to download to a user's computer. Additionally, it will take more time to run, requiring a greater number of frames.
- Outlining as much detail as possible assists in your planning process.

Planning the Slide Show

For the product showcase slide show, each photo should be displayed for four seconds. Additionally, there should be a half-second fade before and after each photo. Therefore, the first photo should fade in or (change opacity) from Frame 1 to Frame 12 because 12 frames is equal to one-half second. Starting at Frame 13, the photo should be displayed at full opacity. That means you need a keyframe at Frame 13. The photo should continue to be displayed until Frame 108 for a total of 96 frames, or four seconds. At Frame 109, the photo should begin to fade out; therefore, a keyframe is needed at Frame 109 to start the fade. The fade should last 12 frames, until Frame 120, so the final keyframe should be at Frame 120. Keyframes for the first photo are needed at Frames 1, 13, 109, and 120. Rather than trying to figure out the correct frames for the other photos, it is easier simply to set all the photos to fade in and out at the same frames and then drag the frames in the Timeline to a new starting point. Although the math may seem confusing, it is much easier to understand when it can be visualized. Consider sketching it out, as in Figure 9, which shows the entire sequence for the first photo. The more times you sketch out a sequence, the easier it is to work out the math in your head. After planning the timing of the animation sequences, you will need to convert the photos to symbols, as you did in Flash Chapter 3. The symbol conversion is necessary because only instances of symbols can be animated to fade.

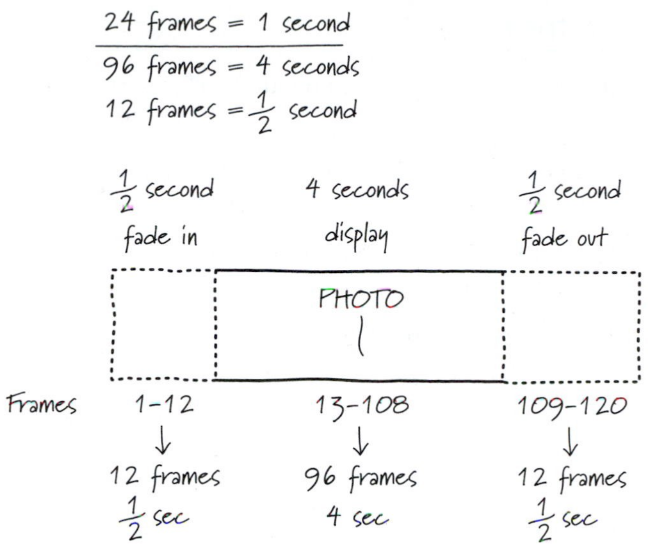

$$\frac{24 \text{ frames} = 1 \text{ second}}{96 \text{ frames} = 4 \text{ seconds}}$$

12 frames = $\frac{1}{2}$ second

$\frac{1}{2}$ second fade in	4 seconds display	$\frac{1}{2}$ second fade out
	PHOTO	

Frames 1–12   13–108   109–120
           ↓   ↓   ↓
      12 frames   96 frames   12 frames
      $\frac{1}{2}$ sec   4 sec $\frac{1}{2}$ sec

Figure 9

To Create Symbols and Instances

The following steps convert the photos on the stage to symbols. Flash requires this conversion because the plan for the animation is to fade objects on the stage, and only instances of symbols can be faded.

1 Click the Flash Properties panel tab to display the Properties panel.

2 On the stage, click the words, Gourmet Olive Oils, to select the JPG image of the text.

3 Click Modify on the Application bar and then click Convert to Symbol to display the Convert to Symbol dialog box.

4 Type `Gourmet Olive Oils` in the Name box, and then change the Type setting to Graphic, if necessary.

5 Click the OK button to convert the imported JPG on the stage to an instance of a symbol.

6 On the stage, click the bottle of pouring olive oil to select it. Repeat Steps 3 through 5 to convert the photo on the Pouring layer to a symbol named Pouring.

7 On the Timeline, click the Visibility button on the Pouring layer to hide the layer so that you can see the underlying layer, Garlic.

8 On the stage, click the bottle of garlic olive oil to select it. Repeat Steps 3 through 5 to convert the photo on the Garlic layer to a symbol named Garlic.

9 On the Timeline, click the Visibility button on the Garlic layer to hide the layer so that you can see the underlying layer, Vanilla.

10 On the stage, click the image of the bottles of vanilla olive oil to select it. Repeat Steps 3 through 5 to convert the photo on the Vanilla layer to a symbol named Vanilla.

11 On the Timeline, click the Visibility button on the Pouring and Garlic layers so that all layers are visible.

To Create Keyframes

The following steps create keyframes on all four imported layers to prepare for the animation.

1 Right-click Frame 13 of the Gourmet Olive Oils layer and click Insert Keyframe on the context menu to insert a keyframe.

2 Right-click Frame 109 of the Gourmet Olive Oils layer and click Insert Keyframe on the context menu to insert a keyframe.

3 Right-click Frame 120 of the Gourmet Olive Oils layer and click Insert Keyframe on the context menu to insert a keyframe.

4 Repeat Steps 1 through 3 on the Pouring, Garlic, and Vanilla layers so that all layers, except Layer 1, have keyframes at Frames 1, 13, 109, and 120 (Figure 10).

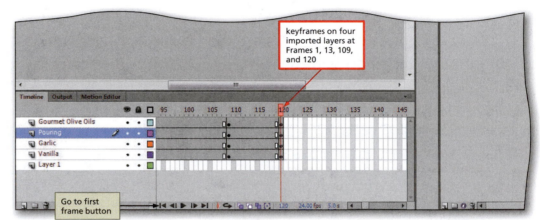

Figure 10

To Change Opacity

The following steps change the opacity of the elements on the stage at Frames 1 and 120 to prepare for the animation.

1 Click the Properties panel to select it.

2 On the Timeline status bar, click the 'Go to first frame' button.

3 On the stage, click the words, Gourmet Olive Oils, to select the instance.

4 On the Properties panel, expand the Color Effect area if necessary, and then click the Style arrow in the Color Effect area to display the color effect options.

5 Click Alpha in the Style menu to select it and then change the Alpha value to 0, if necessary.

6 Scroll the Timeline to the right and click Frame 120 of the Gourmet Olive Oils layer, and then click the words Gourmet Olive Oils on the stage to select the instance.

7 On the Properties panel, set the Color Effect's Style menu to Alpha. Flash will remember the previous setting of 0.

8 Scroll the Timeline to the left until you can see Frame 1 and then click the Visibility button on the Gourmet Olive Oils layer to hide it.

9 Repeat Steps 2 through 8 on the Pouring layer to set the Alpha value to 0 at Frames 1 and 120 of the pouring bottle.

10 Repeat Steps 2 through 8 on the Garlic layer to set the Alpha value to 0 at Frames 1 and 120 of the garlic bottle.

11 Repeat Steps 2 through 8 on the Vanilla layer to set the Alpha value to 0 at Frames 1 and 120 of the vanilla bottle.

12 Click the Visibility buttons for each hidden layer so that all layers are visible.

To Create a Tweened Animation

The following steps create classic tweens on all imported layers to animate the fades.

1 On the Timeline, right-click anywhere between the first two keyframes (Frames 1 and 13) on the Gourmet Olive Oils layer, and then click Create Classic Tween on the context menu to create a tween between Frames 1 and 13.

2 Repeat Step 1 on the Pouring, Garlic, and Vanilla layers to create the initial fade-in animations on all imported layers.

3 Scroll the Timeline to the right until you can see Frame 120.

4 On the Gourmet Olive Oils layer, right-click anywhere between the last two keyframes (Frames 109 and 120), and then click Create Classic Tween on the context menu to create a tween between Frames 109 and 120.

5 Repeat Step 4 on the Pouring, Garlic, and Vanilla layers to create the fade-out animations on all imported layers (Figure 11).

Figure 11

To Move Frames

The following steps move the frames of the Garlic and Vanilla layers to stagger the animation.

1
- Click the 'Go to first frame' button and then click Frame 1 of the Garlic layer to select it.

- Scroll the Timeline to the right until you can see Frame 120, and then SHIFT+CLICK Frame 120 to select Frames 1 through 120 (Figure 12).

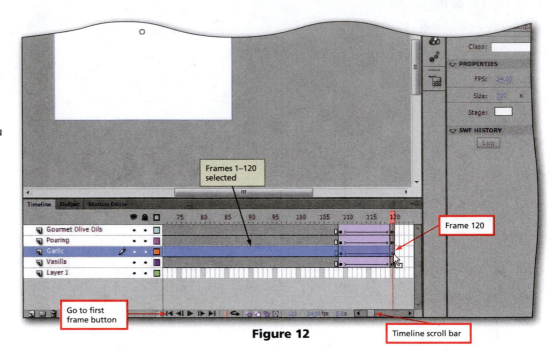

Figure 12

2
- Drag the selected frames to the right, a little at a time, until the Garlic layer's first keyframe moves to Frame 121 (Figure 13).

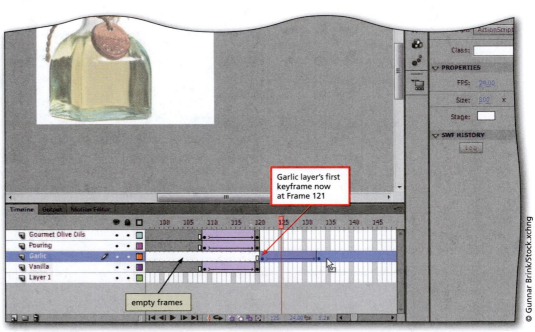

Figure 13

3
- Click the 'Go to first frame' button and then click Frame 1 of the Vanilla layer to select it.

- Scroll the Timeline to the right until you can see Frame 120 and then SHIFT+CLICK Frame 120 to select Frames 1 through 120 (Figure 14).

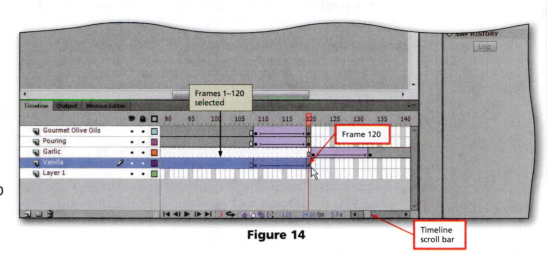

Figure 14

4
- Drag the selected frames to the right, a little at a time, until the Vanilla layer's first keyframe moves to Frame 241 (Figure 15).

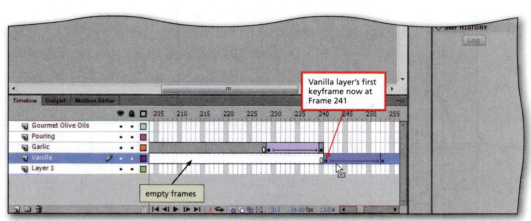

Figure 15

5
- Click the 'Go to first frame' button and then click Frame 1 of the Gourmet Olive Oils layer to move the playhead to Frame 1 (Figure 16).

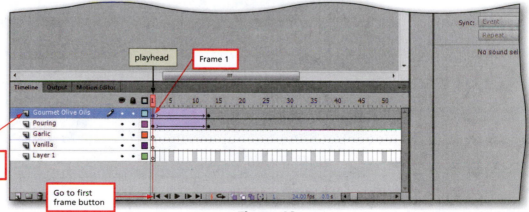

Figure 16

Other Ways

1. Select frames, click Cut Frames on context menu, click destination frame, click Paste Frames on context menu

To Preview the Animation and Save the File

The following steps preview the animation.

1 Press the ENTER key to preview the animation from the stage.

2 Press CTRL+S to save your changes.

Editing Photos within Flash

The Adobe Creative Suite applications offer the benefit of interoperability. If an image that you are using in Flash needs to be edited, there is no need to quit Flash, open the original image in Photoshop, edit it, and reimport it to Flash. Instead, you simply right-click the imported image in Flash's library and select the Edit with Adobe Photoshop CS6 command on the context menu. Flash sends the image to Photoshop, where you can edit the image. When you close the Photoshop window, control is returned to Flash with a prompt to save the file. It is important to note that you cannot edit a symbol. Instead, you must edit the original imported JPG. However, because the symbol is based on the imported JPG, the symbol is updated automatically to reflect any changes made to the imported JPG (Figure 17).

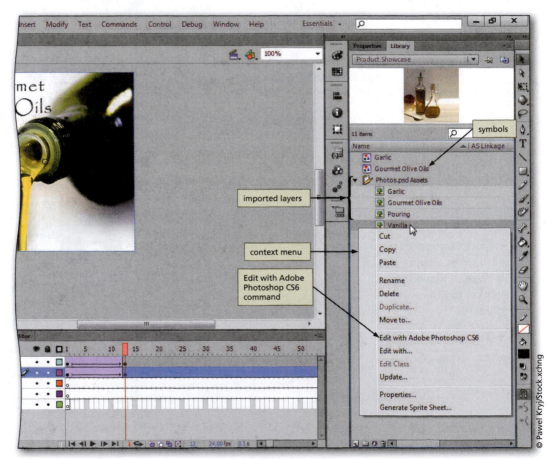

Figure 17

BTW

Virtual Memory
When you use the Edit With Adobe Photoshop CS6 command in Flash, you are using a large amount of memory on your computer system. If Flash is unable to load Photoshop and displays a warning message, close all other open applications and try again.

Editing an image with the Edit with Adobe Photoshop CS6 command creates a permanent change, sometimes called **destructive editing**. You cannot undo your changes. The only way to undo your changes is to reimport the original Photoshop PSD file and replace the edited version.

Although Photoshop's PSD file format supports layers, the more commonly used JPG file format does not. Therefore, if you edit a JPG file, you must flatten or merge any new layers in the image before sending it back to Flash. Recall that flattening an image in Photoshop merges all layers to a single Photoshop background layer. Flattening a layer will eliminate any transparent background. If you need to maintain a transparent background, use the Merge Visible command, which merges all layers into a single layer that maintains a background transparency.

Use the right tool for the job.

Although you can use Flash to do basic bitmap editing, Photoshop excels in this area. Use the best tool for any specific task. Because Photoshop is the best photo-editing tool, it makes sense to edit images with Photoshop rather than with the limited feature set of Flash.

Plan Ahead

To Send an Image to Photoshop for Editing

Recall that each layer in the original Photos.psd file became a separate JPG image in Flash. The following steps send one of those imported images back to Photoshop for editing using Flash's Edit with Adobe Photoshop CS6 command.

1

- Click the Library panel tab to select it.

- Click the triangle to the left of the Photos.psd Assets folder to display its contents.

- Right-click the imported Garlic JPG image to display its context menu (Figure 18).

2

- Click Edit with Adobe Photoshop CS6 to use Photoshop for editing.

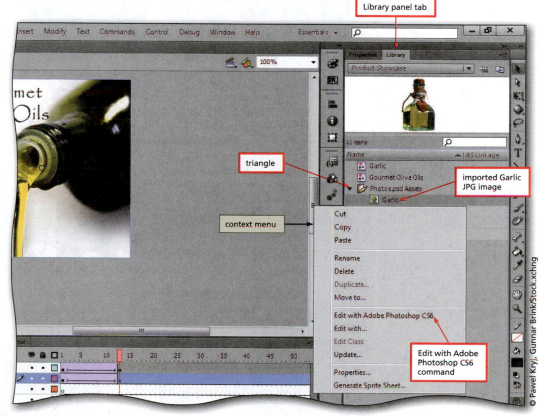

Figure 18

© Pawel Kryj, Gunnar Brink/Stock.xchng

To Edit an Image in Photoshop

The following steps create an adjustment layer to make the bottle redder.

1

● If necessary, click the Adjustments tab to display the Adjustments panel.

● Click the Hue/ Saturation button to display the Properties, Hue/ Saturation panel and create an adjustment layer.

● Set the Hue value to -30 to give the bottle a reddish color (Figure 19).

Figure 19

2

● On the Layers panel, click the Layers panel menu button to display the Layers panel menu (Figure 20).

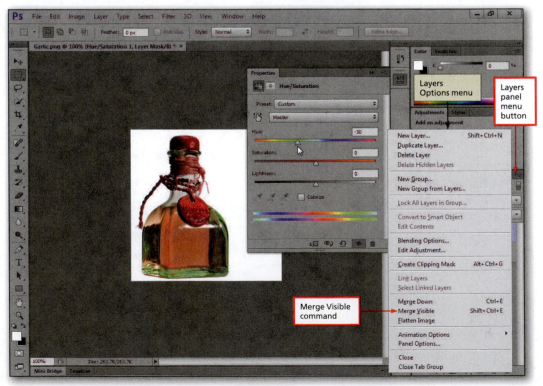

Figure 20

❸
- Click Merge Visible to merge all the layers into a single layer.

- Click the Close button on the document tab to close the file and display a prompt to save your changes (Figure 21).

Q&A

Why am I not using CTRL+S to save the file in Photoshop?

If you press CTRL+S to save your Photoshop file, Photoshop will prompt you for a location to save the PSD file rather than sending the edited JPG file back to Flash.

Figure 21

© Gunnar Brink/Stock.xchng

❹
- Click the Yes button to save your changes and close the image.

Other Ways
1. To adjust hue, click New Adjustment Layer on Layer menu, click Hue/Saturation   2. To merge visible, press SHIFT+CTRL+E

To Examine the Edited File in Flash

The following step returns to Flash to verify the changes you made in Photoshop.

❶
- If necessary, click the Flash button on the Windows taskbar to return to Flash.

- Click the Garlic.png image in the library and verify the color change (Figure 22).

Q&A

Why is my image now stored as a PNG file?

Although Photoshop layers are imported to Flash as JPG images, Photoshop sends your edited image back to Flash in the PNG format. This has no effect on your Flash movie and makes no difference to your work flow.

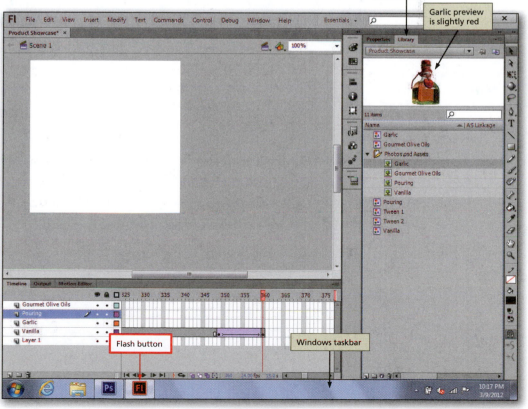

Figure 22

To Preview the Animation Again and Save the File

The following steps preview the animation with the color change.

1 Press the ENTER key to preview the animation and note that when the Garlic bottle image appears in the slide show, it is red instead of green (Figure 23).

2 Press CTRL+S to save your changes.

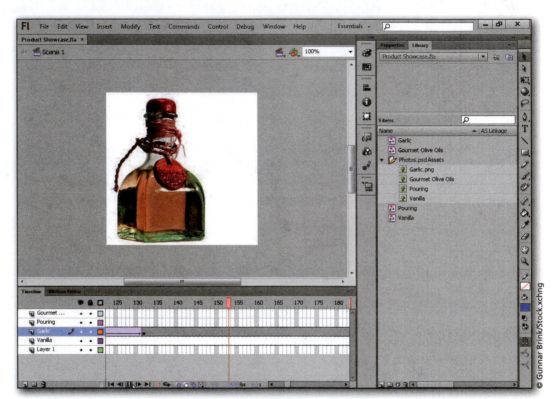

Figure 23

To Quit Flash and Photoshop

The following steps quit both Flash and Photoshop.

1 Click the Close button on the right side of the Flash Application bar to close the window. If Flash displays a dialog box asking you to save changes, click the No button.

2 Click the Close button on the right side of the Photoshop Application bar to close the window. If Photoshop displays a dialog box asking you to save changes, click the No button.

Chapter Summary

In this chapter, you learned to integrate Photoshop and Flash to create one cohesive project. You used Photoshop to edit images and Flash to animate them.

The items listed below include all the new skills you have learned in this chapter:

1. Import a Photoshop Document to Flash (IN1 8)
2. Move Frames (IN1 14)
3. Send an Image to Photoshop for Editing (IN1 17)
4. Edit an Image in Photoshop (IN1 18)
5. Examine the Edited File in Flash (IN1 19)

In the Lab

Lab 1: Morphing Stamps

Problem: As part of a group project to create a mobile application for stamp collectors, your task is to create the initial animation that will appear as the application loads. The animation consists of a blank stamp morphing into a postage stamp, as shown in Figure 24. The initial graphics were created in Photoshop. You will import the Photoshop file to Flash, create the animation, and send one of the Flash graphics to Photoshop for editing while maintaining the transparent background of the graphic.

Note: To complete this assignment, you will be required to use the Data Files for Students. Visit www.cengage.com/ct/studentdownload for detailed instructions or contact your instructor for information about accessing the required files.

(a)

(b)

(c)

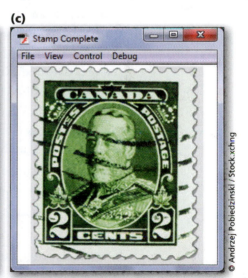

© Matt Palmer/Stock.xchng

© Andrzej Pobiedzinski / Stock.xchng

Figure 24

Continued >

In the Lab *continued*

Instructions: Perform the following tasks:

1. Start Flash and create a new ActionScript 3.0 file. Save the file to the Integration 01 folder with the name `Stamp Complete` in the Flash FLA format.

2. Click File, point to Import, and then click Import to Stage to display the Import dialog box.

3. Navigate to the Integration 01 folder of the Data Files for Students and double-click the Stamps file to begin the import.

4. Uncheck the Background layer. Ensure the 'Convert layers to' menu is set to Flash Layers and that both check boxes at the bottom of the Import to Stage dialog box are checked. Click the OK button to import the Photoshop file.

5. Click the empty Layer 1 in the Flash Timeline to select it and then click the Delete button on Timeline status bar to delete it.

6. Click the Stamp Final layer on the Flash Timeline and then click the Delete button on the Timeline status bar to delete it.

7. Rename the remaining layer Stamp Morph.

8. Right-click Frame 24 and then click Insert Keyframe on the context menu to create a keyframe.

9. Click Modify on the Application bar, point to Bitmap, and then click Trace Bitmap to convert the graphic on the stage into a vector that can be morphed.

10. Change the Color threshold value to 50 and the Minimum area value to 1 and then click the OK button to complete the tracing process.

11. Right-click Frame 48 and then click Insert Keyframe on the context menu to create a keyframe.

12. Press the DELETE key to delete the content of the stage at Frame 48, so that the stage is empty at this frame and ready to receive the other graphic.

13. Click the triangle next to the Stamps.psd Assets folder in the Library panel to display its contents. Click the Stamp Final asset to preview it at the top of the Library panel and notice the stamp is dark red. Right-click the Stamp Final asset and then click Edit with Adobe Photoshop CS6 on the context menu to send the graphic to Photoshop for editing.

14. If necessary, click the Photoshop button on the Windows taskbar to switch to Photoshop. Click the Adjustments tab to display the Adjustments panel and then click the Hue/Saturation button to display the Hue/Saturation controls and create an adjustment layer.

15. Drag the Hue slider to the right until the value is approximately 100 and the stamp turns green.

16. Click the Layers Options menu button to display the Layers Panel menu, and then click Merge Visible to merge the two layers into a single layer that maintains the transparent background.

17. Press CTRL+S to save the changes and then click the Close button to quit Photoshop.

18. If necessary, click the Flash button on the Windows taskbar to return to Flash.

19. Drag the green Stamp Final.png graphic from the library onto the stage. Make sure the entire image fits on the stage.

20. Click Modify on the Application bar, point to Bitmap, and then click Trace Bitmap to convert the graphic on the stage into a vector that can be morphed.

21. If necessary, set the Color threshold value to 50, set the Minimum area value to 1, and then click the OK button to complete the tracing process.

22. Right-click any gray frame between the last two keyframes (Frames 24 and 48) and click Create Shape Tween on the context menu to create a shape tween from Frame 24 to Frame 48.

23. Click the New Layer button on the Timeline status bar to create a layer. Name the new layer, Actions.

24. Create a keyframe at Frame 48 of the Actions layer. Click Frame 48 of the Actions layer and press the F9 key to display the Actions panel. Type stop(); to create a stop action and then close the Actions panel.

25. Press CTRL+S to save the file and then press CTRL+ENTER to test the movie. Close the Stamp Complete testing window after the movie has played, and then quit Flash.

In the Lab

Lab 2: Animating a Checkers Game

Problem: As part of a group project to create a game of checkers for a Web site, your task is to create the initial animation that will display as the game loads. The animation will consist of a checker-board where the checkers appear on the board one after the other at increasing speeds, as shown in Figure 25. The initial graphics were created in Photoshop. You will have to edit the Photoshop file to get it ready to import to Flash. You will then have to import the Photoshop file to Flash and create the animation. Lastly, you will send one of the Flash graphics to Photoshop for editing while maintaining the transparent background of the graphic.

Note: To complete this assignment, you will be required to use the Data Files for Students. Visit www.cengage.com/ct/studentdownload for detailed instructions or contact your instructor for information about accessing the required files.

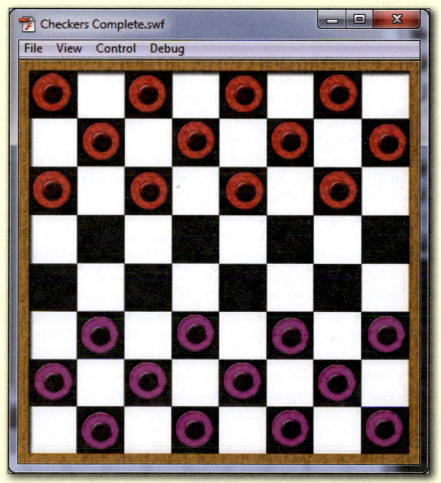

Figure 25

Continued >

In the Lab *continued*

Instructions: Perform the following tasks:

1. Start Photoshop and open the Checkers file from the Integration 01 folder of the Data Files for Students.

2. Rename Layer 1 to Checkerboard, and then save a copy of the file to the Integration 01 folder with the name, Checkerboard for Import, in the Photoshop PSD format.

3. Start Flash and create a new ActionScript 3.0 file. Save the file to the Integration 01 folder with the name, Checkers Complete, in the Flash FLA format.

4. Import the Checkerboard for Import file to the Flash stage, making sure the 'Convert layers to' menu is set to Flash Layers and the 'Set stage size' check box is checked to resize the Flash canvas to match the dimensions of the Photoshop file automatically.

5. Delete the empty Layer 1 in the Flash Timeline.

6. Click the blue checker on the stage and press the F8 key to display the Convert to Symbol dialog box. Type `Blue Checker` for the symbol name and then click the OK button.

7. Click the red checker on the stage and press the F8 key to display the Convert to Symbol dialog box. Type `Red Checker` for the symbol name and then click the OK button.

8. Right-click Frame 32 of the Checkerboard layer in the Timeline and then click Insert Frame to extend the length of the layer.

9. Right-click Frame 32 of the Blue Checker layer in the Timeline and then click Insert Keyframe. Drag the Blue Checker symbol from the Library to the second black square along the bottom row of the checkerboard on the stage.

10. Right-click Frame 32 of the Red Checker layer in the Timeline and then click Insert Keyframe. Drag the Red Checker symbol from the Library to the second black square along the top row of the checkerboard on the stage.

11. Repeat Steps 8 through 10, creating frames and keyframes at Frame 58 and placing a third blue and red checker on the next black square in their rows.

12. Repeat Steps 8 through 10, creating frames and keyframes at Frame 78 and placing a fourth blue and red checker on the next black square in their rows.

13. Repeat Steps 8 through 10, placing checkers on the black squares on their side of the checkerboard until there are three rows of each color. Keyframes should be placed at the following frames: 94, 106, 114, 120, 124, 127, 129, 130.

14. Create a new layer above the Red Checker layer and name it, Actions. Create a keyframe at Frame 130 of the Actions layer. Click Frame 130 of the Actions layer and press the F9 key to display the Actions panel. Type `stop();` to create a stop action and then close the Actions panel.

15. Press CTRL+S to save the file and then press CTRL+ENTER to test the movie. Close the Checkers Complete testing window once the movie has played.

16. Click the triangle next to the Checkers.psd Assets folder in the Library to expand its contents. Right-click the Blue Checker asset and click Edit with Adobe Photoshop CS6 on the context menu.

17. In Photoshop, click the Adjustments panel and then click the Hue/Saturation button to display the Hue/Saturation controls. Change the value of the Hue to 100 so the checker turns purple.

18. Press SHIFT+CTRL+E to merge the visible layers into a single layer that maintains the transparent background. Press CTRL+S to save the changes and then press CTRL+W to close the Photoshop file.

19. Click the Flash button on the Windows taskbar to return to Flash and notice the blue checker is now purple. Press CTRL+S to save the file and then press CTRL+ENTER to test the movie. Close the Checkers Complete testing window once the movie has played.

20. Close the Checkers Complete file. Quit Flash and then quit Photoshop.

1 Creating a New Web Site with Dreamweaver

Adobe product screenshot(s) reprinted with permission from Adobe Systems Incorporated

Objectives

You will have mastered the material in this chapter when you can:

- Start Dreamweaver and customize the Dreamweaver workspace
- Describe the Dreamweaver workspace
- Show and hide panels
- Create a Dreamweaver Web site using a template
- Define a local site
- Add text to a Web page

- Change the format of the text headings
- Add links to a Web site
- Create an unordered list
- Save a Web site
- Check spelling
- Preview a Web site in a browser
- Use Dreamweaver Help

1 | Creating a New Web Site with Dreamweaver

What Is Dreamweaver CS6?

Adobe Dreamweaver CS6, the preferred professional Web site creation and management software, provides a rich user interface with powerful tools. Dreamweaver can be used to design a Web site that is displayed in any browser on multiple platforms, including PC and Mac computers, kiosks, tablets, and smartphones. Dreamweaver's icon-driven menus and detailed panels make it easy for users to add text, images, multimedia files, and links without typing one line of code. Dreamweaver creates code that reflects selections made in the user interface and provides content structure when rendering the page in the browser.

The Adobe Dreamweaver user interface is consistent across all Adobe authoring tools. This consistency allows for easy integration with other Adobe Web-related programs such as Adobe Flash, Photoshop, Illustrator, and Fireworks. Dreamweaver CS6 is part of the **Adobe Creative Suite 6**, a collection of graphic design, video editing, and Web development applications published by Adobe Systems. Dreamweaver CS6 runs on multiple operating systems, including Windows 8, Windows 7, Windows Vista, Windows XP, and Mac OS X. This text uses Dreamweaver CS6 on the PC platform, running the Windows 7 operating system.

Project Planning Guidelines

> The process of developing a Web site that communicates specific information requires careful analysis and planning. Start by identifying the purpose and audience of the Web site and developing a Web page design. If you are working with a client, ask your client to clearly express his or her expectations, such as who will visit the site and how they will use it. The Web page design contributes to the look and feel of the Web site, which includes the amount of text displayed on each page and the format of the text. Details of these guidelines are provided in the "Project Planning Guidelines" appendix. Each chapter in this book provides practical business applications of these planning guidelines.

Project — Small Business Incubator Web Site Plan

You can use Dreamweaver CS6 to produce Web sites such as the Small Business Incubator Web site shown in Figure 1–1. A business incubator is a program that supports start-up companies by providing resources such as office space, and services such as business advice and networking opportunities. A business incubator in Condor, California plans to create the site shown in Figure 1–1 to highlight best practices for small businesses that design their own Web sites. The two-page Small Business Incubator Web site includes the index, or home, page for the Web site and introduces the design elements. The page includes a simple navigation bar in the left column and a main heading followed by a short informational paragraph in the right column. The second page displays a checklist of best practices for designing any small business Web site.

The project in this chapter uses a built-in Dreamweaver layout to create a simple HTML5 page named index as shown in Figure 1–1a. Recall that HTML5 is the most recent standard of Hypertext Markup Language (HTML), the core language for creating Web pages. After entering text into the index page, you will create a second page (Figure 1–1b) named checklist, which includes a bulleted list of best practices for small business Web site planning. Creating a two-page Web site requires a basic understanding of the Dreamweaver user interface, layouts, links, heading sizes, and bullets.

(a)

(b)

Figure 1–1

Overview

As you read this chapter, you will learn how to create the Web page project shown in Figure 1–1 by performing these general tasks:

- Customize the workspace.
- Create a new Dreamweaver HTML5 Web site with two columns.
- Enter text in the Web page.
- Change the format of the headings.
- Add links.
- Save the document.
- Add a second HTML5 page.
- Create a bulleted list.
- Check spelling.
- Preview the Web site in a browser.
- Save the Web site.

**Plan
Ahead**

General Project Guidelines

When creating a Dreamweaver Web site, the actions you perform and the decisions you make will affect the appearance and characteristics of the entire Web site. When creating Web pages, such as the ones shown in Figure 1–1 on the previous page, you should follow these general guidelines:

1. **Review the Dreamweaver workspace window.** Become familiar with the various layouts and available panels.

2. **Define the local site.** Create the local site using Dreamweaver's Site Setup dialog box.

3. **Determine the location for the local site.** Select the location and storage media where you will save the site. Keep in mind that in Chapter 2, you will begin a site and then modify those pages, and add new pages as you progress through this book. Storage media can include a hard disk, USB flash drive, network drive, or cloud computing drive.

4. **Select the words and heading sizes for the text.** Text accounts for the bulk of the content on most Web pages, but Web site visitors often avoid long blocks of text. It is best to be brief. Include headings to organize the text into sections. Use lists whenever possible. Use common words and simple language.

5. **Identify how to format various elements of the text.** Determine which text will be headings and subheadings, paragraphs, and bulleted and numbered lists on the Web page.

6. **Review final tasks.** Prepare to display a Web page to others by adding professional finishing touches such as a Web page title and by checking the spelling of the text.

When necessary, more specific details concerning the above guidelines are presented at appropriate points in the chapter. The chapter also identifies the actions performed and decisions made regarding these guidelines during the creation of the Web site pages shown in Figure 1–1 on the previous page.

Starting Dreamweaver

BTW

Screen Resolution
If you use a screen resolution higher than 1024 x 768, the location of on-screen tools might vary slightly from the book.

If you are using a computer to step through the project in this chapter and you want your screen to match the figures in this book, you should change your screen's resolution to 1024×768. For information about how to change a screen's resolution, read the "Changing Screen Resolution" appendix. The browser used to display the Web page figures is Internet Explorer 9. The browser text size is set to Medium.

To Start Dreamweaver

The following steps, which assume Windows 7 is running, start Dreamweaver, based on a typical installation. You may need to ask your instructor how to start Dreamweaver for your computer.

1

- Click the Start button on the Windows 7 taskbar to display the Start menu.

- Type Dreamweaver CS6 in the 'Search programs and files' text box, and watch the search results appear on the Start menu (Figure 1–2).

Q&A

Why do I have documents and files in my list of results?

Any documents containing the words, Dreamweaver CS6, and any files that have been opened with Dreamweaver CS6 may appear in your list.

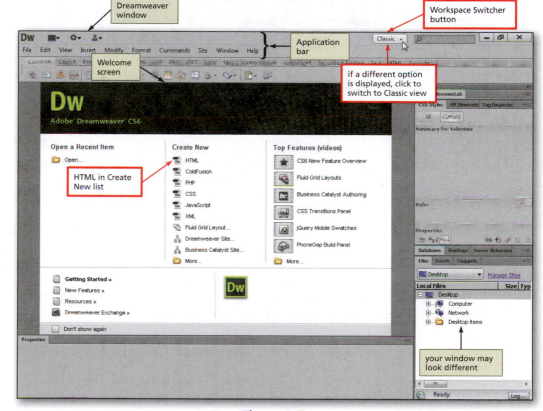

Figure 1–2

2

- Click Adobe Dreamweaver CS6 in the search results on the Start menu to start Dreamweaver and display the Welcome screen.

- If necessary, click the Workspace Switcher button on the Application bar, and then click Classic to switch to the Classic workspace (Figure 1–3).

Q&A

What is the Classic workspace?

Eleven predefined workspace layouts designed for application developers, coders, and Web designers allow you to

Figure 1–3

customize your workspace according to your role or target device. The Classic workspace provides all the tools necessary for a beginning Web designer's needs and omits features for advanced designers and programmers.

Q&A

Why does the Application bar appear on two rows in Figure 1–3?

If your screen resolution is set to 1024 × 768, the Application bar appears on two rows. If you are using a higher screen resolution, the Application bar appears on one row at the top of the Dreamweaver window.

3

- Click HTML in the Create New list to create a blank HTML document.

- If the Dreamweaver window is not maximized, click the Maximize button next to the Close button on the Application bar to maximize the window.

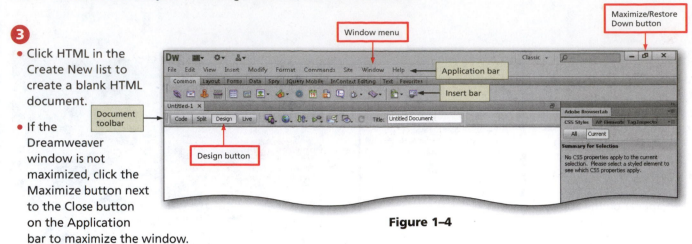

Figure 1–4

- If the Design button is not selected, click the Design button on the Document toolbar to view the page design.

- If the Insert bar is not displayed, click Window on the Application bar and then click Insert to display the Insert panel (Figure 1–4).

Q&A What if a message is displayed regarding default file types?

If a message is displayed, click the Close button.

Q&A What is a maximized window?

A maximized window fills the entire screen. When you maximize a window, the Maximize button changes to a Restore Down button.

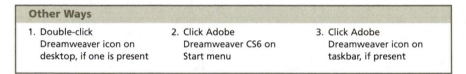

Other Ways		
1. Double-click Dreamweaver icon on desktop, if one is present	2. Click Adobe Dreamweaver CS6 on Start menu	3. Click Adobe Dreamweaver icon on taskbar, if present

MAC For a detailed example of starting Dreamweaver using the Mac operating system, refer to the "To Start Adobe Dreamweaver CS6" steps in the For Mac Users appendix at the end of this book.

Touring the Dreamweaver Window

With the Dreamweaver window open, take time to tour your new Web design environment. The Dreamweaver workspace lets you view documents and object properties. It provides toolbar buttons for the most common operations so that you quickly can make changes to your documents. In Dreamweaver, a document is an HTML file that is displayed in a browser as a Web page. Figure 1–4 shows how the Dreamweaver workspace looks the first time you start Dreamweaver after installation on most computers. To work efficiently, you should learn the basic terms and concepts of the Dreamweaver workspace, and understand how to choose options, use inspectors and panels, and set preferences that best fit your work style.

Dreamweaver Workspace

The **Dreamweaver workspace** is an integrated environment in which the Document window and panels are incorporated into one large application window. To create an efficient, customized workspace, Dreamweaver provides the Web site developer with 11 preset workspace layouts as shown in the Workspace Switcher list in Figure 1–5: App Developer, App Developer Plus, Business Catalyst, Classic, Coder, Coder Plus, Designer, Designer Compact, Dual Screen, Fluid Layout, and Mobile Applications. These workspaces provide different arrangements of panels: Depending on the workspace, some panels are hidden and some appear in different locations in the Dreamweaver window. Each workspace is designed for a different type of Dreamweaver user. For example, programmers who work primarily with HTML and other languages generally select the Coder or App Developer workspace. The Dual Screen option requires two monitors, with the Document window and Property inspector displayed on one monitor, and the panels displayed on a secondary monitor. The Classic workspace contains a visually integrated workspace and is ideal for beginners and nonprogrammers. Select the Mobile Applications view if you want to build an application intended for deployment on a tablet or smartphone device. The projects and exercises in this book use the Classic workspace.

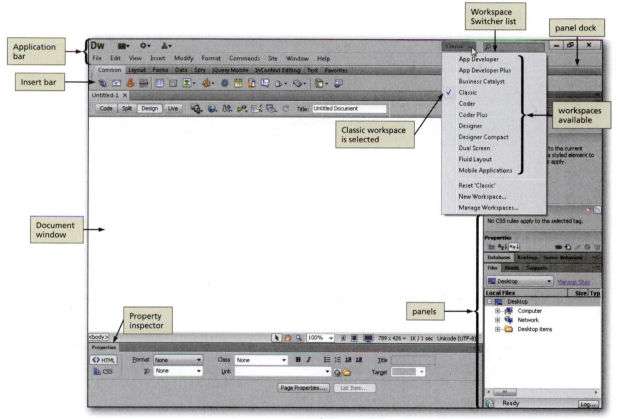

Figure 1–5

In Classic view, the Application bar is at the top of the window, the Insert panel is displayed below the Application bar, the Document window is in the center with the panel dock and panels on the right, and the Property inspector is located at the bottom of the window as shown in Figure 1–5. The following list describes the components of the Dreamweaver workspace:

Application Bar The **Application bar** displays the Dreamweaver menu names and buttons for working with the window layout, extending Dreamweaver, managing sites, switching the workplace layout, searching for help, and manipulating the window. When you point to a menu name on the Application bar, the menu name is selected. When you click a menu name, the corresponding menu is displayed. Figure 1–6 on the next page shows the Edit menu.

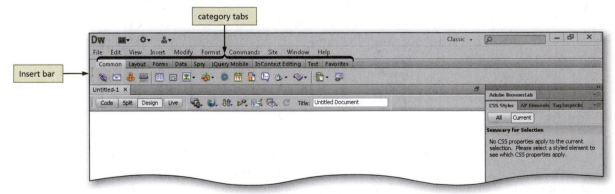

Figure 1–6

The menus contain lists of common actions for performing tasks such as opening, saving, modifying, previewing, and inserting data in your Web page. The menus may display some commands that appear gray, or dimmed — which indicates they are not available for the current selection — instead of black.

Insert Bar Below the Application bar, the **Insert bar** (Figure 1–7), also called the **Insert panel**, allows quick access to frequently used commands.

Figure 1–7

You use the buttons on the Insert bar to insert various types of objects — such as images, tables, links, and dates — into a Web document. As you insert each object, a dialog box allows you to set and manipulate specific attributes of the object. The buttons on the Insert bar are organized into nine categories, such as Common and Layout, which you can access through tabs. Some categories also have buttons with pop-up menus. When you select an option from a pop-up menu, it becomes the default action for the button. When you start Dreamweaver, the category in which you last were working is displayed on the Insert bar.

BTW

Switching from Insert Bar to Panel
If you drag the Insert bar to another part of the Dreamweaver window, it is displayed as a vertical panel instead of a horizontal bar.

Document Tab, Document Toolbar, and Document Window The **document tab** displays the Web page name, which is Untitled-1 for the first Web page you create in a Dreamweaver session, as shown in Figure 1–8. (The "X" is the Close button for the document tab.) The **Document toolbar** contains buttons that provide different views of the Document window (e.g., Code, Split, and Design), and some common operations, such as Preview/Debug in Browser, Refresh Design View, View Options, Visual Aids, and Check Browser Compatibility. The **Document window** displays the current document as you create and edit it.

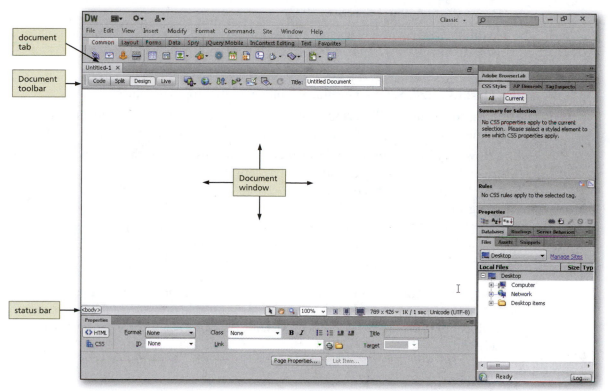

Figure 1–8

When you make changes to a document, Dreamweaver places an asterisk following the file name in the document tab, indicating that the changes have not been saved. The asterisk is removed after the document is saved. The file path leading to the document's location is displayed to the far right of the document tab.

Status Bar The **status bar**, located below the Document window (Figure 1–9), provides additional information about the document you are creating.

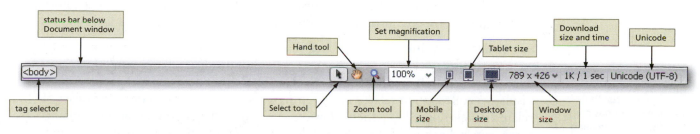

Figure 1–9

The status bar displays the following options:

- **Tag selector:** Click any tag in the hierarchy to select that tag and all its contents.
- **Select tool:** Use the Select tool to return to default editing after using the Zoom or Hand tool.
- **Hand tool:** To pan a page after zooming, use the Hand tool to drag the page.
- **Zoom tool:** Available in Design view or Split view, you can use the Zoom tool to check the pixel accuracy of graphics or to better view the page.
- **Set magnification:** Use the Set magnification context menu to change the view from 6% to 6400%; default is 100%.
- **Mobile size:** Set the Document window to mobile size values, such as for smartphones.
- **Tablet size:** Set the Document window to tablet size values.
- **Desktop size:** Set the Document window to desktop size values.
- **Window size:** Set the Window size value, which includes the window's current dimensions (in pixels). Click this value to display the Window size pop-up menu.
- **Download size and download time:** Refer to this area for the size and estimated download time of the current page. Dreamweaver CS6 calculates the size based on the entire contents of the page, including all linked objects such as images and plug-ins.
- **Unicode (UTF-8):** Refer to this area for the type of text encoding. Unicode is an industry standard that allows computers to consistently represent and manipulate text expressed in most of the world's writing systems.

Property Inspector The **Property inspector**, docked at the bottom of the Document window, provides properties such as the color or font style of a selected object or text in the document. Figure 1–10 shows the default Property inspector when an object is not selected.

Figure 1–10

The Property inspector enables you to view and change a variety of properties for the selected object or text. The Property inspector is context sensitive, meaning it changes based on the selected object, which can include text, tables, images, and other objects. For example, to change the format of a selected heading, you click the Format button in the Property inspector and then select the new format in the list.

Panel Groups Within the panel dock shown in Figure 1–11 on the next page, related panels are displayed in a single panel group with individual tabs. A **panel dock** is a fixed area at the left or right edge of the workspace that hosts a panel group. A **panel** displays a collection of related tools, settings, and options. A **panel group** is a set of related panels docked together below one heading. A panel group typically contains three panels. Each panel provides a wide variety of tools to assist in developing and managing a Web site. For example, the Files panel is used to view and manage the files in your Dreamweaver site.

BTW

Dreamweaver Panels
Dreamweaver has many panels, inspectors, and bars. To open any of them, click Window on the Application bar.

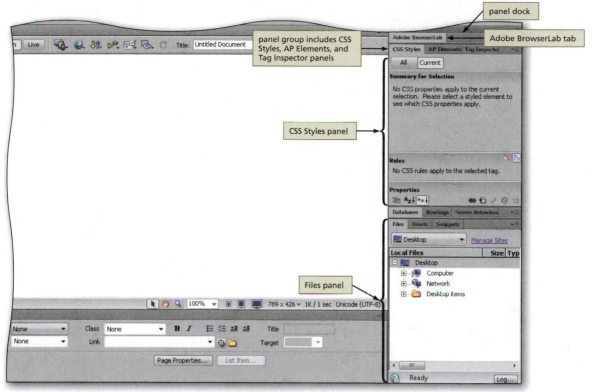

Figure 1–11

Displaying Document Views

The Document toolbar contains buttons that display different views of an active Web page.

Code View In **Code view**, the Document window displays the HTML, CSS, JavaScript, and other server-side (Web programming) language code within a Web page. Figure 1–12 shows the completed source code from the Small Business Incubator Plan Web site. The different parts of the code are associated with certain colors, making it easier to code by hand.

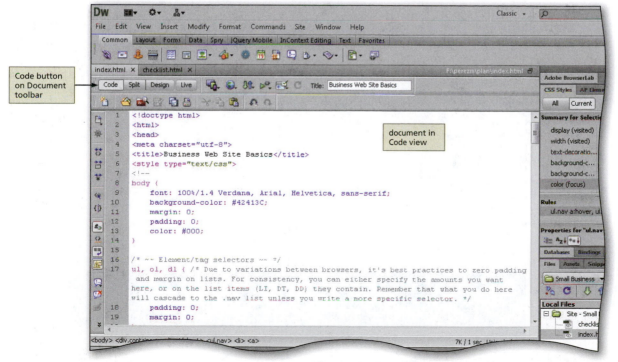

Figure 1–12

Split View **Split view** displays both the source code and the document design simultaneously. Figure 1–13 shows the completed chapter project Web page in Split view. If you add text in the document design pane, the source code is updated immediately.

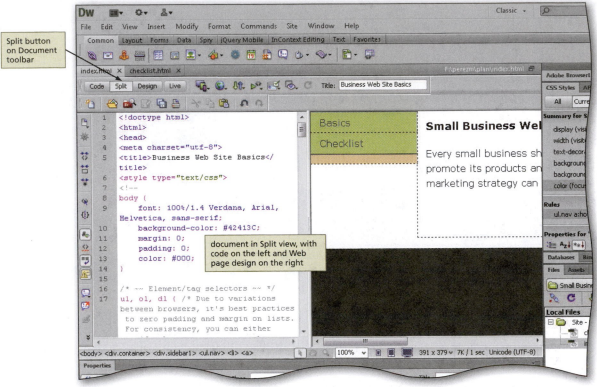

Figure 1–13

Design View The design environment, where you assemble your Web page elements and design your page, is called **Design view**, as shown in the completed project in Figure 1–14.

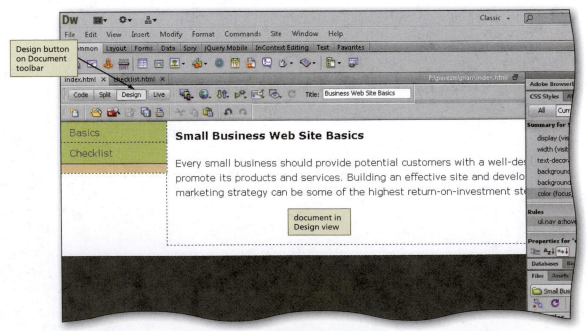

Figure 1–14

Live View **Live view** displays an interactive, browser-based view of the document. This view looks similar to the Design view except it does not support editing functions.

Opening and Closing Panels

The Dreamweaver panels help you organize and modify content using commands and functions. You can customize the workspace to display only the panels you want. Drag a panel by its title bar to move it from its default location and position it where you like, optimizing your Dreamweaver environment. Moving and hiding panels makes it easy to access the panels you need without cluttering your workspace. Each time you start Dreamweaver, the workspace is displayed in the same layout from the last time you used Dreamweaver.

Throughout the workspace, you can open and close the panel groups and display or hide other Dreamweaver features as needed, or move a panel to another location. You use the Window menu to open a panel and its group. Closing unused panels provides an uncluttered workspace in the Document window. You can use the panel options button or a panel's context menu (or shortcut menu) to close the panel or its group. You also can collapse a panel so it takes up less space in the panel dock by double-clicking the panel tab, or you can collapse the entire panel dock so it takes up less space in the Dreamweaver window. In either case, you can expand a panel, panel group, or panel dock to display one or more full panels again.

To Show, Hide, and Move Panels

The following steps show, hide, and move panels.

1

• Double-click the Properties tab below the Document window to collapse the Property inspector (Figure 1–15).

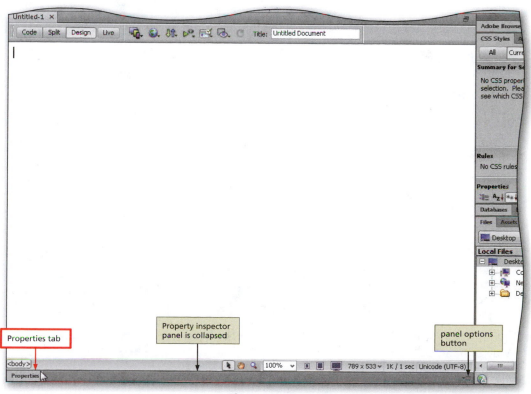

Figure 1–15

2
- Click the Collapse to Icons button in the panel dock to collapse all the panel groups (Figure 1–16).

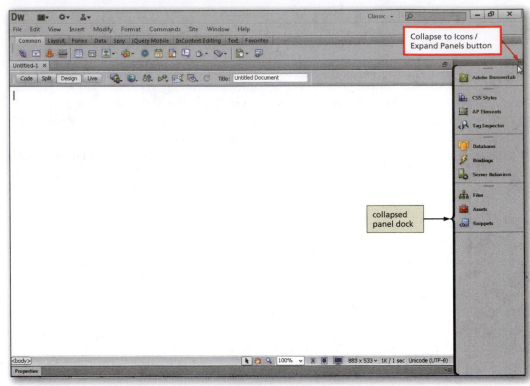

Figure 1–16

3
- Click the Expand Panels button to expand the panel groups.

Q&A

What happened to the Collapse to Icons button?

The Collapse to Icons button and Expand Panels button are in the same location. After you collapse the panels, the button changes to the Expand Panels button so you can expand the panels again.

- Click the Properties tab to expand the Property inspector (Figure 1–17).

Q&A

What is the fastest way to open and close panels?

The fastest way to open and close panels in Dreamweaver is to use the F4 key, which opens or closes all panels and inspectors at one time.

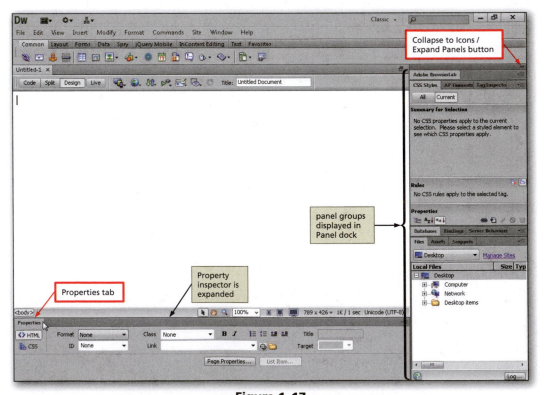

Figure 1–17

4

- Drag the Adobe
  BrowserLab panel
  by its tab to the
  center of the screen
  to move the panel
  to a new location
  (Figure 1–18).

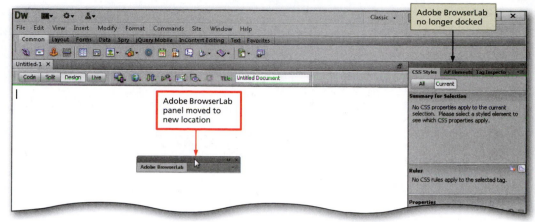

Figure 1–18

Other Ways

1. Click panel options
   button, click Close or click
   Close Tab Group

2. Right-click panel, click
   Close or click Close Tab
   Group

3. Right-click panel, click
   Minimize or click Expand
   Panel

4. Press F4

To Reset the Classic Workspace

After collapsing, expanding, and moving panels, you may want to return the workspace to its default settings. The default workspace, called Classic, displays commonly used panels. The following steps reset the Classic workspace.

1

- Click the Workspace
  Switcher button
  on the Application
  bar to display the
  Workspace Switcher
  menu (Figure 1–19).

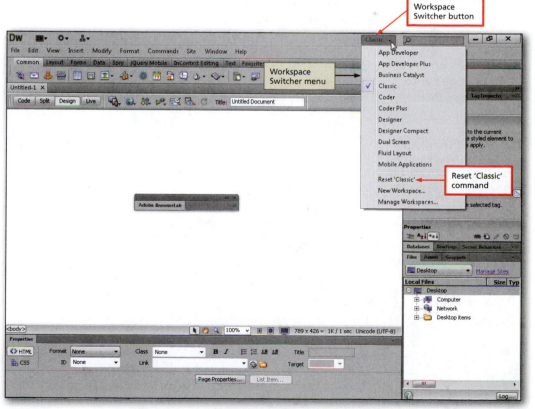

Figure 1–19

2

- Click Reset 'Classic' to restore the workspace to its default settings (Figure 1–20).

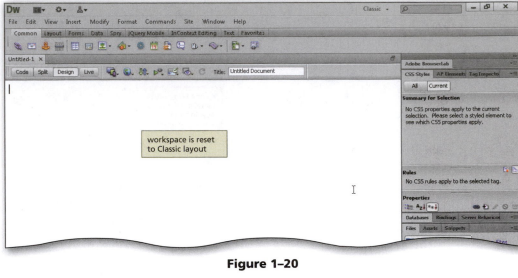

workspace is reset to Classic layout

Figure 1–20

Other Ways

1. On Window menu, point to Workspace Layout, click Reset 'Classic'

To Display the Standard Toolbar

In the Classic workspace, Dreamweaver can display three toolbars: Style Rendering, Document, and Standard. You can choose to display or hide the toolbars by clicking View on the Application bar and then pointing to Toolbars. If a toolbar name has a check mark next to it, it is displayed in the window. To hide the toolbar, click the name of the toolbar so it no longer is displayed.

The Standard toolbar is not displayed by default in the Document window when Dreamweaver starts. As with other toolbars and panels, you can dock or undock and move the Standard toolbar so it can be displayed in a different location on your screen. Drag any toolbar by its selection handle to undock and move the toolbar.

The following steps display the Standard toolbar.

1

- Click View on the Application bar to display the View menu.

- If necessary, click the down-pointing arrow at the bottom of the View menu to scroll the menu.

- Point to Toolbars to display the Toolbars submenu (Figure 1–21).

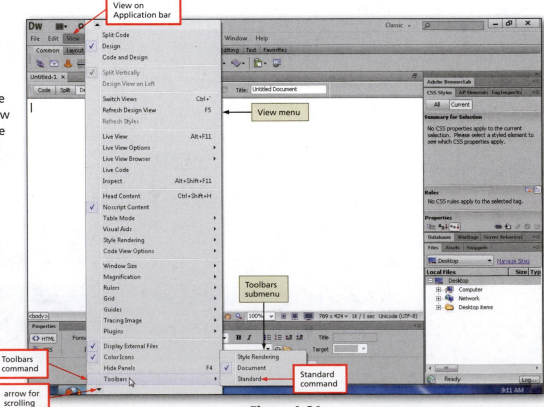

View on Application bar

View menu

Toolbars submenu

Toolbars command

arrow for scrolling

Style Rendering
Document
Standard

Standard command

Figure 1–21

2

- Click Standard on the Toolbars submenu to display the Standard toolbar (Figure 1–22).

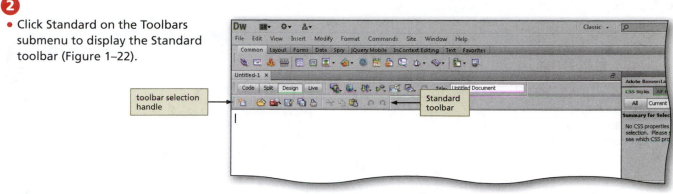

toolbar selection handle

Standard toolbar

Figure 1–22

Other Ways
1. Right-click blank area on toolbar, click Standard

To Access Preferences

In addition to creating a customized environment by selecting a workspace; collapsing, expanding, and moving the panels; and adding toolbars, you can further customize your environment by adjusting your preferences. Dreamweaver's work **preferences** are options that modify the appearance of the workspace, user interactions, accessibility features, and default settings such as font, file types, browsers, code coloring, and code hints. Dreamweaver offers you the flexibility to shape your Web page tools and your code output.

The following steps access Dreamweaver's preferences.

1

- Click Edit on the Application bar to display the Edit menu (Figure 1–23).

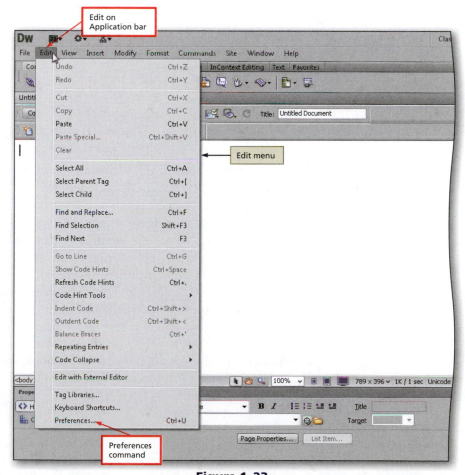

Edit on Application bar

Edit menu

Preferences command

Figure 1–23

2

● Click Preferences to display the Preferences dialog box (Figure 1–24).

Q&A

How do I view the options within each category of preferences?

You can view each option by selecting the category in the left pane to display the options for that category in the main area of the dialog box.

3

● Click the OK button (Preferences dialog box) to close the dialog box.

Other Ways

1. Press CTRL+U

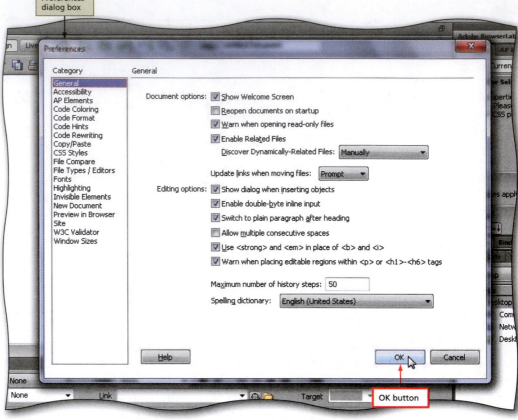

Figure 1–24

Understanding HTML5

Adobe Dreamweaver CS6 supports HTML5, the newest version of HTML. Enhanced features in HTML5 are streamlining Web site design and development so you can create more engaging Web sites, increase Web security, and deploy to multiple devices. You probably have viewed a Web site on a smartphone that was difficult to navigate because the site was not specifically designed for a mobile device. With Dreamweaver and HTML5, you can create an interactive site that will be rendered correctly on a variety of smartphones, tablets, and traditional computers. HTML5 includes native support of video without the use of a plug-in, such as Adobe Flash Player, so that videos play seamlessly on Apple devices, such as an iPad.

When a Dreamweaver page is created, an option called DocType is placed in the first line of HTML code. The **DocType** declaration is not a formatting tag, but rather an instruction to the Web browser indicating in what version of the markup language the page is written. The DocType declaration refers to a **Document Type Definition (DTD)**, which specifies the rules for the markup language so browsers can render the content correctly. For the projects in this book, the DocType will be set to HTML5 to access the latest features of HTML. The first line in an HTML5 document reads: <!DOCTYPE html>.

Understanding CSS3

Working hand in hand with HTML5, Dreamweaver CS6 also supports CSS3, Cascading Style Sheets. CSS3 is the new standard for Web site presentation. Web pages can be designed in two ways:

1. A Web page can contain layout and content information combined in a single HTML file. This option is not recommended because it is difficult to update and maintain such a Web page on larger sites.

2. A Web page can separate content from the layout in two separate files. The content information is coded in the HTML file, but the HTML file does not contain information about how that information is displayed. The appearance, or layout, is stored in a separate file called a CSS file.

A **CSS file** is a simple text file containing style rules that control the appearance of a Web page. Using CSS styles, you can control font size, font color, background, and many other attributes of a Web page, thus reducing a page's file size. In a large Web site that does not use CSS styles, making a formatting revision such as changing the font is very time consuming because each page must be changed individually to use the new font. By using CSS, you can change the font in one line of a CSS file and have the font automatically update throughout the entire site.

In this chapter, a simple text-only site about planning a Web site for a small business displays two basic pages created with a built-in Dreamweaver template that uses CSS. A **template** is a predesigned layout used to create pages with placeholder content. Dreamweaver templates provide a framework for designing a professional page that includes background colors, fonts, and a layout controlled by built-in CSS auto-generated code. In the chapter project, a predefined template with two fixed columns and a left sidebar displaying two vertical columns is used for the layout. Typically, the first vertical column displays a navigation menu while the second vertical column shows the main content of the page. Any predefined style within the template can be customized by changing the corresponding CSS settings.

> **Break Point:** If you wish to take a break, this is a good place to do so. You can quit Dreamweaver now. To resume at a later time, start Dreamweaver, and continue following the steps from this location forward.

Creating a New Site

After touring the Dreamweaver environment, you are ready to define a local site for the Small Business Incubator Web site. When you define a site, you create the folder that will contain the files and any subfolders for the site. The site consists of two pages of text that provide information on basic Web design best practices for small businesses that want to create a Web presence.

Defining a Local Site

Web design and Web site management are two important skills that a Web developer must possess and apply. Dreamweaver CS6 is a site creation and management tool. To use Dreamweaver effectively, you first must define the local site. After a Web site is developed within the local site location, the site can be published to a remote server for access by others on the Internet.

The general definition of a **site**, or Web site, is a set of linked documents with shared attributes, such as related topics, a similar design, or a shared purpose. In Dreamweaver, the term, site, can refer to any of the following:

• **Web site:** A set of pages on a server that are viewed through a Web browser by a site visitor

- **Remote site:** Files on the server that make up a Web site, from the author's point of view rather than a visitor's

- **Local site:** Files on your computer that correspond to the files on the remote site (You edit the files on your computer, often called the local computer, and then upload them to the remote site.)

- **Dreamweaver site definition:** A set of defining characteristics for a local site, plus information on how the local site corresponds to a remote site

All Dreamweaver Web sites begin with a local root folder. As you become familiar with Dreamweaver and complete the chapters in this book, you will find references to a **local site folder**, **local root folder**, **root folder**, and **root**. These terms are interchangeable. This folder is no different from any other folder on your computer's hard drive or other storage media, except in the way Dreamweaver views it. By default, Dreamweaver searches for Web pages, links, images, and other files in the designated root folder. Within the root folder, you can create additional folders and subfolders to organize images and other objects. A **subfolder** is a folder inside another folder. Dreamweaver displays only the files in the root folder and its subfolders when you preview the Web site in a Web browser.

Dreamweaver provides two options to define a site and create the hierarchy: You can create the root folder and any subfolders, or create the pages and then create the folders when saving the files. In this book, you create the root folder and subfolders, and then create the Web pages.

Plan Ahead

Determine the location for the local site

Before you create a Web site, you need to determine where you will save the site and its files.

- If you plan to work on your Web site in various locations or on more than one computer, you should create your site on removable media, such as a USB flash drive. The Web sites in this book use a USB flash drive because these drives are portable and can store a lot of data.

- If you always work on the same computer, you probably can create your site on the computer's hard drive. However, if you are working in a computer lab, your instructor or the lab supervisor might instruct you to save your site in a particular location on the hard drive or on removable media such as a USB flash drive. (This book assumes the Web site files are stored on a USB flash drive.)

Creating the Local Root Folder and Subfolders

You can use several options to create and manage your local root folder and subfolders, including Dreamweaver's Files panel, Dreamweaver's Site Setup feature, and Windows file management. In this book, you use the most common ways to manage files and folders: Dreamweaver's Site Setup feature to create the local root folder and subfolders, the Files panel to manage and edit your files and folders, and Windows file management to download and copy the data files.

To organize and create a Web site and understand how you access Web documents, you need to understand paths and folders. The term, path, sometimes is confusing for new users of the Web. It is, however, a simple concept: A **path** is the succession of folders that must be navigated to get from one folder to another. Because folders sometimes are referred to as **directories,** the two terms are often used interchangeably.

A typical path structure containing Web site files has a **master folder**, called the **root**, and is designated by the backslash symbol (\ ) in the path notation that appears in the Dreamweaver window. This root folder contains all of the other subfolders or nested folders. Further, each subfolder may contain additional subfolders or nested folders. On most sites, the root folder includes a subfolder for images.

For this book, you first will create a local root folder using your last name and first initial. Examples in this book use Mia Perez as the Web site author. Thus, Mia's local root folder is perezm and is located on drive F (a USB drive, which might have a different drive letter on your computer). Next, you will create a subfolder named plan for the Web site you create in this chapter. You will store related files and subfolders within the plan folder. When you navigate through this folder hierarchy, you are navigating along the path. The path to the Small Business Incubator Web site is F:\perezm\plan\. In all references to F:\perezm, substitute your last name and first initial and your drive location.

Using Site Setup to Create a Local Site

You create a local site using Dreamweaver's Site Setup dialog box, which provides four categories of settings. For the Web site you create in the chapter, you only need to work in the Site category, where you enter the name of your site and the path to the local site folder. For example, you will use Small Business Incubator Plan as the site name and F:\perezm\plan\ as the path to the local site. You can select the location of the local site folder instead of entering its path.

After you complete the site definition, the folder hierarchy structure is displayed in the Dreamweaver Local Files list on the Files panel. This hierarchy structure is similar to the Windows file organization. The **Local Files** list provides a view of the devices and folders on your computer, and shows how these devices and folders are organized.

BTW

Dreamweaver Help
At any time while using Dreamweaver, you can find answers to questions and display information about various topics through Dreamweaver Help. Used properly, this form of assistance can increase your productivity and reduce your frustrations by minimizing the time you spend learning how to use Dreamweaver. For instruction about Dreamweaver Help and exercises that will help you gain confidence in using it, read the "Adobe Dreamweaver CS6 Help" appendix at the end of this book.

To Quit and Restart Dreamweaver

The following step quits Dreamweaver and then restarts the program to display the Welcome screen.

1
- Click the Close button in the upper-right corner of the Dreamweaver window to quit Dreamweaver after touring the interface.

- Click the No button (Dreamweaver dialog box) if asked to save changes to Untitled-1.

- Click the Start button on the Windows 7 taskbar to display the Start menu.

- Type `Dreamweaver CS6` in the 'Search programs and files' text box.

- Click Adobe Dreamweaver CS6 in the search results on the Start menu to start Dreamweaver and display the Welcome screen (Figure 1–25).

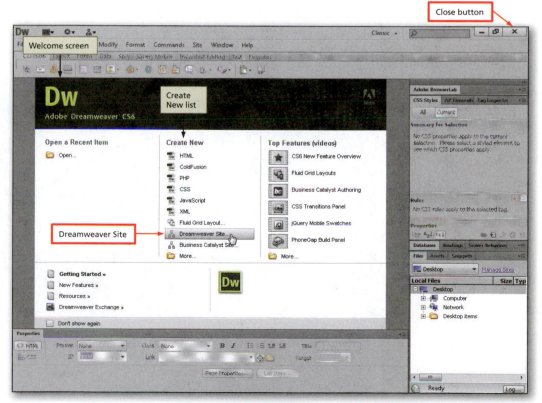

Figure 1–25

To Use Site Setup to Create a Local Site

The following steps define a local site by telling Dreamweaver where you plan to store local files. A USB drive is used for all projects and exercises in this book. If you are saving your sites in another location or on removable media, substitute that location for Removable Disk (F:).

1

- Click Dreamweaver Site in the Create New list to display the Site Setup dialog box (Figure 1–26).

Q&A

Should the name that appears in the Site Name text box be Unnamed Site 2?

Not necessarily. Your site number may be different.

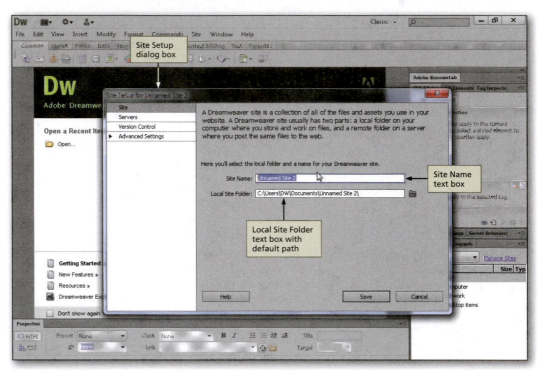

Figure 1–26

2

- Type `Small Business Incubator Plan` in the Site Name text box to name the site (Figure 1–27).

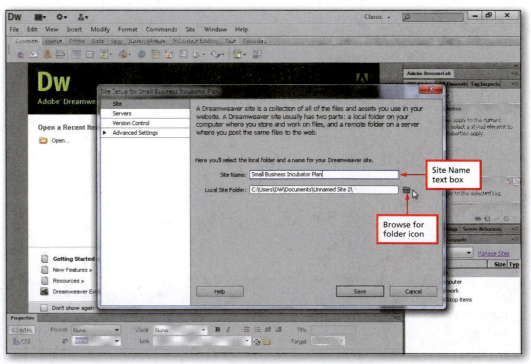

Figure 1–27

3

- Click the 'Browse for folder' icon to display the Choose Root Folder dialog box.

- Click the Select Box arrow to display locations on your system (Figure 1–28).

Q&A

Do I have to save to a USB flash drive?

No. You can save to any device or folder. A folder is a specific location on a storage medium. You can save to the default folder or a different folder.

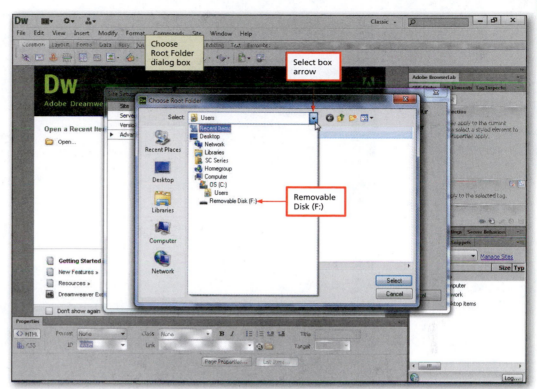

Figure 1–28

4

- Click Removable Disk (F:) in the list, or the name of your storage location.

Q&A

What if my USB flash drive has a different name or letter?

It is very likely that your USB flash drive has a different name and drive letter, and is connected to a different port. Verify that the device in the Select text box is correct.

- Click the Create New Folder button to create a folder for your local site (Figure 1–29).

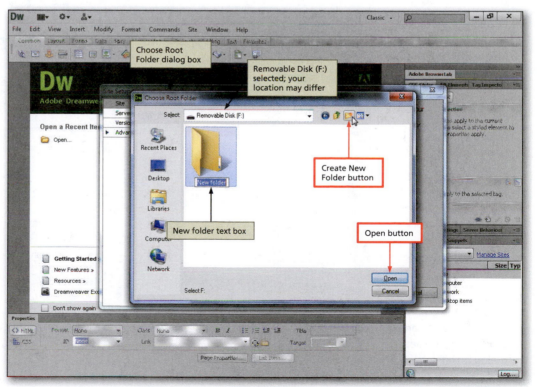

Figure 1–29

5

- For the root folder name, type your last name and first initial (with no spaces between your last name and initial) in the New folder text box. For example, type `perezm`.

- Press the ENTER key to rename the new folder (Figure 1–30).

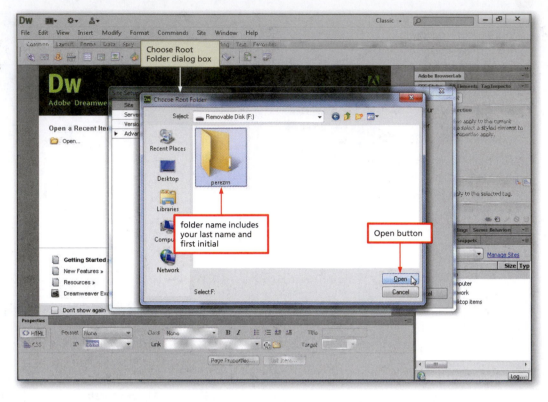

Figure 1–30

6

- Click the Open button to open the root folder.

- Click the Create New Folder button in the Choose Root Folder dialog box to create a folder for the Small Business Incubator Plan site within the folder with your last name and first initial.

- Type `plan` as the name of the new folder, press the ENTER key, and then click the Open button to create the plan subfolder and open it.

- Click the Select button to select the plan folder for the new site and display the Site Setup dialog box (Figure 1–31).

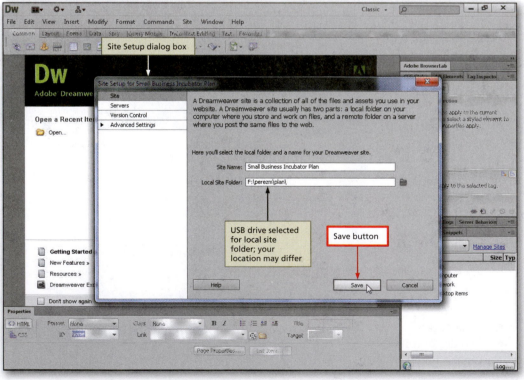

Figure 1–31

Q&A Why should I create a folder on the drive for my Web site?

Organizing your Web site folders now will save you time and prevent problems later.

Q&A Which files will I store in the plan folder?

The plan folder will contain all the files for the Small Business Incubator Plan site. In other words, the plan folder is the local root folder for the Web site.

7
- Click the Save button in the Site Setup dialog box to save the site settings and display the Small Business Incubator Plan site hierarchy on the Files panel (Figure 1–32).

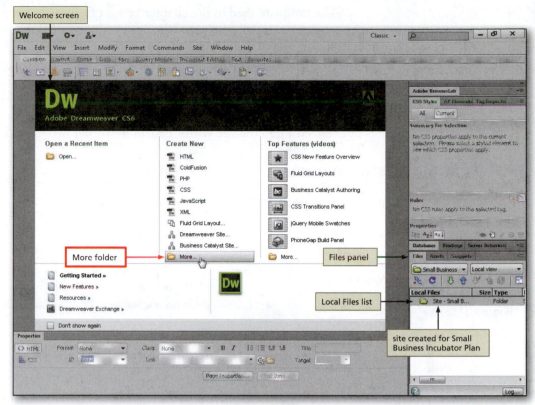

Figure 1–32

Other Ways

1. Site menu, New Site

Selecting a Predefined Template

Dreamweaver CS6 provides templates with built-in layouts to help you quickly create a Web page. The layouts are predesigned pages with placeholder content. The placeholder content is replaced with your own formatted content.

Plan Ahead

Select the words and fonts for the text
Most informational Web pages start with a heading, include paragraphs of text and one or more lists, and then end with a closing line. Before you add text to a Web page, consider the following guidelines for organizing and formatting text:

- **Headings:** Start by identifying the headings you will use. Determine which headings are for main topics (Heading 1) and which are for subtopics (Heading 2 or 3).

- **Paragraphs:** For descriptions or other information, include short paragraphs of text. To emphasize important terms, format them as bold or italic.

- **Lists:** Use lists to organize key points, a sequence of steps, or other information you want to highlight. If amount or sequence matters, number each item in a list. Otherwise, use a bullet (a dot or other symbol that appears at the beginning of the paragraph).

- **Closing:** The closing is usually one sentence that provides information of interest to most Web page viewers, or that indicates where people can find more information about your topic.

The template used in the chapter project displays two fixed columns with an earth tone color design and a DocType defined as HTML5. Dreamweaver provides two types of predefined layouts: fixed and liquid. In a **fixed layout**, the values for the overall width, as well as any columns within the page, are written using pixel units in the CSS file. In a **liquid layout**, the values for the overall width, as well as any columns within the page, are written using percentages in the CSS file. A fixed layout offers a greater measure of control to align items within the fixed columns because the layout is not resized when the site visitor resizes his or her browser window.

To Select a Template Layout

The following steps create a two-column fixed layout with a left sidebar and a DocType defined as an HTML5 page.

1

- Click the More folder icon on the Welcome screen to display the New Document dialog box (Figure 1–33).

Q&A What if I do not see a Welcome screen?

Click File on the Application bar and select New to display the New Document dialog box.

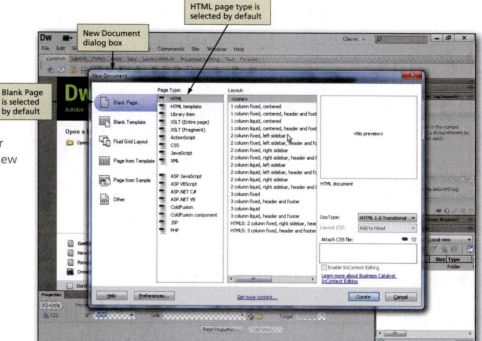

Figure 1–33

2

- Click '2 column fixed, left sidebar' in the Layout column in the New Document dialog box to display a preview of a Web page with two columns.

- Click the DocType button, and then click HTML 5 to change the DocType to HTML 5 (Figure 1–34).

Q&A Do I need to select Blank Page in the left pane and HTML in the Page Type column?

No. Those options are selected by default in the New Document dialog box.

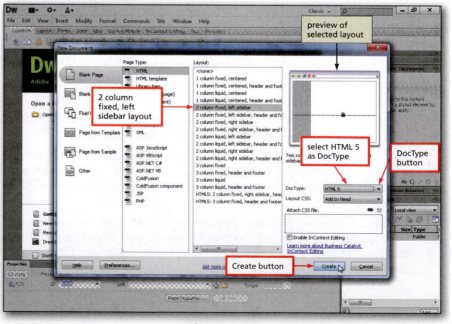

Figure 1–34

3

- Click the Create button to display the two-column fixed layout page in the Document window (Figure 1–35).

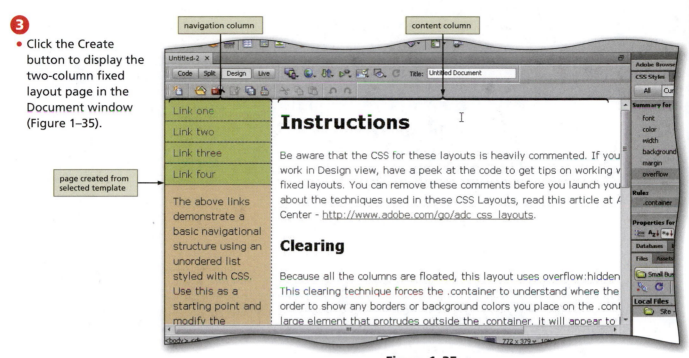

Figure 1–35

To Name and Save the Home Page

The **home page** is the starting point for a Web site. For most Web sites, the home page is named index. This name has special significance because most Web servers recognize index.html (or index.htm) as the default home page. If a folder contains multiple files, the browser determines that the first page to display on a site is the index file. Dreamweaver automatically adds the default extension .html to the file name. Documents with the .html or .htm extensions are displayed in Web browsers. If you have unsaved changes on a Web page, the document tab displays an asterisk after the html extension (index.html*). When you save the page, the asterisk disappears — confirming that your page is up to date in the saved file.

The following steps rename the untitled home page to index.html and then save it.

1

- Click File on the Application bar to display the File menu (Figure 1–36).

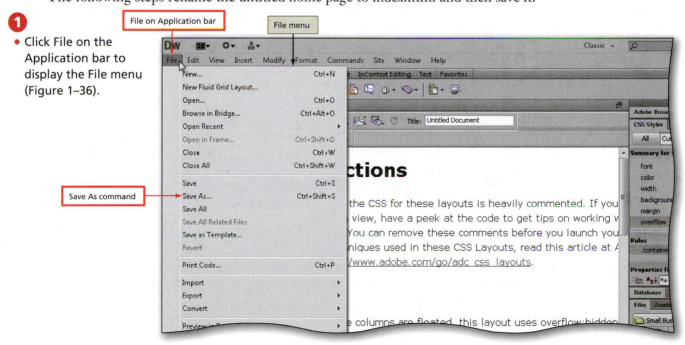

Figure 1–36

2

- Click Save As on the File menu to display the Save As dialog box (Figure 1–37).

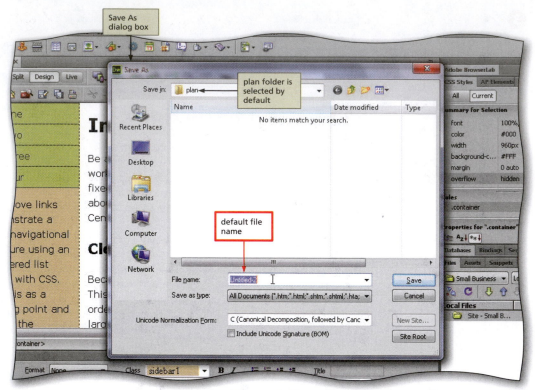

Figure 1–37

3

- If necessary, select the text in the File Name text box, and then type `index` to name the home page (Figure 1–38).

Q&A

Is it necessary to type the extension .html after the file name?

No. By default, Dreamweaver saves an HTML file with the extension .html.

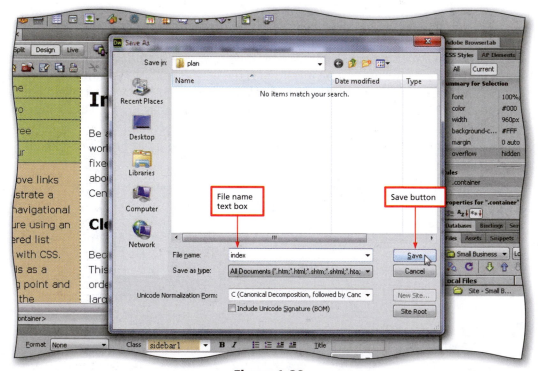

Figure 1–38

 For a detailed example of saving a Web page using the Mac operating system, refer to the "To Save a File in Dreamweaver" steps in the For Mac Users appendix at the end of the book.

4

- Click the Save button (Save As dialog box) to save the home page as index.html and to display the new file name on the document tab (Figure 1–39).

Q&A

What do the icons on the Files panel indicate?

A small device icon or folder icon is displayed next to each object listed on the Files panel. The device icon represents a device such as the Desktop or a disk drive, and the folder icon represents a folder. These icons may have an expand (plus sign) or collapse (minus sign) next to them indicating whether the device or folder contains additional folders. You click these icons to expand or collapse the view of the file hierarchy.

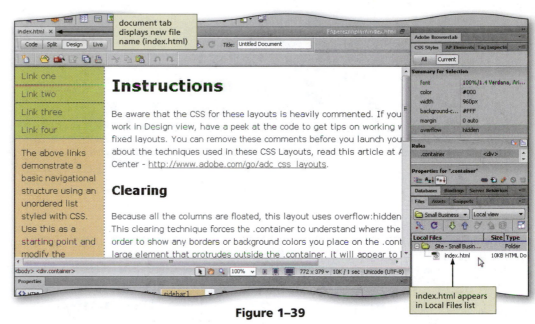

Figure 1–39

To Edit Navigation Link Text

The two columns in the template contain placeholder text instead of an empty page so that you can view how the page will look when displayed in a browser. The left column includes links for navigating from one page to another. Both pages in the Small Business Incubator Plan Web site should display only two links: a Basics link used to display the home page, and a Checklist link used to display the checklist page. The following steps change the link text for the first two links and delete the remaining links in the navigation column.

1

- Drag to select the text, Link one, in the left column of index.html and type Basics to change the text for the first link.

- Drag to select the text, Link two, and type Checklist to change the text for the second link (Figure 1–40).

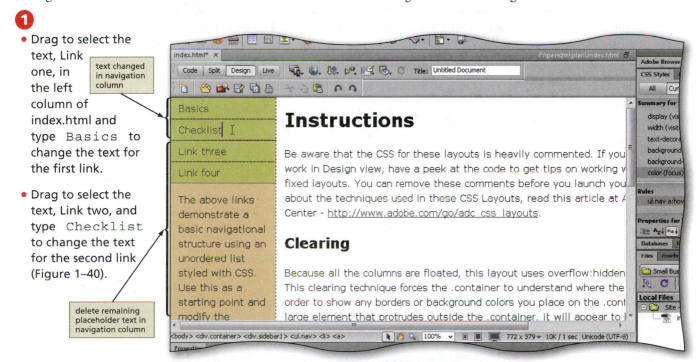

Figure 1–40

- Drag to select the text, Link three, and then press the DELETE key to remove the third link.

- Drag to select the text, Link four, and then press the DELETE key to remove the fourth link.

- Drag to select the paragraph below the links, and then press the DELETE key to remove the placeholder text (Figure 1–41).

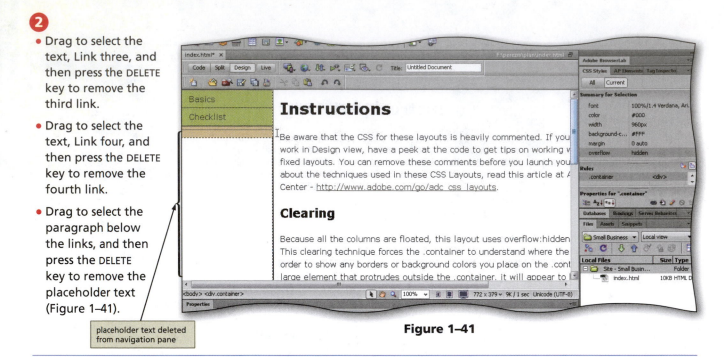

placeholder text deleted from navigation pane

Figure 1–41

To Format Text Using Heading Styles

HTML defines a collection of font styles called **headings** to format the size of text. The advantage of using heading styles to format text that serves as a headline or title is that headings are displayed in relative sizes with Heading 1 <h1> being the largest heading and Heading 6 <h6> being the smallest heading. Any text formatted with Heading 1 is always larger than text formatted with Heading 2. **Formatting** involves setting heading styles, inserting special characters, and inserting or modifying other elements that enhance the appearance of the Web page. Dreamweaver provides three options for directly formatting text: the Format menu on the Application bar, the Text category on the Insert panel, and the Property inspector. In Chapter 2, you will format Web page text using CSS styles. To format the content title in the second column of the index page, you will use the text-related features of the Property inspector.

The Property inspector is one of the panels used most often when creating and formatting Web pages. Recall that it displays the properties, or characteristics, of the selected object. The object can be a table, text, an image, or some other item. The Property inspector is context sensitive, so its options change relative to the selected object.

The following steps edit the text and heading style in the content column.

- Drag to select the text, Instructions, in the right column of the index.html page, and then type Small Business Web Site Basics to change the content title (Figure 1–42).

updated title in content column

Figure 1–42

2

- Drag to select the paragraph below the new title, and then type `Every small business should provide potential customers with a well-designed Web site to promote its products and services. Building an effective site and developing an online marketing strategy can be some of the highest return-on-investment steps you can take.` to change the first paragraph.

- Drag to select the rest of the placeholder text in the content column, and then press the DELETE key to delete the text (Figure 1–43).

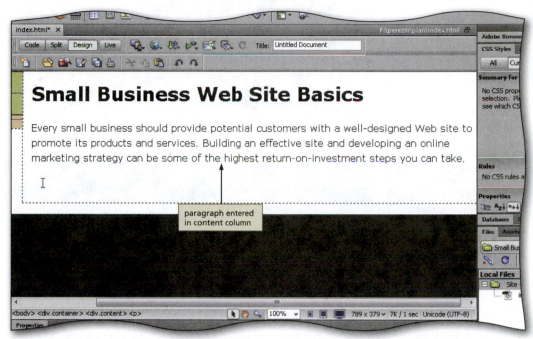

Figure 1–43

3

- Drag to select the content title, Small Business Web Site Basics.

- Click the Format button in the Property inspector to display styles to apply to the selected text (Figure 1–44).

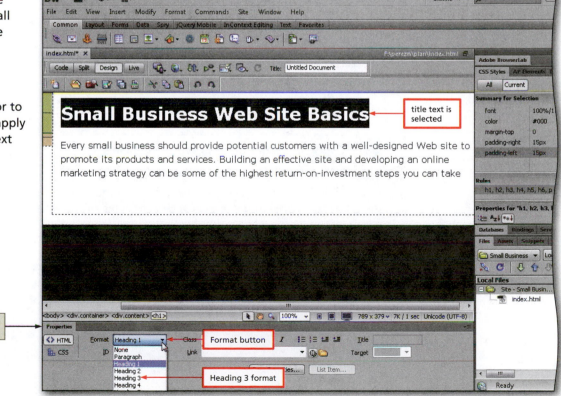

Figure 1–44

4

- Click Heading 3 to apply the Heading 3 style to the content title text (Figure 1–45).

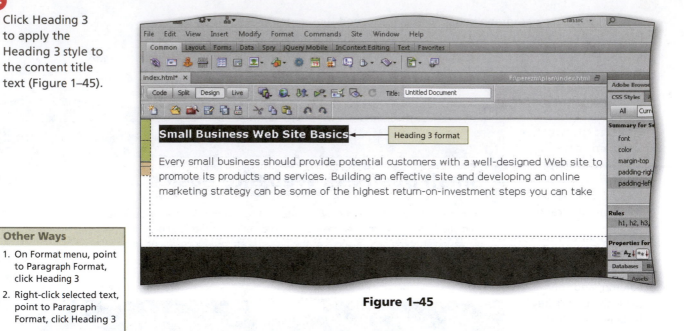

Figure 1–45

To Create a Link

Links allow users to move from page to page by clicking text or other objects. In the Property inspector, the Link box allows you to transform selected text or other objects into a hyperlink to a specified URL or Web page. You either can point to the hyperlink destination by dragging the Point to File button, or browse to a page in your Web site and select the file name. As you drag the Point to File button, Dreamweaver displays a line showing the connection between the Point to File button and the file link. In a browser, when the site visitor clicks the Basics link, the index page should open. The following steps create a hyperlink by dragging.

1

- Select the text, Basics, in the left column of index.html (Figure 1–46).

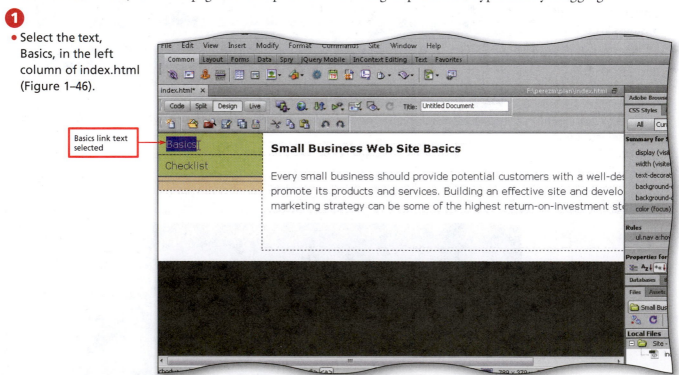

Figure 1–46

2

• Drag the Point to File button in the Property inspector to the index.html file on the Files panel to create a link to index.html (Figure 1–47).

3

• Release the mouse button to complete the link to index.html.

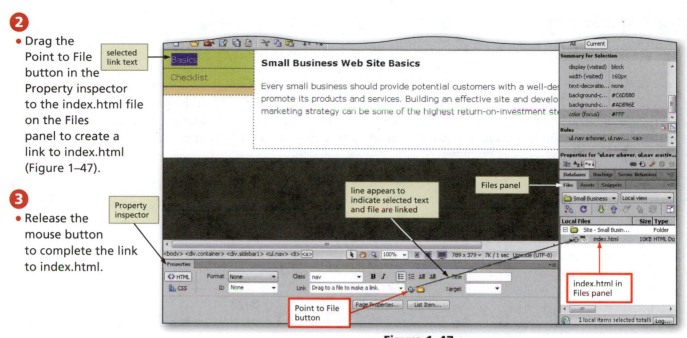

Figure 1–47

Other Ways

1. Type URL or file name in Link box
2. Click Link arrow and select URL

To Save the Home Page

The following steps save the changes to the home page, index.html.

1

• Click File on the Application bar to display the File menu (Figure 1–48).

2

• Click Save on the File menu to save the document.

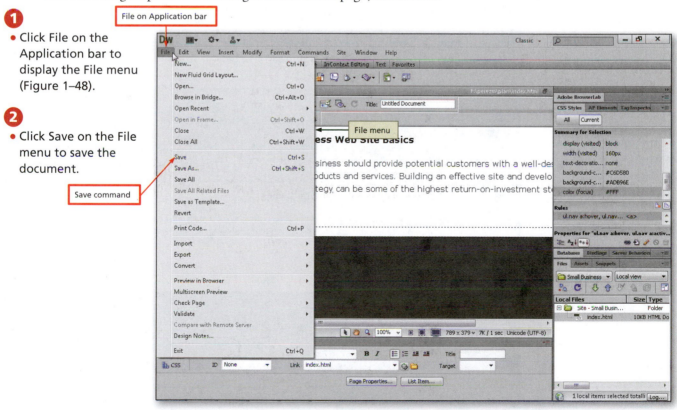

Figure 1–48

MAC For a detailed example of saving a Web page using the Mac operating system, refer to the "To Save a File in Dreamweaver" steps in the For Mac Users appendix at the end of the book.

To Add a Second Page

The first page, index.html, is the model for the second page; in fact, a copy of the first page can serve as the second page. Creating a copy of the first page saves the design time of recreating the page.

The home page (index.html) and the second page (checklist.html) are identical except for the custom text in the content column of each page. As you add pages to your Web site, if your new page is similar to a previous page you created, first save the changes to the existing page, and then save the page again with the new page name, such as checklist.html. The following steps add a second page to the Web site.

1
- Click File on the Application bar to display the File menu.
- Click Save As on the File menu to display the Save As dialog box.
- Type checklist in File name text box to name the second page (Figure 1–49).

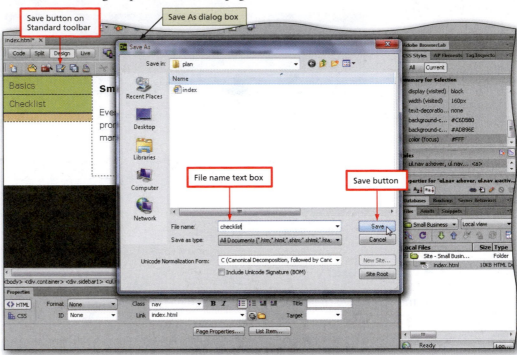

Figure 1–49

2
- Click the Save button in the Save As dialog box to save the second page as checklist.html (Figure 1–50).

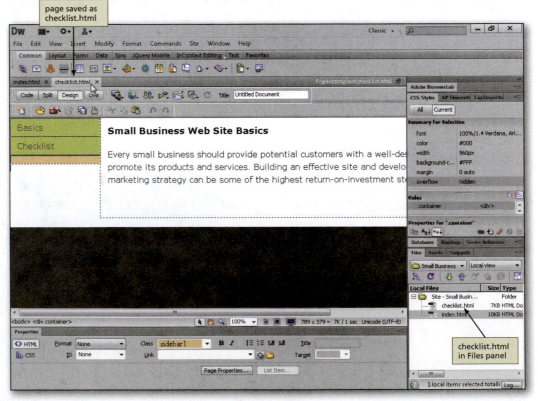

Figure 1–50

To Create an Unordered List

Using lists is a convenient way to group and organize information. Web pages can have three types of lists: ordered (numbered), unordered (bulleted), and definition. **Ordered lists** contain text preceded by numbered steps. **Unordered lists** contain text preceded by bullets (dots or other symbols) or image bullets. You use an unordered list if the items need not be listed in any particular order. **Definition lists** do not use leading characters such as bullet points or numbers. Glossaries and descriptions often use this type of list.

You can type a new list or you can create a list from existing text. When you select existing text and add bullets, the blank lines between the list items are deleted. The following steps edit the checklist.html page to include a new title and a bulleted list of design best practices for a business Web site.

1

- Select the title text, Small Business Web Site Basics, in checklist.html, and then type `Web Site Planning Checklist` to change the title text (Figure 1–51).

Figure 1–51

2

- Select the text in the paragraph below the title, and then press the DELETE key to delete the first paragraph.

- Type `The design and layout of a business Web site should be clean, simple, and professional` and then press the ENTER key to begin a new paragraph.

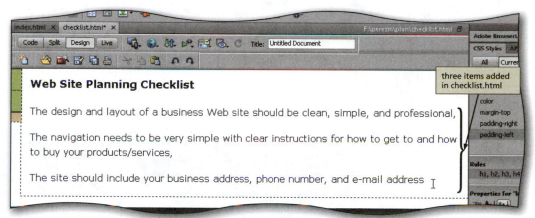

Figure 1–52

- Type `The navigation needs to be very simple with clear instructions for how to get to and how to buy your products/services` and then press the ENTER key to begin a new paragraph.

- Type `The site should include your business address, phone number, and e-mail address` (Figure 1–52).

3

- Drag to select the three checklist items (Figure 1–53).

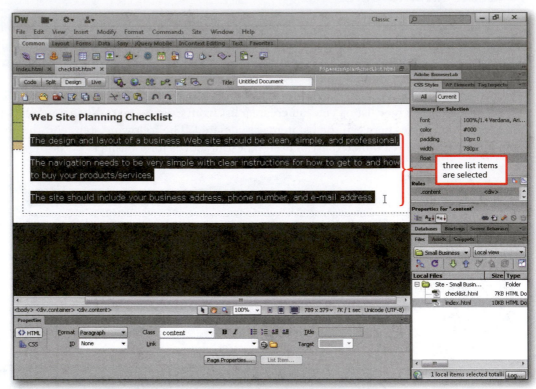

Figure 1–53

4

- In the Property inspector, click the Unordered List button to indent the text and add a bullet to each line.

- Click at the end of the third bulleted line to deselect the text (Figure 1–54).

Q&A

How do I start a list with a different number or letter?

In the Document window, click the list item you want to change, click Format on the Application bar, point to List, and then click Properties. In the List Properties dialog box, select the options you want to define.

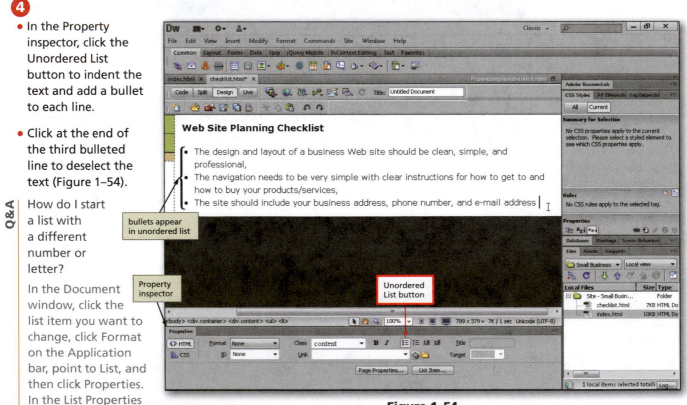

Figure 1–54

Other Ways

1. Format menu, point to List, click Unordered List

2. Right-click text, point to List, click Unordered List

To Add the Links to the Second Page

To complete the navigation, the text, Checklist, in the left column must be linked on both pages to checklist.html. The following steps link the navigation text to the second page.

1

- Drag the horizontal scroll bar at the bottom of the Document window to scroll to the left to display the left column.

- Select the text, Checklist, in the left column.

- Drag the Point to File button in the Property inspector to the checklist.html file on the Files panel to create a link to checklist.html (Figure 1–55).

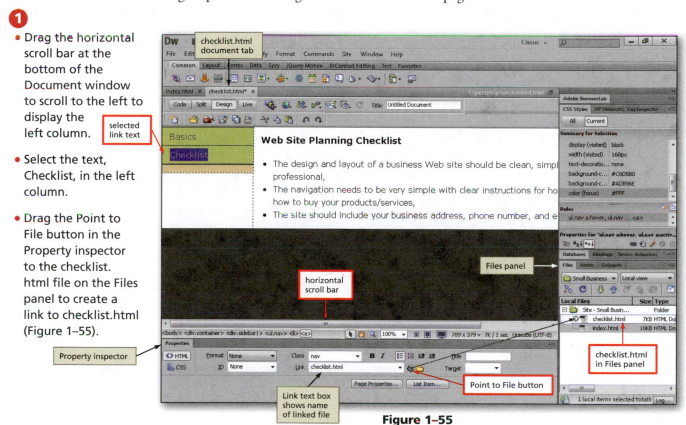

Figure 1–55

2

- Click the index.html document tab to display the index page.

- Drag to select the text, Checklist, in the left column of index.html.

- Drag the Point to File button in the Property inspector to the checklist.html file on the Files panel to create a link to checklist.html (Figure 1–56).

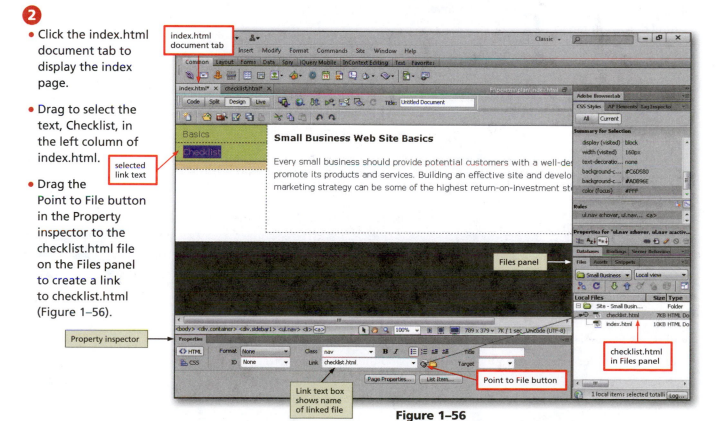

Figure 1–56

To Change the Web Page Title

A **Web page title** helps Web site visitors keep track of what they are viewing as they browse. It is important to give your Web page an appropriate title. When visitors to your Web page create bookmarks or add the Web page to their Favorites lists, they use the title for reference. If you do not title a page, the browser displays the page as Untitled Document in the browser tab, Favorites lists, and history lists. Because many search engines use the Web page title, you should create a descriptive and meaningful name. A document file name is not the same as the page title. The page title appears on the tab of the browser in Internet Explorer 7 and later versions.

The following steps change the Web page title of each page.

- With the index.html page still displayed, select the text, Untitled Document, in the Title text box on the Document toolbar to prepare to replace the text.

- Type Business Web Site Basics in the Title text box to enter a descriptive title for the Web page (Figure 1–57).

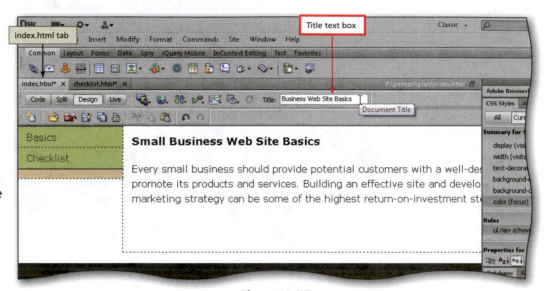

Figure 1–57

- Click the checklist. html document tab to display the checklist page.

- Select the text, Untitled Document, in the Title text box on the Document toolbar to prepare to replace the text.

- Type Business Web Site Checklist in the Title text box to enter a descriptive title for the Web page (Figure 1–58).

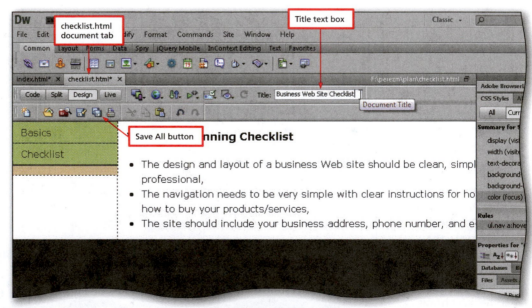

Figure 1–58

3

- Click the Save All button on the Standard toolbar to save both documents.

Q&A What is the difference between the Save button and the Save All button?

When you click the Save button, you save changes only in the displayed document. When you click the Save All button, you save changes in all the open documents.

To Check Spelling

After you create a Web page, you should inspect the page visually for spelling errors. In addition, you can use Dreamweaver's Check Spelling command to identify possible misspellings. The Check Spelling command ignores HTML tags.

The following steps use the Check Spelling command to check the spelling of your entire document. Your Web page may contain different misspelled words depending on the accuracy of your typing.

- Click the index.html document tab.

- Click at the beginning of the document in the right column to position the insertion point.

- Click Commands on the Application bar to display the Commands menu (Figure 1–59).

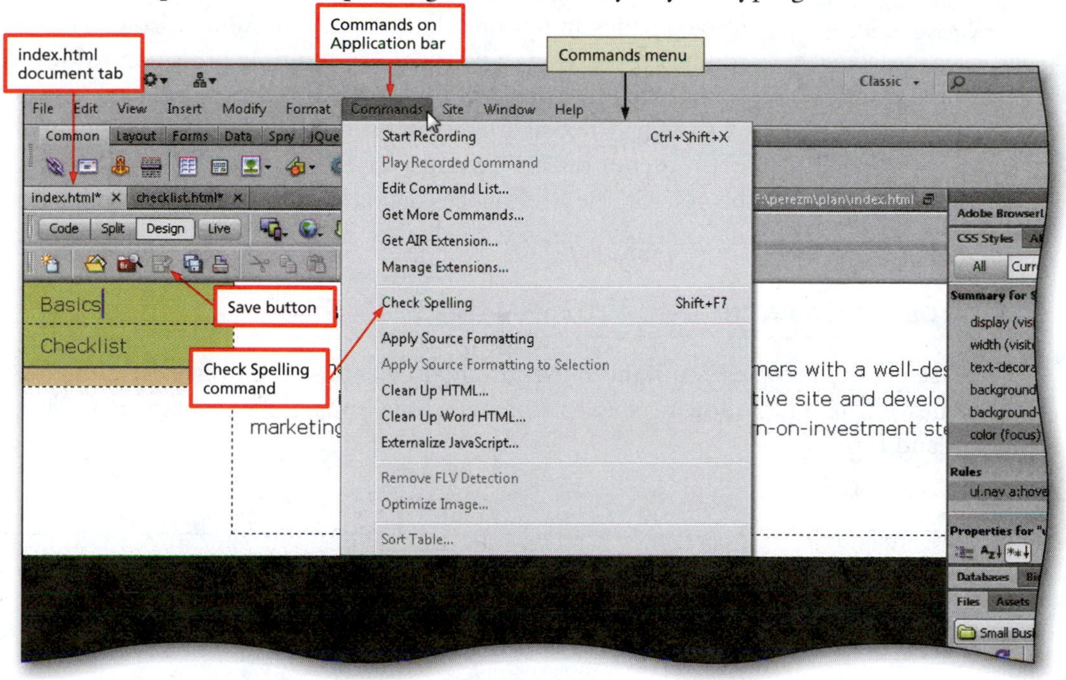

- Click Check Spelling to display the Check Spelling dialog box.

- If a misspelled word is highlighted, click the correct spelling of the word in the Suggestions list or type the correct spelling, and then click the Change button.

Q&A What should I do if Dreamweaver highlights a proper noun or correctly spelled word as being misspelled?

Click Ignore or click Ignore All if proper nouns are displayed as errors.

- If necessary, continue to check the spelling and, as necessary, correct any misspelled word.

- Click the OK button when you are finished checking spelling.

- Click the Save button on the Standard toolbar to save the document.

Figure 1–59

Other Ways
1. Press SHIFT+F7

Previewing a Web Page in a Browser

After you have created a Web page, it is a good practice to test your Web page by previewing it in Web browsers to ensure that it is displayed correctly. Using this strategy helps you catch errors so you will not copy or repeat them.

Review final tasks
Before completing a Web page, perform the following tasks to make sure it is ready for others to view:

- Give your Web page a title.
- Check the spelling and proofread the text.
- Preview the page in one or more browsers so you can see how it looks when others open it.

Plan Ahead

BTW

Quick Reference
For a table that lists how to complete the tasks covered in this book using the mouse, menus, context menus, and keyboard, see the Quick Reference Summary at the back of the book or visit the Dreamweaver student companion site located at www.cengagebrain.com.

As you create your Web page, you should be aware of the variety of available Web browsers. HTML5 can help create more consistency across browsers, but the pages should be tested in each browser platform even if you are using HTML5. Each browser may display text, images, and other Web page elements differently. For this reason, you should preview your Web pages in more than one browser to make sure the browsers display your Web pages as you designed them. Be aware that visitors viewing your Web page might have earlier versions of these browsers. Dreamweaver also provides an option called Preview in Adobe BrowserLab that provides a free online comparison of your page in multiple browsers. **Adobe BrowserLab** is an online service that helps ensure your Web content is displayed as intended.

The Preview/Debug in browser button on the Document toolbar provides a list of all Web browsers currently installed on your computer. You can select a primary browser in the Preferences dialog box. Before previewing a document, save the document; otherwise, the browser will not display your most recent changes.

To Choose a Browser and Preview the Web Site

To select the browser you want to use for the preview, use the Preview/Debug in browser button on the Document toolbar. The following steps preview the Small Business Incubator Plan Web site using Internet Explorer and Firefox.

1
• Click the Preview/ Debug in browser button on the Document toolbar to display a list of browsers installed on your computer (Figure 1–60).

Q&A
Why do I have different browsers listed?

This list displays browsers that are installed on your local computer. If you want to test your page in other browsers, download and install multiple browsers.

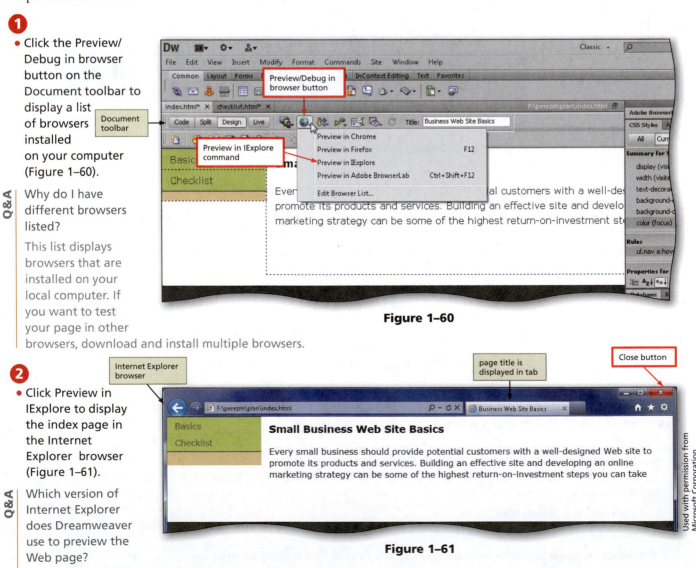

Figure 1–60

2
• Click Preview in IExplore to display the index page in the Internet Explorer browser (Figure 1–61).

Q&A
Which version of Internet Explorer does Dreamweaver use to preview the Web page?

Figure 1–61

Dreamweaver uses the version of Internet Explorer installed on your computer.

3

- Click the Close button on the Internet Explorer title bar to close the browser.

- If the Firefox browser is installed on your system, click the Preview/Debug in browser button again, and then click Preview in Firefox to display the Web page in the Firefox browser.

- Click the Close button on the Firefox title bar to close the browser.

Other Ways

1. On File menu, point to Preview in Browser, click browser of choice

2. Right-click document, click Preview in Browser, click browser

3. F12, CTRL+F12

Dreamweaver Help

The built-in Help feature in Dreamweaver provides reference materials and other forms of assistance. When the main Help page opens, it connects to the Adobe Web site.

To Access Dreamweaver Help

The following step accesses Dreamweaver Help. You must be connected to the Web to complete this step.

1

- With the Dreamweaver program open, click Help on the Application bar to display the Help menu.

- Click Dreamweaver Help to access Adobe Community Help online.

- If necessary, double-click the title bar to maximize the window (Figure 1–62).

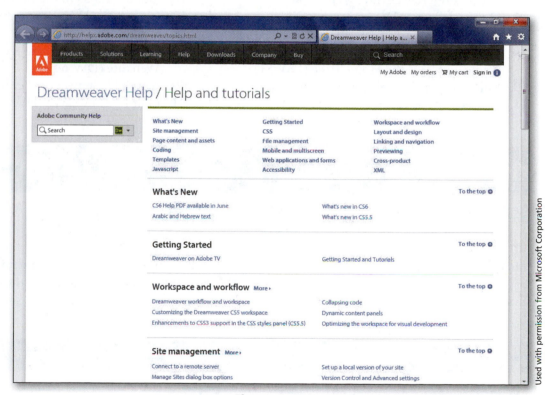

Figure 1–62

Other Ways

1. Press F1

To Quit Dreamweaver

The following step quits Dreamweaver and returns control to Windows.

1

- Click the Close button on the right side of the Application bar to close the window.

- If Dreamweaver displays a dialog box asking you to save changes, click the No button.

Other Ways

1. On File menu, click Exit

2. Press CTRL+Q

MAC For a detailed example of quitting Dreamweaver using the Mac operating system, refer to the "To Quit Dreamweaver" steps in the For Mac Users appendix at the end of this book.

Chapter Summary

In this chapter, you have learned how to start Dreamweaver, define a Web site, and create a Web page. You added a link and used Dreamweaver's Property inspector to connect to another page in the site. You also learned how to use an unordered list to organize information into a bulleted list. Once your Web page was completed, you learned how to save the Web page and preview it in a browser. To enhance your knowledge of Dreamweaver further, you learned the basics about Dreamweaver Help.

The following tasks are all the new Dreamweaver skills you learned, listed in the same order they were presented. For a list of keyboard commands for topics introduced in this chapter, see the Quick Reference for Windows at the back of this book. The list below includes all the new Dreamweaver skills you have learned in this chapter:

1. Start Dreamweaver (DW 28)
2. Show, Hide, and Move Panels (DW 37)
3. Reset the Classic Workspace (DW 39)
4. Display the Standard Toolbar (DW 40)
5. Access Preferences (DW 41)
6. Quit and Restart Dreamweaver (DW 45)
7. Use Site Setup to Create a Local Site (DW 46)
8. Select a Template Layout (DW 50)
9. Name and Save the Home Page (DW 51)
10. Edit Navigation Link Text (DW 53)
11. Format Text Using Heading Styles (DW 54)
12. Create a Link (DW 56)
13. Save the Home Page (DW 57)
14. Add a Second Page (DW 58)
15. Create an Unordered List (DW 59)
16. Add the Links to the Second Page (DW 61)
17. Change the Web Page Title (DW 62)
18. Check Spelling (DW 63)
19. Choose a Browser and Preview the Web Site (DW 64)
20. Access Dreamweaver Help (DW 65)
21. Quit Dreamweaver (DW 65)

Apply Your Knowledge

Reinforce the skills and apply the concepts you learned in this chapter.

Creating a New Web Page

Instructions: Start Dreamweaver. In this activity, you will define a local site, create a new Web page, and save the Web page. Next, you will give the page a title and then add text to the page. Finally, you will format the text and create an ordered list. The completed Web page is shown in Figure 1–63.

Figure 1–63

Perform the following tasks:

1. Use the Site Setup dialog box to define a new local site in the *your last name and first initial* folder (the F:\perezm folder, for example). Type `Apply` as the new site name.

2. Click the 'Browse for folder' icon and navigate to your USB flash drive. Create a new subfolder within the *your last name and first initial* folder and name it `Apply`. Open the folder, select it as the local site folder, and then save the Apply site.

3. Create a new HTML page. Save the new HTML page and type `apply1.html` as the file name.

4. Enter `Web Site Development` as the document title.

5. Type `Web Site Development Steps, Easy as 1-2-3` at the top of the page, and then press the ENTER key.

6. Type `The first step in developing a new Web site is to define a local site. A local site is defined in the Site Setup dialog box.` Press the ENTER key.

7. Type `Once the new site is defined, a new HTML page is created and saved. The new page is typically the home page and the home page is named index.html.` Press the ENTER key.

8. Type `Once the new HTML or home page is created, text is added to the page and then formatted.`

9. Press the ENTER key two times. Type your first and last names.

10. Apply the Heading 1 format to the first line of text.

11. Select paragraphs 2–4, and then click the Ordered List button in the Property inspector to make the text an ordered list.

12. Save your changes and then view your document in your browser. Compare your document to Figure 1–63. Make any necessary changes and then save your changes.

13. Submit the document in the format specified by your instructor.

Extend Your Knowledge

Extend the skills you learned in this chapter and experiment with new skills. You may need to use Help to complete the assignment.

Formatting a Web Page

Note: To complete this assignment, you will be required to use the Data Files for Students. Visit www.cengage.com/ct/studentdownload for detailed instructions, or contact your instructor for information about accessing the required files.

Instructions: Start Dreamweaver. A recreational soccer league wants to teach team managers how to create Web pages using Dreamweaver. The league president created a Web page and asks you to improve it. First, you will enhance the Web page by applying styles, aligning text, and indenting text. Finally, you will make the page more useful by adding links to text. The modified Web page is shown in Figure 1–64.

Continued >

Extend Your Knowledge *continued*

Figure 1–64

Perform the following tasks:

1. Use the Site Setup dialog box to define a new local site in the *your last name and first initial* folder (the F:\perezm folder, for example). Enter `Extend` as the new site name.

2. Click the 'Browse for folder' icon and navigate to your USB flash drive. Create a new subfolder within the *your last name and first initial* folder and name it `Extend`. Open the folder, select it as the local site folder, and then save the Extend site.

3. Using Windows Explorer, copy the extend1.html file from the Chapter 01\Extend folder into the *your last name and first initial*\Extend folder.

4. Return to Dreamweaver and then open the extend1.html document. (*Hint*: Click Open on the Welcome screen.)

5. Select the text in the first line, Customize Your Dreamweaver Interface, and apply the Heading 2 format.

6. Center-align the heading by using the Format menu on the Application bar.

7. Select the paragraph below the first line, starting with "You can customize" and ending with "customize your workspace." Use the Property inspector to apply italics to the text.

8. Select the three lines of text below the paragraph, starting with "Manage windows and panels" and ending with "Set general preferences for Dreamweaver". Indent these three lines of text by using the Blockquote button in the Property inspector or by using the Indent command on the Format menu.

9. In the last line of text, select "Dreamweaver Help". Using the Link text box in the Property inspector, link the following URL to the text: `http://helpx.adobe.com/ dreamweaver/topics.html`.

10. Place the insertion point at the end of the last sentence on the page. Press the ENTER key two times. Type your first and last names.

11. Save your changes and then view your document in your browser. Compare your document to Figure 1–64.

12. Click the Dreamweaver Help link to test your link. If the Adobe Dreamweaver Help site does not open, return to Dreamweaver and verify that you entered the correct URL in Step 9. Make any necessary changes and then save your changes.

13. Submit the document in the format specified by your instructor.

Make It Right

Analyze a Web page and correct all errors and/or improve the design.

Formatting and Checking the Spelling of a Web Page

Note: To complete this assignment, you will be required to use the Data Files for Students. Visit www.cengage.com/ct/studentdownload for detailed instructions, or contact your instructor for information about accessing the required files.

Instructions: Start Dreamweaver. You are working with a neighborhood association that wants to learn about Dreamweaver. An association member created a Web page and asks you to improve it. First, you will enhance the look of the Web page by applying styles, aligning text, and adding bullets. Next, you will make the Web page more useful by adding links to text and inserting a document title. Finally, you will check the spelling. The modified Web page is shown in Figure 1–65.

Figure 1–65

Perform the following tasks:

1. Use the Site Setup dialog box to define a new local site in the *your last name and first initial* folder (the F:\perezm folder, for example). Enter `Right` as the new site name and save it.

2. Click the 'Browse for folder' icon to navigate to your USB flash drive. Create a new subfolder within the *your last name and first initial* folder and name it `Right`. Open the folder and then select it as the local site folder. Save the Right site.

3. Using Windows Explorer, copy the right1.html file from the Chapter 01\Right folder into the *your last name and first initial*\Right folder.

4. Return to Dreamweaver and then open the right1.html document. (*Hint*: Click Open on the Welcome screen.)

5. Enter `Dreamweaver Views` as the Web page title.

6. Apply the Heading 1 format to the first line of text. Use the Format menu to center-align the heading on the page.

7. Apply bullets to the list of views, starting with "Code View" and ending with "Live View".

8. Bold each view name (Code View, Split View, Design View, and Live View).

9. Check the spelling using the Commands menu. Correct all misspelled words.

Continued >

Make It Right *continued*

10. In the last line of text, select "Dreamweaver Help". Using the Link text box in the Property inspector, link the following URL to the text: `http://helpx.adobe.com/dreamweaver/topics.html`.

11. Place the insertion point at the end of the last sentence on the page. Press the ENTER key two times. Type your first and last names.

12. Save your changes and then view your document in your browser. Compare your document to Figure 1–65.

13. Click the Dreamweaver Help link to test your link. If it did not open the Adobe Dreamweaver Help site, return to Dreamweaver and verify that you entered the correct URL in Step 10. Make any necessary changes and then save your work.

14. Submit the document in the format specified by your instructor.

In the Lab

Design and/or create a Web site using the guidelines, concepts, and skills presented in this chapter. Labs are listed in order of increasing difficulty.

Lab 1: Creating a Family Reunion Web Site

Problem: It has been more than 10 years since the entire Hydes family celebrated together. Janna Hydes has decided to coordinate a family reunion and requests your assistance in spreading the word by creating a Web site. Janna has provided you with all of the details about the event, and she asks you to share the information on the site.

Define a new Web site, and create and format a Web page for the Hydes Family Reunion. The Web page as it is displayed in a browser is shown in Figure 1–66. The text for the Web site is provided in Table 1–1.

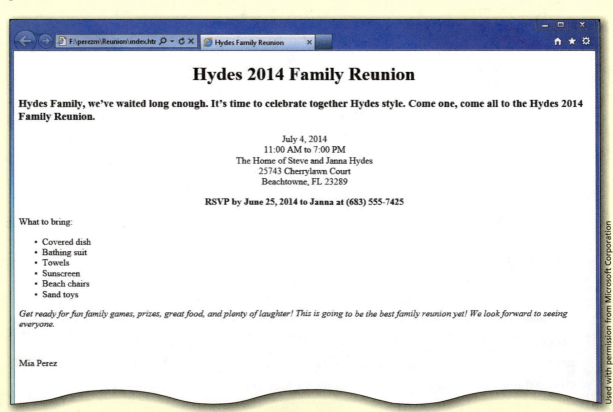

Figure 1–66

Table 1–1 Hydes Family Reunion	
Section	**Text**
Heading	Hydes 2014 Family Reunion
Invitation paragraph	Hydes Family, we've waited long enough. It's time to celebrate together Hydes style. Come one, come all to the Hydes 2014 Family Reunion.
Item 1	July 4, 2014 11:00 AM to 7:00 PM The Home of Steve and Janna Hydes 25743 Cherrylawn Court Beachtowne, FL 23289
Item 2	RSVP by June 25, 2014 to Janna at (683) 555-7425
Item 3	What to bring: Covered dish Bathing suit Towels Sunscreen Beach chairs Sand toys
Closing paragraph	Get ready for fun family games, prizes, great food, and plenty of laughter! This is going to be the best family reunion yet! We look forward to seeing everyone.

Perform the following tasks:

1. Start Dreamweaver. Click Dreamweaver Site in the Create New list to display the Site Setup dialog box. Define a new local site by typing Reunion in the Site name text box.

2. Click the 'Browse for folder' icon to display the Choose Root Folder dialog box. The current path should be F:*your last name and first initial*\\ (substitute the drive letter as necessary). Create a new subfolder in the *your last name and first initial* folder. Type Reunion as the folder name, open and select the Reunion folder, and then save the site.

3. On the Welcome screen, click HTML in the Create New list to create a new HTML page. Save the page and type index.html as the file name.

4. Type Hydes Family Reunion in the Title text box.

5. Type the Web page text shown in Table 1–1. Press the ENTER key after typing the heading and invitation paragraph. For Item 1, press the SHIFT+ENTER keys to insert a line break after each line except the last line. Press the ENTER key after the last Item 1 line. Press the ENTER key after typing each line in Items 2 and 3. Type the closing paragraph.

6. Select the heading text and use the Property inspector to apply the Heading 1 format. Use the Format menu to center-align the heading.

7. Select the invitation paragraph and apply the Heading 3 format.

8. Select all the text for Item 1 and center-align it on the page.

9. Select the text for Item 2, use the Bold button in the Property inspector to apply the Bold style to the text, and then center-align it on the page.

10. Select all the items listed after "What to bring" and use the Unordered List button in the Property inspector to create an unordered bulleted list for the text.

11. Use the Italic button in the Property inspector to apply the Italic style to the closing paragraph.

12. Place the insertion point after the last sentence on the page. Press the ENTER key two times. Type your first and last names.

Continued >

In the Lab *continued*

13. Save your changes.

14. View your document in your browser and compare it to Figure 1–66. Make any necessary changes and then save your work.

15. Submit the document in the format specified by your instructor.

In the Lab

Lab 2: Creating a Recipe Web Site

Problem: Brooke Davis has acquired famous family recipes that have been passed down through generations. She wants to share recipes easily with other family members and friends. You talk to her about setting up a Web site to display the recipes. Because she likes the idea, she asks you to help her get started. You agree to develop the first two pages for her Web site.

Define a new Web site and use a fixed HTML layout to create two Web pages for Davis Family Recipes. The Web pages, as displayed in a browser, are shown in Figure 1–67. Text for the Web site recipe is provided in Table 1–2.

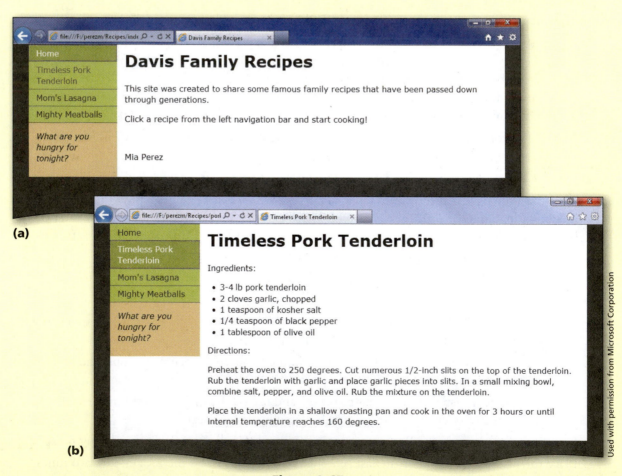

(a)

(b)

Figure 1–67

Table 1–2 Pork Tenderloin Recipe

Section	Text
Heading	Timeless Pork Tenderloin
Ingredients section	Ingredients: 3-4 lb pork tenderloin 2 cloves garlic, chopped 1 teaspoon of kosher salt ¼ teaspoon of black pepper 1 tablespoon of olive oil
Directions section	Directions: Preheat the oven to 250 degrees. Cut numerous ½-inch slits on the top of the tenderloin. Rub the tenderloin with garlic and place garlic pieces into slits. In a small mixing bowl, combine salt, pepper, and olive oil. Rub the mixture on the tenderloin. Place the tenderloin in a shallow roasting pan and cook in the oven for 3 hours or until internal temperature reaches 160 degrees.

Perform the following tasks:

1. Start Dreamweaver. Use the Site Setup dialog box to define a new local site using `Davis Recipes` as the site name.

2. Click the 'Browse for folder' icon to display the Choose Root Folder dialog box. The current path should be F:*your last name and first initial*\\(substitute the drive letter as necessary). Create a new subfolder in the *your last name and first initial* folder. Enter `Recipes` as the folder name, open and select the Recipes folder, and then save the site.

3. On the Dreamweaver Welcome screen, click More in the Create New list. In the New Document dialog box, select Blank Page, Page Type: HTML, Layout: 2 column fixed, left sidebar. Set the DocType as HTML 5 and click the Create button. Save the new Web page using `index.html` as the file name.

4. Enter `Davis Family Recipes` as the Web page title.

5. Delete all of the text in the right column. Type `Davis Family Recipes` at the top of the right column. Press the ENTER key. (If the heading does not appear in the Heading 1 format, apply the Heading 1 format.)

6. Type `This site was created to share some famous family recipes that have been passed down over generations.` Press the ENTER key. Type `Click a recipe in the left navigation bar and start cooking!`

7. Press the ENTER key two times. Type your first and last names.

8. In the left navigation bar, replace the "Link one" text with `Home`. Replace the "Link two" text with `Timeless Pork Tenderloin`. Replace the "Link three" text with `Mom's Lasagna`. Replace the "Link four" text with `Mighty Meatballs`.

9. Delete all of the text below "Mighty Meatballs". Type `What are you hungry for tonight?` Use the Italic button in the Property inspector to apply italics to the text.

10. Save your changes.

11. To create a new document from the existing document, click File on the Application bar and then click Save As. Type `pork.html` as the file name and save the document.

12. Enter `Timeless Pork Tenderloin` as the Web page title.

13. Replace the text in the right column with the recipe text shown in Table 1–2. Press the ENTER key after typing each line or paragraph. (If the Timeless Pork heading does not appear in the Heading 1 format, apply the Heading 1 format.)

Continued >

In the Lab *continued*

14. Select the five items listed after "Ingredients" and use the Unordered List button in the Property inspector to create a bulleted list for the text.

15. Select the text, Home, in the upper-left column. Link it to the index.html page by dragging the Point to File button in the Property inspector to the index.html file in the Files panel.

16. Save your changes and close the pork.html file. The index.html document should be displayed. Select the "Timeless Pork Tenderloin" text in the left column. Link it to the pork.html page by dragging the Point to File button in the Property inspector to the pork.html file in the Files panel. Save your changes.

17. View the index.html page in your browser and compare it to Figure 1–67.

18. Test the link to Timeless Pork Tenderloin and the link to Home. If the links do not work, verify that you properly completed Steps 15 and 16. Make any necessary changes and then save your work.

19. Submit the documents in the format specified by your instructor.

In the Lab

Lab 3: Creating a Business Plan Tips Web Site

Problem: Tyler James is a business consultant who provides his clients with advice about starting their own businesses. He wants to create a Web site with tips for developing a solid business plan. He has hired you to develop his Web site.

Define a new Web site and use a liquid HTML layout to create a Business Plan Tips Web page. The Web page, as it is displayed in a browser, is shown in Figure 1–68. Text for the Web site is provided in Table 1–3.

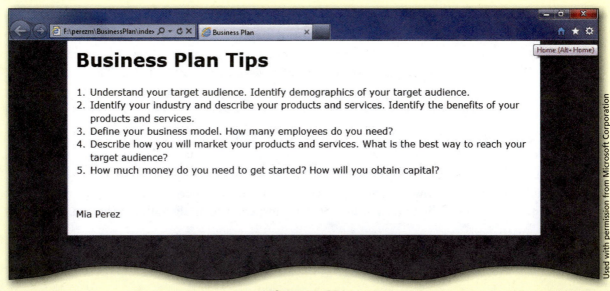

Figure 1–68

Table 1–3 Business Plan Tips

Section	Text
Heading	Business Plan Tips
Paragraph 1	Understand your target audience. Identify demographics of your target audience.
Paragraph 2	Identify your industry and describe your products and services. Identify the benefits of your products and services.
Paragraph 3	Define your business model. How many employees do you need?
Paragraph 4	Describe how you will market your products and services. What is the best way to reach your target audience?
Paragraph 5	How much money do you need to get started? How will you obtain capital?

1. Start Dreamweaver. Use the Site Setup dialog box to define a new local site using `BusinessPlan` as the site name.

2. Click the 'Browse for folder' icon and then create a new subfolder in the *your last name and first initial* folder named `BusinessPlan`. Open and select the BusinessPlan folder, and then save the site.

3. On the Dreamweaver Welcome screen, click More in the Create New list. Create a blank HTML page using the 1 column liquid, centered layout, and HTML5 as the DocType. Save the new Web page using `index.html` as the file name.

4. Enter `Business Plan` as the Web page title.

5. Delete all the text on the page, replacing it with the text shown in Table 1–3. Press the ENTER key after typing each line or paragraph.

6. Press the ENTER key two times after typing the last sentence. Type your first and last names.

7. Select all of the text below the heading and use the Ordered List button in the Property inspector to create a numbered list for the text.

8. Save your changes and then view your document in your browser. Compare your document to Figure 1–68. Make any necessary changes and then save your work.

9. Submit the document in the format specified by your instructor.

Cases and Places

Apply your creative thinking and problem solving skills to design and implement a solution.

1: Protecting Yourself from Identity Theft

Personal

You recently read an article about the growing trend of identity theft. The article has prompted you to create an educational Web site on how people can protect themselves from identity theft. Define a new local site in the *your last name and first initial* folder and name it Protect Yourself from Identity Theft. Name the new subfolder Theft. Create and save a new HTML Web page. Name the file protect. Use your browser to conduct some research on ways to protect yourself from identity theft. Create a heading for your Web page. Apply the Heading 1 format to the title and center-align the title on the page. Below the heading, create an unordered list of 10 different ways to protect yourself from identity theft. Title the document ID Theft. Check the spelling in the document. Include your name at the bottom of the page. Submit the document in the format specified by your instructor.

Continued >

Cases and Places *continued*

2: Creating a Web Site for a Literacy Promotion

Academic

You are in charge of the Literacy Committee at your university. Your mission is to promote reading for enjoyment to university students. You decide to create a Web site to inform students about the best-selling books. Define a new local site in the *your last name and first initial* folder and name it Reading for Fun. Name the new subfolder Read. Create and save a new HTML Web page. Name the file read. Use your browser to conduct some research on current best-selling books. Create a heading for your Web page. Apply the Heading 2 format to the title and center-align the title on the page. Below the heading, create an ordered list of the top 10 best-selling books. Bold three of the book titles. Title the document Reading for Fun. Check the spelling in the document. Include your name at the bottom of the page. Submit the document in the format specified by your instructor.

3: Creating a Web Site for an Accountant

Professional

Your friend is an accountant who wants to create a Web site to advertise his accountant services. You offer to help him develop a Web site. Define a new local site in the *your last name and first initial* folder and name it Accountant Services. Name the new subfolder Accountant. Create and save a new HTML Web page with a 2 column fixed, left sidebar layout. Be sure to select HTML 5 as the DocType. Name the file accountant. Delete the text in the right column. Create a heading for your Web page. Below the title, provide contact information for the accountant services. In the left column, provide links to Home, Services, Costs, and Schedule Appointment. Title the document Accountant Services. Check the spelling in the document. Delete the text below the links in the left column and type your name. Submit the document in the format specified by your instructor.

2 Designing a Web Site Using a Template and CSS

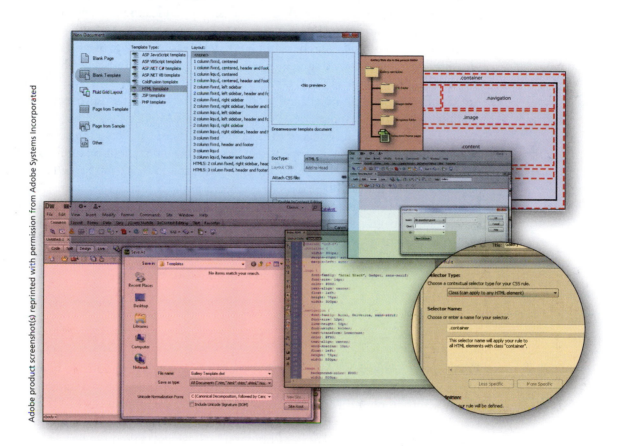

Objectives

You will have mastered the material in this chapter when you can:

- Describe the anatomy of a style sheet
- Describe the types of style sheets
- Create a Dreamweaver Web site using a template and CSS
- Save the HTML template as a .dwt file
- Define the regions of a Web page
- Describe the CSS categories

- Create a CSS style sheet
- Create a CSS rule
- Apply CSS rule definitions
- Create an editable region within a template
- Create a new page from a template
- Preview a Web page using Live view

2 | Designing a Web Site Using a Template and CSS

Designing Web Pages with CSS

By designing a Web page from scratch, you can create a page customized to your exact needs and preferences. A Web site's design provides the first impression of the credibility of an organization. Content is an important part of any site. But if the presentation of that content is not consistent, easy to navigate, and aesthetically pleasing, the site visitor will quickly leave. **CSS**, or **Cascading Style Sheets**, provides the style and layout for HTML content. CSS is the means by which a Web site's presentation is defined, styled, and modified. The newest version presented in the chapter is the CSS3 standard.

To understand the concept of CSS, imagine a chef at a cooking school teaching dozens of students. If the chef spends an hour with each student privately teaching a new cooking technique, the amount of time required to teach this same lesson over and over means it would take days to teach everyone. It makes more sense for the chef to teach the entire class the new cooking technique at once. Similarly, if your Web site has dozens of pages, changing the background color of every single page individually would be very time consuming. But with CSS, you can make one adjustment in the CSS file to display the new background color on every page of the site. CSS allows complete and total control over the style of an entire Web site.

Project — Custom Template and Style Sheet

Designing a professional Web site that appeals to your target audience begins with a plan to define the style of the site, which should suit its purpose and audience. A local family photographer has launched a new Web site using the latest HTML5 and CSS3 standards to market the company's photography services, as shown in Figure 2–1. The Gallery Portrait and Family Photography business (called Gallery for short) requires a site that meets the goals described in its business mission statement: "Our mission is to capture cherished family moments while providing our clients with an unsurpassed photography experience." The Gallery specializes in artistic family and individual portrait photos that capture the different personalities of each subject. You begin the Gallery site in this chapter, and then expand it in subsequent chapters to include information about the company's services, portfolio, pricing, session details, and contact information.

To create a unique and memorable design for the Gallery site, follow the same process that professional Web designers follow when building a site. The Gallery site uses a custom template to establish the layout of the Web pages. Attached to the template is an external style sheet, which uses CSS3 to define the design for each area of the site, including the logo, navigation, main content, and footer areas. An external CSS3 style sheet is the professional standard for styling content throughout an entire Web site. Finally, you create a page based on the template, and then customize the content to suit the first page of the site, shown in Figure 2–1.

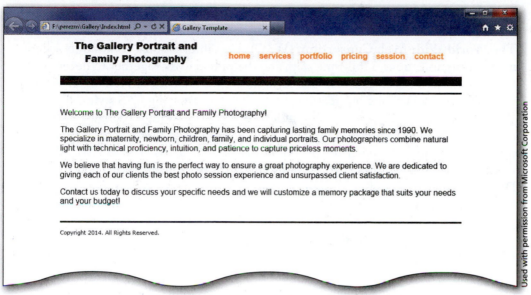

Figure 2–1

Overview

As you read this chapter, you will learn how to create the Web page project shown in Figure 2–1 by performing these general tasks:

- Create a new Dreamweaver HTML5 dynamic Web template.
- Add CSS and image folders.
- Create an external style sheet.
- Add CSS rules to the style sheet.
- Create an editable region in the template.
- Create a new page from the template.

General Project Guidelines

When creating a Dreamweaver Web site, the individual actions you perform and decisions you make will affect the appearance and characteristics of the entire Web site. When creating the opening page for a business Web site, as shown in Figure 2–1, you should follow these general guidelines:

1. **Create an HTML template.** Choose a blank HTML template so you can design a custom layout.

2. **Determine the layout and formatting of the Web site.** Before designing a CSS layout, carefully consider which site structure will convey your message effectively. Maintaining consistency in your page layout and design helps to ensure a productive user experience.

3. **Understand the anatomy of a CSS style sheet.** Recognize the elements of CSS styles.

4. **Create a CSS style sheet.** Define the element properties and values within the CSS style sheet.

More specific details about these guidelines are presented at appropriate points throughout the chapter. The chapter also identifies the actions performed and decisions made regarding these guidelines during the creation of the Web site home page shown in Figure 2–1.

Plan Ahead

Anatomy of a Style Sheet

The **World Wide Web Consortium (W3C)** — an international community where member organizations, a full-time staff, and the public work together to develop Web standards — mandates that CSS style sheets are the core of Web design. When you customize a Web site by creating, modifying, and applying CSS styles, all the Web pages in the site share a consistent look even as the content changes. A **style** is a rule that defines the appearance and position of text and graphics. A **style sheet** is a collection of styles that describes how to display the elements of an HTML document in a Web browser. You can develop CSS style sheets by entering code or by using Dreamweaver's CSS toolset. Designers typically define a style in the style sheet for a Web site and then apply the style to content in many locations throughout the site. Separating style from content means you can change a Web site's appearance easily. If you modify a CSS style, the site updates any content to which you applied that style to reflect the modifications.

A style sheet consists of **CSS rule definitions** that specify the layout and format properties that apply to an element, such as a heading, bullets, or a paragraph. For example, the heading at the top of each page could be defined in a CSS rule stating that this heading always appears as blue, 20-point, underlined text. The term, cascading, in Cascading Style Sheets refers to a sorting order that determines whether one style has precedence over another if two competing style rules affect the same content.

The CSS style sheet shown in Figure 2–2a lays the foundation for the design of the Web page in Figure 2–2b.

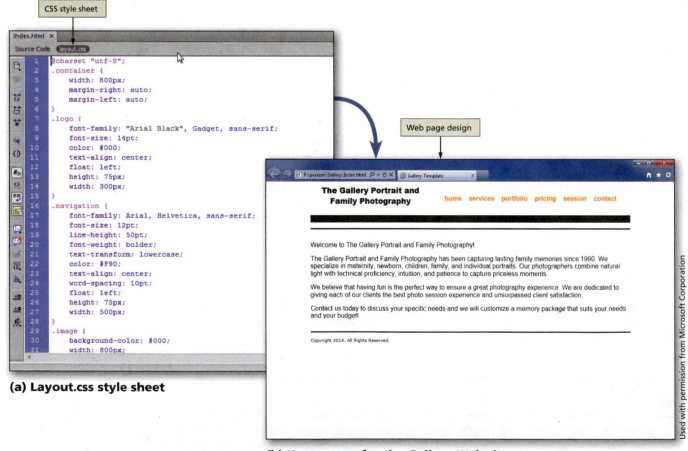

(a) Layout.css style sheet

(b) Home page for the Gallery Web site

Figure 2–2

Because a central style sheet provides the layout code for all pages within the site, style sheets originally were developed in the late 1990s to reduce the size of HTML files. In addition to smaller file sizes, CSS style sheets offer the following benefits, which have changed the architectural design of the Web:

- Faster download times because the styles are separated in a style sheet from the HTML code
- Reduced design expenses because one change in the style sheet updates the entire site
- Improved accessibility for site users who have disabilities
- Improved consistency in design and navigation throughout the site

Understanding the Structure of a Style

A style, also called a rule, uses CSS code to specify how to format an element or a section of a Web page. The anatomy of a style is shown in Figure 2–3. Although Dreamweaver automatically generates the CSS code you need after you make selections in the CSS rules dialog boxes, it is important to understand the elements of a style so you can make additional changes to the code.

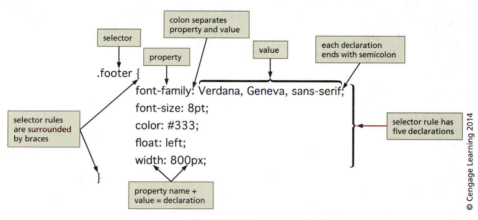

Figure 2–3

© Cengage Learning 2014

Selector   Every CSS style begins with a **selector**, which is the name of the style. The selector informs the browser that a special class or element is styled a certain way. Class selectors begin with a period, as in .content, and ID selectors begin with a hash symbol, as in #right. A **class** identifies a particular region or division on a page, such as the footer, that can be customized. For example, the style shown in Figure 2–3 formats a special class named .footer according to the properties listed within the curly braces. A selector can have multiple properties.

Declaration   Every CSS style also has a **declaration**, which defines the details of a style. In Figure 2–3, the first declaration indicates that the font-family for the .footer selector is Verdana, Geneva, sans-serif. A declaration includes a property and a value, and ends with a semicolon. The .footer selector has five declarations within the curly braces.

Property   A **property** identifies the type of formatting to apply, such as the font family, color, or width. In Figure 2–3, the first declaration is for the font-family property.

Value The **value** of a property specifies the exact formatting to apply. Separate the property and value with a colon. In Figure 2–3 on the previous page, the width property is set to 800 px, indicating that the footer element should be 800 pixels wide. The font-family property has three values: Verdana, Geneva, and sans-serif. The Web site uses the first value, Verdana, if that font is available on the visitor's browser. If Verdana is not installed on the visitor's browser, the Web site uses the next value, Geneva, if that font is available. If the first two fonts are not available, the Web site uses the next value, sans-serif, as a generic font to format the text. Separate multiple values for a property by commas. If a value contains more than one word, place quotation marks around the value.

Declaration Block The CSS style code found between the two curly braces is considered a declaration block within the style sheet.

Identifying Types of Style Sheets

The single selector displayed in Figure 2–3 applies only to the footers throughout the Web site. To create a more comprehensive rule set, use a style sheet to specify a collection of CSS rules as shown in Figure 2–4.

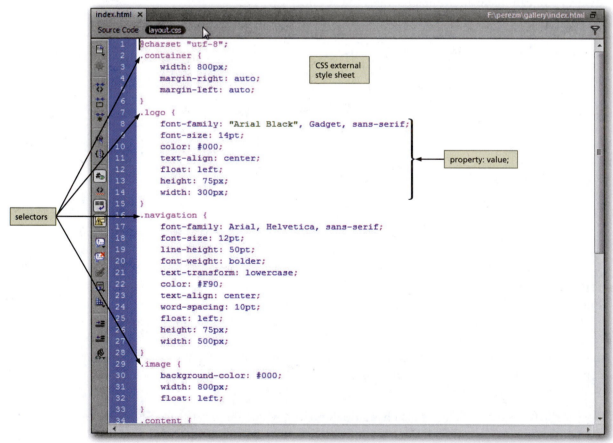

Figure 2–4

The style sheet in Figure 2–4 is an external style sheet. However, you can define CSS rules in an external style sheet, in an internal style sheet, or as inline styles. **External style sheets**, the most commonly used type of style sheet, allow you to store the code for the site styles in a separate document. Dreamweaver takes care of linking the external style sheet to the HTML file by automatically creating code, but you will strengthen your Web designer skills if you understand what is happening under the hood. If you are coding a Web page manually, you need to place a link tag in the HTML code (the content of the page) to attach the external style sheet to the page and apply the style definitions. You typically place code similar to the following example in the HTML <head> section of the page:

```
<link href="CSS/layout.css" rel="style sheet" type="text/css">
<style type="text/css">
```

The **link tag** forms a relationship between the current document and an external style sheet, which is named layout.css in this case. External style sheets are text files with a .css file name extension. An external style sheet is a perfect way to format a large Web site because the styles are applied automatically to all pages in the site. Site management is simple when using an external style sheet because you can update the style in one place in the style sheet and then apply the change throughout the site. Separating the page content from presentation makes it much easier to maintain the appearance of your site.

Another type of style sheet, called an **internal style sheet**, applies formatting styles within an HTML document. In a multiple-page Web site, a single page may have a unique layout that differs from the layouts specified in the external style sheet. You can use an internal style sheet to create a distinct look for this one page only. You embed internal styles in the <head> tag using the <style> tag, as shown in the following HTML code:

```
<head>
<style type="text/css">
body {background-color:navy;}
</style>
</head>
```

This style rule sets the background color for body text to navy. Internal styles take precedence over external styles. If an external style sheet sets the background color of the entire site to light blue, the internal style sheet overrides that rule and displays the background color as navy on this page only. The internal style overrides the external style because the internal style is specific to this single page. HTML pages with internal styles can take longer to load, but the advantage of having one page with its own style rules makes it worthwhile.

The third approach to defining styles is to include inline styles within your Web site. **Inline styles** allow you to insert a style rule within an HTML tag in an HTML page. For example, suppose you want to display only one heading in red. Add an inline style within the heading tag to format the heading, as shown in the following code:

```
<h1 style="color: red;">The Photographer's Gallery</h1>
```

When the inline style code is placed within a tag, it affects that tag only. The other heading styles are not affected by this inline style. Inline styles override external and internal style coding styles. Excessive inline styles can create a slow-loading page that is also difficult to edit, so consider using inline styles very rarely in your site development.

Creating a Dreamweaver Web Template

The design of the Gallery Web site should have a consistent look and feel throughout every page. Instead of using a ready-made design template to create a page as you did in Chapter 1, in this chapter, you create a custom template from scratch. A custom template provides a basic layout for the entire site using design elements that you specify. Templates are best used when you are creating a large site where every page shares the same design characteristics such as the logo, background, font, and arrangement. When you save an HTML page as a Dreamweaver Web Template, Dreamweaver creates a template folder at the root level of the local root folder and generates a **.dwt** file that becomes the design source for all the pages that you generate from it. The .dwt extension stands for Dreamweaver Web Template and is associated with a special type of Web document that adds structure and layout to a page.

Dreamweaver templates have a number of design layout regions, or divisions; some can be edited and others cannot. By creating a Dreamweaver Web Template, you can include editable, unlocked regions for adding content to the page. An **editable region** on a Web page is an area where other Web page authors can change the content. For example, you would locate a calendar of upcoming events in an editable region of a page so that anyone designing the page could modify or update the calendar as necessary to keep it current. A template can also have **noneditable regions**, which are sections with static, unchanging content. By using noneditable regions in a template, you prevent changes to certain areas, such as a navigation bar, and preserve the consistent layout of each page based on the template.

Plan Ahead

> **Create an HTML template**
> Before you create a Web site, you must determine the look and feel of each page in the site. By creating a common template for the site that can be applied to each page of the site, the entire Web site maintains a cohesive, consistent presentation. After creating a template, you use it to create Web pages that share the same layout, style, and content. Place this unvarying content in the noneditable regions of the template. The template also should include editable regions for elements that vary from page to page, such as the page heading and descriptive text. Attach a style sheet to the template so that all the pages created from the template use the same CSS styles.

Organizing the Site Structure

Carefully organizing a business or personal Web site from the start can save you frustration and problems with navigation. You save the Gallery site in a root folder on your USB drive. Within the root folder, you can create additional folders and subfolders to organize images, CSS files, templates, and other objects for the site. In this chapter, you create two folders within the Gallery site to hold the CSS and image resources necessary for the design of the project. After you define a site using Dreamweaver's Site Setup feature, you can create the folder hierarchy shown in Figure 2–5.

In Figure 2–5, the root folder for the Gallery site contains a CSS folder, an Images folder, a Templates folder, and the index.html file, representing the home page that appears when you open the site. An external style sheet named layout.css resides within the CSS folder. When you add images to the Gallery site in Chapter 3, you place them in the Images folder so that when you want to insert an image into a page, you know where to find it. Dreamweaver automatically creates the Templates folder when you save an HTML page as a template file with the .dwt extension. In this case, the Dreamweaver Web Template is named Gallery Template and is stored in the Templates folder.

BTW

Templates Folder
Make sure to keep templates in the Templates folder for a site. Moving a template file detaches the template from a Web page.

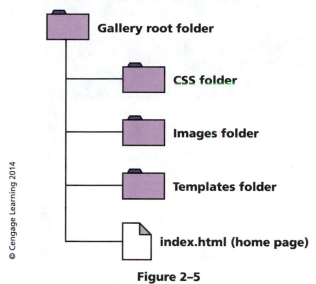

Figure 2–5

To Start Dreamweaver

If you are stepping through this project on a computer and you want your screen to match the figures in this book, you should change your computer's resolution to 1024 × 768 and reset the Classic workspace. For more information about how to change the resolution on your computer, read the "Changing the Screen Resolution" appendix.

The following steps, which assume Windows 7 is running, start Dreamweaver based on a typical installation. You may need to ask your instructor how to start Dreamweaver for your system.

1 Click the Start button on the Windows 7 taskbar to display the Start menu and then type `Dreamweaver CS6` in the 'Search programs and files' box.

2 Click Adobe Dreamweaver CS6 in the list to start Dreamweaver and display the Welcome screen.

3 If the Dreamweaver window is not maximized, click the Maximize button next to the Close button on the Application bar to maximize the window (Figure 2–6).

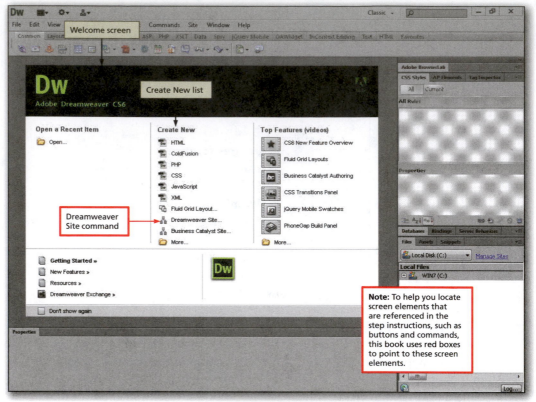

Figure 2–6

To Create a New Site

The following steps create a site named Gallery for the new photography studio Web site.

1

- Click Dreamweaver Site in the Create New list to display the Site Setup dialog box.

- Type `Gallery` in the Site name text box to name the site.

- Click the 'Browse for folder' icon to display the Choose Root Folder dialog box, and if necessary, navigate to your Removable Disk (F:) drive, click the root folder named with your last name and first initial (such as perezm), and then click the Open button to display the subfolders in the root folder.

- Click the Create New Folder button to create a folder, type `Gallery` as the name of the new folder, press the ENTER key, and then click the Open button to create the Gallery subfolder and open it.

- Click the Select button to display the Site Setup for Gallery dialog box (Figure 2–7).

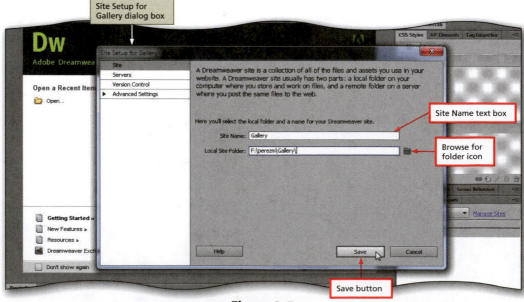

Figure 2–7

2

- Click the Save button to save the site settings and display the Gallery root folder in the Files panel (Figure 2–8).

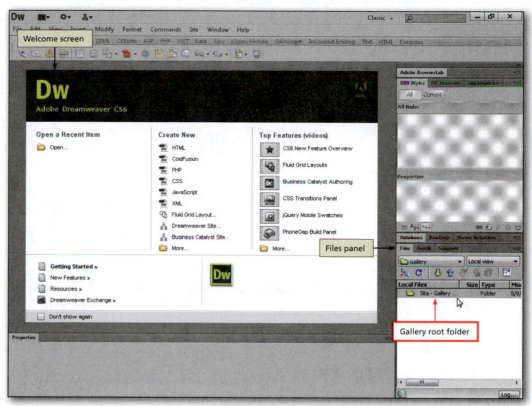

Figure 2–8

To Create Folders for the Image and CSS Files

The Gallery site uses an image file to display a background for the Web pages and a CSS file to set the Web page layout. To make it easy to manage files for a Web site, which can quickly grow to dozens of files, you should store the files in **resource folders**, which are subfolders in the root folder for the site. In each resource folder, store a single type of file. For example, store all the photos, line drawings, backgrounds, and other graphics in the Images folder. Store all the CSS style sheets in the CSS folder. The following steps create two resource folders for the image and CSS files.

1

- Right-click the Gallery root folder in the Files panel to display the folder's context menu (Figure 2–9).

Figure 2–9

- Click New Folder on the context menu to create a new folder.

- Type `CSS` to name the first resource folder in the Gallery site, and then press the ENTER key to create the CSS folder (Figure 2–10).

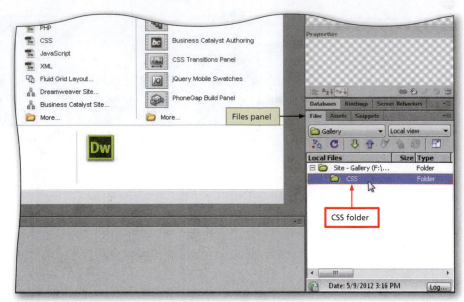

Figure 2–10

- Right-click the Gallery root folder in the Files panel to display the folder's context menu.

- Click New Folder on the context menu to create a new folder.

- Type `Images` to name the folder.

- Press the ENTER key to name the second resource folder (Figure 2–11).

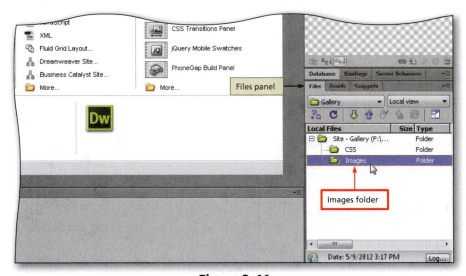

Figure 2–11

To Create a Blank HTML Template

Dreamweaver CS6 provides a blank HTML template with no predefined layout for use in developing a template from scratch. After defining a site, the next step is to design a consistent layout of elements that appear on each page of the site. Save the HTML template as a Dreamweaver Web Template so you can use it to create pages for the site. If you modify the template, you immediately update the design of all pages attached to the template.

To begin a new HTML layout, you use the New Document dialog box, which provides options for creating blank pages, blank templates with liquid and fixed layouts, and blank templates without any predefined layout. After creating a template, you save it with a specific name. By default, Dreamweaver stores the new template in a folder named Templates in the root folder of your site. The following steps create a new blank HTML template.

1

- Click the More folder on the Welcome screen to display the New Document dialog box (Figure 2–12).

What if I do not see a Welcome screen?

Instead of clicking the More folder on the Welcome screen, you can click File on the Application bar and then select New to display the New Document dialog box.

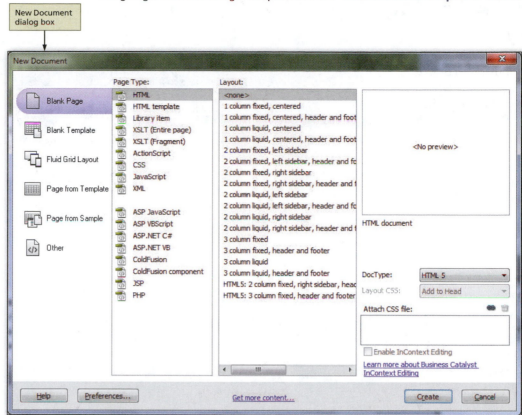

Figure 2–12

2

- Click Blank Template in the left pane to specify you are creating a blank template.

- Click HTML template in the Template Type list to select an HTML template.

- If necessary, click <none> in the Layout list to create a blank HTML template with no predefined layout.

- If necessary, click the DocType button and then click HTML 5 to set the DocType to HTML5 (Figure 2–13).

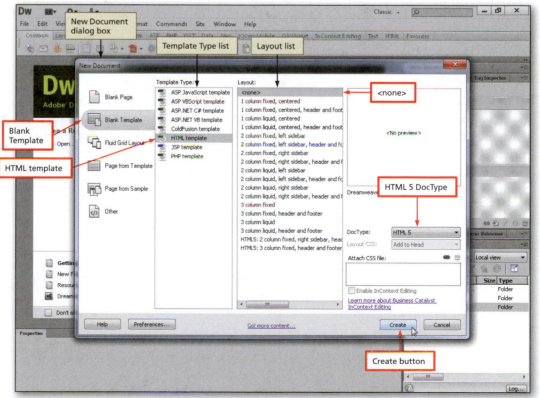

Figure 2–13

● Click the Create
button to display
the blank HTML
template in the
Document window
(Figure 2–14).

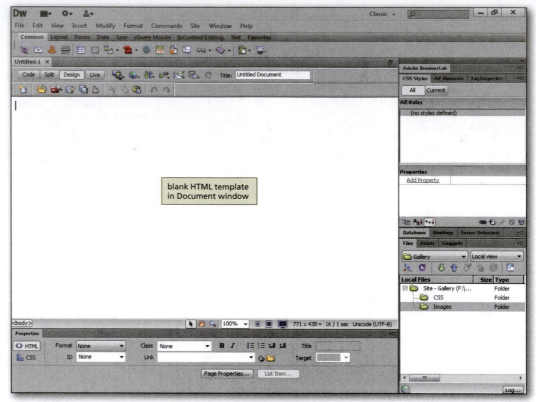

Figure 2–14

To Save the HTML Page as a Template

When you create a template, Dreamweaver uses the name of the site followed by *Template.dwt* as the name of the template, such as Gallery Template.dwt. When saving the template, a dialog box appears reminding you that the template does not have any editable regions. Recall that an editable region is an area in a template that contains text or other objects users can edit. For example, if every Web page based on the template will have a different main heading, include the heading in an editable region. You define editable regions later in this chapter. The following steps save the blank HTML template as a Dreamweaver Web Template.

1

• Click File on the Application bar to display the File menu (Figure 2–15).

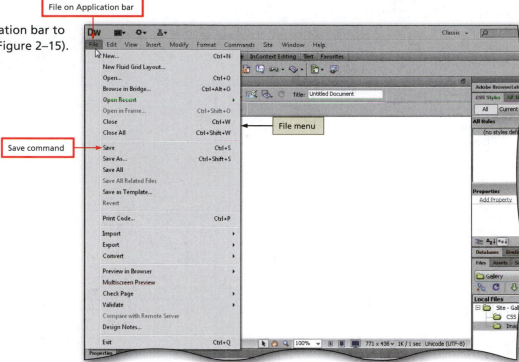

Figure 2–15

2

• Click Save on the File menu to display the Save As Template dialog box.

• If a warning dialog box is displayed, click the OK button to close the dialog box.

• If necessary, click the Site button to display the site list and then click Gallery to select the Gallery site.

• If necessary, select the placeholder text in the Save as text box, and then type `Gallery Template` to name the Dreamweaver Web template (Figure 2–16).

Q&A

Why is the Save As Template dialog box displayed when I select Save on the File menu?

Because this is the first time you are saving the template, Dreamweaver displays the Save As Template dialog box so you can specify a new name for the file.

Q&A

Will the template include editable regions?

Yes. You create the editable regions later in this chapter and in other chapters.

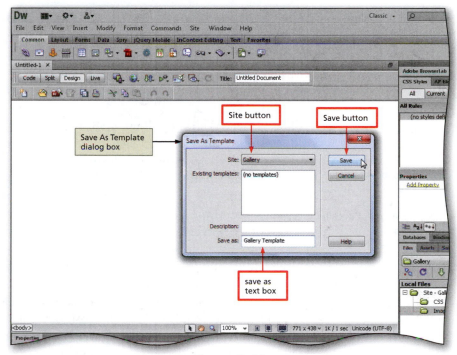

Figure 2–16

3

- Click the Save button to save the Dreamweaver Web template as Gallery Template.dwt in a folder named Templates in the Gallery file hierarchy.

- Click the expand icon for the Templates folder in the Files panel to expand the Templates folder and display the Gallery Template file (Figure 2–17).

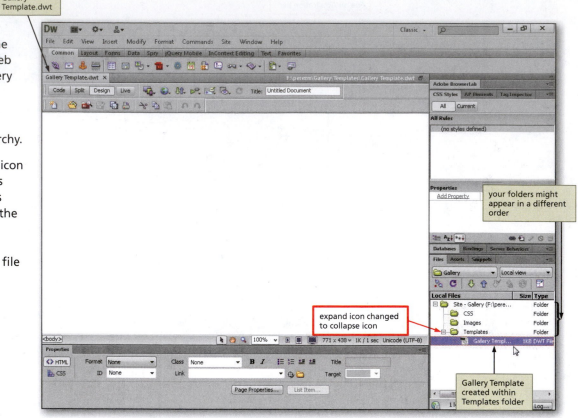

Figure 2–17

Adding CSS Styles

The Gallery Web site will use CSS styles to structure the layout of the pages. Instead of cluttering each HTML page in the site with individual style tags for each element, CSS rules style an element with specified properties such as font type, size, and color throughout the site.

Before you can take advantage of the power of CSS styles, you should organize the content of the Web pages and identify the sections to which you will apply certain types of CSS styles. The most common way to organize content involves dividing the page into different regions, or divisions. Figure 2–18 shows each region of the page sketched during the planning phase of the Web site project. These six regions of the page are the building blocks of the Gallery site design.

The easiest way to format elements within a site is by using specific CSS styles within each region. You can apply positioning and formatting styles to text, images, tables, and other elements in each region. The formatting styles determine the appearance of individual elements by making text in the navigation region, for example, bold, orange, 12-point lowercase Arial text. The positioning styles create simple to complex layouts, arranging blocks of text, graphics, or images on the page. During the design phase of a Web site project, designers often use a wireframe to sketch the layout of the page as shown in Figure 2–18. A **wireframe** is a block diagram that shows the main elements of a Web page layout as boxes with brief descriptions.

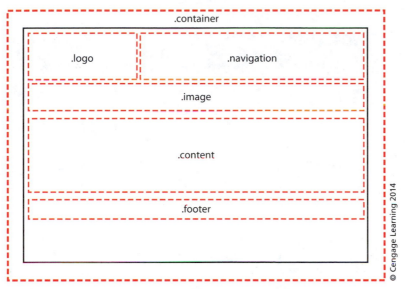

Figure 2–18

Each Dreamweaver CSS layout requires its own style sheet containing each region and the associated style rules necessary to make the layout work. An external style sheet declares style rules for each region, also called a class. Each class selector, identified with a beginning period, specifies a style for a group of elements.

<table>
<tr><td>

Determine the layout and formatting of the Web site
When designing a Web site from scratch, you should consider the types of elements that you must format to create a consistent look across each page in the site. Consider each CSS rule that is needed to format every element:

• Determine the layout of the site, including the location of the logo, navigation, main content area, and footer.

• Plan the formatting necessary for each Web page element to determine the CSS rules for font styles, color, and heading size.

</td><td>

Plan Ahead

</td></tr>
</table>

Recall that CSS is the current standard for formatting Web page elements. In addition, CSS is the standard for Web page layout. Instead of using HTML techniques, which involve tables or frames to structure content, CSS uses the **div tag**, an HTML tag that acts as a container for text, images, and other page elements. When laying out pages with CSS, you place the div tag around text, images, and other page elements to position the regions of content on the page. You can place other tags within a div tag.

BTW

Div Tags
To see examples of div tags used in CSS layouts, you can create a test page from a CSS layout listed in the New Document dialog box.

To Add a Div Tag

Because each region of the CSS layout is associated with a div tag, you need to insert a div tag for each region of content in the Web page or template. The Gallery site has six regions, so you insert six div tags. After naming a div tag, set the CSS rule definitions for the font, position, border, and other properties of that region. The outer region of the Web site, as shown in Figure 2–18, is called the .container class because it contains all the other regions. When adding a div tag, you specify where to store the CSS styles that apply to that region: in this document only, in an existing style sheet, or in a new style sheet. For the first div tag in a page or template, specify a new style sheet. Dreamweaver requests a name and location for the new .css file. In this case, name the new style sheet layout.css and store it in the CSS folder in the Gallery site. The following steps insert a div tag for the container region and save the CSS style sheet.

1

- On the Document toolbar, drag to select the text, Untitled Document, in the Title text box.

- Type `Gallery` as the title of the template page (Figure 2–19).

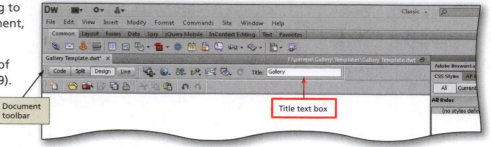

Document toolbar

Title text box

Figure 2–19

2

- Click the Document window, and then click the Insert Div Tag button on the Insert bar to display the Insert Div Tag dialog box (Figure 2–20).

Q&A What is the purpose of inserting a div tag?

You are inserting a div tag to create a division in the Gallery template.

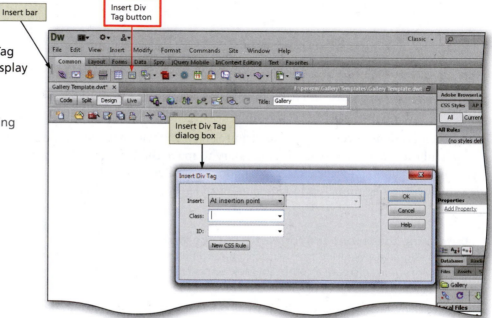

Insert bar

Insert Div Tag button

Insert Div Tag dialog box

Figure 2–20

3

- If necessary, click the Class text box and then type `container` to name the div tag (Figure 2–21).

Q&A Do I also enter a name in the ID text box?

No. You create a div tag as a class or an ID. You can apply a class div tag to any other tag on the page. You can apply an ID div tag only once on a page.

Q&A Should I type a period before the class name?

No. A period is not necessary because Dreamweaver automatically places a period before the class name in the next dialog box.

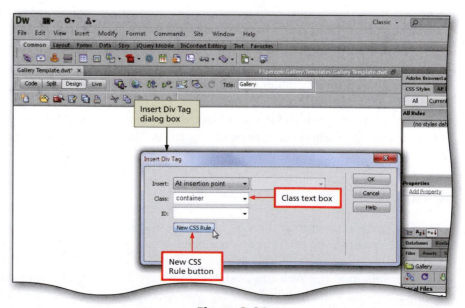

Insert Div Tag dialog box

Class text box

New CSS Rule button

Figure 2–21

4

- Click the New CSS Rule button to display the New CSS Rule dialog box (Figure 2–22).

Q&A What is the purpose of the New CSS Rule dialog box?

Use this dialog box to add a CSS rule that defines the class you created; in this case, the container class.

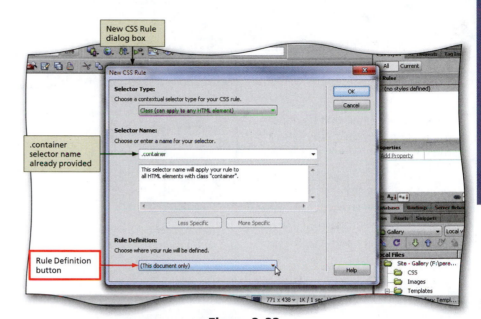

Figure 2–22

5

- Click the Rule Definition button and then click (New Style Sheet File) in the Rule Definition list to select the location in which you want to define the rule, which is in a new style sheet file (Figure 2–23).

Q&A When (New Style Sheet File) is selected, where does Dreamweaver save the CSS style sheet?

When you determine that the rule definition should be saved in a new style sheet, click the OK button to display a dialog box requesting where to save the .css file.

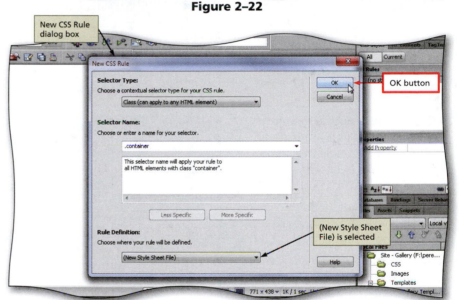

Figure 2–23

6

- Click the OK button to create a new CSS rule for the container region and to display the Save Style Sheet File As dialog box (Figure 2–24).

Figure 2–24

7

- Double-click the CSS folder in the Save Style Sheet File As dialog box to select the file location for the style sheet.

- Click the File name text box and then type layout to name the CSS style sheet within the CSS folder (Figure 2–25).

Q&A Which file type should I select when I save the style sheet?

Dreamweaver automatically selects .css as the default file type.

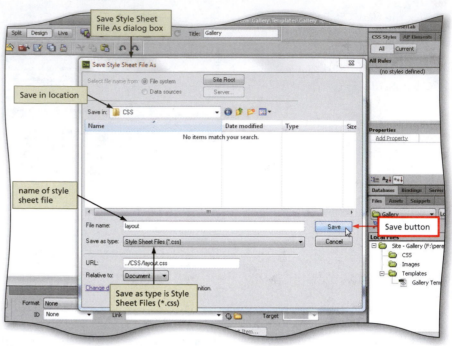

Figure 2–25

8

- Click the Save button to save the style sheet as layout.css and display the 'CSS Rule Definition for .container in layout.css' dialog box (Figure 2–26).

Q&A Why is a CSS Rule Definition dialog box displayed after I save the style sheet?

You use this dialog box to specify the details of the styles to apply to the container region by selecting a formatting category and the appropriate value for each style rule.

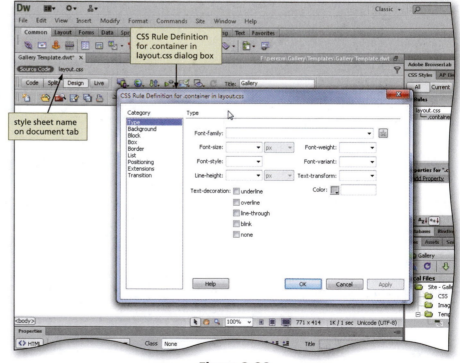

Figure 2–26

Other Ways

1. Click style sheet on CSS Styles panel, click New Rule button

Setting CSS Rule Definitions

The layout.css style sheet contains the CSS rules that define the styles in the Gallery Web site. Instead of entering code by hand, Dreamweaver CS6 provides a CSS Rule Definition dialog box that allows Web designers to define styles easily and effectively for CSS element rules. The CSS Rule Definition dialog box appears when you are creating or modifying styles.

BTW

Creating CSS Rules
Besides using the New CSS Rule button on the CSS Styles panel, you can click the Targeted Rule button on the Property inspector and then click New CSS Rule to create a CSS rule.

Plan Ahead

> **Create a CSS style sheet**
> To create an external style sheet, you need to define which rules to set in each division, or region, of the site. Six div tags with detailed CSS rules change the default settings of the font, color, margins, and other CSS properties. By defining styles in an external style sheet, you can apply the styles in any page in the site connected to that style sheet. Because editing a style in the external style sheet updates all instances of that style throughout the site, external style sheets are the most powerful and flexible way to use styles.

The CSS Rule Definition dialog box in Figure 2–26 consists of nine categories of style rules. Table 2–1 describes each category.

Table 2–1 Categories in the CSS Rule Definition Dialog Box	
Category	**Purpose**
Type	Determines the appearance and format of text for the selected style
Background	Specifies the background color or background images to display as the page background
Block	Provides option styles to space and align text according to your custom settings
Box	Defines the spacing and placement of elements on a page, such as the location of an image within a defined region
Border	Specifies border styles, width, and color values for one or all edges of borders for text, images, and other Web elements
List	Defines list types, custom bullet images, and unique positioning selections
Positioning	Prescribes the placement of CSS elements within the page, which increases a designer's creative control over the appearance of a Web site
Extensions	Determines page breaks for printing and customizes the appearance of elements on the page
Transition	Enables animation changes in CSS values to occur smoothly over a specified duration

To Select CSS Rule Definitions

The .container class within the style sheet provides specifications for the width of the page and for the margin settings. The .container class is the default name for the large container that holds the other classes with the style sheet. In this case, you set the width of the page to 800px. **Pixels (px)** is the measurement unit for setting the dimensions of the container. The measurement value, such as 800, and the unit, such as px, typically are noted without a space between them. The **margin** determines the amount of space to maintain between the container region and the borders of the browser window. Here, you set the left and right margins to auto, which centers the container region horizontally within the browser window. The following steps define the CSS rule definitions for the .container class.

1

- Click Box in the Category list of the 'CSS Rule Definitions for .container in layout.css' dialog box to set the CSS rules for the layout of the container class (Figure 2–27).

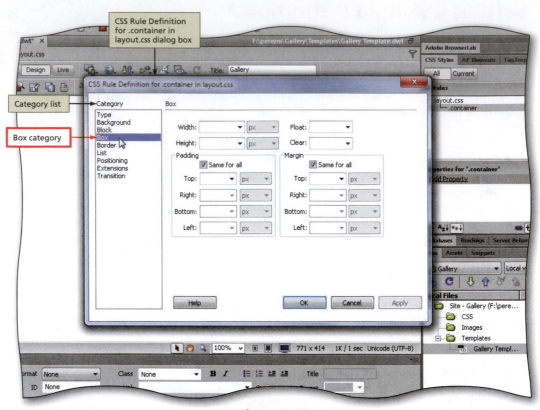

Figure 2–27

2

- Click the Width box and then type 800 to set a width of 800 pixels for the .container class.

- Click Same for all in the Margin section to remove the check mark from the 'Same for all' check box.

- Click the Right box arrow in the Margin section, and then click auto to set the right margin to center automatically within the browser window.

- Click the Left box arrow in the Margin section, and then click auto to set the left margin to center automatically within the browser window (Figure 2–28).

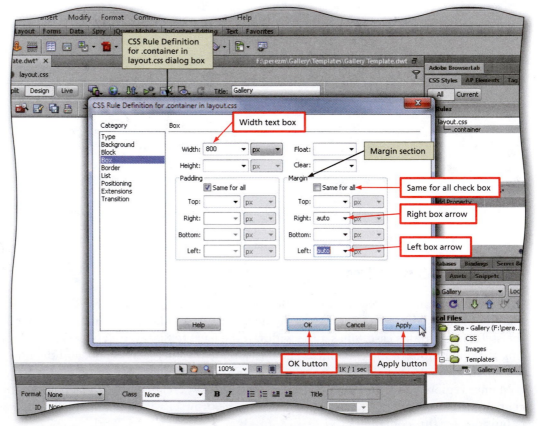

Figure 2–28

3

- Click the Apply button to apply the CSS rules for the .container class within the layout.css file.

- Click the OK button (CSS Rule Definition dialog box) to define the CSS rules for the .container class.

- Click the OK button (Insert Div Tag dialog box) to close the Insert Div Tag dialog box.

- If necessary, select the text 'Content for class "container" Goes Here' in the Document window, and then press the DELETE key to delete the text from the container region (Figure 2–29).

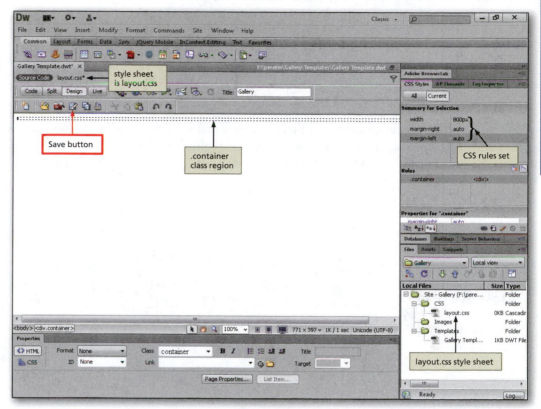

Figure 2–29

Q&A | Why do I click the Apply button instead of the OK button in the CSS Rule Definition dialog box?

Click the Apply button to apply the styles in the current category. You can select another category and then set styles in that category. When you click the OK button, you apply all the selected styles in all the categories.

Q&A | Why are dashed lines displayed in the Document window?

The dashed lines define the region set by the .container class. Later, you define other regions within the .container region.

Q&A | Where are the classes listed for the style sheet?

The classes are listed on the CSS Styles panel on the right side of the Dreamweaver window.

4

- Click the Save button on the Standard toolbar to save your work.

Q&A | What should I do if a dialog box notes that the template does not have any editable regions?

Click the OK button. You will add an editable region later in this chapter. Click the OK button each time this dialog box appears in this chapter.

Other Ways

1. Select class on CSS Styles panel, click Edit Rule button

Break Point: If you wish to take a break, this is a good place to do so. To resume at a later time, start Dreamweaver, if necessary, open the file called Gallery Template, and continue following the steps from this location forward.

To Add the Logo Div Tag and Define Its CSS Rules

A business typically uses its company logo, which can consist of an image and text, to create a recognizable reference to that business. In the Gallery site, the logo consists of the text, The Gallery Portrait and Family Photography, and an image. You add the image in the next chapter. Before you add the text, you define a layout region in the style sheet so you can control the placement and appearance of the region. In this case, you define a region named .logo in the layout.css style sheet to determine the custom arrangement of the Gallery logo. Next, you set the CSS rules for the region by defining the Type property such as font-family and font size, Block properties such as text alignment, and Box properties that set the size of the region. The **float property** determines where text and other objects should float around the region. In Chapter 3, you add an image to the template that should float to the left of the logo. The following steps define the CSS rule definitions for the .logo class.

1

- If necessary in the Gallery template, click within the container region.

- Click the Insert Div Tag button on the Insert bar to display the Insert Div Tag dialog box.

- If necessary, click the Class text box and then type `logo` to name the div tag (Figure 2–30).

How can I tell if I am clicking within the container region?

If the insertion point is within the container region, <div.container> appears on the status bar.

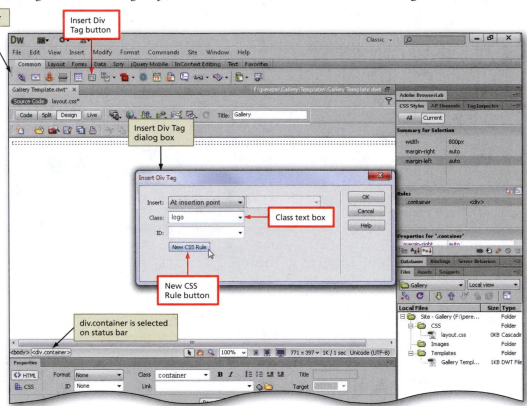

Figure 2–30

2

- Click the New CSS Rule button to display the New CSS Rule dialog box for adding a new CSS rule that defines the logo class (Figure 2–31).

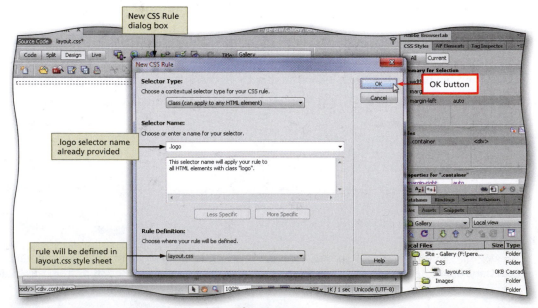

Figure 2–31

3

- Click the OK button to add the .logo selector to the layout.css style sheet and display the 'CSS Rule Definition for .logo in layout.css' dialog box (Figure 2–32).

Q&A Should I create another style sheet for the .logo class?

No. In this case, you save the six style classes within the same style sheet named layout.css.

Q&A How many classes can be added to the style sheet?

You can identify as many classes as you need to define the style of your site.

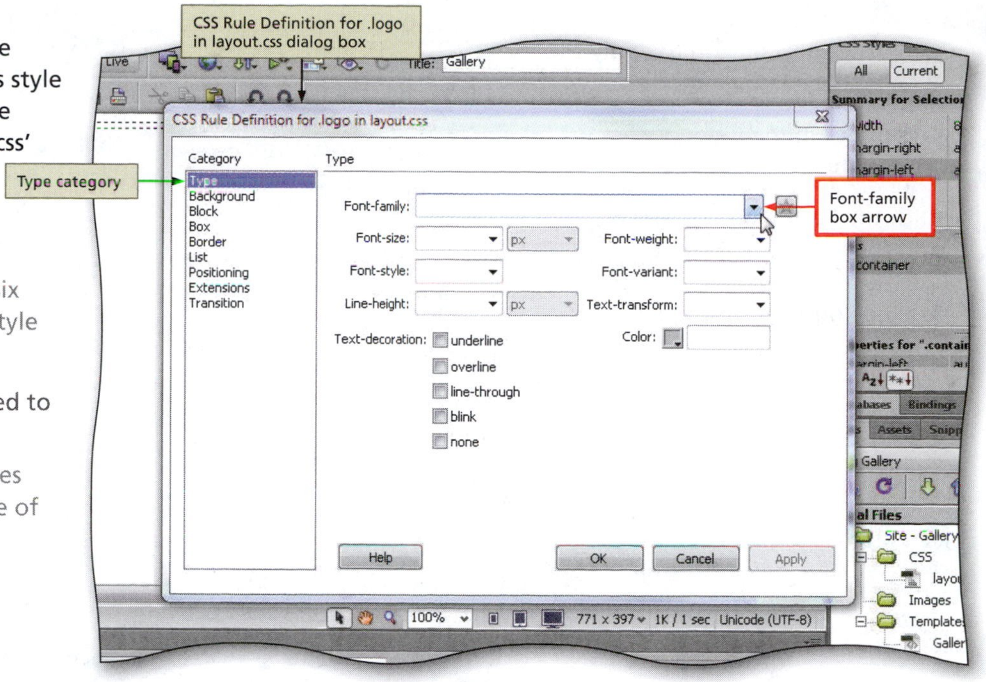

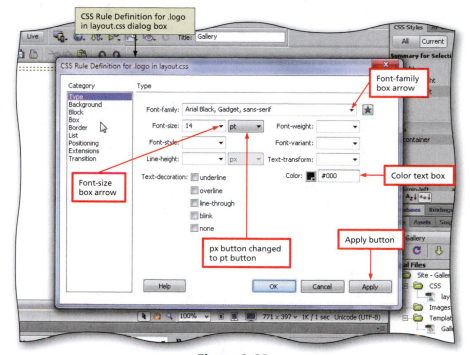

Figure 2–32

4

- If necessary, click Type in the Category list to display the Type options.

- Click the Font-family box arrow and then click 'Arial Black, Gadget, sans-serif' to set the font family for the .logo style.

- Click the Font-size box arrow and then click 14 to set the font size.

- Click the px button next to the Font-size box and then click pt to change the font size units from px to pt.

- Click the Color text box and then type #000 to change the font color to black (Figure 2–33).

Q&A Why is sans-serif or serif typically the last font listed in the Font-family font groupings?

The sans-serif and serif fonts are generic fonts that are displayed on any type of computer.

Q&A Are the px and pt font-size units basically the same?

The px unit measures fonts in pixels and the pt unit measures fonts in points. These units represent different sizes.

Figure 2–33

5

- Click the Apply button to apply the Type settings.

- Click Block in the Category list to display the Block options.

- Click the Text-align box arrow and then click center to set the text alignment for the .logo style (Figure 2–34).

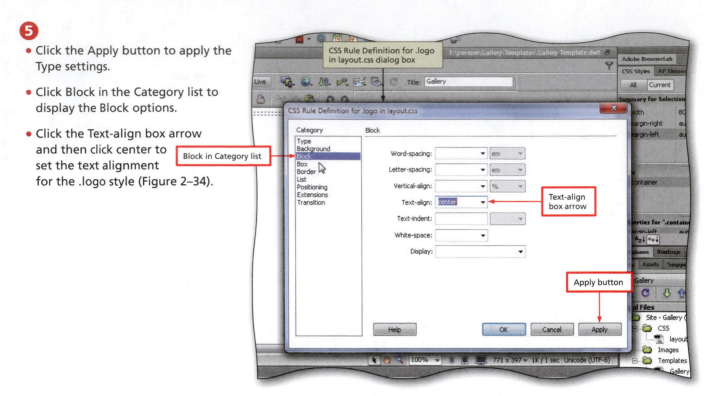

Figure 2–34

6

- Click the Apply button to apply the Block settings.

- Click Box in the Category list to display the Box options.

- Click the Width text box and then type 300 to set the width of the region containing the .logo style.

- Click the Height text box and then type 75 to set the height of the region.

- Click the Float box arrow and then click left to specify that other elements float to the left of elements in the .logo style (Figure 2–35).

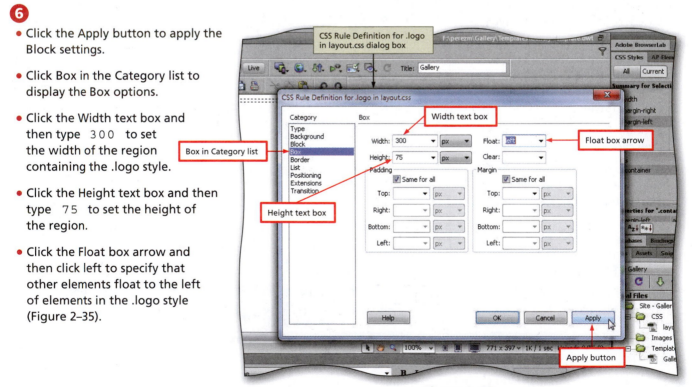

Figure 2–35

7

- Click the Apply button to apply the CSS rules for the .logo class within the layout.css file.

- Click the OK button (CSS Rule Definition dialog box) to define the CSS rules for the .logo class.

- Click the OK button (Insert Div Tag dialog box) to close the Insert Div Tag dialog box and display the .logo class region and its placeholder text (Figure 2–36).

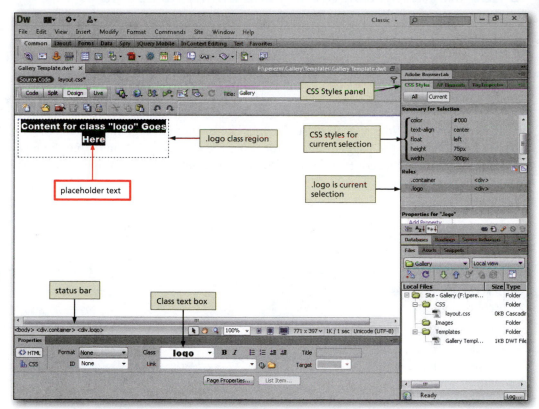

Figure 2–36

8

- If necessary, select the placeholder text 'Content for class "logo" Goes Here' in the Document window, and then type `The Gallery Portrait and Family Photography` to insert the logo text (Figure 2–37).

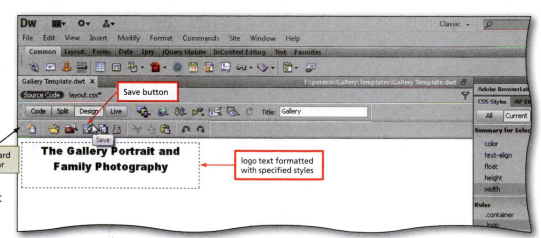

Figure 2–37

9

- Click the Save button on the Standard toolbar to save the template.

Q&A   What should I do if a Dreamweaver dialog box indicates the template does not have any editable regions?

Click the 'Don't warn me again' check box to insert a check mark, and then click the OK button. You specify editable regions later in the chapter.

To Add the Navigation Div Tag and Define Its CSS Rules

Most Web pages have a navigation region that contains links to other pages in the site. Including the navigation region in the Web site template means the navigation links appear in the same place and style on each page, which makes it easy for site visitors to find the links and navigate the site. Web sites typically include navigation links either horizontally across the top or vertically along the left side of each page. Many site designers prefer a horizontal navigation bar at the top of the page because it uses the full width of the page for content instead of crowding the left edge of the page with links, but either design can be effective as long as the navigation provides a strong visual focus. The navigation region for the Gallery site is displayed in the upper-right corner of the page. Similar to defining the logo region, you define the format and position of the navigation region and its contents. The following steps define the CSS rule definitions for the .navigation class.

1

- Click to the right of the .logo region within the document to move the insertion point to the div.container region.

- Click the Insert Div Tag button on the Insert bar to display the Insert Div Tag dialog box.

- If necessary, click the Class text box and then type navigation to name the div tag (Figure 2–38).

Q&A Why does the status bar display <body> <div.container>?

The container region is now selected instead of the logo region.

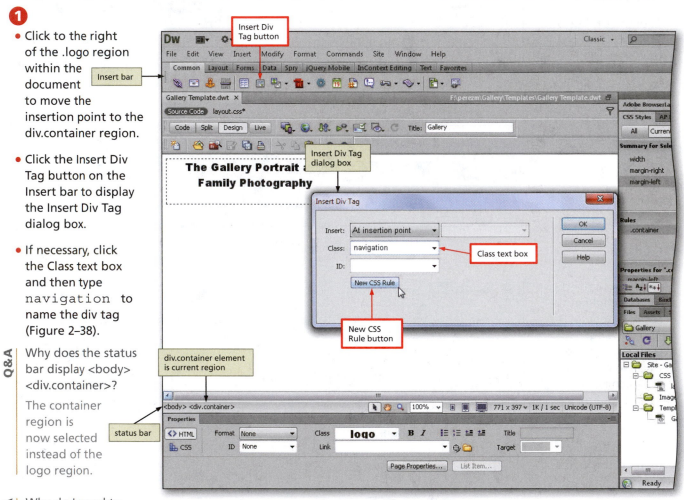

Figure 2–38

Q&A Why do I need to move the insertion point to the div.container region before creating the new navigation region?

You move the insertion point so you can create the new region in the div.container region, which you designed to hold all the other regions. Otherwise, you create the new navigation region in the logo region.

2

- Click the New CSS Rule button to display the New CSS Rule dialog box for adding a new CSS rule that defines the navigation class (Figure 2–39).

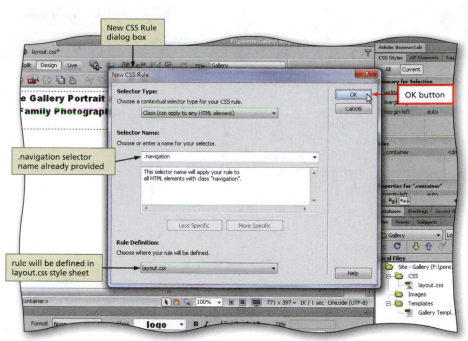

Figure 2–39

3

- Click the OK button to add the .navigation selector name to the layout.css file and display the 'CSS Rule Definition for .navigation in layout.css' dialog box.

- Click the Font-family box arrow and then click 'Arial, Helvetica, sans-serif' to set the font family for the .navigation style.

- Click the Font-size box arrow and then click 12 to set the font size for the .navigation style.

- Click the px button next to the Font-size box and then click pt to change the font size units from px to pt.

- Click the Line-height text box and then type 50 to set the line height to 50.

- Click the px button next to the Line-height box and then click pt to change the line height units from px to pt.

- Click the Font-weight box arrow and then click bolder to set the font to a bolder style.

- Click the Text-transform box arrow and then click lowercase to convert the text to lowercase letters.

- Click the Color text box and then type #F90 to change the style color to orange (Figure 2–40).

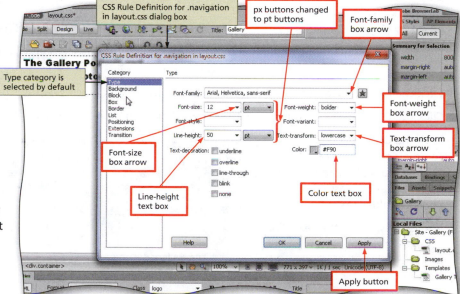

Figure 2–40

Q&A
What does the value, #F90, represent?

The value, #F90, is a hexadecimal number representing a color; in this case, orange. You can enter hexadecimal values in text boxes that request color values, or you can click the color palette button next to the text box to select a color.

- Click the Apply button to apply the Type settings.

- Click Block in the Category list to display the Block options.

- Click the Word-spacing text box, type 10, click the em button, and then click pt to change the word spacing in the .navigation style to 10 points.

- Click the Text-align box arrow and then click center to set the text alignment (Figure 2–41).

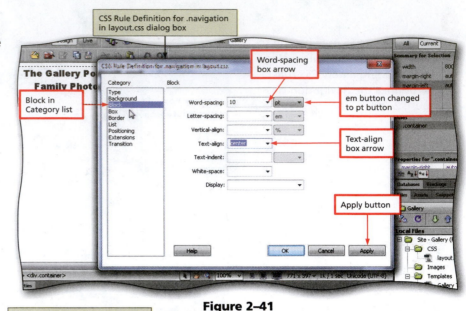

Figure 2–41

- Click the Apply button to apply the Block settings.

- Click Box in the Category list to display the Box options.

- Click the Width text box and then type 500 to set the width of the .navigation region.

- Click the Height text box and then type 75 to set the height of the .navigation region.

- Click the Float box arrow and then click left to change the float property (Figure 2–42).

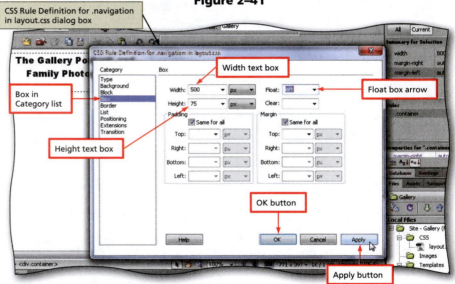

Figure 2–42

- Click the Apply button to apply the CSS rules for the .navigation class within the layout.css style sheet.

- Click the OK button (CSS Rule Definition dialog box) to define the CSS rules for the .navigation class.

- Click the OK button (Insert Div Tag dialog box) to close the Insert Div Tag dialog box and display the .navigation class region and its placeholder text.

- If necessary, select the text 'Content for class "navigation" Goes Here' and then type home services portfolio pricing session contact to enter the navigation text (Figure 2–43).

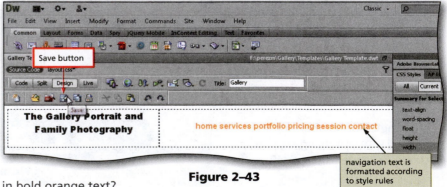

Figure 2–43

Q&A Why does the navigation text appear in bold orange text?

The style rules you just set are applied automatically to the navigation text.

- Click the Save button on the Standard toolbar to save the template.

To Add the Image Div Tag and Define Its CSS Rules

Most Web pages display one or more images to increase the visual appeal of the page. If one image or a certain type of image appears on each page, include an image region in the template so the image appears in the same place and style throughout the site. The pages in the Gallery site eventually will include family and portrait images as samples of photography the company has produced. To display these images consistently on each page, you add an image region to the template and then set its properties. The image region serves as a placeholder for the main images that will be displayed in the Gallery site. The following steps define the CSS rules of the .image class.

- If necessary, scroll right and then click to the right of the .navigation div within the document to move the insertion point to the div.container element.

- Click the Insert Div Tag button on the Insert bar to display the Insert Div Tag dialog box.

- In the Class text box, type image to name the div tag (Figure 2–44).

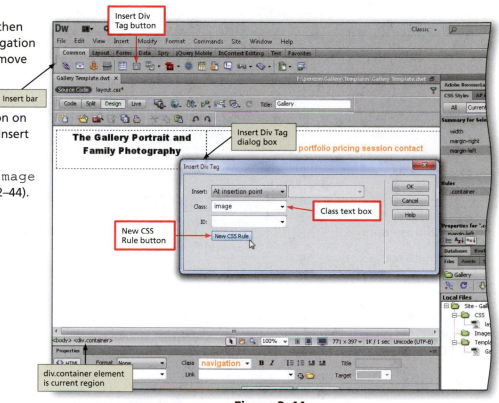

Figure 2–44

- Click the New CSS Rule button to display the New CSS Rule dialog box for adding a new CSS rule that defines the image class (Figure 2–45).

Figure 2–45

- Click the OK button to add the .image selector name to the layout.css style sheet and display the 'CSS Rule Definition for .image in layout.css' dialog box.

- Click Background in the Category list to display the Background options.

- Click the Background-color text box and then type #000 to change the background color of the .image region to black (Figure 2–46).

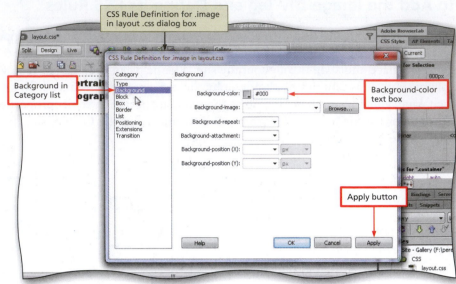

Figure 2–46

- Click the Apply button to apply the Background settings.

- Click Box in the Category list to display the Box options.

- In the Width text box, type 800 to set the width of the image region to 800 pixels.

- Click the Float box arrow and then click left to set the value of the float property (Figure 2–47).

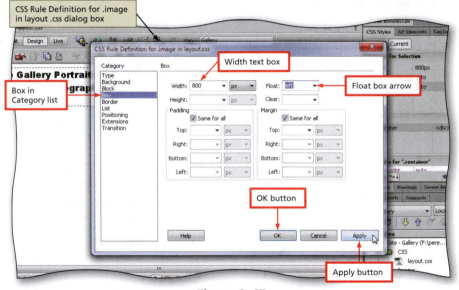

Figure 2–47

- Click the Apply button to apply the CSS rules for the .image class within the layout.css style sheet.

- Click the OK button (CSS Rule Definition dialog box) to define the CSS rules for the .image class.

- Click the OK button (Insert Div Tag dialog box) to close the Insert Div Tag dialog box and display the new image region (Figure 2–48).

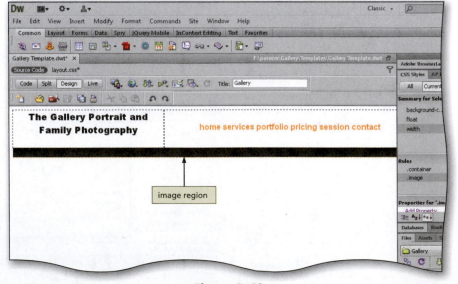

Figure 2–48

To Add the Content Div Tag and Define Its CSS Rules

One way to create a consistent look for a Web site is to include a heading or other text in the same style and place on each page. To achieve this consistency, add a region for the text content to the template, and then specify the style and placement properties in the style sheet. Because each page in the Gallery site will include content such as a heading or other text below the logo and navigation regions, you can add a content region to the template. On the opening page, the content region displays welcome text, but other pages will display different content. For now, you insert the content region with placeholder text and specify the style properties for the region. One new property to enter is **padding**, which specifies the amount of space between the text and its border. The following steps define the CSS rules for the .content class.

- If necessary, scroll right and then click to the right of the .image div within the document to move the insertion point to the div.container element.

- Click the Insert Div Tag button on the Insert bar to display the Insert Div Tag dialog box.

- In the Class text box, type content to name the div tag.

- Click the New CSS Rule button to display the New CSS Rule dialog box for adding a new CSS rule that defines the content class (Figure 2–49).

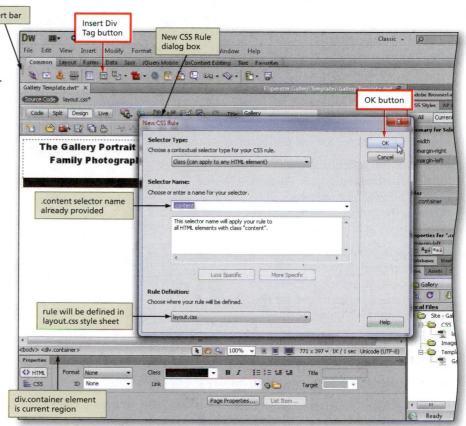

Figure 2–49

- Click the OK button to add the .content selector to the layout.css style sheet and display the 'CSS Rule Definition for .content in layout.css' dialog box.

- Click the Font-family box arrow and then click 'Arial, Helvetica, sans-serif' to set the font family.

- Click the Font-size box arrow, click 12, click the px button, and then click pt to change the units to pt and the font size to 12 points.

- Click the Color text box and then type #000 to change the background color of the .content region to black (Figure 2–50).

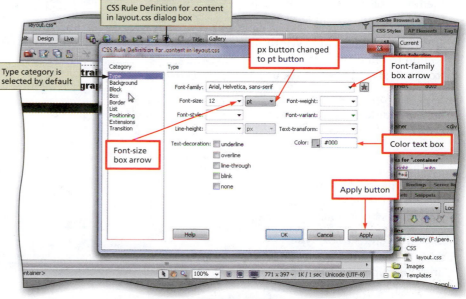

Figure 2–50

3

- Click the Apply button to apply the Type settings.
- Click Box in the Category list to display the Box options.
- Click the Width text box and then type 800 to set the width of the .content region.
- Click the Float box arrow and then click left to set the value of the float property.
- Click 'Same for all' in the Padding section to remove the check mark from the 'Same for all' check box.
- Click the Top text box in the Padding section, type 10, click the px button, and then click pt to change the units to pt and set the top padding to 10 points above the text.
- Click the Bottom text box in the Padding section, type 10, click the px button, and then click pt to change the units to pt and set the bottom padding.
- Click 'Same for all' in the Margin section to remove the check mark from the 'Same for all' check box.
- Click the Top text box in the Margin section, type 10, click the px button, and then click pt to change the units to pt and set the top margin to 10 points.
- Click the Bottom text box in the Margin section, type 10, click the px button, and then click pt to change the units to pt and set the bottom margin (Figure 2–51).

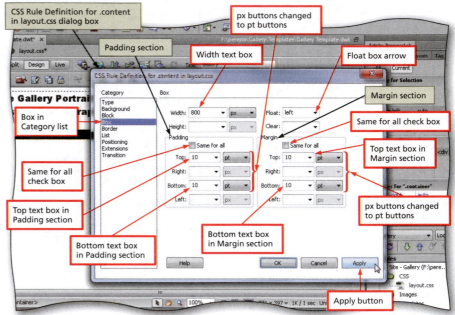

Figure 2–51

4

- Click the Apply button to apply the Box settings.
- Click Border in the Category list to display the Border options.
- Click 'Same for all' in the Style section to remove the check mark from the 'Same for all' check box.
- Click the Top box arrow, click solid, click the Bottom box arrow, and then click solid to select a solid style for the top and bottom borders.
- Click 'Same for all' in the Width section to remove the check mark from the 'Same for all' check box.
- Click the Top box arrow, click medium, click the Bottom box arrow, and then click medium to select a medium width for the top and bottom borders.
- Click 'Same for all' in the Color section to remove the check mark from the 'Same for all' check box.
- Click the Top text box, type #000, click the Bottom text box, and then type #000 to set the color of the top and bottom borders to black (Figure 2–52).

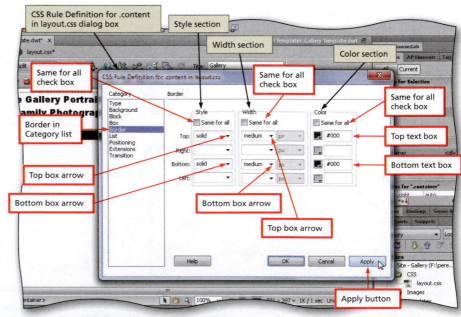

Figure 2–52

5
- Click the Apply button to apply the CSS rules for the .content class within the layout.css style sheet.
- Click the OK button (CSS Rule Definition dialog box) to define the CSS rules for the .content class.
- Click the OK button (Insert Div Tag dialog box) to close the Insert Div Tag dialog box and display the new content region (Figure 2–53).

6
- Click the Save button on the Standard toolbar to save your work.

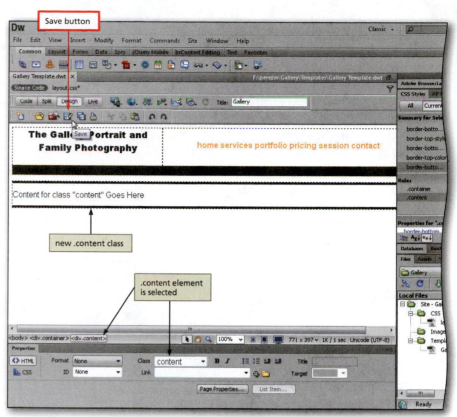

Figure 2–53

To Add the Footer Div Tag and Define Its CSS Rules

The footer of a site typically includes copyright or contact information. The Gallery site displays the year and the copyright information. The following steps define the CSS rules for the .footer class.

1
- If necessary, scroll right and then click to the right of the .content div within the document to move the insertion point to the div.container element.
- Click the Insert Div Tag button on the Insert bar to display the Insert Div Tag dialog box.
- In the Class text box, type `footer` to name the div tag.
- Click the New CSS Rule button to add a new CSS rule that defines the footer class (Figure 2–54).

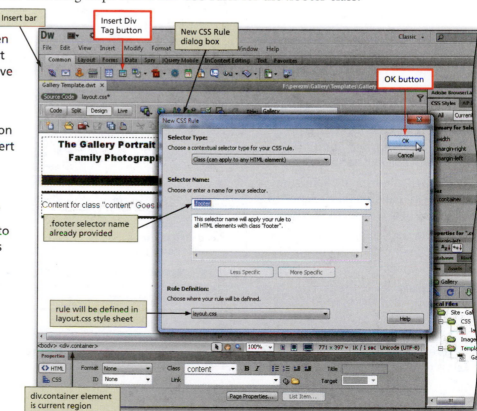

Figure 2–54

2

- Click the OK button to add the .footer selector name to layout.css and display the 'CSS Rule Definition for .footer in layout.css' dialog box.

- Click the Font-family box arrow and click 'Verdana, Geneva, sans-serif' to set the font family.

- Click the Font-size text box, type 8, click the px button, and then click pt to change the units to pt and the font size to 8 points.

- Click the Color text box and type #333 to change the font color of the .footer div region to dark gray (Figure 2–55).

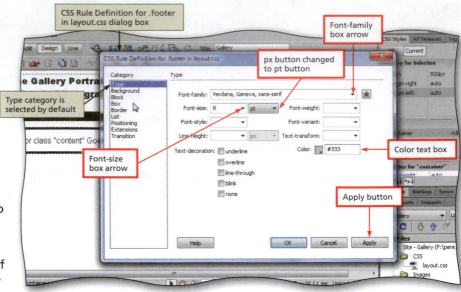

Figure 2–55

3

- Click the Apply button to apply the Type settings.

- Click Box in the Category list to display the Box options.

- Click the Width text box and then type 800 to set a width of 800 pixels for the .footer class.

- Click the Float box arrow and then click left to set the value of the float property (Figure 2–56).

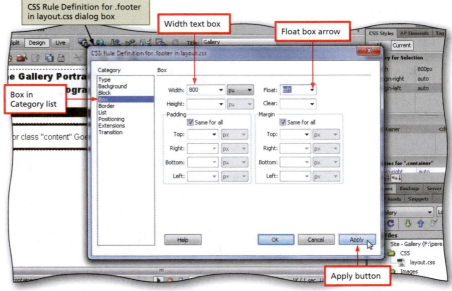

Figure 2–56

4

- Click the Apply button to apply the CSS rules for the .footer class within the layout.css style sheet.

- Click the OK button (CSS Rule Definition dialog box) to define the CSS rules for the .footer class.

- Click the OK button (Insert Div Tag dialog box) to close the Insert Div Tag dialog box.

- If necessary, select the text 'Content for class "footer" Goes Here' and type Copyright 2014. All Rights Reserved. to enter the .footer class text (Figure 2–57).

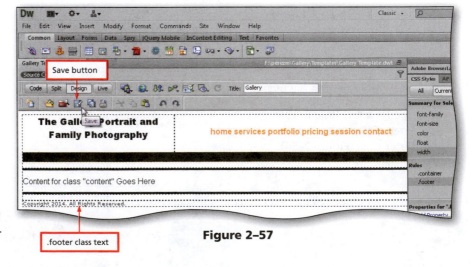

Figure 2–57

5

- Click the Save button on the Standard toolbar to save your work.

Creating an Editable Region of a Template

Recall that the two types of regions you can include in a template are editable and noneditable regions. Noneditable regions, also called locked regions, are the sections of a template that have static, unchanging content, such as a logo or a navigation bar. An editable region on a Web page is an area where other Web page authors can edit the content. As a Web developer, you create editable regions in a template to allow other authors to add or remove information without worrying that they will alter the page layout. This gives you control over the layout of the pages and the template itself. For example, if an element, such as a navigation bar, is exactly the same across the entire site, it should be in a noneditable region of the template. Dreamweaver inserts an element as a noneditable region by default, meaning that no one can edit its content in a Web page based on the template. If a content area contains different information on each page, that content should be an editable region of the template. Because Dreamweaver templates contain no editable regions by default, the next step after creating a template typically is to specify some regions as editable regions so each page in the site can display different content.

To Create an Editable Region

In the Gallery site, the logo, navigation, and footer regions should display the same content on each page. Therefore, they can remain noneditable regions in the template. However, the content region of each page in the Gallery site contains different text. You need to specify that the content region is an editable region in the template so you can display different text on each page. The following steps create an editable region in the template.

1

- Select the text 'Content for class "content" Goes Here' in the content region, and then press the DELETE key to delete the placeholder text.

- Click an edge of the content region to select the region (Figure 2–58).

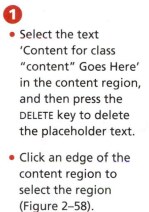

content text deleted

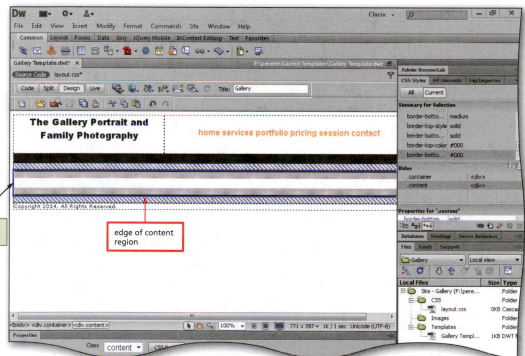

edge of content region

Figure 2–58

2

- Click Insert on the Application bar and then point to Template Objects to display the Template Objects submenu (Figure 2–59).

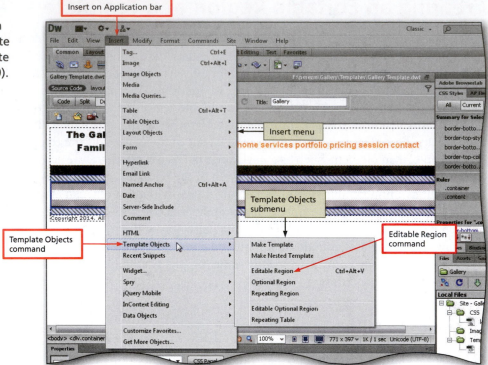

Figure 2–59

3

- Click Editable Region on the Template Objects submenu to display the New Editable Region dialog box.

- If necessary, select the text in the Name text box and then type contentArea to identify an editable region within the content region (Figure 2–60).

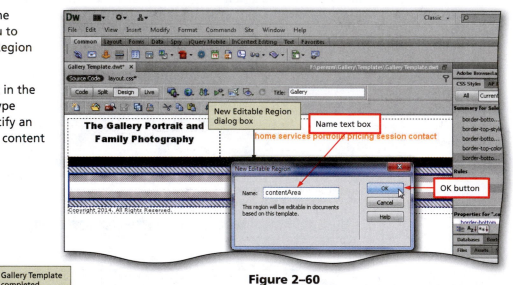

Figure 2–60

4

- Click the OK button to display the editable region.

- If necessary, click in the content region and then type Insert page content here to provide directions to add content to the editable region (Figure 2–61).

5

- Click the Save button on the Standard toolbar to save the completed template.

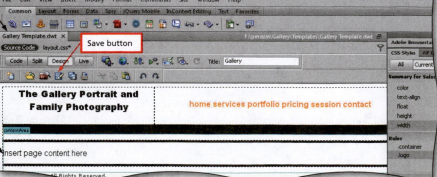

Figure 2–61

To Close the Template

The template is complete, so you can close it. The following steps close the template and display the Welcome screen again.

1
- Click File on the Application bar and then click Close to close the completed template and display the Welcome screen (Figure 2–62).

Q&A

What should I do if an Adobe Dreamweaver CS6 dialog box is displayed?

Click the Yes button to save your changes to the style sheet.

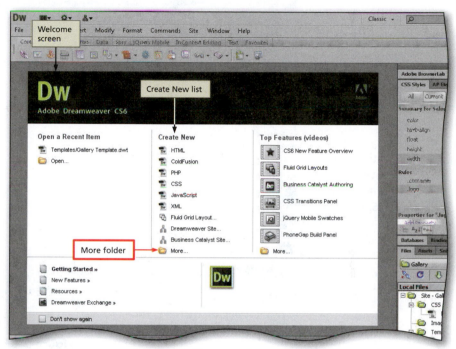

Figure 2–62

Creating a New Page from a Template

After creating and saving a template, you can use it to create Web pages on your site — just as you can create pages based on templates provided with Dreamweaver. To create a consistent site, be sure to associate each page with a template. As you create each new page of the site, you start with the template to establish the layout of the page. The noneditable regions of the template appear on the page as static, unchanging content. For example, if you add navigation, logo, and footer elements to a template, they appear on the Web page you create from the template and cannot be changed. Areas you specified as editable regions in the template appear on the Web page as content or areas you can change.

BTW

HTML and HTM File Extensions

Although Dreamweaver saves Web pages with a .html file extension by default, it can also save files with a .htm extension. Browsers recognize both file types as HTML files. You can set a preference to create pages using one extension or the other by clicking Edit on the Application bar, clicking Preferences, and then clicking the New Document category.

To Create a Page from a Template

To complete this assignment, you will be required to use the Data Files for Students. Visit www.cengage.com/ct/studentdownload for detailed instructions or contact your instructor for information about accessing the required files. The following steps open the Ch2_Home_Content file from the Data Files for Students.

The opening home page of the Gallery site is named index.html. In addition to the template elements, the index page uses the editable region of the template to display an opening message about the Gallery photography services. You add this message to the index.html page by copying text from a student data file named Ch2_Home_Page_Content.txt and pasting the text into index.html. The following steps create a new page from the template and add content to the editable region.

1

- Click More in the Create New list to display the New Document dialog box.

- Click Page from Template in the left pane of the New Document dialog box to create a page from the template.

- If necessary, click Gallery in the Site list to create a page for the Gallery site (Figure 2–63).

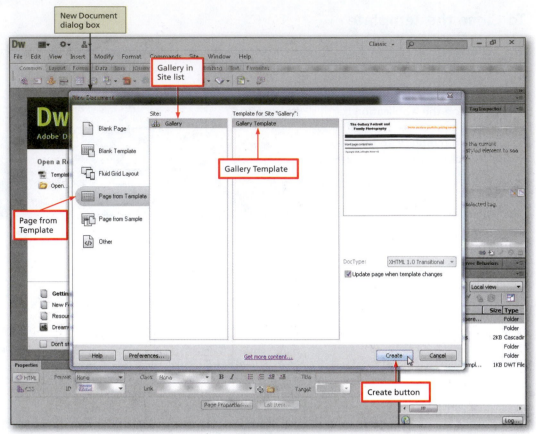

Figure 2–63

2

- Click the Create button to create a new page based on the template for the Gallery site.

- Click File on the Application bar and then click Save As to display the Save As dialog box.

- If necessary, select the text in the File name text box and then type index to name the new page created from the template (Figure 2–64).

Q&A

Which folder should I select to save the index.html file?

Save the home page, index.html, in the root Gallery folder, which is the folder displayed by default in the Save As dialog box. When a browser is directed to the Gallery folder, the browser displays index.html as the opening page.

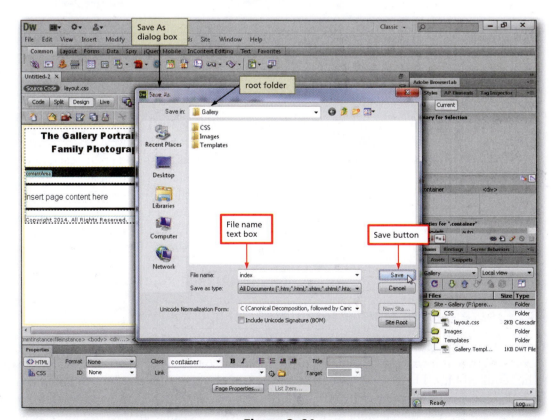

Figure 2–64

3

- Click the Save button to save and open index.html (Figure 2–65).

Q&A

When I move the mouse around the page, the pointer changes to a "not" symbol (circle with a line through it) over some parts of the page. What does this symbol represent in index.html?

The pointer displays a not symbol over the noneditable (locked) regions of the page.

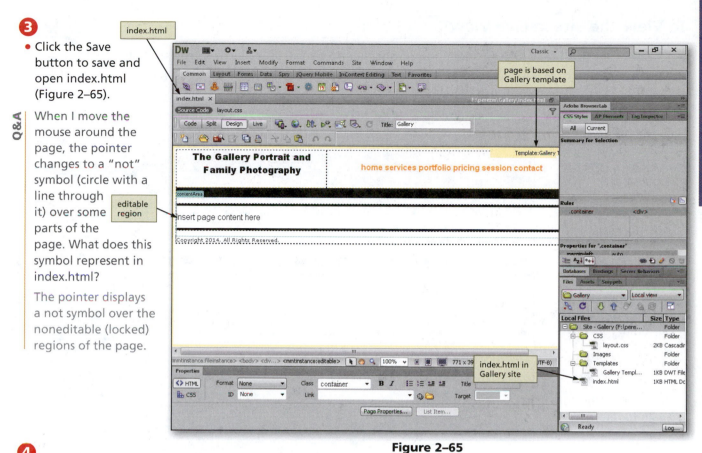

Figure 2–65

4

- If necessary, insert the drive containing your Data Files for Students into an available port. After a few seconds, if Windows displays a dialog box, click its Close button.

- With the Dreamweaver window open, click File on the Application bar, and then click Open to display the Open dialog box.

- In the Open dialog box, navigate to the storage location of the Data Files for Students.

- Click the Chapter 02 folder to display its contents, and then double-click the file, Ch2_Home_Page_Content, to open it.

- Select all the text in the file, click Edit on the Application bar, and then click Copy to copy the text.

- Click the index.html document tab, select the text, Insert page content here, on the index.html page, click Edit on the Application bar, and then click Paste to paste the text you copied (Figure 2–66).

5

- Close the Ch2_Home_Page_Content file.

- Click the Save All button on the Standard toolbar to save the site.

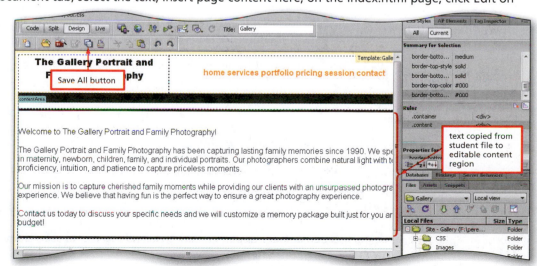

Figure 2–66

To View the Site in Live View

Live view provides a realistic rendering of what your page will look like in a browser, but lets you make any necessary changes without leaving Dreamweaver. The following steps display the page in Live view.

- Click the Live button on the Document toolbar to display a Live view of the site (Figure 2–67).

Experiment

- Click the Code, Split, and Design buttons to view the page in different views. When you are finished, click the Live button to return to Live view.

- Click the Live button again to return to Design view.

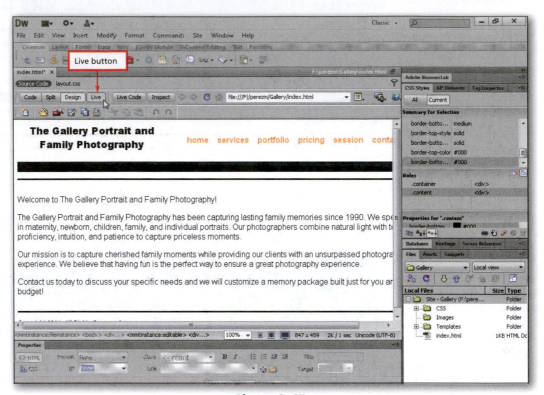

Figure 2–67

To View the Site in the Browser

The following steps preview the Gallery Web site home page using Internet Explorer.

1. Click the 'Preview/Debug in browser' button on the Document toolbar.

2. Click Preview in IExplore in the Preview/Debug in browser list to display the Gallery Web site in the Internet Explorer browser.

3. Click the Internet Explorer Close button to close the browser.

To Quit Dreamweaver

The following steps quit Dreamweaver and return control to the operating system.

1. Click the Close button on the right side of the Application bar to close the window.

2. If Dreamweaver displays a dialog box asking you to save changes, click the No button.

Chapter Summary

In this chapter, you have learned how to create a Web site template using the design building blocks of CSS style sheets. You defined a new Web site, created a Dreamweaver Web Template, and defined regions of the page using a style sheet. You defined each region with CSS rules that provided consistent site formatting. You also learned how to create an editable region within a template. You added a page to the site based on the template and placed text in the editable region. You displayed the completed Web page in Live view and in a browser. The following tasks are all the new Dreamweaver skills you learned in this chapter:

1. Create a New Site (DW 86)
2. Create Folders for the Image and CSS Files (DW 87)
3. Create a Blank HTML Template (DW 88)
4. Save the HTML Page as a Template (DW 90)
5. Add a Div Tag (DW 93)
6. Select CSS Rule Definitions (DW 97)
7. Add the Logo Div Tag and Define Its CSS Rules (DW 100)
8. Add the Navigation Div Tag and Define Its CSS Rules (DW 104)
9. Add the Image Div Tag and Define Its CSS Rules (DW 107)
10. Add the Content Div Tag and Define Its CSS Rules (DW 109)
11. Add the Footer Div Tag and Define Its CSS Rules (DW 111)
12. Create an Editable Region (DW 113)
13. Close the Template (DW 115)
14. Create a Page from a Template (DW 115)
15. View the Site in Live View (DW 118)

Apply Your Knowledge

Reinforce the skills and apply the concepts you learned in this chapter.

Creating a New Web Page Template

Instructions: First, create a new HTML5 Web page template and save it. Next, insert div tags in the template and create a new external style sheet file. Finally, add new CSS rules so that the completed template in Live view looks like Figure 2–68. The CSS rule definitions for the template are provided in Table 2–2.

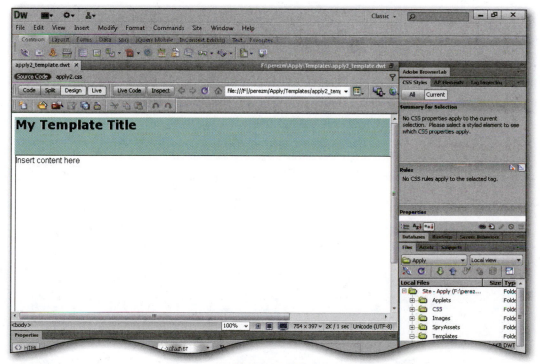

Figure 2–68

Continued >

Apply Your Knowledge *continued*

Perform the following tasks:

1. Use Windows Explorer to access your USB flash drive and create a new folder within the *your last name and first initial*\Apply folder (the folder named perezm\Apply, for example, which you created in Chapter 1). Name the folder `Templates`.

2. Start Dreamweaver. On the Dreamweaver Welcome screen, click the More folder. Create a new document as a blank template, HTML template, with no layout and DocType HTML5.

3. Save the new template in the Templates folder in the Apply root folder. Name the template `apply2_template.dwt`.

4. Insert a new div tag and name the class `container`.

5. Create a new CSS rule and specify that the rule definition will be defined in a new style sheet file. Name the style sheet file `apply2.css` and save it in a new folder named `CSS` in the root folder for the Apply site.

6. Define the CSS rule for the container class according to the settings provided in Table 2–2. Apply and accept your changes when you are finished.

7. Click after the placeholder text in the container and then press the ENTER key to insert a blank line.

8. Insert a div tag within the container. Name the class `header`. Refer to Table 2–2 to define the new CSS rule for the header in Apply2.css. Apply and accept your changes.

9. Replace text within the header div tag with `My Template Title`.

10. Insert a div tag below the header div tag but within the container div tag. Name the class `content`. Refer to Table 2–2 to define the new CSS rule for the content in apply2.css. Apply and accept your changes.

11. Delete the text within the content div tag and insert an editable region. Name the new editable region `Insert content here`.

12. Insert a div tag below the content div tag but within the container div tag. Name the class `footer`. Refer to Table 2–2 to define the new CSS rule for the footer in apply2.css. Apply and accept your changes.

13. Replace the text within the footer div tag with your name. Delete the placeholder text for the container region, and then press the BACKSPACE key to move the header to the top of the container.

14. Title the document `Apply2_Template`.

15. Save your changes and then view your document using Live view. Compare your document to Figure 2–68. Make any necessary changes and then save your changes.

16. Submit the document in the format specified by your instructor.

Table 2–2 CSS Rule Definitions for apply2_template

CSS Rule Definition for .container in apply2.css

Category	Property	Value
Box	Width	1000px
	Right Margin	auto
	Left Margin	auto

CSS Rule Definition for .header in apply2.css

Category	Property	Value
Type	Font-family	Verdana, Geneva, sans-serif
	Font-size	18pt
	Font-weight	bold
Background	Background-color	#9CC
Box	Width	1000px
	Height	75px

CSS Rule Definition for .content in apply2.css

Category	Property	Value
Type	Font-family	Arial, Helvetica, sans-serif
Box	Width	1000px
	Height	400px
Border	Style	solid, same for all
	Width	thin, same for all
	Color	#000, same for all

CSS Rule Definition for .footer in apply2.css

Category	Property	Value
Type	Font-family	Times New Roman, Times, serif
	Font-size	10pt
Box	Width	1000px

Extend Your Knowledge

Extend the skills you learned in this chapter and experiment with new skills. You may need to use Help to complete the assignment.

Attaching an External Style Sheet to a Web Page

Note: To complete this assignment, you will be required to use the Data Files for Students. Visit www.cengage.com/ct/studentdownload for detailed instructions or contact your instructor for information about accessing the required files.

Instructions: A volunteer service organization wants to create a Web site using style sheets. You are creating a Web page for the organization that explains the difference between internal and external style sheets. Apply styles to a page by attaching an external style sheet to an existing Web page. The completed Web page is shown in Figure 2–69.

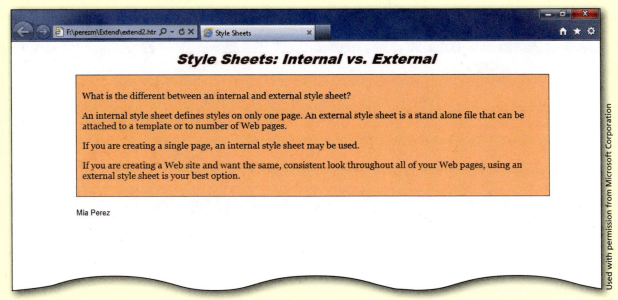

Figure 2–69

Perform the following tasks:

1. Use Windows Explorer to copy the CSS folder and the extend2.html file from the Chapter 02\ Extend folder into the *your last name and first initial*\Extend folder (the folder named perezm\ Extend, for example, which you created in Chapter 1).

2. Start Dreamweaver and open extend2.html.

3. On the CSS Styles panel, click the Attach Style Sheet button to display the Attach External Style Sheet dialog box. (*Hint*: Point to the buttons in the lower-right part of the CSS Styles panel to find the Attach Style Sheet button.) Click the Browse button in the Attach External Style Sheet dialog box, and then navigate to find and then select the extend2.css file located in the CSS folder in the Extend root folder. Add the CSS file as a link, and then accept your changes.

4. Replace the text, Your name here, with your name.

5. Title the document `Style Sheets`.

6. Save your changes and then view your document in your browser. Compare your document to Figure 2–69. Make any necessary changes and then save your changes.

7. Submit the document in the format specified by your instructor.

Make It Right

Analyze a Web page and correct all errors and/or improve the design.

Adding Div Tags and CSS Rule Definitions to a Web Page

Note: To complete this assignment, you will be required to use the Data Files for Students. Visit www.cengage.com/ct/studentdownload for detailed instructions or contact your instructor for information about accessing the required files.

Instructions: A bird-watching club is creating a Web site and wants to know the benefits of using CSS rules. You will create a Web page that lists these benefits. You also will create new div tags and add CSS rule definitions within an existing Web page. The CSS rule definitions for the Web page are provided in Table 2–3. The completed Web page is shown in Figure 2–70.

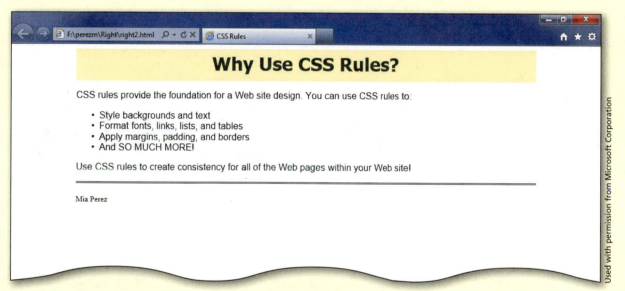

Figure 2–70

Perform the following tasks:

1. Use Windows Explorer to copy the right2.html file from the Chapter 02\Right folder into the *your last name and first initial*\Right folder (the folder named perezm\Right, for example, which you created in Chapter 1).

2. Open right2.html in your browser to view it and note that it currently has no design and no styles applied. Close your browser.

3. Start Dreamweaver and open right2.html.

4. Select all of the text on the page.

5. Insert a new div tag and name the class `container`. Leave the insert type as the default 'Wrap around selection'.

6. Refer to Table 2–3 to define the new CSS rule for the class container. The Rule Definition will be for this document only. Apply and accept your changes.

7. Select the text, Why Use CSS Rules?

Continued >

Make It Right *continued*

Table 2–3 CSS Rule Definitions for right2.html

CSS Rule Definition for .container

Category	Property	Value
Box	Width	800px
	Right Margin	auto
	Left Margin	auto

CSS Rule Definition for .header

Category	Property	Value
Type	Font-family	Tahoma, Geneva, sans-serif
	Font-size	24pt
	Font-weight	bold
	Color	#030
Background	Background-color	#FFC
Block	Text-align	center
Box	Width	800px
	Height	50px
	Top Padding	5px

CSS Rule Definition for .content

Category	Property	Value
Type	Font-family	Arial, Helvetica, sans-serif
	Font-size	12pt
Box	Width	800px
Border	Bottom Style	double
	Bottom Width	medium
	Bottom Color	#000

CSS Rule Definition for .footer

Category	Property	Value
Type	Font-size	10pt
Box	Width	800px
	Top Margin	20px

8. Insert a new div tag and name the class `header`. Leave the insert type as the default 'Wrap around selection'.

9. Refer to Table 2–3 to define the new CSS rule for the class header in this document only. Apply and accept your changes.

10. Select the text below Why Use CSS Rules? beginning with "CSS rules provide" and ending with "within your Web site!"

11. Insert a new div tag and name the class `content`. Leave the insert type as the default 'Wrap around selection'.

12. Refer to Table 2–3 to define the new CSS rule for the class content in this document only. Apply and accept your changes.

13. Select the text, Your name here.

14. Insert a new div tag and name the class `footer`. Leave the insert type as the default 'Wrap around selection'.

15. Refer to Table 2–3 to define the new CSS rule for the class footer in this document only. Apply and accept your changes.

16. Replace the text, Your name here., with your name.

17. Title the document CSS Rules.

18. Save your changes and then view the Web page in your browser. Compare your page to Figure 2–70. Make any necessary changes and then save your changes.

19. Submit the document in the format specified by your instructor.

In the Lab

Design and/or create a Web document using the guidelines, concepts, and skills presented in this chapter. Labs are listed in order of increasing difficulty.

Lab 1: Designing a New Template for the Healthy Lifestyle Web Site

Note: To complete this assignment, you will be required to use the Data Files for Students. Visit www.cengage.com/ct/studentdownload for detailed instructions or contact your instructor for information about accessing the required files.

Problem: In an effort to reduce health insurance costs, your company wants to provide resources for living a healthy lifestyle. You have been asked to create an internal Web site for your company with information about how to live a healthy lifestyle. This Web site will be used as a resource by employees at your company. You thoughtfully have planned the design of the Web site and now are ready to create a template for the site.

Define a new Web site and create a new HTML5 template. Use div tags and CSS rules in your template design. The template in Live view is shown in Figure 2–71, and the final Web page is shown in Figure 2–72. The CSS rule definitions for the template are provided in Table 2–4.

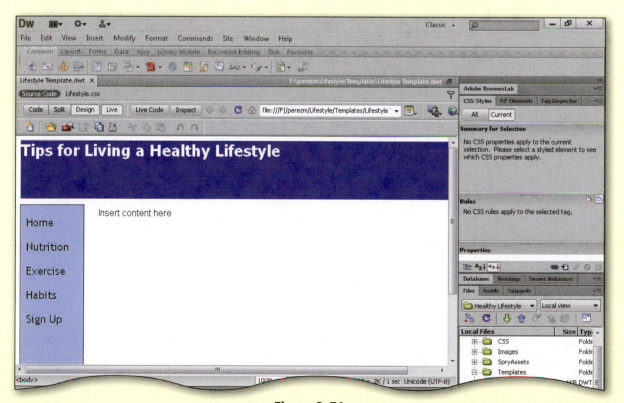

Figure 2–71

Continued >

In the Lab *continued*

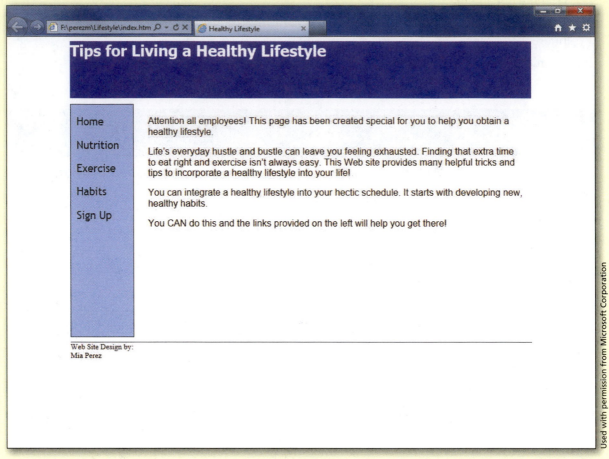

Figure 2–72

Perform the following tasks:

1. Start Dreamweaver. Click Dreamweaver Site in the Create New list of the Welcome screen to display the Site Setup dialog box. Type `Healthy Lifestyle` in the Site name text box.

2. Click the 'Browse for folder' icon to display the Choose Root Folder dialog box. Create a new subfolder in the *your last name and first initial* folder. Type `Lifestyle` as the folder name, select the folder, and then save the site.

3. On the Dreamweaver Welcome screen, click More in the Create New list. In the New Document dialog box, select Blank Template, Template Type: HTML template, Layout: <none>. Set the DocType to HTML5 and click the Create button. Save the new template using `Lifestyle Template` as the file name.

4. Use `Healthy Lifestyle` as the page title in the Title text box.

5. Insert a new div tag and name the class `container`.

6. Create a new CSS rule with a new style sheet file as the location for the rule definition. Name the style sheet file `Lifestyle.css`. Use the Create New Folder button in the Save Style Sheet File As dialog box to create a new folder and name it `CSS`. Save Lifestyle.css within the CSS folder.

7. Refer to Table 2–4 to define the CSS rule for the container. Apply and accept your changes.

8. Insert a blank line after the placeholder text in the container div tag.

9. Insert a div tag within the container. Name the class `header`.

Table 2–4 CSS Rule Definitions for Tips for Living a Healthy Lifestyle

CSS Rule Definition for .container in Lifestyle.css

Category	Property	Value
Box	Width	800px
	Right Margin	auto
	Left Margin	auto

CSS Rule Definition for .header in Lifestyle.css

Category	Property	Value
Type	Font-family	Tahoma, Geneva, sans-serif
	Font-size	20pt
	Font-weight	bold
	Color	#FFF
Background	Background-color	#039
Box	Width	800px
	Height	100px
	Bottom Margin	10px

CSS Rule Definition for .navigation in Lifestyle.css

Category	Property	Value
Type	Font-family	Trebuchet MS, Arial, Helvetica, sans-serif
	Font-size	14pt
	Color	#333
Background	Background-color	#9CF
Box	Width	100px
	Height	400px
	Float	left
	Left Padding	10px
	Right Margin	10px
Border	Style	solid, same for all
	Width	thin, same for all
	Color	#003, same for all

CSS Rule Definition for .content in Lifestyle.css

Category	Property	Value
Type	Font-family	Arial, Helvetica, sans-serif
	Font-size	12pt
Box	Width	650px
	Height	400px
	Float	left
	Padding	5px, same for all
	Left Margin	10px

CSS Rule Definition for .footer in Lifestyle.css

Category	Property	Value
Type	Font-family	Times New Roman, Times, serif
	Font-size	10pt
Box	Width	800px
	Float	left
Border	Style	solid, same for all
	Width	thin, same for all
	Color	#333, same for all

Continued >

In the Lab *continued*

10. Create a new CSS rule. Refer to Table 2–4 to define the CSS rule for the header in Lifestyle. css. Apply and accept your changes.

11. Replace the text within the header div tag with `Tips for Living a Healthy Lifestyle`.

12. Insert a div tag after the header div tag but within the container div tag. Name the class `navigation`.

13. Create a new CSS rule. Refer to Table 2–4 to define the CSS rule for the navigation in Lifestyle.css. Apply and accept your changes.

14. Replace the text within the navigation div tag with the following list, pressing ENTER at the end of each line:

```
Home
Nutrition
Exercise
Habits
Sign Up
```

---

15. Insert a div tag to the right of the navigation div tag but within the container div tag. Name the class `content`.

16. Create a new CSS rule. Refer to Table 2–4 to define the CSS rule for the content in Lifestyle. css. Apply and accept your changes.

17. Delete the text within the content div tag and insert an editable region. Name the new editable region `Insert content here`.

18. Insert a div tag to the right of the content div tag but within the container div tag. Name the class `footer`.

19. Create a new CSS rule. Refer to Table 2–4 to define the CSS rule for the footer in Lifestyle.css. Apply and accept your changes.

20. Replace the text within the footer div tag with `Web Site Design by:`, press the SHIFT+ENTER keys, and then type your first and last names.

21. Delete the placeholder text for the container region, and then press the BACKSPACE key to move the header to the top of the container.

22. Save your changes and then view your template using Live view. Compare your template to Figure 2–71. Make any necessary changes and save your changes. Close the template.

23. Use the New Document dialog box to create a new Web page using the Lifestyle Template. Save the new page using `index` as the file name in the root folder of the Lifestyle site.

24. Replace the text, Insert content here, with text from the Lab1_Content.txt data file.

25. Save your changes and then view the Web page in your browser. Compare your page to Figure 2–72. Make any necessary changes and then save your changes.

26. Submit the documents in the format specified by your instructor.

In the Lab

Lab 2: Designing a New Template for Designs by Dolores

Note: To complete this assignment, you will be required to use the Data Files for Students. Visit www.cengage.com/ct/studentdownload for detailed instructions or contact your instructor for information about accessing the required files.

Problem: You are working as an intern for a Web site design company, Designs by Dolores. The owner, Dolores, is impressed with your Web site design knowledge and asks you to redesign her current site. You are excited about the opportunity to design your first Web site and begin by creating a template for the site.

Define a new Web site and create a new HTML5 template. Use div tags and CSS rules in your template design. The template in Live view is shown in Figure 2–73, and the final Web page is shown in Figure 2–74. The CSS rule definitions for the template are provided in Table 2–5.

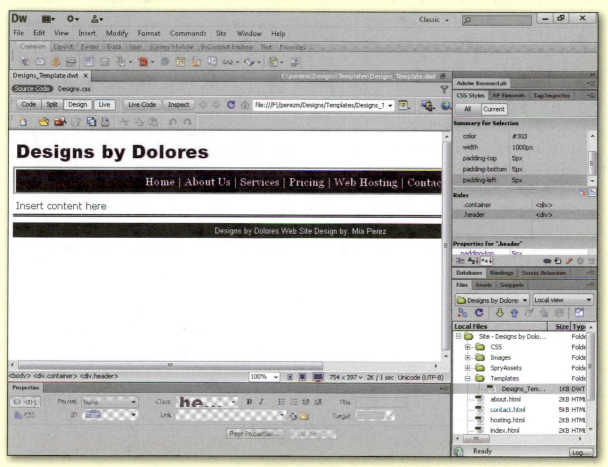

Figure 2–73

Continued >

In the Lab *continued*

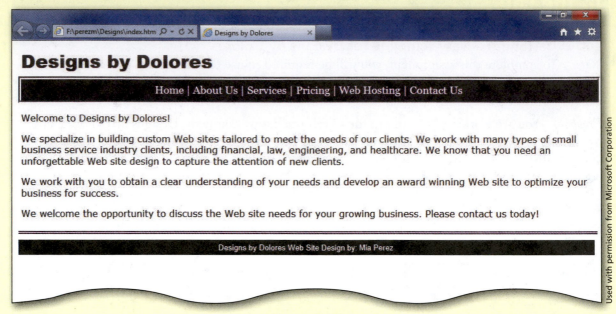

Figure 2–74

Perform the following tasks:

1. Start Dreamweaver. Click Dreamweaver Site in the Create New list to display the Site Setup dialog box. Type `Designs by Dolores` in the Site name text box.

2. Click the 'Browse for folder' icon to display the Choose Root Folder dialog box. Create a new subfolder in the *your last name and first initial* folder. Use `Designs` as the folder name, and then save the folder and the site.

3. On the Dreamweaver Welcome screen, click More in the Create New list. Create a blank HTML5 template with no layout. Set the DocType to HTML5. Save the new template as `Designs_Template` in the Designs by Dolores site.

4. Use `Designs by Dolores` as the page title.

5. Insert a new div tag and name the class `container`.

6. Create a new CSS rule with a new style sheet file as the rule definition. Name the style sheet file `Designs.css`. Save Designs.css in a new folder named `CSS`.

7. Refer to Table 2–5 for the container CSS rule definition.

8. Insert a blank line after the placeholder text in the container div tag.

9. Insert a div tag within the container. Name the class `header`.

10. Create a new CSS rule. Refer to Table 2–5 for the header CSS rule definition.

11. Replace the text within the header div tag with `Designs by Dolores.`

12. Insert a div tag below the header div tag but within the container div tag. Name the class `navigation`.

13. Create a new CSS rule. Refer to Table 2–5 for the navigation CSS rule definition.

14. Replace the text within the navigation div tag with `Home | About Us | Services | Pricing | Web Hosting | Contact Us.`

15. Insert a div tag below the navigation div tag but within the container div tag. Name the class `content`.

Table 2–5 CSS Rule Definitions for Designs by Dolores

CSS Rule Definition for .container in Designs.css

Category	Property	Value
Box	Width	1000px
	Right Margin	Auto
	Left Margin	Auto

CSS Rule Definition for .header in Designs.css

Category	Property	Value
Type	Font-family	Arial Black, Gadget, sans-serif
	Font-size	24pt
	Color	#303
Box	Width	1000px
	Top Padding	5px
	Bottom Padding	5px
	Left Padding	5px

CSS Rule Definition for .navigation in Designs.css

Category	Property	Value
Type	Font-family	Georgia, Times New Roman, Times, serif
	Font-size	14pt
	Color	#FFF
Background	Background-color	#303
Block	Text-align	center
Box	Width	1000px
	Top Padding	8px
	Bottom Padding	8px
Border	Style	groove, same for all
	Width	thick, same for all
	Color	#FFF, same for all

CSS Rule Definition for .content in Designs.css

Category	Property	Value
Type	Font-family	Verdana, Geneva, sans-serif
	Font-size	12pt
Box	Width	1000px
	Bottom Padding	5px
	Left Padding	5px
	Top Margin	10px
	Bottom Margin	10px
Border	Bottom Style	double
	Bottom Width	thick
	Bottom Color	#303

CSS Rule Definition for .footer in Designs.css

Category	Property	Value
Type	Font-family	Arial, Helvetica, sans-serif
	Font-size	10pt
	Color	#FFF
Background	Background-color	#333
Block	Text-align	center
Box	Width	1000px
	Top Padding	5px
	Bottom Padding	5px

Continued >

In the Lab *continued*

16. Create a new CSS rule. Refer to Table 2–5 for the content CSS rule definition.

17. Delete the text within the content div tag and insert an editable region. Name the new editable region `Insert content here`.

18. Insert a div tag below the content div tag but within the container div tag. Name the class `footer`.

19. Create a new CSS rule. Refer to Table 2–5 for the footer CSS rule definition.

20. Replace the text within the footer div tag with `Designs by Dolores Web Site Design by:` and then type your first and last names.

21. Delete the placeholder text for the container region, and then press the BACKSPACE key to move the header to the top of the container.

22. Save your changes and then view your template using Live view. Compare your template to Figure 2–73. Make and save any necessary changes, and then close the template.

23. Create a new Web page using the Designs Template. Save the new page using `index` as the file name in the root folder for the Designs site.

24. Replace the text, Insert content here, with text from the Lab2_Content.txt data file.

25. Save your changes and then view the Web page in your browser. Compare your page to Figure 2–74. Make any necessary changes and then save them.

26. Submit the documents in the format specified by your instructor.

In the Lab

Lab 3: Designing a New Template for Justin's Lawn Care Service

Note: To complete this assignment, you will be required to use the Data Files for Students. Visit www.cengage.com/ct/studentdownload for detailed instructions or contact your instructor for information about accessing the required files.

Problem: You have been hired to create a Web site for a new lawn care company, Justin's Lawn Care Service. You thoughtfully have planned the design of the Web site and now are ready to create a template for the site. You have met with Justin to discuss his needs for the Web site and are ready to start developing the site.

Define a new Web site and create a new HTML5 template. Use div tags and CSS rules in your template design. The template is shown in Figure 2–75, and the final Web page is shown in Figure 2–76. The CSS rule definitions for the template are provided in Table 2–6.

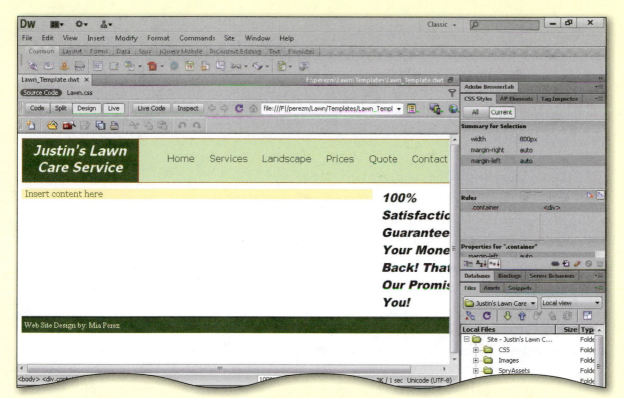

Figure 2–75

Figure 2–76

Perform the following tasks:

1. Start Dreamweaver. Use the Welcome screen to create a new site. Type `Justin's Lawn Care Service` as the site name.

2. Create a new subfolder named `Lawn` in the *your last name and first initial* folder, and then save the site.

Continued >

In the Lab *continued*

3. Create a blank HTML5 template with no layout. Save the new template as `Lawn_Template`.

4. Use `Justin's Lawn Care Service` as the page title.

5. Insert a new div tag and name the class `container`.

6. Create a new CSS rule with a new style sheet file named `Lawn.css`. Save Lawn.css in a new folder named `CSS`.

7. Refer to Table 2–6 for the container CSS rule definition.

8. Insert a blank line after the placeholder text in the container div tag.

9. Insert a div tag within the container. Name the class `header`.

10. Create a new CSS rule. Refer to Table 2–6 for the header CSS rule definition.

11. Replace the text within the header div tag with `Justin's Lawn Care Service`.

12. Insert a div tag to the right of the header div tag but within the container div tag. Name the class `navigation`.

13. Create a new CSS rule. Refer to Table 2–6 for the navigation CSS rule definition.

14. Replace the text within the navigation div tag with `Home Services Landscape Prices Quote Contact`.

15. Insert a div tag to the right of the navigation div tag but within the container div tag. Name the class `content`.

16. Create a new CSS rule. Refer to Table 2–6 for the content CSS rule definition.

17. Delete the text within the content div tag and insert an editable region. Name the new editable region `Insert content here`.

18. Insert a div tag to the right of the content div tag but within the container div tag. Name the class `sidebar`.

19. Create a new CSS rule. Refer to Table 2–6 for the sidebar CSS rule definition.

20. Replace the text within the sidebar div tag with `100% Satisfaction Guaranteed or Your Money Back! That's Our Promise to You!`.

21. Insert a div tag to the right of the sidebar div tag but within the container div tag. Name the class `footer`.

22. Create a new CSS rule. Refer to Table 2–6 for the footer CSS rule definition.

23. Replace the text within the footer div tag with `Web Site Design by:` and then type your first and last names.

24. Delete the placeholder text for the container region, and then press the BACKSPACE key to move the header to the top of the container.

25. Save your changes and then view the template using the Live view. Compare your template to Figure 2–75. Make and save any necessary changes, and then close the template.

26. Create a new Web page named `index` using the Lawn Template.

27. Replace the text, Insert content here, with text from the Lab3_content.txt data file.

28. Save your changes and then view the Web page in your browser. Compare your page to Figure 2–76. Make any necessary changes and then save your changes.

29. Submit the documents in the format specified by your instructor.

Table 2–6 CSS Rule Definitions for Justin's Lawn Care Service

CSS Rule Definition for .container in Lawn.css

Category	Property	Value
Box	Width	800px
	Right Margin	Auto
	Left Margin	Auto

CSS Rule Definition for .header in Lawn.css

Category	Property	Value
Type	Font-family	Tahoma, Geneva, sans-serif
	Font-size	18pt
	Font-weight	bold
	Font-style	italic
	Color	#FFF
Background	Background-color	#060
Block	Text-align	center
Box	Width	200px
	Float	left
	Height	70px
	Top Padding	5px
Border	Style	solid, same for all
	Width	thin, same for all
	Color	#960, same for all

CSS Rule Definition for .navigation in Lawn.css

Category	Property	Value
Type	Font-family	Verdana, Geneva, sans-serif
	Font-size	12pt
	Color	#030
Background	Background-color	#CFC
Block	Word-spacing	15pt
	Text-align	center
Box	Width	590px
	Float	left
	Height	50px
	Top Padding	25px
Border	Style	solid, same for all
	Width	thin, same for all
	Color	#960, same for all

CSS Rule Definition for .content in Lawn.css

Category	Property	Value
Type	Font-family	Georgia, Times New Roman, Times, serif
	Font-size	12pt
	Color	#360

Continued >

In the Lab *continued*

Table 2–6 CSS Rule Definitions for Justin's Lawn Care Service *(continued)*		
CSS Rule Definition for .content in Lawn.css *(continued)*		
Background	Background-color	#FFC
Box	Width	600px
	Float	left
	Right Padding	5px
	Left Padding	5px
	Top Margin	10px
	Right Margin	10px
	Bottom Margin	10px
CSS Rule Definition for .sidebar in Lawn.css		
Type	Font-family	Arial Black, Gadget, sans-serif
	Font-size	16pt
	Font-style	italic
	Color	#FFF
Box	Width	175px
	Float	right
	Top Margin	10px
	Bottom Margin	10px
CSS Rule Definition for .footer in Lawn.css		
Type	Font-family	Times New Roman, Times, serif
	Font-size	10pt
	Color	#FFF
Background	Background-color	#060
Box	Width	795px
	Float	left
	Top Padding	5px
	Bottom Padding	5px
	Left Padding	5px

Cases and Places

Apply your creative thinking and problem solving skills to design and implement a solution.

1: Creating a Web Site Template for Moving Tips

Personal

You recently moved out of your parents' home and, after realizing how much preparation is involved, you have decided to create a Web site with helpful tips and information about the moving process. Define a new local site in the *your last name and first initial* folder and name it

Moving Venture. Name the new subfolder Move. Create and save a new blank HTML template, layout none, and DocType HTML5. Name the file Move Template. Use a div tag to create a class container, and then insert the following class div tags within the container: header, navigation, content, and footer. Create a new CSS rule for each div tag and use a new style sheet file as the rule definition. Name the style sheet file move.css and save it to Removable Disk (F:)*your last name and first initial*\Move\CSS. The container box width should be between 800px and 1000px. Your CSS rule definitions for the other div tags should include a variety of category properties, such as font-family, font-weight, font-size, color, text-align, background, box width and height, and border style. Include a title in the header div tag. Make the navigation a left, vertical sidebar and include Home, Budget, Rentals, Tips, and Contact within the navigation bar. Include an editable region within the content div tag. Include your name in the footer. Title your document Moving Venture. Save the template. Create a new home page for the Web site using the template. Name the home page index. html. In the editable region, include a welcome paragraph that provides a mission statement and summary regarding the Web site's purpose. Submit the document in the format specified by your instructor.

2: Creating a Web Site Template for Student Campus Resources

Academic

You are a volunteer at your college campus library. The library provides print materials regarding various student activities, committees, and campus events. In an effort to reduce printing costs, the library has decided to develop a Web site with this information rather than printing numerous paper copies. You have been asked to design the Web site. Define a new local site in the *your last name and first initial* folder and name it Student Campus Resources. Name the new subfolder Campus. Create and save a new blank HTML template, layout none, and DocType HTML5. Name the file Campus Template. Use a div tag to create a class container, and then insert the following class div tags within the container: header, navigation, content, and footer. Create a new CSS rule for each div tag and use a new style sheet file as the rule definition. Name the style sheet file campus.css and save it to Removable Disk (F:)*your last name and first initial*\Campus\CSS. The container box width should be between 800px and 1000px. Your CSS rule definitions for the other div tags should include a variety of category properties, such as font-family, font-weight, font-size, color, text-align, background, box width and height, and border style. Include the text Student Campus Resources in the header div tag. Make the navigation horizontal, placed below the header, and include Home, Activities, Committees, Events, and Contact within the navigation bar. Include an editable region within the content div tag. Include your name in the footer. Title your document Student Campus Resources. Save the template. Create a new home page for the Web site using the template. Name the home page index.html. In the editable region, include a welcome paragraph that provides a mission statement and summary regarding the Web site purpose. Submit the document in the format specified by your instructor.

3: Creating a Web Site Template for French Villa Roast Café

Professional

You have been hired to design and develop a Web site for a local coffee shop, French Villa Roast Café. Define a new local site in the *your last name and first initial* folder and name it French Villa Roast Cafe. Name the new subfolder Cafe. Create and save a new blank HTML template, layout none, and DocType HTML5. Name the file Cafe Template. Use a div tag to create a class container, and then insert the following class div tags within the container: header, navigation, content, and footer. Create a new CSS rule for each div tag and use a new style sheet file as the rule definition. Name the style sheet file cafe.css and save it to Removable Disk (F:)*your last name and first initial*\Cafe\CSS. The container box width should be between 800px and 1000px. Your CSS

Continued >

STUDENT ASSIGNMENTS

Cases and Places *continued*

rule definitions for the other div tags should include a variety of category properties, such as font-family, font-weight, font-size, color, text-align, background, box width and height, and border style. Include the text, French Villa Roast Cafe, in the header div tag. Make the navigation horizontal, placed to the right of the header, and include Home, About, Menu, Rewards, and Contact within the navigation bar. Include an editable region within the content div tag. Include your name in the footer. Title your document French Villa Roast Cafe. Save the template. Create a new home page for the Web site using the template. Name the home page index.html. In the editable region, include a welcome paragraph that provides a mission statement and summary regarding the Web site purpose. Submit the document in the format specified by your instructor.

3 Adding Graphics and Links

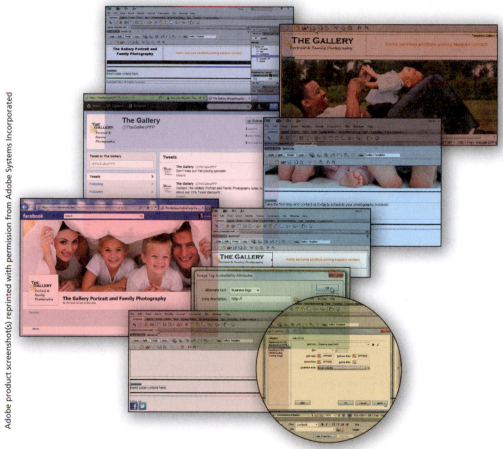

Objectives

You will have mastered the material in this chapter when you can:

- Modify a Dreamweaver template
- Edit a CSS rule
- Add graphics to a template
- Describe image file formats
- Insert images on a Web page
- Describe Dreamweaver's image accessibility features
- Create a Facebook and Twitter presence on the site
- Add images to an HTML page

- Describe the different types of links
- Add a relative link to a template
- Add an absolute link to a template
- Create an e-mail link
- Format a rollover link
- Add a CSS rule to an existing style sheet
- Add an image placeholder and replace it with an image

3 | Adding Graphics and Links

Introduction

A Web page that captures the attention of visitors includes appealing images and easy-to-follow navigation links to other pages within the site. After establishing the initial layout of a site with style sheets, you can add content, including images and links to other pages. The content is the information provided in the Web site, and it should be engaging, relevant, and appropriate to the audience. Some people in the audience may need assistance viewing the site if they have limited vision or other visual impairments, so accessibility issues also should be addressed when developing the site.

By captivating your audience with graphics, you motivate each user to follow the navigation links and investigate the message of your business or topic on your Web pages. A well-designed site includes images that convey the professionalism and focus of the site. As you select each image for a site, remember that a picture truly is worth a thousand words.

Project — Promotional Images

The images displayed on the site for The Gallery Portrait and Family Photography and shown in Figure 3–1 not only are crucial to the design of the site, but also convey the studio's artistic style of photography. Besides increasing the appeal of the Web pages, the images market the Gallery as a business, so they serve as promotion images. Chapter 3 uses Dreamweaver to add pages to the Gallery site and then enhance those pages by including promotion images. The Gallery owners already market the Gallery online through their pages on the Facebook and Twitter social networking sites. Adding Facebook and Twitter image links on the Gallery's Web pages increases customer awareness and brand loyalty.

Edit View Insert Modify Format Commands Site Window

(a) Home Page

© Wavebreak Media Ltd / Shutterstock

(b) Services Page

© .shock / Shutterstock

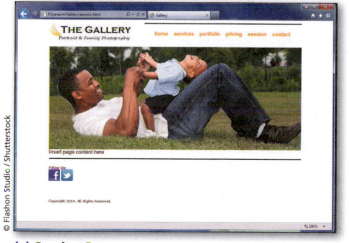

(c) Portfolio Page

© Phase4 Photography / Shutterstock

(d) Pricing Page

© Monika Gniot / Shutterstock

(e) Session Page

© Flashon Studio / Shutterstock

(f) Contact Page

© Serg Ivanov / Shutterstock

Figure 3–1

Overview

As you read this chapter, you will learn how to create the Web page project shown in Figure 3–1 on the previous page by performing these general tasks:

- Modify a template.
- Add images to the site.
- Add pages to the site.
- Connect to social networks.
- Add relative, absolute, and e-mail links.
- Format links.
- Add a new CSS rule to an existing style sheet.
- Add an image placeholder.
- Replace an image placeholder.

Plan Ahead

General Project Guidelines

As you design any Web site, it is vital to consider several factors including the aesthetics of the graphics, the quality of the content, and the ease of the site's navigation. Web sites typically have a home page or an index page, but that does not necessarily mean that all visitors use it to enter the Web site. Generally, with most Web sites, the visitor can enter the site at any point that has a Web page address. This means each page requires links visitors can use to navigate to the other pages. As you modify the home page and add the pages shown in Figure 3–1 on the previous page, you should follow these general guidelines:

1. **Prepare images.** Select your images carefully to make sure they convey the look and feel of your site adequately. Each image placed on the Web must comply with copyright rules. Acquire and then organize your images within the Assets panel. Determine which image goes with which Web page.

2. **Consider accessibility.** Consider how people with accessibility concerns such as visual impairments can use the site and how the site can address these accessibility issues.

3. **Understand the use of social networking sites.** Recognize the value of marketing your site by linking to social networking sites such as Facebook and Twitter.

4. **Identify the navigation of the site.** Consider how each page is linked to other pages within the site. Links also can connect to outside sites and e-mail.

More specific details about these guidelines are presented at appropriate points throughout the chapter. The chapter also identifies the actions performed and decisions made regarding these guidelines during the development of the pages within the site shown in Figure 3–1.

To Start Dreamweaver and Open the Gallery Site

Each time you start Dreamweaver, it opens to the last site displayed when you closed the program. The following steps start Dreamweaver and open the Gallery Web site.

1 Click the Start button on the Windows 7 taskbar to display the Start menu, and then type `Dreamweaver CS6` in the 'Search programs and files' box.

2 Click Adobe Dreamweaver CS6 in the list to start Dreamweaver.

3 If the Dreamweaver window is not maximized, click the Maximize button next to the Close button on the Application bar to maximize the window.

4 If the Gallery site is not displayed in the Files panel, click the Sites button on the Files panel toolbar and then click Gallery to display the files and folders in the Gallery site.

Modifying a Template

The Gallery Dreamweaver Template created in Chapter 1 uses <div> tags to form a number of locked regions and one editable region identified as the content. Recall that Web page designers can edit locked regions only inside the template itself. Editable regions are placeholders for content unique to each page created from the template. The template and other design documents can serve as the Web site **prototype**, a realistic representation of how the new Web site will look and function when it is fully developed. Prototypes can range from a wireframe layout drawing to a working model of the site before it undergoes final development. (A **wireframe** is a sketch that illustrates the arrangement of content on each Web page.) It is best to show a prototype to your customer and ask for his or her approval early in the design process because it is much easier to make changes during the design stages rather than in the final stages of site development.

For the Gallery site, the owners of the studio reviewed the prototype, which you created in Chapter 2. It displays a single photograph with a black background on each page. The Gallery owners want to place unique images on each page of the site to showcase more of the studio's fine photography. They also want to remove the black background and increase the amount of space provided for the images. To meet these objectives, you need to modify the template and insert a second editable region within the image <div> tag. After designing a Dreamweaver template, you can modify any portion of the template to provide more flexibility when updating the site.

BTW

Adobe Tools for Prototypes
You can use Adobe Fireworks or Photoshop to create prototypes and wireframes, especially if you plan to show these mock-ups to clients or others on your Web site development team.

To Open the Gallery Template

Before modifying the Gallery Template file, you must open it in Dreamweaver. The following steps start Dreamweaver and open the Gallery Template.

1 Start Dreamweaver as you usually do, and then click Open on the Dreamweaver Welcome screen to display the Open dialog box. If necessary, navigate to the Gallery site on Removable Disk (F:).

2 Double-click the Templates folder in the Open dialog box to display the contents of the Templates folder (Figure 3–2).

3 Double-click Gallery Template to display the template in the Document window.

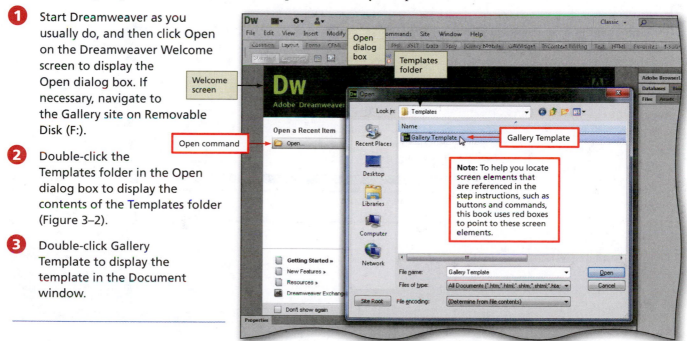

Figure 3–2

To Modify a Dreamweaver Template by Editing a CSS Rule

To edit the CSS rules established in a style sheet or document, you use the CSS Styles panel. You can display the CSS Styles panel in two modes. In **All mode**, the All Rules pane lists the CSS rules defined in the current document and in any style sheets attached to the document. Select a rule to display the CSS properties for that rule in the Properties pane. In **Current mode**, the CSS Styles panel shows style information for the current selection in the document, including CSS properties and rules. In either mode, the bottom of the CSS Styles panel contains buttons that allow you to alter the CSS rules. The button with a pencil icon is called the Edit Rule button, which you use to open a dialog box for editing the styles in the current document or the external style sheet. The layout.css style sheet defines all the styles in the Gallery Template. After opening the Gallery Template and selecting the image CSS rule in layout.css, you can use the CSS Styles panel to edit the background color and box height of the image container to meet the Gallery owner's objectives. The following steps modify the existing template to change CSS rules for the Gallery Web site.

1
- If necessary, click the All button on the CSS Styles panel to display the list of rules defined in layout.css (Figure 3–3).

Q&A

What are the rules listed below layout.css in the CSS Styles panel?

These are the rules you defined in Chapter 2 to design and lay out the template for the Gallery Web site.

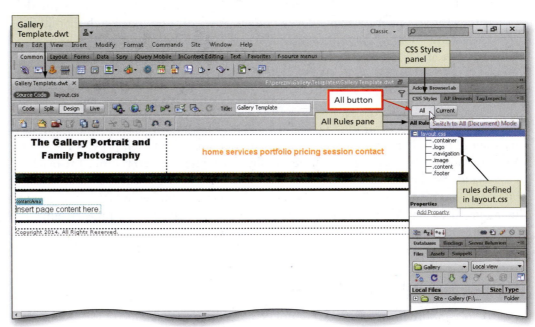

Figure 3–3

2
- Click .image in the All Rules pane to select the .image rule and display its properties in the Properties pane (Figure 3–4).

Q&A

What part of the template does the .image rule format?

The .image rule determines the style of the image region, which is the area with the black background in Figure 3-4.

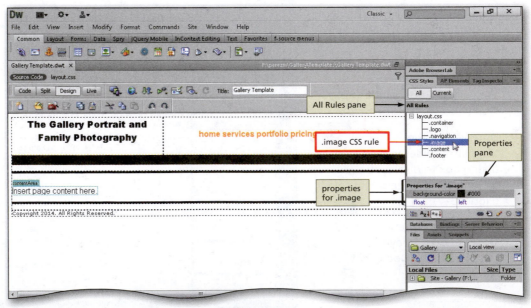

Figure 3–4

- Click the Edit Rule button on the CSS Styles panel to display the 'CSS Rule Definition for .image in layout.css' dialog box (Figure 3–5).

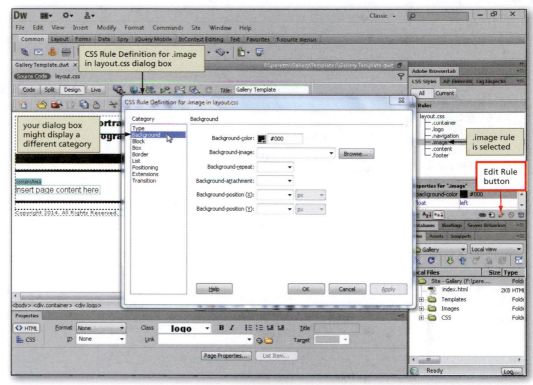

Figure 3–5

- If necessary, click Background in the Category list to display the Background options.

- Double-click the Background-color text box, delete #000, and then press the TAB key to remove the background color of the .image region (Figure 3–6).

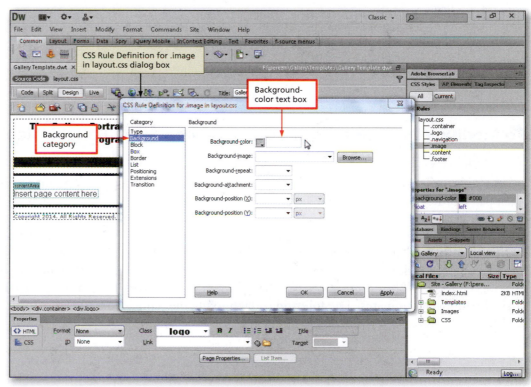

Figure 3–6

5

- Click Box in the Category list to display the Box options.

- Click the Height text box and then type 325 to set the height of the image placeholder to 325 pixels (Figure 3–7).

6

- Click the Apply button in the 'CSS Rule Definition for .image in layout.css' dialog box to apply the CSS rules for .image in the layout.css file.

- Click the OK button in the 'CSS Rule Definition for .image in layout.css' dialog box to modify the CSS rules for .image.

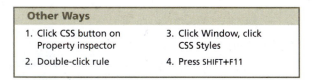

Figure 3–7

Other Ways	
1. Click CSS button on Property inspector	3. Click Window, click CSS Styles
2. Double-click rule	4. Press SHIFT+F11

To Modify a Dreamweaver Template by Adding an Editable Region

When you defined the regions of the Gallery Template in Chapter 2, Dreamweaver inserted them as noneditable, or locked, regions by default. You changed the content <div> container to an editable region so that each page in the Gallery site could include different text. Now that the Gallery owners want to display different images on each page as well, you need to define the image <div> container in the template as an editable region. In a document, Dreamweaver outlines each editable region in blue and displays a small blue tab identifying the region's name. You can determine which regions are not editable in a document by moving the pointer around the Document window. The pointer changes to a "not" symbol (a circle with a line through it) when you point to a locked region. The pointer does not change when you are working in a template because you can modify locked regions in templates. The following steps modify the template to add an editable image region for the Gallery Web site.

1

- Select the text, Content for class "image" Goes Here, in the Gallery Template, and then press the DELETE key to delete the text.

- Click Insert on the Application bar to display the Insert menu, and then point to Template Objects to display the Template Objects submenu (Figure 3–8).

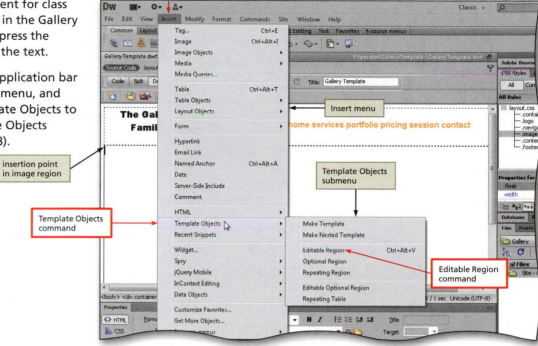

Figure 3–8

2

- Click Editable Region on the Template Objects submenu to display the New Editable Region dialog box.

- If necessary, select the text in the Name text box and then type imageArea to name the new editable region (Figure 3–9).

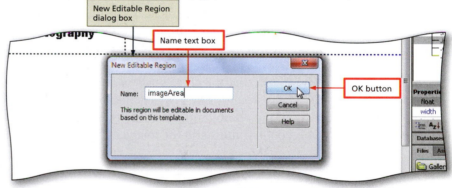

Figure 3–9

3

- Click the OK button in the New Editable Region dialog box to add the imageArea editable region to the template.

- Click the Save All button on the Standard toolbar to save the modified template and display the Update Template Files dialog box (Figure 3–10).

What is the purpose of the Update Template Files dialog box?

When you modify and then save a template, Dreamweaver displays the Update Template Files dialog box so you also can update all of the documents attached to the template. In this case, when you modify the Gallery Template, you can update the index.html document with the same changes.

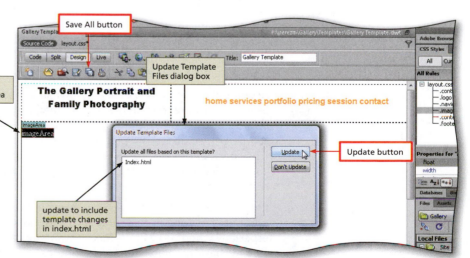

Figure 3–10

4

- Click the Update button to add the imageArea editable region to index.html and display the Update Pages dialog box (Figure 3–11).

5

- Click the Close button in the Update Pages dialog box to update the template and index.html.

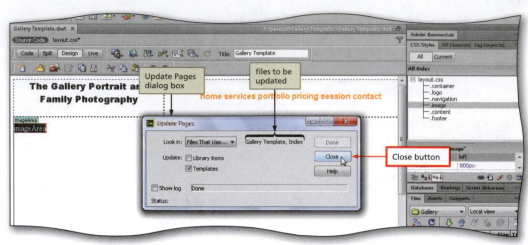

Figure 3–11

BTW

Editing Graphics
After you add a graphic to a Web page, you can use the graphic-editing tools on the Property inspector to fine-tune the image. For example, use the Crop tool to trim the image. Use the Sharpen button to increase the contrast of edges in the image.

Adding Graphics to the Web Site

The graphics that you select for a Web site have the power to create an emotional response in your audience. The best way to create interest in your Web site is to use images that complement the core message of the Web site. Images serve various purposes. For example, you can use photos to illustrate or support content, buttons to provide navigation, logos to identify a company or product, bullets to draw attention to text, mastheads to serve as title graphics, and drawings to add interest to a Web page background. The Gallery site should display photographs that represent the artistic family photography the studio provides. To include these photos in the Gallery site, you first must add the image files to the site's file structure.

Plan Ahead

Prepare images
Before you add images to a Web site, you must determine which images best support the site's mission to attract more traffic to your site. A personal Web site may include images of your friends, family members, or vacation settings taken with a digital camera. Business sites typically feature pictures of the products being sold. Keep the following guidelines in mind as you prepare images for a site:

- **Acquire the images.** To create your own images, you can take photos with a digital camera and store them in the JPEG format, use a scanner to scan your drawings and photos, or use a graphics editor such as Adobe Photoshop to create images. You also can download images from public domain Web sites, use clip art, or purchase images from stock photo collections. Be sure you have permission to reproduce the images you acquire from Web sites unless the images are clearly marked as being in the public domain.

- **Choose the right format.** Use JPEG files for photographic images and complicated graphics that contain color gradients and shadowing. Use GIF files for basic graphics, especially when you want to take advantage of transparency. You also can use PNG files for basic graphics, but not for photos.

(continued)

Prepare images *(continued)*

- **Keep the image file size small.** Use high-resolution images with an appropriate file size for faster loading. Because high-resolution image files are larger, and therefore take longer to download to a browser, use a graphics editor such as Adobe Photoshop to compress image files and reduce their file size without affecting quality. Background images in particular should have a small file size because they often appear on every page.

- **Check the dimensions.** Determine the dimensions of an image file in pixels. You can reduce the dimensions on the Web page by changing the width and height or by cropping the image. Enlarging images generally produces poor results.

As you select images, be aware of copyright laws. **Copyright** is the legal protection extended to the owners of original published and unpublished images and intellectual works. If you have not created the image yourself, you must obtain written authorization to use the image you intend to publish on your Web site unless the image is considered copyright-free. If you purchase images from stock photo collections, which are available at many Web sites, the rights to publish the images are included with your purchase. However, you should read the licensing agreement from each photo collection to determine under what conditions you can publish its images.

Understanding Image File Formats

Graphical images used on the Web fall into one of two broad categories: vector and bitmap. **Vector images** are composed of key points and paths that define shapes and coloring instructions, such as line and fill colors. A vector file contains a mathematical description of the image. The file describes the image to the computer, and the computer draws it. This type of image generally is associated with Adobe Flash, which is an animation program. One benefit of vector images is their small file size, particularly compared to the larger file sizes of bitmap images.

Bitmap images are the more common type of digital image file. A bitmap file maps, or plots, an image pixel by pixel. A **pixel**, or **picture element**, is the smallest point in a graphical image. Computer monitors display images by dividing the display screen into thousands (or millions) of pixels arranged in a **grid** of rows and columns. The pixels appear connected because they are so close together. This grid of pixels is a **bitmap**. The **bit-resolution** of an image is the number of bits used to represent each pixel. There are 8-bit images as well as 24- or 32-bit images, where each bit represents a pixel. An 8-bit image supports up to 256 colors, and a 24- or 32-bit image supports up to 16.7 million colors.

The three most common bitmap image file types that Web browsers support are JPEG, GIF, and PNG.

JPEG (.jpg) is an acronym for **Joint Photographic Experts Group**. JPEG files are the best format for photographic images because they can contain up to 16.7 million colors. **Progressive JPEG** is a new variation of the JPEG image format. This image format supports a gradually built display, which means the browser begins to build a low-resolution version of the full-sized JPEG image on the screen while the file is still downloading so visitors can view the image while the Web page downloads. Older browsers do not support progressive JPEG files.

GIF (.gif) is an acronym for **Graphics Interchange Format**. The GIF format uses 8-bit resolution, supports up to a maximum of 256 colors, and uses combinations of these 256 colors to simulate colors beyond that range. The GIF format is best for displaying images such as logos, icons, buttons, and other images with even colors and tones.

PNG (.png) stands for **Portable Network Graphics**. PNG, which is the native file format of Adobe Fireworks, is a GIF competitor and is used mostly for Web site images. All contemporary browsers support PNG files, though some older browsers do not support this format without a special plug-in.

When developing a Web site containing many pages, you should maintain a consistent, professional layout and design using images throughout all of the pages. The pages in a single site, for example, should use similar background colors or images, margins, and headings.

BTW

Alt Text and Screen Readers
People with visual impairments often use a screen reader to interact with Web pages. The screen reader recites the text provided as alt text to help users interpret the image.

Adding Alt Text to Provide Accessibility

People with visual impairments often use screen readers (speech synthesizers) that can read a text description aloud for each image and let users understand accompanying information about the images. Each image in a Web site should have **alternate text**, also called alt text, that assigns text to the image tag to describe the image. The **alt tag** is an HTML attribute that provides alternate text when nontextual elements, typically images, cannot be displayed. The alt text is considered an accessibility attribute because it provides access to everyone who visits your site. Alternate text always should describe the content of the image. For example, when the screen reader approaches a logo image, the alt tag text may be read as *Company image logo*.

Plan Ahead

> **Consider accessibility**
> After you select images for the site, consider what information the image is conveying as you create each alt tag (alternate text). The text should identify the same information that the image illustrates or communicates.

In addition to assisting people with visual impairments, alt tags can improve navigation when a graphics-intensive site is being viewed over a slow connection. Because the alt text appears before the page begins loading an image, site visitors can make navigation choices before graphics are fully rendered. Alt tags also determine how a search engine locates the content of your site. Search engines can only read text, so images with alt tags allow search engines to match the search description to the site's content, which may aid in search engine rankings. Alt tags are a required element for standards-based HTML coding.

To Copy Files into the Images Folder

Before adding an image to a site, you must add the image file to the file structure of the site. To complete this assignment, you will be required to use the Data Files for Students. Visit www.cengage.com/ct/student-download for detailed instructions or contact your instructor for information about accessing the required files. The following steps copy 12 files from the Data Files for Students to the Gallery site.

- If necessary, insert the drive containing your student data files into an available port. Use Windows Explorer to navigate to the storage location of the Data Files for Students.

- Double-click the Chapter 03 folder, and then double-click the Gallery folder to open the folders.

- Click the contact_image file, or the first file in the list, hold down the SHIFT key, and then click the twitter_image file, or the last file in the list, to select the images needed for the site (Figure 3–12).

Figure 3–12

2

- Right-click the selected files, click Copy on the context menu, and then navigate to the *your last name and first initial* folder on Removable Disk F: to prepare to copy the files.

- Double-click the Gallery folder, and then double-click the Images folder to open the Images folder.

- Right-click anywhere in the open window, and then click Paste on the context menu to copy the files into the Images folder. Verify that the folder now contains 12 images (Figure 3–13).

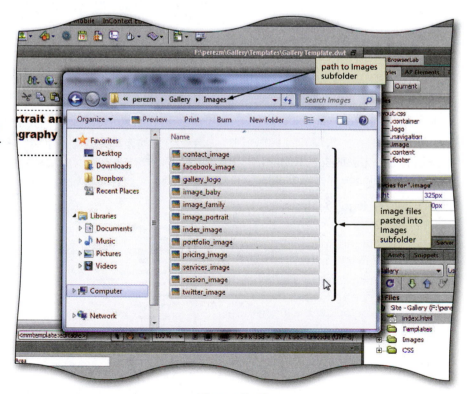

Figure 3–13

To Insert a Logo Image in the Template

Logos increase brand recognition and add visual appeal to any Web page. The Gallery's logo should appear in the upper-left corner of every page within the site to provide consistency to the layout. Instead of using a text logo, an image logo is available for the Gallery site. The following steps insert the Gallery logo into the Gallery Template.

1

- In Gallery Template.dwt, select the text, The Gallery Portrait and Family Photography, in the logo region and then press the DELETE key to delete the text.

- Click Insert on the Application bar to display the Insert menu (Figure 3–14).

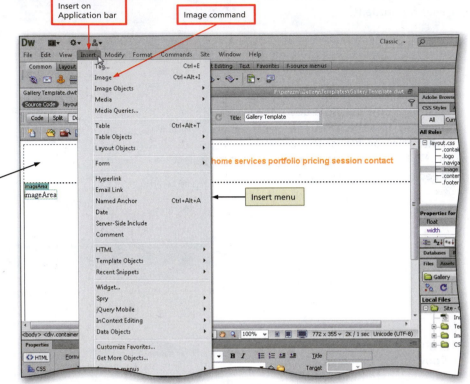

Figure 3–14

2

- Click Image on the Insert menu to display the Select Image Source dialog box.

- Double-click the Images folder to display the image files available.

- Click gallery_logo to select the logo image (Figure 3–15).

Q&A

How long will this image take to load in a browser?

The Select Image Source dialog box lists the file size and approximate download time below the Image preview.

Figure 3–15

3

- Click the OK button in the Select Image Source dialog box to display the Image Tag Accessibility Attributes dialog box.

- In the Alternate text text box, type `Business logo` to add the alt tag necessary for accessibility (Figure 3–16).

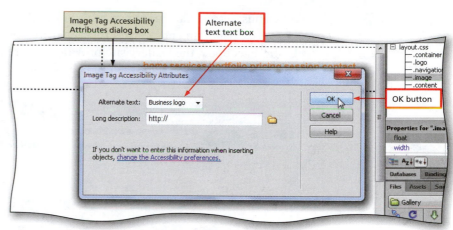

Figure 3–16

4

- Click the OK button to display the Gallery logo image in the logo region (Figure 3–17).

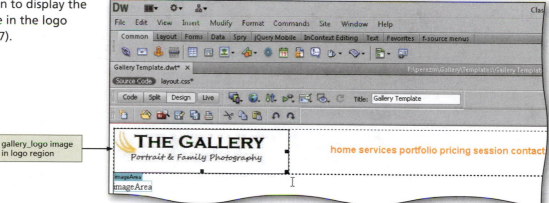

gallery_logo image
in logo region

Figure 3–17

Other Ways	
1. Drag image from Files panel or Assets panel	3. CTRL+ALT+I
2. Right-click image, click Insert	

Marketing a Site with Facebook and Twitter

A **social networking site** is an online community in which members share their interests, ideas, and files such as photos, music, and videos with other registered users. Some social networking sites are purely social, while others have a business focus.

Understand the use of social networking sites
Social networking sites offer a way to promote products and services over the Internet to a larger target audience. Before placing a link to a social networking site on your Web site, a Facebook page and Twitter presence must be established with professional, business-generating content. To establish a presence, join Facebook and Twitter, and then follow the directions on each Web site to post text, images, and links to showcase your organization.

Plan Ahead

Instead of advertising in a newspaper or magazine, many businesses target social networking sites, such as Facebook and Twitter, for their ads. **Facebook** is a social networking site that provides a platform to interact with customers and other businesses that are also members of Facebook. Visitors to a business-oriented Facebook page can engage with their favorite brands and receive product updates. Using Facebook, the Gallery site provides a more personalized, social experience. The Gallery owners have established the Facebook page shown in Figure 3–18.

Figure 3–18

Twitter is a social networking tool for posting very short updates, comments, or thoughts. If you want to receive posts, or tweets, from a Twitter member automatically, you can choose to become a follower of that member. Developing many followers is a goal of most business members. Using the Gallery's Twitter account, shown in Figure 3–19, the studio's owners can post information about special offers and photo packages, and links to the Gallery's Facebook page. Making a positive impression on your Twitter followers is invaluable when growing your business.

Figure 3–19

To Insert Social Networking Icons in the Template

Facebook and Twitter provide specific images for use as icons in other Web sites. Visitors to the Gallery Web site can click the Facebook icon to visit the Gallery's Facebook page, or they can click the Twitter icon to visit the Gallery's Twitter page. The following steps insert Facebook and Twitter icons in the footer of the Gallery Template.

1

- If necessary, scroll down in the Document window, and then click to the left of Copyright 2014 in the footer of the template to place the insertion point directly before the Copyright 2014 text.

- Type Follow Us: and then press the SHIFT+ENTER keys to add text to the footer (Figure 3–20).

Q&A

What is the purpose of pressing the SHIFT+ENTER keys simultaneously?

Pressing the SHIFT+ENTER keys inserts a line break in the Web document. A line break starts a new line without adding blank space between the lines. Pressing the ENTER key creates a new paragraph. Browsers automatically add a blank line before and after a paragraph.

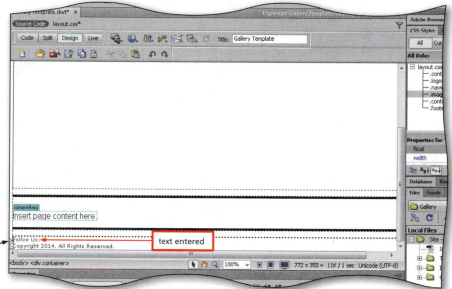

Figure 3–20

2

- Click Insert on the Application bar and then click Image on the Insert menu to display the Select Image Source dialog box.

- Click facebook_image in the Images folder to select the facebook_image file (Figure 3–21).

Q&A

Does the Facebook icon automatically link to Facebook?

No. Later in this chapter, you add a link to the image to connect it to the Gallery's Facebook page.

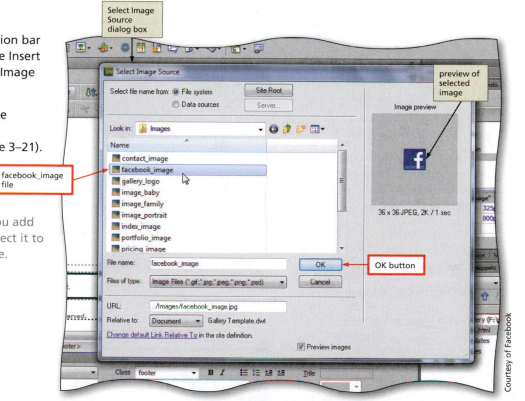

Figure 3–21

3

- Click the OK button in the Select Image Source dialog box to display the Image Tag Accessibility Attributes dialog box.

- In the Alternate text box, type `Facebook icon` to add the alt tag necessary for accessibility (Figure 3–22).

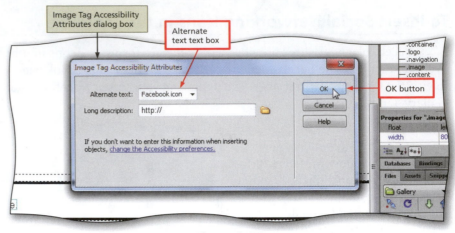

Figure 3–22

4

- Click the OK button to display the Facebook icon image in the footer region.

- Click to the right of the Facebook icon in the footer and then press the SPACEBAR to insert a space.

- Click Insert on the Application bar and then click Image to display the Select Image Source dialog box.

- Click twitter_image to select the Twitter icon in the Images folder (Figure 3–23).

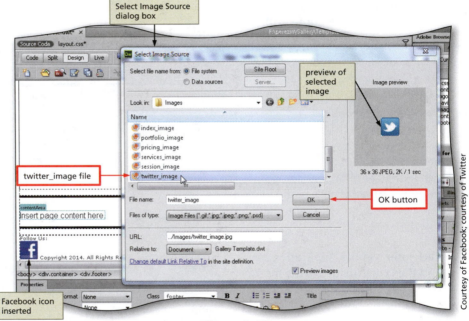

Figure 3–23

5

- Click the OK button in the Select Image Source dialog box to open the Image Tag Accessibility Attributes dialog box.

- In the Alternate text text box, type `Twitter icon` to add the alt tag necessary for accessibility.

- Click the OK button to display the Twitter icon image in the footer region (Figure 3–24).

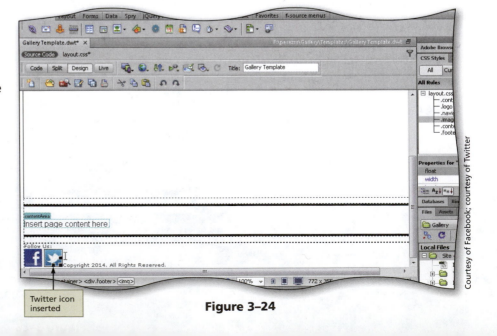

Figure 3–24

- Click to the left of the word, Copyright, in the footer to place the insertion point in front of that text.

- Press the ENTER key two times to create two blank lines between the Facebook and Twitter icons and the Copyright line.

- Click the Save All button on the Standard toolbar to save the template.

- Click Update in the Update Templates dialog box to add the icons to the Gallery Template and display the Update Pages dialog box.

- Click the Close button in the Update Pages dialog box to update the Gallery template and index.html (Figure 3–25).

7

- Click the Close button on the Gallery Template.dwt tab to close the template and display the Welcome screen.

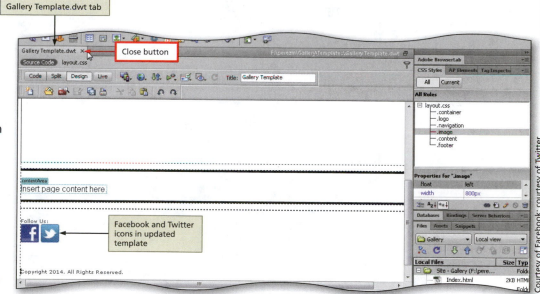

Figure 3–25

To Insert an Image on the Home Page

Because it is the first page most Web site visitors see, the home page must have enough visual interest to catch the attention of visitors and invite them to explore other pages. The following steps insert an image on index.html, the home page.

1

- Double-click index.html in the Files panel to open the index.html page.

- Select the text, imageArea, in the imageArea region and then press the DELETE key to delete the text (Figure 3–26).

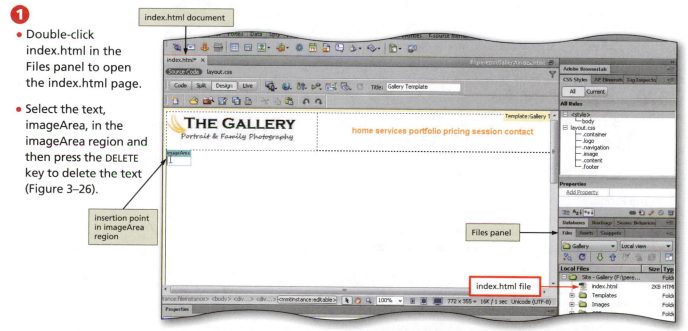

Figure 3–26

• Click Insert on the
Application bar and
then click Image on
the Insert menu to
display the Select
Image Source dialog
box.

• Click index_image
in the Images folder
to select the image
for index.html
(Figure 3–27).

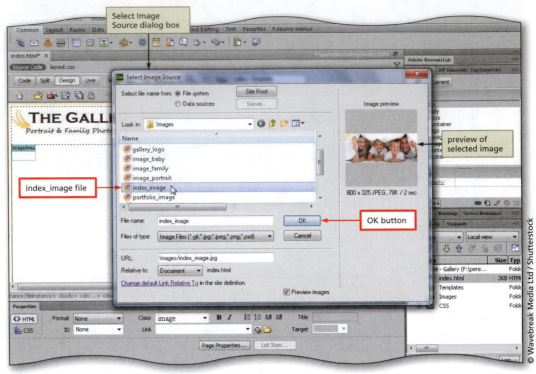

Figure 3–27

• Click the OK button
in the Select Image
Source dialog box
to open the Image
Tag Accessibility
Attributes dialog box.

• In the Alternate
text text box, type
Home family
portrait to add
the alt tag necessary
for accessibility.

• Click the OK button
to display the
index image in the
imageArea region
(Figure 3–28).

Experiment

• Click the Brightness
and Contrast button
in the Property
inspector, and then
click the OK button. Use the slider to change the brightness of the image. When you are
finished, click the Cancel button to return the image to its original state.

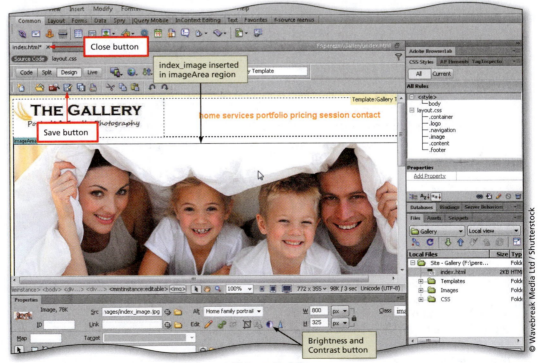

Figure 3–28

• Click the Save button on the Standard toolbar to save your work.

© Wavebreak Media Ltd / Shutterstock

Creating Additional Pages for the Site

After creating the template and home page, the next step is to create the other pages of the Gallery site to which the home page links. The plan for the Gallery site specifies that the site should contain six pages: index.html (the home page), services.html, portfolio.html, pricing.html, session.html, and contract.html. You can design each of these additional pages using the Gallery Template to set the standard structure of the page. If any design change is necessary, you only need to change the template. Dreamweaver then updates all of the pages automatically. The common elements such as the logo, navigation, and footer remain unchangeable, while the editable regions can display different pictures and content on each page.

To Create the Services Web Page

The Gallery specializes in portrait and family photography in a variety of beautiful natural settings throughout the Florida area. These services will be detailed in a page named services.html. The following steps create the services page using the Gallery Template.

1

- Click the Close button on the index.html tab to close the home page and display the Welcome screen.

- Click More in the Create New list to display the New Document dialog box.

- Click Page from Template in the left pane of the New Document dialog box to create a page from the template.

- If necessary, click Gallery in the Site list to create a page for the Gallery site (Figure 3–29).

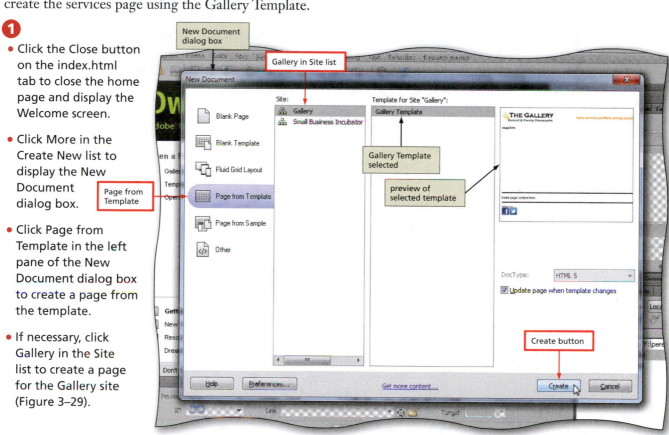

Figure 3–29

2

- Click the Create button in the New Document dialog box to create a new page based on the template for the Gallery site.

- Click File on the Application bar and then click Save As to display the Save As dialog box.

- If necessary, select the text in the File name text box and then type services.html to name the new page (Figure 3–30).

Q&A Which folder should I select when saving the services.html file?

Save the services.html page in the root Gallery folder, which is the folder displayed by default in the Save As dialog box.

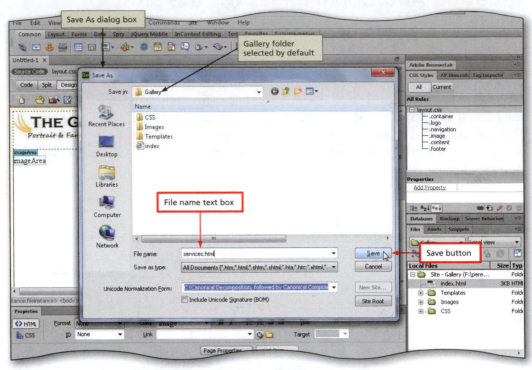

Figure 3–30

3

- Click the Save button in the Save As dialog box to save the document as services.html.

- Select the text, imageArea, in the imageArea region and then press the DELETE key to delete the text.

- Click Insert on the Application bar and then click Image on the Insert menu to display the Select Image Source dialog box.

- If necessary, scroll down and click services_image to select the services image (Figure 3–31).

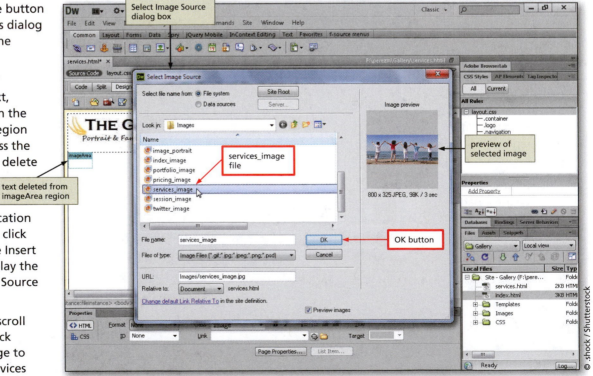

Figure 3–31

© .shock / Shutterstock

- Click the OK button in the Select Image Source dialog box to display the Image Tag Accessibility Attributes dialog box.

- In the Alternate text text box, type Services family portrait to add the alt tag necessary for accessibility (Figure 3–32).

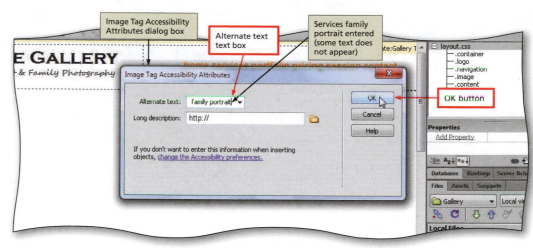

Figure 3–32

- Click the OK button to display the services image in the imageArea region (Figure 3–33).

- Click the Save button on the Standard toolbar to save your work.

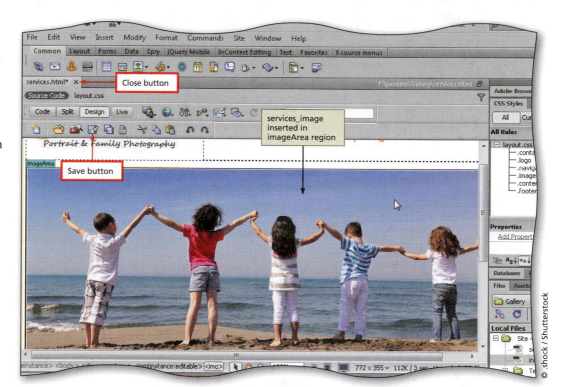

Figure 3–33

To Create the Portfolio Web Page

The portfolio page showcases portraits and family photos in which the personality of the subjects shines through. The following steps create the portfolio page using the Gallery Template.

1

- Click the Close button on the services.html tab to close the services page and display the Welcome screen.

- Click More in the Create New list to display the New Document dialog box.

- Click Page from Template in the left pane of the New Document dialog box to create a page from the template.

- If necessary, click Gallery in the Site list to create a page for the Gallery site (Figure 3–34).

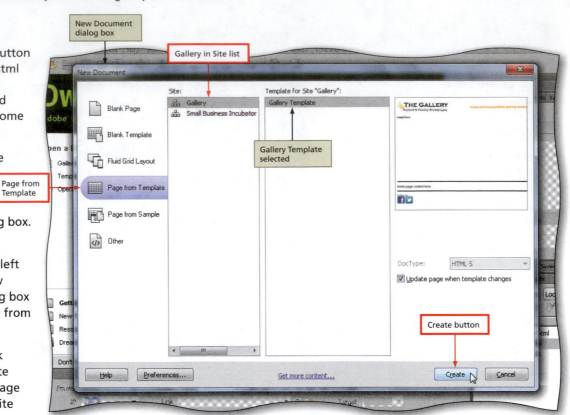

Figure 3–34

2

- Click the Create button in the New Document dialog box to create a new page based on the template for the Gallery site.

- Click File on the Application bar and then click Save As to display the Save As dialog box.

- If necessary, select the text in the File name text box and then type portfolio.html to name the new page (Figure 3–35).

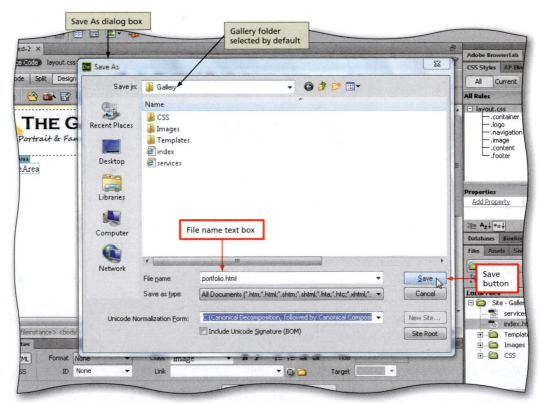

Figure 3–35

- Click the Save button in the Save As dialog box to save the document as portfolio.html.

- Select the text, imageArea, in the imageArea region and then press the DELETE key to delete the text.

- Click Insert on the Application bar and then click Image on the Insert menu to display the Select Image Source dialog box.

- Click portfolio_image to select the portfolio image in the Images folder (Figure 3–36).

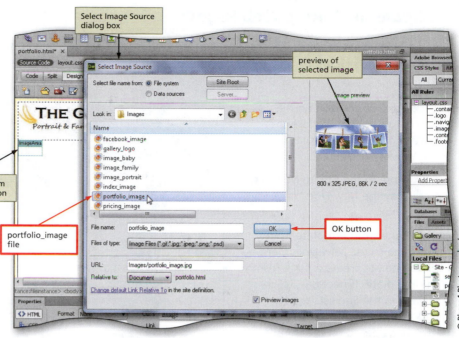

Figure 3–36

- Click the OK button in the Select Image Source dialog box to open the Image Tag Accessibility Attributes dialog box.

- In the Alternate text text box, type `Portfolio family portrait` to add the alt tag necessary for accessibility (Figure 3–37).

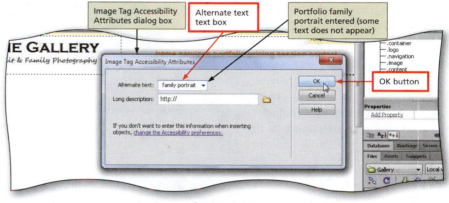

Figure 3–37

- Click the OK button to display the Gallery portfolio image in the imageArea region (Figure 3–38).

- Click the Save button on the Standard toolbar to save your work.

Figure 3–38

© Phase4 Photography / Shutterstock

To Create the Pricing Web Page

The package pricing information for the Gallery will be displayed on the pricing.html page. The following steps create the pricing page using the Gallery Template.

- Click the Close button on the portfolio.html tab to close the portfolio page and display the Welcome screen.

- Click More in the Create New list to display the New Document dialog box.

- Click Page from Template in the left pane of the New Document dialog box to create a page from the template. If necessary, click Gallery in the Site list, and then click the Create button to create a new page based on the template for the Gallery site.

- Click File on the Application bar and then click Save As to display the Save As dialog box.

- If necessary, select the text in the File name text box and then type `pricing.html` to name the new pricing page created from the template (Figure 3–39).

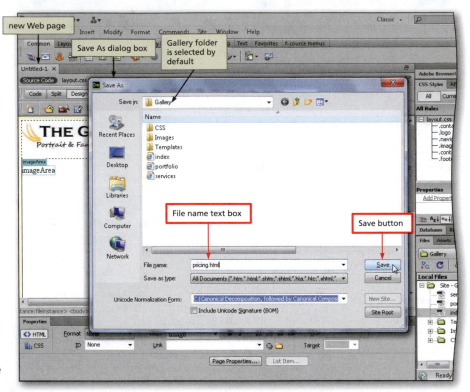

Figure 3–39

- Click the Save button in the Save As dialog box to save the document as pricing.html.

- Select the text, imageArea, and then press the DELETE key to delete the text.

- Click Insert on the Application bar and then click Image on the Insert menu to display the Select Image Source dialog box.

- Click pricing_image to select the pricing image in the Images folder (Figure 3–40).

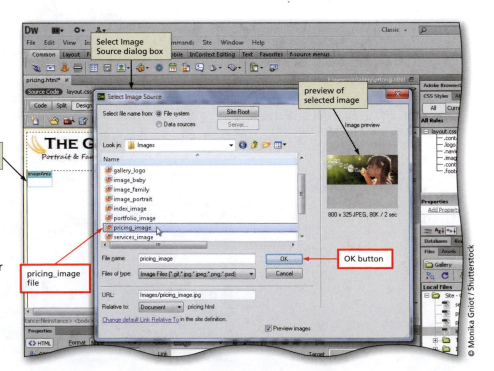

Figure 3–40

- Click the OK button in the Select Image Source dialog box to open the Image Tag Accessibility Attributes dialog box.

- In the Alternate text text box, type `Pricing family portrait` to add the alt tag necessary for accessibility.

- Click the OK button in the Image Tag Accessibility Attributes dialog box to display the pricing image in the imageArea region (Figure 3–41).

- Click the Save button on the Standard toolbar to save your work.

Figure 3–41

© Monika Gniot / Shutterstock

To Create the Session Web Page

Each photo shoot at the Gallery is a memorable experience. To prepare for a one-hour photography session at a selected venue, each client must decide what to wear and what to bring. The session.html page prepares each family for their special photo shoot. The following steps create the session page using the Gallery Template.

- Click the Close button on the pricing.html tab to close the pricing page and display the Welcome screen.

- Click More in the Create New list to display the New Document dialog box.

- Click Page from Template in the left pane of the New Document dialog box to create a page from the template. If necessary, click Gallery in the Site list, and then click the Create button to create a new page based on the template for the Gallery site.

- Click File on the Application bar and then click Save As to display the Save As dialog box. If necessary, select the text in the File name text box and then type `session.html` to name the session page (Figure 3–42).

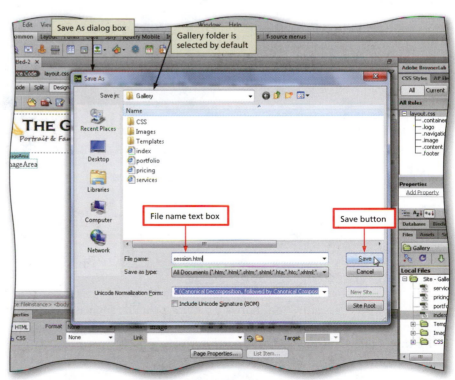

Figure 3–42

- Click the Save button in the Save As dialog box to save the document as session.html.

- Select the text, imageArea, and press the DELETE key to delete the text.

- Click Insert on the Application bar and then click Image on the Insert menu to display the Select Image Source dialog box.

- Click session_image to select the session image in the Images folder (Figure 3–43).

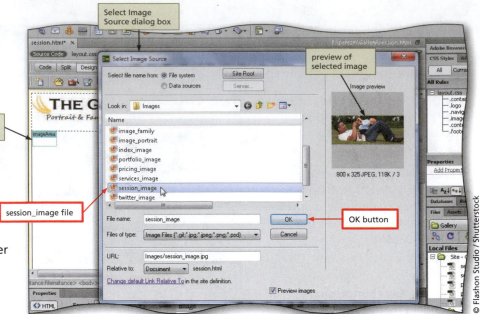

Figure 3–43

- Click the OK button to open the Image Tag Accessibility Attributes dialog box.

- In the Alternate text text box, type `Session family portrait` to add the alt tag necessary for accessibility.

- Click the OK button to display the session image in the imageArea region (Figure 3–44).

- Click the Save button on the Standard toolbar to save your work.

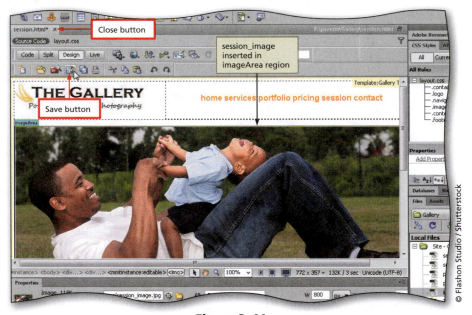

Figure 3–44

To Create the Contact Web Page

Every business site should provide contact details such as location, phone numbers, and hours; and for a photography studio, possible session times also should be included. The following steps create the contact page using the Gallery Template.

© Flashon Studio / Shutterstock

- Click the Close button on the session.html tab to close the session page and display the Welcome screen.

- Click More in the Create New list to display the New Document dialog box.

- Click Page from Template in the left pane of the New Document dialog box to create a page from the template. If necessary, click Gallery in the Site list, and then click the Create button to create a new page based on the template for the Gallery site.

- Click File on the Application bar and then click Save As to display the Save As dialog box. If necessary, select the text in the File name text box and then type `contact.html` to name the contact page (Figure 3–45).

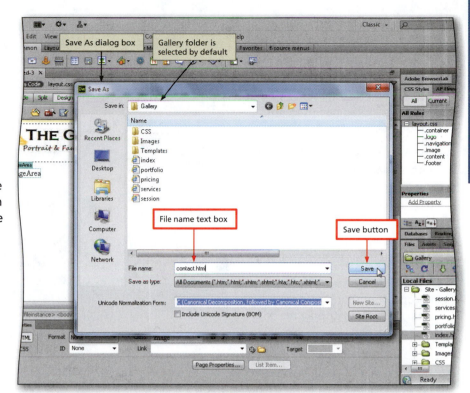

Figure 3–45

2

- Click the Save button in the Save As dialog box to save the document as contact.html.

- Select the text, imageArea, and then press the DELETE key to delete the text.

- Click Insert on the Application bar, click Image on the Insert menu to display the Select Image Source dialog box, and then click contact_image to select the contact image in the Images folder (Figure 3–46).

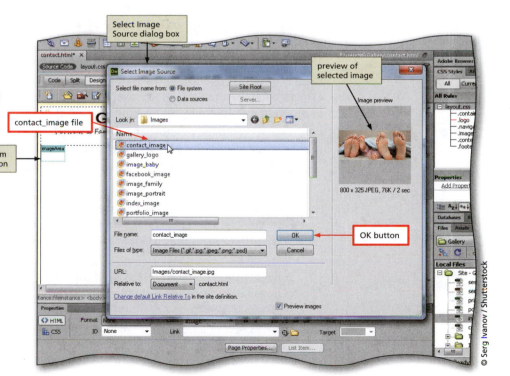

Figure 3–46

© Serg Ivanov / Shutterstock

- Click the OK button to display the Image Tag Accessibility Attributes dialog box.

- In the Alternate text text box, type `Contact family portrait` to add the alt tag necessary for accessibility.

- Click the OK button to display the contact image in the imageArea region (Figure 3–47).

- Click the Save button on the Standard toolbar to save your work.

- Click the Close button on the contact.html tab to close the contact page and display the Welcome screen.

Figure 3–47

© Serg Ivanov / Shutterstock

Break Point: If you wish to take a break, this is a good place to do so. To resume at a later time, start Dreamweaver, and continue following the steps from this location forward.

Adding Links to the Gallery Site

Web site navigation is the pathway people take to visit the pages in a site. Web site navigation must be well constructed, easy to use, and intuitive. Thoughtful and effective navigation tools guide users to other pages on the site and contribute to the accessibility of each page. The fundamental tool for Web navigation is the link, which connects a Web page to another page or file. If you place the mouse pointer over a link in a browser, the Web address of the link appears in the status bar. This location is the Web page or file that opens when you click the link.

Plan Ahead

Identify the navigation of the site
Before you use links to create connections from one document to another on your Web site or within a document, keep the following guidelines in mind:

- **Prepare for links.** Some Web designers create links before creating the associated pages. Others prefer to create all of the files and pages first, and then create links. Choose a method that suits your work style, but be sure to test all of your links before publishing your Web site.

- **Link to text or images.** You can select any text or image on a page to create a link. When you do, visitors to your Web site can click the text or image to open another document or move to another place on the page.

- **Know the path or address.** To create relative links to pages in your site, the text files need to be stored in the same root folder or a subfolder in the root folder. To create absolute links, you need to know the URL of the Web page. To create e-mail links, you need to know the e-mail address.

- **Test the links.** Test all of the links on a Web page when you preview the page in a browser. Fix any broken links before publishing the page.

You can connect to another page using relative links or absolute links. A **relative link** connects Web pages within the site. For example, if a visitor begins on the home page of the Gallery site and clicks the link to the Contact page, the visitor is using a relative link. When you link text or an image to any file listed in the Files panel for the current site, you are creating a relative link. An **absolute link** means that the linked resource resides on another Web site outside of the current one, such as Facebook or Twitter. To create an absolute link, you provide the complete Web site address of the linked resource. For example, to include a link to the home page of the Professional Photographers of America (PPA) Web site, provide *http://www.ppa.com* as the complete Web address.

Another type of link in Dreamweaver is an **e-mail link**, which connects to a particular e-mail address. Clicking an e-mail link starts the user's default e-mail application and then opens a blank e-mail message containing the recipient's e-mail address.

BTW

Creating Links
To create links in Dreamweaver, you can use the Link box, the Browse For File button, or the Point to File button in the Property inspector. You also can use the Hyperlink button on the Insert bar.

To Open the Gallery Template Again

Add links to the Gallery Template so that any documents you create from the template will already contain the links to the other Web pages in the site. When you save the template with the links, Dreamweaver also updates all of the pages based on that template, which is a significant time-saver. The following steps reopen the Gallery Template.

1 On the Welcome screen, click Open to display the Open dialog box with the Gallery folder open.

2 Double-click the Templates folder in the Open dialog box and then click Gallery Template to select the Gallery Template (Figure 3–48).

3 Click the Open button to display the Gallery Template.

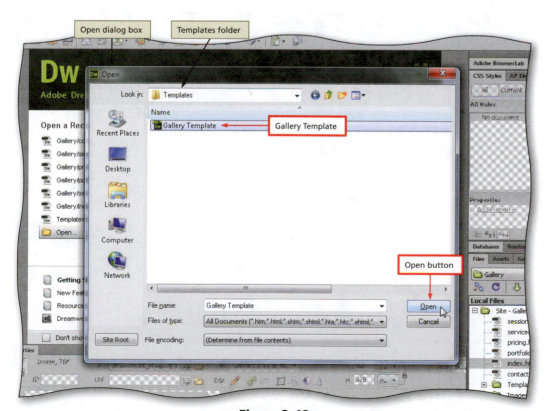

Figure 3–48

To Add Relative Links to the Gallery Template

Visitors can enter the Gallery site through any page within the site, not just the home page. Search engines, links from other Web sites, and bookmarks allow other pages to be used as entry points. Users must find their way around a Web site easily using relative links. You already have used the Point to File button to create links to other pages on the Gallery site. In fact, using the Point to File button is the easiest way to create a relative link. The following steps create relative links to each page within the site.

1
- Select the text, home, in the navigation region of the Gallery Template to select the link text (Figure 3–49).

Q&A Why am I creating a relative link?

You use relative links when the linked documents are in the same site, such as those in your Gallery site.

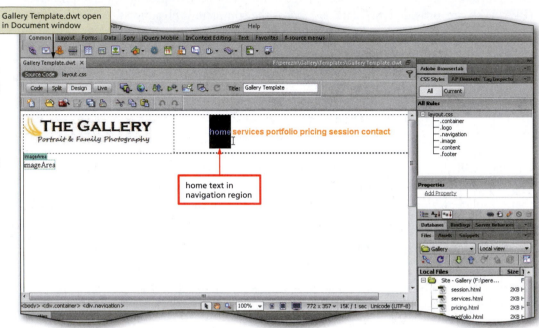

Figure 3–49

2
- Drag the Point to File button in the Property inspector to the index.html file in the Files panel to display a link line (Figure 3–50).

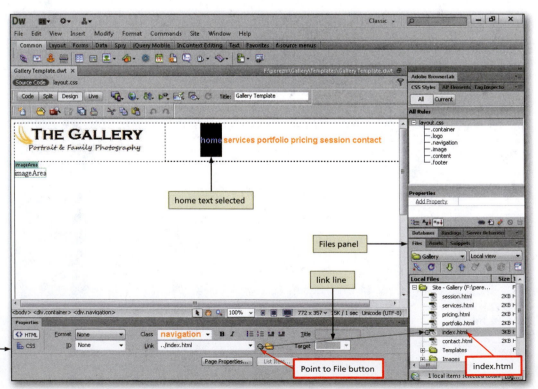

Figure 3–50

3

- Release the mouse button to create the link to index.html.

- Select the text, services, in the navigation region to select the link text.

- Drag the Point to File button in the Property inspector to the services.html file in the Files panel to prepare to create a relative link to services.html (Figure 3–51).

Q&A

Why did the text link for home in the navigation region change to blue underlined text?

Dreamweaver changes all text links to blue and underlines them by default. Later in this chapter, you add a new CSS rule to change the color to yellow and prevent the underlining.

Figure 3–51

4

- Release the mouse button to create the link to services.html.

- Select the text, portfolio, in the navigation region.

- Drag the Point to File button to the portfolio.html file to create a link.

- Select the text, pricing, in the navigation region, and then drag the Point to File button to the pricing.html file to create a link.

- Select the text, session, in the navigation region, and then drag the Point to File button to the session.html file to create a link.

- Select the text, contact, in the navigation region, and then drag the Point to File button to the contact.html file to create a link.

- Click a blank area of the page to deselect the text (Figure 3–52).

Q&A

Why does an icon of a ship's wheel appear from time to time?

That icon is the Code Navigator icon. It often appears when you select text or objects on a page. You can click it to display a list of code sources related to the selection. You don't need to use it in these steps, so you can ignore it for now.

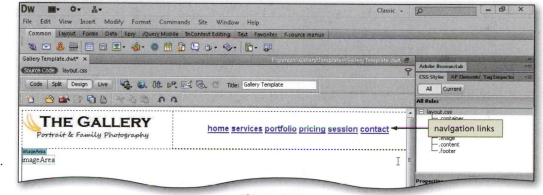

Figure 3–52

Other Ways

1. Type file name in Link box
2. Click Browse For File button in Property inspector
3. On Insert menu, click Hyperlink
4. On Insert bar, click Hyperlink
5. Select text for linking, right-click selected text, click Make Link
6. SHIFT+drag to file

To Add Absolute Links to the Gallery Template

The Gallery site has a presence on Facebook and Twitter, which means the company has set up pages on Facebook and Twitter to promote its photography business. The Facebook and Twitter logos in the footer of the Gallery template each use an absolute link to open the Gallery's pages at Facebook and Twitter. These social networking sites are not part of the Gallery site, so each logo image uses an absolute link to connect to these outside sites. To create an image link, select the image, and then type the Web address in the Link text box. The following steps create absolute links to the Gallery's Facebook and Twitter pages.

1

- If necessary, scroll down in the Document window and then click the Facebook logo in the footer region to select the image (Figure 3–53).

Q&A Can I create links on a new page that doesn't contain any text or images yet?

No. You must select something on a page that becomes the link to another location, so you need to add text or images before creating links. If you want to create links on a new page, it's a good idea to save the page before making the links.

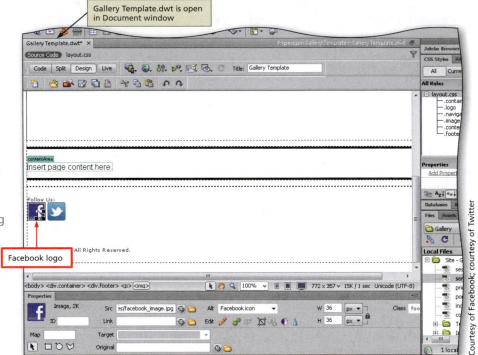

Figure 3–53

2

- Click the Link text box in the Property inspector and then type `https://www.facebook.com/TheGalleryPortraitAndFamilyPhotography` to add an absolute link to the Gallery's Facebook page (Figure 3–54).

Q&A Why does the Facebook address in this step include https:// instead of http://?

A URL that begins with https:// identifies a secure Web site (Hypertext Transfer Protocol Secure). When a user connects to a Web site via HTTPS, the Web site encrypts the session with a digital certificate, which verifies the security of the connection.

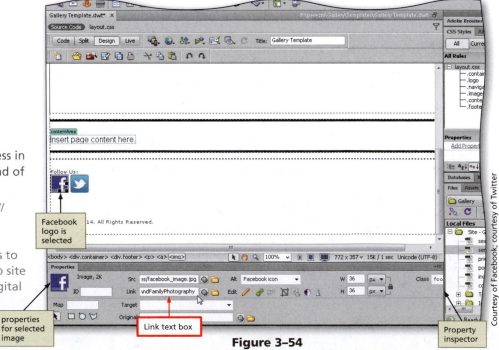

Figure 3–54

3

- Click the Twitter logo in the footer region of the Gallery Template file to select the image.

- Click the Link text box and then type `https://twitter.com/TheGalleryPFP` to add an absolute link to the Gallery's Twitter page (Figure 3–55).

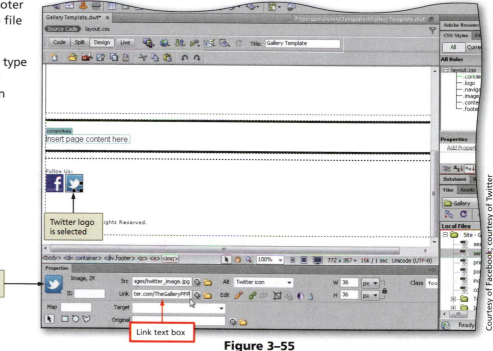

Figure 3–55

4

- Click the Save All button on the Standard toolbar to display the Update Template Files dialog box with six files listed for updating (Figure 3–56).

Q&A Why does the Update Template Files dialog box appear at this point?

After changing the template (in this case, by adding six text links and two image links), Dreamweaver allows you to make the same changes to the documents based on the template.

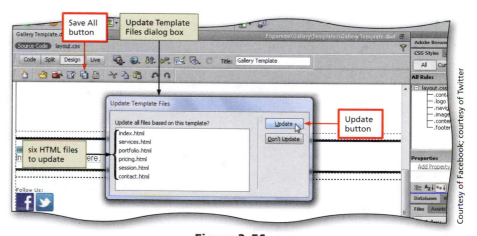

Figure 3–56

5

- Click the Update button to update all of the files based on this template and to open the Update Pages dialog box (Figure 3–57).

Q&A Are all of the links ready to be tested?

The template now includes all of the necessary links to all pages within the Web site and is ready for testing.

6

- Click the Close button to update the HTML pages within the Gallery site.

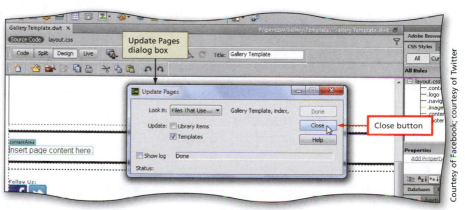

Figure 3–57

To Add an E-mail Link to the Gallery Template

The Contact page of the Gallery site provides a contact phone number and e-mail address. When visitors click an e-mail link, the default e-mail program installed on their computer opens a new e-mail message. The e-mail address you specify is inserted in the To box of the e-mail message header. The following steps show how to use the Insert menu to create an e-mail link on the home page.

1

• Double-click contact.html in the Files panel to open the contact page.

• Select the text, Insert page content here, in the contentArea region, type `Take the` `first step` `and contact` `us today to` `schedule your` `photography` `session!`, and then press the ENTER key to add the contact text.

• Type `(643)` `555-0324` and then press the SHIFT+ENTER keys to add the contact phone number and a line break.

• Type `TheGalleryPFP@` `thegallery.net` to add the e-mail address (Figure 3–58).

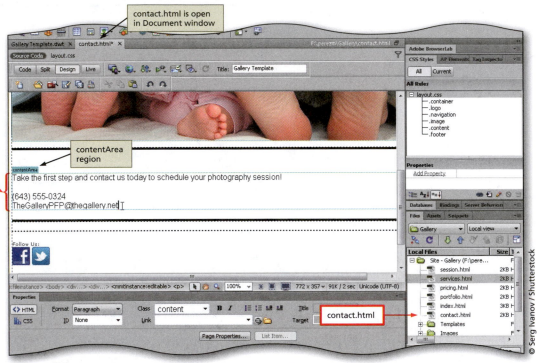

Figure 3–58

2

• Select the text, TheGalleryPFP@ thegallery.net, to select the e-mail address.

• Click Insert on the Application bar to display the Insert menu (Figure 3–59).

 Q&A

Will clicking the e-mail link open my Internet e-mail such as Gmail or Hotmail?

No. You can copy and paste an e-mail address from a Web site into your Internet e-mail. An e-mail link opens automatically only in a local e-mail program such as Outlook.

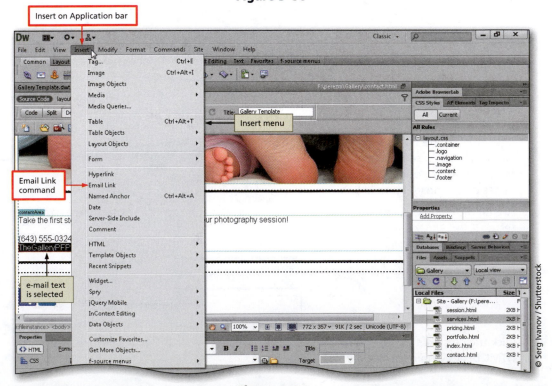

Figure 3–59

• Click Email Link on the Insert menu to display the Email Link dialog box (Figure 3–60).

Q&A

What information does the Email Link dialog box already contain?

The Text and Email text boxes in the Email Link dialog box already contain the display text (the text displayed on the Web page) and the e-mail address (the recipient of the e-mail the user creates).

Figure 3–60

• Click the OK button in the Email Link dialog box to create an e-mail link.

• Click a blank area of the page to deselect the text (Figure 3–61).

Figure 3–61

• Click the Save button on the Standard toolbar to save the contact.html page.

• Click the Close button on the contact.html tab to close the document.

• Click the Close button on the Gallery Template.dwt tab to close the template and display the Welcome screen.

Other Ways	
1. Click Email Link button on Insert bar	2. In Link box, type mailto: followed by e-mail address

Break Point: If you wish to take a break, this is a good place to do so. To resume at a later time, start Dreamweaver, and continue following the steps from this location forward.

Formatting Links

Dreamweaver refers to link text and its colors using the same terms that CSS uses. The color for link text is called the link color. The color of a link after it has been clicked is called the visited color. In the Gallery site, the link color of the text in the navigation region is blue. By default, link text is also underlined in the same color as the text. Adding relative links for the text in the navigation region made the links fully functional. Visitors can click each link to open the corresponding Web page.

To provide more interaction on the site, you can use CSS styles to format the links as rollover text instead of displaying the links in blue with underlining. A **rollover link** changes color when the mouse rolls over it. Rollover links in a Web site design allow you to change or highlight an image or text when the mouse points to it. This change in formatting provides an additional cue indicating that users can interact with the object by clicking it. When a mouse points to the orange links in the navigation area of the Gallery site, the rollover style can change the color to yellow, creating an interesting focal point to draw attention to the navigation links. CSS link styles are classified as page properties, which you can access using the Page Properties button in the Property inspector.

BTW

Rollover Images
Similar to rollover links, you can include rollover images that change when a user points to them on a Web page. To do so, you need two images: the original image, such as a button, and the rollover image, such as the button highlighted. Click Insert on the Application bar, point to Image Objects, and then click Rollover Image.

To Format a Link as Rollover Text

The following steps remove the blue underlining from text in the navigation region and add a rollover style to format the links.

1

- Open the Gallery Template file.

- If necessary, click a blank area of the Gallery Template to deselect any objects.

- Click the Page Properties button in the Property inspector to display the Page Properties dialog box (Figure 3–62).

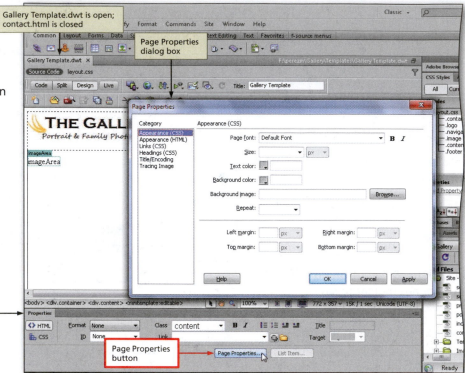

Figure 3–62

2

- Click the Links (CSS) category to display the Links options.

- Click the Link color text box and then type #FF9900 to change the link color to orange.

- Click the Rollover links text box and then type #FFCC00 to change the rollover link text color to yellow.

- Click the Visited links text box and then type #FF9900 to change the visited link text color to orange.

- Click the Underline style button and then click Never underline on the Underline style list to remove the default underline for the link (Figure 3–63).

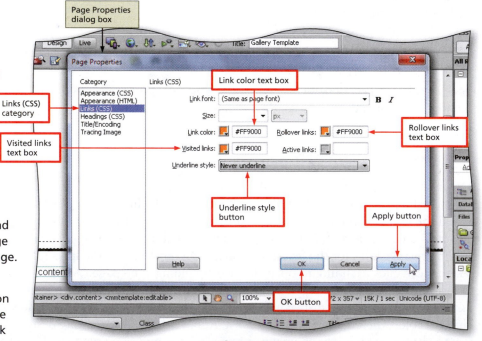

Figure 3–63

 What is a visited link?

Before you visit a page, the link is displayed in a certain color by default. After you visit it, the link changes color. With Dreamweaver, you can set the visited link color to your preference.

3

- Click the Apply button in the Page Properties dialog box to change the link colors of the navigational controls.

- Click the OK button to close the Page Properties dialog box.

- Click the Save All button on the Standard toolbar to display the Update Template Files dialog box.

- Click the Update button to update all six HTML files based on this template and to open the Update Pages dialog box.

Figure 3–64

- Click the Close button in the Update Pages dialog box to close the Update Pages dialog box (Figure 3–64).

To Test the Rollover Links in a Browser

The following steps open and then preview the index.html page in Internet Explorer to test the rollover links.

1 Close the Gallery Template file.

2 Double-click index.html in the Files panel to open the index.html document.

3 Click the 'Preview/Debug in browser' button on the Document toolbar.

4 Click Preview in IExplore in the Preview/Debug in browser list to display the Gallery Web site in Internet Explorer (Figure 3–65).

Figure 3–65

5 Point to each link to view the rollover effect and then click each link to view the pages in the browser.

6 Click the Internet Explorer Close button to exit the browser.

7 Click the Close button on the index.html tab to close the index page and display the Welcome screen.

Other Ways
1. Press F12

Modifying the CSS Style Sheet

When testing the links in the Gallery Web pages, you may have noticed an orange border around the Facebook logo and the Twitter logo. When you changed the link color to orange, the two image links on the Gallery template also were set to include an orange border. As you design a Web site, you may create new CSS rules or change the initial CSS rules in the style sheet for the site. In this case, you can modify a CSS rule to remove the orange border from the image links.

Creating Compound Styles

A compound style applies to two or more tags, classes, or IDs. In Chapter 2, you added a class selector style to the style sheet to identify a region by providing a name that begins with a period such as .logo or .footer. Other selector styles include a tag selector, which redefines an HTML tag such as an h1 heading, and an ID selector, which begins with a # symbol to define a block element such as a paragraph. A **compound selector** is not a different type of selector, but is actually a combination of the different types of selector styles. For example, in the Gallery site, a compound selector style applies to an image element when it is used as a link because you are combining the styles for an image tag selector and for a link.

An **anchor tag** creates a link to another page or document, or to a location within the same page. The anchor tag is <a> and refers to a clickable hyperlink element. The most common use of the anchor tag is to make links to other pages. In the Gallery site, the selector name of the style assigned to the Facebook and Twitter image links includes references to an anchor and an image: a img. The *img* stands for image, and the *a* stands for anchor. The selector *a img* is a compound selector because it combines the anchor tag (a) and the image tag (img) to place (or anchor) an image link at a desired location. To remove the border from the image links, you can use the New CSS Rule button on the CSS Styles panel to add a new CSS rule for the *a img* compound selector.

To Add New CSS Rules with a Compound Selector

To remove the orange border from the Facebook and Twitter image links, you can add a new CSS rule using a compound selector within the layout.css file. The following steps modify the layout.css style sheet to add a new CSS rule for the Gallery Web site.

1
- On the Welcome screen, click Open to display the Open dialog box, double-click the Templates folder, and then double-click Gallery Template.dwt to display the Gallery Template (Figure 3–66).

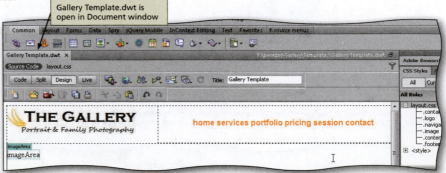

Figure 3–66

2

- Click the New CSS Rule button at the bottom of the CSS Styles panel to display the New CSS Rule dialog box (Figure 3–67).

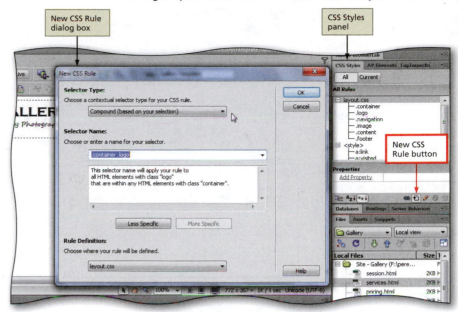

Figure 3–67

3

- If necessary, click the Selector Type button and then click 'Compound (based on your selection)' to create a compound selector type.

- In the Selector Name text box, type a img to create a CSS rule that applies to anchor image elements displayed as links.

- If necessary, click the Rule Definition button and then click layout.css to add the new rule to the layout.css file (Figure 3–68).

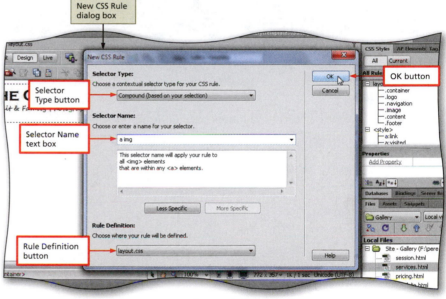

Figure 3–68

4

- Click the OK button in the New CSS Rule dialog box to display the 'CSS Rule Definition for a img in layout.css' dialog box.

- Click Border in the Category list to display the Border options.

- Click the Top box arrow in the Style section, and then click none to remove the default border around the image links (Figure 3–69).

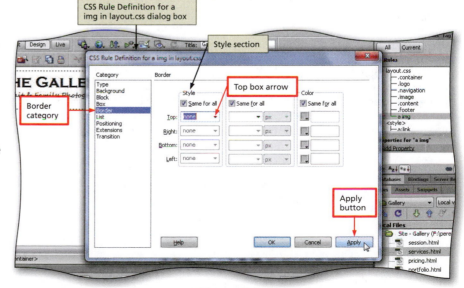

Figure 3–69

5
- Click the Apply button in the 'CSS Rule Definition for a img in layout.css' dialog box to apply the CSS rules for a img within the layout.css style sheet.

- Click the OK button to define the new CSS rule for the image border.

- Click the Save All button on the Standard toolbar to save your work.

- Double-click index.html in the Files panel and then scroll down the page to view the Facebook and Twitter images (Figure 3–70).

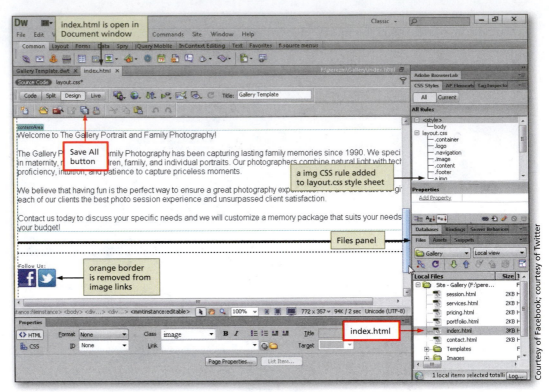

Figure 3–70

Q&A

Why does the orange border no longer appear around the Facebook and Twitter images?

The new CSS rule removed the border from all image links in files attached to the layout.css style sheet.

6
- Close the index page.

Adding an Image Placeholder

After designing an initial Web site for a customer, you may not have access to the final images to complete the pages. For example, the customer might need to take photos of a product still being developed. In this case, you still can complete the design of the Web site. Dreamweaver contains a feature called an **image placeholder**, which reserves space on a Web page for an image during the design process by inserting a temporary photo in its place. A prototype of a Web site may contain image placeholders so the business owner can approve the prototype and the designers can continue working and complete the site. An image placeholder allows you to define the size and location of an image in your design without inserting the actual image. When you replace an image placeholder with the final graphic, the graphic uses the properties of the image placeholder, including the size, which saves you time and preserves the design of the page.

To Define an Image Placeholder

The portfolio page of the Gallery site contains portrait images taken by the photography studio to provide ideas for families to consider when planning their own photo sessions. To provide consistency in the photos, the portrait page can contain three image placeholders, each with a preset size of 150 pixels by 200 pixels. The following steps define an image placeholder on the portfolio page.

1

- In the Files panel, double-click portfolio.html to open the portfolio page.

- Scroll down and select the text, Insert page content here, in the contentArea region, type **Portraits,** and then press the SHIFT+ENTER keys to insert the text and a line break (Figure 3–71).

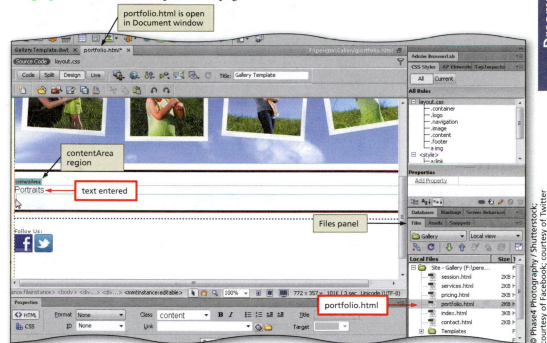

Figure 3–71

2

- Click Insert on the Application bar and then point to Image Objects on the Insert menu to display the Image Objects submenu (Figure 3–72).

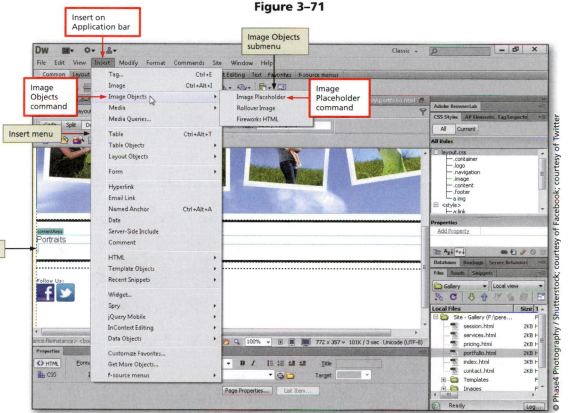

Figure 3–72

3

- Click Image Placeholder on the Image Objects submenu to display the Image Placeholder dialog box.

- In the Name text box, type Portrait to name the image placeholder.

- Select the value in the Width text box and then type 150 to set the width of the image placeholder.

- Select the value in the Height text box and then type 200 to set the height of the image placeholder.

- Click the Alternate text text box and then type Portrait picture to set the alternate text of the image placeholder (Figure 3–73).

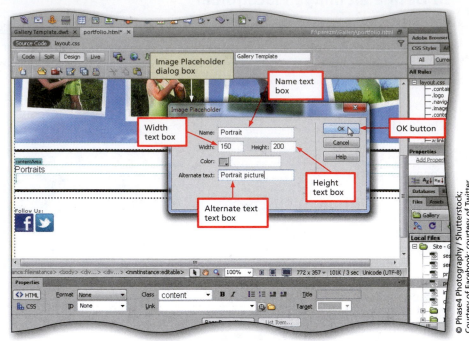

Figure 3–73

4

- Click the OK button in the Image Placeholder dialog box to create an image placeholder named Portrait (Figure 3–74).

Does the image placeholder have to be gray?

No. You can set the color of the image placeholder using the Color button in the Image Placeholder dialog box.

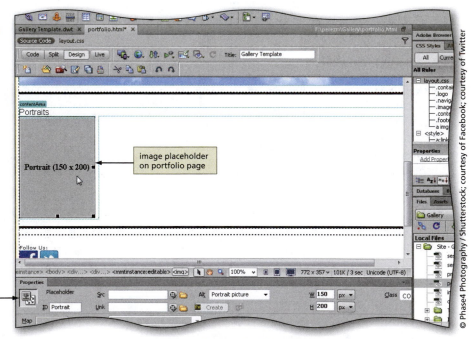

Figure 3–74

© Phase4 Photography / Shutterstock; Courtesy of Facebook; courtesy of Twitter

© Phase4 Photography / Shutterstock; courtesy of Facebook; courtesy of Twitter

Other Ways

1. On Insert bar, click Images button, click Image Placeholder

To Replace an Image Placeholder

The following steps replace the image placeholder with the actual image for the portfolio page.

1

- Double-click the Portrait image placeholder to display the Select Image Source dialog box.

- Click the image_portrait file in the Select Image Source dialog box to select the replacement for the image placeholder (Figure 3–75).

Q&A Why did I insert an image placeholder if I immediately replace it with the actual image?

An image placeholder lets you set properties for an image so you can preserve the page design when you insert a photo or other image. When producing a Web site, you might not have the images as you design the pages. You immediately replace the image placeholder in these steps to practice the technique.

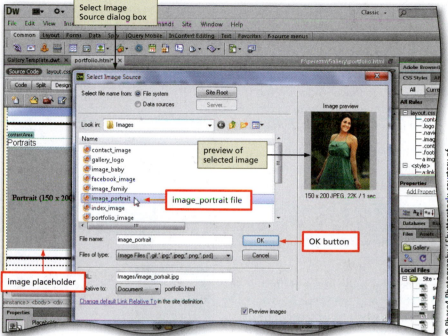

Figure 3–75

© Phase4 Photography / Shutterstock; courtesy of Facebook; courtesy of Twitter; courtesy of Jazmin Diaz

2

- Click the OK button in the Select Image Source dialog box to replace the image placeholder (Figure 3–76).

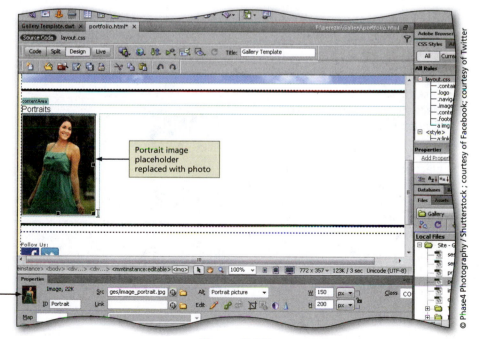

Figure 3–76

© Phase4 Photography / Shutterstock ; courtesy of Facebook; courtesy of Twitter

Other Ways

1. Select image placeholder, click Browse for File button on Property inspector

To Add Image Placeholders

The following steps add two other image placeholders and replacement images.

- Click to the right of the Portrait image to place the insertion point after the image.

- Press the ENTER key, type Family, and then press the SHIFT+ENTER keys to insert the text and a line break.

- Click Insert on the Application bar, point to Image Objects on the Insert menu, and then click Image Placeholder on the Image Objects submenu to display the Image Placeholder dialog box.

- In the Name text box, type Family to name the image placeholder.

- Select the value in the Width text box and then type 150 to set the width of the image placeholder.

- Select the value in the Height text box and then type 200 to set the height of the image placeholder.

- Click the Alternate text text box and then type Family picture to set the alternate text of the image placeholder (Figure 3–77).

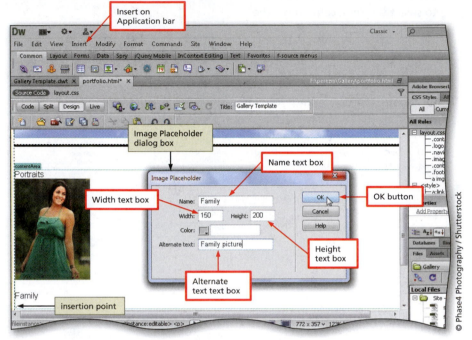

Figure 3–77

- Click the OK button in the Image Placeholder dialog box to create an image placeholder named Family.

- Double-click the Family image placeholder to display the Select Image Source dialog box, and then click the image_family file to select the replacement for the image placeholder.

- Click the OK button in the Select Image Source dialog box to replace the image placeholder (Figure 3–78).

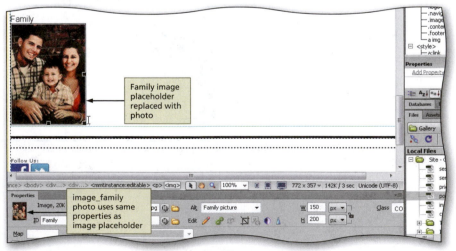

Figure 3–78

- Click to the right of the Family image to place the insertion point after the image.

- Press the ENTER key, type Baby, and then press the SHIFT+ENTER keys to insert the text and a line break.

- Click Insert on the Application bar, point to Image Objects on the Insert menu, and then click Image Placeholder on the Image Objects submenu to display the Image Placeholder dialog box.

- In the Name text box, type `Baby` to name the image placeholder.

- Select the value in the Width text box and then type `150` to set the width of the image placeholder.

- Select the value in the Height text box and then type `200` to set the height of the image placeholder.

- Click the Alternate text text box and then type `Baby picture` to set the alternate text of the image placeholder (Figure 3–79).

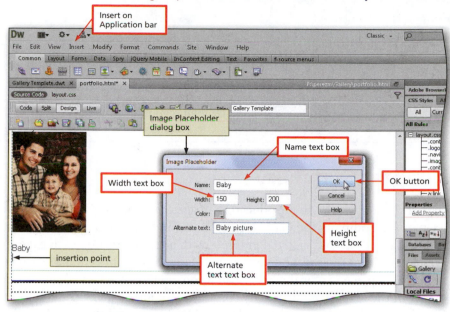

Figure 3–79

- Click the OK button in the Image Placeholder dialog box to create an image placeholder named Baby.

- Double-click the Baby image placeholder to open the Select Image Source dialog box, and then click the image_baby file to select the replacement for the image placeholder.

- Click the OK button to replace the image placeholder (Figure 3–80).

- Click the Save All button on the Standard toolbar to save the Gallery Web site.

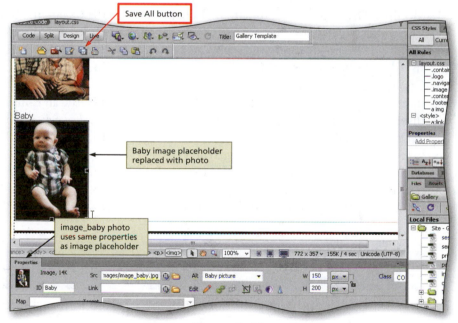

Figure 3–80

To View the Site in the Browser

The following steps preview the home page of the Gallery Web site using Internet Explorer.

1 Click the 'Preview/Debug in browser' button on the Document toolbar to display a list of browsers.

2 Click Preview in IExplore in the browser list to display the Gallery Web site in Internet Explorer.

3 Click each link on the page to test it. Scroll down as necessary to click the Facebook and Twitter image links. Click the Back button in the browser to return to the home page.

4 Click the Internet Explorer Close button to close the browser.

To Quit Dreamweaver

The following steps quit Dreamweaver and return control to the operating system.

1 Click the Close button on the right side of the Application bar to close the window.

2 If Dreamweaver displays a dialog box asking you to save changes, click the No button.

Chapter Summary

In this chapter, you were introduced to images and links and learned how to use placeholders. You began the chapter by modifying the Gallery template to add an editable region for images. Next, you added five new pages to the Gallery site and inserted graphics with alternate text on each page. You also used relative links to link the pages within the site, and you used absolute links connecting to Facebook and Twitter to provide a social networking presence for the site. In addition, you included an e-mail link that visitors can click to contact the owner of the Gallery photography studio. You modified a CSS rule to format all of the links as rollover links. Finally, you added image placeholders to a Web page and then replaced them with photos. The following tasks are all the new Dreamweaver skills you learned in this chapter:

1. Modify a Dreamweaver Template by Editing a CSS Rule (DW 144)
2. Modify a Dreamweaver Template by Adding an Editable Region (DW 146)
3. Copy Files into the Images Folder (DW 150)
4. Insert a Logo Image in the Template (DW 152)
5. Insert Social Networking Icons in the Template (DW 155)
6. Insert an Image on the Home Page (DW 157)
7. Create the Services Web Page (DW 159)
8. Create the Portfolio Web Page (DW 161)
9. Create the Pricing Web Page (DW 164)
10. Create the Session Web Page (DW 165)
11. Create the Contact Web Page (DW 166)
12. Add Relative Links to the Gallery Template (DW 170)
13. Add Absolute Links to the Gallery Template (DW 172)
14. Add an E-mail Link to the Gallery Template (DW 174)
15. Format a Link as Rollover Text (DW 176)
16. Add New CSS Rules with a Compound Selector (DW 178)
17. Define an Image Placeholder (DW 181)
18. Replace an Image Placeholder (DW 183)
19. Add Image Placeholders (DW 184)

Apply Your Knowledge

Reinforce the skills and apply the concepts you learned in this chapter.

Adding Images and a Link to a Web Page

Note: To complete this assignment, you will be required to use the Data Files for Students. Visit www.cengage.com/ct/studentdownload for detailed instructions on downloading the Data Files for Students or contact your instructor for information about accessing the required files.

Instructions: In this activity, you complete a Web page about the Mayan ruins of Tulum located on the Yucatán Peninsula in Mexico. To do so, you add images and a link to an existing Web page. The completed Web page is displayed in Figure 3–81.

Perform the following tasks:

1. Use Windows Explorer to copy the apply3.html file and the Images folder from the Chapter 03\Apply folder into the *your last name and first initial*\Apply folder.

2. Start Dreamweaver. Use the Sites button on the Files panel to display the Web sites created with Dreamweaver and the drives on your computer. Select the Apply site.

3. Open apply3.html. Select the word, Tulum, in the first sentence (not the main heading). Use the Link box on the Property inspector to insert a link to `http://en.wikipedia.org/wiki/Tulum`.

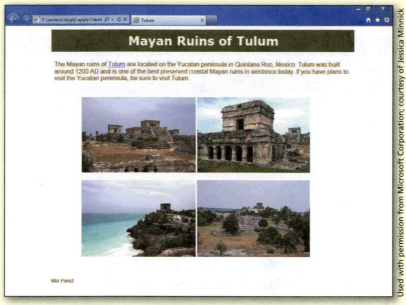

Used with permission from Microsoft Corporation; courtesy of Jessica Minnick

Figure 3–81

4. Double-click the image placeholder Tulum1 to display the Select Image Source dialog box, double-click the Images folder, and then click the tulum_image_1 file to select the replacement for the image placeholder. Click the OK button in the Select Image Source dialog box to replace the image placeholder.

5. Double-click the image placeholder Tulum2 to display the Select Image Source dialog box, and then click the tulum_image_2 file to select the replacement for the image placeholder. Click the OK button in the Select Image Source dialog box to replace the image placeholder.

6. Click to the right of Tulum_image_2, and then press the ENTER key. Use the Image command on the Insert menu to insert a new image, tulum_image_3.jpg. Enter `Tulum Picture 3` as the alternate text.

7. Place the insertion point after tulum_image_3.jpg and press the SPACEBAR. Use the Image command on the Insert menu to insert a new image, tulum_image_4.jpg. Enter `Tulum Picture 4` as the alternate text.

8. Replace the text, Your name here, with your first and last names.

9. Save your changes and then view your document in your browser. Compare your document to Figure 3–81. Make any necessary changes and then save your changes.

10. Submit the document in the format specified by your instructor.

Extend Your Knowledge

Extend the skills you learned in this chapter and experiment with new skills. You may need to use Help to complete the assignment.

Modifying Page Properties

Note: To complete this assignment, you will be required to use the Data Files for Students. Visit www.cengage.com/ct/studentdownload for detailed instructions on downloading the Data Files for Students or contact your instructor for information about accessing the required files.

Instructions: In this activity, you modify a Web page describing sites to visit on Maui. First you modify the page properties by selecting an image to use as a background. Then you establish link colors on the Web page. The page property changes are provided in Table 3–1. The completed Web page is displayed in Figure 3–82.

Continued >

Extend Your Knowledge *continued*

Table 3–1 Page Properties for Extend3.html		
Category	**Property**	**Value**
Appearance (CSS)	Background Image	Use the Browse button to navigate to Images/page_background
Links (CSS)	Link color	#60
	Rollover links	#F60
	Visited links	#009

Perform the following tasks:

1. Use Windows Explorer to copy the extend3.html file and the Images folder from the Chapter 03\ Extend folder into the *your last name and first initial*\Extend folder (the F:\perezm folder, for example).

2. Start Dreamweaver. Use the Sites button on the Files panel to select the Extend site.

3. Open extend3.html. Click the Page Properties button on the Property inspector, and then enter the page properties shown in Table 3–1.

4. Replace the text, Your name here, with your first and last names.

5. Save your changes and then view your document in your browser.

6. Point to the words, Maui and Haleakala National Park, to view the link changes. Click each link and then use your browser's Back button to return to the page to view the link color change.

7. Compare your document to Figure 3–82. Make any necessary changes and then save your changes.

8. Submit the document in the format specified by your instructor.

Figure 3–82

Make It Right

Analyze a Web site and suggest how to improve its design.

Editing CSS Rule Definitions on a Web Page

Note: To complete this assignment, you will be required to use the Data Files for Students. Visit www.cengage.com/ct/studentdownload for detailed instructions on downloading the Data Files for Students or contact your instructor for information about accessing the required files.

Instructions: The Learn HTML Web page provides tips for using HTML5. In this activity, you edit CSS rule definitions for four class selectors in the Learn HTML Web page. The CSS rule definitions for the page are provided in Table 3–2. The completed Web page is shown in Figure 3–83 on the next page.

Table 3–2 CSS Rule Definitions for right3.html

CSS Rule Definition for .container

Category	Property	Value
Box	Width	800px
	Right Margin	auto
	Left Margin	auto

CSS Rule Definition for .header

Category	Property	Value
Type	Font-family	Verdana, Geneva, sans-serif
	Font-size	24pt
	Font-weight	bold
	Color	#C60
Background	Background-color	#FF9
Box	Bottom Margin	5px

CSS Rule Definition for .sidebar

Category	Property	Value
Type	Font-family	Georgia, Times New Roman, Times, serif
	Font-size	14pt
	Font-style	italic
Background	Background-color	#F96
Box	Width	150px
	Height	500px
	Padding	15px, same for all
	Right Margin	10px

CSS Rule Definition for .content

Category	Property	Value
Type	Font-family	Arial, Helvetica, sans-serif
Background	Background-color	#FFF
Box	Width	550px
	Height	500px
	Float	left

Continued >

Make It Right *continued*

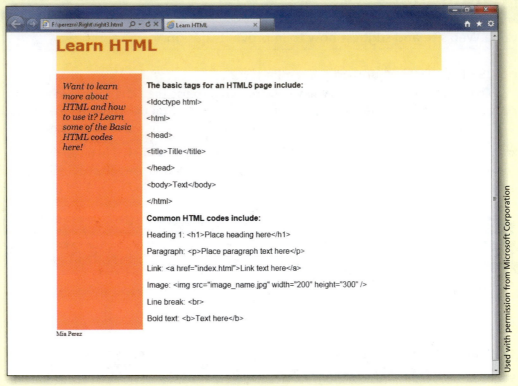

Figure 3–83

Perform the following tasks:

1. Use Windows Explorer to copy the right3.html file from the Chapter 03\Right folder into the *your last name and first initial*\Right folder (the F:\perezm folder, for example).

2. View right3.html in your browser to see its current design, and then close the browser.

3. Start Dreamweaver and open right3.html.

4. Edit the CSS rules for container, header, sidebar, and content. Refer to Table 3–2 to edit the CSS rules for each region. Apply and accept your changes.

5. Replace the text, Your name here, with your first and last names.

6. Save your changes and then view the Web page in your browser. Compare your page to Figure 3–83. Make any necessary changes and then save your changes.

7. Submit the document in the format specified by your instructor.

In the Lab

Design and/or create a document using the guidelines, concepts, and skills presented in this chapter. Labs are listed in order of increasing difficulty.

Lab 1: Adding Images and Links to the Healthy Lifestyle Web Site

Note: To complete this assignment, you will be required to use the Data Files for Students. Visit www.cengage.com/ct/studentdownload for detailed instructions on downloading the Data Files for Students or contact your instructor for information about accessing the required files.

Problem: You are creating an internal Web site for your company that features information about how to live a healthy lifestyle. Employees at your company will use this Web site as a resource for nutrition, exercise, and other health-related tips. In Chapter 2, you developed the template and home page for this Healthy Lifestyle Web site. Now you need to create other Web pages for the site and update the template with links to each page. You also need to modify CSS rules for the template header and navigation, and then adjust link colors and enhance the site with images.

First, use the Lifestyle Template to create Web pages for Nutrition, Exercise, Habits, and Sign Up. Update the Lifestyle Template with links to each page. Next, modify the Lifestyle CSS rule definitions to improve the formatting and design of the pages. Finally, add an image to the Home Web page, and then add images and text to the Nutrition Web page. The revised CSS rule definitions for the header and navigation are provided in Table 3–3. The page property values are provided in Table 3–4. The updated home page is shown in Figure 3–84, and the Nutrition page is shown in Figure 3–85.

Table 3–3 Modified CSS Rule Definitions for Lifestyle.css

CSS Rule Definition Updates for .header in Lifestyle.css

Category	Property	Value
Type	Color	#C30
Background	Background-color	Remove value
Block	Text-align	center
Box	Height	Remove value
	Top Padding	20px
	Bottom Padding	20px

CSS Rule Definition Updates for .navigation in Lifestyle.css

Category	Property	Value
Background	Background-image	Use the Browse button to select navigation_background in the Images folder
	Background color	Remove value
Box	Height	Remove value
Border	Style	Uncheck Same for all
	Top Style	dotted
	Right Style	Remove value
	Bottom Style	dotted
	Left Style	Remove value
	Width	Uncheck Same for all
	Top Width	medium
	Right Width	Remove value
	Bottom Width	medium
	Left Width	Remove value
	Color	Uncheck Same for all
	Top Color	#630
	Right Color	Remove value
	Bottom Color	#630

CSS Rule Definition Updates for .footer in Lifestyle.css

Category	Property	Value
Border	Top Width	thin
	Top Style	solid
	Top Color	#333

Continued >

In the Lab *continued*

Table 3–4 Page Properties for Healthy Lifestyle Pages		
Category	Property	Value
Links (CSS)	Link color	#C30
	Rollover links	#690
	Visited links	#C30
	Underline style	Show underline only on rollover

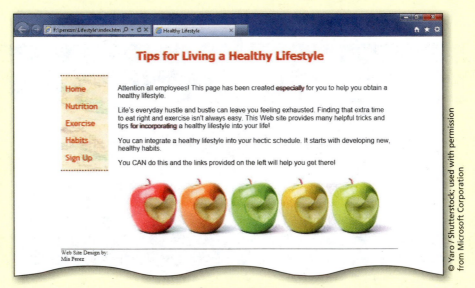

Figure 3–84

© Yaro / Shutterstock; used with permission from Microsoft Corporation

Figure 3–85

© Ronald Sumners / Shutterstock; used with permission from Microsoft Corporation

Perform the following tasks:

1. Use Windows Explorer to copy the Images folder and the nutrition.txt file from the Chapter 03\ Lab1 folder into the *your last name and first initial*\Lifestyle folder (the F:\perezm folder, for example).

2. Start Dreamweaver. Use the Sites button on the Files panel to select the Healthy Lifestyle site.

3. On the Dreamweaver Welcome screen, click More in the Create New list. In the New Document dialog box, select Page from Template, Site: Healthy Lifestyle, and Template for Site "Healthy Lifestyle": Lifestyle Template. Save the new Web page using `nutrition.html` as the file name. Close the file.

4. On the Dreamweaver Welcome screen, click More in the Create New list. In the New Document dialog box, select Page from Template, Site: Healthy Lifestyle, and Template for Site "Healthy Lifestyle": Lifestyle Template. Save the new Web page using `exercise.html` as the file name. Close the file.

5. Use the same method as in Steps 3 and 4 to create two more Web pages, using `habits.html` and `signup.html` as the file names. Close the files.

6. Open the Lifestyle Template.dwt file.

7. Select the word, Home, in the navigation bar. Use the Point to File button on the Property inspector to create a relative link to index.html. (*Hint*: You may need to use the scroll bar on the Files panel to scroll down and view the index.html file.)

8. Select the word, Nutrition, in the navigation bar. Use the Point to File button on the Property inspector to create a relative link to nutrition.html.

9. Select the word, Exercise, in the navigation bar. Use the Point to File button on the Property inspector to create a relative link to exercise.html.

10. Use the same method as in Steps 8 and 9 to create a link from the Habits text in the navigation bar to the habits.html file, and from the Sign Up text in the navigation bar to the signup.html file.

11. Use the Edit Rule button on the CSS Styles panel to edit the CSS rules for the header, navigation, and footer in Lifestyle.css. Refer to Table 3–3 for the updated values. Only update the values listed in the table; keep the other values the same. Apply and accept your changes.

12. Click the Page Properties button on the Property inspector and refer to Table 3–4 to change the page property values. Apply and accept your changes.

13. Click the Save All button on the Standard toolbar to save your changes. Click the Update button in the Update Template Files dialog box. Click the Close button in the Update Pages dialog box. Close the template.

14. Open index.html.

15. Place your insertion point after the last sentence in the content area and press the ENTER key. Use the Image command on the Insert menu to insert home_image. Use `Home image` as the alternate text.

16. Save your changes and view the document in your browser. Compare your document to Figure 3–84. Make any necessary changes, save your changes, and then close index.html.

17. Open nutrition.html.

18. Replace the text, Insert content here, with the text in the nutrition.txt file. Use the Unordered List button on the Property inspector to create an unordered list for the five lines of text below the paragraph, beginning with "Include plenty of…" and ending with "…your portions".

19. Place your insertion point after the last list item and press the ENTER key. Use the Unordered List button to remove the bullet. Use the Insert Image command on the Insert menu to insert the nutrition_image picture. Use `Nutrition image` as the alternate text.

20. Use the Format menu on the Application bar to center-align the picture.

21. Save your changes and view the document in your browser. Compare your document to Figure 3–85. Make any necessary changes and save your changes.

22. Click the links on the navigation bar to view the other pages, and to confirm that each item on the navigation bar is linked to the correct page. Make any necessary changes and then save your changes.

23. Submit the documents in the format specified by your instructor.

In the Lab

Lab 2: Adding Images and Links to the Designs by Dolores Web Site

Note: To complete this assignment, you will be required to use the Data Files for Students. Visit www.cengage.com/ct/studentdownload for detailed instructions on downloading the Data Files for Students or contact your instructor for information about accessing the required files.

Problem: You are creating a Web site for Designs by Dolores, a Web site design company. The site provides information about the company and its services. In Chapter 2, you developed the template and home page for the Designs by Dolores Web site. Now you need to create the Web pages for the site, insert a logo, and update the template with links to each page. You also need to modify the link colors and enhance the site with images.

First, use the Designs Template to create Web pages called About Us, Services, Pricing, Web Hosting, and Contact Us. Update the Design Template with links to each page. Next, modify the Lifestyle CSS rule definitions to improve the formatting and design of the pages. Finally, add text and an image to the About Us Web page. The revised CSS rule definitions for the header, navigation, content, and footer are provided in Table 3–5. The page property values are provided in Table 3–6. The updated home page is shown in Figure 3–86, and the About Us page is shown in Figure 3–87.

Table 3–5 CSS Rule Definition Updates for Designs by Dolores

CSS Rule Definition Updates for .header in Designs.css		
Category	Property	Value
Type	Font-family	Remove value
	Font-size	Remove value
	Color	Remove value
Box	Top Padding	Remove value
	Bottom Padding	Remove value
	Left Padding	Remove value

CSS Rule Definition Updates for .navigation in Designs.css		
Category	Property	Value
Background	Background-color	#036

CSS Rule Definition Updates for .content in Designs.css		
Category	Property	Value
Box	Left Padding	Remove value
Border	Bottom Color	#036

CSS Rule Definition Updates for .footer in Designs.css		
Category	Property	Value
Type	Color	#333
Background	Background-color	#FC0

Table 3–6 Page Properties		
Category	**Property**	**Value**
Links (CSS)	Link color	#FFF
	Rollover links	#FF0
	Visited links	#FFF
	Underline style	Never underline

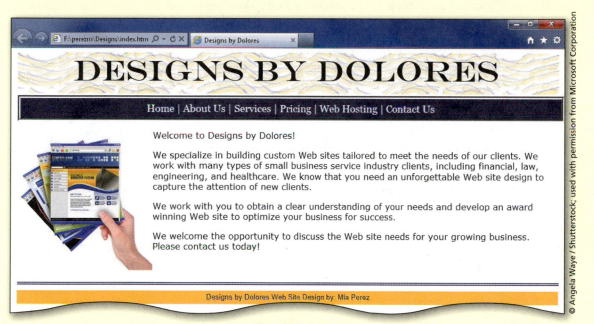

Figure 3–86

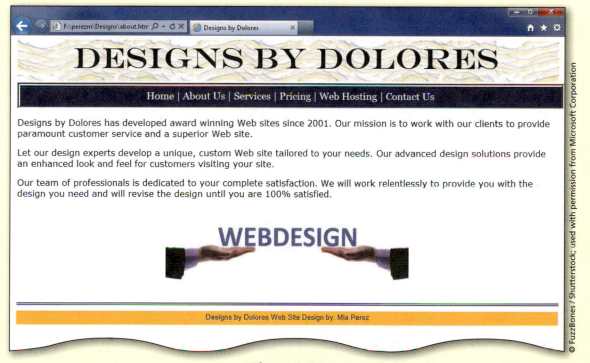

Figure 3–87

Continued >

In the Lab *continued*

Perform the following tasks:

1. Copy the Images folder and the about.txt file from the Chapter 03\Lab2 folder into the *your last name and first initial*\Designs folder (the F:\perezm folder, for example).

2. Start Dreamweaver. Use the Sites button on the Files panel to select the Designs by Dolores site.

3. Create a new Web page using the Designs Template. Save the new page in the root folder for the Designs site using `about.html` as the file name. Close the file.

4. Use the same method as in Step 3 to create four more Web pages and use `services.html`, `pricing.html`, `hosting.html`, and `contact.html` as the file names.

5. Close all open documents, and then open Designs Template.dwt.

6. Select the word, Home, in the navigation bar. Use the Point to File button on the Property inspector to create a relative link to index.html.

7. Select the words, About Us, in the navigation bar. Use the Point to File button to create a relative link to about.html.

8. Use the same method as in Steps 6 and 7 to create links for Services, Pricing, Web Hosting, and Contact Us.

9. Use the Edit Rule button on the CSS Styles panel to edit the CSS rules for the header, navigation, content, and footer in Lifestyle.css. Refer to Table 3–5 for the updated values. Only update the values listed in the table; keep the other values the same. Apply and accept your changes.

10. Delete the text, Designs by Dolores, in the header. Insert the designs_logo image in the header. Use `Business logo` as the alternate text.

11. Click a blank area of the page, and then click the Page Properties button on the Property inspector and refer to Table 3–6 to change the page property values. Apply and accept your changes.

12. Save your changes to the Designs Template and the Designs.css file. Update the files that use the template and then close the template.

13. Open index.html.

14. Place your insertion point to the left of the word, Welcome, in the content area. Insert the home_image image. Use `Home image` as the alternate text.

15. Right-click the image, point to Align on the shortcut menu, and then click Left to left-align the image.

16. Place your insertion point after the last sentence, Please contact us today!, and then press the ENTER key.

17. Save your changes and view the document in your browser. Compare your document to Figure 3–86. Make any necessary changes, save your changes, and then close index.html.

18. Open about.html.

19. Replace the text, Insert content here, with the text in about.txt.

20. Insert the about_image picture after the last paragraph, use `About image` as the alternate text, and then center-align the picture on the page.

21. Save your changes and view the document in your browser. Compare your document to Figure 3–87. Make any necessary changes and then save your changes.

22. Click the links on the navigation bar to view the other pages, and to confirm that each item on the navigation bar is linked to the correct page. Make any necessary changes and then save your changes.

23. Submit the documents in the format specified by your instructor.

In the Lab

Lab 3: Adding Images and Links to the Justin's Lawn Care Service Web Site

Note: To complete this assignment, you will be required to use the Data Files for Students. Visit www.cengage.com/ct/studentdownload for detailed instructions on downloading the Data Files for Students or contact your instructor for information about accessing the required files.

Problem: You are creating a Web site for a new lawn care company, Justin's Lawn Care Service. The Web site will provide information to customers, including descriptions of services and pricing. In Chapter 2, you developed the template and home page for the Justin's Lawn Care Service site. Now you need to create the Web pages for the site, add a logo to the template, update the template with links to each page, modify the link colors, and enhance the site with images. You also will modify the CSS rule definitions.

First, use the Lawn Template to create Web pages for Services, Landscape, Prices, Quote, and Contact. Update the Design Template with links to each page. Next, modify the Lawn CSS rule definitions to improve the format and design of the pages. Add a logo and an image to the template, and then set an image as the page background. Finally, add images to the Landscape Web page. The revised CSS rule definitions for the header, navigation, content, and footer are provided in Table 3–7. The page property values are provided in Table 3–8. The Landscape page is shown in Figure 3–88, and the Contact page is shown in Figure 3–89.

Table 3–7 Updated CSS Rule Definitions for Justin's Lawn Care Service

CSS Rule Definition for .header in Lawn.css

Category	Property	Value
Type	Font-family	Remove value
	Font-size	Remove value
	Font-weight	Remove value
	Font-style	Remove value
	Color	Remove value
Background	Background-color	Remove value
Box	Top Padding	Remove value

CSS Rule Definition for .navigation in Lawn.css

Category	Property	Value
Type	Font-weight	bold
Background	Background-color	Remove value
Border	Style	Remove value (keep Same for all box checked)
	Width	Remove value (keep Same for all box checked)
	Color	Remove value (keep Same for all box checked)

Table 3–8 Page Properties

Category	Property	Value
Appearance (CSS)	Background image	Use the Browse button to select background_image in the Images folder
Links (CSS)	Link color	#030
	Rollover links	#090
	Visited links	#030
	Underline style	Show underline only on rollover

Continued >

In the Lab *continued*

Figure 3–88

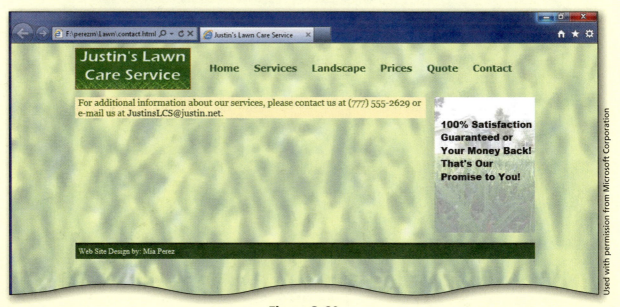

Figure 3–89

Used with permission from Microsoft Corporation

Perform the following tasks:

1. Start Dreamweaver. Use the Sites button on the Files panel to select the Justin's Lawn Care Service site.

2. Use the Lawn_Template to create the following Web pages: `services.html`, `landscape.html`, `prices.html`, `quote.html`, and `contact.html`. Save and close each new Web page.

3. Open Lawn_Template.dwt. Add the appropriate relative links to Home, Services, Landscape, Prices, Quote, and Contact in the navigation bar.

4. Edit the CSS rules for the header and navigation in Lawn.css. Refer to Table 3–7 to modify the values. Apply and accept your changes.

5. Replace the text in the header with the lawn_logo image. Use `Business logo` as the alternate text.

6. Replace the text in the sidebar with the sidebar_image. image. Use `Sidebar image` as the alternate text.

7. Add page properties as specified in Table 3–8. Apply and accept your changes.

8. Save your changes to the Lawn Template and the Lawn.css file. Update files and then close the template file.

9. Open landscape.html.

10. Replace the text, Insert content here, with `Landscaping Ideas`.

11. Press the ENTER key and then insert the landscape1 and landscape2 images. Press the SHIFT+ENTER keys and then insert the landscape3 and landscape4 images. Press the SPACEBAR to separate the images that appear on one line. Use `Landscape image 1`, `Landscape image 2`, `Landscape image 3`, and `Landscape image 4` for the alternate text, respectively.

12. Click to the right of Landscape image 4, press the ENTER key, and then type `Plants and Flowers` below the landscape images.

13. Press the ENTER key and then insert the plant1, plant2, plant3, plant4, and plant5 images. Press the SPACEBAR to separate the images. Use `Plant image 1`, `Plant image 2`, `Plant image 3`, `Plant image 4`, and `Plant image 5` for the alternate text, respectively.

14. Save your changes and view the document in your browser. Compare your document to Figure 3–88. Make any necessary changes and save your changes.

15. Open contact.html.

16. Replace the text, Insert content here, with `For additional information about our services, please contact us at (777) 555-2629 or e-mail us at JustinsLCS@justin.net`.

17. Add an e-mail link, `JustinsLCS@justin.net`, to the e-mail text.

18. Save your changes and view the document in your browser. Compare your document to Figure 3–89. Make any necessary changes and save your changes.

19. Click the links on the navigation bar to view the other pages, and to confirm that each item on the navigation bar is linked to the correct page. Make any necessary changes and save your changes.

20. Submit the documents in the format specified by your instructor.

Cases and Places

Apply your creative thinking and problem solving skills to design and implement a solution.

1: Adding Web Pages and Links for Moving Venture Tips

Personal

You have created the home page for Moving Venture Tips and now need to create the other Web pages for the site. After creating the pages, you will add links to the pages from the navigation bar on the Move Template. You have decided to modify the font color and background color for the

Continued >

header and navigation. You also want to modify the page properties by adding link colors. You also will add an image to the Rentals page. Use the Move Template to create Web pages for Budget, Rentals, Tips, and Contact. After creating these pages, link the text in the navigation bar to each page in the site. Modify the CSS rules for the header by changing the type color and background-color. Modify the CSS rules for the navigation by changing the background-color, border style, and box width. Add page properties for Links (CSS) by defining a color for the link color, rollover links, and visited links. Add text about rental information to the Rentals page. Create an Images folder and save it within the Move root folder. Add an image to the Rentals page. Check the spelling using the Commands menu and correct all misspelled words. Submit the document in the format specified by your instructor.

2: Adding Web Pages, Images, and Links for Student Campus Resources

Academic

You have created the home page for Student Campus Resources and now need to create the other Web pages for the site. After creating the pages, you will add links to the pages from the navigation bar on the Campus Template. You have decided to modify the font color and background color for the navigation. You also want to modify page properties by adding a background color and link colors. You also will add text and an image to the Activities page. Use the Campus Template to create Web pages for Activities, Committees, Events, and Contact. After creating these pages, link the text in the navigation bar to each page in the site. Modify the CSS rules for the navigation by changing the type color, background-color, and border colors (if you have borders). Modify the CSS rules for the content by changing or removing the box height. Modify the CSS rules for the footer by changing the font-family and color (in the Type category). Add page properties for Appearance (CSS) by defining a background color. Add page properties for Links (CSS) by defining a color for the link color, rollover links, and visited links. Add text describing student activities information to the Activities page. Create an Images folder and save it within the Campus root folder. Add an image to the Activities page and center-align the image on the page. Check the spelling using the Commands menu and correct all misspelled words. Submit the document in the format specified by your instructor.

3: Adding Web Pages, Images, and Links for French Villa Roast Café

Professional

You have created the home page for French Villa Roast Café and now need to create the other Web pages for the site. After creating the pages, you will add links to the pages from the navigation on the Cafe Template. You have decided to modify the font color for the navigation, and the background color and padding for the content. You also want to modify the page properties by adding a background image and link colors. You also will add an image to the Home and About pages. Use the Cafe Template to create Web pages for About, Menu, Rewards, and Contact. After creating these pages, link the text in the navigation bar to each page in the site. Modify the CSS rules for the navigation by changing the type color. Modify the CSS rules for the content by changing the background color and adjusting the box padding. Add page properties for Appearance (CSS) by defining a background image. Add page properties for Links (CSS) by defining a color for the link color, rollover links, and visited links. Add text to the About page. Add text to the Contact page and include an e-mail link. Create an Images folder and save it within the Cafe root folder. Add an image to the Home page and right-align the image on the page. Add an image to the About page and center-align the image on the page. Check the spelling using the Commands menu and correct all misspelled words. Submit the document in the format specified by your instructor.

Inserting Flash and Photoshop Files in Dreamweaver

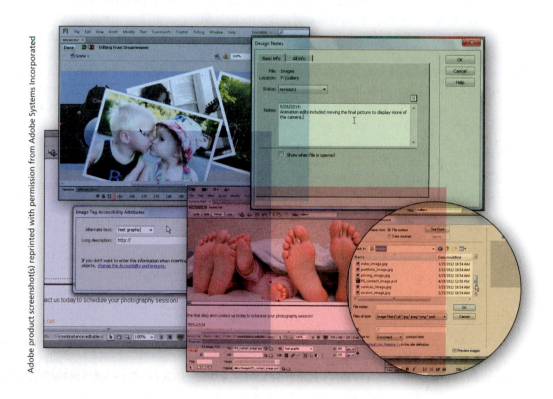

Objectives

You will have mastered the material in this project when you can:

- Describe the need to integrate Dreamweaver with Flash and Photoshop

- Insert a Flash movie into a Dreamweaver Web page and play it

- Use Dreamweaver's Edit in Flash tool

- Edit a movie and return it to Dreamweaver

- Link a Photoshop image in Dreamweaver

Inserting Flash and Photoshop Files in Dreamweaver

Introduction

One of the advantages of using Dreamweaver is the integration it has with other programs in the Adobe Creative Suite and the consistent user interface. Because you now have learned the basic editing capabilities in all three applications — Photoshop, Flash, and Dreamweaver — this chapter shows you how to integrate those applications by importing a Flash movie and a Photoshop file into a Dreamweaver Web site.

In addition to the ease of inserting images and content created with Flash and Photoshop, you also can edit an image or file in its original editor after you insert it in a Dreamweaver document. For full integration, you must have all of the applications installed on your computer. As you learned in the first integration chapter, roundtrip editing ensures that code updates are transferred correctly between applications. This applies to Dreamweaver as well.

Plan Ahead

General Project Guidelines

When creating a project, the actions you perform and decisions you make will affect the appearance and characteristics of the finished product. As you import objects into Dreamweaver, such as the ones shown in Figure 1, you should follow these general guidelines:

1. **Use animations purposefully.** Animation and graphics should serve a purpose. Choose animations and graphics as carefully as you do any other element of your Web site or your marketing approach. Remember that visitors will form an impression of your product and your company based on what you show them, so use graphics carefully.

2. **Create smart objects.** Keeping your Web site or publication up to date with the most recent copy or graphic is an important design tool. A smart object, embedded and linked to its source, allows you to update without importing again. It also standardizes the most recent version of a file occurring in multiple places.

3. **Create or update design notes.** Design notes are separate files associated with an element or graphic in Dreamweaver. These editable files can be used to record a range of information about the project, such as explanatory notes, date stamps, tasks still needing to be done, and so on. Use design notes to keep track of the source file, who created and edited it, and its status.

When necessary, more specific details concerning the above guidelines are presented at appropriate points in the chapter. The chapter also will identify the actions performed and decisions made regarding these guidelines during the creation of the edited project shown in Figure 1.

Project — Inserting a Flash Movie and a Photoshop Smart Object

Animation and high-end graphics add realism and dimension to Web pages. Animations, also called movies, attract attention to advertisements and add value to content pages. Using graphics and animation appropriately on a Web site can illustrate a concept, product, or service more clearly.

In this project, you will import a Flash movie into a Dreamweaver Web site and then edit the movie from Dreamweaver. You also will import a Photoshop file into the Web site and roundtrip it in Dreamweaver. Finally, you will create a design note, which stores information about the edits and dates them. Editing files from Dreamweaver will create a link between applications that will generate automatic updates to the Web site. You will use the Gallery Web site created in the Dreamweaver portion of this book. If you did not create the Gallery Web site, see your instructor for ways to complete this project. Figure 1a shows the imported movie in its finished state. Figure 1b shows the graphic after Photoshop editing.

a) Services page with embedded movie

b) Contact page with edited smart object

Figure 1

Overview

As you read this chapter, you will learn how to import the movie in Figure 1a on the previous page and edit the graphic shown in Figure 1b on the previous page by performing these general tasks:

- Import a Flash movie into Dreamweaver.
- Edit a Flash movie.
- Import Photoshop files into Dreamweaver.
- Create a smart object link.
- Create a design note.

To Copy Files into the Images Folder

Before adding a Flash movie and Photoshop image to a site, you must add the files to the file structure of the site. The following steps copy three files from the Data Files for Students to the Gallery site on your file storage location. Visit www.cengage.com/ct/studentdownload for detailed instructions or contact your instructor for information about accessing the required files. If you did not create the Gallery Web site, see your instructor for ways to complete these steps.

1 Navigate to the location of the Data Files for Students.

2 Double-click the Integration 02 folder to open it.

3 Click the Movie.swf file, and then SHIFT+click the Movie.fla file and the PS_contact_image.psd file to select all of the images and movies needed for the site.

4 Right-click the selected files, click Copy on the context menu, and then navigate to Removable Drive (F:), or the location of the Gallery folder you created in Dreamweaver Chapter 3, to prepare to copy the files.

5 Double-click the Gallery folder, and then double-click the Images folder to open the Images folder.

6 Right-click anywhere in the open window, and then click Paste on the context menu to copy the files into the Images folder (Figure 2).

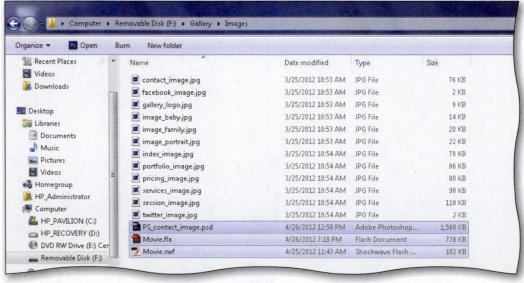

Figure 2

Integrating Dreamweaver and Flash

Dreamweaver has many commands that help you import, edit, and play Flash files. Because of the close integration of all the Adobe CS6 applications, many of the Flash commands are built into Dreamweaver's menu system and panels. For example, the Import command on the Dreamweaver menu bar has a Media submenu with commands to import various types of Flash animations. Once an animation is imported into Dreamweaver, the Property inspector has both a Flash Edit button and a Play button.

To Open the Services Page in Dreamweaver

The following steps open the services.html page in the Gallery Web site that you created in Dreamweaver Chapter 3. If you did not create the Gallery Web site, see your instructor for ways to complete these steps.

1 Start Dreamweaver.

2 Press CTRL+O to display the Open dialog box. If necessary, navigate to the Gallery site on Removable Disk (F:), or the location of your Gallery folder.

3 Double-click the services.html file to display the page in the document window (Figure 3).

Figure 3

To Delete the Image

The following steps delete the current image on the services.html page in preparation for importing a Flash movie.

1 Click the image in the imageArea to select it.

2 Press the DELETE key to delete the image (Figure 4).

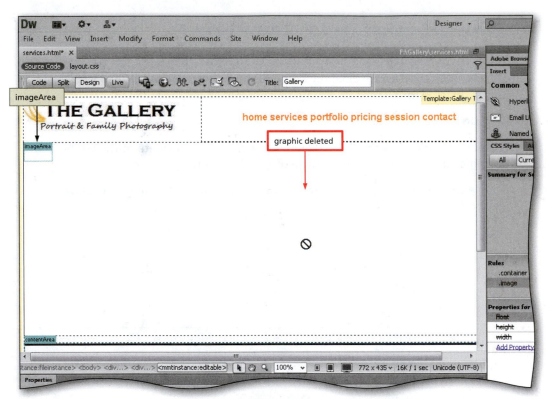

Figure 4

To Import a Flash Movie

Recall that the source document of a Flash animation or movie has the file extension of FLA, and can be opened and edited using Adobe Flash. A movie whose purpose is to play on the Web commonly has a file extension of SWF. The following steps use the Dreamweaver Import menu to import a Flash movie in the SWF format. Dreamweaver allows you to create accessibility settings, such as an alt tag, when you import the movie. Recall than an alt tag is an HTML attribute that provides alternate text when nontextual elements, typically images, cannot be displayed or when the picture is accessed by a screen reader.

1

• With the insertion point still located in the imageArea, click Insert on the menu bar and then point to Media to display the Media submenu (Figure 5).

Q&A

What is the purpose of the FLV command?

FLV files are special Flash files offering high rates of compression to deliver longer videos over the Internet.

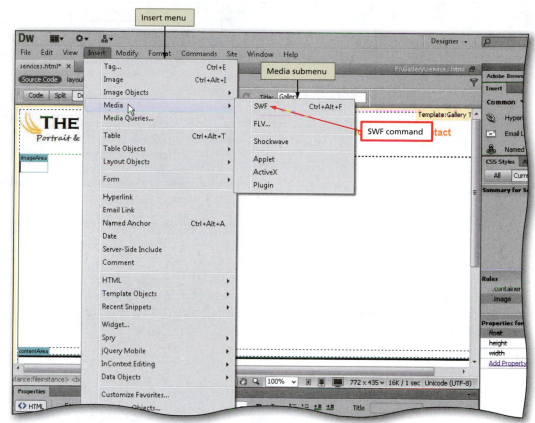

Figure 5

2

• Click SWF to display the Select SWF dialog box.

• Double-click the Images folder to display its contents (Figure 6).

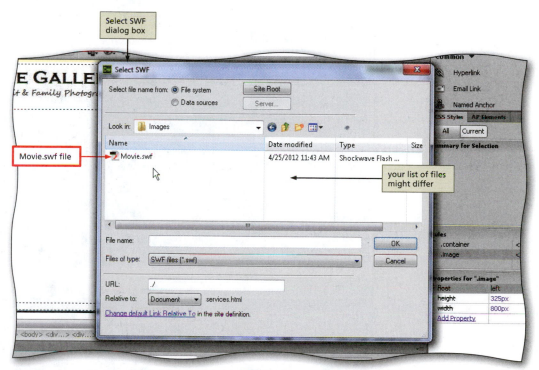

Figure 6

3

- Double-click Movie.swf in the list to begin the process of inserting the movie.

- When Dreamweaver displays the Object Tag Accessibility Attributes dialog box, type `camera movie` in the Title text box (Figure 7).

Q&A What is the purpose of the Access key and Tab index text boxes?

Entering a single letter in the Access key text box allows the Web site visitor to access the movie with a CTRL key combination. You can use the Tab index text box to set a tab order when you have other links and form objects on the page and need the user to tab through them in a specific order.

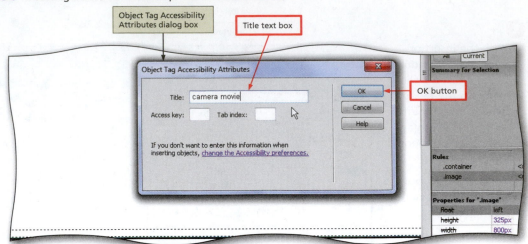

Figure 7

4

- Click the OK button to insert the movie and display a Flash placeholder image (Figure 8).

Q&A I do not see the movie. Did I do something wrong?

No. Dreamweaver displays the placeholder until you play the movie.

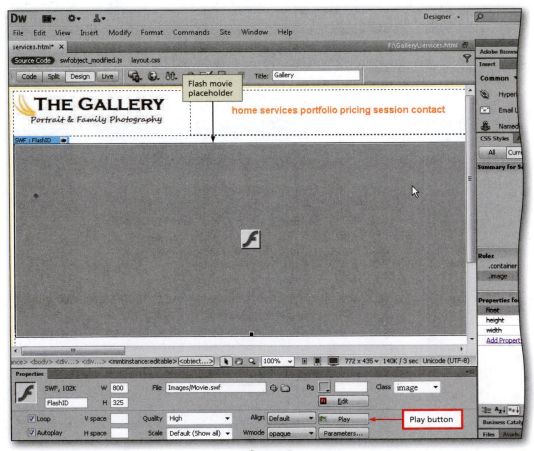

Figure 8

Other Ways

1. Press CTRL+ALT+F, navigate to desired folder, double-click desired file

2. Click Media on Insert panel, click SWF, navigate to desired folder, double-click desired file

To Play the Movie in Dreamweaver

The following steps play the movie in Dreamweaver.

- With the Flash movie placeholder still selected, click the Play button on the Property inspector to play the movie. If Dreamweaver asks you to save the page and dependent files, click the Yes button (Figure 9).

Q&A

My browser wants to install a new Flash player. Should I allow that?

You will have to decide if you want to install the latest version of the Flash player for your browser. Consult your instructor about the installed version.

🔍 **Experiment**

- Click File on the menu bar, point to Preview in Browser, and then click the browser of your choice. Watch the movie playing in the browser.

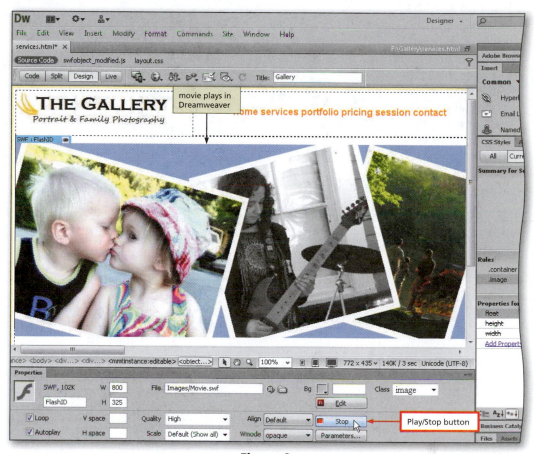

Figure 9

2

- When the movie is done playing, click the Stop button.

Other Ways
1. Select movie placeholder, press CTRL+ALT+P

To Edit the Movie

You would like to see more of the camera at the end of the movie; therefore, you must edit the movie so that the entry of the last picture does not cover the image of the camera completely. The steps on the next page edit the movie. The Flash Edit button automatically opens Flash and loads the FLA file.

1

- Click the Flash Edit button on the Property inspector to begin the process of opening Flash.

- When the Locate FLA File dialog box is displayed, navigate to the Images folder of the Gallery site on your storage location, if necessary (Figure 10).

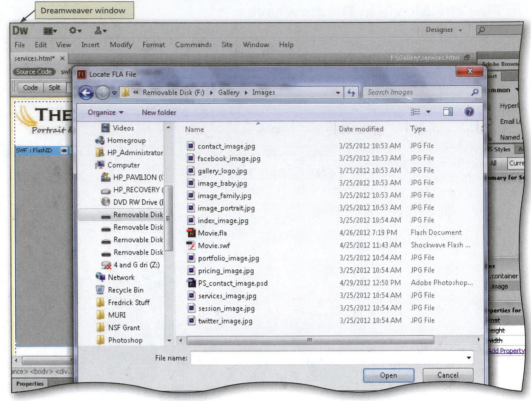

Figure 10

2

- Double-click the movie.fla file to open it in Flash. Maximize the window, if necessary (Figure 11).

Figure 11

3

- If necessary, click the 'Go to last frame' button on the Timeline status bar to prepare for adjusting the final location of the photo.

- On the stage, drag the picture of the two children to the right and slightly down, so that more of the camera is showing (Figure 12).

 Experiment

- Drag one of the points on the path to change how the image travels through the animation. Preview the animation by pressing the ENTER key. When you are done, press CTRL+Z twice to undo the path change.

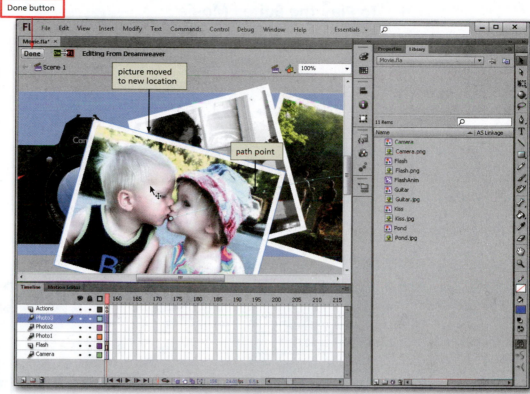

Figure 12

4

- Click the Done button to return the edited movie to Dreamweaver (Figure 13).

- If Flash is still running, click the Flash button on the Windows taskbar, and then click the Close button on the Flash title bar.

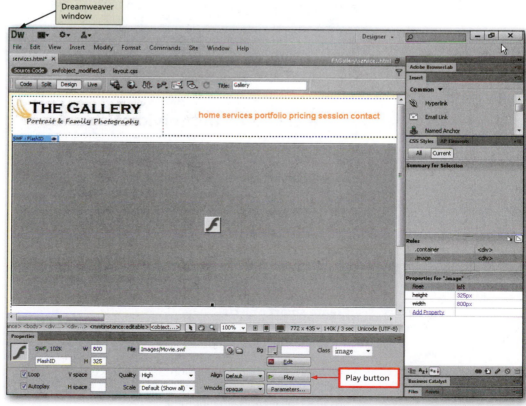

Figure 13

Other Ways

1. Right-click image, click Edit With Flash

To Play the Edited Movie

The following step plays the movie again to confirm that the camera is now visible in the background.

1 Click the Play button on the Property inspector to play the movie (Figure 14).

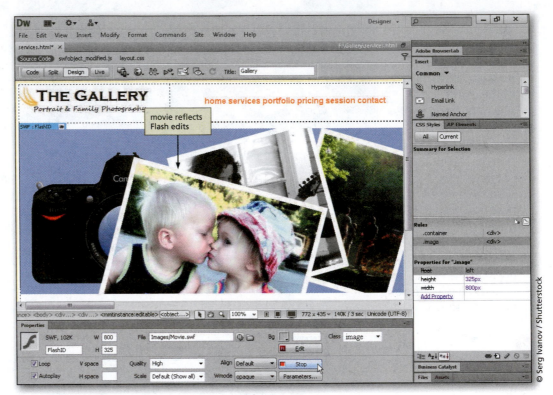

Figure 14

To Save and Close the Services Page

The following steps save the page with the edited animation and close the file.

1 Press CTRL+S to save the page.

2 Press CTRL+W to close the document without quitting Dreamweaver.

Plan Ahead

Create smart objects.
A smart object graphic is embedded and linked to its source, rather than simply inserted or copied. When planning your graphics, it is better to create a smart object; that way, if anyone updates the graphic, you have the ability to import the most recent version into your Web site or publication. Smart objects especially are useful for graphics that commonly change, such as those with updates (price, date, or personnel) or when logos, products, or services are modified.

Integrating Dreamweaver and Photoshop

The tight integration among the Adobe Creative Suite applications allows you to edit any image on your Dreamweaver Web page using Photoshop as an editor. Dreamweaver displays a Photoshop Edit button on the Property inspector when an image is selected. You also can create a smart object when you import a Photoshop image into Dreamweaver. A **smart object** is an image that is embedded and linked to its Photoshop source, rather than simply inserted or copied. By creating a smart object, any changes to the original Photoshop image are available to Dreamweaver and consequently appear on the Web page. Dreamweaver uses a smart object badge, displayed in the upper-left corner of the image, to indicate that the image is linked to a source file. A green badge indicates the most recent version. A green and red badge indicates a new version exists in Photoshop and the Dreamweaver version of the image needs to be refreshed. On the contacts page of the Gallery Web site, you will import a Photoshop image, edit it, and then update or refresh the link.

To Open the Contact Page in Dreamweaver

The following steps open the contact.html page in the Gallery Web site that you created in Dreamweaver Chapter 3. If you did not create the Gallery Web site, see your instructor for ways to complete these steps.

1 In the Dreamweaver window, press CTRL+O to display the Open dialog box.

2 Double-click the contact.html file to display the page in the document window (Figure 15).

Figure 15

To Delete the Image

The following steps delete the current JPG image in preparation for changing the image on the contact.html page.

1 Click the image in the imageArea to select it.

2 Press the DELETE key to delete the image.

To Import a Photoshop Image

The following steps import the Photoshop version of the graphic to create a smart object. When Dreamweaver imports Photoshop files (PSD files), you have the option of optimizing the image and preparing it for the Web. You also can add alternative text and a hyperlink if desired.

1

- With the insertion point still located in the imageArea, click Insert on the menu bar, and then click Image to display the Select Image Source dialog box.

- Double-click the Images folder to display the list of images.

- Scroll as necessary in the Name box to display the PS_contact_image.psd file (Figure 16).

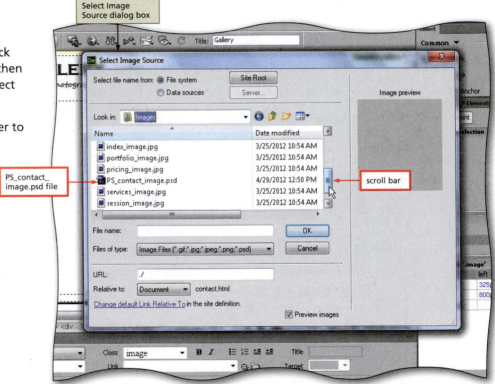

Figure 16

2

- Double-click the PS_contact_image. psd file to select it and to display the Image Optimization dialog box (Figure 17).

Q&A Should I change any of the optimization settings?

No. The default files will use a JPG image with a quality setting that allows for fast downloading.

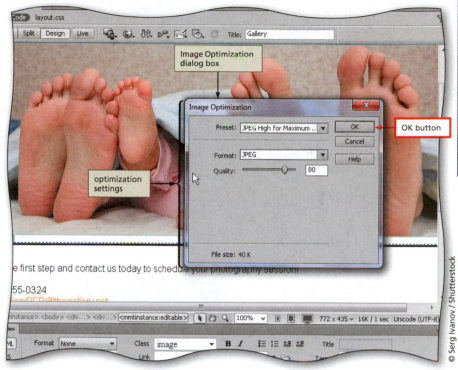

Figure 17

© Serg Ivanov / Shutterstock

3

- Click the OK button to display the Save Web Image dialog box.

- Double-click the Images folder to open it (Figure 18).

Q&A Why do I need to save?

This step saves the optimized file as a JPG on your storage device. As a smart object, Dreamweaver will update both the JPG and the PSD files automatically with each edit.

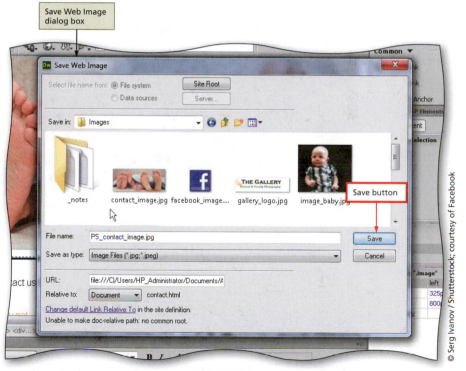

Figure 18

© Serg Ivanov / Shutterstock; courtesy of Facebook

4

• Click the Save button to save the Web image and to display the Image Tag Accessibility Attributes dialog box.

• Type `feet graphic` in the Alternate text box (Figure 19).

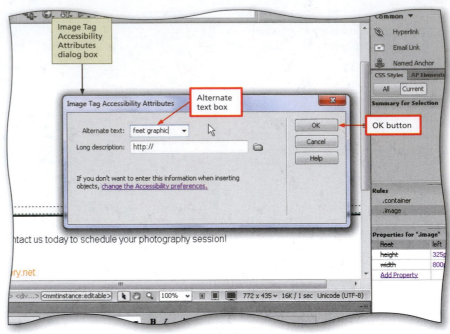

Figure 19

5

• Click the OK button to accept the optimization and file settings for the new image (Figure 20).

Q&A

Should I see a change on my screen?

The file might look the same temporarily, but it will be linked to an editable Photoshop file and update automatically.

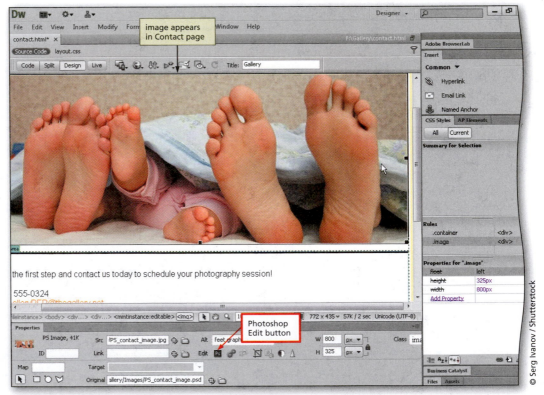

Figure 20

© Serg Ivanov / Shutterstock

Other Ways

1. Press CTRL+ALT+I, navigate to image, click OK button, enter alternate text, click OK button

To Edit a Photoshop Image

You need to update the image for the contact.html page of the Gallery Web site to reflect recent changes. The following steps edit the PSD image to display the changes and to take advantage of the smart object link for future updates.

1

- Click the Photoshop Edit button on the Dreamweaver Property inspector to access Photoshop (Figure 21).

Q&A My interface color scheme is darker than the one in the figure. Did I do something wrong?

No. Someone might have reset your color scheme. You do not need to change it; however, if you want a lighter color scheme, see Photoshop Chapter 1 for ways to reset the color of the interface.

Figure 21

2

- On the Photoshop Layers panel, click the visibility icon on the pink gradient layer to display the pink gradient layer in the workspace (Figure 22).

3

- Click the Close button on the Photoshop title bar. If Photoshop prompts you to save the file, click the Yes button to save the file and return to Dreamweaver.

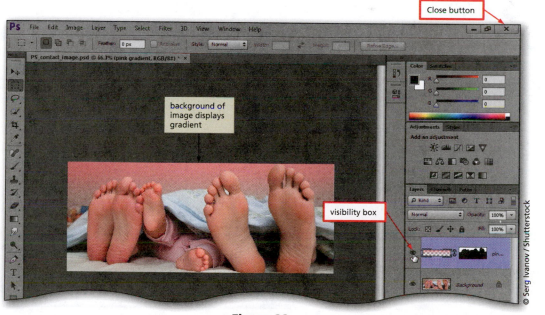

Figure 22

Other Ways

1. Right-click image, point to Edit With, click Photoshop, edit image, close file

To Update a Smart Object

The following steps update the smart object created by linking Dreamweaver and Photoshop.

1

- Scroll left in the document window until you see the smart object badge in the upper-left corner of the image.

- Right-click the image to display the context menu (Figure 23).

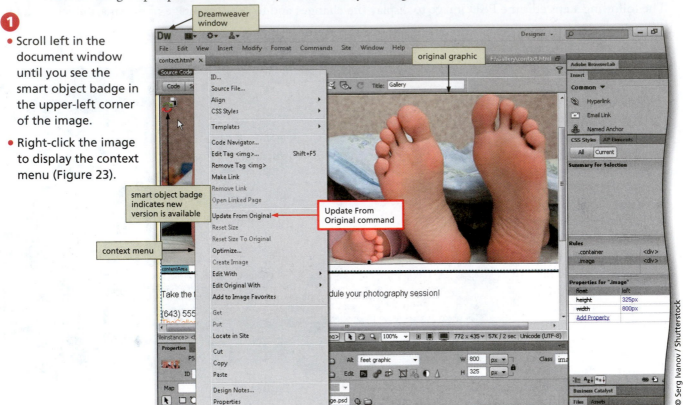

Figure 23

© Serg Ivanov / Shutterstock

2

- Click Update From Original on the context menu to update the image (Figure 24).

Q&A Does the smart object badge change?

Yes, the smart object badge is now green, indicating that the most recent version is displayed. You might have to scroll the document window to the left.

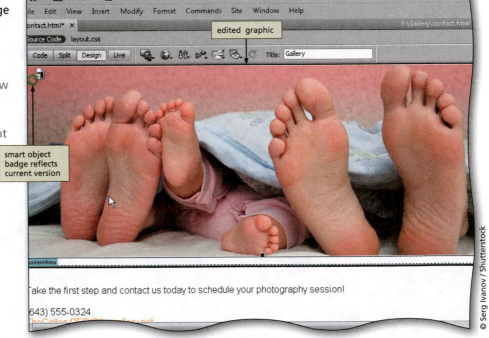

Figure 24

© Serg Ivanov / Shutterstock

Other Ways

1. On Property inspector, click Update From Original button

To Save and Close the File

The following steps save the contact.html file with the new smart object image and close the file.

1 Press CTRL+S to save your changes.

2 Press CTRL+W to close the file without quitting Dreamweaver.

Design Notes

Dreamweaver projects can contain **design notes,** which are small files that contain information about a graphic or other element in a Dreamweaver Web site. You can add a design note yourself, or use the one that Dreamweaver creates when you import a graphic. You can use design notes to store element information such as the edit date, the kind of edits, or the location of the file — information that you do not want to be visible to visitors of the Web site. Dreamweaver also relies on design notes for product integration, allowing Dreamweaver to locate the source document for an imported image or movie. During the import process, Dreamweaver design notes record references to the original PSD, PNG, or FLA files, which are automatically imported into the site along with any Web-ready files such as GIF or SWF files. In addition to location information, design notes contain other pertinent information about exported files, such as scripts for hot spots or rollovers, link status, as well as individual images in a table or movie.

> **Create or update design notes.**
> Dreamweaver automatically creates a design note when you edit a linked file or a movie in Flash. Other times, you can create your own design notes when you need to keep track of the status to include details about images or objects, such as the source files, who created them, or where you can get additional files and information. Design notes do not appear to Web site visitors, so you can use them for information you cannot save in the file itself. It is a good idea to create a design note for every graphical element in your Web site.

When you import the file into Dreamweaver, Dreamweaver creates a folder named _notes in the same folder as the imported file in which the design note is stored.

To Open a Design Note

The following steps open the design note that Dreamweaver created when you imported the Flash movie.

1

- In the Dreamweaver window, press CTRL+O to display the Open dialog box.

- Navigate to the location of your Gallery folder.

- Double-click the Images folder to open it.

- Double-click the _notes folder to display its contents.

- Click the 'Files of type' button and then click All Files (*.*) in the list (Figure 25).

 Q&A What does the extension MNO stand for?

It stands for Macromedia Note Object and is the legacy extension for design notes. MNO is a second extension added to the file name and extension of an existing object in Dreamweaver.

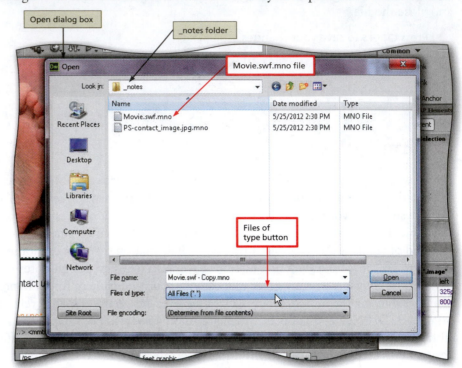

Figure 25

2

- Double-click the Movie.swf.mno file to open it (Figure 26).

Q&A What are the tags in the design note?

In this specific design note, Dreamweaver records the XML data and information about data type and the location of the associated source file.

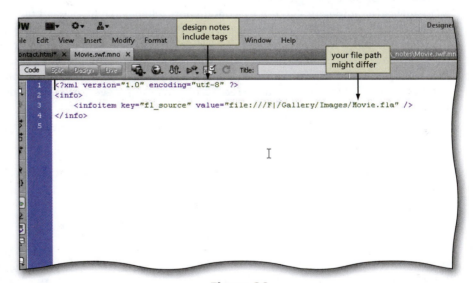

Figure 26

Other Ways

1. On File menu, click Open, navigate to desired folder, double-click design note file

To Edit a Design Note

Dreamweaver allows you to tag a design note with one of eight prestored **status** adjectives, such as revision1, beta, and needs attention, among others. The following steps edit the status of the design note, adding the current date and comments about the associated element. To use design notes, your Dreamweaver site must exist. See your instructor for ways to set up your pages as a Dreamweaver site, if necessary.

- Click the Files tab to display the Files panel.

- Right-click the Images folder and then click Design Notes to open the Design Notes dialog box.

- Click the Basic info tab, if necessary.

- Click the Status button to display its list (Figure 27).

Q&A

What is the purpose of the 'Show when file is opened' check box?

If you check the 'Show when file is opened' check box, the Design Notes dialog box will appear when you open the MNO file, saving you the step of opening it from the Dreamweaver File menu.

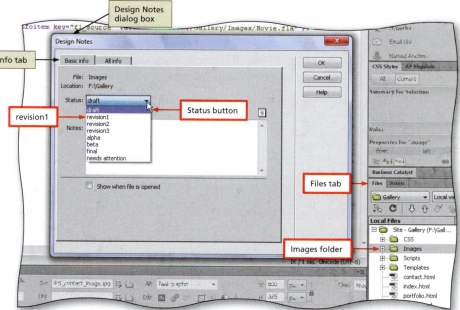

Figure 27

- Click revision1 to select it.

- Click the Insert date icon to display the date of the edit in the Notes box.

- Click below the date in the Notes box and then type `Animation edits included moving the final picture to display more of the camera.` to insert a comment about the update (Figure 28).

🔎 Experiment

- Click the All info tab and notice that the information from the Basic info tab has been transferred. Future revisions to the design note also will appear on the All info tab.

❸

- Click the OK button to close the Design Notes dialog box and save the design notes edits.

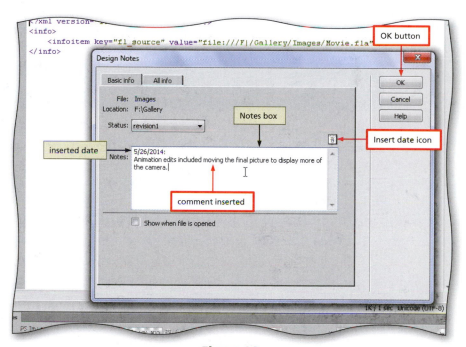

Figure 28

Other Ways

1. With Images folder selected, click File on menu bar, click Design Notes, edit status, click OK button

2. Right-click image, click Design Notes, edit status, click OK button

To Close the Design Note File

The following step closes the design note file.

1 Press CTRL+W to close the file.

To Quit Dreamweaver

The following steps save the contact.html file with the new smart object image, and quits Dreamweaver.

1 Press CTRL+S to save the file with the same name.

2 Press CTRL+Q to quit Dreamweaver.

Chapter Summary

In this chapter, you learned to integrate Dreamweaver with Flash and Photoshop to insert a Flash movie and a Photoshop smart object.

The items listed below include all the new skills you have learned in this chapter:

1. Import a Flash Movie (IN2 6)
2. Play the Movie in Dreamweaver (IN2 9)
3. Edit the Movie (IN2 9)
4. Import a Photoshop Image (IN2 14)
5. Edit a Photoshop Image (IN2 17)
6. Update a Smart Object (IN2 18)
7. Open a Design Note (IN2 20)
8. Edit a Design Note (IN2 21)

In the Lab

Lab 1: Editing a Photoshop Image

Problem: You decide to crop the picture of the baby on the portfolio page of the Gallery Web site, in order to focus on the baby's face.

Instructions: Perform the following tasks:

1. Start Dreamweaver and press CTRL+O to display the Open dialog box. If necessary, navigate to the Gallery site on Removable Disk (F:), or the location of your Gallery folder.

2. Double-click the portfolio.html file to display the page in the document window.

3. Scroll down to display the picture of the baby. Click the picture to select it.

4. On the Property inspector, click the Photoshop Edit button to open the picture in Photoshop.

5. Press the z key to activate the Zoom Tool and zoom to 200%.

6. Press the c key to activate the Crop Tool. Drag the lower-center cropping handle to include the baby's upper body and arms (Figure 29).

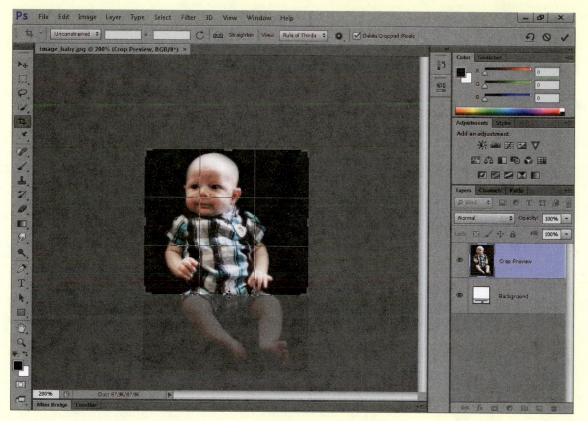

Figure 29

7. Press the ENTER key to commit the crop.

8. Click the Close button on the Photoshop title bar. When Photoshop prompts you to save the file, click the Yes button. When Photoshop prompts you to accept the JPEG options, click the OK button.

9. In the Dreamweaver window, right-click the picture and then click Update From Original to update the image.

10. On the Property inspector, select the text in the Width text box and then enter the value shown in the Height box to create a square picture.

11. Press CTRL+S to save the file again.

12. Press CTRL+Q to quit Dreamweaver.

In the Lab

Lab 2: Creating a Design Note

Problem: You decide to create a design note for the image on the pricing page of the Gallery Web site. The design note should contain your name, the date of your edits, and plans for future animation.

Instructions: Perform the following tasks:

1. Start Dreamweaver and press CTRL+O to display the Open dialog box. If necessary, navigate to the Gallery site on Removable Disk (F:), or the location of your Gallery folder.

2. Double-click the pricing.html file to display the page in the document window.

3. Right-click the graphic of the girl blowing bubbles and then click Design Notes.

Continued >

In the Lab *continued*

4. Change the status to revision1.

5. Insert the current date using the Insert date icon.

6. Click the Notes box, press the ENTER key twice, and then type `The name of this file is pricing_image. It is a JPG file. It was edited by Joy Starks. Future plans include animating the bubbles.` to insert a comment (Figure 30).

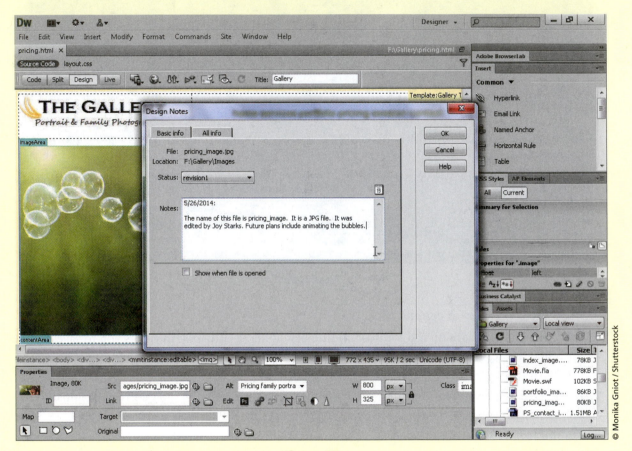

Figure 30

© Monika Gniot / Shutterstock

7. Click the OK button to close the Design Notes dialog box.

8. Press CTRL+S to save the file again.

9. Press CTRL+Q to exit Dreamweaver.

Appendix A

Project Planning Guidelines

Using Project Planning Guidelines

The process of communicating specific information to others is a learned, rational skill. Computers and software, especially the Adobe Creative Suite (CS6), can help you develop ideas and present detailed information to a particular audience.

Using Adobe CS6 you can edit photos, create animations, and design state-of-the-art Web sites, among other things. Computer hardware and productivity software, such as Adobe CS6 reduces much of the laborious work of drafting and revising projects. Some design professionals use sketch pads or storyboards, others compose directly on the computer, and others have developed unique strategies that work for their own particular thinking and artistic styles.

No matter what method you use to plan a project, follow specific guidelines to arrive at a final product that presents an image or images clearly and effectively (Figure A–1). Use some aspects of these guidelines every time you undertake a project, and others as needed in specific instances. For example, in determining content for a project, you may decide an original graphic would communicate the idea more effectively than an existing photo. If so, you would create this graphical element from scratch.

Determine the Project's Purpose

Begin by clearly defining why you are undertaking this assignment. For example, you may want to correct camera errors and adjust image flaws. Or you might want to create a graphic for a specific publishing or marketing purpose. Once you clearly understand the purpose of your task, begin to draft ideas of how best to communicate this information.

Analyze Your Audience

Learn about the people who will use, analyze, or view your work. Where are they employed? What are their educational backgrounds? What are their expectations? What questions do they have? Design experts suggest drawing a mental picture of these people or finding photographs of people who fit this profile so that you can develop a project with the audience in mind.

PROJECT PLANNING GUIDELINES

1. DETERMINE THE PROJECT'S PURPOSE
Why are you undertaking the project?

2. ANALYZE YOUR AUDIENCE
Who are the people who will use your work?

3. GATHER POSSIBLE CONTENT
What graphics exist, and in what forms?

4. DETERMINE WHAT CONTENT TO PRESENT TO YOUR AUDIENCE
What image will communicate the project's purpose to your audience in the most effective manner?

Figure A–1

By knowing your audience members, you can tailor a project to meet their interests and needs. You will not present them with information they already possess, and you will not omit the information they need to know.

Example: Your assignment is to raise the profile of your college's nursing program in the community. Your project should address questions such as the following: How much does the audience know about your college and the nursing curriculum? What are the admission requirements? How many of the applicants admitted complete the program? What percent of participants pass the state nursing boards?

Gather Possible Content

Rarely are you in a position to develop all the material for a project. Typically, you would begin by gathering existing images and photos, or designing new graphics based on information that might reside in spreadsheets or databases. Design work for clients often must align with and adhere to existing marketing campaigns or publicity materials. Web sites, pamphlets, magazine and newspaper articles, and books could provide insights of how others have approached your topic. Personal interviews often provide perspectives not available by any other means. Consider video and audio clips as potential sources for material that might complement or support the factual data you uncover. Make sure you have all legal rights to any photographs you plan to use.

Determine What Content to Present to Your Audience

Experienced designers recommend writing three or four major ideas you want an audience member to remember after viewing your project. It also is helpful to envision your project's endpoint, the key fact or universal theme that you wish to emphasize. All project elements should lead to this endpoint.

As you make content decisions, you also need to think about other factors. Presentation of the project content is an important consideration. For example, will your brochure be printed on thick, colored paper or transparencies? Will your photo be viewed in a classroom with excellent lighting and a bright projector, or will it be viewed on a notebook computer monitor? Determine relevant time factors, such as the length of time to develop the project, how long editors will spend reviewing your project, or the amount of time allocated for presenting your designs to the customer. Your project will need to accommodate all of these constraints.

Decide whether a graphic, photograph, or artistic element can express or emphasize a particular concept. The right hemisphere of the brain processes images by attaching an emotion to them, so in the long run, audience members are more apt to recall themes from graphics rather than those from the text.

Finally, review your project to make sure the theme is still easily identifiable and has been emphasized successfully. Is the focal point clear and presented without distraction? Does the project satisfy the requirements?

Summary

When creating a project, it is beneficial to follow some basic guidelines from the outset. By taking some time at the beginning of the process to determine the project's purpose, analyze the audience, gather possible content, and determine what content to present to the audience, you can produce a project that is informative, relevant, and effective.

Appendix B

Graphic Design Overview

Understanding Design Principles

Understanding a few basic design principles can catapult you to the next level of digital artistry. Beyond knowing how to use software, a graphic designer must know how to create effective and readable layouts no matter what the product type. In this Appendix, you will learn the design principles, color theory, typography, and other technical knowledge required to create usable and successful graphic designs.

A major goal in graphic design work, whether for print or Web page layout, is to guide the viewer's eyes toward some key point. Another major goal of design work is to convey a certain emotion — a project can have the effect of making the viewer feel relaxed, energetic, hungry, hopeful, or even anxious. By implementing a few basic principles of design, you can control your viewers' physical focus so they look where you want them to look as you steer them toward a desired emotion. Design principles typically include the following:

- Balance
- Contrast
- Dominance
- Proximity
- Repetition
- Closure
- Continuance
- Negative space
- Unity

Balance

Visual elements can be **balanced** within a design, with visual elements distributed in a horizontal or vertical arrangement. Unbalanced designs can cause viewers to feel anxious or uncomfortable, or even like they are falling sideways out of their seats. Balance may be achieved symmetrically or asymmetrically. Symmetrical balance mirrors a visual element to achieve equilibrium (Figure B–1). Asymmetrical balance can be achieved by balancing a small, dark element with a large, light element (Figure B–2) or balancing one large element with several smaller elements (Figure B–3).

with symmetrical balance, the left and right halves are mirror reflections, and the two trees, which are identical in size and shape, balance the composition

Figure B–1

left-heavy design with sparse right sidebar that is too white to add much weight

balanced design with a darker right sidebar adding weight to the right side

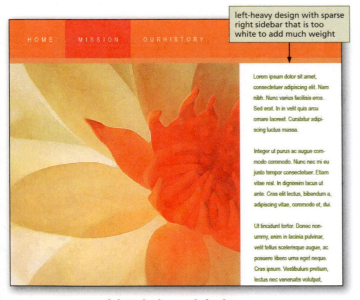

(a) Unbalanced design

(b) Balanced design

Figure B–2

large photo at right is asymmetrically balanced by the multiple small thumbnails on left

Figure B–3

Contrast

Contrast describes the visual differences between elements; it adds variety to a design and helps to draw the viewer's focus. Differences in color, scale, quantity, or other characteristics of visual elements help to achieve contrast. The element that is different from the others draws the viewer's attention. In Figure B–4, the words in white contrast against the other words on the page, and the viewer's eye is drawn to the contrasting sentence.

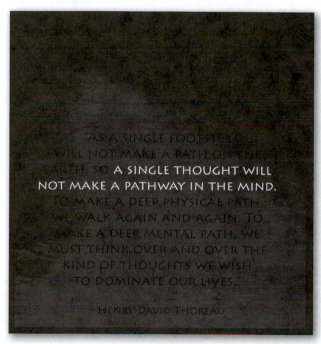

Figure B–4

Dominance

Dominance is a critical principle in controlling viewer focus. The dominant element in a design is the one to which a viewer's eyes and attention usually move first. An element's position within a design or its contrast to other elements can establish dominance. If you want your viewer to focus on a certain area of your design or on a specific design element, make it dominant, like the yellow V.I.P. banner in the discount card shown in Figure B–5, which grabs your attention with its contrasting color, even though it is not the largest element in the design.

Figure B–5

BTW

Dominant Object Placement
Placing an object at a certain location within a grid, such as the intersection of thirds or slightly above and to the right of center, helps to establish dominance.

Proximity

Proximity describes the relative space between elements. Related elements should be close to each other. Headings should be close to their related paragraph text, and product names should be close to their photos and prices. As shown in Figure B–6, when related items are not within close proximity of each other (Figure B–6a), the viewer might not know the items are related. When elements are too close, the design looks cluttered and text can become difficult to read. Strive for balance in your proximity, as in Figure B–6b.

(a) Items without proximity are not clearly related

(b) Items with close proximity are clearly related

Figure B–6

BTW

Natural Repetition
Repetition occurs naturally in the petals around a flower, patterns on snakeskin, and polygons on turtle shells.

Repetition

Repeating a visual element helps to tie a design together. **Repetition** of color, shape, texture, and other characteristics can help to unify your design (Figure B–7), create patterns, or impart a sense of movement. Most Web sites repeat a design theme across all the pages so users know they are on the same site as they navigate from page to page. Repeated colors and layouts help to unify the overall Web site design.

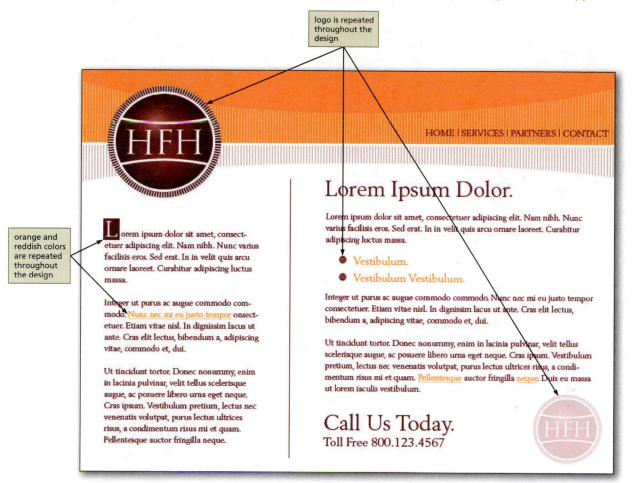

Figure B–7

Closure

Not everything in a design must be composed of solid lines. Composing objects from small parts and spaces allows a design to breathe and creates visual interest. Under the concept of **closure**, the human brain will fill in the blanks to close or complete the object (Figure B–8).

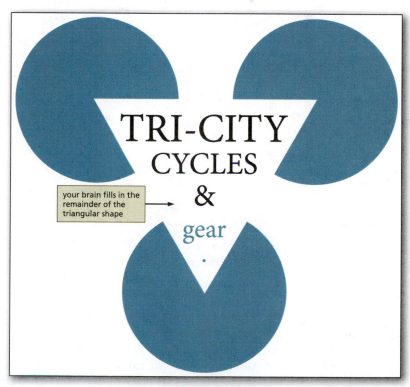

Figure B–8

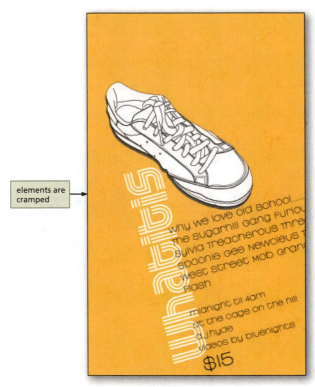

large dominant dancer captures your attention and her arms direct your eyes straight to the message

Figure B–9

Continuance

Once a viewer's eyes start to move across a page, they tend to keep moving — and you can exploit this **continuance** to guide their eyes exactly where you want them to go. A dominant object can capture the viewer's initial focus, and diagonal lines within that dominant object can guide the viewer's eyes toward the focal point of your design (Figure B–9).

Negative Space

Negative space refers to the space in your design that does not contain information, or the space between elements. For example, the space between the vertical heading and descriptive text or the space between a logo and the vertical heading, as shown in Figure B–10, is negative space. Without negative space, your design will feel cluttered, and viewers will have difficulty identifying on the focal point. Note that negative space, also called **white space**, literally does not translate to "white space," as negative space does not have to be white (Figure B–10).

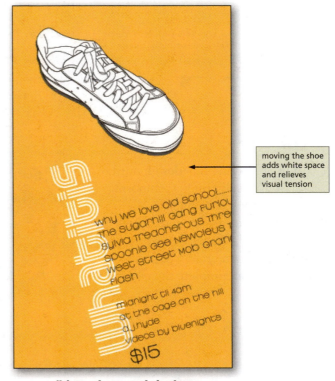

elements are cramped

moving the shoe adds white space and relieves visual tension

(a) Cluttered design   **(b) Uncluttered design**

Figure B–10

Unity

Unity refers to the concept that all elements within a design work well together to form a whole. The individual images, textures, text, and negative space join together to create a single unified message or meaning. Unity can be created by applying a combination of basic design principles. Balanced elements alone do not produce a visually appealing design. The same is true for elements with appropriate proximity and negative space, good contrast, or clear dominance. No single design principle is responsible for a pleasing design. Instead, the combination of these principles creates a single unified design. Without unity, a design degrades into chaos and loses meaning. Of course, that is not a bad thing if chaos is the intentional message.

Layout Grids

A graphic designer needs to know where to place elements within a document or Web page. The use of grids makes it easy to align objects to each other and can help with balance and proximity. You can apply any of the many standard grids to Web page layouts or print layouts for standard paper sizes. One very popular grid system uses thirds, which is derived from the golden ratio.

Rule of Thirds and Golden Ratio The rule of thirds specifies that splitting a segment into thirds produces an aesthetically pleasing ratio. The rule of thirds is derived from a more complex mathematical concept called the golden ratio, which specifies segment ratios of long segment divided by short segment equal to about 1.618 — which is close enough to the rule of thirds that designers typically apply the rule of thirds rather than break out their calculators (Figure B–11).

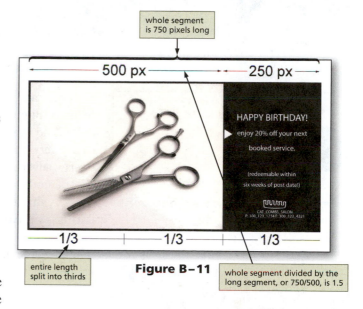

Figure B–11

Color Theory

Color can have a profound effect on the overall message a design conveys. Certain colors evoke specific emotions, and the way colors are combined can make the difference between readable copy and copy that is unable to be read.

Color Properties

Before you begin to work with color, it is important to understand the properties of color, which include hue, saturation, shade, tint, and value.

Hue refers to the tone, or actual color, such as red, yellow, or blue. Many color theorists interpret hue to mean pure color. A pure color, or hue, can be modified to create color variations. A basic color wheel, shown in Figure B–12, displays hue.

Saturation refers to the intensity of a color. As hues become less saturated, they create muted tones and pastels as they approach gray. As hues become more saturated, they appear very bright (Figure B–13).

Figure B–12

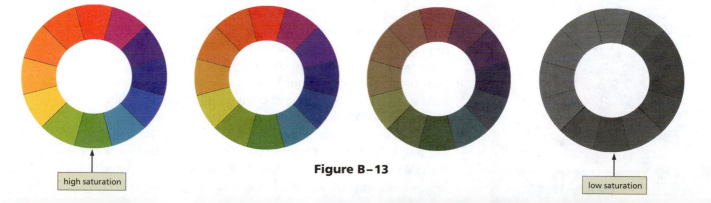

Figure B–13

desaturated hues can have calming effect

Figure B–14

oversaturated hues can be hard on the eyes

Figure B–15

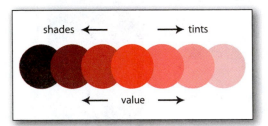

shades ⟵   ⟶ tints

value

Figure B–16

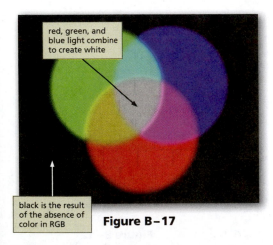

red, green, and blue light combine to create white

black is the result of the absence of color in RGB

Figure B–17

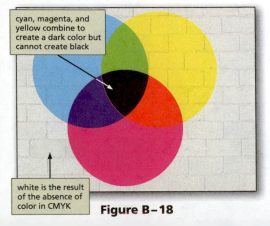

cyan, magenta, and yellow combine to create a dark color but cannot create black

white is the result of the absence of color in CMYK

Figure B–18

Desaturated colors can produce mellow tones and evoke calm feelings (Figure B–14). Oversaturated colors can produce neon-like colors and cause excitement (Figure B–15). Sometimes it is appropriate to use very bright colors, such as in a picture book for children or a high-energy advertisement for a sports drink. Other times, bright, saturated colors produce the wrong feeling for your work.

A **shade** is a mixture of a hue and black, producing a darker color. A **tint** is a mixture of a hue and white, producing a lighter color. A color's **value** describes its overall lightness or darkness. A tint has a higher value, while a shade has a lower value (Figure B–16). Mixing a hue with its shades, tints, and variations of saturation can lead to very harmonious color combinations.

Color Modes

A color mode describes the way in which colors combine to create other colors. The most commonly used color modes are RGB, CMYK, and LAB. Each mode has its strengths and weaknesses, and each is appropriate for a specific type of work.

The **RGB** color mode mixes red, green, and blue light to create other colors. Computer monitors and TV screens use the RGB color mode. All images used on a Web site must use the RGB color mode because few Web browsers can display CMYK images. RGB is an additive color mode, meaning colored light combines (light waves are added) to create other colors. The absence of all color in the RGB mode results in black. As colored light is added, white is created, as shown in Figure B–17. RGB is also device dependent, because the colors you see depend on the viewing device. Different computer screens will display colors in the same photograph differently due to variances in the manufacturing process and component wear over time. Do not waste your time trying to get your Web site to display the same exact colors consistently from computer to computer. It is not possible.

The **CMYK** color mode mixes physical cyan, magenta, yellow, and black pigments (such as ink) to create other colors, and is used in color printing. CMYK is a subtractive color mode. The absence of all color in the CMYK mode results in white light, and, as colored pigment is added, light wavelengths are absorbed or subtracted, creating color (Figure B–18).

Cyan, magenta, and yellow alone cannot create black; thus, the need for pure black in the CMYK mode.

Unlike RGB and CMYK, which combine individual well-defined colors, the **LAB** color mode combines levels of lightness with two color channels, a and b. One color channel ranges from green to magenta, while the other includes blue through yellow. By combining color ranges with lightness values, LAB is able to closely approximate the true human perception of color and thus is able to produce more colors than either RGB or CMYK. This makes it an ideal color mode for photographers wanting to have access to every possible color in a photograph. LAB typically is used during photographic retouching and color correction. The image then is converted to RGB or CMYK for use with electronic media or print.

BTW

LAB
LAB is sometimes written as L*a*b for lightness, color channel a, and color channel b.

Psychological Considerations of Color

Colors can evoke both positive and negative emotions in people, and the influence of a color can differ among individuals and cultures. While the effect of color on people is not an exact science, there are some generalities.

White often is associated with cleanliness, purity, and hope. Doctors and brides in most Western cultures wear white. However, white is associated with death and mourning attire in some Eastern cultures. White is the most popular background color and offers great contrast for highly readable dark text.

Black often is used to represent evil, death, or mourning, but also mystery, intelligence, elegance, and power. Black text on a white background is the easiest to read.

Red is used in Western cultures to signify love, passion, and comfort — but also is used to represent sin, anger, hell, and danger. Use dark reds to imply indulgence or fine living and brownish reds for designs dealing with Thanksgiving, harvest, or the fall season in general.

Green symbolizes many positives such as growth, tranquility, luck, money, ecology, environmentalism, and health, but it also symbolizes jealousy. Green can have a calming effect.

Blue often is cited as the favorite color by men. Like green, it evokes feelings of calmness and serenity. Blue implies authority, stability, loyalty, and confidence. However, it is one of the least appetizing colors, as there are few naturally blue foods. It also is associated with sadness and bad luck, as evidenced in blues music or phrases like "I've got the blues."

Yellow generally makes people happy. It is a highly visible and active color. However, too much yellow can lead to frustration and eye fatigue. Babies cry more in yellow rooms. Avoid using yellow as a page background and use it instead in smaller areas to draw attention.

Print Considerations for Color

The printing process cannot reproduce every color. Gamut refers to the range of printable colors, and colors that cannot be printed are said to be *out of gamut*. If an out of gamut color exists in your document, the printer you are using simply will get as close to it as it can — but it will not be exact. Depending on the printer you have installed, the actual color produced can vary. Photoshop identifies out of gamut colors in the Color Picker with a small icon. If your document contains out of gamut colors, you have two options: change or replace the out of gamut color with one that is in gamut; or accept that the final print may not be exactly what you expected.

Web Considerations for Color

When working with color for the Web, the most important thing to remember is that colors will appear differently on different computers. Web sites look similar, but not exactly the same, from computer to computer. Years ago, Web designers used only the **Web-safe colors**, which was a set of 216 colors that supposedly appear the same on all monitors. This was due to the limitations of video subsystems at the time, as computer monitors could display only 256 specific colors. Microsoft Windows supported 256 specific colors, and Apple Macintosh supported a different 256 colors. Of the two sets, 216 were the same across both platforms; these 216 became the **Web-safe palette.** However, designers soon realized that only 22 of those 216 were truly the same between Windows and Macintosh; this subset was called the **really Web-safe colors.**

Photoshop displays a warning in the Color Picker for non-Web-safe colors. Modern computers (as well as cell phone browsers) can display millions of distinct colors, so limiting yourself to 216 Web-safe colors is no longer a necessity. In fact, it is extremely limiting, because the 216 Web-safe colors are generally very bright or very dark with few choices for pastels or saturation and value variances. Most designers do not use Web-safe colors for their designs.

Relativity

A color's relative lightness/darkness value can appear different depending on what other color neighbors it. The gray block in Figure B–19 looks lighter when against the brown background and darker when against the light yellow background. Keep this in mind as you choose background/foreground relationships. A certain hue (or tint or shade) might look great when it is by itself, but you may not be so fond of it when used in close proximity to another certain color.

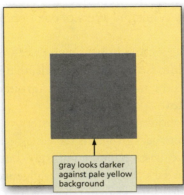

gray looks lighter against brown background

gray looks darker against pale yellow background

Figure B–19

Color Schemes and Matching

Choosing colors that work well together and enforce the design's message can be challenging but worth the effort. Successful color matching requires an understanding of **color schemes**, which simply describes an organized method of matching colors based on their positions on a color wheel. The color scheme can make or break a design.

Figure B–12 on page APP 9 displayed a color wheel. While there are various color wheel models, the most popular uses the primary colors red, blue, and yellow (Figure B–20a). Primary colors combine to create the secondary colors green, orange, and purple (Figure B–20b). A primary and a secondary color combine to create a tertiary (third level) color (Figure B–20c). More complex color wheels can include gradients to show varying saturation, tints, and shades (Figure B–21).

(a) Primary colors

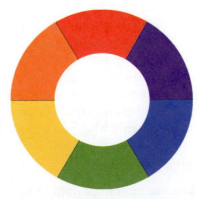

(b) Secondary colors

(c) Tertiary colors

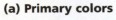

Figure B–20

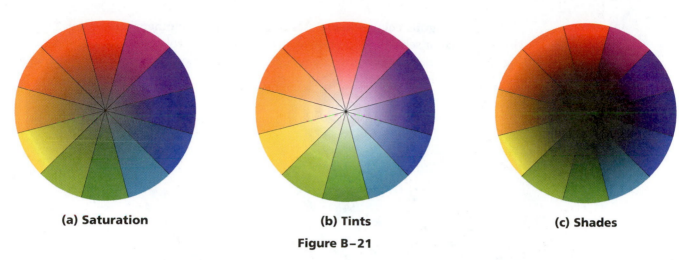

(a) Saturation   **(b) Tints**   **(c) Shades**

Figure B–21

Color Schemes   A **monochromatic color scheme** is one that uses a single hue with a variety of shades and tints (Figure B–22). This is an easy color scheme to create. While a monochromatic color scheme can appear soothing, the lack of hue variance can leave it looking a bit boring.

BTW

Color Scheme Web Sites

Stand-alone color scheme software programs are available for purchase, but Adobe offers a free online service at kuler.adobe.com that lets you browse color schemes created by other users, modify them, and create and save your own.

you are invited...

Figure B–22

A **complementary color scheme** uses colors directly across from each other on the color wheel. Their high contrast can look vibrant but also can be hard on the eyes. Avoid using complementary pairs in a foreground/background relationship, as shown in Figure B–23. Adjusting the saturation or substituting tints and shades makes this color scheme more workable.

bright complementary colors do not work well in a foreground/background relationship

adjusting the arrangement of the colors or using a variety of values or saturation can help

you are invited...

you are invited...

Figure B–23

An **analogous color scheme** uses colors next to each other on the color wheel. This color scheme is generally very appealing and evokes positive feelings (Figure B–24). Be careful not to choose colors that are too far apart. A very wide range of analogous colors can appear mismatched.

Figure B–24

The **split-complementary scheme** uses a base color and, instead of its direct complement, the two colors on either side of its complement (Figure B–25). This scheme offers a lot of hue variance, and therefore excitement. However, if all the hues are overly saturated, split-complementary colors can be very harsh. Try keeping one hue saturated and use tints, shades, or desaturated colors for the rest of the scheme.

Figure B–25

Other color schemes such as triadic, tetradic, neutral, and an infinite number of custom schemes also exist. Using a color matching resource such as software or a Web site is a good way to help you get started choosing colors and allows you to experiment to see what you and your client like.

Typography

Typography is the art of working with text. Perhaps the two most important factors for graphic designers to address when working with text are visual appeal and readability. A dull text heading will not entice viewers to read the rest of the advertisement, but a text heading that looks beautiful can be useless if it is not readable (Figure B–26).

Readability

Readability is the measurement of how comfortable or easy it is for readers to read the text. Many factors contribute to overall readability. Commonly accepted readability factors include the following:

- Large text passages written in lowercase are easier to read than long text passages in uppercase.

- Regular text is easier to read than italicized text.

- Black text on a white background is easier to read than white text on a black background.

- Legibility affects readability.

- Line length, letterforms, and appearance all influence readability.

HONEY BEE BODY CARE

flat and unappealing

visually appealing and easy to read

elegant, but difficult to read

Figure B–26

Before learning the details of readability, you must understand some type basics. A **font** is a set of characters of a specific family, size, and style. For example, the description Times New Roman, 11 points, italic is a font. What most people consider a font is actually a **typeface** (Times New Roman, in this example). A font represents only a single specific size and style within a family, while a typeface is a set or family of one or more fonts.

Legibility refers to the ease with which a reader can determine what a letter actually is. If readers cannot figure out the letter, they cannot read the text, resulting in low readability and failed message delivery. The difference between legibility and readability is subtle. Figure B–27 shows an exit sign — something that needs to be legible.

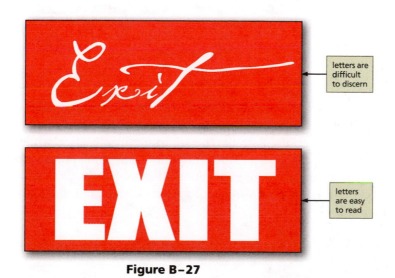

letters are difficult to discern

letters are easy to read

Figure B–27

BTW

PLEASE DO NOT YELL
Not only is typing in all uppercase difficult to read, but it connotes yelling at your reader.

Line length refers to the physical length of a line of text. When lines are too long, the reader's eyes can get lost trying to go all the way back to the left side of the page to find the next line. There is no conclusive magic number for how long a line of text should be. Optimal line lengths differ for adults and children, and for people with dyslexia and without. The best choices for line length differ based on the media of the message; printed newspapers, books, text on a Web site, and the subject lines in an e-mail message all require different line lengths. Some studies recommend line lengths based on physical lengths in inches, while other studies recommend a maximum number of characters per line. However, many designers follow the guideline that line lengths should not exceed 70 characters (about two-and-a-half alphabets' worth of characters).

Typeface Categories

Typefaces are organized into several categories, including serif, sans-serif, script, and display. Serif typefaces include additional appendages, while sans-serif typefaces do not (Figure B–28). It is generally accepted that large passages of serif text in print are easy to read, while sans-serif text is easier to read on a Web page. Because headlines are typically short, either serif or sans-serif is appropriate. Varying the headline typeface style from the body copy typeface style is an effective method of adding some visual excitement to an otherwise dull page of text. Script typefaces look like handwriting, and display typefaces are decorative.

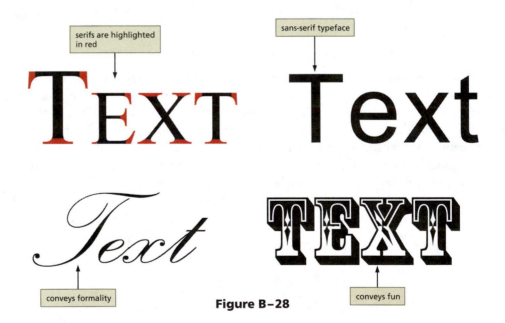

Figure B–28

In addition to differences in readability, the choice of a serif, sans-serif, or other typeface can help to create an emotion much like the selection of a color scheme. Wedding invitations often use a script typeface to signify elegance, while headlines using display typefaces can grab a reader's attention. The same phrase written in different typefaces can have different implications (Figure B–29). Similarly, differences in the size, weight (boldness), or spacing of a typeface also can influence emotion or meaning (Figure B–30).

You are invited ← typeface implies a fancy party or elegant gathering

typeface implies the event will be fun, zany, or whimsical → **You are invited**

Figure B–29

you are asked to remove your shoes, but you are still made to feel welcome ↓

you are being ordered to remove your shoes, and emphasis on REMOVE may cause resentment ↓

Remove shoes before entering

REMOVE SHOES BEFORE ENTERING

Figure B–30

Designing for Web versus Print

Graphic designers must be aware of subtle differences in how print and Web projects are created and perceived when designing for these media. While many design principles are common to both, it takes a different mindset to successfully create a design for either medium. Print designs are static, as the layout never varies from print to print (though differences in color may appear due to inconsistencies with the printer or printing press). The appearance of Web designs can vary, depending on the device used to view them. Some print designers struggle with the device dependency and fluidity of Web page designs. Some Web designers unnecessarily concern themselves about accommodating fluid or shifting content when designing a print advertisement.

Device Dependency and Fluidity

The main differences between print and Web design are related to device dependency and fluidity. Web pages are **device dependent**, meaning that the appearance of the page varies depending on the device (computer, cell phone, or PDA) on which they are viewed (Figure B–31). Discrepancies in monitor color calibration, screen resolution, and browser window size can affect how a Web page appears to the viewer. Colors can change, objects can shift, and text can wrap to a new line on different words from one device to another. In comparison, a newspaper or magazine looks the same no matter where it is purchased or where it is read. Designers can work with Web programmers to design pages for different devices.

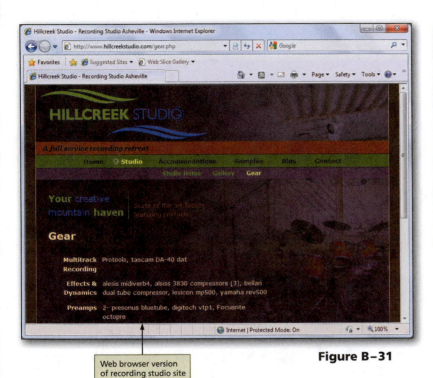

Web browser version of recording studio site

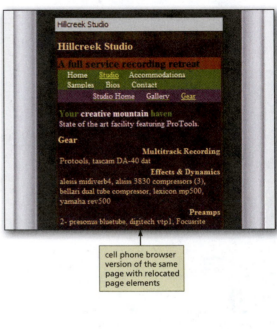

cell phone browser version of the same page with relocated page elements

Figure B–31

Pixels, Dimensions, and Resolution

A pixel is the smallest element of a digital image. Magnifying an image reveals the individual pixels (Figure B–32). A pixel, unlike an inch or centimeter, is not an absolute measurement. The physical size of a pixel can change depending on device resolution.

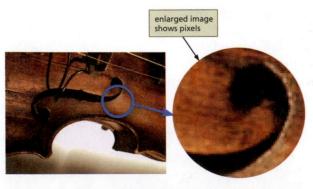

enlarged image shows pixels

Figure B–32

As you learned in Chapter 1, resolution refers to the number of pixels displayed on a computer screen. More pixels gives greater detail. When referring to an image file, the phrase, document dimensions, is used to describe the number of pixels in the file. For example, a document might have the dimensions of 450 × 337, meaning it contains 450 pixels across and 337 pixels vertically, for a total of 151,650 pixels. File size is directly related to document dimension. The more pixels there are in a document, the larger the file size.

When used to describe an image file, the word, resolution, also is used to describe the printed output. The print resolution is given in pixels per inch (PPI); for example, 72 PPI or 300 PPI. PPI is a linear measurement: 72 PPI means that, when printed, the output will contain 72 pixels across every linear inch. If the document dimensions were 450 × 337, those 450 horizontal pixels would print in groups of 72 PPI, resulting in a printout just over six inches wide (Figure B–33). If the resolution, but not the dimensions, was increased to 300 PPI, then those same 450 pixels would print in groups of 300 per inch, producing a final output about 1.5 inches wide.

Key points to remember when working with resolution are:

- A pixel is not a static measurement. Pixels change in size. They get smaller or larger to fill an inch as defined in the PPI setting.
- Changing the resolution of an image file has no effect on the file size. It affects the physical size of the printed output.
- Changing the document dimensions does affect the file size.

When printing documents, printers create each individual pixel with a group of microscopic dots of ink (or toner or other pigment). The number of dots a printer can generate is measured in dots per inch (DPI). People sometimes incorrectly use the term DPI when they really mean PPI. A printer with a resolution of 2400 DPI means it can squeeze 2400 dots of ink (not pixels) into a single inch. The more dots used to create a pixel, the truer color each pixel can have — resulting in a higher quality print.

450 px wide at 72 ppi

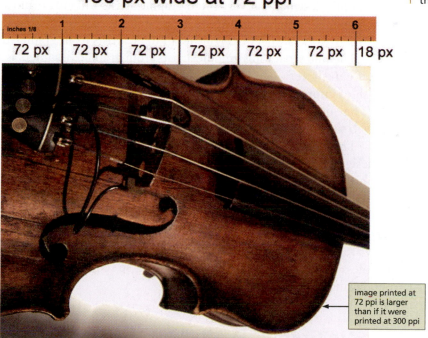

image printed at 72 ppi is larger than if it were printed at 300 ppi

450 px wide at 300 ppi

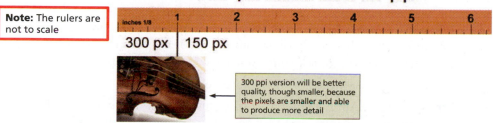

Note: The rulers are not to scale

300 ppi version will be better quality, though smaller, because the pixels are smaller and able to produce more detail

Figure B–33

A common misconception related to creating image files is that all graphics for use on the Web should be created at a resolution of 72 PPI. However, because PPI affects the output of printing only, the PPI setting has no effect on the screen display of an image.

It is common practice to save Web images at 72 PPI, not because it optimizes images for the Web, but because the 72 PPI myth so widely is believed.

Working as a Graphic Designer

The business world offers many opportunities for people with creativity and an eye for design. From automotive design to fashion to advertising, the need for talented graphic artists is vast. Many industry experts believe there are generally three levels of professionals working in the graphics field: graphic artists, graphic designers, and people who own graphics editing/design software.

Graphic artists typically receive extensive schooling as art majors and know a lot about design principles and art history. However, schooling does not necessarily mean formal education in a school environment. A graphic artist can be self-educated. The key to the "artist" designation revolves around a personal need to creatively express oneself beyond that of producing commercial work for hire. While graphic artists work with software, they typically also produce art with more traditional media such as paints, pencils, fiber, metals, or other physical materials. Graphic artists may hold the same job as a graphic designer, but very often graphic artists will create and sell their own original artwork. This personal drive to create and the resulting independent production of original artwork is what distinguishes graphic artists from graphic designers.

The line separating graphic artists from graphic designers is a fine one. A **graphic designer** often is knowledgeable about design principles and may possess a wealth of information about art history, but not all graphic designers are graphic artists. They usually create design products for others, such as brochures, advertisements, or Web sites, using software, but do not create their own original works.

The third category of graphic designers includes people who own and use graphics design software for various purposes. This category, **software owners**, is not a true graphic design designation. Simply owning a copy of Photoshop or knowing how to use a certain software program does not make you a graphic artist/designer. Whereas artists and designers understand principles of design, effective use of color, and possess a certain degree of artistic ability or raw talent, design amateurs rely on the power of the software to help them create projects. Of course, it is possible for an amateur to become a professional designer or artist — but doing so requires education and training, not just purchasing a software suite.

Jobs in Graphic Design

An understanding of design principles and software skills opens the door to many opportunities in the professional graphics industry. Jobs for graphic designers range from freelance work and self-employment to full-time careers with advertising agencies, Web design firms, print houses, software companies, or the marketing team within an organization such as a school or commercial or nonprofit business. Perhaps the most important questions to ask yourself when considering a job in this field are:

- Do I want to work for myself or for someone else?
- Am I truly an artist? Am I creative? Or do I simply follow direction well, understand basic design principles, and know how to use graphics software?
- What is my preferred medium — physical (print) or electronic (Web, software interface)?

Once you have secured a position in the graphics field, you will be assigned projects that will call on your design skills and other abilities.

Design Projects

A successful project always begins with solid planning. Proper planning helps you to stay focused and reduces the potential for wasted time and money — both yours and your client's. A project plan must specify the following aspects of the project:

- Scope of design work
- Roles and responsibilities of designer and client
- Expectations and specifications for final product, including time frame

When you and your client agree on the scope of the work and are clear on what the final product should look like, you as the designer know exactly what it is you need to produce. It is better to take the time to plan a project before sitting down with the Creative Suite applications, so you have a good idea of what to do once you start the software.

Client and Designer Roles

Both the client and the designer have specific jobs. Defining and agreeing on these roles is crucial for the success of the collaboration.

Simply put, the client must clearly communicate his or her expectations. Clients often need help articulating their wants and needs, and the designer must be able to help draw this information from the client. Additionally, the client must be available to provide feedback when the designer offers a draft for feedback or proofing. A client's responsibilities include the following:

- Clearly communicate the needs of the project
- Provide timely and constructive feedback
- Trust the designer's expertise
- Pay the bills on time

Aside from the obvious (creating the product), the designer also is responsible for making sure the client knows their own responsibilities and avoids poor design choices. Sometimes, a client will request something that is just bad — like certain colors that do not work well together or make text unreadable. The designer is responsible for respectfully steering the client away from the bad options and toward a better alternative.

In a highly competitive job market, you must determine what sets you apart from your competition. A potential client might choose one designer over another not because one is a better or more creative artist, but simply because they like the other designer more.

Customer service is part of your job, as well. Treat your client and your client's time and money with respect, be personable, and appreciate your client, and you will have more to offer than your competitors will. In addition to meeting the responsibilities previously defined, you should do the following:

- Be on time to meetings
- Meet or beat your deadlines so you do not submit work late
- Be able to explain your design choices
- Ensure adherence to copyright law

Defining the Project

As a designer, you must understand you are acting in the role of a hired hand — not an artist with complete creative control. You are being hired to create what your client wants, not what you necessarily prefer. While you need to educate your client as to best practices in design, ultimately the client is paying the bill, so he or she has the final word when it comes to making decisions.

Specifying Project Details

Project details should be discussed with the client and agreed upon before any design work begins. One detail to consider is what the client needs for files. For example, does the client require a 300 PPI TIF file or a layered Photoshop file? How will the files be delivered? Will they be sent by e-mail, burned to a CD and mailed, or downloaded from a Web site or FTP server? Additionally, a timeline of deliverables should be stated. A first draft of the design should be sent to the client for approval by a certain date, and pending timely client feedback, the final version should be delivered by the project deadline. The client may have a desired time frame, and the designer must be able to deliver the work within that time frame. Sometimes a compromise must be reached.

Collecting Materials

Existing materials help to speed up the design process. If you are hired to create a Web site or brochure, ask your client for copies of their existing promotional materials, such as a business card, letterhead, or logo. Ask your client what they like and dislike about these materials and if the product you are creating should be stylistically similar. This approach can prevent you from going down the wrong path, inadvertently creating something the client does not like or need. Additionally, you will need to collect any photographs your client has earmarked for the project.

Next, you must gather other assets for the project; specifically, high-quality artwork and photographs.

Original Artwork   If you have the raw artistic ability or own quality camera equipment, you can create your own original artwork or take your own photographs if you are a professional-level photographer. You can outsource some of this work to professional artists or photographers — just be sure to get your client's approval for the cost. Your other option is to use stock art.

Stock Art   **Stock art** includes existing artwork and photographs that can be licensed for use. The cost of a single picture can range from zero to several thousand dollars, depending on the source and license restrictions. Realistically, you should expect to pay between $5 and $40 for each print-quality digital file if you cannot find free sources.

Stock art is commercially available from many companies, most with a Web presence — meaning you can download images or purchase whole collections of stock art on CD or DVD from a Web site. Thousands of companies sell commercial stock art online. Some of the most popular resources are fotosearch.com, corbis.com, and gettyimages.com.

When searching for stock art, be sure to seek out **royalty-free images**. Images that are royalty free can be reused without paying additional fees. For example, you could spend $100 to purchase an image that is not royalty free and use it on a Web site. If you want to use the same image in a brochure or another client's Web site, you might have to pay another fee to reuse the image. Royalty free means that once the initial payment is made, there are no re-usage fees.

If you do not want to pay anything for your images, look into finding **public domain** artwork or photographs. Images in the public domain are completely free to use. The only trick is finding quality artwork in the public domain. Whereas commercial stock art Web sites typically have millions of high-quality images from which to choose, public domain stock art Web sites often have far fewer choices. Public domain stock art sites include Flickr, Morgue File, and Uncle Sam's Photos.

Other Licenses   There are usage licenses allowing free unrestricted use of images, audio, video, text, and other content similar to that of the public domain. These licenses include Copyleft, Creative Commons, education use, fair use, GNU general public license, and open source. The definitions of these alternative licenses read like a law book, but it is helpful to recognize the names. Laws related to these licenses allow for limited use of copyright-protected material without requiring the permission of the copyright owner. If you find images or other content offered as one of these alternatives, there is a good chance it will be completely free to use.

Whatever the source for your images, be sure to read the license and usage rights and restrictions carefully. No matter your source for artwork, you need to document its origin. The documentation serves two important purposes. First, it provides a record of the image's origin in case you need to get additional similar artwork. Second, it provides peace of mind should you or your client ever face legal action for copyright infringement. The documentation does not have to be fancy; it can simply be a list of where an image is used in a project and where that image was acquired.

Summary

Successful design uses the principles of balance, contrast, dominance, proximity, repetition, closure, continuance, negative space, and unity. The properties of color include hue, saturation, shade, tint, and value. Color modes include RGB for Web images, CMYK for images you intend to print, and LAB for access to the largest color space possible when working with digital photographs. Adherence to Web-safe colors is unnecessary. Colors can have emotional implications and should be used in harmony with neighboring colors. Color schemes include monochrome, complementary, analogous, and split-complementary.

Typeface selections can affect text readability, as can line lengths. Typefaces are organized into several categories, including serif, sans-serif, script, and display. The same Web site can look different from one monitor or computer to another.

Pixels per inch (PPI) determines the number of pixels printed per inch and affects the printed size of an image only, not how it appears onscreen or its file size. Higher PPI settings produce better quality printouts but have no effect on how an image appears onscreen. Dots per inch (DPI) refers to printer capabilities and defines how many dots of ink a printer can print in a linear inch. Pixel dimensions, not image resolution, affect how large an image appears on-screen and the size of a file.

Working in graphic design can incorporate a range of creative roles; working with clients in a design role requires specifying project expectations and the responsibilities of both designer and client.

In the Lab

1: Evaluating Advertisements

Instructions: This appendix discusses many features and characteristics that you can evaluate with regard to graphic design. Find a color advertisement in a magazine and create a table similar to the following, using the design principles described in the appendix. Write a few sentences about each of the topics, using appropriate terminology; be specific about the parts of the advertisement you are discussing. Include a copy of the advertisement when submitting this assignment to your instructor.

Name of Magazine:
Type of Product or Service Advertised:
Balance:
Contrast:
Dominance:
Proximity:
Repetition:
Closure:
Continuance:
Negative space:
Unity:

In the Lab

2: Creating a Personal Brand

Instructions: You would like to create graphics and documents that display your own special flair and style, for social media, your e-portfolio, and your Web site. In preparation, you would like to decide on color and font schemes.

Create a custom color scheme. Decide if you want to use a complementary, analogous, or split-complementary scheme. Assume black and white, and then choose two accent colors that fit your scheme. Use a color panel from one of the applications, or use a color wheel from the Web to identify the colors by their color number. As an alternate scheme, select one of your chosen accent colors and find three shades or tints of that color for use in a possible monochromatic publication.

Choose a custom font scheme. Select a strong bold font for headings and a body font with contrasting ornamentation and typeface. Use Photoshop's Type Tool options bar and Characters panel to identify the names of the fonts.

Make a list of all of your choices and submit it in the format suggested by your instructor. For extra credit, create a publication or graphic using your custom schemes.

Appendix C

Publishing to a Web Server

Publishing a Web Site

Once you have created a Web site, you need to make it available to its intended audience. The discussion in this appendix is generally appropriate for small business and personal Web sites. Keep in mind that midsized and larger businesses typically publish their sites using their own dedicated Web servers; however, the concepts are the same. Publishing a Web site, also called going live, involves four general steps:

1. Select a Web hosting company.
2. Choose and register a domain name.
3. Publish your Web site files to a Web server.
4. Associate your domain name with your nameserver.

Web Hosting Companies

For your Web site to be available to users or visitors, it must reside on a special computer called a Web server. A Web server is a computer connected to the Internet, with Web server software installed. It is the Web server software that makes files stored on a computer available as a Web site. Although anyone with a computer can download and install Web server software at no cost, configuring Web server software is a complex process best left to experts. A **Web hosting company**, or **Web host**, is a company that offers Web hosting services. Web hosting companies rent space on their Web servers for you to store your Web site.

How to Choose a Web Host

Choosing a Web host begins with research. Read about Web hosts online and in technology publications. Keep in mind however, that online reviews of Web hosting companies often are biased or sponsored. Reviews are biased negatively as it is human nature to complain when you do not like something, but fewer people take the time and energy to write a review when they are pleased with a product or service. A review is biased positively when the review is sponsored by the Web hosting company itself — meaning either the Web host owns the review Web site or it purchases advertising on the review Web site, potentially influencing the display of positive reviews.

Once you have identified a few potential Web hosts, you should compare their features and test their tech support policies, as described later in this appendix. Recommendations from friends or colleagues are also important to consider when choosing a Web host. Choosing a host is an important consideration that should not be rushed.

Before choosing a Web hosting company, you should decide whether you need shared hosting or dedicated hosting and review the services and features outlined in the section that follows.

Dedicated and Shared Hosting

When a single Web server hosts a single Web site, the arrangement is called **dedicated hosting**. Dedicated hosting allows the client and the Web site full access to all of the server's resources, such as the processor, memory, and hard drive space (Figure C–1a). Unfortunately, dedicated hosting is expensive, sometimes costing several hundred dollars or more per month.

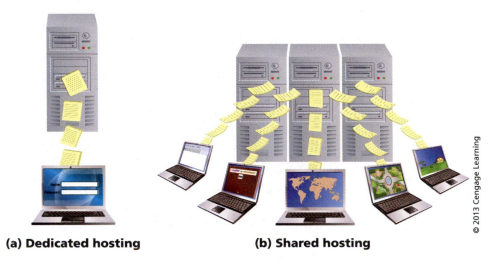

(a) Dedicated hosting   **(b) Shared hosting**

Figure C–1

© 2013 Cengage Learning

Shared hosting refers to multiple Web sites sharing a single Web server or a bank of Web servers (Figure C–1b). Shared Web servers host many, sometimes thousands, of individual Web sites that reside on the same server. Those Web sites share the server's processor, memory, hard drive space, and other computer resources. A reputable Web host has powerful Web server computers that can handle this kind of load, as well as the expert staff to configure the computers and Web server software. The disadvantage to shared hosting is that you do not get all the power of the server to yourself, as you do with dedicated hosting. The advantage is that shared hosting is very inexpensive, often just a few dollars a month. Most small business and personal Web sites use shared hosting.

Hosting Services and Features

The following paragraphs outline some of the more important features to consider when choosing a Web host (Figure C–2).

Disk Space   Web site pages (HTML documents) are small files that do not take up much storage space; however, other files, such as images, Flash movies, or other video and audio files used on your site, can be quite large. A typical image file used on a Web site may be as large as 50 kilobytes. A Flash movie file may be several thousand kilobytes. If your Web site files are larger than the disk space available to you, your Web site will not fit on the server. Choose a Web hosting plan that offers unlimited disk space.

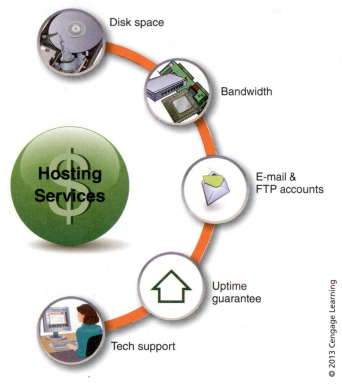

© 2013 Cengage Learning

Figure C–2

Bandwidth Every time a user connects to your Web site, your files are transferred across the Internet to the user. **Bandwidth** refers to the number of bytes your Web site is sending across the Internet. A **byte** is approximately equivalent to one character — a **kilobyte** is 1,024 bytes. The more users that connect to your site, or the larger your files are, the more bandwidth you use. Some Web hosts disable your Web site if you exceed the allotted bandwidth for your account, whereas other Web hosts charge you additional fees for overages. Choose a Web hosting plan that offers unlimited bandwidth.

E-mail Accounts To maintain professionalism, it is best to have an e-mail address that uses the same name as your Web site. For example, if your Web site is www.MyWebSite.com, it is best to have e-mail addresses such as info@MyWebSite.com or contact@MyWebSite.com rather than MyWebSite@hotmail.com or MyWebSite@gmail.com. Having an e-mail address that uses the same name as your Web site increases brand and name recognition — and is more likely to drive people to your site. Some hosting plans offer fewer than five e-mail accounts, which can be problematic if you need e-mail addresses for many more employees, for example. Choose a Web hosting plan that offers an adequate number of e-mail accounts for your site's needs.

FTP Accounts To copy your Web site to a Web server, you must connect to the Web server using software called an FTP client. **FTP** stands for **File Transfer Protocol**, which is a method of copying files between computers across the Internet. Because multiple people may be working on the Web site and updating files, each person should have his or her own FTP account for security purposes. If several people use the same FTP account, passwords may be changed inadvertently, making it impossible for the others to log on. Individual FTP accounts also help track who added, updated, or deleted files from the Web site. Choose a Web hosting plan that offers an unlimited number of FTP accounts.

Other Hosting Considerations
You might want to ask potential Web hosting companies about their financial strength, their physical security, their disaster recovery plan, and how long they have been in business.

Cost Shared hosting plans typically cost anywhere from $0.99 to $15 per month. The most expensive plans are not necessarily the best, nor are the least expensive always the best value. You can find excellent features from a reputable Web host such as webhostinghub.com or hostgator.com for about $6 per month. Choose a Web hosting company whose costs offer the best value for the services offered.

Setup Fee Some Web hosting companies charge a setup fee of $20 or more just to set up a new account. Choose a Web host that does not charge a setup fee.

Uptime Guarantee **Uptime** is the amount of time your Web site is available. Ideally, you want your site available 100 percent of the time; however, sometimes computers crash, hard drives become damaged, or other components in a computer cause it to stop working. When this happens on a Web server, Web sites residing on that server are not available. The reliability of the service is an important consideration. Choose a Web host that offers at least a 99.9 percent uptime guarantee to ensure that your Web site is always available.

Tech Support Tech support can be offered in a variety of ways. Make sure you choose a Web host that offers e-mail, phone, and online chat support 24 hours a day, seven days a week. It is a good idea to test the tech support service of a hosting company before signing up for an account. Sales and billing departments are usually excellent about taking phone calls and responding to e-mails, but you are not likely to need to reach those people once your account is active. Call tech support and see how long it takes them to answer. E-mail tech support and see how long it is until you receive a response. Ask a basic question such as, "What is the typical wait time before receiving a response from your tech support?" Some $0.99 per month hosting plans seem like a good deal until you encounter a problem. If you cannot reach tech support, or they reply with a generic programmed response as if they are reading from a script, that $0.99 per month cost may not be such a great deal after all. Choose a Web hosting company that offers 24-hour support, short wait times, and quick turnaround for e-mail questions.

Domain Names

Every computer connected to the Internet is assigned a unique number, called an **Internet Protocol (IP) address**, which identifies the computer. An IP address is used when one computer needs to contact another computer. For example, when a user opens a Web browser and types the name of a Web site, such as cengage.com, his or her computer actually connects to the Web server by using the IP address of the Web server. Because IP addresses are difficult to remember, most sites use a domain name such as cengage.com. A **domain name** is a combination of letters and numbers that names a Web site for locating purposes; it is the part of the URL that follows the **protocol designation** such as http:// and any **subdomain** listing such as www (Figure C–3). The user's computer automatically matches the domain name with the IP address in order to connect to the Web server. You need to choose a domain name carefully, and purchase, or register, your domain name to work in conjunction with your Web hosting company. You will learn how to register a domain name later in this appendix.

IP Addresses
An IP address typically is four decimal numbers separated by periods. However, as these numbers are being exhausted rapidly, a new eight-number IP address, using a hexadecimal notation, is being advocated by the Internet Assigned Numbers Authority (IANA).

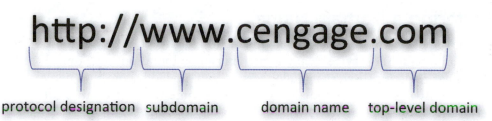

protocol designation   subdomain   domain name   top-level domain

Figure C–3

Choosing a Domain Name

Choose a domain name that is easy to spell, easy to type, and easy to remember. Your domain name might have to fit on a business card, and some users will need to type it into their Web browser's Address bar. Avoiding domain names that are lengthy or complicated is a good approach. A **top-level domain** (**TLD**) is the last part of a Web site's name. For example, .com, .org, .net, and .edu are all top-level domains. When choosing a domain name, you need to decide which top-level domain is best for your site. Table C–1 describes a few of the more popular top-level domains that you are likely to use.

Table C–1 Top-Level Domains		
Top-Level Domain	**Eligibility**	**Description**
.biz	Anyone can register	Intended for businesses as an alternate to .com
.com	Anyone can register	Originally intended for for-profit businesses, .com has become the most popular top-level domain
.edu	Only educational institutions may register	Used by educational institutions
.info	Anyone can register	No prescribed theme or orientation
.org	Anyone can register	Originally intended for nonprofit organizations

In most cases, you should choose to use .com if possible because it is the most familiar to people.

BTW

Domain Availability

After you choose a domain name, you need to make sure that no one has chosen that domain name already. You can use a Web site that will check for you, such as godaddy.com or checkdomain.com, or you can type the domain name with its subdomain and top-level domain into a browser's URL text box and see similar Web sites. Keep in mind that some sites may be registered but

Registering a Domain Name

You **register**, or purchase, a domain name through a company called a domain name registrar service. Many registrars can be found online. Some of the most popular registrar services include register.com, godaddy.com, and networksolutions.com. By registering a domain name, you become the registrant, or official owner of the site name (Figure C–4).

Figure C–4

Expect to pay anywhere from $10 to $30 per year for domain name registration. After the domain name is registered, you must renew it yearly. If your domain name registration expires, your Web site no longer will be available to the public.

Many registrars also offer Web hosting, and conversely most Web hosting companies offer free domain name registration. However, avoid this temptation to consolidate services. It is best to keep them separate. Register your domain through one company, and host your Web site with a different company. For any number of reasons, you might want to change Web hosting companies. By registering the domain name with a company other than your Web host, you easily can associate your domain name with any current hosting company.

DNS

The **Domain Name System** (**DNS**) is a system that associates or connects a domain name with a Web server (Figure C–5). Computers on the Internet called DNS servers, or **nameservers**, store these associations in a database. The final step in making your Web site available is associating your domain name with the Web server so that when someone opens a browser and types www.YourWebSite.com, that user's computer can find the Web server that hosts your site.

Domain Name System

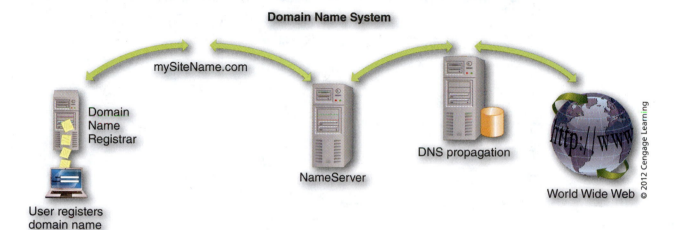

Figure C–5

Some hosting companies associate your domain name for you; others require you to do it yourself. To associate your domain name with your Web server, obtain the name of your nameserver from your Web hosting company. Then go into your domain name registrar service account and update your domain name with the name of the nameserver. As every registrar's Web site is different, you might need to contact the registrar's tech support to learn where to make the nameserver change. Once you have updated your domain name to use a specific nameserver, your domain name will be **associated** with your Web server. This allows the user's Web browser to link to your Web site when a visitor types your domain name in his or her Web browser.

DNS Propagation

There are thousands of nameservers all over the world, and when one is updated, all of the other nameservers receive an update with the new information. The updating process of the nameserver database, across all DNS servers on the Web, is called **DNS propagation**. After you make a change to your nameserver setting, it can take up to 72 hours for that change to propagate, meaning that your Web site might not be available during those three days. Several companies, including whatsmydns.net and viewdns.info, offer instant checking of DNS propagation (Figure C–6 on the next page). DNS propagation is a feature to consider when evaluating potential Web hosts.

BTW

Web Address Forwarding
Web forwarding, also known as domain forwarding, allows you to associate or redirect multiple domain names to a single Web address. For example, if you mistakenly type `google.org` or `google.biz`, a domain forwarding will take you to google.com automatically. You can increase the number of hits to your Web site by including multiple extensions, misspellings, and common typos in your domain name forwarding.

Figure C–6

Copying Files using FTP

Once you have contracted with a Web host, registered your domain name, and associated your domain name with a nameserver, you need to copy your files to the Web server using FTP client software. Some Web design software, such as Dreamweaver, includes a built-in FTP client (Figure C–7). You also can purchase FTP client software, or use free software such as FileZilla or SmartFTP.

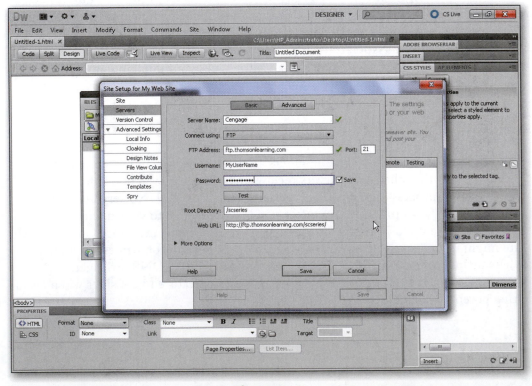

Figure C–7

Copying Files

The process of copying files to the Web server is straightforward, but first you must have four pieces of information from the Web hosting company. Although all FTP clients have slightly different interfaces, they all allow you to specify these four pieces of information:

1. Host name: The name of the Web server. This is usually the same as your domain name, but your Web host should provide an alternate name to use until DNS propagation is complete.
2. Username: The name you use to log on to the Web server.
3. Password: The password you use in conjunction with the username.
4. Remote folder: The name of the folder on the Web server to which you copy your files.

The Web hosting company should provide all this information in an e-mail message. If this information is not provided to you by e-mail, you should contact the hosting company's tech support.

Once the information is entered, you can connect to the Web server and copy your files from your computer to the Web server, by either dragging and dropping, or by clicking a Move button. The process of copying files from your computer to another computer, such as a Web server, is called **uploading**. Copying files from another computer to your computer is called **downloading**. With FTP software and the proper user permissions, you can upload your Web files to publish them and download your Web files to edit them as necessary.

BTW

Viewing Server Files
Your Web hosting service might allow Windows Explorer-based copy and paste techniques for copying files to your Web server. With the correct FTP URL, you can use a browser to log into your files. Your browser might display a message such as, "On the menu, click View, and then click Open FTP Site in Windows Explorer."

Chapter Summary

Publishing a Web site to a Web server requires research and preparation. Prior to publishing, you must select and hire a Web hosting company. Consider both technical and support offerings provided by the Web host before you decide on a company. You must acquire a domain name through a domain name registrar and associate it with a Web server for DNS propagation. Finally, publishing the Web files involves uploading files to your Web server using FTP.

Publishing to a Web Server

1: Choosing a Web Hosting Company

Instructions: This appendix recommends several features and characteristics to measure when choosing a Web hosting company. Research Web hosts — online at reputable sources and in technology publications. Find at least four different Web hosting companies and create a table similar to the following, using the criteria described in the appendix.

Company name				
Web site				
Dedicated or shared?				
Disk space				
Bandwidth				
E-mail accounts				
FTP accounts				
Cost				
Setup fee				
Uptime guarantee				
Tech support				

Publishing to a Web Server

2: Choosing a Domain Name

Instructions: You have taken a job as an intern with a consulting firm that helps start-up businesses create a Web presence. Your boss has asked you to recommend three appropriate domain names for a small hobby store named Hobby Express. Their specialty is model railroading, but they also sell puzzles, craft kits, art supplies, and strategy games.

Using the recommendations in this appendix, research domain names that are not currently used. Choose an appropriate top-level domain and an effective domain name that is easy to spell, easy to type, and easy to remember. Write a paragraph for each of the three recommendations explaining why you chose the domain.

Appendix D
Using Adobe CS6 Help

This appendix shows you how to use Adobe CS6 Help. At anytime, whether you are accessing a specific application currently or not, there are ways to interact with Adobe CS6 Help and display information on any Help topic. The help system is a complete reference manual at your fingertips.

Adobe CS6 Help

Adobe CS6 Help documentation is available in several formats, as shown in Figure D–1 on the next page. The first format is a Web-based help system that was introduced in Chapter 1. If you press the F1 key or choose Help from the application's Help menu, Adobe Community Help appears in your default browser. You then can use the Web page to search for help topics. The Adobe Community Help page also contains many other kinds of assistance, including tutorials and videos. Your computer must be connected to the Web to use this form of Help.

A second form of Help is available as a PDF file. Again, pressing the F1 key or choosing Help on the application's Help menu opens the Adobe Community Help page on the Web. Then, you can click the Help PDF link to open a searchable help documentation, specific to each CS6 application, in book format. You can save this help file on your storage device, or continue to use it on the Web. If you prefer to view documentation in print form, you can print the Adobe CS6 Help PDF file for your application.

Adobe CS6 Help displays two main panes. The left pane displays a search system. The right pane displays help information on the selected topic. Help displays a topic navigation system on the left, and pages from Help documentation on the right.

Using Help

The quickest way to navigate the help system is by clicking topic links on the Help pages. You also can search for specific words and phrases by using the **Search box** in the upper-left corner of the Adobe Community Help Web page. Here you can type words, such as *layer mask*, *hue*, or *file formats*; or you can type phrases, such as *preview a Web graphic*, or *drawing with the Pen Tool*. Adobe Community Help responds by displaying search results with a list of topics you can click.

Here are some tips regarding the words or phrases you enter to initiate a search:

1. Check the spelling of the word or phrase.
2. Keep your search specific, with fewer than seven words, to return the most accurate results.
3. If you search using a specific phrase, such as *shape tool*, put quotation marks around the phrase — the search returns only those topics containing all words in the phrase.
4. If a search term does not yield the desired results, try using a synonym, such as Web instead of Internet.

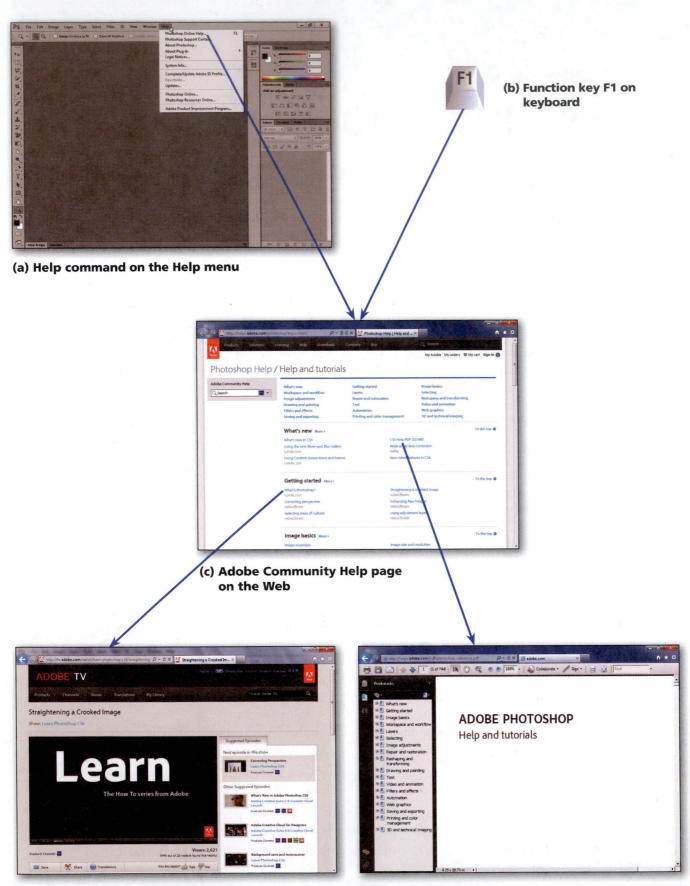

(a) Help command on the Help menu

(b) Function key F1 on keyboard

(c) Adobe Community Help page on the Web

(d) Sample video and tutorial page

(e) Help in PDF format

Figure D – 1

To Access Adobe Online Help

The following step opens Adobe Help. Although the steps show Photoshop, the process is the same for the Flash and Dreamweaver.

- With one of the Adobe CS6 applications running on your system, press the F1 key to display the Adobe Community Help window.

- When the Adobe Help window is displayed, double-click the title bar to maximize the window, if necessary (Figure D–2).

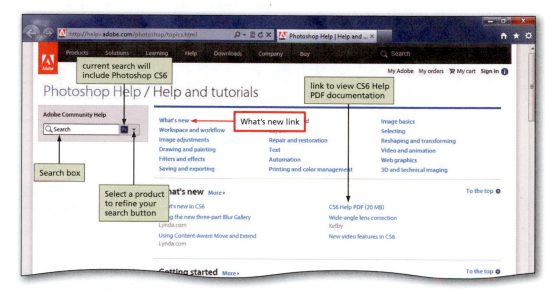

Figure D–2

To Use the Topics List

The Topics List is similar to a table of contents in a book. Adobe updates the topics on a regular basis, so your Topics List will look different. The following steps use the topics list to look up information about what is new in CS6.

- Click the topic, What's new in CS6 to display its contents (Figure D–3).

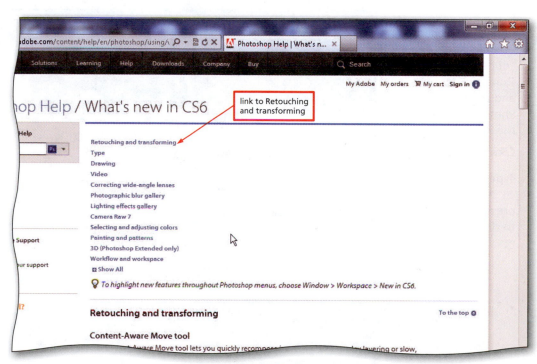

Figure D–3

- Click the link, Retouching and transforming, to display information about the new retouching tools (Figure D–4).

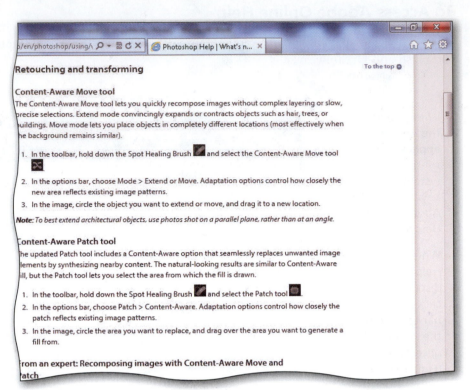

Figure D–4

To Use the Adobe Community Help Search Box

The following steps use the Search box to obtain useful information by entering the keywords, ruler origin.

- Click the 'Select a product to refine your search' button, shown in Figure D-2, and then choose Photoshop in the list.

- Click the Search box.

- Type ruler origin and then press the ENTER key to display the search results (Figure D–5).

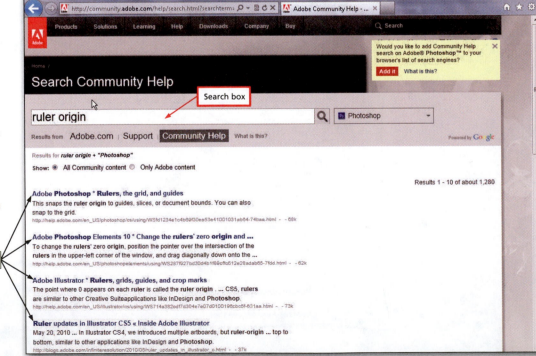

Figure D–5

- When the list of Help topics is displayed, click Adobe Photoshop* Rulers, the grid, and guides, or a similar topic in your list.

- Scroll as necessary to display the Change a ruler's zero origin topic (Figure D–6).

Experiment

- Click the 'Select a product to refine your search' button and choose a different application. Enter a topic of interest to you in the Search box and then press the ENTER key.

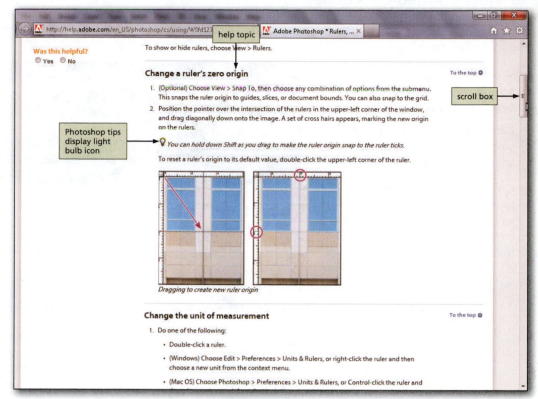

Figure D–6

At the top of each Help page, subtopics are displayed as links. On the left, Help displays feedback option buttons. At the very bottom of each Help page is a place for online discussions. A light bulb icon indicates a Help tip.

If none of the topics presents the information you want, you can refine the search by entering another word or phrase in the Search box.

To View a Video on Adobe TV

Using Adobe CS6 Help while connected to the Web, you can view online videos and tutorials, as done in the following steps.

- Scroll as necessary to display the Search box at the top of the page.

- Click the 'Select a product to refine your search' button and then choose Dreamweaver in the list.

- Click the Search box and then type `adobe tv web fonts` to enter a search topic. Press the ENTER key to search for the video (Figure D–7).

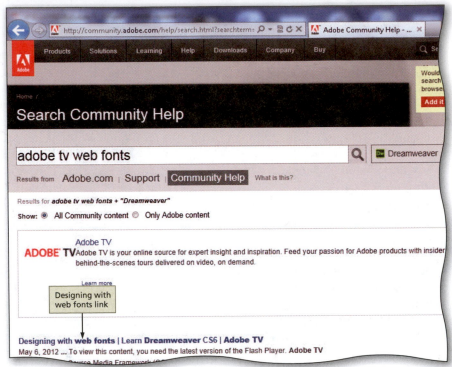

Figure D–7

2

- When Help displays the topics, click the link, Designing with web fonts, or a similar link to open the page. The video will start automatically (Figure D–8).

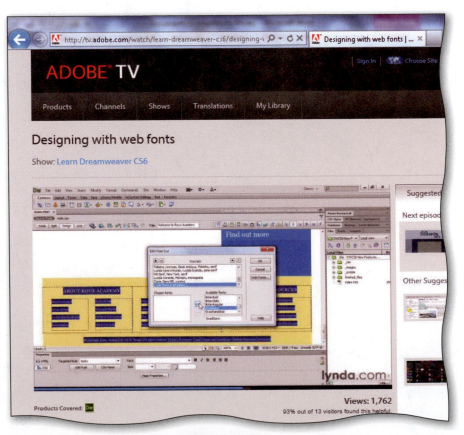

Figure D–8

3

• When the video is finished playing, click the Close button on the title bar of the browser window to quit Help. (Figure D–9).

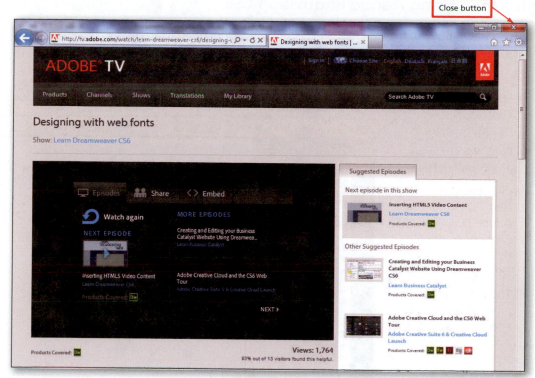

Figure D–9

Using Adobe CS6 Documentation

Using Adobe CS6 is a complete set of documentation for using the Adobe CS6 products. The PDF file is organized into topics with a table of contents like a regular book. You can access Using Adobe CS6 by clicking the link on the Adobe Online Help page.

To Open Using Adobe Photoshop CS6

The following step opens Using Adobe Photoshop CS6 from the Adobe Online Help page. You will use Adobe Acrobat to view the documentation. The steps for opening Help from within the other applications are similar.

1

- Start Photoshop if necessary.

- Press the F1 key to access online Help.

- Click the link, CS6 Help PDF in the Adobe Online Help window, to open the documentation. (Figure D–10).

Q&A

The file would not open because I do not have Adobe Acrobat on my system.

See your instructor for ways to access the file.

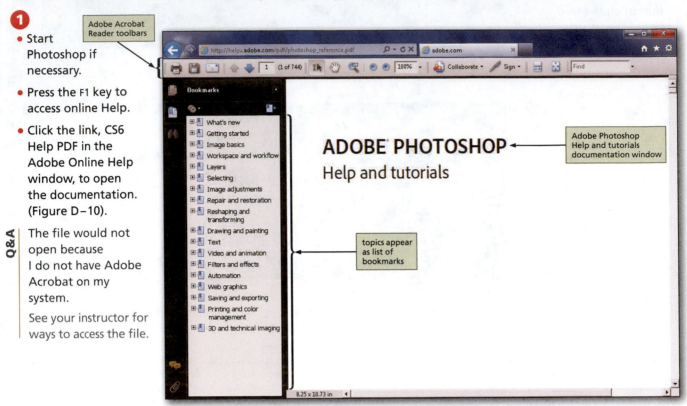

Figure D–10

To Navigate the Documentation by Bookmark

The following steps use the left pane of the documentation window to find information related to color.

1

- With the Adobe Photoshop Help and Tutorials documentation file still displayed, click the plus sign next to the words, Image Basics and then click About color, to display the topics (Figure D–11).

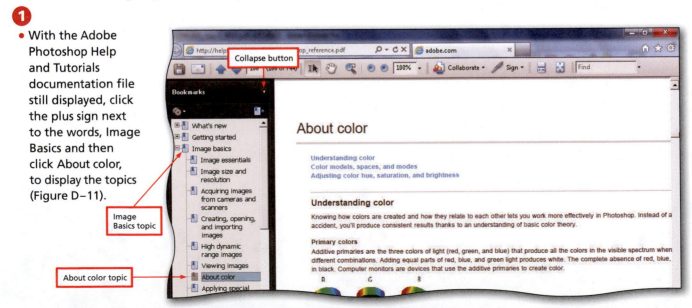

Figure D–11

2

- Click the bookmark, Understanding color, to display the information on the right side of the window.

- Click the Collapse button to hide the Bookmark pane (Figure D–12).

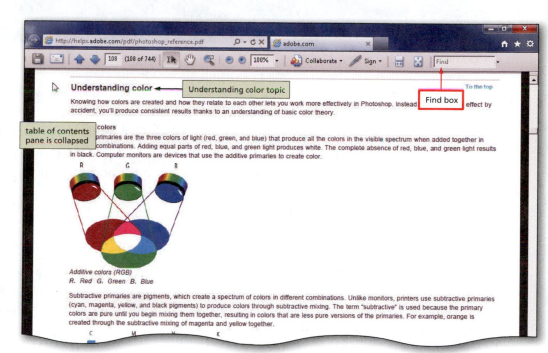

Figure D–12

To Use the Find Box

The following step searches the documentation for information about the topic, knockout options, using the Adobe Acrobat Find box.

1

- With the Using Adobe Photoshop CS6 documentation window still displayed, click the Find box in the Adobe Acrobat toolbar and then type **knockout options**.

- Press the ENTER key to search for the term (Figure D–13).

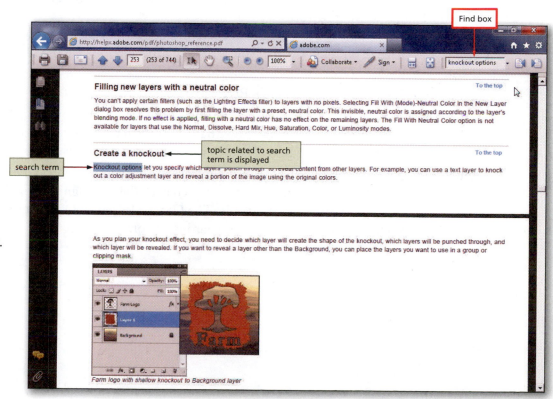

Figure D–13

Use Help

1: Using Adobe Flash Help on the Web

Instructions: Perform the following tasks using Adobe Online Help.

1. Click the 'Select a product to refine your search' button and then choose Flash CS6 in the list. Type **pen tool** in the Search box and then press the ENTER key.

2. When the topics are displayed, click the topic, Adobe Flash Professional* Drawing with the Pen tool.

3. One at a time, click two additional links and print the information. Hand in the printouts to your instructor. Use the Back to previous page and Forward to next page buttons to return to the original page.

4. Use the Search box to search for information on alignment. Click the Adobe Flash Professional* Arranging objects topic in the search results. Read and print the information. One at a time, click the links on the page and print the information for any new page that is displayed.

5. Use the Search box to search for information on tutorials. Navigate to a tutorial of your choice and follow the directions. Write three paragraphs describing your experience, including how easy or difficult it was to follow the tutorial and what you learned. Turn in the paragraphs to your instructor.

6. Close Adobe Online Help.

Use Help

2: Using Adobe Dreamweaver CS6 Documentation

Instructions: Use the Using Adobe Dreamweaver CS6 documentation to understand the topics better and answer the questions listed below. Answer the questions on your own paper, or hand in the printed Help information to your instructor.

1. To access the Dreamweaver CS6 documentation, start Help from the Dreamweaver application, or click the 'Select a product to refine your search' button and then choose Dreamweaver CS6 in the list.

2. Click the link to view the CS6 Help PDF.

3. Use the Adobe Dreamweaver Help and tutorials PDF documentation to find help on snapping. Use the Find box, and enter **use snapping** as the term. Click the search result entitled, Use snapping, and then print the page. Hand in the printouts to your instructor.

4. Use the Adobe Dreamweaver Help and tutorials PDF documentation and expand the bookmarks, if necessary. Navigate to the topic CSS, and then click the plus sign to expand the topic. Scroll in the Bookmarks panel to display the topic, The CSS Styles panel. One at a time, click each link and print the page. Hand in the printouts to your instructor.

Appendix E

Using Adobe Bridge CS6

This appendix shows you how to use Adobe Bridge CS6. Bridge is a file exploration tool similar to Windows Explorer, but with added functionality related to images. Bridge replaces previous file browsing techniques, and now is the control center for the Adobe Creative Suite. Bridge is used to organize, browse, and locate the assets you need to create content for print, the Web, and mobile devices with drag-and-drop functionality.

Adobe Bridge

You can access Adobe Bridge from Photoshop, Flash, Dreamweaver, or from the Windows 7 Start menu. Adobe Bridge can run independently from the Creative Suite applications as a stand-alone program.

To Start Bridge Using Windows

The following steps start Bridge from the Windows 7 Start menu.

- Click the Start button on the Windows 7 taskbar to display the Start menu.

- Type **Bridge CS6** as the search text in the 'Search programs and files' text box, and watch the search results appear on the Start menu (Figure E–1).

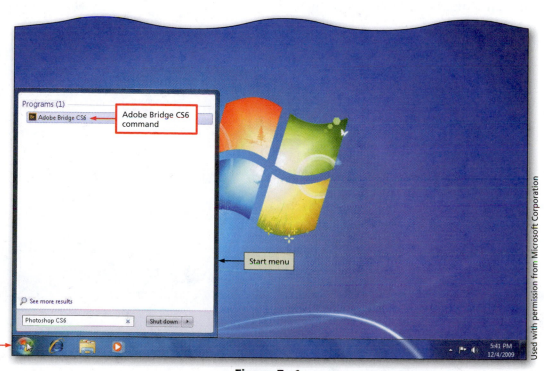

Figure E–1

2

- Click Adobe Bridge CS6 in the search results on the Start menu to start Bridge.

- When the Bridge window is displayed, double-click its title bar to maximize the window, if necessary.

- Click Computer on the Favorites panel, if necessary (Figure E–2).

Other Ways

1. In individual CS6 applications, click File on Application bar, click Browse in Bridge

2. Press ATL+CTRL+O

Figure E–2

To Reset the Workspace

To make your installation of Bridge match the figures in this book, you will reset the workspace to its default settings in the following step.

1

- Click Window on the menu bar, and then point to Workspace to display the Workspace submenu (Figure E–3).

- Click Reset Workspace on the Workspace submenu.

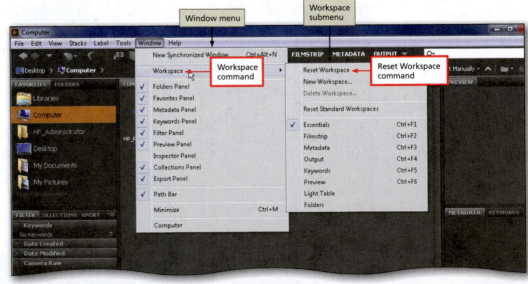

Figure E–3

Other Ways

1. Press CTRL+F1

The Bridge Window

The parts of the Bridge window are displayed in Figure E–4. The window is divided into panels and includes a menu bar, a toolbar, and a status bar.

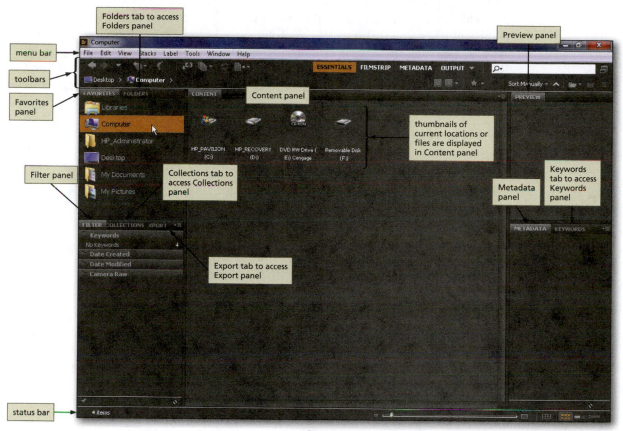

Figure E–4

The Panels

Several panels are displayed in the Bridge workspace in default view. To select a panel, click its tab. You can change the location of the panels by dragging their tabs. You can enlarge or reduce the size of the panels by dragging their borders. Some panels include buttons and menus to help you organize displayed information.

Favorites Panel   The Favorites panel allows quick access to common locations and folders, as well as access to other Adobe applications. You can click a location to display its contents in the Content panel.

Folders Panel   The Folders panel shows the folder hierarchy in a display similar to that of Windows Explorer. You can click the plus sign to expand folders and the minus sign to collapse them.

Content Panel   The Content panel is displayed in a large pane in the center of the Bridge window. The content panel includes a view of each file and folder, its name, the creation date, and other information about each item. The Content panel is used to select files and open folders. To select a file, click it. To open a folder, double-click it. You can change how the Content panel is displayed on the Bridge status bar.

Preview Panel The Preview panel displays a preview of the selected file that is usually larger than the thumbnail displayed in the Content panel. If the panel is resized, the preview also is resized.

Filter Panel The Filter panel is displayed in the lower-left region of the Bridge window. The Filter panel includes many categories of criteria used to filter or control which files are displayed in the Content panel. By default, three categories are displayed when you first start Bridge: Keywords, Date Created, and Date Modified. As you click files, the criteria categories change to include metadata that is generated dynamically depending on the file type. For example, if you click an image in the Content panel, the Filter panel includes criteria such as camera data. If you click an audio file, the criteria include artist, album genre, and so on.

Collections Panel The Collections panel is displayed in the lower-left region of the Bridge window. **Collections** are a way to group photos in one place for easy viewing, even if the images are located in different folders or on different hard drives. The Collections panel allows you to create and display previously created collections, by identifying files or by saving previous searches.

Export Panel The Export panel is displayed in the lower-left region of the Bridge window. The panel helps with saving and uploading to photo-sharing Web sites, including Facebook, Flickr, and Photoshop.com.

Metadata Panel The Metadata panel contains metadata information for the selected file. Recall that metadata is information about the file including properties, camera data, creation and modification data, and other pieces of information. If multiple files are selected, shared data is listed such as keywords, date created, and exposure settings.

Keywords Panel The Keywords panel allows you to assign keywords using categories designed by Bridge, or you can create new ones. The keywords help you organize and search your images.

Toolbars and Buttons

Bridge displays several toolbars and sets of buttons to help you work more efficiently (Figure E–5).

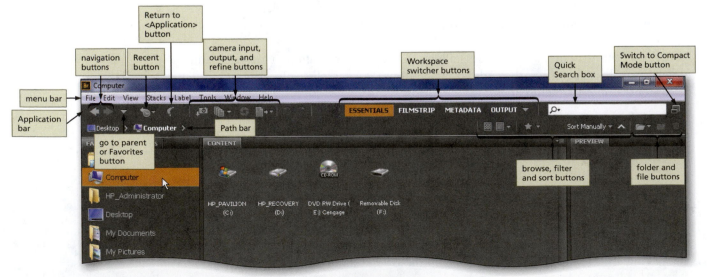

Figure E–5

Menu Bar   The menu bar is displayed at the top of the Bridge window and contains commands specific to Bridge.

Application Bar   Below the menu bar is the Application bar, which includes the navigation buttons, file retrieval and output buttons, buttons for switching workspaces, and other buttons to search for files.

Path Bar   The Path bar displays the path for the current file. To the right of the Path bar are shortcut buttons to help you work with your files. Browse, filter, and sort buttons change the display in the Content panel. The 'Create a new folder' button inserts a new folder in the current location. The rotate buttons are active when an image file is selected in the Content panel. The Delete item button deletes the selected item.

Status Bar   At the bottom of the Bridge window, the status bar displays information and contains buttons (Figure E–6). On the left side of the status bar is information regarding the number of items in the current location and how many files are selected, if any. On the right side of the status bar, the Thumbnail slider sets the size of the thumbnails. To the right of the slider are four buttons used to change the display of the Content panel, including the 'Click to lock thumbnail grid' button, the 'View content as thumbnails' button, the 'View content as details' button, and the 'View content as list' button.

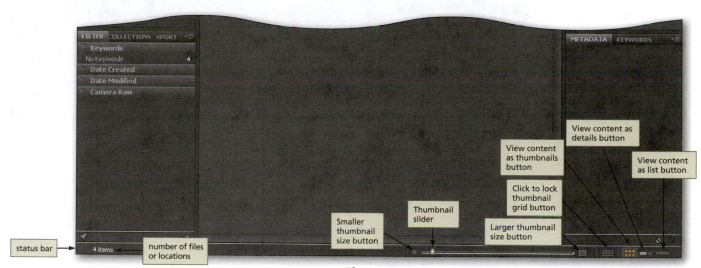

Figure E–6

Bridge Navigation and File Viewing

The advantages of using Bridge to navigate through the files and folders on your computer system include an interface that looks the same in all folders, the ability to see the images quickly, and the ease with which you can open the files in each application or other image editing software. Besides the four kinds of displays represented by the Workspace switcher buttons on the right side of the status bar, Bridge offers several other configurations or layouts of the workspace accessible on the Workspace submenu on the Window menu (Figure E–3 on page APP 46).

To Navigate and View Files Using Bridge

The following step navigates to the Data Files for Students to view files. Visit www.cengage.com/ct/studentdownload for detailed instructions or contact your instructor for information about accessing the required files. You then will use the Workspace switcher buttons to view the Content panel in different styles.

- In the Content panel, double-click the location associated with the Data Files for Students.

- When the folders and files are displayed, double-click the Photoshop folder, and then double-click the Chapter 01 folder to display the files (Figure E–7).

 Experiment

- One at a time, click each of the workspace buttons on the options bar and note how the Content panel changes.

Figure E–7

Other Ways

1. To view Filmstrip workspace, press CTRL+F2

2. To view Metadata workspace, press CTRL+F3

3. To view Output workspace, press CTRL+F4

4. To view Keywords workspace, press CTRL+F5

5. To view Preview workspace, press CTRL+F6

Duplicating Files
Bridge also offers a Duplicate command on the Edit menu (Figure E–8) that makes a copy in the same folder. Bridge renames the second file with the word, Copy, appended to the file name.

Managing Files

If you want to move a file to a folder that currently is displayed in the Content panel, you can drag and drop the file. The right-drag option is not available. If you want to copy a file, you can choose Copy on the Edit menu, navigate to the new folder and then choose Paste on the Edit menu. At anytime you can press the DELETE key to delete a file or folder, or right-click and then click Delete on the context menu. To rename a photo in Bridge, right-click the file and then click Rename. Type the new name.

To Copy a File

The following steps copy a file from the Data Files for Students to a USB flash drive using Bridge.

1

- With the Chapter 01 folder contents still displayed in the Content panel, click the Case 1-2 Tubing thumbnail to select it.

- Click Edit on the menu bar to display the Edit menu (Figure E–8).

 Experiment

- Choose a picture and then use one of the rotate commands on the Edit menu to rotate the image. Press CTRL+Z to cancel the rotation. When you are done, click Edit on the menu bar.

Figure E–8

2

- Click Copy on the Edit menu.

- In the Favorites panel, click Computer.

- When the Computer locations are displayed in the Content panel, double-click Removable Disk (F:) or the drive associated with your USB flash drive.

- Click Edit on the menu bar, and then click Paste to display the copy in its new location (Figure E–9).

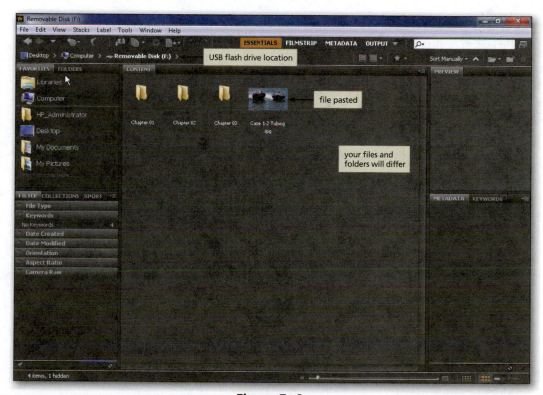

Figure E–9

Other Ways

1. To copy, press CTRL+C
2. To paste, press CTRL+V

Metadata

A popular use for Bridge allows you to assign metadata to files. Metadata, such as information about the file, author, resolution, color space, and copyright, is used for searching and categorizing photos. You can use metadata to streamline your workflow and organize your files.

Metadata is divided into categories, depending on the type of software you are using and the selected files. The category File Properties includes things like file type, creation date, dimensions, and color mode. IPTC Core stands for International Press Telecommunications Council, which is data used to identify transmitted text and images, such as data describing the image or the location of a photo. Camera Data (Exif) refers to the Exchangeable Image File Format, a standard for storing interchange information in image files, especially those using JPEG compression. Most digital cameras now use the Exif format. The standardization of IPTC and Exif encourages interoperability between imaging devices. Other categories may include Audio, Video, Fonts, Camera Raw, and Version Cue, among others. You can see a list of all the metadata categories and their definitions by using Bridge Help.

To Assign and View Metadata

The Metadata Focus workspace makes it easier to assign or enter metadata for photos. In the Metadata panel, you can click the pencil icon to select fields of metadata, or you can move through the fields by pressing the TAB key. The following steps enter description and location information for the selected file.

1

- Click the Case 1-2 Tubing thumbnail to select it.

- In the Metadata panel, move the mouse pointer to a location just right of the field names. When the mouse pointer changes to a double-headed arrow, drag to the right to display more of the words.

- Drag the left border of the Metadata panel to widen the panel itself.

- In the Metadata panel, scroll down to the IPTC Core area.

- Click the arrow next to the heading, IPTC Core to expand the area if necessary (Figure E–10).

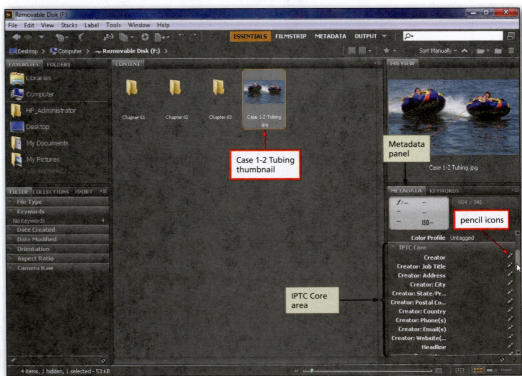

Figure E–10

Adobe CS6 Appendix E

2

- Scroll down to the Description field and then click the pencil icon to the right of the Description field. Type **Tubing Adventure** as the description.

- Scroll as needed and then click the pencil icon to the right of the Sublocation field. Type **Raccoon Lake** as the location.

- Press the TAB key, Type **Rockville** as the city.

- Press the TAB key. Type **Missouri** as the state (Figure E–11).

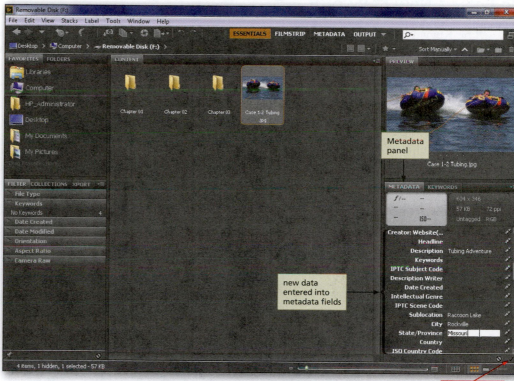

Figure E–11

3

- Click the Apply button at the bottom of the Metadata panel to assign the metadata to the photo.

- Click File on the menu bar and then click File Info to display the Case 1-2 Tubing.jpg dialog box, and verify the Description field (Figure E–12).

- Click the OK button to close the dialog box.

  Experiment

- Click each of the thumbnail buttons on the Bridge status bar to see how they change the display.

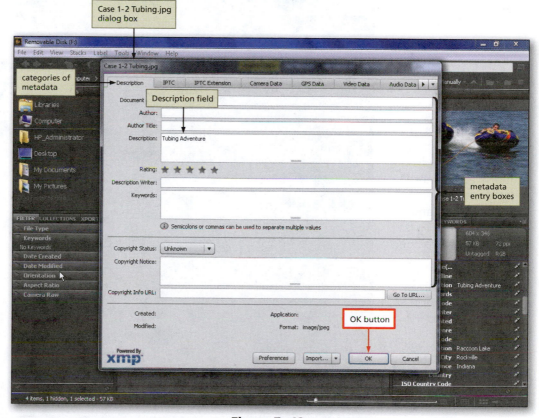

Figure E–12

To Enter a New Keyword

The Keywords panel lets you create and apply Bridge **keywords** to files. Keywords can be organized into categories called **sets.** Using keywords and sets, you identify and search for files based on their content. To assign keywords, you click the box to the left of the keyword in the Keywords panel, as shown in the following steps.

1

- With the Case 1-2 Tubing image still selected, click the Keywords tab to display the Keywords panel.

- Right-click the word, Places, to display the context menu (Figure E–13).

Figure E–13

2

- Click New Sub Keyword on the context menu.

- When the new field is displayed in the Keywords panel, type **Missouri** and then press the ENTER key to create the new item in Places.

- Select the photo again in the Content panel, if necessary.

- Click the check box to the left of Missouri to assign a Missouri keyword to the picture (Figure E–14).

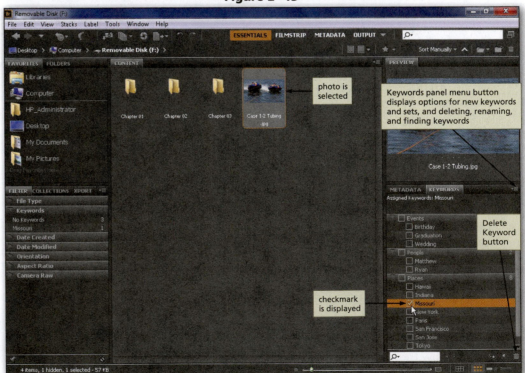

Figure E–14

To Rate a Photo

A rating system from zero stars to five stars is available in Bridge to rate your images and photos. A rating system helps you organize and flag your favorite or best files. Many photographers transfer their digital photos from a camera into Bridge and then look back through them, rating and grouping the photos. You can rate a photo using the Label menu or using shortcut keys. Once the photo is rated, stars are displayed below or above the file name depending on the workspace view. To change a rating, click Label on the menu bar and then either increase or decrease the rating. To remove all stars, click Label on the menu bar and then click No Rating. In some views, you can change a rating by clicking stars or dots that display below the thumbnail. You can remove the rating by clicking left of the stars.

The following step adds a rating to a photo file in Bridge.

1

- With the Case 1-2 Tubing image still selected in the Content panel, press CTRL+3 to assign a three star rating (Figure E–15).

Q&A

How do you remove the stars if you change your mind?

Click to the left of the stars in the Content panel, or press CTRL+0 (zero) to remove the stars.

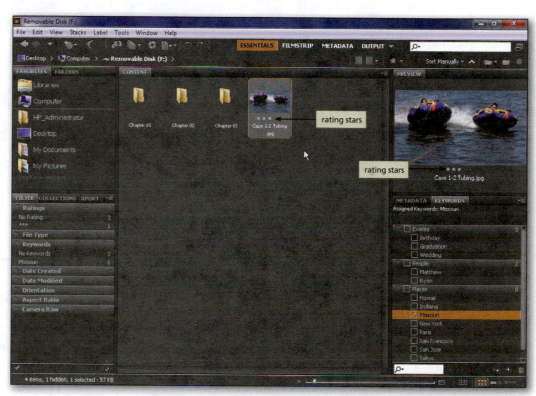

rating stars

rating stars

Figure E–15

Other Ways

1. On Label menu, select desired rating

To Label a Photo with Color Coding

Another way to group photos in Bridge is to use a color coding system. Bridge provides five colors with which users can label or group their photos. Each color has a category keyword that can be used to group photos. Keywords such as Approved, Second, or Review are used in photojournalism to indicate the status of the photo for future usage. Some companies use the colors for sorting and selecting only. The steps on the next page add a green color indicating approval to the Case 1-2 Tubing image using the menu system. Shortcut keys also are available for labeling photos with color coding. You can edit the words associated with the various colors. To do so, press CTRL+K to enter Preferences and then click Labels in the left navigation pane.

1

- With the Case 1-2 Tubing image still selected in the Content panel, click Label on the menu bar to display the Label menu (Figure E–16).

 Q&A

Can I change the colors associated with each label status?

No. Beginning with the Select command on the Label menu and going down, the colors are red, yellow, green, blue, and purple, respectively.

Figure E–16

2

- Click Approved to choose a label status.

- If Bridge displays a dialog box, click its OK button to apply the color (Figure E–17).

Q&A

Where will I see the word, Approved, that I chose from the Label menu?

In the Essentials workspace, you only see the green color around the rating. If you click the Metadata workspace switcher button, the status itself is displayed.

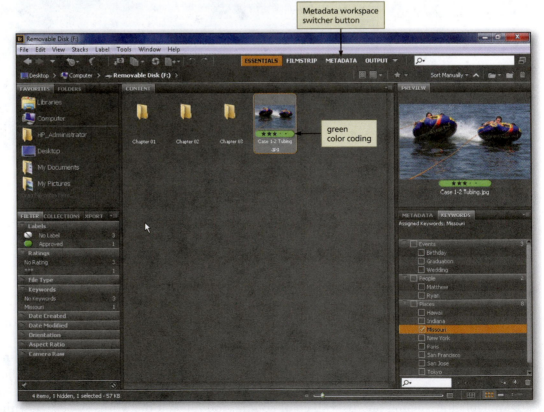

Figure E–17

Other Ways

1. For green color coding, press CTRL+8

Searching Bridge

Searching is a powerful tool in Bridge, especially as the number of stored image files increases on your computer system. It is a good idea to enter keywords, or metadata, for every image file you store, to make searching more efficient. Without Bridge and the search tool, you would have to view all files as filmstrips in Windows, and then look at them a screen at a time until you found what you wanted.

Using the Find Command

In Bridge, you can enter the kind of data or field that you want to search, parameters for that field, and the text you are looking for using the Find command. For example, you could search for all files with a rating of three stars or better, for files less than 1 megabyte in size, files with Indiana as their location, or files that begin with the letter, m.

BTW

Saving Ratings
Color coding and ratings are portable to other computers only when photos have embedded extensible markup platform (XMP) storage space. Otherwise, the colors and ratings are stored in your system's cached memory.

BTW

Flash & Dreamweaver
Both Flash and Dreamweaver files can be rated and color coded. You can follow the exact same steps, just select a Flash file or a Dreamweaver file in the Content panel.

To Use the Find Command

The Find dialog box displays many boxes and buttons to help you search effectively. In the following steps, you will look for all files with metadata that includes the word, lake.

1
- Click Edit on the menu bar, and then click Find to display the Find dialog box (Figure E–18).

Q&A

How do I search in other locations?

Click the Look in box arrow and choose a preset location, or click the Browse command on the list to navigate to the desired location.

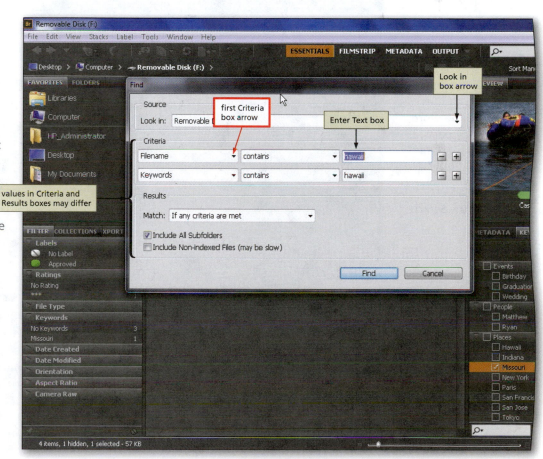

Figure E–18

2

- If necessary, click the first Criteria box arrow, scroll down as necessary, and then click All Metadata to search all of the metadata fields.

- Press the TAB key twice, and then type **lake** in the Enter Text box to enter the criteria (Figure E–19).

Experiment

- Click the second Criteria box arrow, to view the choices for delimiting the criteria. When you are finished, click contains.

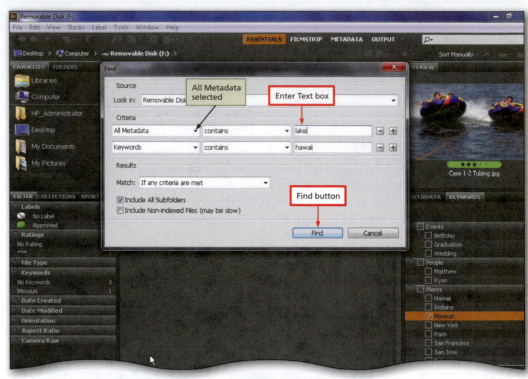

Figure E–19

3

- Click the Find button to display all files that have the word, lake, in any part of their metadata (Figure E–20).

- Click the Cancel button in the Search title bar.

Q&A

Can I search for types of images?

Yes, click the first Criteria box arrow, and then click Document Type. The third Criteria box then lists types of images from which you may choose.

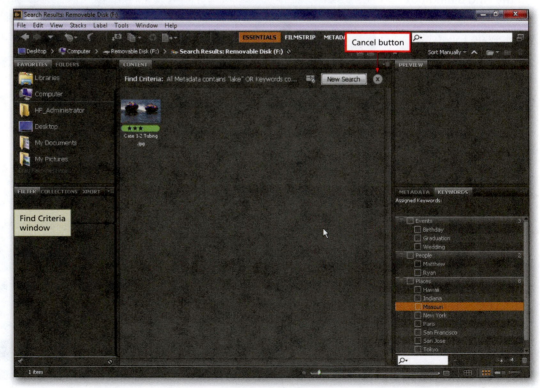

Figure E–20

Other Ways

1. Press CTRL+F, enter search criteria, click Find button

The plus sign to the right of the search boxes in the Find dialog box allows you to search multiple fields. You can add additional criteria by clicking the plus button. For example, if you needed to find photos that were created last winter from your vacation in the Rockies, you could search for the date in the first line of boxes, and then enter a description in the second line of criteria boxes to narrow your search even further in the second line of boxes (Figure E–21). When clicked, the Match box arrow allows you to match any or all criteria.

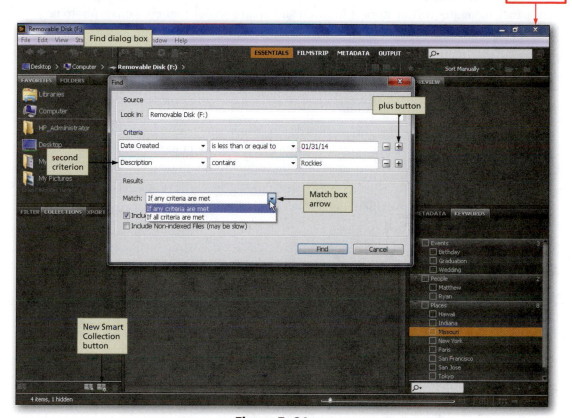

Figure E–21

Bridge offers you a way to save common searches as a **collection** for use later. For example, if you were working for a grocery wholesaler who stores many files for artwork in advertising, searching for pictures related to dairy products would be a common search. Looking through folders of images for pictures of milk or cheese would be very time consuming. To create a stored, search collection, click the New Smart Collection button and enter your criteria. Bridge then allows you to name the search. To display stored collections, click Collections in the Favorites panel. Then to perform the search again, double-click the collection. With metadata and collection searches, Bridge saves a lot of time.

To Quit Bridge

The final step quits Bridge.

1 Click the Close button on the Bridge title bar.

Using Bridge with Photoshop

1: Assigning Metadata

Instructions: You would like to assign metadata to some of the photos you worked on in previous chapters in this book.

1. Start Bridge. When the Bridge window is displayed, click Computer on the Favorites panel. In the Content panel, navigate to your storage location and open a folder that contains a photo or image file.

2. Click to select a file in the folder. In the Metadata panel, scroll down and click the pencil icon next to the word, Description. In the description box, enter a short description of the image. Scroll as necessary to click the Description Writer box. Enter your name. Enter Metadata for two other fields such as your e-mail address or location.

3. With the first photo still selected, click the Keywords tab. When the Adobe Bridge dialog box appears, click Apply to apply the changes you just made in the Metadata panel. On the Keywords tab, click to place a check mark next to any keywords that apply to the photo.

4. Scroll to the bottom of the keywords list. Right-click the Other Keywords category and then click New Keyword on the context menu. When the new keyword box appears at the top of the panel, type a new keyword relating to the selected.

5. Repeat Steps 2 through 4 for each photo in the Content panel of the Bridge window.

Using Bridge with Flash

2: Searching for Flash Files

Instructions: You would like to define a Smart Collection for some of the Flash files you have created.

1. Start Bridge. Navigate to Removable Drive (F:) or the location of your storage device.

2. Click the Collections panel to select it, if necessary.

3. Click the New Smart Collection button to open the Smart Collection dialog box. Choose the criteria of Document type, equals, and Flash Document. Click the Save button.

4. In the Collections panel, name the smart collection, My Flash Files.

Using Bridge with Dreamweaver

3: Rating Web Pages

Instructions: You would like to rate some of the Dreamweaver files you have created.

1. Start Bridge. Navigate to the location of a Dreamweaver file you created in a previous chapter.

2. Select an HTML file. In the Preview panel, right-click the file and then click Open on the context menu to preview the Web page. When you are finished examining the Web page, close the browser window to return to Bridge.

3. Assign a rating to the file on a scale from 1 to 5. On the Label menu, click the number of stars that corresponds to your rating. Repeat the process for another Dreamweaver file. Choose your favorite Dreamweaver file in the folder and right-click the file in the Content panel. Click Add to Favorites on the context menu.

4. Consult with at least three other members of your class to compare your ratings.

Appendix F

Changing Screen Resolution

This appendix explains how to change the screen resolution in Windows 7 to the resolution used in this book.

Screen Resolution

Screen resolution indicates the number of pixels (dots) that the computer uses to display the graphics, text, and background you see on the screen. The screen resolution usually is stated as the product of two numbers, such as 1024×768. That resolution results in a display of 1,024 distinct pixels on each of 768 lines, or about 786,432 pixels. The figures in this book were created using a screen resolution of 1024×768.

To Change Screen Resolution

The following steps change your screen's resolution to 1024×768 pixels. Your computer already may be set to 1024×768 or some other resolution.

1
- If necessary, minimize all programs so that the Windows 7 desktop is displayed.

- Right-click the Windows 7 desktop to display the desktop shortcut menu (Figure F–1).

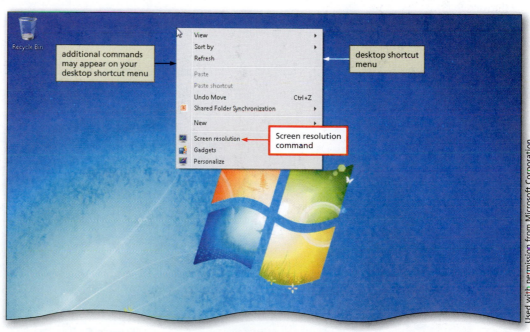

Figure F–1

● Click Screen resolution on the shortcut menu to open the Screen Resolution window. Maximize the window if necessary (Figure F–2).

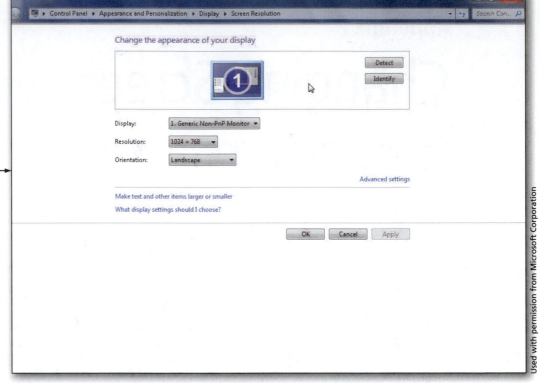

Figure F–2

● Click the Resolution button to display the list of available resolutions (Figure F–3).

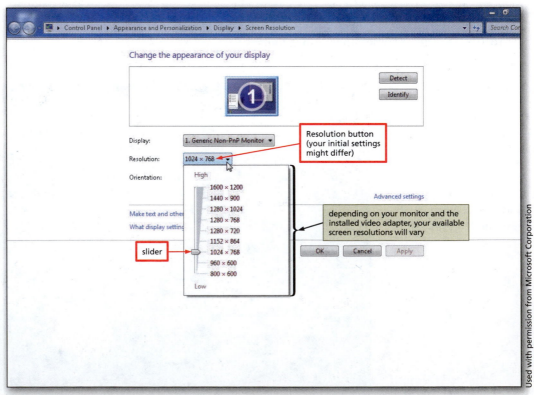

Figure F–3

4

- Drag the slider in the Resolution list so that the screen resolution changes to 1024 × 768, if necessary (Figure F–4).

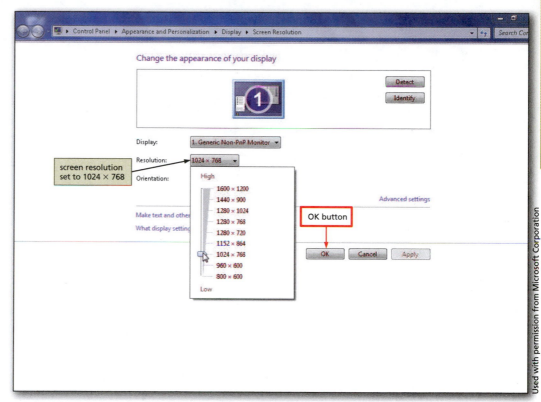

Figure F–4

5

- Click outside of the list to close the list. Click the OK button to change the screen resolution (Figure F–5).

6

- If Windows displays the Display Settings dialog box, click the Keep changes button to accept the changes and return to the Desktop.

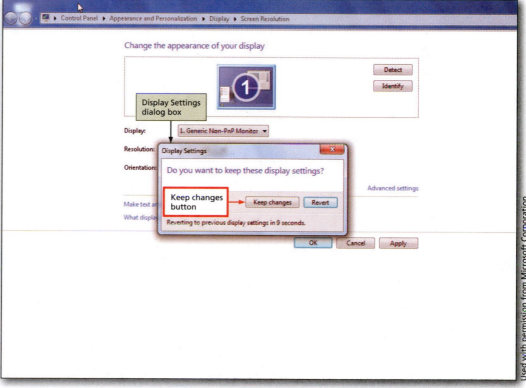

Figure F–5

Appendix G

For Mac Users

For the Mac User of this Book

For most tasks, little difference exists between using the Adobe Creative Suite 6 with the Windows 7 operating system and using it with the Mac OS X Lion 10.7 operating system. With some tasks, however, you will see some differences, or you might need to complete the tasks using different steps. This appendix demonstrates how to start an application, open a file, create a folder and save a file, close a file, display the application menu, and quit an application, using Adobe Creative Suite 6 and the Mac operating system. To illustrate these tasks, this appendix uses samples from Photoshop, Flash, and Dreamweaver. The tasks can be accomplished in other Adobe programs in a similar fashion.

Keyboard Differences

One difference between a Mac and a PC is in the use of modifier keys. **Modifier keys** are special keys used to modify the normal action of a key when the two are pressed in combination. Examples of modifier keys include the SHIFT, CTRL, and ALT keys on a PC and the SHIFT, CMD, and OPT keys on a Mac (Figure G–1). The CMD key sometimes is referred to as the APPLE key.

PC modifier keys

(a) PC keyboard

Mac modifier keys

(b) Mac keyboard

Figure G–1

Adobe product screenshot(s) reprinted with permission from Adobe Systems Incorporated

Table G–1 explains the keystroke equivalencies. For instance, if PC instructions tell you to press CTRL+T to perform a task, Mac users would press CMD+T. In addition, many Mac menus display shortcut notations using symbols to represent the modifier key.

Table G–1 PC vs. Mac Keystroke Equivalencies		
PC	**Mac**	**Mac Symbol**
CTRL key	CMD key	⌘
ALT key	OPT key	⌥
SHIFT key	SHIFT key	⇧

To Start an Application

The following steps, which assume Mac OS X Lion 10.7 is running, start an application based on a typical installation. You might need to ask your instructor how to start an Adobe application for your computer. The figures in the following steps use Photoshop; however, the steps are similar in Flash and Dreamweaver. To start another program, substitute the program name in Step 1.

1

- Click the Spotlight button on the Mac desktop to display the Spotlight box.

- Type the name of your application, such as Photoshop CS6, as the search text in the Spotlight text box and watch the search results appear (Figure G–2).

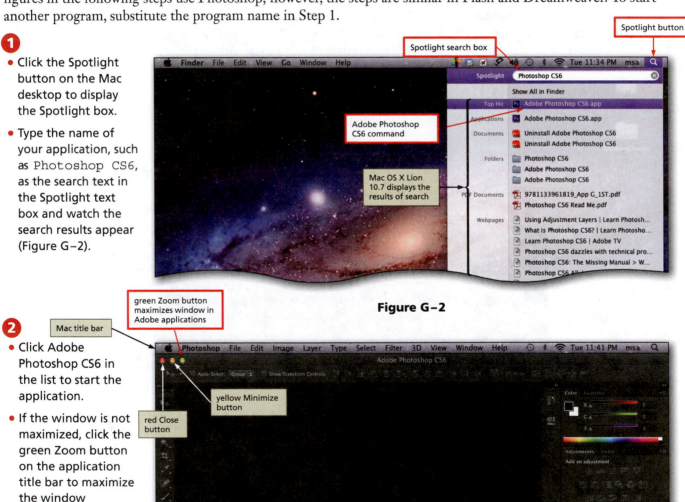

Figure G–2

2

- Click Adobe Photoshop CS6 in the list to start the application.

- If the window is not maximized, click the green Zoom button on the application title bar to maximize the window (Figure G–3).

Figure G–3

Q&A

Does the PC version of Photoshop have a title bar?

No. On the PC platform, Photoshop and Flash have an Application bar that combines the menu and clip controls. Dreamweaver CS6 has a title bar and a menu bar. In all three applications, the clip control functions — minimize, maximize, and close — are inherited from the operating system, and are placed where the system user would expect to find them.

③

• Follow the instructions in Photoshop, Flash, or Dreamweaver Chapter 1 of this book to reset the workspace and settings. The Preferences command in Photoshop on a Mac is located on the Photoshop menu, not the Edit menu.

Other Ways	
1. Click Finder icon in Dock, navigate to applications, locate Adobe Photoshop CS6, double-click icon	2. Click Photoshop icon on Dock

To Open a File

To complete this assignment, you will be required to use the Data Files for Students. Visit www.cengage.com/ct/studentdownload for detailed instructions or contact your instructor for information about accessing the required files. The following steps open a file from the Data Files for Students.

The figures in the following steps use Photoshop; however, the steps are similar in Flash and Dreamweaver. To open a file in another application, substitute your application name in Step 3 and the file name in Step 4.

①

• Start your application, if necessary.

• Click File on the title bar to display the File menu (Figure G–4).

Q&A

What does it mean when Adobe includes multiple symbols in the shortcut key notation?

Multiple symbols mean that you must hold down several keys. For example, a notation of ⌥ ⌘ O on the menu would mean to press and hold the OPTION and COMMAND keys while you press the O key. Written instructions might say press OPT+CMD+O.

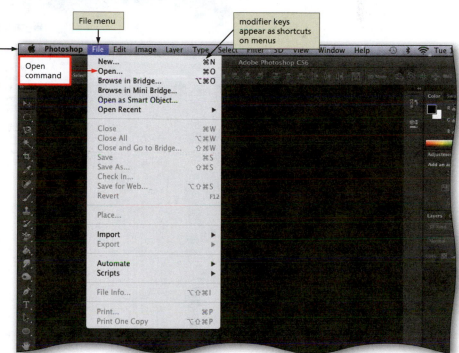

Figure G–4

2

- Click Open on the File menu to display the Open dialog box.

- Click the Where button to display a list of the available storage locations on your system (Figure G–5).

🔍 **Experiment**

- Click a location on the Favorites panel on the left side of the Open dialog box and watch the Where button change. Click the Where button.

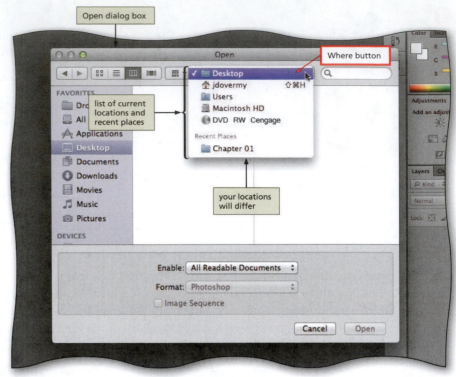

Figure G–5

3

- Click the drive associated with the location of the Data Files for Students. (Figure G–6).

- Navigate to the Photoshop folder, and then the Data Files for Students folder.

Q&A

What is the default location shown in the Open dialog box?

By default, the Open dialog box shows the first 10 items in the folder or volume last used during an open or save process. You can use the Icon view, List view, Column view, or Cover Flow view buttons to change the way the contents are presented. Cover Flow view allows you to see the contents of a file as a thumbnail.

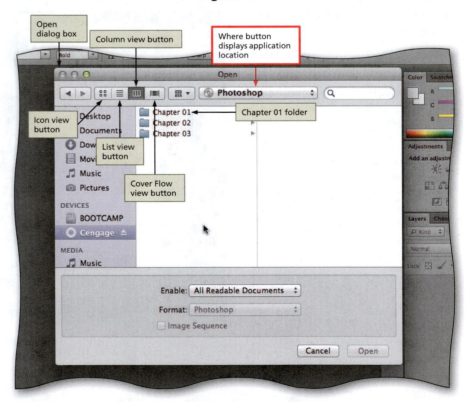

Figure G–6

4

- Double-click the Chapter 01 folder.

- Click the file you want to open, in this case Eagle.jpg, to select it (Figure G–7).

5

- Click the Open button to open the selected file and display the open file in the application's workspace.

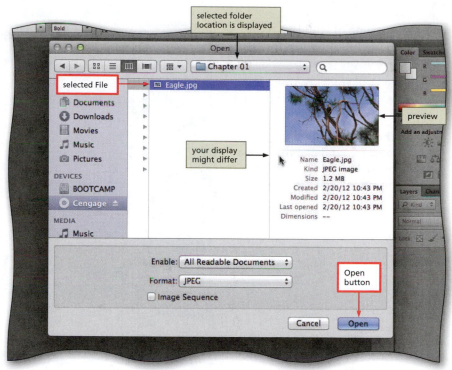

Figure G–7

Other Ways

1. Press CMD+O, select file, click Open

To Create a Folder and Save a File

After editing a file, you should save it. The following steps create a folder on a USB flash drive and save a file. The figures in the following steps use Flash; however, the steps are similar in Photoshop and Dreamweaver.

1

- Start your application and open a file.

- With a USB flash drive connected to one of the computer's USB ports, click File on the title bar to display the File menu and then click Save As to display the Save As dialog box.

- Type the name of your file in the Save As box to change the file name. Do not press the RETURN key after typing the file name.

- Click the Save in button to display the list of available locations (Figure G–8).

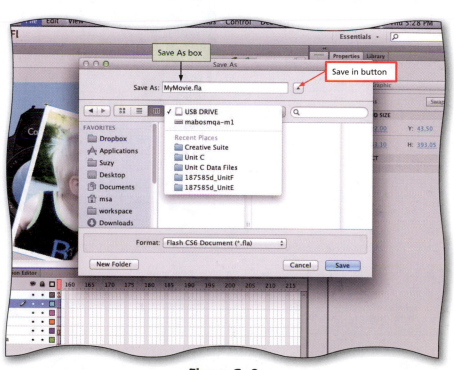

Figure G–8

- Click the name of your USB flash drive, in the list of devices to select that drive as the new save location.
- Click the New Folder button to create a new folder on the selected storage device.
- When the new folder appears, type a new folder name to change the name of the folder, and then press the RETURN key (Figure G–9).

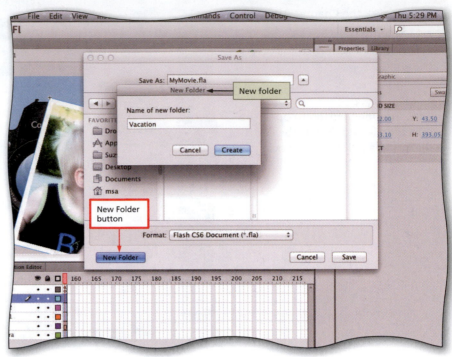

Figure G–9

- If necessary, click the new folder to open it.
- If necessary, click the Format button to display the list of available file formats. Choose the format appropriate for your application and purpose (Figure G–10).

- Click the Save button to save the document on the selected drive with the new file name.

Figure G–10

Other Ways

1. Press SHIFT+CMD+S, choose settings, click Save button

To Close a File

The figures in the following steps use Dreamweaver to close an open file; however, the steps are similar in Photoshop and Flash.

1

- Start your application and open a file.
- Click File on the title bar to display the File menu (Figure G–11).

Q&A

Is the File menu different on a Mac?

The File menu is basically the same. The commands might be grouped in a slightly different manner. The File menu does not contain the Exit command as it does on a PC. You will learn in the next steps that the Exit command is on the application menu, in this case the Dreamweaver menu.

2

- Click the Close command on the File menu to close the current open file without quitting the application.

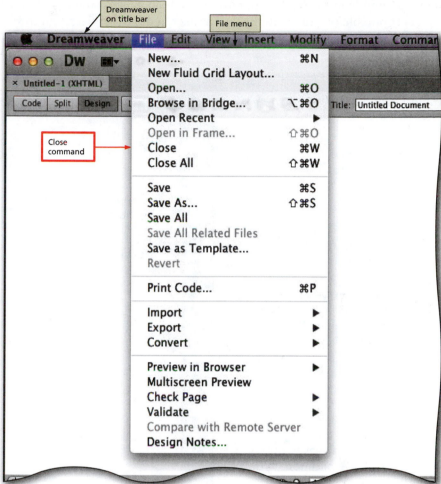

Figure G–11

Other Ways
1. Press CMD+W

To Display the Application Menu and Quit the Application

Using the Mac operating system, Adobe CS6 includes a unique application menu to the left of the typical menu used in Windows. This application menu includes commands that you find in different locations on a PC, the most notable of which are the preferences, options, services, and the Quit command for each application. The following steps open the application menu for Dreamweaver; however, the steps are similar for Photoshop and Flash.

1

- Start your application and open a file.

- On the title bar, click the application name, in this case Dreamweaver, to display its menu (Figure G–12).

Q&A

What does the Services command do?

Mac OS X includes a Services submenu in many applications for tasks such as looking up a word in the dictionary, rotating an image, sending an e-mail, or compressing a video. Any Service installed on your Mac that manipulates files related to your application will be displayed on the Services submenu.

2

- Click Quit Dreamweaver, or the name of your application, to quit the application.

Q&A

Can I click the red Close button to quit the application?

The red button closes the application window, but the application will continue to run until you quit the application.

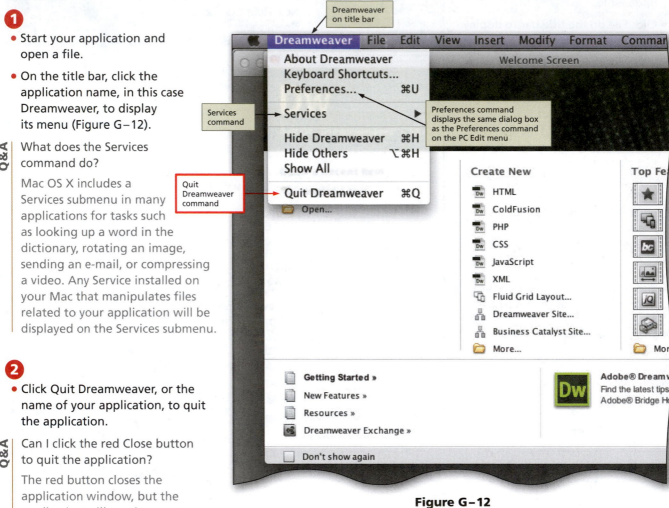

Figure G–12

Other Ways

1. Press CMD+Q
2. On Dock, click and hold mouse button, on context menu, click Quit

Index